ROBE
HAW

A BIOGRAPHY

Blanche d'Alpuget was born in Sydney in 1944, and worked as a journalist in Australia and the UK before going to live in Indonesia in 1966 and later Malaysia. She lived abroad for nine years, in South-East Asia and Europe, continuing to write for various newspapers and journals.

Her first book, *Mediator*, was published in 1977. A biography of Sir Richard Kirby, it arose from the interest she shared with him in Indonesian affairs and like *Monkeys in the Dark*, her novel set in Indonesia and published in 1980, it received critical acclaim. *Turtle Beach*, her second novel, set in Malaysia, was published in 1981 and won the Sydney PEN Golden Jubilee Award, the *Age* Book of the Year Award, the South Australian Government's Bicentennial Award for Literature and the Braille Book of the Year Award.

Robert J. Hawke grew out of the study of his career that Blanche d'Alpuget had to undertake for the biography of Kirby. It was written with the assistance of a two-year Senior Fellowship from the Literature Board. In 1983 it won both the NSW Premier's Award and the Braille Book of the Year Award. This book has led to her work in progress, a novel set in Israel.

Schwartz
Penguin Books

ROBERT.J. HAWKE

A BIOGRAPHY
by
Blanche d'Alpuget

SCHWARTZ
PENGUIN BOOKS

Penguin Books Ltd, Harmondsworth, Middlesex, England
Viking Penguin Inc., 40 West 23rd Street, New York, New York 10010, U.S.A.
Penguin Books Australia Ltd, Ringwood, Victoria, Australia
Penguin Books Canada Ltd, 2801 John Street, Markham, Ontario, Canada L3R 1B4
Penguin Books (N.Z.) Ltd, 182–190 Wairau Road, Auckland 10, New Zealand

First published by Schwartz Publishing Group
in conjunction with Lansdowne Press, 1982
This edition published by Penguin Books Australia in association
with Schwartz Publishing Group Pty Ltd, 1984
Reprinted 1984
First published in Great Britain by Penguin Books 1985

Printed and bound in Great Britain by
Cox & Wyman Ltd, Reading
Typeset in Sabon

For my father, Lou d'Alpuget, with affection

Contents

Acknowledgments

I am deeply indebted to many people for providing me with material for this book. I wish to thank Sir Peter Abeles, Jose Aguiriano, Reo Allen, Gil Appleton, Lila Baillie, Kate Baillieu, Jim Baird, Lily Ballard, Ephraim Bar-Schmuel, Rhonda and Ron Blake, Francis Blanchard, Elizabeth Brenchley, Maggie Broadbent, Geoff Brown, Senator John Button, Helga Cammell, Sir Roderick Carnegie, Bernard Cherrick, Dr Colin Clark (for a letter), Professor Manning Clark, Dr Harry Cohen and June Cohen, Justice Judith Cohen, Peter Coleman, David Combe, Sir John Crawford, Chris Crellin, Col Cunningham, Sir George and Lady Currie, Cliff Dolan, Barry Donovan, John Ducker, G.L. Duffield, Don Dunstan, Sir John Egerton, H.E. Michael Elitzur, Senator Gareth Evans, Coral and George Fisher, Charlie Fitzgibbon, Bernard Fortin, Gwen Geater, Ray Geitzelt, Saadia Gelb, Rev. Allan George, Professor Jim Hagan (for books), Professor Keith Hancock, Albert Hawke, Rev. Clem Hawke, Dr Ron Hieser (deceased), Bob Hogg, Clyde Holding, Beatrice Holt, Rev. Clarence Hore, Jock Innes (for a letter), Bill Kelty, Pat Kennelly (deceased), H.E. Abraham Kidron and Shoshana Kidron, Sir Richard and Lady Kirby, Jack Knight, Eddie Kornhauser, I.L. Lagergren, Bill Landeryou, Harry Leece, Isi Leibler, Bill Leslie, Sam Lipski, Jennie McLellan, David McBride, Mr Justice McClelland, Gail and Rod Madgwick, Heribert Maier, Isadore Magid, Bruce Masters, Gwen May, Sir John Moore, Paul Munro, Robin Morison, Joe Morris, Amal Mukherjee, Peter Nolan, Zvi Netzer, David Pearce, Shimon Peres, George Polites, Oliver Popplewell, Professor John Poynter, George Poyser, Ben Rabinovitch, Dr Don Rawson, Peter Redlich, Oscar de Vries Reilingh, Doris Rhodes, Joe Riordan, Mr Justice Robinson, George Rockey (deceased), Bob Rogers (for letters), Ben Same, Saul Same, Prof. Geoffrey Sawer, Mike Schildberger, George Seelaf, Dr N. Shavit, Jim Shea, Michael Siew (for letters), John Simonds, Jean Sinclair, E.F. Sivyer (for letters), Dr Bob Smith, The Rt. Hon. Michael Somare (for letters), Harold Souter, Don Stewart, Prof. Sam Stoljar, The Hon. Tony Street, Ari Tel-Shahar, Mr Justice Toohey, Uniting Church parishioners in Bordertown and Maitland, Barry Watchorn, Senator John Wheeldon, Sir Frederick Wheeler (for books), David White, Professor David and Marjorie White, The Hon. Gough Whitlam, Kelvin Widdows, Edgar Williams, Ian Willis (for books), Ralph Willis, Terry Winter (deceased) and Beryl Winter, Francis Wolf, Meg and Jules Zanetti, Patsy Zeppel.

I thank, too, the staff of the current information section of the Parliamentary Library, especially Bobbie Sluyters and Margaret Healy; the staff of the National Library, especially Leoni Warne and Mark Cranfield; and the librarian of the ACTU, Anne Wilson.

A group of four friends, whose expertise is in psychology and political science, were unfailingly generous with their time and their libraries. Many of the insights and ideas in this book are thanks to them. I am especially grateful to Dr Michael Epstein, a child psychiatrist; Professor Ross Martin and Dr Angus McIntyre of La Trobe University; and Dr Graham Little, of Melbourne University. Dr Epstein and Dr McIntyre also had the dubious pleasure of putting up with me as a houseguest for weeks at a time, in Melbourne. Carol Treloar and Ruth Dewar were similarly generous with accommodation in Melbourne and Adelaide, as were Harry and June Cohen and George and Glen Browne in Perth, Sandra Alexander and Nick Herd in Sydney, and Mark Pierce in Tel Aviv. I thank also Margaret and Harry Leece for accommodation in Paris, and Kelvin Widdows for accommodation in Geneva. Travelling costs for this book were large: the hospitality of these people, most of whom had never met me before I arrived on their doorsteps, was of great help in keeping my expenses down. H.E. David Goss and Ann Goss from the Australian Embassy, Tel Aviv, and Jim Shea, from the US Embassy, Tel Aviv, were kind to me beyond the bounds of diplomacy. I wish to thank also staff of the ILO, especially John Simonds, who arranged my programme there, and staff of Histadrut, especially Ephraim Bar-Schmuel, for arranging my programme and taking me on a tour of Israel.

I could not have begun this book had it not been for the Literature Board of the Australia Council: it provided me with a two-year senior writer's grant to live on while I was researching. My publisher, Morry Schwartz, gave me a handsome advance to meet travelling costs.

The book could not have been brought to conclusion without the help of three women: Tess van Sommers, my psychological companion, who, as ever, advised and encouraged me; Elizabeth Douglas, who edited the manuscript with great care; and Jan Bourke, who typed it beautifully. I thank them all. I am grateful, too, to Jean Sinclair, the personal assistant of R.J. Hawke, for spending so much time in passing messages to him from me, and in finding research material; and to John Ducker for reading the manuscript.

My mentor and friend, Peter Ryan, of Melbourne University Press, also read the manuscript for me when he was very busy, and when I had reached a stage of exhaustion and despondency. There was great pressure of time in producing the book: chapter by chapter, in the later stages, it was edited and marked up as it was written. This speedy delivery caused in me a sort of post-natal depression during the fortnight's break between finishing writing and waiting for typesetting to begin, and I was overcome with doubts. Peter Ryan's encouragement, arrived like a basket of flowers in winter.

Finally, I thank my husband, Tony Pratt, for his patience, and my son, Louis Pratt, who, for a nine-year-old, takes great care of his mother.

Foreword

There is a school which holds that biographies of the living should not be written, because they cannot be honest. Indeed, the problems confronting the biographer of a living subject are daunting, especially if — as in the case of R.J. Hawke — the writer knows that much of what she reveals about her subject may be used and misused against him, in his lifetime, perhaps to the detriment of a career that is in mid-term. Such considerations have also concerned Hawke. It is a mark of his candour and integrity that he has permitted me, as an authorised biographer, to write about him critically and often unflatteringly and that, in the tradition of his spiritual ancestor, Cromwell, he is willing to be presented 'warts and all'. The only area I have avoided is a discussion of the Hawke children, whose privacy has already been invaded over many years. I have omitted information about the children at the request of Hazel Hawke. Her desire to protect them, and not to have re-published matters which have already appeared in the Press, has been a price worth paying for her help and unflinching frankness, both in giving information and in reading the manuscript for accuracy of detail. I have been guided by her perceptions a great deal, while exercising the responsibility to reach my own conclusions.

It is, surely, one of the most unnerving experiences in any life to have the past loom up, made solid in words. When Sir Richard Kirby first read the manuscript of the biography I had written about him, he exclaimed, 'Oh, God. I feel like a full frontal nude!' Hawke made a similar remark in the same situation: 'This is traumatic — like seeing your face in a mirror with a thousand facets. Some of the images seem to me grotesque.'

I have taken the view that there is no single truth to be told about something as complex and shifting as a fifty-year life span, but rather many truths, from various perspectives which, when viewed together, reveal the dimensions of personality. To do this I have had to rely on people who have known Hawke at different stages of his life. Throughout the book I have allowed them to speak for themselves about him, offering opinions which, sometimes, are contradictory but out of which, I think, a coherent pattern emerges.

While the great drawback to biographies of the living or recently dead is the problem of candour — and, under Australian law, libel — an advantage lies in the wealth of information that may be collected, either from the subject or from those people who have known him or her. Importantly, too, friends, enemies and relations can provide a heavy counterweight to the subject's self-view. In Hawke's case their assistance to me has been crucial, for he is a man of dominating personality and persuasiveness and one, moreover, whose legal training has enabled him to confound critics with dextrous, logical argument. I make no claim to have been able, at all times, to withstand the force of Hawke's self-perceptions, but I have tried to present them as his own, by giving them as transcripts of his descriptions of situations, and where possible, presenting different views. The book is full of voices, for it is largely an oral history.

The use of oral history — in plain language, interviews — overcomes to some extent a major difficulty in writing about twentieth-century lives: lack of documentation. Telephones, radio, television, the whole world of audio-visual technology, has altered us so much: people have abandoned, for example, the custom of committing their intimate thoughts to letters and diaries, the documents which were once the primary source of a biographer. But oral history is only a partial solution — for what the middle-aged man recalls, let us say, about his parents is, generally, different from what the child, writing a diary, may have thought of them and may have later, unconsciously, built in to his behaviour in reaction to those thoughts. Again, the recollections of people who knew the subject in childhood are an important counterweight.

A particular problem created by the telephone is that much historically relevant communication is given over to it in the adult's career, where once the same transactions would have been made in writing. Oral history helps bridge the gaps — sometimes inadequately, sometimes much better than any written record: the Nixon White House tapes are, so far, the most celebrated example of the superiority of an oral record to a formal, written one. Wherever possible I have tape-recorded interviews.

I did some early work on this book in mid-1979 but did not turn my full attention to it until the beginning of 1980. At the time Hawke was still, as he described it later, 'climbing the mountain' — that is, struggling with his drinking problem. By the time I began writing, in mid-1981, he seemed to have conquered the mountain. By now he has been a teetotaller for two years. Much of this book is the story of Hawke's battle with alcohol. Much of it also is the story of a life contending with what I have called 'a dream' — that is, Hawke's ambition to be the political leader of his country. I have labelled it a dream not to suggest unreality, but because it is an aspect of something that is larger and vaguer than the specific goal of political leadership, and is, rather, a yearning towards unity. The vision has come and gone throughout his life, like a recurrent dream that is part of a broader field of emotion. Intertwined with it are other 'dreams' — International House, the ACTU enterprises, peace in the Middle East — whatever their focus, all of them flowing out from the same powerful source.

One of the Hawke family dreams was so like gossamer that I felt I could not include it in the text, but record it now: Hawke's father told me that his favourite chapter of the Bible concerned the Building of the Temple, explaining, 'David planned it, but it was his son, Solomon, who executed it'. It was only when this biography was almost complete that Hawke learned that his father had been an office holder of the ALP and in youth had wanted a political career himself.

At the time I began research Hawke had decided to try to live out his ambitious vision of political leadership. That, and his recent struggle with drink, have given a shape and motifs to the book which may well, from the longer view, seem artificial. A life of Hawke written posthumously would perhaps give a very different emphasis to the themes of alcohol and ambition — or what may be termed hedonism and social integration. This is, therefore, a partial life and will be to some people an example of the wrong-headedness of not only attempting the biography of a living subject but of one in mid-career.

I think it has been worth writing, for a number of reasons: one, obviously, is the intrinsic interest of the subject. Another is that it has provided an opportunity to trap information which otherwise will vanish as its living sources die, information about a social institution for which I feel profound respect (and often irritation): the Australian trade union movement. Frustrating and foolish as it sometimes is, I believe the freedoms of our society are carried on its shoulders.

Blanche d'Alpuget
May 1982, Canberra

Postscript: In less than a year our political landscape has been transformed: in May 1982 the Australian mainland had only one Labor government and Malcolm Fraser bestrode the continent with such authority that it seemed the Faustian pact his Party had made to gain power in 1975 could stretch forward, without horizon. Today there are five Labor governments in Australia, and Hawke is Prime Minister. His personality, as delineated in the following pages, has changed in emphasis in the past three years: the process of struggle and suffering which leads to wisdom and which began in Hawke in the late 1970s has produced a man at peace with himself, prepared, finally, for the task to which he was trained. Or, as it may appear now, was destined.
B d'A
March 1983, Jerusalem

Chapter One

R.J. Hawke was born, on the brink of the Great Depression, into a family and background that would seem rightly to have belonged not to the twentieth but to the early nineteenth century. People have come to see him as a worldly man, one who has built an international reputation for courage and who is now striving for the highest position of power in his country. What is forgotten, or has been grasped only fleetingly, is that he was reared in the narrowest of social enclaves: in small town, fundamentalist Christianity. The stresses set up in him by bursting free of that rigid mould, while retaining many of its values, have created an unusually complex personality.

The Hawkes accepted the popular meaning of the name Robert: 'Of shining fame'. His mother, who said she had moments of acute awareness resembling precognition — she would sometimes press her fingers to her temples and say, 'Oh! I've just had a flash!' — chose the name for him before he was born, sure that it would be suitable.

Ellie Hawke already had one son whom she loved passionately and she hoped that the second baby would be a girl. Her craving for a daughter was immoderate. But when she took out the Bible each day, keeping a vow she had made in childhood, she told friends and relations that she was astonished how often it fell open, as if by design, at the early chapters of Isaiah, and how her eye was drawn to the verses foretelling the birth of great sons — The sign of Immanuel and The Prince of Peace: 'For unto us a child is born, unto us a son is given: and the government shall be upon his shoulder . . .'

Ellie had spent nearly a decade, since the birth of her first child, Neil, wishing to have another, a daughter. But in that time she had only a miscarriage. At last she consulted a doctor and took his advice to have an operation; by early 1929, soon after the family moved to Bordertown in

South Australia, she was pregnant once more. At first she planned to call the new baby Elizabeth. However, when it seemed that the Bible kept leading her to Isaiah, Ellie began to feel that she was being given a sign, and told people, 'I think it's another boy'.

She and her husband, Clem, believed that events are planned by God. When, in the pre-dawn hours of 9 December 1929, in the darkness before a scorching summer day, she again gave birth to a son, they felt that the baby in some indefinable way was different from others, and that he was a destined instrument of the Lord.

Clem Hawke recalled:

> Even the matron in the hospital said, 'There is something special about this baby'. He was very beautiful. But there was something else, perhaps the configuration of his features or the way he moved in his crib. People felt it. When we had him christened a few months later by Dr Keik, my former theological teacher, Keik said, 'This is a *special* child'. Shakespeare summed it up: 'There is a divinity that shapes our ends, rough hew them though we may'. The same thing applies to destiny, I believe. We thought he was destined for a great future, even then.

The baby was christened Robert James Lee. James was the name of his paternal grandfather; Lee was his mother's maiden name.

Edith Emily Lee (as Ellie had been christened) was a woman who was outstanding in her community before she was thirty. Half a century later, when she was dead, there were people in the country towns of South Australia who recalled her as a force that had changed their lives for the better. Mostly they were women who, as girls, had come under the spell of Ellie's mission in life: to educate girls to be independent, forthright and teetotal. She encouraged these qualities in boys, too, but had a special tenderness for her own sex and its oppressions. She was not a feminine woman: by temperament she was impatient, aggressive and dogmatic. Physically she was plain-featured, although her smile was remarkably beautiful — 'She made you feel as if the world had lit up', a student recalled. She was of average height for a woman of those days, and slim, but strongly-made: Ellie had splendid health for almost eighty years, and the energy of a racehorse. Those who loved Ellie remembered her with a mingling of affection and awe; beside her, other women appeared timid, enervated and dishonest. She would not tell or tolerate 'even a white lie, for the sake of making social relations easier'. Many found her frankness intolerable, as later others were to find the frankness of her son unacceptable. All her life Ellie lived in a rage of activity, even in childhood exhausting herself, collapsing temporarily, 'then jumping up and saying, "I'm right now!" and rushing off on some new project'. A brother-in-law said, 'Ellie was a woman who lived two years in every one'. She was the daemon, the driving force, in her son's life.

Clem Hawke was its star of navigation.

Many of the puzzling characteristics of Robert Hawke, much of his apparently paradoxical behaviour, can be traced to the fact that, in time, he rejected much of his early training, and to another fact — that from birth he was subjected to two strong, contrary forces: physically and temperamentally his parents were, in important aspects, opposites.

Clem was tall and slight, strikingly handsome, whimsical, diplomatic and flirtatious. His daughter-in-law recalled, 'Clem could make you feel as if you were the most interesting person he'd ever met in his life'.

He and Ellie were Celts, both with grandparents born in Cornwall who had immigrated to the copper fields of South Australia in the middle of the nineteenth century. Both had been reared as Methodists, both came from an age when worldly ambition and spiritual virtue existed in harmony and both, in their own ways, were agitators. They wanted to change the world by exhortation. Beyond that their social similarities went no further.

Clem left school at twelve and had worked on a milk run then had been apprenticed to a blacksmith. His family was poor; his father, a Kapunda copper miner, was 'Labor from his toenails to his hair roots'.

Ellie had completed high school and teachers' college. Her family was prosperous and politically conservative. Her father, Will, who had begun life in poverty, became a wheat and barley farmer in the Yorke Peninsula and, in middle age, was able to afford the luxury of a trip 'home' to his ancestral village in Cornwall. He arrived there dressed in top hat and tails.

Methodist rectitude in the Lee household ruled the smallest details of daily life: Ellie, who could not tolerate idleness, was raised in the belief that it was wicked to knit on the Sabbath, for example. In her social milieu there were those who regarded playing-cards as toys of the Devil, and who would go without sauce for their Sunday lunch rather than break the Sabbath ruling against work, by drawing the cork from a sauce-bottle.

In Will Lee's youth the fires of Methodist revivalism had swept the South Australian copper fields, arousing ancient passions:

> Unless one lived with [the miners] in those revival days it would be impossible to appreciate such scenes as occurred. Those were the days when preachers spoke of Hell with an absolute belief in it as the abode of damned souls. It can be imagined what an effect the denunciation of sinfulness would produce on the uneducated 'man with a past'. Swearers, blasphemers, drunkards, men with loud voices and boisterous in their excesses were caught up in the tide of revivals . . . One evening [a preacher] became so overwhelmed with holy rage at those who had crucified Christ that he unconsciously turned and spat over in the western corner of the church.[1]

In Will's adulthood those fires still smouldered beneath his roof and in his talks as a lay preacher there was an echo of that old, sulphurous fury with the unrighteous.

James Hawke, in contrast, was an unemotional Methodist; the social properness, which was a strong characteristic of the Lee household and which never left Ellie, was less noticeable among the Hawkes. They were church-goers, but nothing could quench the reckless gaiety and playfulness of the tribe of seven Hawke children. 'We Hawkes had a streak of devilry', one said. Others remember, 'You could not be in the door five minutes before Millie [one of Clem's sisters] would say, "Right! Now for a game of cards!" '

The Lee family had the Victorian passion for public duty, for helping others who, being less determined, less strong, less faithful to the Lord's command-ments than they, had met misfortune. Will, a man of quick and fiery temper, had been 'a bigoted Methodist and a bigoted Tory', but he was also 'the most generous man in the world'. He had literally given itinerant men, whom he housed and fed when they called at his farm, the shirt from his back. Having retired comfortably from the land Will Lee ended his days working in a cement factory and giving his wages to the needy. He dropped dead while helping a farmer plant a crop. Energetic determination was the mark of the Lees.

Optimism was the mark of the Hawkes: it flowed into them from the gospels and from the Labor movement. Of the five Hawke boys, two became ministers of religion, four attempted political careers, and one became Premier of Western Australia. An uncle, Dick Hawke, was a Labor candidate in Kapunda, 'but couldn't win against the farmers'. A Hawke cousin else-where in South Australia became a Country Party Member of Parliament. They had quick wits, the Celtic flair for oratory, and were born agitators, wanting to sculpt, from the public emotion they could arouse, the public will to reform society. 'The Hawkes had to use their voices — in politics or from the pulpit', Clem said. 'They had to spread the good news.'

Clem and Ellie both believed that the purpose of existence was a life of unity with God resulting in practical good works. Ellie, who like her father was a lay preacher, had struggled against convention for the right to have an education and a career as a teacher, so that she might educate others. Clem had been weighted down by poverty, unable to plot a course, and by eighteen had held half a dozen ill-paid, unskilled jobs. He was Secretary of the Kapunda branch of the Australian Labor Party and began to dream of a career in Labor politics. He wrote to the Premier of South Australia about the possibility of an urban seat if he moved to Adelaide, but before he had decided to act on the Premier's advice (to contact the Trades Hall), Clem was drawn in a different direction.

By now he was working on a paper-run and was always keen to arrive at the house of Kapunda's Baptist minister, the Rev. Mr John Murray, who had two pretty daughters. Clem spent a good deal of time chatting to them. At length, Mr Murray invited him inside for conversations of a more serious nature. Soon afterwards, on a wintry night, Clem was totally immersed in the cold font of Mr Murray's church to emerge a Baptist, ready to become a home missionary.

Two years later, by the time he met the schoolteacher Edith Emily Lee (and re-named her Ellie), Clem had left the Baptist church and returned to Methodism. He was now a Methodist home missionary, stationed at Forster on the River Murray in South Australia.

Ellie was in charge of her third school, at Forster. Her sisters had accepted the lot of farmers' daughters: they had left school at thirteen and stayed home to help their mother, but Edith Emily had been 'education mad' from early childhood.

Within days of meeting Clem Hawke, Ellie was much attracted to the charming young preacher, five months her junior, uneducated, unordained and with political views which for her were radical and for her father verged on treachery: the Hawkes were anti-conscriptionist.

For his part Clem was fascinated — as others were to be either fascinated or angered — by Ellie's strength of character, her forthright manner, her physical vitality, and her sense of purpose.

Hawke said of his parents, 'Mum just loved dad. He was the boss, but there beside him was this incredibly strong woman. And she would tend to take over. As a minister's wife mum was unbelievably supportive — it was like having two ministers for the parish.'

In June 1920, a year after they met, Clem and Ellie were married, in Thebarton Methodist Church, Adelaide. In the meantime Clem, who was only twenty-two, had changed churches once more — this time, permanently. He had joined Congregationalism, the church that, as a radical puritan sect, had inspired Cromwell, the Pilgrim Fathers, Milton and Bunyan. It was committed to social equality (including the ordination of women) and the authority of the laity over the clergy. Of all Christian churches, it seemed to Clem, the Congregational was the most liberal, least dogmatic, least concerned with wickedness, most optimistic, and the closest in its functioning to Labor's vision of the Brotherhood of Man.

In time, Clem converted Ellie to Congregationalism, but the old fire-and-brimstone pungency of outback South Australian Methodism, with its emphasis on sin and backsliding and its history of grim decorousness shot through with flares of revivalism, seems never completely to have left her. Ellie retained her Methodist indignation against the unrighteous, the slothful, the dishonest, the weak. Hawke was to learn from his mother that 'it would be sinful — she didn't use the word, but she conveyed the idea — sinful if I did not use my talents'. Clem took a gentler view of the world.

A few weeks after marriage Ellie became pregnant and her teaching career had to be abandoned. Her first child was born at Houghton in the Adelaide Hills where Clem, still unordained, had been invited by the congregation to become their minister. Ellie named the baby John (after her favourite brother) and Neil, a name whose popular meaning, accepted by the Hawkes, is 'champion'. He was known by his second name. From the beginning Ellie doted on him. Hawke said later, 'Neil was *her* son, her first-born, her favourite. He'd had nine years to be her son, before I came along.'

The family moved to New Zealand for a couple of years (where Clem was ordained) then back to South Australia, to Renmark. Here Ellie returned to teaching. 'Education is the key to the world', she told her pupils. 'Read, read, read. Learn, learn, learn. God gave you a brain — you're meant to use it. If you haven't got a book to read, get a dictionary and learn a page of it each day.' Although she was impatient with adults, she was patient and loving with children, and, longing for a daughter of her own, she lavished affection upon parish girls, whom she treated as favourite nieces, and upon favourite nieces, whom she treated as daughters. Around 1926 she asked a sister to give her one of her daughters to rear. The sister refused.

When Ellie became pregnant again in 1929 she knew, from medical advice, that the second baby would be her last. Half a century later Hawke recalled, uneasily, 'My mother wanted me to be girl. She used to say, "You were meant to be Elizabeth". That used to annoy me. I thought she was silly to say it, because I was me! Bob.'

From his early years his relationship with his mother was complex, even problematic, affected by his awareness that he had disappointed her in one area that he was incapable of changing — his sex — and also by the knowledge that, almost in recompense for his unwelcome gender, she had great expectations of him. In young adulthood he 'often shouted at Ellie', a relation said. The test of wills between them had a primal history and was perhaps the seed, developed later by Hawke's physical weakness and illnesses, of his striving to become powerful.

It took him half a century to make a sort of peace between the warring states within him, a confrontation that arose from his biological maleness on one side, and on the other, the phantom Elizabeth against whom he, Bob, had to fight from the beginnings of life. A defiant masculinity was a central aspect of Hawke's personality: its battles for ascendancy were to be played out through displays of swashbuckling virility — in language, sporting prowess, aggressive competitiveness, and through many invasions into enemy territory: in common speech, through womanising.

Ellie, for her part, quickly adjusted, at least superficially, to the disappointment of another son: to her it was God's will and she bowed to it. The boy, she decided, would be reared to social duty of a high order and his efforts would be recognised and honoured. When Hawke was in his early twenties she told his fiancée, 'We called him Robert because it would sound good later, when he became Sir Robert'.

Hawke was made a Companion of Australia, an honour superior to knighthood, in January 1979.

Chapter Two

Heaven lay around Hawke in his infancy. He was reared in a country manse in a quiet way of life deeply rooted in tradition, the seasons accentuated by church festivals, the year divided according to divine significance. It was a world rounded and harmonious.

The community in Bordertown was still snug, not yet touched by the financial crash of the previous April. The Tatiara district, of which Bordertown is the centre, is one of the richest agricultural areas in Australia. In the late 1920s the town was booming: people there only read about the disasters in the cities. Scullin, who had been Prime Minister for two months, had, in the second week of December, just offered the State premiers £1 million for road work to provide employment. In the New South Wales coalfields the nation's greatest industrial dispute in the twentieth century, a lockout by employers, was dragging on and the miners and their dependants were half-starved. Police occupied the towns of the Hunter coalfields, scab labour was employed, a miner was shot dead, others were injured. But in Bordertown the only signs of depression were the scores of travel-soiled men jumping from trains then hanging around the railway yards, alert for a beckoning finger from one of the farmers loading his produce on the trains. 'It was a good year for hay, 1929. You could get any amount of labour', an oldtimer remarked sardonically.

The Congregational parish was the largest in the district, exceeding the Methodists; Clem and Ellie were among the town's élite. Ellie was considered a snob by some parishioners, 'because she was educated — heddykated we used to say — and was a schoolteacher. It was something to be a school-teacher in those days. I felt she looked down on people who weren't heddy-kated.' The 'Congs', as they called themselves, were in a mood as expansive as their district's in the late 1920s. When the horse selected for Clem's use on pastoral calls proved troublesome the laity decided, boldly, to buy him a motorcar. It was a 1927 four-door, cloth-top Chevrolet and cost £150. With wheat selling at only a little less than its 1925 price and sheep still doing well, the parish could afford it. It could afford, too, to keep the minister's table supplied with mutton, butter and milk and his hearth with firewood. Ellie grew the best vegetables in town — 'lettuces, even in winter!' people remembered, fifty years later.

The manse was a four-roomed house of local limestone with high ceilings and a lean-to at the back for the kitchen, laundry and bathroom. A croquet green was across the road and a couple of minutes walk away was the church, also of limestone. Although it was built in the late nineteenth century it had the friendly, candid symmetry of Georgian architecture. It has been internally renovated in recent years, but in those days its most striking feature was an arch painted on the wall at the head of the nave, lettered in blue, gold and black, with the motto *He Who Watches Over Israel Slumbers Not Nor Sleeps*. Israel — sung about, spoken of, yearned for — glowed as a portentous presence at the heart of spiritual life. Israel was a distant, shining land, enigmatic and ageless, a link between the living and the dead, the present and the past, God and man. 'I vividly recall', a woman wrote to Hawke years later, 'watching your mother basking in pride when a piece of the Holy Land was named after her son for his great humanitarian efforts . . . she had tears in her eyes listening to the sermon and speech given by your father on that glorious day in Israel . . . one of the happiest that you could have provided for them in their lives.' Israel had entered Hawke's life before he could speak, for Ellie took him to church from birth.

It was in church that parishioners first noticed how he was being reared. 'The trouble was', a Bordertown man complained, 'his mother wouldn't smack him. He'd be up there in the front, wriggling and throwing things on the floor, or yelling. He was completely undisciplined. It wasn't fair to Clem, trying to give the sermon, when there was a baby disrupting things. I used to want to knock his block off.' In the twenty-five years Hawke lived with his parents he was never once struck by either of them. 'I was', he said, 'dreadfully spoiled'. The spoiling came from both parents, especially from Hawke's father.

Clem adored his second son. He said,

> From early on I felt special affinity, a drawing towards Bobbie. It's a mysterious thing — Ellie had it with Neil. It's something that just happens sometimes in families — you remember Joseph and the coat of many colours? His father felt it. You can't say it's right or wrong to have a favourite child . . . Bobbie had an outflowing magic about him.

He bathed and dressed this baby, things he had not done for Neil, and Hawke's earliest memories were all of 'love — an overwhelming love. I can't describe how passionately my father loved me; I was just dad's boy.'

The relationship between father and son, which was so intense that Ellie worried about their dependence upon each other, equipped Hawke for life with the capacity to feel and, without embarrassment, to express love for his own sex. It also seems to have cast the emotional die that patterned his later relationships with other men: Hawke is intensely loyal and uncritical of his friends and in return evokes from them an unusual fondness, a paternal indulgence. All his closest men friends have been older than Hawke, either in years or in worldliness; all have had Clem's desire to give of themselves to him. Men have lent him their houses to entertain in, their motorcars to ride in, their yachts to holiday on; they have come to his kitchen to cook his meals; to sit at his bedside and amuse him when he was ill; they have taken him shopping and chosen his clothes. George Rockey, a co-builder of Australia's largest transport company, TNT, was a type of father to Hawke in the late 1970s. When Rockey was dying in 1981 and too weak to walk much, he worried about Hawke's health and his wardrobe: 'I send Bob to my tailor now, so his suits are good. But I'm not satisfied about his socks — I must take him to the proper place for underwear', he said. Sir Peter Abeles, Rockey's senior business partner, is another very close friend. A journalist recalled going to dinner one evening with Hawke and Abeles:

> Sir Peter gave Bob the keys to his Rolls Royce. Bob drove it, laughing his head off, like a kid with a fantastic toy . . . I was in business by myself at the time, and in financial difficulties. A couple of days later I got a phone call from Abeles, whom I barely knew. He chatted for a while, then said, 'I think I could help you, if you would like'. I was staggered — he was offering me 25 grand at 5%. Finally I asked, 'Why are you doing this?' He replied, 'Oh well, we both have a very close friend', and the penny dropped. He knew Bob and I had been mates for thirty years, so that made me somebody he would help, because of his affection for Bob.'

Throughout Hawke's life men have been drawn by 'the outflowing magic' that Clem felt — and encouraged — and have responded to it by behaving like fathers or doting uncles. (Hawke called Rockey 'Uncle George', and Rockey signed himself by this name on letters to Hawke.)

It seems as if, in his earliest years, an emotional stage were set and roles allotted to actors, and that the play was performed again and again. While this welded psychological bonds of great strength between Hawke and his friends the son-parent configuration of relationships became, with Hawke's increasing age, inappropriate — even undesirable — for it was holding part of his personality in limbo. Men and women only a few years older than Hawke called him 'The Boy' when he was in his late forties; he was treated, by intimates, as a boy who needed adult care and guidance. The role began to exasperate Hawke, and his friends.

Clem's special son, however, was also Ellie's special baby, a gift to her from God. But the intensity of affection between father and son tended to challenge her status with the child, and later events in the family were to cause whatever incipient competition there may have been between the parents to develop into rivalry for the boy. A relation recalled, 'Bob could play his family off against each other: he was the centre of attention and the adults competed for him'. This was, perhaps, the origin of Hawke's later extraordinary success in getting publicity: he had learned, when very young, how agreeable it was to be a cynosure, and in adulthood had an inner need to recreate — before a bank of television cameras, or a roaring crowd — the emotional landscape of earlier years. 'Publicity is one of the things that keeps you going in politics', another politician remarked. 'The days when Bob's been all over the news-papers and the television I've seen him smiling. And sad, when he wasn't.'

Given the circumstances of his birth perhaps it was to be expected that his parents would rear him more tenderly than his elder brother. Certainly the difference in parental treatment of the Hawke boys was profound: Neil had few of the indulgences allowed to Bobbie. Before he was a teenager Neil was punished for misdemeanours 'with a hiding from me once a fortnight — and that's when he was good', Ellie said; sometimes Clem gave him the strap. In his teenage years, in school holidays, Neil worked as a farmhand. Hawke took his first holiday job when he was at university.

Bordertown parishioners remembered Neil as a quiet, well-mannered boy yet Clem and Ellie both fondly described him as a young firebrand, physically reckless and deaf to caution, while Hawke, they said, was a quiet, angelic child with whom they could reason. Perhaps both accounts are accurate, from different perspectives. But as Hawke grew older he developed some of the characteristics that his parents attributed to their elder son. Most people want their children to live for them the lives they cannot: it may be that at an unspoken level the Hawkes encouraged their sons to break free of the extreme decorousness of genteel, *petit bourgeois* parish life, while insisting that they maintain the essence of Christian values.

Clem took Bobbie on rounds of the parish and by the time the child was three he had begun to model himself actively on his father: a bleary box-brownie photograph of 1933 shows Hawke, hands raised, preaching to an old woman lying on a cane *chaise longue* in her garden. She was too ill to attend church; Hawke had announced, 'I'm going to cheer you up, like my dad'.

Clem said,

> We taught him the whole time, not only by talking to him, but also by the practical life we lived . . . In the Congregational church we had no creeds as such — the only creed I'll accept is the Apostles — but we built religion around the human side of Christ's ministry. And, of course, the divine side. We built it around His example — giving counsel to the

dejected and the despairing, healing the sick, putting out a social programme for the betterment of the world. What's the use of preaching the gospel to a man with an empty stomach! It's all pie in the sky, when what he wants is pie now.

The crash came to Bordertown in 1931: wheat dropped to 2s. 7d. a bushel and oats to 1s. 3d. A dozen eggs sold for 3d. Hawke was too young to remember the boom years and knew only the period of struggle and misery for farmers. Childhood memories of his parents' friends talking about low prices, bad seasons and bankruptcies affected him strongly, instilling in him attitudes to rural life that were much more sympathetic than is normal among urban Labor movement officials. Country people noticed the difference: in 1979, in a national survey, farmers and cattlemen voted Hawke their first choice of leaders.

With the Depression Clem and Ellie had to work much harder. On Sundays there was a special collection known as the Distress Fund. Ellie made meals from what she had to hand in the kitchen for the swagmen who came to her door, and would offer the manse's spare room to people in need of lodging for a night, or for weeks. The ethic of hospitality transmitted to Hawke: his own household, friends commented later, resembled a motel, with all sorts of people making themselves at home there. 'Bob's the easiest touch in the world', a man said of Hawke in middle age. 'I've seen real rogues, people you wouldn't look at, nudge him for a loan. He's gullible, like that.' It was a family characteristic: Clem and Ellie once loaned most of their savings to a woman in distress, never to see the money again. Hawke recalled, 'I used to be angry with my mother sometimes, watching her give money to characters whom even I knew were telling lies'.

Clem was considered an outstanding minister because of his pastoral work: while other churches' congregations diminished in Bordertown during the Depression, the numbers in the Congregational parish grew. 'He had the gift of listening', a parishioner recalled. 'He would never reject anyone. One day he ate seven afternoon teas, rather than discourage people from telling him their troubles by turning down their food.' During these years when Hawke was his father's shadow, visiting with him the houses of the dejected, despairing and sick, he was absorbing attitudes that were to stay with him long after he had rejected the Congregational as his church and Christianity as his faith: he was learning to dream of a future career in which he would be able to benefit humanity directly and practically. He was also acquiring his father's habits — especially sympathetic listening, one of the most useful skills for a politician and a negotiator. Chris Crellin, Hawke's chauffeur-bodyguard during his latter years at the ACTU, recalled,

I used to watch Bob at social functions. The way he could listen to people was brilliant: he'd cock his head on one side, like he does, and would stand there letting them bash his ear for half an hour. Whether he was really listening or not, I don't know. But he always looked as if he were following every word they said. Getting him to leave a place was impossible. He'd say 'Goodbye' and two hours later would be only ten feet closer to the door, listening to some story about a kid needing a job or somebody's aunty from India wanting a visa for Australia. When he'd finally get in the car he'd have a pocketful of bits of paper with people's names on them, people he was going to try to help. It was a never-ending thing. People would eat him up.

Hawke puts high value on what may be termed his pastoral skill. To a question about which of the thousands of newspaper articles about him he liked most, he replied, 'There was one in the mid-1960s, by Richard Hall. He said I was "a good listener". I was proud about that.'

While Clem's long suit was fellow-feeling, Ellie's was action. In Bordertown she was inaugural secretary-treasurer of the primary school welfare club; she gave lessons in handicrafts and divinity; she was an office bearer of the Girl Guides; she trained the children's choir; she worked for the Women's Christian Temperance Union. She was often in conflict with the parents of girls she was teaching because, with the crash, farmers were taking their daughters out of school and putting them to work as farmhands or housekeepers.

Before Ellie was married she had angered her sisters by resisting farm housekeeping; married, she maintained the view that housework should be shared by husband and wife, and so it was: Clem did half the chores. Ellie rescued several girls from manual drudgery by having them live in the manse. Parishioners had a respectful caution for what was known around town as 'the sharp edge of Mrs Hawke's tongue'.

There was never enough occupation for Ellie and in Bordertown she took up croquet, becoming an office bearer of the club. She had been a keen tennis player but found croquet more mentally stimulating — 'tennis lacks skill', she declared — and in later life croquet became 'Ellie's second religion'. Hawke said, 'Croquet! The politics and rules of croquet that we used to get at home were enough to drive you bloody mad. It seemed to be the most important thing in the world.' He too plays croquet with enthusiasm; he once chased Margaret Whitlam across the green at the Prime Minister's Lodge, waving his mallet at her when she beat him on a shot and whooping, 'I've got to win! You know I've got to win!' As a university friend remarked vividly, if not quite accurately, 'Bob was his mother — inside out'.

At the beginning of 1933 the family made an important decision. Neil, who was eleven, was sent to boarding school. Ellie was determined that he should have the best possible opportunities so he was enrolled at King's College, a Baptist and Congregational school in Adelaide. Neil's departure from home turned Hawke, in effect, into an only child. His 'spoiling' increased.

In 1935 Clem was called to his next post in the Yorke Peninsula town of Maitland. The congregation there knew nothing about their new minister and his wife, with the exception of a detail that had drifted across hundreds of miles of pasture, bush and desert: 'The Hawkes have a terrible kid'.

Hawke was not yet five. Already a motif in his life was emerging: people saw him as untamed, a disruptive element, an outsider who would have to prove himself before he would be accepted.

Chapter Three

Hawke was a highly-strung child. Before the upheaval of moving to Maitland he had been robust, but in the new environment, with a humid climate, he stopped growing at a normal rate and was often ill with respiratory tract infections.

He was sent to school in Maitland, where he was known as Little Bobbie, and was regularly bashed-up — according to fellow pupils — because he started most of the fights himself. It seems he disliked school at first. 'I'd see him going off in the morning with his satchel on his back, bawling his head off all the way down the street', a townswoman said. His friends, after a time, were boys several years his senior, who acted as elder brothers, and his closest friend was one who was considered socially inappropriate for the minister's son. This was Reo Allen, one of the nine red-blooded offspring of the local truck-driver. The Allen boys were handy with their fists. Reo, who later worked in a factory in Adelaide, said, 'I was a kind of protector for Little Bobbie — anybody who punched him had to fight me. He was a real small kid, but a brainy bugger — if you'll excuse the expression.' Teasing girls, including a young woman teacher at whom they would shout insults in the street, was a favourite pastime.

Hawke was consistently top or next to top of his class, his rival being the headmaster's daughter. 'The fact was', he said, 'I had a head-start, because my parents read to me'.

What they read was significant. For both Clem and Ellie the Bible was the foundation of education. While Hawke was still too young to be introduced to the complex beauty of the King James translation, he was raised on a bowdlerised work, Hurlbut's *Story of the Bible*: 'The Complete Bible Story, running from Genesis to Revelations, Told in the Simple Language of To-day for Young and Old, Profusely Illustrated with Colour Plates and Half-tone Engravings'. In the charmed circle of family love, Clem, reading to Hawke at bedtime, introduced to his son's mind images of heroes that were to stay with him for life.

Hurlbut's is a handsome volume. The colourful frontispiece shows David, small and barefoot, barely more than a child, alone, facing a huge bearded man who has the advantage of standing on higher ground. Goliath is magnificently armoured in brass shining like gold: breast-plate, helmet, leggings. Behind him on a hill, registering amused disdain for David, lounge the bejewelled princes of the Philistines. The caption reads, 'David's plan to fight the giant did not need any armour, but did need a quick eye, a clear head, a sure aim and a bold heart'. David was one of the many saviours who entered Hawke's imagination in childhood. Years later, describing his career as an industrial advocate, he said, 'I'd look up at the other end of the Bar table, crowded with silks and their juniors, able to buy the best economic advice in the country — they were *black* with money for research — and there I'd be, just me, and I used to think, "Jesus Christ, it's David against Goliath!" '

But the favourite character of Hawke's childhood was Samson, whose story is told in Hurlbut as 'The Strong Man: How He Lived and How He Died', accompanied by black-and-white engravings of the young Samson slaying a lion; Samson beguiled by Delilah; Samson, aged and terrible, destroying the Philistines and himself in the temple of their fish-god, Dagon. Hawke knew the Samson story word for word and shared with him one circumstance: both were Nazarites. Like Samson, Hawke had been pledged by his mother to God as one who would never drink alcohol. In Bordertown Ellie had adopted as her consuming interest the work of the Women's Christian Temperance Union and had enrolled Hawke in its children's branch, the Band of Hope.

The WCTU is a women's movement with a proud history. It was the cause around which nineteenth century feminists gathered in the USA, the UK and the British colonies. Suffragettes wanted the vote so as to be able to bring in prohibition, for alcohol then, as now, was the single greatest catalyst for wife-murder and assault, child bashing and other domestic brutality. The WCTU's motto is 'Agitate, Educate, Legislate' — a motto Hawke was to apply himself throughout his career.

Ellie had shouldered the cause of abstinence with indignation. A parishioner recalled that one afternoon he was taking tea in the manse when she gave him a lecture about the dangers of cigarettes (also disapproved of by the WCTU). After some time Clem, who was listening attentively, unbuttoned his jacket and discreetly held it open for the parishioner to see, in an inside pocket, a packet of Capstans. Clem gave the faintest smile, re-buttoned his jacket and returned his attention to Ellie's remarks. Twenty years later members of the Lee family at Christmas lunch found that Ellie had placed beneath each festive bon-bon a WCTU pamphlet about the dire effects of drink.

She was an effective lay-preacher — 'Ellie would always pluck at your heart-strings', a relation said — but whatever success she had with reforming outsiders, the response from those closest to her was rebelliousness. A niece upon whom she doted (the one she had wanted to adopt) put brandy in the Christmas trifle. A woman who lodged with the Hawkes and who, as a Methodist, disapproved of smoking herself, once smoked a cigarette in Ellie's presence, to defy her. Hawke became a heavy drinker.

In Maitland, parishioners who had heard that Hawke was 'a terrible kid' did not alter their opinion so much as expand it. He was terrible, but he was also lovable. Mothers, in particular, found him endearing — very friendly, full of wit, fun and daring. On Saturday night he would go off to the pictures by himself, while Ellie fretted, 'What's the use? I can't stop him.'

An honorary member of the household in Maitland, Gwen Geater, said:

> Bobbie was one of those kids that you had to make up your mind with, or he'd dominate you. I put him over my knee more times than I can count. It was the only way . . . Clem had taught him to play cricket and on Sundays, when Clem was busy, if you wouldn't play cricket with Bobbie there was no peace. He'd drive you mad until you gave in. But he was so lovable — full of fun, and affectionate. I loved my Robert.

Miss Geater was fourteen years Ellie's junior, her closest friend and co-worker in the WCTU. She was a woman of feminine, dark-eyed good looks and was the dearest of Ellie's 'daughters'. Clem's predecessor in Maitland had been a bachelor; the manse was run-down and church activities which fall to a minister's wife had not been performed. Ellie set out to revolutionise the parish — in short order she had organised the women into building a civic garden to celebrate South Australia's sesquicentenary, for example — but this extra work left her with less time than usual for running her household. Within a couple of weeks of arriving in Maitland she had said to Miss Geater's mother, 'You've got three daughters and I've got none. Give me one of yours', and Gwen had been given over to Ellie as a helpmate.

While many parish women, like Miss Geater, recalled Hawke with affection and often looked after him — Ellie worked a healthy 60 to 80-hour week — his mother was the single important female presence he remembered. He had no grandmother or aunt whom he saw often and doted upon; he could not recall a woman teacher influencing him.

Ellie filled the manse with women and girls; she was forever busy with them on parish or civic activities: women, it seems, entered Hawke's life as rivals for his mother's attention, probably compounding whatever hostility he already felt towards females, on account of 'Elizabeth'. For many years during adulthood there was a certain undertow of ruthlessness in Hawke's treatment of women, in marked contrast to his tolerance and affection for men.

His attachment to his father was still intense. Once, when Clem was called from Maitland to Melbourne to discuss the possibility of becoming a minister there, Hawke announced, 'I can't live without him. Send a telegram for him to come home. I'm going to die.' When Clem was not around and Hawke's contact with the world — even, as he experienced it, with life itself — was broken, the child retreated into nervous, almost hysterical demanding and isolation. 'As a child I had few friends', he said. 'Dad was enough for me. I didn't want anyone else.'

Already one of the paradoxes of Hawke's life was beginning to reveal itself: he had an acute need to belong (to his parents, especially Clem) and an equally strong desire to avoid control (by Ellie and others). The shape of his later political career was beginning to show its outline: the man of the Left who refused to observe the Left's ideology, the labour leader who rejected the authority of The Labor Leader. Speaking of his childhood friendships Hawke observed: 'I was a loner. I wasn't interested in anyone else. I didn't depend on anyone else — I had no need for anyone else. I had my own views about life, I knew what was in my head.' Hawke's identity as a non-conformist was coming to life.

Meanwhile — perhaps because of the telegram episode — Ellie had begun to caution Clem about the pitch of emotion between him and Bobbie. Hawke recalled, 'My mother said dad and I loved each other too much, in the sense that I expected too much of him, and he of me.'

When the family had moved to Maitland in 1935 it had been into a large manse set in a wilderness. Ellie was famous for her gardening and, without reticulated water, she transformed what Hawke called 'that desert of a manse' into an oasis of flowering shrubs, fruit trees and vegetables. There was a tennis court attached to the grounds, adding to the sense of spaciousness Ellie had created. They might have stayed in that town or others in South Australia for years, with Hawke in due course being sent to boarding school in Adelaide. But the summer of 1938-39 shattered the Hawkes' beneficent small world of weekdays spent in good works and Sundays in praise of God and the Holy Land.

That summer was a terrible one for the whole nation. There was the longest heatwave in living memory and bushfires consumed the countryside from Queensland to Tasmania. From Europe there rumbled rumours of war.

Seventy people died during the fires in Victoria; as well, babies died from dehydration and old people from heat prostration. The Adelaide Hills exploded in flames on Black Friday in January; factories had to close; the city ran out of soft drinks and ice, and food was scarce.

Neil Hawke — who had been dux of King's College and had recently landed a job in the State Treasury (at a time when unemployment for young people was running at 20%) was one of those who tried to cool off at an Adelaide novelty, the indoor Unley Crystal Pool. He, like Hawke, loved swimming; he was a fine, manly lad, used to fending for himself and was already living up to the 'champion' of his name. Neil was swimming in competitions and had won prizes in bicycle racing.

The heatwave continued into February. On the 18th Ellie's mother, Matilda, died, aged seventy-seven. At her funeral in Adelaide Ellie and Clem noticed that Neil was pale and quiet. Two days after they had returned to Maitland a telephone call from Neil's landlady told Clem and Ellie that he had been taken to hospital with fever, headache and convulsions. Clem returned immediately to Adelaide. From there he rang Ellie to tell her to come urgently: Neil had meningitis. He had almost certainly contracted it from the Unley pool.

The progress of meningitis is horrific to witness. Headache and convulsions are followed by loss of normal motor functions, destruction of personality, and distortion of the face as purulent liquid from the meninges overflows the cranium, in pints, and forces its way into the tissues of the face. The body wastes to bone as the head enlarges.

For forty-eight hours Clem and Ellie prayed by Neil's bedside. Next morning the drought broke in South Australia with one of the heaviest rains in living memory; it was also the coldest February day in Adelaide for more than thirty years. In the early hours of the following day hospital staff telephoned the Hawkes to come quickly. They set out into the cold, wet night, but by the time they arrived Neil had died.

Chapter Four

They were optimistic people, trusting in God's mercy, and their response to Neil's death was an heroic manifestation of their faith.

Clem planted a wooden cross on the grave in the Mitcham cemetery, Adelaide, and placed a death notice in the *Adelaide Advertiser*:

> HAWKE, on 27 February at a private hospital. John Neil, dearly beloved elder son of Rev. A.C. and Mrs Hawke, Congregational Manse, Maitland . . . 'The golden bowl is broken'.

They returned to Maitland. A parishioner said, 'We thought Clem was made of stone. He showed no emotion whatsoever but went on with his work as if nothing had happened.' For Ellie, sadness was 'too deep for tears . . . [In sixty years] I don't think I ever saw the wife cry', Clem said.

People were astonished then, and afterwards, by how the Hawke family habitually eschewed any discussion of emotional pain, of anything that might be considered 'morbid'; how they and their surviving son denied the existence of personal distress. Hawke had been trained in contempt for wickedness. As the Hawkes rejected Satan, so they rejected the negative aspects of Neil's death and waited for the Lord to reveal to them why He had gathered in a young soul. Hawke never inquired into the nature of his brother's death, never visited his grave or even discovered where he was buried — although he had loved Neil who, Clem said, 'hero-worshipped Bobbie and would rush to play ball with him as soon as he came home from school'.

For a man of emotional make-up, as Hawke is, the family taboo against dwelling on anything negative was a contradiction of nature. His later life was remarkable for moments when 'negative' emotions, kept at bay, would abruptly crowd upon him: Hawke would suddenly roar with anger, or begin to weep.

Hawke has no memory of his mother crying when she returned home, but he realised she was devastated: 'Totally devastated. I don't have a vision of wailing — she wasn't behaving irrationally or anything like that — but I just knew that she was deeply hurt, that she'd lost something that was irreplaceable . . . I had these two problems in childhood: my mother wanted me to be a girl, and then her son died, and I had, somehow, to replace him.' The paradise of his early childhood had been broken: the life he had known as 'dad's boy' was finished; his father had changed — Clem urged the child to turn his affections towards his mother, who awaited him with open arms, and acute anxiety. But as Hawke himself recognised, he could not really replace Neil as Ellie's son: he was a sort of impostor.

Relations said, 'When Neil died Ellie turned all her attention on to Bob. She over-indulged him. She was terrified she would lose him, too.' Indeed, within days of Neil's death Hawke became ill with fever and it was feared that he, too, had meningitis. But it was only one of his stress-related viral attacks.

As for Clem, the grief he had suppressed wore him out, and when parishioners noticed that his natural diplomacy had turned to melancholy aloofness they feared that he was on the path of a nervous breakdown. A fellow Congregational minister who visited Maitland in mid-1939 urged Clem to get away, to start a new life, and offered to arrange a transfer to Western Australia. Hawke remembered the move as 'Joy! As if it were yesterday, this enormous, enormous joy of going on a train across the centre of Australia.'

Clem's new church was in West Leederville, a lower-middle-class suburb of Perth, and within a few weeks the family had found a cottage on the rise of Tate Street, Leederville. Their new home had a meagre front garden, a generous back garden, five rooms, a screened-in back verandah, stained glass kookaburras set in glass panels in the front door and a porthole window in the hall. When Hawke became a householder he showed his affection for the landscape of childhood by choosing a house which carried echoes of the Maitland manse and the Tate Street house: it had a tennis court and a porthole window.

There were no fringe benefits in the West Leederville parish — no rent-free manse, no motorcar, no firewood or food from the farms of parishioners. Clem's wage was the same as that for an unskilled labourer; suddenly life was frugal. For Hawke it was to become cut off from happiness as well, for in 1941 Clem enlisted in the AIF as a pastor. Within six months Hawke was in a second physical decline. He was still small for his age, with poor chest development and skinny limbs. He suffered repeatedly from attacks of sinusitis.

With Clem away, Ellie took in as boarders the wife of a Methodist minister who had also enlisted, and her son, but there was friction between the two women. The boarder recalled,

In the evening she'd bring home from the WCTU a lot of pamphlets and over the tea-table she would give the boys lectures on drinking and smoking. I used to think, 'Oh, no. She'll drive them to it!' Ellie was still grieving over Neil — not openly, but there was an atmosphere in the house. She had kept some of his clothes and sometimes I'd see her open the wardrobe and bury her head in them.

To Hawke and others Ellie, who was a pacifist, remarked after the outbreak of war, 'God took Neil to spare him from shedding blood. Neil would have enlisted, if he'd lived.' The boarder felt that, 'She would be looking for Neil for the rest of her life'.

Ellie had flung herself into WCTU work in Perth and at night was often out at meetings or overseeing a hostel for homeless girls. At home, the other woman complained,

> She wouldn't discipline Bob, who used to be quiet for long periods then have outbreaks of deliberate naughtiness. Ellie would say to me, 'Oh, you speak to him'. She was out — it seemed sometimes every night of the week — and I'd have to put him to bed. He'd always want a bit of love at bedtime — he was a devil of a kid, he'd whinge and whinge until he got his own way, but he was very affectionate. The cat would be there in bed with him, hidden under the blankets. He wasn't allowed to sleep with the cat but every night, sure enough, there it would be. When I'd find it he'd roar with laughter.

In this early period in Perth he developed a resentment for the WCTU, 'because I thought it took up too much of mum's time, almost to my detriment'. He also began to manipulate his parents by throwing tantrums. On the weekends when Clem was due home on leave Hawke would stand at the front gate, staring up Tate Street for the first sight of his father walking down from the trolley bus. He had, he recalled, 'a tremendous tantrum, an unbelievable tantrum on my twelfth birthday, when dad came home on leave and they wouldn't take me to a pirate movie, but went off to see *Pygmalion*'. Where once there had been 'overwhelming love', anger was now intruding more and more into Hawke's life. A sense of powerlessness had overtaken his existence, exaggerated by ill health.

During these years of severe upheaval for the family Hawke's health became so poor as to seem chronically afflicted. He had won a scholarship to Perth Modern School in 1942, but did not excel there. 'I was sickly in the first year at Mod. In my second year I seemed to be sick all the time.' There was a lot of physical fighting at the school and Hawke, smaller and weaker than other boys, got the worst of it. A fellow pupil remembered him as 'very thin, with a pinched look. He was sharp-featured and had a hatchet face for a small boy.' Finally in 1944 Ellie, having exhausted other remedies, took him to a naturopath. The man recommended fasting, then a high-fibre diet with few dairy products, eggs or meat. To this day Hawke has thanked him for 'a total transformation. I became very strong. My body seemed to develop enormously quickly. I took great pride in my physical development — I could mix it with the other kids. I remember the feeling of joy in growing strong, of having a great feeling of confidence that no one physically worried me any more.' One unusual effect was that his hair, which had been straight, became thick and wavy. He had reached puberty, and was enveloped by an ecstatic sense of completeness, as if sexual definition as a male, as Bob, had brought a surge of power. Another pupil, Robin Morison, recalled Hawke after his 'total transformation': 'Bob was one of those often involved in punch-ups. He was very pugnacious. He didn't have a lot of girlfriends — he seemed more interested in sport and being tough than in chasing girls. Also, he did not suffer fools gladly, even then. He would abuse kids for asking silly questions and wasting the class time. He was a real tough-guy.' Hawke recalled,

> Adolescence was a *good* time ... The old masturbation syndrome hit me about the same age as everyone else. I felt guilty about it, I suppose — perhaps more than average guilt. But it didn't detract from the enjoyment. I found it a startlingly interesting new dimension to life. In an embarrassed sort of way dad pushed a couple of books about sex at me. I reckoned I knew as much about it as he did — and I was probably right! ... I was seventeen or eighteen before I learned about menstruation, and then it came as a terrible shock. I had a mixed-up, unreal, funny reaction. It convinced me that kids should have proper sex education when they're young.

With adolescence Hawke's yearning for Clem's physical presence abated: he no longer stood at the front gate waiting for his father. He said, 'I was a little boy when he enlisted, and a young man when he was demobbed'.

It was Ellie who had got Hawke into Perth Modern School. She had wanted Hawke, like Neil, to attend a private school, 'because that would make a better person of one. There was an element of snobbery in mum, an élitist thing. A private school was a proposition I resisted very stoutly and dad was my ally in that, so we won the argument.' When Ellie discovered that Perth Modern School was academically élite, accepting each year only the top primary students in Western Australia, she coached Hawke to win a place at it.

> She sat down beside me every afternoon and would say, 'Come on. You've got to work and work and win that scholarship.' She taught me to work hard and she planted in me the idea that if I did work, I could do it. I enjoyed the lessons well enough, but I found the keeping-at-it tedious ... I have a hedonistic streak. To get things done I have to determine my priorities, or I spend too much time on things that aren't relevant ... After I won the scholarship, I didn't study. I treated school as a sleigh-ride. I had fun.

Having fun is a serious business for Hawke. His parents were keen bridge players and approached the card table with a gleam of purposefulness in their eyes. Ellie especially always strove to do well whatever she undertook — when she went to a film she would mentally grapple with the plot and characters afterwards — and she played to win. Hawke played bridge, tennis, ping-pong and billiards and loved crossword puzzles. Fun took its most sublime form, at school, in cricket. He said, 'Somehow dad had instilled in me, when I was about four, a love of cricket. When we'd gone on holidays back to his family home at Kapunda he had spent hours tossing me a ball to bat . . . God invented cricket.'

He strove to excel as a cricketer; whenever he could, Clem would attend his matches. Hawke was a batsman and wicketkeeper, and when he was chosen for the First XI he fantasised about becoming a Test cricketer.

> There was a prize of a bat for anyone in the First XI who could make 100 runs in a final-year game. In the five years I'd been at Mod nobody had won the bat. The match came, and I'd made 93 runs and I thought, 'This is it! I'm going to crack the record!' I knew how proud dad would be if I won it. Then Cyril Calcutt, who taught maths-science, bowled a ball that pitched outside the leg stump, and I went to hook the thing and was given LBW. There was no way in the world I was out! By God, I was so annoyed. I was enormously disappointed. It was, really, one of the biggest disappointments of my schooldays . . . One of my only real regrets is that I didn't learn to bat well until I went to Oxford and had coaching. If only I could have learned when I was younger!

Perth Modern School has acquired a high reputation over the years because of its numbers of outstanding pupils, but while the school's intellectual material was first class the education it offered in Hawke's day was, in the opinion of an alumnus, 'limited'. Its atmosphere was authoritarian, its subjects career-oriented: it was a show-case for the intellectually competitive. 'Mod was an exam factory', in the view of John Wheeldon, one of its former pupils, later a Labor Senator and a minister in the Whitlam Government.

> It was good for kids who were willing to knuckle down to the system, who were highly-motivated. A lot of kids there were from very poor families. Doing well at Mod was their passport into the middle class. But for boys like Bob and me, who knew we would attend university and enter a profession, it was not an encouraging atmosphere in which to extend our minds.

The ornaments of education — drama, painting, music, literature — were not much regarded at the school. Wheeldon continued: 'We had few extra-curricula activities, compared with the better private schools. Passing exams was all that mattered to the headmaster — he even disapproved of our attending ABC Youth Concerts, because in his opinion they were a waste of time.'

Hawke's cultural tastes remained undeveloped at high school; he acquired no interest in the arts, nor did he develop a love of reading for pleasure: reading was for self-improvement. The puritan attitude that fiction was basically a waste of time seems to have affected him. In adulthood Hawke's middle-class friends were often surprised that a man of his intellect and education read so few novels, and that when he did read one it was to pass the time while travelling, and therefore usually some light, racy yarn.

At school Latin became symbolic of high culture for Hawke, and Latinate English became his style — so much so that the satirist, Barry Humphries, in a skit in the 1970s, announced that all trade union officials now used the word 'indicate' instead of 'said' because Bob Hawke had taught them to. Hawke said, 'If I were an educational dictator I would make Latin compulsory. It's a great aid to the development of logic.' He was already committed to 'useful' learning. Unsurprisingly, therefore, he did not feel the shortcomings of Mod keenly, as Wheeldon did. But like Wheeldon and many other pupils, he disliked, almost hated, the headmaster. With this man Hawke had his first major crisis with authority, and would have been expelled — for a prank during a chemistry lesson in third year — but for Clem's intervention. Wheeldon recalled, 'The headmaster was a Labor man. In my youth I was a dedicated Liberal, largely because of him. He left me with an abiding dislike of any sort of State control of anything, which I've found, even as a socialist, rather difficult to overcome.' Hawke was a Labor sympathiser at school and did not allow his dislike of the headmaster to influence his politics. He said,

> The best lesson I had from school was the development of scepticism about authority as such. I realised there wasn't such a thing as goodness in authority, that its goodness or badness depended upon the people who wielded it. That became very much part of my conscious belief and is still deeply ingrained in me.

Perth Modern School crystallised in Hawke's mind ideas that had a long history in his behaviour — rejection of control, 'the minister's son showing he was independent'.

Despite Ellie's protests he joined the school cadets but then found himself rejecting the commands of his senior officers and, after three years of training, was still a private. Only three boys, another being Wheeldon, managed to remain privates.

Wheeldon recalled that Hawke

> . . . already had that larrikin streak. Since then I've seen him be abrasive with people, but he has never been with me. I've always had the

impression that he is a warm-hearted fellow. As a boy he was already very interested in politics, as I was — the whole school had a high awareness of current affairs. Debating was one of the few extra-curricular activities that the headmaster encouraged. Hawke took a leading role in a debate on some current event, which was held before the assembled school. He was a good debater, even then . . . I remember us one afternoon, when we were fourteen, talking for at least an hour about the American trade unions. The Communists had tried to blow up the car of Walter Reuther of the United Auto Workers, and we talked about the problems of trade unions — how they had to deal with the employers *and* the Communists. He was always very interested in events of that type.

The stimulus to Hawke's interest in politics was a change in family circumstances: a new member had joined the Hawke circle, with profound effect. Clem's favourite brother, Albert, who at the age of sixteen had taken over Clem's job as Secretary of the Kapunda ALP, was reunited with him in Perth. Albert, also known as Bert, was already a minister in the Western Australian Government and was being groomed for the premiership. He was a professional politician of high calibre, combining skill in administration with power and wit as an orator. He had a quick mind and a charmingly suave manner. Ellie, who had been tepid towards Labor, was converted. Clem, who had been obliged to keep quiet about his political sympathies in the conservative towns of South Australia, could now indulge his youthful enthusiasm. A Hawke household was once more Labor 'from toenails to hair roots'.

Albert, who had no son of his own, came each week to dine and play bridge with Clem and Ellie who, under Clem's influence, had years ago abandoned the idea that knitting on Sundays was a sin and that playing cards was another. Albert made Hawke his favourite nephew and became the boy's political mentor. It was a piece of sweet fortune for Hawke: first, to have a mentor; second, to have such a good one. Uncle Albert became a critical figure in Hawke's development and later success. A schoolboy friend of Hawke's said, 'His uncle showed Bob that there was a wider world, that life was not all about God, and he introduced Bob into that world'.

In 1945 when the Prime Minister, John Curtin, died Albert was asked to stand for Curtin's seat of Fremantle. His backers were confident that he could, after the departure of Chifley, become the next Leader of the ALP. But Albert rejected the opportunity in favour of the certainty of becoming premier of Western Australia and lived afterwards with a lingering regret, shared by Clem and Ellie. In 1979, when Hawke was agonising about entering federal Parliament, Uncle Bert took hold of him and said, 'Is another Hawke going to squib it?'

When Bert passed up his chance in 1945 he, Clem and Ellie turned their hopes on the boy. From the time the family had moved to Perth and Ellie had become a Labor enthusiast, she had begun to say she wished that Hawke would have a political career. She enrolled him when he was fourteen in classes for the Art of Speech, a subject not taught in State schools. It was the training ground for orators. The nineteenth century canon that oratory was *the* political skill still prevailed — if not in the minds of politicians, certainly with large sections of the electorate, and particularly with Ellie Hawke. Her son was already showing the effects of a family background in which both parents were public speakers and where an insistence on fluency, in Clem's case, and accuracy in Ellie's, ruled daily life. (An exasperated niece once snapped at Ellie, 'We don't have to speak grammatically to get into the Kingdom of Heaven, Aunt!') From the time Hawke was twelve Ellie had been saying, only half jokingly, to relations, 'Bob will be prime minister one day — he has the gift of the gab'. Gradually the idea became family lore: Hawke *would be* prime minister. Robin Morison recalled that in his final years of high school,

> Hawke would often tell people he was going to be prime minister. Max Newton, who along with Hawke was the other most flamboyant boy at school, was very irritated by Hawke's saying this, and used to be sarcastic about it. He'd walk into class and say, 'The Prime Minister is coming' or 'He's just told me *again* that he's going to be prime minister . . .'

Hazel Hawke said of the family in the 1940s, 'The idea [that Bob would be prime minister] was always around'.

Clem had been demobbed in 1945. During his four years in the AIF he had been in daily contact with men of a type he had seldom before encountered. They were swearers, blasphemers, womanisers, heavy drinkers, agnostics, atheists. Hawke said, 'The experience had a big effect on dad. He was a liberated man.' Clem had begun to read psychological works to help him with counselling these wild, tough men; he had begun to drink alcohol with them; he had more liberal attitudes to social behaviour; the benign sophistication that was so noticeable in his later years began to settle upon him. But his occasional glasses of beer were anathema to Ellie and for the first time there were sharp arguments at home. Money was scarce. In the AIF Clem's pay had been better than it ever was in civilian life, but now he was out of a job because his West Leederville church had gone to another minister, and it would be a year before a second church, at Subiaco, became available to him. In the meantime he worked in an insurance company. Ellie returned to teaching. Sometimes she upbraided Clem for 'weakness'. As had happened in thousands of other families during the war, she had become accustomed to being the head of the household, and readjustment was difficult.

Hawke looks back on the period from Neil's death to Clem's placement in a second Perth church as one of 'dislocation'. Contemporaries of his, who also had developed from children into young men under the guidance of their mothers, nevertheless found his family environment extraordinary. One said, referring to 1945 when he first met Hawke,

> Ellie would talk of nothing but her marvellous son. It was always Bob Hawke, Bob Hawke — and God. And the necessary connection between them. Sometimes you would see a look of embarrassment on Clem's face when Ellie was going on and on about Bob's ability. When he came home from school he had to make an accounting to her of how he had done that day. She drove him. When there were exams there was a great discussion about why he had come sixth or seventh, not first. In Ellie's mind Bob was not God simply because he was not old enough to be God. She instilled in him the Inevitability Syndrome — that inevitably he would be the best. He had no idea that his upbringing was unusual . . . For Ellie there was just Bob Hawke — the rest of the world was simply other people around him.

Hawke, however, did not respond to his mother's urgings to shine academically and to begin to fulfil his destiny. He matriculated at the end of 1946 with a good pass but one which, for Perth Modern students, was only average, and enrolled in Law at the University of Western Australia. There had never been any doubt at home that he would attend university. Living in Perth made the process easier, for the University of Western Australia was, then, the only free university in the country. Hawke had no special reason for choosing Law. It just seemed 'a useful sort of course'. He started at university with a vision of himself as a good-average student and a sportsman.

Six months later something happened that was to transform his life.

Chapter Five

Belonging to organised community groups was natural for people as highly socialised as the Hawkes. One of the first things Hawke did on entering university was to join the Labor Club. Another was to begin playing first-grade cricket. And a third was to join the Student Christian Movement. He was a deacon of the Subiaco church and was considered an outstanding chairman of meetings — years later his political enemies would acknowledge sourly his effectiveness as a chairman, their expressions brightening as they remarked, 'And that's something he can't do on television'.

At seventeen Hawke was still thin, almost skinny; his limbs were slender and he had small, well-shaped hands which he was in the process of disfiguring through playing cricket. His face was bony but agreeable, with a broad well-formed mouth and wide-set greenish eyes that were both alert and candid. He had caught, from Ellie, the habit of moving them restlessly, and also had the trick of quizzically raising one eyebrow. His hair, which had been reddish-blond in childhood, had turned dark brown and was luxuriantly curly; it and his lustrous olive skin were his most attractive physical features and then and later he lavished attention on both, keeping his hair groomed and his suntan in finest condition. A university friend said, 'One day he came to watch a cricket match, wearing shorts, and sat stroking his leg, looking at it as if he loved it. He was a narcissist.' Hawke said of himself, at the end of school days, 'I was proud of my good, strong body', and has never disguised his vanity about his hair and his skin. In later life he would ask women, 'What do you like best: my brains or my curly hair?' — or would say, 'Look at my beautiful suntan'. For all this, Hawke was not a handsome boy and good looks did not come to him until he was in his forties, when his hair turned into a magnificent grey wolf's ruff and his face was sculpted with experience. In youth his attractiveness to others, male and female, was his personality. With adults he was a friendly, conventionally well-mannered, straight-laced religious lad. He had not tried drinking or smoking, he disapproved of gambling — and continued to do so until he was almost forty — and he tried to uphold the virtues of social duty and reform that he had learned at home. With his peers he was high-spirited, quick-witted and a flirt. Few girls knew how to deal with his aggressive *badinage*. Meg Zanetti, a fellow pupil in Art of Speech, recalled, 'He was very cocky. I just couldn't cope with his teasing.'

The terrible kid was now the brash youth. Hawke said of himself as a teenager, 'I was obnoxious in many ways. I was self-confident, and that can come out as brashness.' Hawke did not confine his brashness to girls. Sectarian issues were important on the campus in the late 1940s, and as a Protestant Hawke was sharp in his criticism of other streams of Christianity. John Toohey, a fellow Law student, recalled that he spent much of Law I in defending his Roman Catholicism against Hawke's jibes: 'All those stories about nuns and priests, and what happened behind the walls of the convent at the top of Tate Street — Bob brought them all out'.

Student politics were also of great importance at the university. Robert Menzies, six years out of office, was gradually evolving 'the Liberal philosophy', in opposition to the creeping authoritarianism that had come to infect Labor during its years as the wartime government and later as the instrument of post-war reconstruction. The international success of Communism during the 1930s and now, more dramatically, in the 1940s, was influencing politics everywhere, and at the University of Western Australia its strength was heightened by the numbers of ex-servicemen and women on campus. The year 1947 was the peak for ex-service enrolments and these older students brought to the campus a special worldliness and toughness. 'They were the stars, in class and on the playing fields', Toohey said. 'The university was more radical and adult at that time than it was for years later. Student politics were much influenced by events in Eastern Europe.'

When Hawke joined the Labor Club he was

quickly disillusioned with the Club as such. It clearly wasn't an ALP Club, it was more a Communist Club. At the time Russia seemed to embody a lot of good things: a better society, a fairer one, a more egalitarian one. None of us knew the evil that was being perpetrated there. I was never attracted to Communism, although I had much more sympathy towards it then than I have now. In the Labor Club I felt there was a subterfuge, that they were taking positions which were detrimental to the Labor Party. So I was forthright in expressing my views. I didn't have any feelings of reticence, as a freshman, about getting up in debates and being pretty forthright and critical. By the end of that year I'd left the Labor Club and set up the ALP Club, and was its first president[1] . . . I had a capacity to get into arguments, and to influence people.

His style, developed through debating at Mod and attendances at State parliamentary debates, was already militantly rationalistic: he was beginning to learn to use logic as a weapon. Ellie, however, was not as impressed by it as some others were. When Hawke entered university he clashed with her over the logic of driving a motorbike.

Sweeping along the northern river foreshore of Perth there is a large reserve of bushland, King's Park, which separates the commercial centre and the university from the small, neat suburbs to the north and west. In the 1940s public transport from West Leederville to the university detoured around King's Park, involved several changes of trolley bus and took at least half an hour. The alternative was to drive through the park, taking no more than ten minutes. Hawke said he needed a motorbike to get to university. Ellie argued that motorbikes were dangerous, and Clem agreed with her. It was a question of safety, not money. From her salary Ellie paid for the family's modest luxuries.

Throughout Hawke's childhood it had been a matter of honour for her that, although family finances were always straitened, he was never to be allowed to feel disadvantaged.

It was a big thing with mum that I should not want for anything. It was part of that sense of security that I always had — I knew that if I had some reasonable request that I wouldn't be knocked back. When it was clear that I really wanted a new bicycle, there was a new bicycle. When I got into the First XI I wanted a bat. So I got a bat. At university, about the motorbike, I had the logic of geography on my side. Of course it wasn't just that. A motorbike was — oh, big deal! I kept on and on about the logic of it. Finally, dad came round.

Outvoted, Ellie capitulated.

Hawke was given a black Panther which, from the outset he rode, according to a contemporary, 'hunched forward, staring straight ahead, never looking to right or left, and convinced he was riding it well'. In the second term holidays Hawke was riding the Panther through King's Park, returning from the university library. It was a stirring early spring day, but he felt off-colour and had taken several analgesic powders. He was still suffering attacks of sinusitis and, more recently, tonsillitis. He remembers the bike going into a skid, being thrown from it and landing hooked through with agony. He lay on the side of the road, screaming with pain. After some time a passing motorist took him to hospital. Apart from bruising, Hawke had no sign of injury but was in unbearable pain: 'I was screaming and screaming, it was so unspeakable. I thought, death would be marvellous. I'd have deliverance from this.' Injections eased his agony down to a black labyrinth. Inside it he was left, entombed.

Medical staff began tests. Some internal injury had occurred when he had hit the ground and his abdomen had smashed against a metal stand (for the motorbike) which he had been carrying inside his windcheater. At 8 o'clock that night Jack Knight, a boy Hawke played tennis with and a close friend, talked his way into the ward. Knight recalled,

> I'd seen the colour of death on my grandparents when they were dying. It's a deep grey. Bob was that same colour. He was conscious but in too much pain to talk and just lay there cursing and moaning. Ellie was fussing. She talked continuously when she was distressed, to cover up her emotions — it was as if emotions were too dangerous, you could keep them away by talking.

Twenty-four hours after he was injured Hawke was anaesthetised and woke up some hours later with an L-shaped wound, seven inches by seven inches alongside his navel, and no spleen. It, along with blood vessels, had been ruptured. He said,

> I can remember at one point my parents talking about the motorbike and how they cursed their decision to allow me to have it. When I came to after the operation next day I can dimly remember them talking to the surgeon and saying they blessed him for having saved me. I'd been on the critically-ill list for several days. Time is vague — I have a vision of my mother weeping over me. I think it was after the operation that I realised what an enormous sense of tragedy dad and mum would feel, losing their only son. I was acutely aware of how close to death I had been, and I got this sense that the Lord had spared my life. I can't overstate how important that accident was. It was the total turning-point of my life.

Emotionally, Hawke had had an experience of priceless value: he had faced death, and won.

At the same age Neil, in whose shadow Hawke had lived, had been defeated. There, in the anguish of his parents, was proof that he was no longer an impostor but the centre of both their lives. For all of them, there was another level of meaning, one which transcended the ordinary world, for the Hawkes believed implicitly that God always acted with design. By threatening, then relenting over, Bob's life, they all felt that He had given them a sign. Hawke had forgotten or had never been told about the signs Ellie had read in the Bible before he was born: now he too believed he was an instrument chosen by the Lord.

> From very early mum had told me I had great talents and that it was a duty to use them. It would be sinful — she didn't actually use the word, but she conveyed the idea — sinful, if I didn't use these talents. And

there it was: The Parable of the Talents. Like the bad servant whom God had punished, I hadn't been using my talents. I hadn't taken school seriously; I hadn't taken university seriously. Lying there in hospital I decided I was going to live my life to my utmost ability, that I'd push myself to my limits.

And so, at seventeen, he was re-born. The sense of invulnerability, the prizes, the physical injuries, the soaring optimism, the last-minute timing, the grandiose schemes, the breathtaking stamina and equally astonishing bouts of idleness, the wild sober and drunken sprees, the fearless espousal of causes, the honours, the love affairs, the nobility of heart, the thousands of friends and the murderous enemies, were all to follow.

Chapter Six

'He fascinated me. He fascinated everyone.' Jules Zanetti, a Sydney journalist, was talking about Hawke aged eighteen to twenty-four. 'It was a foregone conclusion that Bob was going to be prime minister. I took it absolutely seriously — we had long conversations about it — he would be prime minister and I would be his Press officer. There was magic in the way he could get you to believe in things. It was an ability to manipulate. He had it then.' Hawke had had it since early childhood; by his late teens the lovable devil-of-a-kid had the gift of creating in his friends an eagerness to please him while, tormentingly, he went his own way. There was a subtle imbalance in all his relationships: somehow, he was always the more important partner. Hawke's life as a captain with lieutenants to do his bidding was under way. Zanetti continued, 'With us, it was a love-hate relationship. Somehow, we've always kissed and made up . . . The bastard!'

Zanetti, a returned serviceman almost two years Hawke's senior, met him at university. Other friends, who had known Hawke from schooldays, say they found no change in him after the motorbike accident, but what seems clear from his own testimony is that there had been an inner transformation. At school, when Hawke had talked of becoming prime minister, he was speaking a part created for him by Ellie. Now, he was writing the drama himself: he had taken over her dream for him as his own. He spent the next five years, after his escape from death, in pursuit of the prizes which he now believed it was his duty and destiny to win. His confidence was boundless: any defeat he treated as a temporary, quirkish set-back to be cast, after a period of sharp dejection, away from him. Then and later ebullient — even reckless — confidence became the Hawke style: he projected an image of the young man questing for glory and adventure, guided by the courage of high endeavour. A university tutor said, referring to Hawke aged about twenty, 'Bob had charisma at a time when most Australians didn't know the word existed'.

Hawke had not developed steady scholastic habits at school but had allowed himself to be forced to learning by Ellie who, in the very act of urging him to work, was also reinforcing the family belief that he was especially gifted. Even when most intensely mentally engaged Hawke's 'streak of hedonism' was present: he studied with his Persian cat draped around his neck. The gifted child (an intellectual aristocrat) has no need to apply himself to sensible, constant effort: he can succeed against the odds, with a burst of concentration. At Modern School Hawke had despised 'swots'. He still did. At university he set out to invent a way of becoming a top Law student — the top Law student — without diminishing his cherished status as extraordinary. His solution, arrived at, it seems, unconsciously, was alarming. 'He needed pressure', a friend said.

> He would let things slide until the examinations were upon him, then would study frantically. And he would almost always come down with sinusitis or tonsillitis just before exams, so that he would have to push himself even harder, to make up for the time lost while he was ill. Bob comes alive under pressure.

Many students study only at the last moment, but their aim is merely to pass. Hawke was different, in that his aim was, by daring failure, to leap to triumph. A certain air of 'You, dark forces, do your damnedest — and I'll beat you!' has clung to him ever since. Daring has recurred throughout his career. 'The mistake the Socialist Left made', an ALP official said, reflecting on the downfall of the Stop Hawke campaign of the late 1970s, 'was to triple-dare him, to threaten him with extinction. He took on the dare.'

Hawke had missed most of the third term Law lectures as a result of his accident but chose not to ask for posts. He sat for all but one of his examinations at the normal time, and passed. Although he would need to take honours in every subject in each successive year (to make up for the passes in first year) he believed he would graduate with first class honours in Law. John Toohey, later a distinguished judge, competed each year with him for top position and was, finally, the only student to graduate *cum laude*. Toohey said, 'Bob was very disappointed when he missed the First. He expected to get it — he always anticipated winning, and he wanted to carry off all the prizes.'

While Hawke wanted to be a top Law student, many of the practices of lawyers and many of the traditions of the law disgusted him. Soon after beginning the course he had told Clem he would not enter the profession:

> I felt a lawyer was very much a hired hand who was prepared to argue the case whatever his view, and I found that offensive. I also thought there was a fair degree of pretension about the law, that it tried to invest itself with some intrinsically glorious majesty, as such, as The Law. And I could never be persuaded of that. I thought the law was an instrument

of society and it could be and should be an instrument for a better society, but that it could be a very evil thing — it could be used to condone things that couldn't and shouldn't be condoned.

At twenty-one he had a second class honours degree in Law; he was a first-grade cricketer; a delegate to the ALP State conference (where Albert continued to coach him, and Hawke to show his independence of mind by referring loudly to the Labor Party State President as 'that baldy old bastard'). He was an active member of the Student Christian Movement; President of the Congregational Youth Fellowship; and President of the students' Societies Council. He had an urge to be involved, a rushing embrace of the world. A university friend said that Hawke, at twenty-one, showed 'an impatience, an eagerness to get to the point, whether it were of observation, principle or joke'. And, alongside that, he had a patient determination to equip himself for his long-term goal of leading the country. He decided to do a second — Arts — degree, majoring in economics, 'because if one were interested in government a knowledge of economics was sensible'. He also decided to earn some money. He took a job in the Vacuum Oil Company as a trainee executive and studied part-time for a year. He disliked his job, which he found 'pointless', that is, it had no social value, and he missed the expansiveness of university life. In 1951 he resigned from Vacuum Oil and returned to university full-time, gathering his strength for a final effort to plant his flag at the summit of student life: he wanted to become president of the Guild of Undergraduates and to win the Rhodes Scholarship for Western Australia. He said that since his third year of Law 'it had become obvious that I was within that small range of students who would be relevant candidates for the Rhodes. A number of people mentioned it to me — student colleagues, and Dr Rossiter [the Warden of Wesley College and a member of the University Senate] very strongly suggested it to me.'

Zanetti by now was editor of the university newspaper, Pelican, and became Hawke's publicist in the campaign to make him president of the Guild:

> Bob wanted to be president because he wanted to bring in reforms. It wasn't a question of power for power's sake — he was totally sincere in wanting to use power for the public good. He was also totally determined about getting it. Presidency of the Guild was a huge step towards the Rhodes. Bob sat down and drew up a blueprint for action. He had two power bases, the ALP Club and the Student Christian Movement. I used to tell him he was a hypocrite, that he couldn't possibly still be a believer, that he was just using the SCM for votes.

Zanetti himself was known as 'an operator'. His bargain with Hawke for 'putting Bob's smiling face on the front page of Pelican time after time' was that, once Hawke was president he would get Zanetti a vote — as against just a seat — in the Guild.

In 1951 Hawke ran for president and won the position with the support of both the ALP and the Liberal Clubs. His old friend Jack Knight was a Liberal activist and helped to carry Liberal support for Hawke, who became, in Zanetti's view, 'the best Guild president we ever had'. In the opinion of the Vice-Chancellor, [Sir] George Currie, Hawke was

> . . . absolutely top-notch. He was almost the perfect president so far as a vice-chancellor was concerned. He was gentlemanly, co-operative and charming, and among the presidents was outstanding for his sense of responsibility. He was a natural leader. By tradition all the presidents of the Council had to be of outstanding character, and all-rounders at the university. Hawke was innovative and an excellent chairman of meetings. He was well-spoken in those days. He had a distinctly Australian voice, but it was not harsh . . . It was hard to make the connection between that man and the one we saw on television later, being rude and obviously having had too much to drink. I suppose those things were there in him then, but were never called forth.

As Guild president one of Hawke's first official duties was to welcome the freshers of 1952. His speech (published by Zanetti in *Pelican*) shows how strong, still, was his manse conditioning, and his slight uneasiness about it:

> You are coming from the somewhat restraining atmosphere of the secondary school into an environment which gives you every possible opportunity to develop your intellect, character and personality. You will find a comparative lack of discipline external to yourself — to a large extent you have become your own disciplinarians. This, of course, involves distinct responsibilities to yourself, to those by whose sacrifices it has been made possible for you to attend the uni., to your fellow students, and finally to the whole society of which we are all a part . . . I would ask that you keep an open mind on all things, rid yourself of bias or preconceived prejudices and accept the intellectual responsibility of thinking clearly. If you do this you will find that at the end of your university career its main purpose will have been achieved — you will be equipped for worthwhile citizenship and to give a lead to those who may be less fortunate than yourselves. I apologize for the fact that the above sounds most sermon-like . . .[1]

Hawke had been elevated, as the university's representative student, into an unfamiliar social milieu of dignitaries, local and foreign. The State Governor, Sir Charles Gairdner, was guest-of-honour at many university social events and it was Hawke's duty to help to entertain him, to sit at the top table, dance with Lady Gairdner, deliver speeches of welcome and of thanks. The Governor liked him enough to invite him to Government House for weekend tennis. The Vice-Chancellor, 'a bloke I loved', and his wife invited Hawke to afternoon teas. These social contacts were important for Hawke's most ambitious scheme as Guild president.

He had become friendly with some of the foreign students, in particular a Singhalese boy, a Buddhist who was lonely and missing his family, probably suffering what is now recognised as culture shock. Hawke invited him home and encouraged him to treat the Tate Street house as his own. In 1951 two Asian students had hanged themselves, and in early 1952 a third was taken to hospital with a nervous breakdown. The plight of foreign students stirred up Hawke's compassion: for him the next logical step was to do something practical, to rescue them.

He first founded an Australian-Overseas Student Club, then on 9 April 1952 gave an afternoon tea for 'overseas students to exchange ideas and impressions and discuss a few of the problems associated with entering our university'. Slowly, the idea of building an International House emerged, and in August 1952 Hawke launched the concept with characteristic ebullience. The building would cost, he announced, £150,000, and 'the bulk of this sum will — we hope — come from Asian countries, grants from the Australian [federal and WA] governments and American foundations like the Rockefeller Institute'.[2] He flung himself into publicising and fund-raising. Sir Charles Gairdner agreed to become patron of the appeal; there was an impressive ceremonial opening; *Pelican* ran front-page stories about it; Hawke badgered the Western Australian news media for publicity; there were sporting competitions, a gala ball, male and female beauty contests, a huge fête . . . all in vain.

International House was the first of his doomed enterprises, a forerunner to the failures he would experience as President of the ACTU. The inner pressure of his optimism preserved in Hawke a naivety about the goodwill of others which was later to cause astonishing misjudgments. Only £2,200 of the £150,000 was raised for International House. He said,

> I had the feeling that if I could have gone into it earlier and been able to stay there longer we could have got it off the ground. I was disappointed that my concept of it came to me too late for me to have a chance to really get it going. There was some opposition to it, some on racist grounds, some feelings that it was a threat to new or existing colleges, but I think the problem was one of apathy and non-appreciation of the idea, rather than of opposition. I thought that the idea was so obviously good and sensible and right that it would get a momentum of its own. Well, it didn't.

Another student said, in the sour tone of envy that Hawke's contemporaries were increasingly beginning to use when they spoke of him, 'The trouble was, International House was all Bob's idea. He hogged the limelight.'

It was during the International House appeal that Clem and Ellie first had real cause for alarm about their son's behaviour. Hawke had been to the Guildford house of a businessman to ask for a donation; the man had offered him spirits and Hawke had arrived home drunk.

In 1949 he had been unable to withstand the pressure of his peers any longer and at a Law Faculty dinner had drunk a glass of beer. After about a week of illicit drinking he had come home one evening, told Ellie he wanted to talk seriously to her, and after the dishes were cleared away, sat at the table and confessed. He told her that not only had he begun to drink, but also that he was not going to stop. Their discussion was a long one and 'not very pleasant'. It ended with Ellie saying, 'I'm glad, at least, you had the honesty to tell me'.

It is a mark of the faith and strength of this extraordinary woman that she forced herself to endure her son's drinking. She prayed daily that he would stop, but she did not make scenes with him about it. Reflecting years later, when Ellie was dead, Hawke said with intense sadness for the anguish he had caused her, 'She learned to live with it. Better than I did.'

As a product of several generations of teetotallers it is possible that Hawke had no physiological resistance to alcohol and may even have been allergic to it at first. According to a student drinking companion,

> After two glasses of beer he would be whacked or throwing up in a way I've never seen before — it was an incredible cacophony, you'd think the whole world, including his feet, was coming up. But Bob was determined to improve as a drinker, as he was determined to improve at everything he did.

Hawke drank moderately for about two years, but as his tolerance improved his intake increased: 'Mum could see that I was still working extremely hard; I hadn't become "a dissolute young man". There was never any drink in the home and I never drank at home. There was never any flaunting in front of her.' But he was beginning to get drunk often, and in 1952, at a National Union of Australian University Students meeting in Melbourne, went off for a boozy weekend, returned late and still drunk on Monday morning, and thereby missed the chance of the highest position for Australian university students, presidency of NUAUS. The Right-wing lobby was able to convince the centre group, whose support Hawke needed, that he was too wild for the job. Twenty years later this opinion was to become a national refrain.

Jack Knight said:

> Bob had a terrific fear of Ellie catching him drunk. I used often to get him into bed — he was sleeping on the back verandah — and we'd creep around the side of the house. There was a watertank there where he could have a wash. Then I'd get him up the steps, through a fly-wire door and into bed. I was scared about Ellie catching us, too. She would have blamed me for leading Bob astray.

Gradually Hawke was able to hold his liquor better and in 1952 he won a university speed drinking competition, organised by Zanetti, by downing three schooners of beer in 9.3 seconds. Within a few years the world was to know of Hawke's prowess with alcohol: at Oxford he drank 2½ pints of beer in 12 seconds and was entered in the *Guinness Book of Records*. In competitions for long-distance drinking, however, he was a failure; Zanetti carried off the prizes. He, too, had come from a teetotal background and remarked wistfully in 1980, 'We worshipped the grog'.

Ellie's determination to endure and not to discuss Hawke's drinking became a cause of sometimes unbearable tension for her. One day when he was late returning home to meet a friend she became increasingly jittery. At last she fled into another room, flung herself on the floor and wailed. Almost thirty years later the household tension about alcohol and the family taboo on speaking about emotional distress had not lessened. In 1977 Kate Baillieu, a television journalist, was waiting at the Tate Street house to interview Hawke *en famille*. Baillieu had made the gaffe of bringing as a present to Clem and Ellie a bottle of whisky. They had laughed and explained they did not drink. Hawke was late. Everyone there knew that he had been drinking heavily the night before but although the subject had been raised by Baillieu's inappropriate present, no mention was made of this. Ellie became more and more agitated, talking constantly, until she suddenly said to Baillieu, 'You know, he has blackouts'.

In this highly-charged atmosphere it was inevitable that Hawke should begin leading a double life. On one side there was the gregarious student leader, already sexually experienced, a beer-garden king who when indignant would throw punches. On the other there was the minister's son who abhorred violence, who went to church on Sundays, was a deacon, taught Sunday school and helped to organise wholesome holiday camps and hymn-singing social evenings.

Because there was apartheid between the hymn-singers and the drinkers most people knew him only in one role. Because he could establish rapport so strongly with his companions of the hour, the whites, as it were, could not believe that he loved the blacks just as much. Those of his drinking contemporaries who did know about Hawke's religious life were baffled by the paradox they saw, and believed that his Christianity was bogus.

It was an older man, a tutor in the English Department at the University of Western Australia, Bob Rogers, who recognised that Hawke, in public, dressed in camouflage. Rogers, who influenced Hawke strongly, wrote:

It was the beer-garden Hawke only whom I knew, for a time — extrovert, bursting with boisterousness and vigour. For a time, but not for long. The passing show of Saturday afternoon football, of holding a charismatic court, was a sideline; his bar-room friends were just side-kicks. We began to indulge, even on licensed premises, in serious inquiries, albeit seeing the comic dimension of so many academic issues. So I was surprised one morning to be severely reprimanded by the management of the hotel in which we frequently drank, for I am, generally speaking, inoffensive, certainly so in my cups. But I was upbraided as the friend of the bloke who had offered to change the publican's face. When I saw Hawke later I asked him why he had threatened to punch the publican. Bob replied that I ought to know.

The evasion intrigued me and in it lay, upon reflection, the key to an essential part of Bob. The publican represented an aspect of the Australian Way of Life which sends Hawkey up the wall. Wherever the type within a type occurs — used-car salesman, medical practitioner or P.R. consultant — Hawke senses someone *on the take*. And that he truly resents. Because Bob can so successfully perform as the voluble extro-vert, the inner Hawke is underestimated and misunderstood. That is, the Hawke who sits and judges and loathes the operator — whatever his mask of *bonhomie* or of service — who is on the cheap grab.

Shortly, I was to graduate formally from knowing the bar-room to meeting the carefully hidden private Hawke. Bob was uneasy. 'You are . . . you aren't . . . of course, you don't have to.' It was an invitation to meet his parents, to spend an evening playing bridge at their house.

Mr Hawke welcomed me — he was tall, lean, clean, not flowery and not to be trifled with. I met his strong handshake with deep misgivings. Our bridge party was all-male: I was to partner Jack Knight. The booze Jack and I had organised for later was in the boot of my old-fashioned bomb. We sat down for our game: the tang of austerity dominated the card table and I had the feeling that Mr Hawke was observing me, rather than I, him. Yet he was completely self-contained and when the conversation touched on personalities in student politics, he showed something of disdain for those in the scrabble for power. Somehow, Clem Hawke intruded as a presence, gently, persuasively, intelligently, as, I suggest, he pervaded his son's life. Increasingly, I lost interest in the cards as they were dealt.

At supper, Mrs Hawke fussed over sandwiches, cakes and soft drinks. I was offered beer, presumably a concession to me as a practising Catholic. I felt as though I were accepting something unhygienic (and certainly unnecessary). I yielded, under pleasant, hospitable pressure and Bob, the unashamed hypocrite, condescended and accepted a small glass, too.

We had a bit of trouble starting my old bus and Bob was called out to give it a heave. He approached readily, suddenly remembered what was in the boot, then shunned my car as though it were a den of iniquity. I can still recall the look of distaste on his face as we left. Looking back, that perhaps was another key: the distaste of the party-goer who sees through the shallowness, the artificiality, the falsity, and despises those who take grog-ons seriously. Bob was tugged in two directions. He could see no reason for not joining the cultivated carefreeness of *bonhomie* and its amusing revelations and he had nothing but disgust for the emptiness behind it. He saw *bonhomie* as an aspect, a tool to be used.[3]

Already, apocryphal stories were circulating about Hawke on campus. One was that when not selected for the first-grade cricket team he had called a meeting, stacked it, had the selectors dismissed and installed new ones who promptly selected him. Within a few years the aura of success, the myths, the unspoken envy surrounding Hawke was so great that they combined to create an impenetrable disguise, and he became, increasingly, a puzzle. Rogers was the last man to see Hawke, as it were, alive.

In 1949 Hawke had defied a second major taboo of his background: he had lost his virginity. A university friend recalled, 'He could always line up girls, for himself and his friends. It was a case of "You provide the beer and I'll bring the girls", and we'd be off to the sand-dunes with a couple of blankets.' Another friend said, 'Bob was always on the look-out for love-nests. He was a great key collector. If you found a door locked to which he had a key, you'd know Bob was in there with some girl.'

But while Hawke was, and continued to be, a womaniser, he had only one special love: his co-religionist, childhood acquaintance and fiancée, Hazel Masterson. Hazel was the girl Hawke trusted, the one who shared his dreams and would help him realise them. She was the younger daughter of a modestly well-to-do accountant, a man who was a staunch conservative and secret philanthropist. Unknown even to his family, Jim Masterson had for years made a habit of giving money to battlers. He had been a battler himself — his family was poor and he had come to the city and worked his way through night school. Hazel Masterson had grown up with the values of kindliness and social duty that had inspired the Lee household. She was five months older than Hawke, the same age difference between Ellie and Clem, and like them, she and Hawke met through the church. Hazel was a good musician and became a church organist at Subiaco and a focus for many of the Congregational youth activities, where she was always in demand as a pianist. In her later teenage years she was secretary of the Congregational Youth Fellowship while Hawke was its president. For both of them this was an ideal division of labour and one which became their settled *modus operandi*: Hawke the public figure; Hazel the administrator. In all their life together Hawke has never paid household bills nor made a decision about its organisation.

Their courting began in the church community and continued in their parents' homes: 'The influence of home was very strong on us', Hazel said. Hawke recalled, 'Hazel was a vibrant person. She was interested in the church, music, tennis, and after a bit, me.' She was as emotional as Hawke, had a lively wit and among friends was full of irrepressible laughter. One recalled, 'I once travelled with Hazel in a small jet aeroplane and something would set her off — a remark, or a funny memory — and out would come this wonderful whoop of laughter. The other passengers would start grinning, and after a while the whole plane was in fits, everyone laughing because Hazel had.' She was very good looking with fair hair and pale eyes and a fine, strong bone-structure in which could be seen the blood-lines of a Czechoslovakian Jewish grandmother. Among strangers, however, she was often shy and Hawke's university friends considered her 'withdrawn'. Some noted, later, 'sometimes a great sadness in her eyes'. Hazel was working as a stenographer and 'in the student community she felt at a disadvantage', Jules Zanetti said. He called her The Mouse, until he got to know her better when, like others, he realised she was 'a great girl, a lovely girl'.

She and Hawke had started going out together (on the Panther) in 1948. In the early summer of 1949 Hawke had made a formal call upon Jim Masterson to ask his permission to marry Hazel. Masterson had reservations: Hawke was only nineteen, he was a political radical — in Masterson's terms — and he had no apparent intention of settling down to earning a living and supporting a wife in the comfort that her father had provided. Masterson's doubts were similar to Will Lee's thirty years earlier, but greater, and in the end just as futile: 'We were madly in love. We were off our beans about each other', Hazel said. They were engaged. Ellie at last had a real daughter she could mother. A friend recalled,

> Ellie would bring them a cup of tea in bed on Saturday mornings and cluck about how sweet it was that Bob and Hazel were having a brotherly-and-sisterly cuddle. A cuddle! Ellie knew her son and she was determined he was not going to run off the rails with some girl she'd never met. She was delighted to have Hazel staying at Tate Street weekend after weekend, as a magnet to keep Bob at home. They were a terrific couple. People would talk about Bob-and-Hazel — 'We've invited Bob-and-Hazel, Bob-and-Hazel were there'.

As events turned out their engagement was to be almost of Biblical length: it lasted six years.

In 1951 Hawke was a candidate for the Rhodes Scholarship, and failed. He was a candidate again in 1952, and in November that year was awarded the prize. A few weeks later he set out by P&O ship from Fremantle to represent the Congregational Church at a world conference of Christian Youth in South India. Clem and Ellie, Hazel, friends and parishioners farewelled him with pride, for he was the most distinguished student of his day in Western Australia, honoured by the church, the State and his peers.

He went off blithely, unaware that the summer sapphire of the Indian Ocean was carrying him towards a spiritual storm.

Chapter Seven

Hawke says of his childhood and youth,

> I accepted unquestioningly that God was the centre of everything. And
> it satisfied me. In later childhood I remember having uncomfortable
> thoughts about where did God actually live? What was Heaven? What
> were its limits, shape and nature? What was involved after death — did
> people have their actual form in Heaven or Hell? But the substance of
> my faith wasn't in question. Subconsciously only I was beginning to feel
> uneasy about my total theocentric explanation of things.

In Perth in the 1940s church attendances were still high. A pupil at Modern
School estimated that at least half the pupils attended church services and
Sunday school. The difference between Hawke and his contemporaries in
religious matters was the breadth of his knowledge of the Bible, hymns, and
rites of the church, and the depth of his emotional commitment to Christianity. It was part of the cluster of his imperial loyalties: self, family and church
were linked. At university he began to encounter minds as vigorous as his own
but with different ideas about religion — specifically Roman Catholics.
Hawke argued with them vehemently. 'At university I became more conscious of uneasiness. One of the great joys of student life was the long
theological arguments I used to have with Roman Catholics. Catholics fascinated me. I sought them out.'

One was John Toohey; another a philosophy lecturer, Selwyn Graves, who
had been an adult convert; and a third was Bob Rogers, an upper-middle-
class 'Evelyn Waugh type of Catholic', ten years Hawke's senior, the man
Hawke had invited home to play bridge. The three were active members of
the Newman Society, Hawke said.

In our discussions certain questions would arise from propositions I put which challenged their dogma. They were able to say, and I was able to agree, that if you were astringent about some of those propositions you found a challenge to your own beliefs. I challenged papal infallibility. The Catholics argued back: How can you believe in the Virgin Birth, the raising from the dead and so forth? They asserted that the whole Protestant position was far too waffly and subject to the truth being what one wanted the truth to be, and that their dogmatism, far from being a weakness, was a strength. And, in a sense, I could see the logic in that: if there was going to be a Christian religion, then there had to be some parameters to what was the truth. The logic that followed from my questioning of Catholic dogma started to nibble, very slightly, around the edge of my own belief . . . I felt some guilt, but not burdensome guilt, about defying some of the moral laws of the church, but really I regarded those laws as irrelevant to the realities of existence. I didn't want to burn the church on that account. In fact, I've never wanted to burn the church . . . I didn't discuss these ideas with dad because more than anything I didn't want to hurt him. I loved him so much, and I thought he might feel hurt.

At the age of twenty-three when Hawke embarked for India he was still a practising Christian who took the good government and welfare of the church seriously. The conference in India was to be a strategic exercise for Christian soldiers — or so he believed.

He knew nothing of India — that 'functioning anarchy', as Galbraith described it. He was an emotional young man, prone to moral indignation and the urge to give comfort to the depressed, the despairing and the sick. Like his parents he had a desire to rescue. His trust in the church was centred upon its succour. And he was travelling towards the most outrageously afflicted society on earth, where the very concept of effectively relieving distress was maddening. In India, skeletons walk about in the streets.

The ship berthed in Colombo 'which was a shock'; he then travelled by train and boat to Madras, 'a greater shock', and took a plane to Travincore Cochin and finally a bus to the conference centre, Cottyam. (Travincore Cochin became later Kerala State.) Three hundred Christians from different countries, including a large Indian contingent, were gathered in Cottyam. The conference complex was close to a bishop's residence which had spacious grounds shaded by large trees and maintained by a staff of sweepers. The local Christians financially dominated the country round about. Hawke noticed with gathering indignation that there was a sharp class distinction between them and the poor, disregarded multitude of Hindus. However, he was still cheerful, as usual: 'The experience of meeting people from all over the world was terribly exciting and stimulating to me'. Pastor Niemoller of Germany was the main speaker, and a good one; accommodation — in school dormitories — was comfortable and, most importantly, Hawke was not suffering the gut infections which were enfeebling scores of other visitors. He had decided not to take risks with his health and would eat nothing but cashew nuts and bananas.

As the conference continued his moral indignation with his co-religionists increased:

> The culmination for me started to come towards the end of the conference. The Communist Party in the area was very strong, the strongest in India as a result — as I worked it out — of the activities of the Christian church. The church had created through their mission schools the highest level of literacy in India and the Communist Party had taken advantage of this to swamp the district with cheap literature. Communist proselytising was very much simplified by literacy. The Party had organised an enormous rally and those in charge of our conference had issued an edict that none of us were to have anything to do with it. Of course, I took absolutely no notice of that, and went to the rally, and was taken up on the dais to meet the leaders. Their appeal to the people was so relevant! I forecast then that Kerala would be the first Communist State in the British Commonwealth, and I was right. Back at the conference centre there was some resentment that I'd gone to the rally. It was said I'd given comfort to the Communists by being present. A part of the whole unreality of the situation was the fact that the Communists had their propaganda on sale very cheaply, and even the Russian classics, beautifully bound, for unbelievably low prices. In contrast, a Bible cost twenty times as much.
>
> A few days after the rally the Christmas celebrations began. There were two things that happened. The first was a great feast held in the grounds of the bishop's residence. Tables were groaning, groaning with food, and people were gorging themselves, while just a few yards away there were hundreds of the poor staring in through the bishop's fence, looking at us and our food. Then, on Christmas Eve there was an open-air service and afterwards Christmas parties in the homes of the Christians from Cottyam, to which we were invited. People were singing hymns and carols and the one that stuck in my mind was 'The World to Christ We Bring, Christ to the World We Bring', and it all seemed so bloody unreal and hypocritical. I wandered down to the village. It was hot during the day but became cool after sunset. The people who lived in the street had already settled down for the night; they were lying on the pavements with bits of rag pulled over themselves to try to keep warm. There was one little kid — he had a beautiful face with huge eyes — lying there with an older girl. He looked terribly miserable. It all suddenly jarred in my mind. There were those comfortable Christians up the road singing about bringing Christ to the world,

and the world to Christ, and here *was* the world. And to the Christians they seemed to be totally irrelevant as the Christians were irrelevant to them.

I went back to the dormitory and got a windcheater and took it down to the little girl for her baby brother. She put it on him. They thought it was the greatest thing that had ever happened — and it was nothing to me, in terms of material possessions. The whole conjunction of circumstances sickened me.

On Christmas Day there were more services and more irrelevancies and the conference broke up a couple of days later. I made my way from there with a young Anglican minister to Bangalore and Mysore, by bus and train, and back to Madras by train. We deliberately went third class. In Mysore and Bangalore the contrast between wealth and poverty, which I thought I'd seen, really hit me. We saw the palaces of princes and rajahs. In one, the stables had been converted to garages — there were twenty-five bloody motorcars and the palace was lit up at night with light bulbs all over it, while all around there were people begging and half-starved . . .

We arrived in Madras at dawn and were met by a local Christian, who owned a newspaper. People were just waking up, scores and scores of them lying in the shit and filth of the gutters. The newspaper owner took us off to lunch with a relation of his. He was driving a great flash car and on the way the relation asked how he liked his new car. Our host complained bitterly because there was something wrong with one of the doorhandles. Well, that jarred just a little with me.

I left India and returned to Colombo, where I was the guest of a Singhalese student I knew in Perth. They were Buddhists, their house was in the grounds of a temple, and the atmosphere of the household was very peaceful and unbelievably gentle. I talked a lot about Buddhism with them, and they took me up to a temple in the hills, in Kandy, where I met the monks and talked to a very old abbot, who explained more about Buddhism to me. I found Buddhism fascinating. Their concept that you progress towards the ineffable through a number of existences seemed to me much more intellectually satisfying than the Christian belief that you come just once and are cast into circumstances maybe of great wealth or of great moment, but that you come to God or don't come to God on the basis of that one life. The logical attraction of Buddhism after the devastating experience of India was a further part of my breaking down. I was never on the point of embracing Buddhism but I found, and still find, it infinitely more satisfying than the Judeo-Christian philosophy.

When I got back to Australia customs officials seized the Communist literature I'd bought in Cottyam, including pamphlets which purported to prove the use of germ warfare by the Americans in the Korean War. I was pretty savage about my rights to bring into the country Communist literature [the Menzies Government had failed in 1951 to have the Australian Communist Party outlawed] and the next day a Commonwealth car arrived at Tate Street with some embarrassed-looking blokes who returned all the stuff to me.

Clem, with the Hawke characteristic of discounting the existence of distress, described his son as 'emotional' when he returned from India: 'I've only twice seen Bob emotional', he said. 'The first time was when he'd been to India. The second time was after the war in Israel.'

Hawke was experiencing a crisis of loyalty: he was disgusted with his church, but his church and his father were inextricably linked.

> I talked about the politics, rather than the religious doubts, to dad. Religion was his total life. I didn't want to say anything that might make him think it was all a charade or a joke or an unreality . . . Looking back, I can see that time in India and Ceylon was the turning point, but it was still a process which took a long time to work itself out. I continued going to church, with decreasing enthusiasm. It was years before I said to myself, 'I'm an agnostic'. I've never said 'I'm an atheist' — it's an illogical statement, I think.

Bob Rogers, who unwittingly had hastened the attrition of Hawke's faith, noticed how tense and defensive he was on return from India. Hawke rang Rogers and asked, in an urgent tone, to meet him at the students' pub, the Nedlands Hotel. When Rogers entered, 'Hawkey pretended not to notice that I had come in and talked energetically to people he could not stand and finally threw me an aside — "Let's go somewhere else." '[1]

Once they were alone together Hawke's furtiveness eased and he explained to Rogers how shaken he had been by his experience of India's appalling conditions. Again, Hawke expressed his political and humanitarian horror, not his religious doubts. But Rogers had an inkling that there was more involved, for he gently reminded Hawke that the existence of distress and oppression was not an argument against Christianity, that Christ himself had lived in such a society. Rogers wrote:

> India seemed to spark off in Bob the role of a secular missionary, the Humanist who burns to reduce the store of so much socially-induced human misery. 'It would be so simple if . . .' And I think that Bob does divide us into the Goodies and the Baddies. The Goodies are those who, either actively or as spectators, support reducing the level of human misery; the Baddies, those who, motivated by privilege or gain, do nothing to impede the war on human suffering.

That I have portrayed him as a missionary does not exclude the proposition that some missionaries can be ruthless and have flashes of irritation, in Bob's case, an irritation caused by those who, he considers, befog or arrest the campaign against human distress. Such irritation can cut across party or union affiliations and baffle those who try to pinpoint his position in the political spectrum.[2]

It was, however, to be another five years before Hawke would find an arena in which to express his secular missionary zeal, and that was in the Australian Conciliation and Arbitration Commission.

A few weeks after his return from India Hawke had to report on the Cottyam meeting to a Congregational conference in Adelaide. He went there *en famille*, with Clem, Ellie and Hazel, who was present in her own right, as a Western Australian delegate. There were a couple of hundred Congregationalists attending; Hawke was asked to address a plenary session.

> I wanted to be able to do it well, in a way which had a message, and not a destructive message, about my doubts. On the afternoon before I was to speak I went off into the bush by myself and thought and prayed. I had an intense desire to be helped. I prayed for help. What was going on inside me was a torment — those great doubts I had were doing something. I prayed again that night, in bed. I wanted to emphasise the things said at Cottyam about Christian concern, but I was in terrible doubt about the relevance of Christian belief, and in doubt about the concern that Christians *should* have for others. I was in a torment about the two aspects I had seen. When I began to speak something extraordinary happened. I felt something unknown — a capacity in myself which I had never suspected — it was as if it were not I speaking but someone else. My speech was brilliantly articulated — I had never been able to speak like that before — and it had enormous impact, people were moved in a way in which I've never been able to repeat — oh, just once it happened again, at an ALP meeting in late 1979. In Adelaide I had the feeling that something unique had happened, that there had been a response to my request for help.

A missionary jumped up and said, 'Thank God for Bob Hawke!'

That day in Adelaide was probably Hawke's last as a Christian; it was his first as a political agitator: he had swept the mood of the conference round from one of a condemnation of the expense involved in sending representatives to India to approval of the decision, and wild ovation.

He returned to Perth, to study and tutor in economics and to wait out the seven months until he was due to take up his Rhodes Scholarship. He had lived five years convinced that the Lord had touched him with His hand; now this conviction seemed questionable. Hawke's next five years were unsettled. He was in the full flower of his youth and his life on the surface appeared joyous, full of novelty, mad-cap gaiety, intellectual challenge. However, an older man who got to know Hawke during this period remarked, 'I thought he was a soul in torment'.

Chapter Eight

On the day in November 1951 when Hawke learned he had not been chosen as the Western Australian Rhodes Scholar for 1952 he went to the cinema with Hazel. Later he could not remember what film they had seen but Hazel recalled the evening vividly. The movie, chosen at random, had turned out to be about a Rhodes Scholar; their outing was acutely painful. But within days Hawke had shaken off his disappointment and decided to re-apply the following year.

As events unfolded, he was to be glad that he had at first failed to win the Rhodes. With hindsight he was able to see in the one-year delay to his ambition the origin of his career as a labour leader: the delay gave him a chance to complete his Arts degree, majoring in economics; this in turn determined the nature of his study at Oxford, which linked to his further research at the Australian National University, which led him to the attention of officials of the Australian Council of Trade Unions.

Rhodes had specified in his will the qualities he desired in scholars: 'Literary and scholastic attainments; qualities of manhood, truth, courage, devotion to duty, sympathy for and protection of the weak, kindliness, unselfishness and fellowship; exhibition of moral force of character and of instincts to lead and to take an interest in his fellows, physical vigour, as shown by fondness for and success in manly outdoor sports'. They also had to be bachelors.

Hawke could not be credited with literary attainments but he possessed all the other attributes, plus another: a nose for pretension. Cecil Rhodes offended Hawke's deepest social beliefs. He regarded Rhodes as a colonial exploiter who, having amassed a great fortune from cheap black labour, had found it convenient to distribute his wealth posthumously to children of the upper middle class. Hawke's opinion of Rhodes Scholars was not high, either. He wanted to win the Rhodes Scholarship because it was there for the winning, and would enable him to study abroad. He had applied also for a scholarship to an American university and would have been equally happy with that, he said, but the Rhodes was decided first.

Hawke made no secret of his contempt for Rhodes (and Rhodes Scholars in general) but did not explain his reasoning. He rarely does: for him, people are either trained to perceive social evil, as he is, in which case no explanation is necessary — or they are not, in which case explanation is futile. Furthermore, Hawke demands of his friends that they psychologically bond with him, spontaneously and without need for words — a demand which is often too great. Other students found his expressed disdain for Rhodes combined with his eagerness to win a Rhodes Scholarship paradoxical and even improper. Repeatedly during his career Hawke's 'sort of terrific conceit, which won't allow him to share his mental processes', (as a close friend described it), was to cause misunderstandings and misjudgments.

The final interviews of the short-list candidates took place on Friday 28 November 1952 at Government House. Six tense young men waited in an ante-room for the secretary, Josh Reynolds, to call them inside for the decisive meeting with the selection committee. It was made up of Sir Charles Gairdner; the acting vice-chancellor, Professor N.S. Bayliss; and five other men, most of them former Rhodes Scholars. Hawke was friendly with the chairman (Gairdner) and the secretary. In the opinion of contemporaries he had cultivated the friendship of Reynolds, who was warden of St George's College, by taking holiday jobs at the university. It was an accurate assessment but to picture it — as some contemporaries did — as self-interested deviousness is too cynical. From schooldays Hawke had worked at relating to others and had seen relating as work: the milkman, the corner-store shopkeeper and the Dean of Law were all subject to Hawke's self-aware desire to be liked. Clem operated in exactly the same way.

Hawke recalled,

> I was second or third to be called in and was asked one question — I've forgotten what. Then this bloke, a lawyer, said to me: 'Mr Hawke, one of the important considerations in the mind of The Founder' — you were supposed to genuflect at the mention of The Founder — 'and one of our responsibilities, is to have a concern for what a Rhodes Scholar will do. If we were to award you a scholarship, what would you do in later life?' I said, 'I don't know. I don't wish to practise Law. The only answer I can give you is that it would be some sort of public service, by which I don't mean that I would necessarily go into *the* Public Service.' And he said, 'Come, come, Mr Hawke. You *must* have an idea.' And I said to him again, rather sharply, 'I'm sorry, but that is all I can honestly say. I just don't know. Perhaps within that definition of public service I would want to do some academic work, but I can't help you more than that.' And he then came back at me again and said that wasn't good

enough. So I turned to the Governor and said to him, 'I've answered the question honestly and to the best of my ability. And I resent the insinuation that I'm not being forthright about it. And I haven't come here to have my honesty impugned!' I really went off. I was then asked some other questions, by others, which I answered genially and then I was shown out, thinking, 'Oh, well. I've blown it.' The other blokes asked me how I'd done and I said, 'Aw, a bit of fun'.

Then the fateful moment came. Old Josh came out again and said, 'The committee would like to see Mr Hawke'. I went in and the Governor walked round from behind his chair to greet me and said, 'Bob, we read all the references before we interview the candidates. I must tell you that my inclination was that you were the person for it.' Then he added quietly, 'If I had any doubts about it, your replies to that character confirmed my previous opinion'. And that was it. I'd won.

In the months between winning and embarking for England Hawke had another serious injury. He was run down by a cart-horse and had his thigh ripped open. Again he lost a lot of blood and when he was injected with penicillin in hospital suffered anaphylaxis, a violent allergic reaction that is often fatal. He had fallen off the motorbike a couple more times; he had been struck in the face by a cricket ball — a week after a young man, playing on the same pitch, had been killed by a ball — and brought home to Ellie covered in blood. Physical injuries were becoming a way of life. Pushing himself to his limits — even flinging away the idea of limits — Hawke suffered over the years broken wrists, sprained ankles, torn ligaments, smashed fingers, cuts, contusions and temporary paralysis from spinal injury.

There was, too, emotional hurt. He was deeply in love with Hazel but their marriage had been delayed and delayed and now he was leaving her. They wanted to have children. Their friends were already parents. A six-year engagement was cause for derision — as Hazel had accepted for some time and Hawke was accepting now, for the first time. In the days before his departure he was overcome with angry sadness, forced to realise that his career, his commitment to duty-and-destiny, would for years, or forever, over-ride their private lives. Hazel welcomed her role as helpmate in Hawke's life, and along with Ellie had become his abiding champion and protector. But he was struck dumb, as he always is when distressed, gripped by a sense of horror and dishonour at delay. He had seen, for a moment, his selfishness and what burdens he was imposing upon both of them.

He had already what Hazel later called 'a battery of defence mechanisms', and only those close to him had a vague uneasiness that something was disturbing him, as Bob Rogers revealed in this description of a party. It was the biggest of a round of farewells, the guests including everyone from the university Young Liberals (the future Liberal leader, Billy Snedden, was a guest) to the Communists, and was held in Rogers' house. He wrote:

The party was one of the merriest I have ever attended. We were disturbed by the police (who had received a complaint about noise) but that was the only jarring note in the saturnalia. Bob was gay, beaming: it seemed to be one of those moments in his life when he felt that jollity could go on forever. So I was surprised when, awakened by my bladder at about six in the morning, I found Bob on his knees in the kitchen scrubbing the floor. I told him to stop making a fool of himself and leave the floor as it was. He refused. I offered to help. He told me to get out. So I left him to enjoy his puritanical conscience in his own way. About ten, someone called in to take Hawkey for a swim. I checked the house. It had been meticulously tidied. About 2 o'clock there was a call from the pub. Remnants of the party were having lunch or breakfast there. Hawkey said he needed a shower and came back to my place.

He reappeared sometime later dressed in a very conservative fashion and complaining of hunger. He refused to drink. I should have smelt a rat. Bob said he needed to get across to Subiaco in a hurry, so I drove him over. On the way we discussed some of the intellectual foibles of our guests and I asked him casually, but somewhat to the point, 'Where are we going?'

'Just drop me off in Rokeby Road', he said.

I said, 'Yes, but where are *you* going?'

As we were nearly at Rokeby Road he had to come clean: the Congregational Youth were giving him a grand farewell starting at 6 o'clock. I was entranced! I made a quick check and knew I was shaved and moderately well-dressed. I then expressed my pleasure at going to a Congregational Youth dinner. I had never been to one and I looked forward to the occasion very much. I looked forward to the opportunity of attempting to fathom . . . We had reached the Congregational Hall.

'You are not coming in', Bob said.

'What!'

'You smell of *drink*.'[1]

On Saturday 15 August 1953 Hawke was to set sail for England. He had, as usual, neglected his preparations until it seemed he would miss the boat. As usual, too, friends and relations rallied round and Hawke himself had an eleventh-hour burst of intense activity and somehow, amid alarums and confusion, he got on board the *Dominion Monarch* in time, with his papers in order and some money borrowed from a parishioner to help with small luxuries while abroad.

He was so broke that when he had won the Rhodes Scholarship he had been able to afford only the cheapest passage, and had booked on a rust-bucket called the *Mooltan*, known jocularly as the Smallpox Ship. But during 1953 one of the windfalls that were to become normal for him occurred: the Shaw Savill line reverted to a pre-war policy of giving free return first-class berths to Rhodes Scholars. Instead of travelling in a six-bunk cabin below the waterline next to the engine-room of the Smallpox Ship he sailed in a state-room of the well-found *Dominion Monarch*. He enjoyed himself inordinately and, having stayed up until three in the morning at a party following a call at the Canary Islands, caught a chill, had to be carried ashore in England and was taken by ambulance to Southampton Hospital, with pneumonia.

The college he had chosen at Oxford was University, one of the cheaper, smaller colleges. He had picked it for its price and because he was attracted by the work of a don there. Hawke said,

> There had been earnest discussions back at the University of Western Australia about which was the oldest of Oxford's colleges — Merton or Univ. [An Oxford joke has it that King Arthur founded University.] When I first arrived and got shown to my rooms I was quite sure which was the oldest — University was, and I had the oldest rooms in it. In the bedroom there was a washstand with a bowl which my scout, Ernie, who was 180 years old, would fill each morning with warm water. The bathroom was downstairs. There was a coal fire, which Ernie used to light, and that left the room warm enough to freeze your balls. And there was some dreadful old furniture and a piece of bald carpet on the floor. My first impression was that it was all so bloody ancient and so unfunctional a place in which to live. But the sheer beauty of Oxford, the tradition as much as the beauty, hits you as soon as you arrive there — Magdalen and All Souls and Balliol.

On the whole, however, the mystique of Oxford, which in the 1950s was still considered the most significant university in the world, affected him little. 'I thought there was a fair degree of bullshit about Oxford. There was a lot of pretension and genuflecting to the glories of tradition. People called the terms Trinity, Michaelmas and so on. I called them First, Second and Third.'

He was quickly nicknamed 'Digger'. Graham Freudenberg wrote in *A Certain Grandeur*:

> Robert James Lee Hawke may prove to be the first completely modern Australian politician. He was the only Australian to have left Oxford more convincedly Australian than before he went there. Oxford had much the effect on Hawke as Cambridge had on Lee Kuan Yew a decade before; both learnt that there was nobody better than them there, but that their destiny lay absolutely at home. Hawke, in his generation, was the most significant of those who learned in England to patronise the English, as the English had patronised the Australians for six generations.[2]

Because Hawke had failed to win the Rhodes on his first attempt he had completed all but one unit of a Bachelor of Arts degree while in Perth, and he took the examinations for this at the end of 1953 at Oxford. The normal course for Rhodes Scholars with a background in Arts-Law is Politics, Philosophy and Economics — PPE. But Hawke now had two graduate degrees and gaining a third seemed tiresome. He was bored by the work, older than other PPE students and homesick: 'I had a feeling of pointlessness. It was winter, cold, intensely lonely. I used to go back to my grim little monk's cell at night . . . Not having something to which I felt strongly attached — to compensate for the security I'd known for the whole of my life — made it worse. Nothing in my work was exciting and challenging.' Again he was fretting himself into a decline.

After a month or so he wrote to Hazel and asked her to throw in her job and join him as soon as she could. She replied that she had booked to arrive at Tilbury in December 1953, and sent him money to buy a van in which they could tour England and Europe the following spring. Hawke was so elated at the prospect of seeing Hazel again that on the morning he set off to meet her at Tilbury his concentration lapsed, the van went into a spin . . . Fortunately, there was no traffic.

With Hazel's arrival Hawke was renewed and Oxford became 'the happiest years of my life'. After a couple of weeks he had decided to cut his losses, abandon PPE and take up postgraduate work. He wanted to do a piece of original research but he had already lost too much time to write a doctoral thesis, so he opted for the lesser degree of Bachelor of Letters. He was mentally casting about for a topic which would marry his legal and economic work and which would be 'relevant to Australia', when one unusually bright winter morning he went to the library at Rhodes House and stood looking around at the shelves:

> It was fantastic! There was a full set of Commonwealth Arbitration Reports, a complete set of Hansards, a complete set of the Convention debates and a complete set of the newspapers of the 1890s — the period of the Great Strike that had spawned arbitration. And there were all the relevant history books. It suddenly clicked! I'd study the Australian arbitration system — how wages were determined.

Afterwards he thought of that instant when something had pinched at him as another signpost of destiny.

Dr Colin Clark was then at Oxford directing the Institute of Agricultural Economics and agreed to become Hawke's supervisor. Their first contact was cordial and Hawke was excited (as he wrote to his financial benefactor, the parishioner who had lent him money and was to lend more) about having as supervisor 'certainly one of the foremost economists in the world today, and recently arrived from Australia, where during the past years he has been intimately acquainted with the economic situation and Government decisions at a high level'.[3]

With hindsight, Hawke's enthusiasm was ironic: Clark had been the economic advisor to E.J. Hanlon's Labor Government in Queensland but in early 1952 his relationship with the premier had ruptured over the issue of a green revolution — a central concept of the National Catholic Rural Movement — in Queensland. Hawke was unaware that Clark had experienced the crisis of adult conversion to Roman Catholicism; that he had been deeply attracted by the spiritual qualities of the Rural Movement and, realising the impracticality of some of its programme, had set about developing a workable economic scheme appropriate to its social concepts. Inflation in Australia was severe by 1952; Clark urged a brake on further industrialisation in favour of intensive settlement of the land; lower tariffs; and the abolition of automatic quarterly adjustments of the basic wage (to help combat inflation). He proposed that the adjustment-for-inflation system of wage fixation be replaced by productivity-geared wage increases. Clark was one of the few economists in the world who understood productivity-gearing at the time. Unknown to Hawke, Clark's concepts, transmitted through the network of Catholic intellectuals in Australia, and applied without deep understanding of economics, had just caused a revolution in wage fixation. In 1954 the name Santamaria meant nothing to Hawke. He was, however, a little uneasy about some facets of his supervisor's personality: 'He is an ardent R.C.', Hawke wrote, 'and in some respects this tends to colour his work. I am sure that during the course of my study under him there will be differences of opinion, but at all times I should be sure of stimulating supervision'.[4]

The stimulating supervision transmuted into an almighty row.

Clark believed he was to supervise an economics thesis which would be titled, as he recalled later, The Economics of Wage Arbitration.[5] But Hawke wrote at the time, 'the topic for research is Wage Determination in Australia'.[6] Clark was expecting an economics thesis; Hawke was researching politics and history.

They continued to see each other for a couple of months until a day in second term when Clark, whose conversation is scintillating but whose manner can be cold and abrasive, lost patience with his student. Hawke said:

> I had just discussed with him my ideas on the development of the arbitration system with special reference to the concept of the basic wage. And then, Clark staggered me. He said, 'Mr Hawke, that is a matter that would be of no interest to me, but what is more important, it would be of no interest to the University of Oxford'. Me being me, I didn't accept that. I said, 'It may be of no interest to you, but there's no reason to believe it would not be of interest to the University of Oxford'. And I left.

Hawke had now had two false starts. His confidence was shaken by Clark's remark that his thesis would be of no interest to Oxford — for it suggested he would fail to get his degree — and he was indignant. 'I find it difficult', he wrote, 'to be at all unbiased when speaking of the man . . . an individual who regards an interview with a student as an opportunity for a pedantic exercise in which he delivers himself of certain pronouncements with an air of papal infallibility, and you have the feeling that if you attempt to push your own ideas you run the threat of excommunication.'[7] Clark's opinion of Hawke, as he expressed it to friends, was disdainful, particularly of Hawke's ability with economics. The units of economics in Hawke's Arts degree had not equipped him for the high-level economic research which Clark expected and he used later to refer to Hawke as 'that economic drongo'.

The wardens of University College and Rhodes House found a new supervisor for Hawke, the Professor of Government and Public Administration at All Souls, K.C. Wheare, an Australian and former Rhodes Scholar. Wheare's field was Constitutional Law. He was considered one of the outstanding legal intellects of his time and was a kindly, diffident man, assuring Hawke he knew nothing of the development of the basic wage — perhaps Mr Hawke would teach him?

> It was well into second term before this was all sorted out. I was tremendously excited about doing major research for the first time in my academic life, and I had the added edge now that I wanted to demonstrate that Clark was wrong. I had thought the man must be mad, bonkers. *Later* I discovered what it was all about. Clark was the economic advisor to Santamaria. He was the evil genius behind the 1952-53 basic wage case decision — had just, in fact, been involved in butchering the basic wage, and here was a young man wanting to come in and research it!

Hawke never forgave Clark. In Oxford the stage had been set for his passionate assault upon the wage decisions of the Australian arbitration system.

Meanwhile, his decision to become a researcher had altered the way he looked at Oxford itself. He began to appreciate it as a sanctuary of freedom and tolerance. To the east, Europe was struggling out of the rubble of war, and across the Atlantic the United States was deranged with McCarthyism. At home the ALP was boiling with sectarian hatreds, and Liberalism, in its 'first, fine careless rapture', was persecuting its political enemies. In the town of Oxford itself, in the tea shops, young men with crewcuts and sky-blue uniforms were a constant reminder that Europe and America now awaited nuclear war with the Soviet Union, for the airmen came from a base a few miles out of town, from which bombers armed with nuclear warheads flew on exercises twenty-four hours a day. But in the colleges Communists held professorships and walked the quadrangles with the springy steps of free men. The University of Oxford seemed, Hawke said, 'an island in a mad world'. In the safety of isolation he had, for the first time ever, the opportunity to please himself entirely.

> I'd made a deliberate decision before I went there to put a moratorium on politics, student and party, because I knew that when I went back to Australia I'd be deeply involved in politics, probably for the rest of my working life. I decided to enjoy Oxford, but on my terms. I picked my friends in a way which had no care of the future. I had all kinds of relationships, just for relationship's sake — a pleasure I've never been able to have in any other two years of my life since.

His companions ranged from Sir Howard Florey (who developed penicillin), to a Dorset policeman. For no cost he indulged in a pleasure which he could not afford in Australia: he joined the Royal Air Force Reserve and learned to fly.

Hawke's friends (who had noted the way he piloted land transport) predicted that he would kill himself in an aeroplane. It was, however, his motor vehicle, the van known around Oxford as The Fornicatorium, that led to trouble. In late 1954 he was at an Air Squadron dinner where one of the guests became paralytically drunk. With the help of another student, Jimmy Allan, Hawke drove the boy home and put him to bed. It was after midnight, pouring with rain, and Hawke himself had been drinking. A police car followed the van back to the squadron party then, as Hawke got out, the police seized him and accused him of stealing the van. The ancient, once murderous, town-versus-gown feeling in Oxford was still strong and police harassment of students was common. Hawke was loud in his indignation. The commandant of the squadron had to be called out to vouch that the van was not stolen, and that seemed the end of the matter. But a few days later the police called on Hawke with a summons for dangerous driving.

Already he was something of a hero, a Wild Colonial Boy, to sections of the student community, particularly those in the sporting club, Vincent's. On the day his case was to be heard his friends packed the gallery of the magistrate's court. Hawke had not expected that the police would lie under oath, but they did. He was convicted, fined £40stg and had his licence suspended for six months. His supporters heckled the police and the magistrate, and a number of them were arrested and charged with contempt. The case was reported locally, and in the Western Australian Press, under the headline 'Rhodes Scholar on Dangerous Driving Charge'. Hawke said, 'I felt terribly ashamed. I was also very angry — it was a cook! I decided to appeal, and if I lost the appeal to throw it in and go home.'

At the University of Western Australia Hawke had never joined in student pranks, and had given the impression to contemporaries that 'he thought such things were beneath him'. But at Oxford in November 1954 he was again caught by the police as he attempted to steal a street lamp. He was convicted and fined £5stg.

His second conviction complicated his appeal against the first. Hawke engaged a barrister, Oliver Popplewell, for the appeal. Popplewell wanted to bring up as evidence of Hawke's driving experience his previously clean driving record, but if he were to do this the police would bring forward Hawke's conviction for attempted theft. This had been such a footling matter that it had not attracted the attention of the Press; Clem and Ellie were unaware of it. 'Bob was very anxious that his parents shouldn't get to hear about the street lamp', Popplewell said, and took instructions from Hawke to present the case in a different way. The police had said that Hawke had put his arm out the rolled down driver's window and made a vulgar gesture at them. But the driver's window could not be rolled down, for it was made up of one fixed and one sideways sliding glass panel. Hawke told Popplewell to ask the police: How far was the van's window down when the defendant put his arm through it and made the gesture? As events turned out, the Constable said the window was three-quarters to fully down; the Sergeant that it was fully rolled down, and this time their perjury was revealed.

The appeal was heard in the Oxford Quarter Sessions in March 1955 before Mr A.C. Longford, the Deputy-Recorder. The main witness for Hawke was Jimmy Allan, a cricket Blue and also a member of the Worcester College rugby team, which on the day of the appeal was playing an inter-college final. To Popplewell's and Hawke's horror, when Allan was called he did not appear. The session was adjourned. Popplewell had not yet questioned the police.

A few minutes later Allan arrived breathless, covered in mud, and without a tie. An apocryphal story circulated later that he had come into court wearing a Hawk's tie — the Hawk's Club being the Cambridge rival of Vincent's. Popplewell 'washed him and brushed him up a bit and put a tie on him', and Allan entered the box.

The Deputy-Recorder was testy about the adjournment and demanded why Allan was late. When Allan admitted he had been playing rugby Longford became even more irritated and upbraided the young man for wasting the court's time. Allan had a Scots temper and replied it was important that he play, because it was the first time his college had been in Cupper's final. The case seemed lost. Longford glared, then abruptly asked, 'Which college?'

On hearing that it was Worcester, Longford's manner changed: 'That was my father's college', he said wistfully.

Popplewell recalled, 'And from that moment on everything Jimmy Allan said was accepted by the judge. The police's lie was exposed, their reliability was destroyed and we romped home, with costs, and had an enormous party that evening in Vincent's.'

After this troublesome period Hawke settled once more to 'enjoying my academic work beyond description and playing cricket to saturation point'.

His working method was already established. It was a system of alternating intense pressure and *détente*. A don described it later:

> In summer he drank excessively, wenched excessively, played cricket excessively. We thought he was going to the dogs. When winter came, he stopped drinking, stopped wenching, and studied excessively. We thought he'd do himself an injury from over-work. But when summer came he forgot the library, returned to his girls and his beer. That was Digger for you.[8]

Hawke said, 'I had only three terms in which to prepare a 70,000 word thesis'. In fact, he had five, but his determination to play and his need for pressure made the other two a mental blank. As co-workers were to discover later, when Hawke has decided on a period of indolence it is impossible to cajole him out of it or to coax him into consideration of serious matters. Conversely, when he has marshalled his attention to a problem, he refuses to be distracted from it, and gives the impression that he has not only intellectually but physically entered into it.

Because it is a method that lacks administrative planning, to be effective it needs immense energy, a hit of inspiration, and some luck. Many people agree with Hawke's own assessment that he is lucky, but half his luck is boldness.

As a cricketer at Oxford Hawke was unlucky. He was twelfth man in the Oxford team, and although he toured the counties for months he was never called upon to bat and so failed to win a full Blue. But academically he had good fortune. In 1955 he won a six-week scholarship to the Institute of American Studies in the Schloss Leopoldskron, Salzburg, for a residential course in American industrial law and relations. Leading American academics and bureaucrats in the field of industrial relations conducted the lectures. Among them were the head of the Bureau of Labour Statistics and the Director of Community Affairs from the Jewish Labour Committee, Ben Seligman, who became later Professor of Economics at the University of Massachusetts. Seligman was attracted to Hawke and 'took me under his wing, another father-figure thing, I suppose'. Like other men who felt a desire to indulge Hawke, Seligman was tolerant of his protégé's harum-scarum behaviour and took it in his stride when, as Hawke's host at a performance of *The Magic Flute*, his guest fell asleep.

Hawke had his usual last-minute administrative chaos when his thesis was due to be handed in. As usual, friends rallied around and the work was finished in time. In December 1955 he presented himself in Schools for the *viva voce* on his topic, which was titled, 'An appraisal of the role of the Australian Commonwealth Court of Conciliation and Arbitration with special reference to the development of the concept of the basic wage'. It broke new ground and has survived for a quarter of a century as an introductory text for students of the history of industrial law. The Salzburg work had enabled him to include a comparison between the Australian system of wages arbitration and the American system of collective bargaining. He had gained from Wheare an understanding of the Australian Constitution and its weaknesses, and a desire to see it reformed. 'When I arrived for the *viva* the chairman said, "Mr Hawke, you're in the fortunate position of knowing more about your subject than any of us". They complimented me on the thesis. We had a genial yarn and that was it. I was a Bachelor of Letters.'

Hawke's thesis is not so much the work of an intellectual, in the sense of a theorist, as of a forceful intellect, a honed, logical mind concerned with practicalities. The last paragraph reads: 'At the time when it was becoming a nation Australia made a bold experiment [by establishing the arbitration system]. If the experiment . . . has become an inadequate instrument of self-realisation, Australia should recognise the fact and, equally boldly, seek to improve the instrument."[9] These written thoughts of a post-graduate student are, at heart, a politician's speech. Aged twenty-six and unemployed, Hawke was addressing not his English examiners, but the Australian people.

His two insouciant years were over. When he arrived back in Perth in the summer of 1956 he discussed with Albert Hawke the possibility of a seat in Parliament.

Hawke's maternal great grandfather, John Lee, 1834-1911

Will Lee, Hawke's maternal grandfather, 1859-1922

Will Lee's bible class: Ellie is seated beside him, second from left; his youngest child, Lila, is seated on his other side

Above: Ellie, aged 20

Right: Clem Hawke, aged 20

Below: Albert Hawke, the best man, Ellie, Clem and a bridesmaid

Bobbie, Bordertown, 1930

Bobbie, Bordertown, 1933

Bobbie, aged four

Clem, Bobbie, Ellie and Neil, in Bordertown

HERE'S BAKER BOB
RIGHT ON THE JOB

Bobbie selling hot cross buns

Above left: Clem and Bobbie, 1941

Above: Ellie Hawke

Left: Ellie, aged about 75

Hawke and Hazel on the Panther

Hawke and Hazel: engagement photograph

University of Western Australia, about 1952

Hawke and Ellie packing for his trip to Oxford

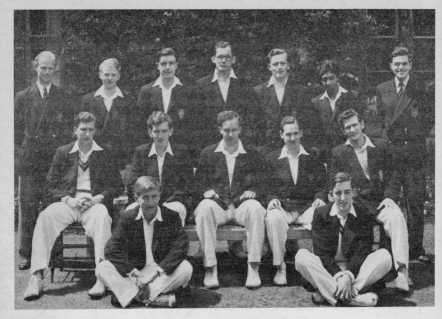

The University College, Oxford, Cricket XI, 1954: *back row:* K. Baber, I. Morgan, V. Lees, E. Thomson, J. Dunne, N. Corea, B. Jones; *middle row:* T. Horn, P. Wilcox, R. Prentice, N. Colwell, R. Hawke; *front row:* J. Duncan and A. Monro.

Hawke and Hazel standing in Red Hill,

Chapter Nine

Hawke's youthful fantasy about becoming prime minister seemed, he said, when he cast a condescending backward glance at it in the summer of 1956, to be no more than that: a fantasy of youth. Examining the same idea again, with his Uncle Bert, he believed it *could* be realised: 'I talked to him in terms of a political career and obviously, if I had a political career, I would want to go to the top'. No seat was immediately available and anyway Hawke's formal education was incomplete: he had won a research scholarship to the Australian National University which he was committed to take up in the early part of 1956. At the ANU he was to write a doctoral thesis on the basic wage; he would be the first Ph.D. student in the Faculty of Law there. But before he began a new stretch as a student he had a different commitment: now that the enforced bachelorhood of the Rhodes Scholarship was behind him he was free to marry Hazel.

Their wedding was in Trinity Church, Perth, on the afternoon of 3 March, a day with temperatures higher than 100°F and the air heavy with an approaching thunderstorm. A guest recalled: 'We were all dressed up and perspiring. Hawke's Uncle Bert gave the toast to the bride and groom and it felt like eight hours, though it probably only went on for forty minutes. It was a hot and long reception and there was only lemon cordial to drink.'[1]

Hazel, whom the family described on ordinary days as 'bubbly', was laughing as she came out of the church on Hawke's arm; in their wedding photographs he is looking at her with a grin of rapt smugness. After a honeymoon on the coast at Yallingup they set out, broke and still owing the money borrowed for Oxford, for University House, Canberra.

In 1956 the national capital was an expanse of paddocks, bush and mountains surrounding a cluster of suburbs and government buildings. Kangaroos did not hop in the main street but they were a common sight on the edges of town; magnificent parrots — black and sulphur-crested cockatoos, galahs, rosellas and lorikeets — visited domestic and public gardens in noisy flocks. There was no lake then and few restaurants outside the modest hotels and clubs. For entertainment at night there were the pubs, a couple of cinemas and the Blue Moon Cafe in Civic, specialising in fried things. The Australian National University, almost at the centre of town, was a dozen buildings, some fibro huts, playing fields, lawns and bushland. 'We were used to small towns. We enjoyed Canberra', Hazel said.

University House was, by the standards of the city and the times, de luxe accommodation. It was new, attractively designed and centrally heated. Few of those who lived there liked it. There were no cooking facilities in its apartments and meals were taken in a communal dining-room; its rules were strict and quirkish: pregnant women were not allowed to be residents, for example. The Master of University House, Professor A.D. Trendall, was a man of extremely tidy habits who, on entering a scholar's apartment, would immediately begin to straighten up piles of books or other articles lying out of place. There were no undergraduates in residence but amorous liaisons on the premises were against the rules. 'It was run like a girls' boarding school', complained a senior academic. 'The rules *made* people break out.' In due course Hawke broke out in spectacular fashion.

The Hawkes' next door neighbours were Peter Coleman and his wife, Verna. Coleman, who later had a distinguished career in journalism and a less distinguished one in NSW Liberal politics, was at the time uncertain of his future. He had attended the London School of Economics, had been a teacher in the Sudan, and had come to the ANU to read social philosophy. On his first day there he felt uneasy with the university's atmosphere, which he described as 'flab Lib-Lab', and with University House, and was already doubting his decision to live there when, after a few hours, he met Hawke.

> Bob was pleasantly atypical — he had an intense vitality. He was obviously a man from a wider world and was a most interesting and lively person. I thought, 'Oh, here's somebody to be friends with!' We chatted for a bit, then he turned round and shouted, 'Hizel' in that nasal, West Australian voice, and she came over. She seemed like a jolly, country girl — good humoured, with a very flat voice . . . I envied Bob's sense of direction. His academic work had been of a piece, it all fitted together. He was a man following his star.

They had not long been residents in University House when, in the same week, Hazel and Verna Coleman discovered they were pregnant. Both couples had to move: from University House to the university-owned flats in Masson Street, Turner, where again, they were neighbours.

Hawke was delighted by the prospect of fatherhood and wanted his first child to be a son. 'He was so insistent about having a son that he gave the impression that Hazel's destiny in life was to be his wife and to have his son — something which I, then a bachelor, found extremely odd', a fellow scholar recalled. In January 1957 Hazel gave birth to a daughter, whom they christened Susan Edith, and called Susie. 'When we saw her we were overboard!' Hawke said. He was an extravagantly affectionate father and treated friends to descriptions of the undreamed of wonders of Susie — her first smile, the eruption of teeth, crawling. When she was about a year old he was in Melbourne and telephoned Hazel in Canberra; the person who overheard his conversation was astonished: 'He didn't even say hullo to Hazel, but as soon as she answered the phone demanded, "Is Susie walking yet?"'

Hawke responded to the role of head of family with a burst of domesticity modelled on Ellie's example as a gardener. He set out to grow the best vegetables in Canberra, where the months of frosts and dry summers make the going hard. 'Supposedly it was to save money, but he treated it as a challenge and grew things that would have won prizes in a horticultural show', Coleman said. 'He used fish and vegetable compost and would go around the local fish and fruit shops collecting their detritus. It was like farming — squalid and hard work. We were fascinated to watch him spending days digging in fishheads and fishguts, out in the sun.' The Colemans were also intrigued by the periodic appearance of a local Congregational minister, who came to mow Hawke's lawn. Hazel remarked later, having observed for years the phenomenon of people eagerly offering themselves to Hawke's service, 'Bob's supporters do everything for him — except blow his nose'.

Coleman continued,

> Bob had charm, even charisma: the word was just coming into common use then. There was always a group of people around him, at the ANU usually younger students, who would do what he wanted. While I was very attracted to him I was also repelled — that is too strong a word — uneasy, about being with him when he was in his 'public figure' role, performing, being the hail-fellow-well-met centre of a fan club.

Hawke had been at the ANU only a few weeks when the position of scholar's representative, with a seat on the university council, came up for election. Coleman encouraged him to stand and 'he walked in'. Hawke was also involved in a political discussion club and played first-grade cricket. He had been a lusty, wild-hitting batsman before he left Australia; at Oxford he was described as overly confident and impatient, hooking too soon. He said, 'I had natural talent as a cricketer, but it was undeveloped until I had coaching at Oxford'. The ANU had only two first-grade cricketers playing for the Australian Capital Territory, one of them Hawke. Some observers thought that the effect of coaching had inhibited him so that now, in place of his full-blooded swipes at the ball, he was 'a bit of a prod and poke man', determined to avoid getting out but not yet master of the Zen-like cricket of England. 'In those days Australians played effective cricket; the English achieved grace', the ANU historian (and cricket buff), Manning Clark, said.

One day, however, playing for the ACT in Newcastle, Hawke had a second experience of what seemed supernatural grace:

> Something happened — I felt as if I were out of my body. I was hitting the ball and I suddenly knew that I couldn't miss it — every ball was coming straight to the bat. They changed bowlers and went through contortions to try to get me out but I just hit them and hit them — fours and sixes — until I was 78 not out. There was a New South Wales talent spotter there and he rushed over and talked about selection trials for me, said I should try out for a non-metropolitan team. I told him that wasn't me out there, it was somebody else playing. Next game I was out for a duck.

Within months of arrival in Canberra Hawke's ascendancy was established; he was, in the words of Ross Martin (later Professor of Political Science at La Trobe), 'the student star'. But in January the following year his high standing with the university establishment was swiftly and vigorously lowered.

A gathering of bishops was staying at University House on the night of a party there, at which Hawke was a guest. A professor who was host to the bishops got out of bed to complain that the noise was preventing his guests from sleeping; he ran into Hawke. There is an ornamental lily pond at University House which was known then, because of the pride Trendall took in it, as The Master's Pond. Hawke offered to throw the professor into The Master's Pond. Later that night, accompanied by a group of admirers, Hawke went swimming in it. Next day the professor lodged a complaint against Hawke with the Vice-Chancellor; Hawke resigned from the university council. Had he not done so he would have been dismissed.

This was only one of many escapades. 'We used to see Hazel crying', Coleman said.

> She was very supportive of Bob, you always knew that she felt he was a *special person*, that he had a great career ahead of him, and she would become upset when he was getting into scrapes that could damage his future. She used to say, 'It's Oxford all over again'. I often saw her take him to task, in a good-humoured way, about his behaviour. In those days Bob talked freely about the rows with the police he'd had at Oxford, and his great beer-drinking competition. Later he preferred not to mention those things and got angry with me for writing about them.

In Canberra Hawke became friends with two of the town's great characters: Max Newton and Dr Ron Hieser. Newton had been Hawke's verbal sparring partner at Perth Modern School and was considered along with another pupil, John Stone (who became Secretary of the Treasury), to be an intellectual phenomenon. Newton had been to Cambridge and taken a First in economics and in Canberra was working as a journalist for the John Fairfax group. Hawke had not liked him at school, where Newton was known as 'a swot'; their friendship in Canberra was unstable and electric with challenge. Together with Ron Hieser, Hawke's closer friend, they drank in the back bar of the Canberra Hotel. Both Hieser and Newton had a touch of genius: Newton had a brilliant career as an economic journalist then became the publisher of a newspaper of vulgar titillation for several years before getting a new lease of life in his fifties, as one of the outstanding economic writers in the USA. Hieser worked on the development of econometrics in Australia, but became an alcoholic invalid in his fifties, and died before he turned sixty. Hieser had left school at fifteen, had various jobs, joined the Communist Party, spent five years in the AIF and was, by the late 1950s, a Left-wing member of the ALP. He already had a gargantuan appetite for liquor of all types and for argument; he was broken-hearted over the disarray within the ALP and had embraced the politics of despair — a subject over which he and Hawke constantly disagreed. He found Hawke 'completely uninterested in theory — he knew as much about Marx as the average journalist: Bob was a practical politician'. Hawke considered Hieser's despair useless and self-indulgent. Manning Clark recalled, 'They were an inseparable trio for a while. They came to play ping-pong at my house one day, rushing in together — it was like a huge snowball flying through the door — then rushed out together in a sort of ballet.' Hieser, who was eight years Hawke's senior and capable of bettering him in argument, was in the opinion of many a bad influence on Hawke.

John Knight, Hawke's old friend from Perth who had helped him win presidency of the Guild by bringing in Liberal Club votes, had also moved to Canberra and was working in the Treasury. He recalled:

> I earned £28 a fortnight clear — we were all broke in those days and who ever had money spent it. One Friday in a non-pay week Bob rang me at 2 o'clock in the afternoon and invited me to join him and Ron Hieser in the pub. I told him I couldn't leave work. Hieser then came on the line and demanded that I come to the pub. Ron was much more aggressive than Bob — he was aggressive drunk or sober. When I told Ron I was broke he slammed the phone down. About an hour later I looked up to see Bob and Ron standing beside me, both of them in jolly spirits. 'Give us five quid', Bob said. I told him I was skint. Ron bellowed, 'Whaddya mean, you've got no money? They don't pay you enough! Where's Lennie?' *Lennie* was Lenox Hewitt [later Sir Lenox], a first assistant secretary of the Treasury. At that stage, as a base-grade clerk, I regarded class elevens as gods. My boss, Laurie Burgess [later President of the Superannuation Board] was an eleven. Burgess called me over and told me to make my friends leave the office. I pleaded with

them, and after a while they disappeared. Then a bit later there was a commotion from the direction of the *sanctum sanctorum*, the first assistant secretary's office. Bob and Ron had gone to the men's lavatory, removed all the paper towels and rolls of lavatory paper and made a carpet with it, stretching from the lavatory, along the corridor and into the office of Hewitt's stenographer, up to Hewitt's door. They had stationed themselves there and were refusing to leave until they had spoken to Hewitt about his economic management in general and my low wages in particular. We tried threatening, then pleading, with them. It was no good. They finally left when Burgess handed over £5. It took me weeks to repay him.

Hieser was close to the Labor leader, Dr H.V. Evatt, and introduced Hawke to him, mentioning that Hawke was doing research work for the Australian Council of Trade Unions. Hawke said, 'Evatt asked me, "How can you work for the ACTU? They're the Groupers — there are Clerks [Union officials] and Ironworkers on its executive." I replied, "You don't avoid the ALP because there are some people in it with whom you disagree", and went on to have a violent argument. I told him I thought he was bloody mad.' Already Evatt's extraordinary memory was beginning to fail, but it was not realised then that a tragic mental decay was overtaking him. Hawke had been right: Evatt, always eccentric, was going mad.*

Some time after his first meeting with Evatt, Hawke and Hieser were in Melbourne together and attended a celebration in the Richmond Town Hall for the federal Member for Yarra, Jim Cairns, who had just been awarded his doctorate. Evatt was presiding. He, Hawke, Hieser and some others moved on to the Windsor, which at that time was the leading hotel in Melbourne. Evatt, who had been a High Court judge, had another argument with Hawke, on this occasion about Constitutional Law. At some stage he left and Hawke and Hieser continued drinking until about 2 a.m. On the way out they came across a corridor of rooms outside the doors of which hotel guests had placed their shoes to be cleaned. 'Look how these rich bastards demean the workers!' Hawke said. He and Hieser rushed up and down the corridor rearranging all the pairs of shoes, placing brown ones with black ones, long ones with short ones, until there was not a matching pair in the corridor. When they discovered they had three odd shoes left over they threw them down the lift-well.

Some months later Hawke and Hieser were again in Melbourne, drinking in a bar alongside some supporters of the National Civic Council, the body organised by B.A. Santamaria to maintain his anti-Communist campaign in

---

* In the late 1970s people were astonished when Hawke, as President of the ALP, insisted that a Labor research fund be named The Evatt Foundation. Fund-raisers objected, 'We won't get a penny out of business for Evatt's memory'. Hawke replied, 'He deserves the honour. You'll have to work harder.'

the trade unions, and one closely associated with the Democratic Labor Party. The split in the ALP was recent. Hieser and Hawke, ostensibly having a private conversation, talked loudly and provokingly about the NCC, until the other men wheeled around with their fists up. They ran out to a back lane, pursued by the NCC men, one of whom had marked down Hawke and was aiming to king-hit him. Hawke, who has never learned to box (and who abhors physical violence on principle, but when drink-taken would sometimes forget), leapt away, fell and crashed his forehead on the street, splitting open an eyebrow. The NCC men fled. Hieser took Hawke to Royal Melbourne Hospital, where the casualty doctor on duty was Chinese. Hieser said,

> Bob's presence of mind was beautiful. He was covered in blood and he looked up at the doctor and asked, 'Are you from Taiwan? Or Formosa?' The doctor murmured, 'Taiwan'. Bob cocked his good eyebrow at me and said, 'Hit by the NCC. Stitched by the Kuomintang!' Basically, Bob was straightlaced, but he had an imp inside him which leavened the conventional lump . . . Oh, I *envied* his vitality.

Hawke's persona took on its mature form at the ANU. To male contemporaries — and the university was largely a male world — he presented the image of an excessively virile, vigorously intelligent, part-larrikin Australian mate. He was febrile in his boisterousness: indeed, a sort of fever seems to surround Hawke often when he is in company — even *badinage* on the telephone with friends will make him sweat. He was humorous and aggressive, and hectoring in debate. The ANU was self-consciously an intellectual meritocracy and Hawke's determination to be a winner further encouraged in him the style of an intellectual bully. Coleman said,

> He was a formidable opponent in his area of specialisation and he was very well-informed on political matters, but in social philosophy he was a lightweight, and always regarded as one. Argument with Bob was not an intellectual excitement, for his intellect was limited, as were his interests — he had, for example, no interest in literature, the theatre or music, except for pop music. *Li'l Abner* and *Reedy River* were two popular musicals in those days; Bob had the records. I watched him one day play *Reedy River* about twenty times . . . It was his personality that was impressive. A strong, attractive personality.

Hawke was given to outbursts of sarcasm, or worse, when thwarted in argument. One night at a party he became so irritated by a scholar who was refusing to accept the logic of his case that he shoved her backwards into a wall, roaring, 'I'll bang some sense into you!' His friendship with Coleman was finally ruptured a few years after leaving the university when, during a night of political discussion, Hawke lost all patience with Coleman's now solid Liberal views and, according to Coleman, ordered his German Shepherd dog to drive Coleman from the house. Hawke has no memory of this incident. Whatever did happen, Coleman was not bitten nor threatened by the German Shepherd, with whom he was on good terms. He said,

> Hazel was almost in tears, and saying, 'Oh, Bob!' After that Bob put his arm on my shoulder and said, 'Well, Coley, we had a good barney, eh?' It was an attempt at the old winning mateyness. I don't mind a man who loses his temper. It was not his sooling the dog on to me that did it, but I realised I no longer knew the private man . . . [On the other hand] even at the ANU Bob had that soothing, mediator's ability that became famous later. Two of our neighbours at Masson Street, both of them academics, and one a philosopher, had a row over some domestic issue and by agreement they called Bob in to settle it for them.

Few people at the ANU glimpsed 'the carefully hidden, private Hawke' that Bob Rogers had discovered at the University of Western Australia. But older men sensed that beneath the public image there was a different personality. One such observer was a resident in University House, who often heard Hawke arriving late at night at the door of Emily Sadka, a Sephardic Jewess who had lived in Western Australia and had been to Oxford. She was about ten years Hawke's senior and was a woman of rare strength of character, visually enforced by exaggeratedly Semitic features which gave her a frightening appearance. She died young. A friend of Sadka's recalled,

> Emily had a great sense of Biblical morality: This is Just, this is Unjust. She talked not like an orthodox Jewess but like an emancipated Jewess stepping out of the Bible. She was reticent, but at critical moments she would speak and when she did she spoke the Law of Moses. She was a retributionist: she wanted people to be punished for their sins, she demanded that they walk in the lee of Mount Sinai. Emily had an appeal to people who had a serious interest in life; she herself had a particular feeling for robust Anglo-Saxon men of intellectual quality.

Nobody imagined that Hawke and Sadka were having an affair: they were not. Her neighbour said,

> I would hear Bob whispering 'Let me in, Emily' late at night after he had spent the day boozing with his low-down friends — they could give you the low-down on anyone and were full of cynicism. Bob would come along, after that company, to Emily. It was touching how anxious he was to talk to her. I thought he was a soul in torment, looking for purification.

This observer had realised that beneath Hawke's gregarious machismo there was what Rogers had seen, a sterner character who sat in judgment and loathed the sharp operator — who was, sometimes, himself. What Hawke shared with Sadka was a system of values built upon the teachings of the Hebrew prophets: they could talk to each other in a private grammar.

One of Hawke's closest older friends — 'a bloke I loved' — was Sam Stoljar, then a Reader in Law at the ANU. Stoljar revelled in the excitement of ideas and had been on the lookout for Hawke from the time he arrived in Canberra because Professor Wheare had written from Oxford recommending Hawke to Stoljar as a man of great ability. Stoljar said,

> The flighty playboy would make fifty thousand circles around Emily's door before he would knock. Bob was not a playboy at heart. In spite of all his childishness, frivolities, pranks and drinking, and being a wild man — in spite of all these things he was sound at the core. There was a constancy to his convictions, he had a basic maturity. Along with the scandals he caused at the university — really, vastly innocent things — there was his concern for the public good. He was a man of energy, an improver of human life. To be a scholar in the ivory tower of your study required the kind of devotion that Bob does not have — all his interests led him away from the sleepier, less energetic, lazier if you like, academic's devotion. Bob had to *do things* . . . People recognised that he was not destined for our quiet world. One evening in a philosophy talk this question was set by the lecturer: 'On the day that Bob Hawke is Prime Minister of Australia can I say with certainty that I will still be a scholar?'

Uncertainty about the academic life had beset Hawke a few months after his arrival at the ANU, but he attacked his studies vigorously. His supervisor, Professor Geoffrey Sawer, said: 'I was very satisfied with my first Ph.D. student — Bob was hard-working and although he would go on benders they never interfered with his academic progress'. Hawke's discontent was twofold: the unhurried pace of academic life frustrated him, and epistemologically his thesis topic was unattainable. Sawer explained:

> When Bob started his research he was sure he had a picture in his mind as to how to delineate the basic wage concept, but his great problem was that his topic was beyond the reach of anyone attempting to make a conceptual, as against a psychological, analysis of why the learned judges decided this or that. Matters he had set out to analyse simply defied analysis. The intellectual tool Bob had cultivated up till then — logic — would not serve his purposes. He simply *had* to change his topic, but it took him a long time to realise this and admit that his original vision was faulty.

Many scholars, economists in particular, have gone quietly mad with frustration or performed acrobatic leaps of sophistry in trying to apply to wage arbitration the rules of their discipline. The arbitration system is a social institution, like marriage, and can be just as wayward in rational terms. At the time Hawke was attempting, from a distance, to develop theories about its workings, the wage-fixing system was undergoing a particularly stormy and irrational period. When he finally became a part of the drama he did more than any other man, except the founder of wage fixing, Mr Justice Higgins, to force logic upon it.

A third cause of discontent with life as a student presented itself to Hawke in early 1957: he attended his first basic wage case.

At the University of Western Australia he had been inspired, he said, by an account of the career of Clarence Darrow, the great American lawyer and civil rights fighter, who had shown him 'what you could do, *against the odds*, if you were intelligent, articulate, and tough'. Rejecting the practice of law as personally offensive and morally indefensible yet moving towards a career as an academic lawyer, Hawke had suddenly, in the Arbitration Commission, come face to face with a branch of legal practice that roused his deep instincts to serve the community. Here was the real world, the practical forum where, for good or ill, human lives were affected. But he was held back on the sidelines, looking on, while barristers and Queen's Counsel argued the cases.

A roundabout path had led Hawke to the Arbitration Commission in 1957.

In mid-1956 the Australian Council of Trade Unions had called a special congress with two items on the agenda: atomic testing at Monte Bello Island and union policy on the basic wage and federal arbitration system which, under the chief judgeship of Sir Raymond Kelly, had been through a revolution.

The arbitration system had exercised three functions: it protected unionists against bread-line wages; it periodically adjusted the income of unionists; it prevented and settled industrial disputes.

The protective function was fulfilled by the basic wage — the minimum that an unskilled man could be paid — which had been established in 1907 and since 1921 had been indexed for inflation. Every three months cost-of-living adjustments were made to it, automatically. The adjustments were a small, continuous check on the redistribution of income away from unionists, via price rises.

The large adjustment of income occurred at long, irregular intervals when it was widely believed that a new plane of prosperity had been reached in the nation. The primary large adjustment came through a basic wage inquiry; a secondary large adjustment occurred through a margins inquiry, the margin being that money paid for skill and added to the (unskilled) basic wage to make a single pay-packet. Basic wage inquiries were marathon affairs lasting usually a year or more and occurring on average once a decade. During them arguments were made about 'the capacity of the economy to pay' and the 'needs' of a family of man, woman and 'about three children'. There was no precise way of measuring either capacity or needs; the unions on one side and the employers on the other argued for their measurements then the arbitration judges struck a compromise between them. During the Depression the arbitration system adjusted income by reducing unionists' wages by 10%.

Dispute settlement, the system's third function and the only one required of it by the Constitution, took up most of its time. The prevention and settlement of industrial disputes formally occurred when 'paper' disputes over the basic wage and margins arose; very frequently real disputes arose, and these were settled by the judges and commissioners conciliating the parties or, if conciliation failed, arbitrating. If the disputants flouted arbitration they were punished. Depending upon the temperament of the federal government, arbitration judges were empowered by legislation to punish with fines, prison or banishment — that is, deregistration. Higher wage rates for a certain industry or group of workers nearly always resulted from the settlement of a dispute. Together, the system's three functions made up a fourth which, it can be argued, was its most important: it damped down the tendency to envy in the community. As the Australian Communist Party recognised more quickly than others, this softening effect of arbitration diminished the vehemence of socialism. Put crudely, the arbitration system has helped to keep radical and reform parties out of office in Australia.

The system had jogged along since 1904, always under attack from one vested interest group or another, and being respected for its activities — until 1950.

By a fluke that year a radical judge, Alf Foster, raised the basic wage from £7 to £8, an increase that by its magnitude staggered the employers and the Government, and gave joy to the unions. Foster had led a mutiny on the Bench against the new Chief Judge, Sir Raymond Kelly. Kelly, too, was a radical, but a conservative one. Like Foster, who had been described by the Press as 'the red judge', Kelly was a social engineer. He was a member of the South Australian Roman Catholic Establishment, a man of gentle though authoritarian nature, eccentric and wholly well-meaning. He was emotionally attracted, like Dr Colin Clark and thousands of others, to an idea that came into vogue in the late 1940s in Australia — although it was as old as the existence of cities. It was a vision of paradise regained: on a small farm, in a life of simplicity, voluntary frugality and communion with God. The mills of industry were to Kelly as dark and satanic now as they had ever been; he saw them as sucking the souls out of men's bodies.

Unlike other enthusiasts of the ideology of the National Catholic Rural Movement, however, Kelly was in a position to make changes to the lives of millions of workers. He believed that 'Foster's £1', as it was known, was a national disaster; a cause of inflation; and an encouragement for the industrial workforce to grow and, therefore, soullessness to increase. He determined to undo the damage he saw.

In 1953, in dramatic and secret circumstances, Kelly presided over a Bench of judges that revolutionised the role of the arbitration system, openly institutionalising it as manipulator of the Australian economy.* The coup was startlingly simple: like all coups, merely a matter of abolishing one set of rules, declaring another and establishing new managers. The Bench that year abolished automatic quarterly cost-of-living adjustments; it declared that henceforth wages — money wages not real wages, which were falling — would rise only when the economy had capacity to pay and *that* decision would be made by the managers of this new scheme for the distribution of cash, the judges in arbitration. This extraordinary power to decide upon the basic necessities of life for the workforce was vested in men who knew almost nothing about economics, not even how they could measure 'capacity to pay' in any sensible fashion or if, indeed, it was measurable. Nor were they familiar with poverty. Sociologically, the judgment was a stimulant to envy. One example: all the States except South Australia decided to maintain automatic adjustments; within three years workers under State awards were earning on average 19s. a week more than workers under federal awards, doing the same work, often in the same shop.

The 1953 decision convulsed the trade union movement. It had stripped workers of their protection against inflation — which had reached 22.5% in 1951 — and had given nothing in return, except the demand for legal fees. If the unions wanted wage rises awarded in future they would have to employ a Queen's Counsel — Kelly did not care for mere barristers in his court — and hope that his arguments would persuade the judges that the economy had 'capacity to pay'. The tables had been turned for Foster's £1 and the employers gloated: they could not measure capacity to pay any more than the judges could, but the employers could scare the Bench by crying Bankrupt! And did.

As if all this were not unwelcome enough to the unions they then learned from their legal advisors that the 1953 judgment was written in such a way as to make it invulnerable to attrition. It was a monster of a document, knotted together with such ingenuity that the unions would have to persuade a future Bench to disown it *in toto*, for half measures were useless. After the unpredictable behaviour of the arbitration Bench in recent years another major swing of judicial minds would have raised the most serious questions; it was, therefore, most unlikely that the judges would have the nerve to disown the 1953 decision. The unions tried to persuade them to in 1956, and failed.

Meanwhile, the Government had become alarmed by the bitterness in industrial life caused, in part, by the 1953 judgment, in part by the authoritarian and punitive atmosphere that the system breathed, under Sir Raymond

---

* In 1947 Foster had noted that the Arbitration Court judges were 'the economic dictators of Australia'.

Kelly. In early 1956 the Government, using as its excuse the Boilermakers' Case,[2] split the Arbitration Court, removing the power to punish with fines and prison to a new body, the Industrial Court. It gave the economic functions and those for prevention and settlement of industrial disputes to another newly-created institution, the Conciliation and Arbitration Commission. Mr Justice Foster, who was now seventy, believed that because of his seniority he should be made head of the Commission, but to his anger a younger judge, Richard Kirby, got the job. From the outset relations within the Arbitration Commission were strained.

Foster abhorred the 1953 judgment. Kirby, a man of more passive nature, had publicly associated himself with it, although privately the judgment embarrassed him. In 1956 Kirby presided on the Bench which refused the unions' application to overturn the 1953 decision; he presided and refused again in 1957, 1958, 1959 and 1960. Foster believed that Kirby was naive and had been tricked by Sir Raymond Kelly in 1953; that Kirby's continued support for Kelly's handiwork was caused by embarrassment and timidity. Kirby was certainly a very different Chief Judge[3] from his predecessor, Kelly; he described himself as 'an underdog's man' and by temperament was a peacemaker. Hawke was making his first live contact with the arbitration system in a promising new era.

The ACTU special congress of 1956 was to discuss trade union tactics on award wages in the wake of the revolution that had taken place. Hawke asked if he might attend, was welcomed, given a seat on the platform and introduced to the President, Albert Monk, and the Secretary, Harold Souter. He said, 'It became clear to the executive of the ACTU that I knew more about the basic wage than anyone else in the country'. Souter, who had heard about Hawke through Horrie Brown, an ANU economist who had appeared for the ACTU in the 1950 basic wage case, invited him to assist by supplying historical and legal research for the first case to be argued, in early 1957, under the new annual system established by the Conciliation and Arbitration Commission.

Souter's invitation, however, was not the honour it might seem: then and later the stinginess of the trade union movement kept its peak council short of funds so that Souter was always on the alert for academics with a Labor movement bias who were willing to donate their expertise. He had been the ACTU research officer and advocate himself, but since moving into the Secretary's job there had been no replacement. Instead the ACTU briefed a Queen's Counsel to present its cases, so that what was skimped on research was spent on fees for a silk, his junior and instructing solicitors. The ACTU advocate was Richard (later Sir Richard) Eggleston, a man whose arguments were faultless in logic and presented with exquisite lucidity of thought and whose knowledge of economics was unique in the legal profession. He was an acknowledged leader of the Melbourne Bar. For years he attempted to explain to the Bench that if 'capacity to pay' meant anything, it meant an increase in productivity. It seems strange now, when the concept is widely understood, but in the 1950s the legal profession in general greeted the terminology of economics with distrust and ridicule, inspired, one must suppose, largely by the intellectual snobbery that tends to attach to legal training. In 1950 and 1953 barristers had derided the work of Horrie Brown, who had developed an index for measuring productivity; in his 1950 judgment Kelly had dismissed Brown's work as fanciful.

Eggleston's instructing solicitor was Bob Brodney of Maurice Blackburn and Company, a firm that had advised the unions for more than thirty years and had its offices in the ACTU building, which was across the road from the Melbourne Trades Hall and next door to that other hub of trade union life, the Lygon (later the John Curtin) Hotel.

Eggleston opened the 1957 case but had to depart shortly afterwards for an employers' brief in the Privy Council, 'and that', in the words of Sir John Moore (the second President of the Conciliation and Arbitration Commission), 'was the beginning of the end of Dick Eggleston as far as the ACTU was concerned'. Eggleston left carriage of the unions' argument to his junior, who lacked Eggleston's flair and authority. Hawke sat in court during the case and recalled, 'My material was butchered by the junior! I suffered the tortures of the damned.'

Keith Hancock, another young academic whom Souter had asked to assist with economic research, said, 'Bob took a particularly severe view of the way the case was handled. In comparison, the employers' junior, Lindsay Williams, was continually feeding stuff to their silk, Drew Aird. Bob said the relationship between Eggleston and his instructing solicitor was irrelevant and totally inefficient.'

In 1958 Hawke again assisted with legal and historical research for the unions' wage case and again suffered a ferment of indignation. Hancock (later Professor, and Vice-Chancellor of Flinders University) had found Hawke:

> Well-mannered and civilised. On one of his visits to Melbourne he stayed with my parents, who were most impressed by what a nice, quiet, refined boy he was. My mother was particularly charmed by him. He was obviously very intelligent and could grasp any type of argument quickly, including economic argument. I remember watching him do a very difficult crossword puzzle, full of historical and literary clues. Perhaps it's a comment on how naive I was, but Hawke seemed to me sophisticated and cultured. I later began to think he was a Jekyll and Hyde character, when I heard some of the stories about him at the ANU.

Hawke similarly puzzled the Bench of the Arbitration Commission. Kirby recalled that in 1957 and 1958 the judges had watched him and had been impressed by his enthusiasm and vitality:

> He was very fresh-faced and we thought he was only twenty-two or three. On occasions he was unable to sit still and we could see he was nearly going mad with frustration, wanting to jump up and have a say. We used to watch him with some curiosity and amusement, and wonder who this young cove was. One day he suddenly stepped into my chambers, introduced himself as a research scholar and started asking questions as if he were entitled to, ignoring the fact that I was of judicial rank and deciding a matter that he was involved in. He had that academic's snobbery that he was entitled to badger anyone, and did so in a somewhat iconoclastic fashion, to knock you off your perch a bit. He asked what qualifications I thought each member of the Bench had for deciding very important questions of national economics. I told him we were chaps with trained minds, we picked up as much economics as we could, but I didn't go into any detail because he didn't make me feel I wanted to tell him. I went on to say that on a full Bench we did our best to work as a team, which amazed him and inclined him to ridicule. He said, 'How can you be a team, when you're talking about economics?' It was something like a confessional. Finally I told him it was no good discussing the matter any more. I thought him brash and almost rude, but the overwhelming impression was that I couldn't come to grips with him.

Besides ruffling the feathers of the Chief Judge, Hawke had unwittingly bumped into the internal politics of the Arbitration Commission: Kirby was *trying* to create a team, but he and Foster were not on speaking terms. The débâcle of 1950 had arisen because Foster and Sir Raymond Kelly were not speaking. (A third silence between judges, in 1965, was to have the most far-reaching effect on Hawke's career — and the Australian economy.)

Meanwhile, Hawke had also prodded Kirby on that other vulnerable area — the lack of economic expertise on the Bench. It was an inauspicious first encounter for both men.

By early 1958 Hawke had collected a mass of material for his thesis, he was already a part-time lecturer in Law at the Canberra University College, and he had been offered a senior lectureship at the University College, to divide his time between teaching industrial law in the Law Faculty and industrial relations in the Economics Faculty. He said, 'I had been going from one academic niche to another, it all had a logic about it, but I felt that somehow the academic life wasn't dragging out of me all that it could'. Increasingly he had been spending his time at the ACTU. Peter Coleman wrote of Hawke in this period:

> I met him in the Lygon Hotel, Melbourne, that unofficial Labor head-
> quarters opposite Trades Hall and next to the ACTU. There, beneath
> faded framed pictures of old Labor leaders, present-day union officials
> and politicians gather to intrigue or get drunk. (The Groupers go to the
> Dover down the road.) Somehow we ended up at a party thrown, I
> think, by the Fuel and Fodder Workers' Union in Trades Hall, and after
> a few speeches about the old days, some songs about the Bush, the Wild
> West, and the Deep South, and a good deal of beer, Bob Hawke drove
> me home.
>
> As we shot along St Kilda Road, Hawke sat hunched grimly over the
> wheel peering through rimless glasses. At the Junction he swung, as it
> were, into orbit and without reducing speed spun around the circus
> about ten times looking for the right turn-off. Each time, as we sped past
> it, I called out, 'There it is! There!' — each time too late.* Then,
> apparently by a mixture of luck and intuition, he suddenly shot off at a
> tangent up the street leading to my flat. I last saw him disappearing . . .
> at the maximum speed.
>
> Without straining things too much, the whole incident seems sym-
> bolic of Hawke at the time. Pugnacious, ambitious, full of confidence,
> in a hell of a hurry but not certain which way to turn and certainly not
> listening to anyone who wanted to advise him.⁴

One evening in mid-1958 Hawke was at an ACTU dinner in Usher's Hotel, Sydney, when late in the evening the President, Albert Monk, came over to him and put an arm around his shoulders. 'Albert was a man who erected big fences around himself. He didn't want close friends, he didn't want intimacy — he was frightened of it', Hawke said.

> But when he'd had a fair bit to drink he would relax. And when he did
> make an intimate gesture, because it was so unusual, it had a strong
> impact. So, he put his arm around me and what he said came out of the
> blue:
> 'We'd like you to be our research officer. What about it?' It seemed as
> if suddenly everything was falling into place, as if it were a culmination
> of all that had gone before, so that, in an inexorable way, everything
> had been leading up to that moment: I knew more about the basic wage
> system than anybody else. I was uniquely well-equipped to do the job.

* Hawke maintained at the time, and later, that Coleman had hyperbolised, 'to give substance to what he wanted to say — that I did not know where I was going. He grossly exaggerated.'

He was to work for about two years at the ACTU, preparing and arguing wage cases in the Arbitration Commission; Monk and Souter presumed that after that he would return to academic life. Their plan was that he should act as a bell-wether for the unions among other academic lawyers and economists. 'We envisaged that we'd employ him for a couple of years, then replace him with someone else from the universities and in time would build up a group of academics who were interested in and sympathetic to us, and that they would spread knowledge of wages arbitration throughout the university system', Souter said. Capturing Hawke, domesticating him and setting him to work was to become the fierce obsession of many people; many of them have been disappointed, at least in their original hopes. Souter, who had persuaded Monk to hire Hawke, was soon to discover that he eluded control.

Although Hawke was certain that the ACTU job was his destiny, he did not accept immediately. Instead he began a process which, at other important times in his life, he was always to repeat: he lobbied, he built up a power-base of supporters, so that when he left the ANU he did so on an indefinable but strength-giving cloud of others' hopes and good wishes. He succeeded, too, in persuading Sawer that he should be re-awarded a fellowship to complete his doctorate when the ACTU sojourn was over. Sawer said:

> He asked my advice about the ACTU job, saying it was the sort of work he would love doing and that, living in the atmosphere of unions, he could be even more effective than Eggleston. I believed that had Bob gone to the Bar he would have made a brilliant jury advocate, and in my opinion, the Arbitration Commission *needed* a jury advocate. I urged him to take it.

There were many other scholars whom Hawke infused with enthusiasm for the prospect of his new role; Sawer and they shared an opinion that working for the unions would be a ladder into politics for Hawke. 'It was exciting', Coleman said, 'to know somebody who was spoken of as a future prime minister'. The university community believed it was watching a drama unfold towards a denouement which they, the select, knew in advance.

For their part Monk and Souter had successfully lobbied the rest of the ACTU executive to accept Hawke. Their efforts were necessary because at the time the great influx of manual workers' children into universities — the 'gentrification', as it has been called, of the working class — had not begun and trade union circles were proudly anti-academic. Higher education was both frightening and cause for derision; the blue-collar ethos laid down that things working class and union were so unknown and unimaginable to an educated man from the middle class as to be beyond his comprehension or sympathy. The words 'intellectual' and 'academic' were often pejoratives for which 'pooftah' or 'pansy' could be synonyms. Hawke, aged twenty-eight, with education from three universities, never having earned his living — by union standards — in his life, was an astonishing employee for the ACTU. In his twenty-one years with that organisation he never completely overcame the class prejudice that first greeted him; initially, it was a prejudice of the Right.

When his appointment was announced the pubs buzzed with curiosity, scepticism and some loud ridicule about the outsider. Tom Dougherty, an old enemy of Monk and the mogul of the giant Australian Workers' Union (which was still not affiliated with the ACTU and had attempted to murder it at birth), scoffed in his union's journal 'From Eggleston to Egghead'. Doubts about Hawke's capacity to represent the tribe were such that the ACTU executive became nervous and established advisory panels of unionists to help him. Then Mr Justice Foster, who was to be one of the three judges Hawke would face in his first big case, sent word to Monk that he was much displeased about the change of advocates. Foster had not decided a basic wage case since 1950; he wanted, as he explained later, to overturn the 1953 decision but for that to happen he needed arguments to be presented to him with the utmost authority and persuasion. He wanted Eggleston, not some young man who was not even a barrister but had been plucked from a university course. Monk decided that, after all, Eggleston had better be the advocate. But Souter and some Left-wing members of the executive had become convinced that Hawke could and should present the case. After a couple of weeks of uncertainty, their view prevailed.

Hawke's test was to attempt what Eggleston had failed to achieve in three years of trying: to slay the monster of 1953.

For a boy raised on David and Goliath it was the perfect start to a career.

Chapter Ten

The living representative of Hawke's enemy was the Chief Judge in industry, Richard (later Sir Richard) Kirby, President of the Conciliation and Arbitration Commission. Kirby was the only judge sitting in 1959 who had sat on the notorious Bench of 1953. He had chosen for this year's basic wage case himself, Alf Foster and Frank Gallagher, the latter a judge who had never before sat on a basic wage case, and who did not share Foster's radical social views. Gallagher, therefore, could be relied upon to side with Kirby. It followed that Hawke's main task was to persuade Kirby to see the wrongheadedness of the 1953 judgment and of his decisions to uphold it in 1956, 1957 and 1958. But instead of persuasion Hawke mounted an assault of unparalleled aggressiveness upon the Chief Judge's actions.

'He is a man', Kirby said, 'of religious fervour'.

If the ranks of Gideon have to be slaughtered he will up and into 'em, boots and all. He has a great religious strength inside: there's something in Bob that makes him give everything he's got, and he's just not a practical bloke . . . He would not try to persuade. He characterised me as a villain and a fool for the 1953 decision and for refusing to go back on it since then, and he wanted confession and repentance. He hectored me. He knew his case inside out — Gar Barwick is the only other cove I've known who speaks from knowledge the way Bob Hawke does. But Barwick was a great persuader. Bob just couldn't bring himself to think, How can I persuade these judges to go my way? It was an underlying streak of puritanism in him: I had to change my mind and into the bargain admit I had been a bloody fool and a crook as well. He could have said, 'You can be pardoned for suspending the automatic adjustment system in 1953, but you should restore it as soon as you can, and it doesn't matter, Your Honour, about the subtle philosophy, just do the practical thing now, be pragmatic'. That's what a good advocate at the Bar would have come out with. Eggleston aside, I'd rank Bob Hawke above any of the silks who appeared before us, but he employed bad tactics. It's part of the honesty of the man, of course — he would not tell a lie, he would not pretend he thought I was a decent chap and those decisions of mine had been an aberration. He was determined to rub my nose in the dirt. If only he'd shown me a way that we could get out of that '53 decision, how we could rationalise it.

The Commission in those days was housed on the rising slope of Little Bourke Street, directly across the road from the High Court. It was a modern informal court: the building was new, the courtrooms appointed with nondescript pale timber furnishings, the judges and barristers wore neither wigs nor robes. Hawke made his first appearance, highly strung, restless in his gestures, continually pacing as he addressed the Bench above him, rolling on the sides of his shoes, gesticulating, swivelling his eyeballs to show impatience and flicking his eyebrows up and down as if they were attached to strings. 'He danced on his brief', a barrister said. Hawke was in the continuous motion of high nervous energy, his body language intensifying the message of his speech, all delivered in a rat-a-tat-tat of sentences bursting at up to 220 words a minute — too fast for all but the best shorthand writers — and in a very loud voice. It was said that union officials several blocks away in the Trades Hall could hear his submissions. But while there was an appearance of informality in the court, traditions died hard. The judges were used to, and expected, deference from advocates. Even Foster, the radical, had complained bitterly when the system was split in two in 1956 and powers of punishment were removed to the Industrial Court: 'They can throw inkwells at us and we'll be powerless to stop them!' Hawke's attacks upon Kirby and other judges of the cases from 1953 to 1958 would have, a few years earlier, had him put out of court, at the least; Kelly would have gaoled him for contempt. Kirby and Gallagher were scandalised by Hawke; Foster, fighting with Kirby, abhorring the 1953 decision and regarding himself 'as the Godfather of any union man who appeared before us', was delighted. Foster had a mane of white hair and eyebrows described as better than Menzies'; beneath them his dark eyes flashed with pleasure as he listened to Hawke attacking the Chief Judge.

On the first day of the case Foster had begun the morning by sniping at Hawke; before 4 o'clock that afternoon he was actively barracking for him from the Bench. The hostility between Foster and Kirby was obvious to all those in court and increased the pain that Hawke's arguments were causing the President of the Commission, but Hawke did not soften. He showed in that case a pattern of behaviour that was consistent throughout his career as an advocate and as a politician: he fought without mercy until he had won; as soon as defeat was conceded he became magnanimous; he would not humiliate a conquered enemy.

Throughout the 1950s the employers had used as a witness a businessman and company secretary, R.P. Truman, whose evidence had been the bane of the unions. Early in the case Hawke claimed he would in due course discredit Truman's evidence, to which Kirby remarked, 'Mr Truman . . . can always very ruggedly defend himself', to which Hawke replied, 'We'll see about that'. His attack on Truman was devastating, demonstrating that what he said now, and had said for years, was wrong. Truman's word was left supported by only one shred of evidence — figures which he said he had checked with the Commonwealth Bank. During a lunch adjournment Hawke rang the bank and discovered that Truman's claim was inaccurate. Kirby, now embarrassed, said the bank's statement ought to be authenticated. Hawke offered to do this by calling the bank official to whom he had spoken. At this, the employers' advocate, Drew (later Mr Justice) Aird announced that Hawke's word was sufficient. Aird had realised that his witness's evidence was fallacious, as Hawke said it was, and was admitting defeat. Truman would never again be used as a witness. But Foster wanted the employers — and by extension, Kirby — publicly humiliated and demanded that Hawke go ahead and call the bank official. To Foster's anger, Hawke refused.

At the ANU Hawke had become friendly with the economist, Horrie Brown, who had helped the ACTU for a decade and had spent a week in the witness box during the 1953 case under such strain that he had later suffered a heart attack. It was Brown who had recommended to Souter that the ACTU employ Hawke. Brown was an extremely gentle, softly-spoken man, loved by all who knew him. 'He was my mentor', Hawke said. Before the case began Hawke spent hours with him, mastering the concepts of productivity measurements. Brown was not well enough to be a witness himself, but he put Hawke in contact with another academic economist, Eric (later Professor) Russell of Adelaide University, who was. A third economic advisor for Hawke was Wilf Salter, an old friend from the University of Western Australia. Together the three men spent hundreds of hours with Hawke, teaching him economics. 'It was like having a university degree course in a matter of weeks. It is impossible to state adequately the assistance those blokes gave me — I just could not have done what I did without them', Hawke said.

Hawke probably knew no more economics than Eggleston, but Eggleston was a full member of the legal fraternity and a sort of mental huff had overtaken the arbitration judges at the idea that a legal brother could speak with authority on something which they did not understand. The Bench had consistently refused to allow Eggleston to put economic arguments to it. Suddenly, with Hawke — a legal outsider who, since he was not a barrister, was not entitled to and was never accorded the polite address of 'Learned Friend' — the reasons for objecting to economic arguments from the Bar table vanished. There was no discussion: Hawke simply stood in court and addressed the judges as both a legal and economic expert. And from him, they accepted it. It was an extraordinary change, and the first step to winning his case and to bringing logic to bear on wage fixation.

Besides demanding that automatic quarterly adjustments be reinstated, Hawke's brief also demanded that the basic wage be increased for gains in productivity. He hammered at the judges that productivity was a substitute for the nebulous term 'capacity to pay'; he produced evidence that since 1953 productivity had increased by 10% and that therefore real wages ought to have increased 10%. Instead, real wages had fallen by 5%. Foster, who had little idea of what productivity was at the beginning of the case, was intrigued and continually interjected with questions. Kirby, for the first time understanding the enormity of the effect upon unionists of the 1953 decision, was appalled. He said,

> Bob did something that Eggleston was never able to do. He belted economic understanding into our heads. He stood there and lectured us for hours, like a schoolmaster, which I must say I did not like. Until then I'd shared the general view that productivity was a combination of efficiency and co-operation — an untidy sort of thing. He galvanised my interest in economics; I became determined to learn as much about it as I could. While I was seething with resentment against him, and spurred into hostility with Alf Foster at the time, Hawke had made me realise with his economic arguments that we had not only allowed wages to fall behind prices, but also that we had allowed them to fall behind capacity, which was the very basis of our decision.

Kirby could not bring himself to overturn the 1953 decision, but Hawke had persuaded him to take a critical step towards reform: he decided that the basic wage must be increased to at least the level it would have been had automatic adjustments not been cancelled. Foster wanted the reintroduction of automatic adjustments and an increase in the basic wage of £1. Gallagher, as expected, sided with Kirby in refusing automatic adjustments, and wanted to increase the basic wage by only 10s. Kirby struck a deal: the judges increased the basic wage by 15s., bringing it to 2s. more than if the old system had not been ruined.

It was a magnificent victory for Hawke, and instantly established him with the trade union rank and file as a brilliant advocate. He had arrived in the wage-fixing arena at the luckiest of moments: the Arbitration Commission was not yet three years old; the conceptual underpinnings of wage fixation were in need of reform; he had a Chief Judge open to rational argument and vulnerable to the plight of 'the underdog'; and, most importantly, the economy was surging ahead in the great wave that had swelled up at the end of the war and was rolling forward — to crash, in 1974.

Hawke had only a few weeks' respite before his next case began. This was the first margins case to be heard for five years. It was particularly challenging, because for the first time Hawke was 'getting right up to the work face', as he put it: learning what actually happened in shops. His brief had two strands: that the economy had 'capacity to pay' and that because the arbitration system had kept margin awards artificially low for several years (Kelly's influence, again), a parallel system of over-award payments had sprung up and spread, and that therefore the Commission ought to be realistic and award to unionists 'the going rate'.

For evidence about 'the going rate' Hawke produced more than a dozen union officials as witnesses; among them were John Ducker, then a lowly organiser for the Iron Workers, and Cliff Dolan, from the Electrical Trades Union. 'The long-haired intellectual', as Hawke was still characterised, impressed Dolan with his confidence in dealing with senior opposing counsel and his trade union witnesses. They became friendly. No friendship sprang up between Hawke and Ducker, although Ducker was one of Hawke's most effective witnesses. He said, 'If there was an option open to John between drawing a long bow or a short one, he went for the long bow every time. He was a dedicated winner — tough and hard and aggressive, and he obviously had a future, though at the time he was a very minor figure.' Ducker, who was born in Yorkshire and speaks with a strong, expressive accent, had in due course the power to do more than most to nobble Hawke. If Ducker had had his way Hawke would not have become President of the ACTU. Later, Ducker helped to save Hawke's political life.

The employers' advocate in the 1959 margins case was Cliff (later Mr Justice) Menhennitt, a Queen's Counsel and an aggressive barrister. He and Hawke quickly established a dislike for each other and their submissions and cross-examinations became punctuated with snarling and snapping. Hawke won another major victory in the margins case, securing an increase in awards of 28%.

His success in the two cases made him in the eyes of the trade union movement a phenomenon. Another employers' barrister, Jim (later Mr Justice) Robinson, said, 'He had the reputation of being a giant killer. The results he had put on the board in the two cases of '59 were unbelievable in terms of what had gone on since 1952-53.'

Hawke was treated as a celebrity in trade union circles. Officials now referred to 'the brilliant advocate'; his Rhodes Scholarship became a matter of communal union pride, and Hawke tactfully stopped revealing his scorn for Cecil Rhodes and Rhodes Scholars; his string of degrees was remarked upon with a certain puzzled favour instead of derision. Suddenly, employing 'an intellectual', as the trade union movement and industrial journalists insisted on describing Hawke, seemed an interesting idea. Jim Baird, the industrial officer of the Amalgamated Metal Workers and Shipwrights Union, who at the time was a research officer for the militant Boilermakers' Society, recalled,

Bob was the only person I knew in the trade unions at a national level who had any tertiary education at all. He set out to introduce into the trade union movement arguments about economics. Looking back, it was economics of a modest level, but I can understand why: few people knew what economics was in those days. We [the Left] saw him as a good thing . . . There was a tradition in the trade union movement of making assertions and allegations, but we'd run into people who had tertiary education, who required us to *prove* our claims. And that was where the change in trade union thinking started to take place. It was one of the things Bob was able to do for the trade union movement: he made union arguments logical, reasonable and provable. He didn't always win, but he set in train that process. The days of wild assertions have gone.

Thanks to Hawke's successes, within a few years individual trade unions began to employ their own 'intellectuals' — either men and women with university training or tradesmen who were taken 'off the tools' and given time to read and think. This trend would probably have occurred anyway; it is certain that Hawke's example encouraged it, and that as advocate he gave to the Australian trade union movement something of as much value as money: a bold reinterpretation of ideas.

The employers were aghast at Hawke's success. He had persuaded the Commission to increase the national wages bill by £130 million — or £150 million, as the *Sydney Morning Herald* editorial writers said, or perhaps £165 million, as Peter Coleman claimed in the *Observer* — and was quickly dubbed Mr Inflation. The Commonwealth Treasury was known to be furious with the Commission. In the basic wage case of 1960, the Commonwealth, represented by Eggleston, departed from its practice of presenting neutral economic evidence and openly opposed the unions' case, saying that a wage increase would cause curtailment of plans for industrial expansion, weaken the confidence of overseas investors and cause a rapid spiralling of costs and prices. Hawke, who was asking for a 22s. increase in the basic wage, was so stunned by Eggleston's submission that he momentarily thought he had misunderstood it. When his former teacher replied that indeed the government stood against him, with the employers, Hawke snapped, 'This has never been done before'.

The Commission awarded an increase of only 5s.; it refused quarterly adjustments.

Hawke took the decision as a bitter defeat. He said, 'In 1959 the judges had been malleable. Suddenly the dead hand of Menzies' conservatism descended. I was very crooked on the Commission for the 1960 decision, crooked on the system . . . I'd been in the centre of Labor politics. I think the 1960 decision was a factor in drawing me to the Left.'

Left and Right, applied to the trade union movement, are terms which came into use from the late 1950s, to replace the earlier categories of Grouper and anti-Grouper. It is impossible to give a watertight definition of Right — people, and unions, could be Right on most issues but Left on others — but, in the broad, the Right was the child of the Groupers plus all those who so disapproved of the Communist Party (although they may have been anti-Grouper) that they supported the Menzies Government's strident anti-Communism. The Right of the trade union movement stretched from the NCC and the DLP to the centre of the ALP. The Left was everyone else. But in Victoria the Left was Lefter: radical and militant. Hawke's style fitted the Left (although the further Left disliked not only the workings of the Arbitration Commission, but also its very existence, and logically should have disapproved of Hawke as part of 'the system'). From the time he joined the ACTU the Left treated him with interested curiosity, then support, then wild enthusiasm. He was for the Left a positive, progressive force. The Right, natural xenophobes — their political ancestors had invented the White Australia policy — thought of him as an outsider and therefore dangerous. After 1959 the Right treated Hawke with grudging admiration. His defeat of 1960 brought them *schadenfreude*. On a personal level the Right found Hawke's lack of deference to the Bench improper and destabilising of a system which they supported though often disagreed with, but again on a personal level many Right-wing union leaders were vulnerable to Hawke's charm. However, once Hawke had been marked by the Left as *their* man he was fair game for the Right, for the two power blocs battled for territory continually. Hawke, always anxious to belong to a social group, was drawn into the embrace of the Left.

By the early 1960s there were widespread rumours that he was a Communist. Even Ellie got to hear of them and, on a trip to Melbourne, took her son aside to ask if he had become a Communist. Hawke was so irritated that he replied only, 'I'm not a card-carrying member'. In some of the employers' ranks a canard circulated that Hawke, a crypto-Communist, had as his real aim the shattering of the capitalist system — which he would accomplish by bankrupting it with wage increases. David McBride, who became a member of the Industries Assistance Commission after many years as industrial advocate for the Electrical Trades Union, recalled that an employers' representative said to him, 'When I saw you and Bob Hawke kicking a football at lunch-time I realised he was just a human being. I'd thought he was a Com.' The man went on to make it clear he had considered Hawke a manifestation of evil. Throughout Hawke's career this theme of evil was to recur as people projected their fears on to him.

They were able to do this, in part, because of the intensity, 'the religious fervour', of Hawke's nature. When he had moved to the ACTU he had finally broken the psychological bonds of theism and Congregationalism; the spiritual struggle that had begun in adolescence was over. 'It was soon after I moved to Melbourne', he recalled, 'that I realised: "I am an agnostic".'

The trade union world has always been for the most committed of its members 'a religion'; Hawke entered it with the fervour of a convert. It was a slight change in emphasis only for the excessively combative Christian scholar to become the excessively combative rescuer of the workers — fired up, in 1960, by the indignation of defeat.

Increasingly, Hawke espoused the causes of the Left. In trade union circles he supported unity tickets — that is, Labor candidates and Communists standing together for election to union office. In ALP circles, which for historical reasons were more venomous and personal in Victoria than in other States, Hawke associated himself with the Left's position of anti-American-ism and a belief in a whole range of demons: the CIA, Santamaria, the Australian Security Intelligence Organisation (which he believed, as did others, had opened a file on him), class enemies, and, of course, Archbishop Mannix, who during the 1958 election campaign had achieved new heights for the rhetoric of guilt-by-association with his declaration: 'every Communist and every Communist sympathiser in Australia wants a victory for the Evatt Party'. Hieser recalled, 'When we drove past Raheen, Mannix's residence, Bob shook his fist and roared at it'.

Kirby, who already greatly admired Hawke's mind, recalled that he was acutely embarrassed by him around this period when, one night at a dinner party given by the United States Consul General, Hawke and some trade unionists were openly contemptuous of their surroundings. The Consul General's residence had a splendidly appointed dining-room, with Aubusson carpets and other sumptuous fittings. Kirby said,

> The present Bob Hawke would be interested in them as civilized appur-tenances, but then he and the other union fellows were contemptuous, almost swaggeringly rude, making snide remarks to each other in voices that were easily overheard. I'd been to numerous functions of that rather grand nature with trade union teams and they had always behaved properly. The next day the Consul General rang me and in the course of conversation said, 'I hope I did not offend your young com-panions'. I apologised for them.

At another dinner Hawke shouted at Kirby's wife when she could not, momentarily, recall Hazel's name. He saw Kirby at the time, he said, 'as the big Chief Judge, the member of the Establishment', and once, when drunk, bailed up Lady Kirby to demand, 'Why does your husband hate me?'

Ralph Willis, who in late 1959 joined the ACTU as research assistant, recalled that Hawke was brusque and initially intimidating and that nothing in his behaviour suggested that he was the darling son of a devout household. But, as usual, older men knew intuitively that Hawke's gentle side could be evoked by a fatherly approach. In the trade union movement one such man was Jock Innes, who met Hawke in the Lygon Hotel just after he had begun work at the ACTU and 'took me under his wing'. Innes used to refer to Hawke as 'my other son'. His real son was Ted, one of Hawke's boon companions, then an official of the Electrical Trades Union, later a federal parliamentarian. In the Arbitration Commission Hawke attracted another father-figure: Mr Justice Foster.

During the 1959 basic wage case Foster sent a note to Hawke asking for a meeting when the case was over. Foster lived three minutes' walk away from Hawke, in Sandringham, and a regular Sunday morning visit from the advocate to the judge was established. While Innes, Terry Winter and other senior trade union men had taken it upon themselves to educate Hawke in union lore, explaining to him the complexity of alliances and rivalries, Foster performed the same function for Hawke about the arbitration system. Hawke said,

> Alf had a very considerable affection towards me, and an enormous sense of gratitude. The first thing he said when I went to his house was how thrilled he was that I had understood the disastrousness of the 1953 judgment and had been so astringent in my analysis of it. He regarded it as his mission to change that judgment, and he had thought it was going to be a pretty lonely mission. Then I turned up.

When Foster learned from Hawke that Dr Colin Clark had rejected his thesis subject, the old man was gleeful. He told Hawke something of which he had been unaware during the 1959 case: 'That Clark was the economic guru to Santamaria. And that Santamaria had *worn the carpet thin* — Alf's exact phrase — going in and out of Sir Raymond Kelly's office before the 1953 case!'

When in 1961 Hawke returned to his assault upon the 1953 judgment he did so with the fire of avenging a personal injury. It was one of his greatest performances, in Australia, as an advocate.

Hawke's instant success in his career and his need to become one with the trade union brotherhood was achieved, predictably, at the expense of his family life.

He and Hazel, because of their small-town backgrounds, had felt nervous about living in a city as large as Melbourne. They decided it would be more enjoyable if they lived near the water, and if they had their own house. Hawke made it a condition of joining the ACTU that he be lent the deposit for buying a house. Harold Souter, the ACTU Secretary, recalled, 'Bob was amazing for a lawyer. He just looked at the contract and said, OK. It was Hazel who did all the bargaining.' It was Hazel who did everything — she was the foundation of Hawke's support system. She said, 'He had a very difficult job ahead of him and I was determined there would be no chink in his armour'.

Within a few days they had bought a cottage in Keats Street, Sandringham, a pleasant but then unfashionable bayside suburb, half an hour's drive from the city. They were too much in debt to afford a refrigerator or furniture, even a bed, and slept on a mattress on the floor. Hazel made cupboards, bookshelves and a wardrobe out of appleboxes; she bought a second-hand stove for £7 from which she was still scrubbing grease in February 1959 when their second child, Stephen, was born. Ten Innes, an electrician by trade, rewired the house; Wally Curran, of the Meat Employees Union, laid cement — an ironic fact, for by 1971 Hawke and Curran detested each other.

School aside, Hawke's childhood had been devoted to a life of games and religion and he never developed the practical skills of boyhood — carpentry, mechanical understanding, a basic knowledge of physics and management of finance. His only domestic skill was gardening and, when he was older, some cooking. Unless a piece of machinery fed the imagination — like an aeroplane, or a yacht (Hawke learned to sail) — it bored him, so much so that at the age of fifty he would stand squinting and puzzled at the printed instructions on the lid of an automatic washing-machine or some other electrical appliance, as if at a script written in Greek. He never paid household bills, or concerned himself about his overdraft or tried to administrate — even to getting his newspapers delivered — as long as there was someone around to do it for him. Jean Sinclair, his personal assistant in later years at the ACTU, became so used to Hawke's complaints that filing cabinets were stuck or electric kettles did not work or addresses were lost that she would wonder aloud sometimes how he managed to dial a telephone.

Hawke's major foray into the handyman field while at Keats Street was to build a carport: he cubed instead of squared the quantities of sand and cement he would need and for weeks afterwards the pavement was blocked by a sand dune. 'If he built a hen-house it would fall down!' Hieser exclaimed, not quite accurately for Hawke went on to assemble a splendid aviary for Susan (after Hazel had shown him how). But that was a labour of love, and for living things. Hieser's brother-in-law, the Melbourne University research scientist, Bill Mansfield, built Hawke a fence.

From the day Hawke began work at the ACTU his family life became, he said, 'unusual'. He had to work extremely long hours; to overcome the prejudice against him and to make himself as effective as possible as an advocate he needed to rub shoulders with unionists. This meant spending hours yarning and joking in the smokey, smelly, red-linoed and cream-walled 'Trades Hall office' — the Lygon Hotel. He was rarely home. The running of the household and raising of the children fell almost entirely to Hazel. She was a skilful manager and liked the traditional role of mother and chatelaine, although as she said later, 'No one will ever know how difficult it was'. It was to become more difficult. By the time his children were teenagers Hawke was so over-committed to work and to his vast network of relationships that his family had to arrange appointments to be able to discuss problems with him.

But in his early years at the ACTU part of Sunday, at least, was a family day and throughout the summer months Hawke, Innes, Mansfield, and David White (another research scientist) together with their spouses and children, played tennis and had barbecues.

White, later a professor at Melbourne University, recalled, 'Bob was out to win at tennis. You'd be walking back from the net towards the base line when his next ball would come whizzing past your head.'

At the time Hawke joined the ACTU its public image was at best sketchy. There were two full-time officials, Monk and Souter, and an executive which was elected at biennial congresses and made up of trade union leaders drawn from the State Trades and Labour Councils and various industry groups. The Trades and Labour Councils, which mesh with State Labor Party machines and are in some States the real centres of ALP power and patronage, operate as the State branches of the ACTU. Monk and Souter aside, the members of the executive owed allegiance first to their unions or Trades and Labour Councils. The ACTU was a body for residual loyalty.

Against the bitter opposition of the huge, sprawling Australian Workers' Union, the trade union movement had created the ACTU in 1927 as a co-ordinating instrument; a negotiator during major strikes; and as a national representative of the movement to government, to overseas union groups, to the International Labour Organisation, and so forth. Its single constitutional objective is: 'The socialisation of industry, i.e. production, distribution and exchange', an aim to which it has merely paid lip service. The union movement in Australia is highly-fragmented; constantly distracted and enervated by Left-Right power struggles and intra-bloc rivalries; jealous; underfinanced; and used to an easy life — in the sense that in the twentieth century it has been protected by the arbitration system from the protracted wars with employers which are waged in a collective bargaining system. Under collective bargaining a union must have the funds to pay its members to strike for three months at a stretch;* in Australia the majority of strikes last only a day. The ACTU was then and still is only of sporadic use to unions. They kept it broke by paying tiny fees for its upkeep, and in non-congress years often not paying at all. The ACTU is an inherently weak organisation, with no machinery for enforcing its decisions upon its affiliated unions. Its authority springs from the moral force of solidarity — with the occasional trip or plum job, arranged through a Trades and Labour Council or the Conciliation and Arbitration Commission, to reward an especially helpful union official or to get rid of a mischievous one. But in the main it is powerless

---

* Technological change has made collective bargaining much easier; by the 1970s a few hundred workers, in the oil industry, for example, could bring the nation to a halt. This trend will continue.

to give patronage or to punish, except with public shaming and isolation from the rest of the trade union movement.

Albert Monk, a great and very astute man in Australian industrial life, kept the organisation going and prevented an outright split in the movement in the 1950s — when the ALP split — by a combination of diplomacy, cunning and stubbornness. The Grouper unions, like the Ironworkers, Clerks and Shop Assistants, were not expelled nor encouraged to leave the ACTU voluntarily, because of Monk's determination to keep the movement whole.

He had the short rotund figure and round pudding face of a music hall grocer; he wore pebble-lens spectacles, had a wall-eye, and mumbled. Monk's manners were old fashioned and rather courtly, particularly with women whom, as a breed, he found intimidating. He disliked publicity and hated appearing on television.

Monk was committed body and soul to the trade union movement, to getting a fair deal for the working class. He had come to Australia from England at the age of eight, in 1908; at his roughneck school he had been abused and beaten up for his appearance and his accent. The unemployment of the 1930s burned an ineradicable fear into his mind — 'For Albert the Depression ended the day he died'[1] — and from then on he did all in his power to prevent its recurrence; this meant increasing the productive capacity of the Australian economy and, from 1949, co-operating with anti-Labor governments to achieve their economic goals. In 1956 the wharfies publicly denounced him as 'a scab' and 'Holt's Holiday Home Boarder' (Harold Holt being the Minister for Labour). Monk was highly strung, although this rarely showed in his enigmatically bland appearance. Before congresses his hands would tremble and his whole body seemed to shake with nervousness until the moment when he took the platform to give his presidential address, which he delivered in an inaudible mumble, to awed silence. Monk ran the congresses dictatorially: any motion of which his executive disapproved he ruled lost on the voices, and left it up to the floor to demand a division. By the 1960s he was an alcoholic and would make ten or more quick forays each day out of the back door of the ACTU and into the Lygon for a nip of whisky. He had a thousand acquaintances but few intimates, although many men who worked closely with him held Monk in loving admiration, and all respected him.

Monk left the administration of the ACTU entirely to Souter. The Secretary, unlike Monk who had never been a blue-collar worker but had started his career as a shorthand writer, had been a fitter by trade and had risen through the ranks to become in the 1940s the industrial advocate of the militant Amalgamated Engineering Union, sire of the Amalgamated Metal Workers and Shipwrights Union. Souter came from a South Australian Seventh Day Adventist background and remained a teetotaller and non-smoker; he drank neither tea nor coffee. His wholesome regime showed in his appearance: he was small, lithe and energetic. Even in his sixties he had a bright-eyed, boyish air which went well with his salty, though decorous, turn of phrase. Souter's integrity was a byword in industrial life, as was his commitment to the movement. In the 1960s when the giant Australian Workers' Union was negotiating affiliation with the ACTU Souter drank two whiskies with the AWU bossman, Tom Dougherty — who regarded other liquids as fit only for bathwater or for babies — and the next day was blinded with headache. He had a thankless task in running an organisation which was always under-financed and under-staffed, and which he had taken on without training in administration when the previous Secretary, Reg Broadby, was dying. In the twenty years Souter was Secretary of the ACTU employees and executive members complained frequently that he was secretive and refused to delegate. He was an administrator who finely constricted his own life and sought to constrict the lives of others. Being teetotal was an immense social disadvantage to him in the trade union world, with its obsession with the idea of 'a man's man', defined and revealed in the boozy, tactile fraternity of the pub. 'A sarsparilla drinker', (Sir) Jack Egerton said of Souter, his voice thick with disdain. Souter was all fastidiousness: alert, clear-eyed, clean and lean — an alien. His relationship with Hawke was, from the outset, uncomfortable.

Until 1952 the ACTU had been housed in a nook in the Melbourne Trades Hall, a Victorian elephant of a building with Doric columns, fifteen-foot ceilings and a wholly impractical internal distribution of space. In 1952 it moved across the road into a two-storied red brick box of its own, with a flat roof and floors so badly laid that in the upper storey they rose and fell in waves. There was no furniture upstairs and Hawke at first had a cubby-hole with a desk and telephone on the ground floor. His arrival brought the staff to six — Monk and Souter, their secretaries, and a junior, Jennie McAlpine — and upset their tiny, cosy nest. McAlpine recalled, 'The whole atmosphere changed when Bob arrived, and even before he arrived. We all worked at ordinary desks, but Harold said now that The Young Man was coming the women would have to have modesty boards on the fronts of their desks, so that The Young Man wouldn't look at our legs.' McAlpine was to work for Hawke, but when he moved upstairs, through lack of space on the ground floor, Souter 'would not allow me to move up, too, because we would be alone together'. McAlpine was a teenager and a devout Baptist; from the outset Hawke treated her like a kid sister and re-named her Susie, after his daughter. 'Susie' McAlpine had never tasted alcohol and when, towards Christmas in 1958, the other secretaries planned to introduce her to drink, Hawke wrote her an *Ode to a Plot*, which ran in part

> But even worse now comes to light
> They plan to get young Susie tight
> Who is to blame for this foul plot
> To turn young Sue into a sot?

The temptress holder of the evil apple
None other than our Tessy Chapple . . .
   [who worked for Souter]
But Susie now has been forewarned
Before the evil day has dawned
Now these females cannot harm her,
Saved by her knight in shining armour.

He signed it, The Knight.[2]

Despite Hawke's chivalrous attitude to 'Susie', Souter remained suspicious, for Hawke's reputation for wenching was already known. A few months later Souter threatened them both with the sack for working alone together (on preparation of the 1959 basic wage case) on a Sunday. Bad feeling between Hawke and Souter was now firmly established, and was to grow. The atmosphere in the ACTU office, which had been good-natured, turned sour; by the time Ralph Willis joined the staff a year later there was 'a very unpleasant atmosphere in the place'.

'Susie' left the ACTU in 1962 to get married, but she continued to visit the office, to chat and show off her children. In the late 1960s she went to tell Hawke some terrible news. She said,

> We'd been talking for a while when Bob said, 'What have you really come to tell me, Susie?' and I broke down and told him that I had been diagnosed as suffering multiple sclerosis. He came round to me and put his arms around me, then he got very angry. He said 'Why you? You've done nothing wrong in your life! You've been a church-goer, you don't smoke, you don't drink . . . !' I thought he was angry with God. That night he rang me to say he had arranged with a Professor of Medicine to do new tests on me. Two weeks later I got the results: they were negative. I went in to tell Bob and he saw the smile I was wearing as I came through the door, and he began to cry with relief. We both sat there blubbering.*

There was no properly organised library in the ACTU and throughout 1959 Hawke was without a research assistant. Because the basic wage cases began in February he was working most intensively during the humid Melbourne summer. He said,

> The conditions were frightful. Because of the flat roof the temperature in my office used to reach about 120° F. The way I had to discipline

---

* In 1973 'Susie' was running down the street to help a neighbour who has having a domestic crisis, when 'everything went haywire'. She has been partially crippled since.

myself for work and sleep was remarkable. I'd leave home at four or four-thirty in the morning and work for five hours before going into court. I taught myself to lie on the floor and sleep during the lunch adjournment, then could return fresh to court. I'd have a nap again in the late afternoon, and work into the night. The pressure was unbelievable. In the peak periods it was seven days a week, eighteen hours a day, for several weeks. But that ability to catnap was a tremendous advantage. Ever since I've been able to sleep anywhere . . . Eggleston had taught me that as long as I was prepared I need not be nervous in court. But I had to be right on top of it, because once I got on my feet I was totally vulnerable. I had to be on top of all the statistics, all the theories, and prepared to answer questions that were flung at me from the Bench, or that came from the Bar table — from employers or the Commonwealth — and they had all the resources in the world. The work had the beauty for me of a very concrete relevance to society. I think the joy of that carried me through.

It was obvious by the end of the year that Hawke had to have help. Ralph Willis (later the Member for Gellibrand) was employed, and 'Susie' was allowed to move upstairs now there was a chaperon. Willis was another 'intellectual': he had an economics degree and had been working in the Department of Labour, but he had the advantage of being the son of a Boilermakers' Society official who was universally respected in the trade union movement. Willis recalled,

I had nicked out of work to a phone box in Bourke Street to ring Bob and ask him how I should apply for the job. He was brusque. He said, 'Do what you're doing now — organise a time to come and see us'. He gave the impression that he didn't give a damn whether I came or not. At the interview he made it clear that I would have to work bloody hard, and that was fully borne out. When cases were on they consumed our lives: we'd have a few beers in the evening, then return to the office for more hours of work. Bob used to write out his own notes, but he didn't read from them. His method was to prepare notes in a way which allowed him to expound upon them at great length. Once, in the 1964 case, he spoke for a whole day on only three lines of notes . . . It used to amaze me that he would walk out of the Arbitration Commision, having talked on one plane all day, step into the Lygon and swap yarns with blokes from the wharf, as easily as with barristers. His key attribute as a union official and a politician is probably that ability he has to relate to all levels. He really enjoyed mixing with unionists: he could spend hours listening to their stories. During his years as advocate he established a huge network of friendships through those pub contacts, and became known as 'a good guy' . . . Bob used to get drunk, but in those days he was a good drunk — he'd get into spirited arguments, and could always argue logically no matter how much he'd had to drink and he could still drive a car relatively safely.

An oddity of Hawke's drinking was that he did not have 'normal' hangovers: in his whole life he has never had a headache. Hieser, who stayed overnight with Hawke often, complained, 'He'd get up, after maybe an hour's sleep, bright-eyed and bushy-tailed and asking for his breakfast, when the rest of us were barely able to speak'.

After his defeat in the 1960 basic wage case Hawke partly recouped his dignity with a South Australian basic wage case later that year. The employers were presenting an ingenious and apparently logical argument that wages in the State should be reduced because of a lower cost of living there. Hawke had a flash of insight about the fault in his opponent's logic, which concerned 'the going rate'; confirmed his guess, and won the case. The next national hearing was set for early 1961 before Kirby, Ashburner and Moore, the latter a new judge who had appeared as advocate for the Commonwealth during 1959. Ashburner was regarded by all sides as the most conservative member of the Bench. He had been an advocate for the meat industry employers and had held some briefs for shipping companies and BHP. He was a former Rhodes Scholar. The employers, who had panicked after Hawke's successes in 1959 and dropped their usual counsel, Drew Aird, had hopes of sympathy from Ashburner. Moore was an unknown quantity. For the 1961 case the employers engaged a highly regarded common law Queen's Counsel from the Melbourne Bar, Dr E.G. Coppel. As they went into court photographs were taken: Coppel, white-haired, wearing rimless half-moon spectacles and with a dignfied demeanour, looked like a headmaster standing beside a bright senior boy. Hawke was grinning, as slim as a whippet, his pompadour of dark hair gleaming, and his eyes too — for he was about to eat Dr Coppel.

Hawke's brief was the same as before: that the cost of living adjustments should be restored so that real wages could keep pace with prices, and that gains in productivity be substituted for 'capacity to pay' and distributed to the community as an increase in the basic wage. This year he had extra psychological strength on his side: anger about the 1960 decision, and knowledge of Santamaria's role in the 1953 decision which, for the third time, he would be attempting to have overturned. He also had a trump card, a witness, Sir Douglas Copland, an economist who had been prominent in Australian public affairs in the 1930s and 1940s. During the war Copland had been advisor to Curtin and was known as the economic ruler of the nation. He had been Ambassador to China and High Commissioner in Ottawa; he was the first vice-chancellor of the Australian National University; he had nine doctorates; he had assisted the Victorian Employers' Federation in establishing an economic research project and was a director of it; he had coined the phrase 'milk-bar economy' for post-war Australia. He was a big, vigorous man with a large voice which in economic matters carried as if ringing down from Mt Olympus.

Under questioning from Hawke in the witness box Copland gave evidence that since 1953 productivity had risen by 19.5% and wages by 18%; he agreed with Hawke's suggestion that the lack of cost-of-living adjustments was an injustice to the lower level of wage earners; he also agreed that he could not see how the economy would be injured if automatic adjustments were resumed.

Dr Coppel had called as a witness a senior lecturer in economics at Melbourne University, Dr J.O.N. Perkins. In the economic fraternity news had already spread that Hawke, because he understood economics, was much harsher than the ordinary barrister in cross-examination, and that his technique of taking a statement and tearing it into small, verbal shreds, and the sheer violence of the aura around him when he was battling with a witness caused embarrassment and intimidation. When Coppel announced his witness, Perkins, Hawke immediately requested the right of cross-examination on broad economic issues. Earlier in the case Hawke had cross-examined a leading agricultural economist, Keith Campbell, on broad economic issues and had overwhelmed him. Perkins considered for a few minutes outside the courtroom then announced that he would not be questioned on matters outside his field of expertise, and therefore would not appear. The practice of calling economic experts was over: Hawke had created a situation where his opposition would have, like him, to speak with authority.

Coppel knew little about wage fixing or economics. For the employers the case was, in the words of his junior, 'disastrous'.

Unexpectedly, Hawke had turned up a second trump card. His opening address lasted three days and was directed at the Bench in highly personal terms, a characteristic of his debating which, in later years, won him hundreds of arguments — and no friends. He told the Bench: 'You have perpetrated this situation . . . You have inflicted hardship upon thousands of people . . . Do not delude yourselves . . .' Ashburner, a traditionalist, was offended by Hawke's hectoring and abusive tone and asked Kirby, as Chief Judge, to rebuke him publicly. Kirby refused. On the first day of the hearing a group of railway workers had marched on the Commission, made a row, then ranged themselves along the back of the court in such a way that letters pinned to their lapels had spelt out the message WE WANT MORE DOUGH. The Chief Judge's salary was almost ten times the basic wage. When Kirby announced, 'I am afraid we will have to adjourn' (because of the railway men) Hawke snapped at him, 'It's not something *you'd* know about'. Kirby was fearful that if he rebuked Hawke he would be so pugnacious in his response that the only option would be to put him out of court. That would inevitably lead to demonstrations, questions in Parliament and so forth. With the Chief Judge sitting in furious silence, Ashburner decided to act. On his third day of non-stop talking Hawke burst out: 'It is indisputable that in real terms the output of goods and services has increased, but this Commission, particularly in that nonsense in the Annual Leave judgment . . .' Ashburner interjected, 'I wish you would not distract me by using those adjectives, such as "absurd", words like "nonsense" and so on'.

> HAWKE: I am using it in the strictly literal sense of 'non sense'.
> ASHBURNER, J: It does distract my attention from the substance of your argument.
> HAWKE: If it has that effect, Your Honour, there is certainly not much use in pursuing it because I do not want to distract Your Honour from what I was saying. I will contain my feelings.[3]

Hawke had abruptly realised his error, and an area for advantage: he had engaged Ashburner in personal debate — the judge had come forward and Hawke could now wrestle with him, one-to-one. Ashburner was the only member of the Bench unfamiliar with the arguments already enunciated in 1959 (Moore had heard them as counsel for the Commonwealth that year) and Hawke, having flushed him out, concentrated upon pursuing him. George Polites, who had recently been appointed as Secretary of the Australian Council of Employers' Federation, said with a giggle, 'It was sick-making. Hawke talked to Ashburner like a Dutch uncle.' Hawke also wore his Oxford tie, an accessory which Ashburner, who liked to wear *his* Oxford tie, noted with approval.

The transcript of the case is full of questions from Hawke such as 'Does Your Honour appreciate my argument?' and 'Does Your Honour have any further reservations about this, because I can see that it is obviously a fundamental matter?' and 'I do not know whether Your Honour, Mr Justice Ashburner, has any reservations still to which you might like me to address myself?' Ashburner knew so little of economics that at one stage the whole Bar table had to suppress a convulsion of laughter when His Honour asked about 'the London funds', at that time a term synonymous with Australia's international reserves. The employers argued that the success of Australia's export earnings, reflected in the London funds, was fuelling inflation in Australia. 'How', asked the Judge, 'can the money be in London and be used in Australia at the same time?' It took counsel almost an hour to explain the significance of high reserves. To his credit and to the credit of the system Ashburner was prepared to reveal his ignorance.

Hawke's address in reply lasted twelve days. Sir John Moore recalled,

> He'd reached a stage where he physically couldn't stand, except by hanging on to the lectern. He was leaning over it, supporting his weight on it, and still talking to us. We were adjourning at regular intervals because his voice was giving out. I could see from where I was sitting on the Bench that he had kicked his shoes off and was standing there in his

socks, just barely able to go on, but still arguing very forcefully. He was an extraordinarily strong debater.

Sheer will-power and belief in his cause carried Hawke through and evoked his habitual lapses of tact — he referred to some of Kirby's judgments as 'pathetic', 'completely fallacious', 'objectionable', and accused the Commission of being cowardly. But it had been a magnificent performance: he had finally convinced the Chief Judge he must confess and repent for the 1953 decision, and he had won the minds of Ashburner and Moore. The reform of the system that Hawke had demanded so precociously, in Oxford, was about to take place.

The decision, which was unanimous, increased the basic wage by 12s. and decreed that in future it would be adjusted annually in line with the cost-of-living index, and triennially for increases in productivity. The onus would be on the employers to prove that this should not happen.

In the trade union movement, Hawke was a hero. The employers ground their teeth.

He spent some of his next year abroad, as a delegate to the Duke of Edinburgh's study conference in Canada, and later studying the effects of Britain's entry into the European Economic Community. In early 1963 he argued another margins case against yet another advocate the employers were trying out, and achieved a pleasing result. But while his career had reached a peak, Hawke was now in trouble with Monk and Souter and at home his family life was under strain. Both problems were due, in part, to his success.

From his first heady achievements in 1959 he had been in demand as a speaker at public functions. By May 1960 Monk, Souter and some Right-wing members of the ACTU executive were alarmed at the tendency for Hawke to be presented as a spokesman for the ACTU, and the question of the public statements of the Council's research officer became a matter for executive debate. Its discussion split, as ever, on Left-Right lines. Souter had forbidden Hawke to speak publicly about ACTU policy; there had been a row over an airfare; the ACTU junior vice-president, Bill Evans, of the Left, had asked Hawke for material to use in a speech but Souter had instructed Hawke not to supply it. Evans required Souter to defend himself, which he did, with the support of the Right-wing boss of the NSW Labour Council, Jim Kenny. The issue was settled, with bad tempers all round, to burst forth again a year later. In June 1961 Hawke attended the annual State Labor Party conference and in intemperate language attacked Sir Raymond Kelly (whom he once described, according to the *Financial Review*, as 'that Irish pig farmer'), the Democratic Labor Party and B.A. Santamaria for combining to defeat quarterly adjustments. Santamaria issued a denial of his involvement with Kelly; Senator McManus, the leader of the DLP, issued a demand for an apology. Monk was so angry with Hawke he issued a statement saying that

Hawke had been attending the ALP conference as a representative of the Theatrical Employees' Association, not the ACTU. In ALP and Left-wing trade union circles the row increased Hawke's celebrity status and his opportunities for more agitating. He was asked to appear on television, a medium he was learning to master; newspapers pestered for interviews — and met him in different moods: the Melbourne *Sun* in 1963 described Hawke as, 'softly spoken, quiet'. Life as a minor celebrity had an electric edge of excitement. There were more hours of jubilant exchange in the pub, more late nights with boon companions, more boon companions — for Hawke could be 'best mates' with thirty people at once — and his days see-sawed with the thrill of new friendships, new exquisite moments of fun and rapport. Repeatedly, when people attempt to describe why hours passed with Hawke seem magically charged with humour and play, they fall back to saying, 'He's just such *fun*'. But he was drinking too much and at home arguments were frequent.

Hazel had given birth to a third child, Rosslyn, in November 1960 and by July 1963 was 28 weeks pregnant with a fourth. Hawke used often to tell 'Susie', 'I'm going to have seven children — the Biblical number'. On 1 August Hazel was out shopping when she felt the pangs of premature labour. She was taken to the closest hospital where an emergency caesarian section was performed. The new baby was a fine-looking black-haired boy, but he had to be kept in a humidicrib while Hazel, who was very ill after losing pints of blood, was too weak to see him. Hawke told her, 'He's a really strong baby — wait until you see his beautiful little chest!' To Hawke's delight she suggested that the new boy should be named Robert James. As events turned out, Hazel never saw her fourth child.

Within hours delight turned to anxiety, then despair. The baby, seven weeks premature, was dying. Hawke sat for twenty-four hours beside his crib watching him sink away from life. Hazel was too ill to leave hospital and Hawke, with one companion for support, saw Robert James buried, then arranged for Hazel to recover at the house of their tennis friends, David and Marjorie White. In the first days of shock he wept frequently and began to drink himself into oblivion. As always when deeply distressed he became speechless and immobilised — he could not talk out his feelings, he would not return to the grave. Indeed, it was almost twenty years and Hawke was a different man before he could say, one day in 1981, 'I think I'll go and visit Robert'. On a Saturday afternoon about a fortnight after Hazel returned home he was to go to the football and insisted that she accompany him. They set out by taxi but had not gone far when Hawke had what Hazel described as 'a frightening attack: he was disoriented, felt paralysed and thought he was dying'. She took him straight to hospital. He was suffering alcoholic poisoning.

He was still ill from his self-punishment and Hazel was in the early stages of a long period of grief when, a few weeks later Hawke was pressed to begin his political career in earnest. He was attending an ALP dinner in a Melbourne hotel when Albert McNolty, Secretary of the Victorian Labor Party, made a point of sitting next to him.

The Prime Minister, Robert Menzies, had won the 1961 election by only one seat and since then had been on the alert for an issue which would excuse him holding another, premature election. Since 1961 the economy had recovered; unemployment, which had been 2.8%, was once again negligible; and, most importantly, the ALP had recently committed one of its breathtaking public gaffes. Arthur Calwell, the Leader, and Gough Whitlam, the Deputy-Leader, had been photographed late at night standing in the street under a lamppost, hunched in overcoats against the cold, waiting to be informed of a decision of the Party's 36-member federal conference of which they, although the Party's foremost public representatives, were not members. The photograph had been published under the heading '36 Faceless Men', a popular term for the conference delegates, and had done the ALP immense damage, with its suggestion of sinister, unknown forces manipulating Labor's parliamentary politicians like puppets. Since 1951 when Menzies' legislation to ban the Communist Party had been defeated, due largely to the efforts of the former Labor Leader, H.V. Evatt, Menzies had claimed that the ALP was ruled by 'outside forces'. Had he taken the photograph himself he could not have had a more dramatic illustration for his claims. Then, in early October 1963 the ALP, or rather the Leader, Calwell, compounded the gaffe by asking the federal executive to give a ruling on State aid for non-government schools. State aid is Australia's most ancient and bitter political issue. Obligingly — for the Prime Minister — the ALP federal executive ruled against State aid.

Menzies called a snap election for 30 November 1963.

In addition to a domestic issue he had an external one: President Sukarno of Indonesia, the Great Leader of the Revolution, the Father of the Nation, the Champion of Islam, Field Marshal and Supreme Commander of the Armed Forces, President for Life, etc., had just launched Confrontation of Malaysia. In September Sukarno's denouncement of Britain's manipulation of Asian affairs had been so enthusiastically received that Jakarta mob had razed the British Embassy. Effigies were burnt, cars thrown into canals. Sukarno was depicted in Australia as a dangerous lunatic, Joe Stalin in a black velvet fez. The electorate was encouraged to believe that at any moment a multitude of Indonesian soldiers would turn their attention to the south. The Australian government, having played a part in stimulating fear, promptly offered to assuage it. Menzies announced that Australia was buying a fleet of long-range, low-altitude bomber aircraft of the most contemporary design, then called the TFX, later famous as the F111. With these, Australia could bomb Jakarta. The Defence Minister, Athol Townley, was despatched to Washington to lay a deposit on the table for these dashing war machines. It was not explained to the public that it would be at least eight years before they would be built and airworthy. Malaysia and Indonesia would be friends and

Sukarno would be an invalid prisoner-of-State long before the first F111 had a chance to crash. But meanwhile, Menzies had a cause.

Hawke said, 'I remember as though it were yesterday: Albert McNolty sat beside me and began to heavy me about standing'. McNolty had already done Hawke a favour: he was an official of the Sheet Metal Workers' Union, of which Hawke was a member-of-convenience, for as ACTU advocate he formally appeared for the metal trades unions. Hawke had asked McNolty to get him a 'good deal' on a refrigerator and one day a brand new refrigerator had been delivered to the house as a gift. Hawke continued:

> His argument was simple. He said, 'Look, we can win government this election, we need only to hold the seats we've got and win a couple more. Corio is one we should win. You are a national figure now. You could win Corio. You've got a duty and an obligation to the whole Labor movement. You're a marvellous advocate, no one can do what you've been doing. *But*, winning government is more important. You can do it.' I was not very thrilled about the idea. Hazel and I talked it over. Next day I talked to Harold [Souter] and Albert [Monk] about it and said I felt I had an obligation to run, that it was a matter of duty. They were understanding, and gave me leave.

Within days Hawke had been formally selected as the candidate for Corio, a mixed rural and industrial seat south-west of Melbourne with its centre the city of Geelong. It was held by the Minister for Shipping, Hubert Opperman, an Olympic champion cyclist who was called Oppy by his constituents. Hawke would need a 3.4% swing to unseat him.

Hazel said, 'We were both still very sick and sorry people. The election campaign was a necessary and practical commitment. It helped us, in some degree, to cope with the grieving.'

Once Hawke had overcome his reluctance he mentally changed gears; he shut the baby's death out of his mind and set out to become a parliamentarian.

Chapter Eleven

'If I'd had another week of campaigning, I would have won', Hawke said later. Time is always his enemy. But it is doubtful, given the events of October-November 1963, that an extra week on the hustings would have put Hawke in Parliament as the Member for Corio. The election campaign began with the assassination of President Diem of South Vietnam and ended with the assassination of President Kennedy of the United States; by 23 November not just the electors of Corio but the whole Western world was appalled and yearning for security. People, in those circumstances, do not dismiss conservative governments. The nation in 1963 clung to Menzies as a child to its father's leg.

Hawke polled 748 more primary votes than Opperman, creating a swing to Labor of 3% in an election which brought a national 3% swing away from the ALP and when its vote in Victoria as a whole dropped to 40.3%, with 12.4% of first preferences going to the DLP. His result was excellent, in the circumstances, but it was not good enough: after the distribution of DLP preferences he had only 22,456 votes to Opperman's 25,666. 'Who brought this Communist in here?' a member of the Corio Club had demanded when he saw Hawke being introduced around the clubhouse. Hawke's sponsor, a local businessman, had strode forward and knocked the calumniator down. It was a nasty campaign.

It began badly for Hawke, with resentment of him among the local Party faithful. The rulers of the Victorian ALP, the central executive, were dissatisfied with the two Corio men who had put themselves forward for the seat and on the eve of selection of candidates (having secured Hawke's promise to run), announced that nominations had been re-opened. They gave the early election as their excuse for bending the rules. They then selected Hawke. An outsider. George Poyser, in 1963 the Assistant Secretary of the Victorian ALP, former Secretary of the Geelong Trades Hall Council (and later a Labor

Senator), was appointed Hawke's campaign manager. He said, 'There was a lot of resentment that the executive had behaved in this way and a lot of resentment against Hawke who, Party members felt, had been imposed upon them. I went down to Corio with a feeling of dread.'

Enthusiastic local members are essential in election campaigns: they do the chores — the letter-box drops, the handing out of advertisements, the lending of their motor cars, the cheering at meetings. There was only a month in which to campaign. Poyser said, 'Hawke had to be sold to the Party faithful before we could sell him to the electorate at large. The key to it was that he was a Rhodes Scholar and a working-class advocate. We pushed the Rhodes Scholar line and within a week Bob had 100% of the local organisation behind him.' But meanwhile, Opperman's machine had caught the scent of ALP discontent about the outsider and began to press hard on the 'local man' issue. A few weeks earlier the football team of the city of Geelong had played in the Victorian Football League grand final. Football is a matter of life and death to Victorians who each winter become maddened, in their tens of thousands, as the grand final approaches. Opperman had made a highly publicised dash by air and road from Brisbane to arrive in time to see Geelong beat Hawthorn for the premiership. He still glowed, locally, from the heroes' reflected glory. Hawke gave an undertaking that if elected he would live in Corio, but a promise was not enough to quieten the clamour of criticism, so the Party rented him a house in Portarlington. Hazel and the children moved down from Melbourne. She was still 'easily upset', as campaigners noticed, and not well enough to play a public role; 'I fed the troops', she said. Here again the Opperman machine had an edge: his wife was politically active and campaigned continually for her husband among local people she had known for years. Hawke's own health was a worry. While an inside group knew that he was recovering from alcoholic poisoning and grief, and described this to others as 'a bit of a chest problem', there was doubt whether he would be able to stand up to the campaigning. 'Every day there was a factory-gate meeting, each evening he went around the clubs and at weekends he met the football enthusiasts. We had to make him a byword in Geelong very quickly; he had to be given the maximum exposure to the electorate', Poyser said. A sense of pathos is never far from the ALP and was expressed in the slogan Hawke's managers wrote: 'Bob's standing for you — give him a seat'. Opperman, in contrast, ran on the virile message, 'Performance not Promises! Your man is Opperman.'

On 5 November the Press was forecasting the possibility of a Labor victory. On 6 November Calwell, in what he described as 'a red-blooded, face-to-face Australian political meeting open to all comers', launched Labor's campaign, promising a 5½% increase in economic growth, a revolution in education, a vigorous housing drive, tax concessions, improved social services, and a nuclear-free zone in the Southern Hemisphere. Menzies, who had perfected the appearance of lofty good temper with fools and such confidence in the job he was doing that he could afford a gentlemanly indolence, replied that the ALP was either promising 'roaring inflation' or intended to increase taxes. A nuclear-free zone was a 'suicidal proposal', he sighed. He had smacked at Calwell as if dislodging a gnat. He would open his own campaign a week later — on television.

The Corio campaign managers knew their candidate. Hawke was, above all, a debater and one suited to the unexpected and dashing. Poyser arranged to fill the Geelong West Town Hall with television sets; Menzies' speech would be screened to the audience gathered for Hawke, then he and Gough Whitlam would reply to it — as if they were both in debate with the Prime Minister. It was a clever piece of theatre which very few politicians would be capable of carrying off. While Menzies was speaking Hawke scribbled out only an opening paragraph:

> You have witnessed tonight in the speech of the P.M. the most amazing piece of hypocrisy in post-war Australian political history. This man *came to office on a hoax* — to put value into the £1 — and will now be thrown out of that office as a political burglar, a man completely lacking in integrity. The *millionaire* in words is starkly revealed as poverty-stricken in ideas . . . By their deeds shall we know them. . .'

Hawke had guessed, accurately, that Menzies would again, as he had in 1961, adopt as his own a number of Labor policies.

It was a night of strong assertions and superlatives: Whitlam told the audience of 750 Labor supporters that Hawke had 'greater industrial experience than any man in Australia'. With two fast-on-their-feet agitators on stage the evening went with zest.

But earlier that day, on 12 November, the DLP candidate, J.J. Mahoney, had been reported at length in the *Geelong Advertiser* for a speech he had made to the local Polish community, during which he had dwelt upon the Indonesian peril. Mahoney had said that the election was the most vital ever to be held in Australia and that it was a question of 'safeguarding the nation's future'. It was necessary therefore that policies relating to defence and foreign affairs be placed above all else, otherwise coming generations might be forced to 'live in slavery'. He continued, 'Under the leadership of Dr Sukarno this threat is inspired by nationalistic tendencies, but Communism is helping to ferment and incite Sukarno's lust for power. The children of Australia cannot vote in this election: their future rests upon the votes of older people.' Two days later the *Advertiser* reported him saying, 'Once the millions of Asia spill over into Australia this country cannot defend itself . . .' The *Advertiser*, owned by the local Douglas family and managed by a former sea-captain who had married into the clan, was conservative. Poyser had been complaining to its management about bias since 1949. He said, 'It did no good. They would not give equal space, equally displayed, to Labor, but they raised no objections to running our advertisements, full-page, if we liked.' Hysteria in the electorate was building up and was thoroughly reported by the local paper. When Opperman opened his campaign a few days after Hawke he was continuously heckled for an hour and a half. He attacked Hawke as Left-wing and made repeated references to the sinister '36 faceless men'. The slurs about the ALP and Communism were everywhere, especially on local radio broadcasts aimed at housewives.

Hawke's health gave way and he had to spend three days in bed. Hazel recalled being enraged and mortified as she listened to gentle radio voices appealing to her, the mother in the home, to save her children's lives by refusing to vote for Labor. Hawke said,

> The Catholic Church was very very strong, and I remember one incident vividly: [Senator] Pat Kennelly, a devout Catholic, came down to campaign. There was an opening of a big new hall in one of the Catholic parishes on a Saturday and it was suggested he and I should go along there. The DLP had been putting out the most monstrous stuff about the Party generally and about me — that the Party was under the control of Communists and I was a disguised Communist. And this afternoon as we walked through the crowds little kids of eleven and twelve pointed at me and Pat, saying 'Communists, Communists, Communists'. Pat nearly wept. He couldn't believe the Church was doing that.

However, Hawke had already established a swing, and was holding it. He had also had a stroke of luck: the shipping, coal and hotel magnate, R.W. Miller, held a grudge against Opperman and wanted him sacked as Minister for Shipping. Opperman had refused to grant permits to Miller's ships to operate on the Australian coastal trade, while granting permits to ships flying flags of convenience and owned, mostly, by the major oil companies. Miller saw his chance in Hawke and offered to support his campaign financially. Poyser said,

> We kept the Miller money separate from the official Labor accounts, so that it did not appear in any of the books. We were frightened that the Liberals would accuse us of over-spending. We worked through a Mr Taylor in Miller's office. We would ring him up, tell him how much a full-page advertisement or a radio ad. would cost, and the cheque for the exact amount would arrive next day.

Huge advertisements about Hawke began to appear in the *Advertiser*, and Hawke, who is always at home with debate on specifics, began to castigate Opperman for his handling of the Shipping portfolio. The Minister was piqued into reply, saying Australia could not afford to establish its own shipping line for carrying import and export cargoes.

On 20 November Hawke addressed a lunch-time meeting of factory workers at Alcoa, telling them, 'Australia must move positively and quickly to establish an overseas shipping line', and that the country was being held to ransom by the Overseas Shipping Conference, which decided the freight charges to be imposed on Australian exporters. On the same day the Miller *Canopus* sailed into the port of Geelong. The crew lowered a huge piece of cloth, which covered almost one side of the ship, with an advertisement painted on it urging a vote for Hawke. The next day there was a half-page advertisement in the *Advertiser* saying, 'The Labor Movement Welcomes R.W. Miller's *Canopus* to Geelong, The First Australian Owned Tanker To Enter Corio Bay With An Australian Crew'. There was a picture of Hawke and one of the tanker. Hawke repeatedly challenged Opperman to debate with him face-to-face, but the Minister wisely declined and instead rode around Corio on his bicycle. He had said in one speech that there were six Communists among Labor's '36 faceless men'; the Labor machine was demanding stridently and futilely that he retract the statement. Opperman was so hard pressed by Hawke that he left the electorate only once during the campaign and had ministerial documents sent by car to Geelong for signing.

By the morning of 23 November, a week before polling day, Hawke was running away with the seat. His handbills announced:

> His outstanding academic career . . . He has conducted all recent major cases before the Arbitration Commission which have resulted in INCREASES in the BASIC WAGE and MARGINS and THREE WEEKS ANNUAL LEAVE. His recent international experience. His armed services experience. Bob Hawke flew as a pilot with the Oxford University Air Squadron of the ROYAL AIR FORCE VOLUNTEER RESERVE .
>
> Sport: An all-round sportsman . . . played 1st grade cricket . . . toured with the Oxford University side. He has YOUTH — EDUCATION —EXPERIENCE —VIGOUR —INTEGRITY.[2]

The electorate had been lavishly papered with these bills. Once Hawke had been accepted by the Party he had stirred such enthusiasm that scores of volunteers had joined his campaign and five times had filled the letter-boxes of Corio with campaign leaflets. When Harold Holt, the Federal Treasurer, had challenged anyone to name a country more prosperous than Australia Hawke had challenged Holt to debate the Government's economic management. Holt had declined. Hawke said, 'None of them would debate. I talked about defence and international affairs, but basically I talked about economics. I tried to tell the story about the attack on living standards via wages and wages policy that was involved in the Menzies' Government approach. I had the authority of my position as ACTU advocate.'

Then, in the late morning of Saturday 23 November the forward rush of enthusiasm hit a wall: President Kennedy had been shot dead. It was as if the planet had lurched in its orbit.

Poyser heard the news over the radio in the Geelong Trades Hall and thought, 'Nationally, we can't win'. Hawke, who'd been told early that morning, was stunned, but remained optimistic. The old campaigners, however, knew that a different message was necessary now that people were frightened. New, full-page advertisements of Hawke were made, picturing, for the first time, Hazel and the children all seated together on a settee and announcing, 'Bob Hawke the Family Man'.[3]

Labor was in retreat. By 25 November the Party's defence policy had been swept away. In Brisbane Calwell announced that Labor's nuclear-free Southern Hemisphere idea had been misunderstood; that in a war the USA would 'give Australia nuclear arms'; and that 'we, the ALP, would use any weapon to defend Australia if attacked'. Menzies smiled and pointed out that he had already ordered TFX aircraft, which 'rounded off the largest and most ambitious re-equipment programme in the peace-time history of Australia'. Hawke said,

> The atmosphere the Libs created in that post-Kennedy assassination period was unbelievable. They had B-47 bombers flying over Australia; there was constant talk about 'the Asian hordes', as some people chose to refer to the Indonesians, and about the F111s. Menzies was brought down to Corio on the day before the election to speak at the Ford factory. There had never been so many police in the area — police were wandering around with rifles, on the roofs of buildings, and they went through the lockers in the factory — there was supposed to be an assassination threat to Menzies. The atmosphere was electric. At the Ford meeting people were expecting to see Menzies shot. And they had conjured up the whole bloody thing!

Poyser recalled Menzies' address to the Ford workers: 'He had turned up surrounded by police. In the crowd some joker ignited a cracker he had in a cigarette packet. When the thing went bang people's faces turned white.'

By election day the polls showed that Labor would lose. In Corio there were police stationed at the booths. The *Geelong Advertiser* that morning ran an editorial spurning Labor's 'gaudy bait' and noting, 'Mr Opperman in his younger days was idolised by Geelong and district people as a world famous figure in sport . . . The electorate is not likely to forsake him now.'

By 10 o'clock that night television commentators announced that Menzies was back in government, while in a maverick result Bob Hawke had beaten the Minister for Shipping. Hawke said,

> People around me were saying, 'Hey, you've won it!' I found George Poyser, who knew how every booth in the electorate had to vote for us to win. He used the East Geelong High School booth as his litmus test: if my vote was of a certain percentage there, I would be in. I told him

everyone thought I'd won and he replied, 'Well, you haven't. The figures from East Geelong High School are not good enough.'

It was a week before the result was officially known. Opperman, in accepting victory, commented with spleen on the ALP expenditure and Miller's generosity to Hawke's campaign: 'Never has so much been spent in so short a time by so varied interests to effect a defeat'.

Hawke said, 'It was a disappointment — I don't like losing anything I do — but I knew I had achieved an enormous result. And I had something to go back to that I was very much involved in and deeply committed to.'

The basic wage case for 1964 was due to open in ten weeks, with a new young advocate representing the employers. In the Conciliation and Arbitration Commission the dawn was breaking for what was later called 'the heroic age of advocacy'.

The wage fixation changes of 1961 had been, in the words of the Chief Judge, Sir Richard Kirby, 'a great reformative step'. They had worked in relation to prices in 1962 and 1963 and now it was time for the triennial review of productivity. If that went smoothly, the unions could begin to relax: they would have a whole package of wages adjusted to prices and productivity: their decade-long fight against the decision of 1953 would have succeeded; and they would have a planned, stable system for the allotment of money logically intermeshed with the Australian economy. At least, in theory.*

Hawke approached the 1964 case with confidence. The economy was booming, with international reserves of £840 million — higher than ever before; there had been a 40% increase of exports of manufactured goods compared with the same period twelve months earlier, and it followed upon the increase in margins and annual leave that Hawke had won in 1963. The employers could not cry Bankrupt! A new mood of buoyancy was sweeping the nation, summed up in the title of a recently-published book, *The Lucky Country*. Unemployment was negligible. People swollen with abundance went on diets of grilled rump steak. We had never had it so good and we were going to have it better, for the drum beats of the mining boom were already audible in the distance. London was swinging. Western Europe (and Japan) danced and shrieked with Beatlemania. In America, Kennedy's Camelot was changing into Lyndon Johnson's Great Society, which would see an end to poverty, inequality, ignorance. The heady, golden sixties were underway.

The wage case for that year reflected the confidence and good temper of the

---

* In practice, supply and demand dictate wages and salaries. Employees in fast-growing industries or shops, and militants, get 'over-award' pay and, in the professions, increased fees.

times. It was a friendly, humorous case, with the Bar table and the Bench swapping jokes and passing notes about the cricket scores. It ended in Sydney with the Chief Judge and the two leading advocates boozing together, and later Hawke and the employers' new man, Jim Robinson, dancing *pas de deux* in the foyer of Menzies Hotel at 4 o'clock in the morning.

A few weeks later the full Bench gave its decision: the basic wage would be increased by £1 to take account of price and productivity increases.

The unions were jubilant. The employers' counterpart to Albert Monk, George Polites, invented a judges' jingle which did the rounds of all the industrial relations pubs: 'The economy in the round is sound — we'll give a pound!'

The night before the decision was given the Defence Minister, Senator Paltridge, had told Parliament that the United States had been pressing Australia to join more actively in supporting the sagging anti-Communist front in South Vietnam, and that Australia would therefore be sending military instructors to help out the American military instructors already in the country. His statement was the proverbial cloud no bigger than a man's hand. In the wage case, too, there had been a little cloud: it was called the total wage. The employers wanted it; the unions rejected it, and so did the Bench. But it kept on growing. 'The heroic age of advocacy' between Hawke and Jim Robinson was the battle for the total wage, which opened in 1964. The economic nightmare of Australian wage fixation, which came to a climax in 1974 and again in 1981, began then.

Wage fixation and its economic consequences is a highly complicated — and controversial — area which only a full-length book could adequately cover. For brevity, one can give this equation: under the system of basic wage and margin an annual pay packet was made up of, say, £1,000 basic wage and £1,000 margin, increased one part at a time, with a lag of several years for margins' increases. With a total wage the annual paypacket is still £2,000, but it is increased at one blow. If a flat-rate increase is awarded the lesser-paid worker tends to catch up with the better paid. Better-paid workers want percentage increases, for it takes no talent in mathematics to realise that, say, 10% of £2,000 is greater than 10% of £1,000. The most militant unions are the craft unions, and they are better paid; therefore, over a period of time, they will tend to get their own way and have percentage increases awarded. This means that the highly-paid workers will be even more highly paid in relation to the poorly paid. Relativities are badly disturbed; envy arises — the fitter earns more so the labourer demands more and the brain surgeon puts up his fees. Taxation swallows most of the gain, but more of the brain surgeon's, so he hires a lawyer/accountant to figure out how to pay less tax. Governments discover they needed the extra tax wealth all along and spend it on causes appropriate to their political priorities; this creates resentment in half the electorate. The result is bad temper, high wages, cheating, and huge tax returns to the government. Prices increase — for whatever reason (drought in the wheat belt, a consumer fad) — and the fitter demands a wage rise.

The employers had designed their total wage argument with a different scenario in mind. They wanted the total wage increased only for gains in productivity. But for the unions productivity increases are mere gravy. Their meat is prices and their measuring stick is the consumer price index, which is expressed in percentage terms. Australia ended up with a total wage increased for prices at a time of low productivity movements.

George Polites, the Executive Director of the Australian Council of Employers' Federation (ACEF), has the credit for designing the case for the total wage but had no hand in the botched-up way it was applied in law. Polites had come to the Employers' Federation in 1959, having worked his way up from industrial advocate for the Victorian employers to the job of Personnel Director of the then small but ambitious transnational company, Utah, before becoming the dynamo of organised employers. He is short, energetic, full of nervous energy and shrewdness, his speech terse and humorous, prickling with shafts of epigrammatic wit. He had been dissatisfied with the advocacy of Drew Aird but the internal politics of the ACEF had prevented him from making real reforms until the annual leave case of 1963. That year he had persuaded his colleagues that a young barrister he had spotted in the South Australian basic wage case of 1960, a case known as 'The South Australian Employers versus The World', was the man to establish against Hawke. Polites' protégé was Jim Robinson, a barrister four years Hawke's senior, who had not, as was customary for the employers' counsel, taken silk. He was, like Hawke, a son of the manse.

Polites had a stroke of genius in promoting Robinson, for he was an opponent whom Hawke could not dislike, could not regard as a personal enemy — as he had, so notably, Cliff Menhennitt. (A few months earlier, in the 1963 margins and annual leave case, clashes between Hawke and Menhennitt had filled the courtroom with emotional lightning, causing pain to observers and judges.) As well, Robinson was malleable: Polites, as his mentor, was to be the phantom general directing his young warrior's fight.

Robinson was slim, blue-eyed, with delicate almost faun-like features and, although aggressive in court, was a man of instantly-recognisable good nature and good humour. Like Hawke he had the faculty of becoming, in a few seconds, a boy again — Kirby used to call him Peter Pan — and his boyishness, which was whimsical, complemented the naughty innocence of Hawke's sudden reversions to childhood play. His manner was languid; his speech finely modulated and slow, touched, as was Hawke's, by Biblical allusions. Robinson's mother had alarmed her wealthy family by marrying a missionary and going off to China. Robinson was born there. His childhood was characterised by the external chaos of the war-lord period and the internal control of a stern, anaemic Christianity. He had grown up with evening prayers and daily Bible readings, church four times on Sundays and caveats against the sin of worldliness. His father was formidable — 'a headmaster in another form'. Robinson said, 'There was no smoking, no drinking, no lipstick for girls, no movies — Hollywood was the work-place of the Devil — no radio on Sundays. Even the *Women's Weekly* was a bit *risqué*.' At the age of twelve he had come to Australia, and rebelled — by breaking Sabbath observance and, in secret, playing sport. Hawke was fascinated that Robinson had defied the church so young. Having discovered the similarities of their childhoods they were charmed by each other and spent hours discussing how they should rear their own children with greater liberty than they had known. Robinson was particularly attracted to Hawke's relationship with Clem and Hawke's openly-expressed affection for men he admired. By 1964 they were already warm friends. Hawke had loathed some advocates on ideological grounds: Robinson was non-political. 'Jim didn't believe he was going to save the nation, like Cliff Menhennitt. I often thought he wouldn't mind taking a case for our side', Hawke remarked. Robinson was already in Hawke's debt: in the 1960 case one of the employers' witnesses had gone to Hawke and suggested that Hawke cross-examine his evidence in a certain way, which would discredit it. Hawke had dismissed the man and so as not to distress Robinson — who was on trial for his future career — had waited until the case was over before telling him about the perfidy. Robinson said, 'That remains with me twenty years later as being what typified Bob's integrity'. From that case on they had bonds of trust: to save time and work they exchanged the names of witnesses, and witness statements, and later gave warning of procedural changes although, as Robinson said later,

> Bob played the game straighter than we did. He would as a matter of course give us as much notice as possible of procedural points. We would consider the length of notice we'd give him as part of our tactics. Perhaps it made no practical difference, because Bob thrived on surprises, but it was an article of faith with him that he never sought to take advantage of trust. And he never complained about not receiving identical treatment from me and George.

Since he had taken over as head of the employers' body Polites had become determined that its traditional argument to the Commission, a brief he described as 'no increase, no time, no how', must be changed. He thought the employers' refusal to concede any award wage increase, in a time of full employment and strong economic growth, was sterile and unreal — and ultimately damaging. While employers asserted fiercely in court that they could afford not a penny more in wages, outside court they were already paying large over-award rates as they competed among themselves for labour. The unions, therefore, regarded the employers' submissions as exercises in hypocrisy.

The employers had come to behave like hapless virgins in court — and wantons outside — and regarded the unions as bent upon rape, in court and out. Polites recognised how bad for industrial relations this situation was and determined that there must be some rapprochement between desire and its rebuff, that some award wage permissiveness was in order. He fought hard in the employers' councils to persuade his colleagues that it was in their best interest to give something — and to ask for something in return — instead of having the process of exchange accomplished by *force majeure*. His solution, unveiled by Robinson in the 1964 case, was the New Look Wages Plan. With it, the employers were offering to increase wages in line with productivity increases; they asked in return for the abolition of the basic wage and margin system and its replacement by a total wage. Welding the two-part system into one would prevent the unions having 'two bites of the cherry', as it was commonly described — that is, winning an increase in the basic wage then topping this up with an increase in margins, using as a major reason the disturbance of relativities.

The unions could never agree to the New Look Wages Plan, for it ruled out cost of living adjustments and without them any inflation would shrivel the value of wages. It would be back to the days of Sir Raymond Kelly. At the time neither side imagined that over a period of years the Arbitration Commission would mediate the issue by giving the employers part of what they wanted and the unions part of what they wanted, and that the final result would be a hybrid, a total wage adjusted for inflation, not productivity. Productivity could drop to zero, but if inflation were 10% wages would be increased by 10%, or almost that amount — and that is what happened, and what institutionalised the wage crises of the 1970s and early 1980s. In 1964 the word 'stagflation' did not exist.

The day after Robinson revealed the New Look Wages Plan there was a big union rally in Melbourne, addressed by many officials, including Albert Monk. It passed a resolution: 'This meeting is emphatic that the move to abolish the basic wage is no more than an attempt to satisfy further the selfish demands of employers and from which no benefit can possibly result to any member of the work force'. The meeting called on workers to 'support the basic wage struggle'. In court Hawke poured scorn on the total wage and productivity gearing of it, summoning to his aid the work of the Attorney-General, Garfield Barwick. In 1961 Barwick had prepared a White Paper on restrictive trade practices in Australia which showed that a system of monopolies and inhibitions upon free trade existed. Hawke argued that these practices, long outlawed in other countries, rendered invalid the employers' theory that wages be increased only in line with productivity increases, for the theory depended upon the free working of the market. He was, during these years, already developing the idea that was to sweep him to national prominence later, when he set out to break retail price maintenance.

Hawke had a receptive audience for his case. The Bench for 1964 was Kirby, Gallagher, Moore and John [later Sir John] Nimmo, the last a new judge who had come to the jurisdiction only a month before. Hawke knew he could rely upon Kirby and Moore to uphold the 1961 judgment, and probably Gallagher. Even if the decision were split 2-2 the Chief Judge would have a casting vote, so whatever Gallagher and Nimmo decided, Hawke could not lose. He was at his most relaxed and agreeable in court that year, confident of a victory and not required to engage in the verbal brutality of cross-examination. After 1961, when Dr Perkins had decided he would not face cross-examination from Hawke, the employers had abandoned the habit of calling witnesses. The transcript is scattered with flashes of humour and some unexplained adjournments, when in fact proceedings were halted so that Hawke and Robinson could go to Kirby's chambers to listen to the cricket. At the end of the day Hawke and Robinson would have a beer in the Beaufort Hotel on the corner of Queen and Little Bourke Streets, where they burlesqued their performances in court, acting out imagined conversations between the judges about how each advocate had behaved. Robinson recalled,

> The thing I remember most about Bob in those days was his enthusiasm for debate, on any topic. Whether in court or out, he always had a view — a strong, well-articulated view, on all subjects. And he thrived on debate . . . His style of advocacy sought to force a response from the Bench so that the members would become involved, rather than just listen. Once the response came he switched from formal advocate to informal debater. You could almost hear him say, 'Now I've gottcha!' It was the tactic he had used so successfully with Ashburner, in 1961. Kirby was difficult to corner, and when cornered would wax wrathful, but Moore could be drawn into a discussion. We both used a variation of the technique with a commissioner, Terry Winter [who for technical reasons was part of a second Bench simultaneously hearing the 1964 case]. Winter would ask a question when Bob or I was addressing and the one of us concerned would straight-faced say something like, 'I'm glad you asked that question, Mr Commissioner, it shows a shrewd appreciation of the argument I was putting and with the benefit of that observation I can move now directly to the development of a related issue'. And then without answering the question we'd simply resume our submissions. Bob and I used to joke about this in the Beaufort and picture Winter going home that night, wondering, 'What was it that I asked that was so brilliant?'

Another aspect of Bob's advocacy was its apparent credibility. In the 1963 margins case I sarcastically referred to him as 'the golden prophet of economic analysis'. This was, of course, to suggest that he really had feet of clay. Bob presented to the Bench his more difficult economic propositions like a big game fisherman showing off his personal trophies. How then could one doubt the authenticity of such a presentation! If a judge were bold enough to question Hawke's reasoning Bob would take his argument step by step, stopping to ask, 'Does Your Honour follow me so far?' I could never bring myself to do that, but it was sickeningly effective. You see, unless the judge said, 'No. I'm not satisfied — what about XYZ?', Bob felt he'd won him over. It worked more often than not. Even today there's no other advocate who does that in the same way as he can. Every question is an absolute plus to him; he uses a question as a catalyst to embellish his arguments, and the embellishments fit — they sound arguable. That is a very complete forensic skill.

Predictably, for a man who aimed at the brilliant coup and had little patience for detailed planning, Hawke was not so outstanding as a tactician. He was more generous — or naive — than his opponents in the exchange of information. He had a fixed hatred of Kelly and returned repeatedly to Kelly's wickedness, lecturing the Bench about old cases until 'Hawke's historical exercise' became a standing joke and Robinson would suggest languidly that there could be nothing of any moment in the rest of what Mr Hawke had to say, since he had spent two days giving a history lesson. This was a technique that Hawke had learned from Eggleston and did not abandon, presumably, because he so loved to be right — as Sir John Moore described it later, 'banging my head against a wall and saying, "You're a bloody nong!" ' The judges were often noticeably bored by Hawke's long harangues on times past and wrong decisions. In the employers' camp George Polites was a born tactician. He planned for Robinson not only the preliminary points, the order of addresses, the nature of the case, its length and how to counter Hawke's arguments, but also such details as whether to avoid splitting Robinson's case over a weekend. Robinson said, 'Bob was less concerned with the peripheral matters surrounding a case: he went for the jugular'.

By 1964 the President of the Commission, Sir Richard Kirby, had overcome his initial hostility to Hawke and treated him and Robinson as favourite nephews. He had come to expect cheekiness and intemperate language from Hawke in court and out. When the case ended in May, in Sydney, Hawke, Robinson and Kirby were invited to an employers' function held at a golf club, and happened to be sitting together in an alcove. Robinson said,

Bob was calling Kirby 'Dick This' and 'Dick That'. I never called him anything but Your Honour, or Judge or Sir Richard and Bob got irritated by this. He said, 'For Christ's sake, Jim, be a man. Call him Dick.' And I said — we'd been drinking since 11 o'clock that morning, and it was now about 8 at night — 'Now, look here, Bob, that is my choice. I will call him what I want. I might even call him "ya old bastard", but I won't call him Dick.' Kirby sat there, listening to us arguing and highly amused by the pair of us.

Within less than a year Kirby's avuncular tolerance for Hawke was to become a major factor in an industrial relations scandal, the national wage case of 1965. This case, Hawke's worst defeat, led directly to his decision to run for the presidency of the ACTU.

The seeds of the 1965 judgment, which equalled in notoriety the decision of 1953, were planted in 1964. Although Hawke won a victory in gaining an extra £1 for unionists, its award was made on a decision split between Kirby and Moore on one side, and Gallagher and Nimmo on the other, and to make it law Kirby had to exercise his right of casting vote. On the question of *how* wages should be determined, Kirby, Moore and Gallagher upheld the principles of the 1961 decision; Nimmo rejected them. Since Nimmo was new to the jurisdiction his action was discounted. It should not have been. It was the first public sign that inside the Conciliation and Arbitration Commission a challenge to the authority of the President was evolving. There was a complex of reasons for it; one major one was anger about Kirby's failure to restrain Hawke. Three judges at least — Gallagher, Nimmo and Sweeney — all deplored Hawke's lack of respect, his 'dyslogistic' mode of address, as they called it; his contempt for 'the majesty of the law'.

The whole system had been shaken by his style. Even when most polite Hawke talked man-to-man or even teacher-to-man — 'like a Dutch uncle' — to the Bench. Kirby said, 'While he wouldn't persuade, he was totally honest. Other coves would try to mislead you, but Bob would never, either to strengthen his case or to preserve it from weakness, lie or mislead us. He was like the good little boy who would always own up.'

Among the employers and the more conservative union officials there was grave concern about Hawke's style, for he had set a fashion in tough-talking which other young union advocates were copying, and they were not always as honest, or logical, as Hawke. In 1963 the Electrical Trades Union called an officers' meeting at which one of the agenda items was: Should an industrial advocate be aggressive? The question was decided in the affirmative only after long debate. There were many less formal arguments. George Polites said,

We took a conscious decision not to embrace Bob's style of advocacy. We thought it was bad in itself, and bad for the system . . . There was a double standard, anyway. Robinson could never have got away with the violent language accepted from Hawke. In his opening submission in 1964 I instructed Jim to needle the Bench, accusing it of having 'a bet both ways'. Kirby became enraged. He called Jim 'a disgrace to your principals' and demanded an apology. I refused to let Jim apologise in the way Kirby had asked. What he had said was nothing compared to the extravagance of Hawke, of his personalised attacks. Bob had the Bench *in terrorem*.

The question of 'Hawke's style' was spreading.

The 1964 decision was given in June; in July Hawke went to Western Australia to argue for a £3 1s. increase in the State basic wage. In the opinion of observers he angered the arbitrator by his forcefulness. The awarded increase was only 3s.

While in Perth Hawke appeared on television and, asked about Labor's failure in the 1963 election, replied that the Party had been 'inefficient in enunciating its principles in terms of the needs of present-day society'. Within a decade members of the ALP would be able to point to a hundred similar statements from Hawke, his supporters quoting them as examples of honesty and clear-thinking, his enemies as instances of contempt for the rules of solidarity.

There were already small signs that Hawke, while a man of the Left, did not fit snugly into its mould. One was his house. In 1964 he and Hazel had sold the Keats Street cottage and bought a two-storied orange brick house in Royal Avenue, Sandringham, a street of large and expensive residences owned by business and professional people. There was nothing working class about the place, from its price — £17,250 — to its tennis court. It was well beyond Hawke's means, for he was earning only a little more than £2,000 annually. The house had been on the market for eighteen months without attracting a buyer and, although imposing outside was, according to Hazel, 'a soulless place inside, painted battleship grey'. Hawke had fallen in love with its tennis court: it was a piece of his childhood recreated to have a house with a tennis court attached. The owner agreed to sell the house for £12,250 and allow Hawke a year's option to buy the tennis court for £5,000. 'My bank manager took a tremendous gamble and agreed to give me a huge overdraft', Hawke said. As a financial proposition for the bank Hawke had one advantage: in 1963 the Sydney *Sun* had published a story referring to, 'R.J. Hawke, the Communist industrial officer of the Waterside Workers' Federation'. (The name should have been Norm Docker.) Hawke sued for libel. One week before his option on the tennis court was due to expire the settlement, for £1,000, came through. It was the first of many. Hawke continued to spend his libel settlements on improvements to the house, or in reducing his debts. In later years he would lead guests to 'the Frank Packer swimming pool' and 'the Maxwell Newton sauna bath', but he does not know how much over the years he has won in libel cases, for his lack of interest in handling financial matters is total. He said, 'I had no qualms about libel settlements. The people gathered at the other end of the Bar table to oppose me were earning in *one day* what I earned in a year. I reckoned I deserved the extra cash.' In the 1960s the grandness of the Royal Avenue house excited comment among trade union friends, even though it was half-furnished. 'Most people said it looked as if we couldn't afford to live in it — the curtains were rotting and all the furniture was second-hand', Hazel recalled. In those days the adverse comments were mere ribbing.

Besides the house, another sign that Hawke felt free of the bonds that were willingly, even exultantly, worn by other people of the Left was his choice of friends. From his first years out of school Hawke had enjoyed friendships across the political and social spectrum: Jules Zanetti had been intrigued that Hawke, after tea with the Governor, would go to the pub to yarn with men in blue singlets — or *vice versa*. There had always been some version of hymn singers and boozers, thesis and antithesis, with *his* life as the synthesis. But it was years before the trade union movement realised that Hawke had many friendships, and a second life, among 'the ruling class'.

In the 1960s one of these friends was Rod (later Sir Roderick) Carnegie, known from Oxford, where he had been a famous oar. Carnegie was a young man on his way to the top in business, already the Australian principal of the American consulting firm McKinsey & Co. They met for lunch every three months or so. Carnegie said,

> I found his views on the overall society interesting. I think we shared a common belief that Australia was a country that had to find its own independent identity. The issues that concerned him were: What does it mean to be an Australian? What does Australia stand for? Should Australia depend upon the tradition of great and powerful allies? Whether totally-owned foreign companies were good for Australia, or not? Were we developing the country in a way that was most appropriate? He was concerned about the way in which society tried to work together on issues.

These were all matters to which Carnegie, over the years, has also addressed himself. He continued,

> I remember at one lunch we got into disagreement about Menzies. Bob took the line that Menzies would be ultimately assessed as a very bad prime minister, and while I could agree with part of what he was saying, I thought he was not providing a balanced point of view. Among the older members of the community, who were just coping with the shock of England entering the Common Market, and other changes in relationships — the Suez Canal, for instance — I can see how Bob would have come across as a radical person.

By the late 1970s Hawke's friendship with Carnegie and other captains of industry was public knowledge, and the cause of fury in trade union and Left-wing circles. It was thought to demonstrate a change of personality in Hawke, a corruption. In fact, while his attitudes have changed over the years, his behaviour has remained consistent. The boy who did not accept the authority of his headmaster, or the intrinsic majesty of the law, or the church's bans on alcohol and sex, or the drinker's bans on the church, or the judiciary's demands for respectful language, rejected too the authority of his political colleagues to define how he should live.

As an advocate Hawke was about to face his biggest crisis with authority, in the national wage case of 1965. The result was a personal disaster, sweeping away six years of his work. Nationally, it was disastrous also, for the 1965 decision crumpled the trust that both the trade union movement and the employers had vested in the wage-fixing system.

Authority was at the heart of the 1965 case: the authority of legal traditions; the authority of the Chief Judge; the authority of employers of labour. Industrially, the challenge to authority had already begun. After more than a decade of quietude when there had been a minimum of industrial unrest, and most of that on the wharves, in the boom year of 1964 men and women members of blue- and white-collar unions began to demand their share of increased prosperity, by going on strike. Railwaymen and wharfies, mannequins and public servants, struck work and the year had drawn to a close on a note of rising industrial discord.

The employers did not wait, as was usual, for the unions to go through the legal process necessary to create a national wage case but took the initiative and brought on the case themselves. They had decided to apply again in 1965 for the total wage. As a tactic, they were going to carp at the Bench about the increasing turbulence of industrial life — which, they were to submit, the total wage would calm. The idea was a piece of Polites' wizardry.

The Bench for 1965 was Kirby, Moore, Gallagher, Sweeney and Nimmo. Kirby and Moore, Polites knew, viewed strikes as a fact of life in a buoyant economy; the other judges believed strikes were preventable.

The hearing opened in late January but did not get properly under way until 2 March, with Robinson instead of Hawke appearing first. He tendered fifty-seven exhibits, many of them leaflets and articles from union journals which urged demonstrations by members to influence the Commission's decision. One exhibit, the 'militant's blueprint', was an outline for a strike campaign for higher wages. Robinson said,

> We culled the unions' own publications, because they had the ring of their own free minds, and were absolutely delighted to find an editorial, the 'militant's blueprint'. We were using it to scold the Bench for granting £1 in 1964 and were using it, even more importantly long

term, to achieve the total wage. In early cases we had produced dozens of examples of nastiness from the trade union movement. But the reaction on a new mind [that is, Mr Justice Sweeney] to national wage proceedings was quite dramatic — greater than we had expected. I don't think anybody really *in* the industrial relations jurisdiction would have taken any of the material as gospel without discounting it. What unions say and what they do is different. There was an unworldly reaction from the Bench.

It was obvious early in the hearing that some judges viewed militant behaviour with disfavour. For Sweeney and Nimmo this reaction was understandable, for they were new to industrial relations and unused to the belligerent coloratura of union rhetoric. Gallagher, however, was one of the most experienced industrial lawyers in the country. But he held strong views on law and order and had a reputation for being the most outspoken member of the Commission on the subject of strikes. Robinson added, 'It's fair to say that Gallagher was always capable of responding to that sort of material — an emotive response'. Robinson was offering a 6s. increase in wages, for productivity increases, to be made to a total, not a basic, wage.

He was followed by John Kerr, Q.C., representing the Commonwealth. Hawke disliked Kerr, who had an impressive head of prematurely white hair, and a falsetto voice. When he swept into court Hawke would remark loudly, 'Here comes Goldilocks', or, 'The Liberace of the Law . . .' Kerr's submission stated that any wage increase in 1965 'would be fraught with danger' but was silent on the Commonwealth's attitude to the total wage — to Hawke's considerable irritation. Hawke's brief was to apply for an increase of between 12s. and 15s. in the basic wage for an increase in prices and productivity, and to object to the request for a total wage. For the first time since 1953 the unions were *not* demanding reinstatement of automatic adjustments, such was their faith in the Commission.

Polites, who said later, 'Hawke never understood Gallagher, and neither did Kirby', had shrewdly assessed the psychology of all the actors: Robinson was totally prepared and confident. The minefield had been laid and Hawke strode manfully into it.

Hawke said, 'There clearly was a determination on the part of three members of the Bench not to do me, but to do Kirby and Moore, and that meant having me as an object of considerable dislike. It was an incredible performance. They behaved totally unjudicially.' Polites added, 'Bob made up his mind he had lost the case right at the start'.

Before the hearing began the Melbourne Trades Hall Council had circulated a pamphlet reading: 'We ask workers in all factories, shops, offices, depots, etc. to elect and send representatives in a continuous stream to fill the Conciliation and Arbitration Commission's chamber during the hearing of claims. DO IT NOW! '

Hawke's opening address was smothered by the shouts of his supporters, proceedings had to be adjourned and Hawke had to give an undertaking that there would be no more rumpus. On his first day he clashed with Gallagher; Kirby rebuked him; then he clashed with Sweeney when he referred to the 1953 judgment as 'infamous'; then with Gallagher again over the question of strike campaigns. Gallagher, a warm-hearted and emotional man, was losing his temper with Hawke, who had already affronted him and Nimmo by attacking them for their dissent from the prevailing decision of 1964. Hawke accused the Commonwealth of 'flagrant and blatant dishonesty' for not stating plainly that it neither supported nor opposed the total wage. Kerr, when he had a chance to reply, was scathing about Hawke's 'extravagant language'.

Early in the case there were lively, amicable exchanges between Hawke and Sweeney, who arrived each day with an index of transcripts of earlier cases and was taking an acute interest in Hawke's submissions. Sweeney was known as 'a lawyer's lawyer'; increasingly, he began to debate with Hawke, to raise queries, to demand further proof. The hearing had moved to Sydney on 16 March, to Temple Court where, across the corridor, a royal commission was in progress. Hawke was speaking so loudly that he disrupted its proceedings and a note was sent in asking that he lower his voice; he was also speaking so fast that the shorthand writers could record him for only ten minutes at a time. His voice had broken down in earlier cases; on Hawke's fifth day of talking, to an increasingly irascible Bench, George Polites nudged Robinson and said, 'They're after him. He'll lose his voice in a minute.' Hawke needed a week to recover his voice. He returned full of fight. On 6 April there was another rumpus when 200 wharf labourers picketed Temple Court and stood in the street shouting, 'We want wage justice!' so loudly that their voices penetrated to the hearing, on the building's third floor. After an hour Kirby announced the case was adjourned and police were summoned. The next morning there was a police guard, for the wharfies as they had prepared to move off under orders had shouted, 'You wait! The women are coming tomorrow.' The atmosphere was jittery in expectation of a female demonstration. Hawke assured the Bench there would not be another onslaught, male or female, but Kirby decided that the police guard should remain. Hawke launched back into an attack upon Gallagher and Nimmo, and an attempt to defend to Sweeney the principles of the 1961 judgment which, for days, the judge had been disparaging. The exchanges between Hawke and Sweeney were becoming increasingly splenetic and at the lunch adjournment a group of union officials, including David McBride and Cliff Dolan, took Hawke aside and said, 'Look mate, go easy. He's getting under your guard.' After lunch Hawke had been speaking for only a few minutes, directly to Sweeney, when this exchange took place:

> HAWKE: I think Your Honour will see that there is a classic illustration of the sort of stupidity, if I may say so with respect to the tribunal at the time, that they were getting themselves into.

SWEENEY, J: It is a very different thing to say 'with respect'. If you want to be consistent, you should delete the 'stupidity' reference or the 'respect'.

HAWKE: In that case, I would prefer to delete the 'with respect'.

SWEENEY, J: You please yourself, as far as I am concerned.

HAWKE: Yes, I will please myself, Your Honour.[4]

The atmosphere was electric. Along the Bench faces were pale with anger. Kirby sat in silence, and after what seemed a lifetime, Hawke began speaking again.

Sweeney had clearly rejected the 1961 wage-fixing principles that Hawke had fought for over years; Nimmo had rejected them in 1964 and would do so again. That left Gallagher.

At 10 a.m. on 28 June in the Conciliation and Arbitration Commission Building in Melbourne, the Number 1 courtroom was packed with union and employer officials and journalists waiting to hear the decision. The judges trooped in, sat, then Kirby, his voice shaking with distress, announced that their decision was split, and to the disbelief of his audience continued, 'The majority view will be given by Mr Justice Gallagher on behalf of other members of the Bench'.

It was fifteen years since a Chief Judge had been rolled.

As Gallagher read the judgment on behalf of himself, Sweeney and Nimmo the shock in the courtroom turned to dismay. The majority decision did not do the one thing which by law a wage case is required to do: settle an industrial dispute. Hawke had lost shatteringly: the 1961 principles, which the unions had so deeply trusted that they had not even asked for automatic adjustments, were gone.

The judgment rejected the unions' formula of prices and productivity. It adopted 'capacity to pay' but rejected the employers' formula for measuring capacity — productivity. It refused to increase the basic wage at all, but awarded an additional 6s. to margins, calculated, strangely enough, on the productivity formula. It rejected a total wage, but decided that in future basic wage and margins cases be heard simultaneously, which was tantamount to making the acceptance of a total wage inevitable. It adopted the view that wage increases should be compatible with price stability. It condemned a strike in Mt Isa and the waterside workers' campaign against involvement in the Vietnam War. It pointed out that strikes reduced the capacity of the economy to pay higher wages, inflicted hardship on the general body of employees and asserted that a policy of strike action was diametrically opposed to arbitration, and that strikes were a calamity for the whole community.

Within minutes of the court adjourning, militant union officials were demanding that the ACTU demonstrate the anger of the movement by calling a national strike. An emergency executive meeting was arranged for the following week.

Cliff Dolan recalled,

> Bob was absolutely furious. I sat through the whole case and right from
> the word Go it had been obvious that Sweeney and Nimmo had a
> prejudice against him. There was no doubt, if you were in that court-
> room, that they were out to get him. His submissions were as good as
> ever, but he'd lost the case before it started. However, we all still
> expected a certain amount of justice. There was no justice in the
> decision . . . A big group of us had discussions, going on until the early
> hours of next morning, about what he could do. Bob was looking for
> some way to appeal the decision.

There is no appeal against decisions of a full Bench. Nevertheless Hawke
called on Kirby in chambers and asked him to overturn the decision. Kirby
refused.

In some shops workers had downed tools immediately on 29 June; there
were scores of wild-cat strikes and the large Communist-led Amalgamated
Engineering Union began churning out pamphlets titled, 'Arbitration Be
Damned'.

When the ACTU executive met, Hawke addressed it for an hour about the
legal possibilities. After another five hours of discussion the executive decided
not to call a national strike and directed Hawke to apply for a review of the
1965 decision. Kirby rejected his application, mentioning in passing that
judgments need not be 'treated as dogma which cannot be departed from in
the future. Indeed the contrary is the case.' It was as good as a promise that,
one way or another, the 1965 decision could be reversed but that legal niceties
would have to be observed. Meanwhile, Hawke's detractors on the Right-
wing of the union movement and among the employers were laughing up
their sleeves. In those circles it was held that Hawke had mismanaged the
1965 case and brought calamity on his own head.

Hawke's commitment to a career in the trade union movement had waxed
and waned for six years. He had begun work as ACTU advocate with a
determination to force reforms in wage fixation, and with his eye on Parliament. When he had been rebuffed in 1960 his commitment had taken a
further vigorous leap. By 1963 it had relaxed once more. Abruptly in 1965
defeat converted ambivalence to a consuming passion to achieve reform.
Within weeks of Kirby's refusal to overturn the decision Hawke had made
two resolutions: 'I got hold of that judgment , which was both incompetent
and devious, and I determined I would go through it, paragraph by paragraph, sentence by sentence, word by bloody word — and destroy it!' He had
also decided to become the next President of the ACTU.

When the news got round industrial relations circles, which it did quickly,
for Hawke confides his plans in many, including journalists, some people

laughed out loud. The ACTU was a blue-collar organisation; Monk aside, its executive was made up of men who had worked their way up from 'the tools' to jobs within their unions and finally to the top of the union tree. Conventional wisdom of the Right, which controlled the ACTU, had it that *only* a union official could aspire to replace Monk. For an employee and former academic, like Hawke, the ambition seemed as risible as a donkey in the Melbourne Cup. Hawke said, 'Albert and Harold never let me forget that I was only an employee'. Eighteen months earlier when a member of the ACTU executive had suggested the presidency idea to Hawke he had laughed himself and replied, 'I wouldn't have a feather to fly with'. What he needed was a machine.

In the spring of 1965 Hawke began assembling a machine that would drive him forward into the President's job.

Chapter Twelve

Hawke had two recognised, potent skills to counterbalance his handicap as a trade union outsider: one was his capacity to establish rapport — the vast network of friends, the 'good guy' of the pub — the other was his ability as a debater, which at this stage of his career he was restricted to using, in the main, as a wages advocate. Heated and welded together by the fire of moral conviction these skills made Hawke a political agitator, a man who could emotionally bond with an audience and shape the response of huge numbers of people. But only success would give him the chance to address huge numbers of people; meanwhile, he had to rely upon stretching the range of his rapport with trade union officials, whom he could meet face-to-face, and upon establishing himself as a champion in the minds of the rank and file through his skill as a wages advocate. The authority of his position as ACTU advocate had been important in the Corio election; it would be critical in the ACTU presidential election because Hawke had nothing else that was concrete to point to — no trade, no time as a shop steward or as an organiser, no experience as a union negotiator, no proof that he was authentically of the trade unions and should be their leader.

He turned his attention to advocacy with determination in late 1965. He had two great challenges: one was the wage case of 1966. It was a matter of personal vindication and was vital to his aspirations for the presidency. The other was the 'Local Officers Case', the first major wage case to be held in Papua New Guinea. This was for Hawke a fight against racism — and as such, an issue of Good against Evil. He lost the New Guinea case, but he had a galvanising effect upon political awareness in the territory, and when he left it was amid shouts from white colonialists that he was a rabble-rouser, and from black indigenes that he had given them courage and shown them skills to use in the quest for independence.

In the spring and early summer of 1965, before either of these cases began,

Hawke was already busy, with a beer glass in his hand, lobbying people to support him as the next president of the ACTU. Ray Geitzelt, a formidable Left-wing numbers man in New South Wales, remembered that it was close to Christmas time, in the Lygon, when Hawke first talked to him about his ambition, using the exhortation-cum-threat, 'If blokes like you won't support me, I might as well go back to the ANU!'

David Combe, a young but already influential figure in the South Australian Labor Party, who in late 1965 was working on the staff of the State Attorney-General, Don Dunstan, recalled, 'I was looking forward to meeting Bob, but having heard that he was the son of a Congregational minister and knowing what the Congregational church is like in South Australia, I assumed he didn't drink. It was 100° on the day I went to the airport to pick him up and I was determined to have a beer.' Combe is a tall, friendly man, a Prince Alfred College boy whose speech has a distinctive South Australian plumminess; he was Federal Secretary of the ALP from 1973 to 1981. He continued,

> I thought I'd say to him, 'Look, you can have a lemon squash, but I must have a beer'. Then this rough little diamond came along and said, 'Bob 'awk. You lookin' for me?' and I said, 'Oh, yes. David Combe. Delighted to meet you, Mr Hawke.' And he said, 'Listen, I don't bloody-well know about you, but I gotta have a beer!' So we went to the nearest pub, then to my place and had another, then we stopped at a couple of pubs on the way to his hotel. And we seemed to strike a tremendous rapport, straight off. He was very open to me about his ambition to be President of the ACTU, and asked me to sound people out, to try to find support. And I did that for him . . . It was an idea that was totally offensive to a lot of trade union blokes at that stage. I would talk to union officials, saying how outstandingly competent he was — on that first night I met him a group of us ended drinking all night and Bob didn't have more than half an hour's sleep, but the next morning he delivered the speech he'd come to make, without a note, and it was brilliant. We brought him back to Adelaide to speak again, and made sure there were heaps of trade unionists in the audience, so they could judge themselves how impressive he was. It was a case of breaking down barriers among people whom he would not have a chance to get to know personally, people who would be participating within the forums of their own unions, as to how they'd vote as ACTU Congress delegates.

Some weeks before either of these direct approaches Hawke had already, obliquely, begun his campaign: in late August 1965 he had attacked the federal Budget on television, speaking as ACTU advocate, and had so inspired some of his friends who were industrial journalists that they had written articles speculating that he was being groomed for the presidency.

While the whole Hawke family spontaneously felt the need to 'use their voices, to spread the good news', Hawke himself also had a highly developed sense of the usefulness of the news media. His success in using the Press and television was so great largely because publicity — being the centre of attention — corresponded perfectly with a major element in his personality, laid in infancy and childhood. Hawke had mesmerised his parents: he relished and had the knack of mesmerising. As his personal assistant, Jean Sinclair, commented later, 'It was cruel to watch Bob with journalists. They were lambs to be slaughtered. He's so complex, and so defensive, that there was never one who got close to understanding him.'

A few weeks after the President-to-be stories had appeared Albert Monk, flanked by George Polites and another senior employers' representative, Doug Fowler, arrived in the chambers of Sir Richard Kirby. They were there to lodge a formal complaint, on behalf of organised labour and organised capital, about the ACTU advocate. Kirby recalled,

> I couldn't understand what Albert was getting at, initially. He shifted from foot to foot and mumbled behind his hand. I can still see the smirk on George Polites' face — he'd taken a step or two back and was standing behind Albert. Albert finally said, 'Look here, young Hawke is getting too big for his boots. We want you, as President of the Commission . . .' It was some footling thing about an adjournment I'd granted Bob, which he had not first cleared with the ACTU. George's eyes were shining — he was almost bursting with suppressed laughter.

Monk was sixty-five, but he had given no sign about when he might retire, and Harold Souter was his obvious successor as President. The war of nerves had begun, and was to last another four years. In the meantime, Hawke had to recoup his losses of 1965 in the 1966 wage case.

At the ACTU biennial Congress of August 1965 the militant Left of the trade union movement had demanded a new wages policy: the Left wanted to abandon the prices and productivity argument and to replace it with a submission for a 'living basic wage'. The 'living basic wage' was new only in name; it was the old 'needs' concept which Mr Justice Higgins, the philosopher-king of wages arbitration, had made famous in the Harvester Judgment of 1907 when he had referred to the needs of 'a man, wife and about three children . . . living in frugal comfort in a civilized community', and had thus begun the whole process of centralised wage fixation in Australia. In the image of that family group of little battlers there is something peculiarly appealing — there is pathos, courage, and solidarity. Higgins himself had decreed that such a basic wage should be 'sacrosanct, beyond the reach of bargaining'. His words were engraved on the hearts of the trade union movement and on those of the electorate at large. During the Depression, a judge who was required to reduce the basic wage publicly described his job as 'disgusting'. The Harvester Judgment was a great piece of law; it was also a grand piece of nonsense, for it supposed the male worker was married and sire of three children — which was pure fiction. By 1920, as a commission of inquiry discovered, all these notional marriage beds had produced 2,100,000 phantom children;[1] by 1965 Australia's population, if one went on the Harvester Judgment, would have rivalled Indonesia's. However, the official of a male-membership trade union who will publicly acknowledge this little curiosity of wage-fixation has not yet been born. One practical effect of the Great Law was that women could not, while the basic wage existed, get equal pay — *logically*, because working women were not — or had no right to be — supporting spouses and three children. Another effect, obviously, was that the single man was very much 'over-paid'.

While the definition of the basic wage created a gross injustice to working women (the influence of which is still evident, in the 1980s), and has been a factor in youth unemployment, it has had another egregious effect, for it mixed together the concept of employee and of citizen. Trade unions were established for a specific purpose: to get the best possible conditions for the working man, through bargaining with employers. There have always been paternalistic employers who have, like kindly feudal lords, cared for their employees' security throughout life. But the Harvester Judgment, the very foundation of wage fixation, institutionalised feudal thinking: by it, the employer was required to bargain with the whole man — the worker producing goods, the citizen raising a family. This system can work very well — for example, in Japan, where the roots of feudalism have never been severed and are the support structure for a mighty industrial tree. But in Australia, matters which in a democracy *should* be dealt with in regard to the whole nation — for example, accident compensation and superannuation — have been made the responsibility of employers. As for the unions, they are mentally and emotionally so accustomed to mixing up the concept of worker and citizen that it seems to them as proper as a law of nature. The corollary is that there is little reason for this vast number of working people to elect governments which will diminish the relationship between labour and capital, sever the feudal bonds, and take responsibility for the welfare of the whole citizenry. The very effectiveness of trade union bargaining makes federal Labor governments unnecessary for the trade union movement. Liberal-Country Party governments have known this for a long while, and have known, too, that the responsibility for reform can be carried lightly.

Meanwhile, particularly for the Left of the trade union movement, it is now unacceptable *not* to mix up worker-and-citizen.

At the ACTU Congress of 1965 the Left demanded that a 'living wage' of £22 a week, some £7 higher than the existing basic wage, become the new ACTU policy. Hawke, already beginning to build upon the support of the

Left-wing for his presidency campaign, gave an impassioned speech of opposition. He said, 'I was told beforehand that I would prejudice my position with the Left, but I thought, too bad — they are wrong and I am going to say so'. Sir John Moore commented later,

> I think he personally very deeply believed in trying to improve wages and conditions, but that is overlain by his understanding of economics. He understands that if wages go too far, other economic results happen, which may not be good for the country, and he has to balance those two things. Inherent in everything he does is a strong sense of trying to look after the ordinary person.

Hawke defended the 'prices and productivity' formula at Congress while personalising his address in such a way as to make a vote against 'prices and productivity' a vote against his competence as an advocate. It was a ploy he was to use time and again: at heart, an unconscious emotional manipulation. The Left's proposal was defeated. A decade later Left-wing union officials were to recall the arguments they had had with Hawke — in the public forum of the 1965 Congress and privately, in bars — about ACTU wages policy and to think that they had misjudged him all along: at the very moment when he was gathering them to his cause, when they were falling in love with him, he was, in disguise, 'just a pragmatist'. The danger is always there for the man who, even unwittingly, sculpts from the emotion of his supporters a response which, without emotion, they would not give: when the love affair is over, when they reflect in solitude, they believe themselves robbed. The passionate hatred the Left came to feel for Hawke should be seen in the context of the see-saw's crash from the heights of rapport — infatuation — and the use that Hawke made of it, thudding down to resentment.

The 1966 case, which because of the complicated nature of the competing union and employer claims was called the Basic Wage, Margins and Total Wage Cases, began in February 1966 before Judges Wright, Gallagher and Moore, and Commissioner Winter. Kirby had put Sweeney and Nimmo off the Bench and, diplomatically, himself.

The new presiding judge, Syd Wright, had been in the 1930s and 1940s the employers' greatest advocate and when he had been elevated to the Bench in 1951 there had been rejoicing in their ranks. But Syd, a man of mischievous wit which was enhanced by a deep, melodious voice, had, on becoming Mr Justice Wright, abruptly appalled his former patrons. He declared he was a child of the working class himself and was for the employers what John Kerr became for Gough Whitlam — in the words of one of Wright's former clients, 'the worst appointment we ever had'.

The case got properly under way on 8 March, when Hawke — appearing for the Electrical Trades Union, the Amalgamated Engineering Union, the Blacksmiths' Society, the Boilermakers' Society, the Federated Moulders'

Union, the Sheet Metal Workers, Agricultural Implement and Stovemaking Industrial Union, and the Miscellaneous Workers' Union — began his opening address. He had been sitting in the sun in his back garden, watching his children playing, when he had made the decision that he would go through the 1965 judgment 'word by bloody word — and destroy it!' The hour was now approaching.

His opening address lasted for three weeks, a display of stamina which, in itself, was extraordinary. For the first week Hawke concentrated on the function of the Conciliation and Arbitration Commission as defined by law, which, he submitted, it had not been properly exercising:

> . . . the overwhelmingly important issue which you must decide in these proceedings: what is the function and charter of this Commission . . . ? Is it to be a tribunal for the prevention and settlement of interstate industrial disputes . . . Or are [you] going to abandon and substantially submerge that function in an attempt to assume and discharge primarily the role of an economic sub-legislature . . . trying to create and sustain a favourable economic climate . . . ?

He was gingerly in his criticisms of Gallagher: '. . . we do not necessarily identify with that [1965] judgment a representation of Your Honour's complete position on these basic issues . . .' Again he performed 'Hawke's historical exercise', to the considerable interest of the presiding judge, Wright, who had not heard it all before. Gallagher grew restive when Hawke gave quick jabs at the 1965 judgment; however Hawke remained circumspect in his replies to the judge, sprinkling 'with respects' through every answer to him. But on 15 March, the first day of the second week, Hawke got into his stride, and the fight between him and Gallagher was on, for Hawke had begun his destruction of the 1965 judgment and in terms of the 'fools and crooks' who had written it. After the lunch adjournment Wright exercised the responsibility of the presiding judge by saying: 'Mr Hawke, you have been invited to criticise quite freely; you realise that. But I would suggest to you that words like "blithely" and "outrageous" do not help your case at all.'[2] Hawke withdrew the words and five minutes later used 'blithely' again. By 16 March the transcript was studded with Hawke's sarcasms: 'now this remarkable statement', 'what sense can one make of a judgment which does this?', 'the Commission has come to a hopeless position', 'what meaning can this sort of language have?', 'literally non sense', 'in my unceasing search in trying to make sense of these things, I went to my dictionary', 'now this is a completely objectionable sentence', 'one is certainly indebted for the increase in the fund of knowledge which is involved in this next sentence', 'but the next paragraph is equally objectionable'. By lunch-time the following day Hawke had goaded Gallagher into a rage and the judge burst out:

I place on record that this is a wanton, reckless statement which should never have come from a senior advocate before this Commission. It is the sort of statement you expect from the lips of some Domain Demosthenes or a Hyde Park Cicero. It is absolutely unworthy of you and it is absolutely untrue.

HAWKE: Then it will probably be necessary to pursue that after lunch, Your Honour.

GALLAGHER, J: You please yourself about that.

HAWKE: Yes, I shall.[3]

The court adjourned. After lunch Hawke returned, still determined to overwhelm Gallagher with shame for the 1965 decision, but taking a different tack, and one which, if anything, was more intimidating.

HAWKE: I have a job to do, not for Hawke . . . it is not Hawke speaking, but the representative of all those people . . . 80% of the Australian population.[4]

Already he had begun the political leader's practice of referring to himself in the third person, as an instrument through which the voice of the people is heard.

On 18 March the court adjourned because Hawke had again infuriated Gallagher by referring to the 1965 judgment as a 'diatribe' and 'absolute humbug'. When the judges returned to their Bench Hawke was required to assure them that he was not imputing personalities. On 22 March, when Hawke was still continuing his attack on the 1965 judgment, Wright was moved to say: 'Mr Hawke, there will have to be some limit as to which we can conduct a post-mortem on last year's proceedings, you know . . . I would ask you to spare us everything you can as regards the past.'[5]

Hawke continued his opening address on 23, 25, 29, 30 and 31 March, and then the Commission, punch-drunk, adjourned for a couple of weeks. Perhaps the attention of Jim Robinson and George Polites had wandered during Hawke's marathon forensic autopsy (which Polites described as 'the hypnotic approach — if you say it often enough, people will believe it'). At some stage before Hawke had begun his third week of talking, he had been at Melbourne airport and had bumped into his old friend Keith Hancock, who was now Professor of Economics at Flinders University. Before going to different flights, they had a quick chat during which Hancock, who had been an advisor to the Vernon Committee, told Hawke that he had, since writing a chapter on wages for the Vernon Report, changed his mind, and that he had made a speech to the Victorian Chamber of Manufactures about his revised ideas on wages. He gave Hawke a copy of his speech and, on 23 March, Hawke referred to it in the Commission and offered to make copies of

Hancock's speech available to the Bench. Somehow, Robinson and Polites overlooked the warning sign. Robinson began his opening address on 21 April, complimenting the Commission for its 'courageous' 1965 decision — and the next day made the first of many references to the Vernon Report, for its chapter on wages had numerous points in common with the 1965 decision, and substantiated the employers' claims.

The Vernon Report was one of the great controversies of the mid-1960s. To counter criticism of government actions which were said to have led to the economic recession of 1961, Menzies had in 1963 established a Committee of Economic Inquiry, under the chairmanship of Sir James Vernon, Chairman of the Colonial Sugar Refinery, and including Sir John Crawford, Director of the Research School of Pacific Studies at the ANU, Professor Peter Karmel, Dr D.G. Molesworth and K.B. Myer — a distinguished selection of leaders from the fields of business and academia. Their report, which had inquired into Australia's demography, employment, basic resources, savings, imports, exports and likely growth patterns, was one million words long. It had been tabled in Parliament in September 1965 and had embarrassed the Government — and angered the Treasury. There was heated argument for and against its recommendations, with comments being sought from overseas economists and with every newspaper editorialist in Australia dashing into print about which of its one million words should be considered sacred, which profane. Inside the hubbub there was a still, quiet centre: the Prime Minister, Sir Robert Menzies, was exercising a prerogative of power: inertia. In the long run, Menzies ignored the Vernon Report.

On the next day of sitting Robinson talked at length about the Vernon Committee and tendered, as his ninth exhibit, a report on its chapter which dealt with wages. It looked like an ace for the employers. But Robinson and Polites had just made an egregious tactical mistake with Exhibit R 9. They had cornered Hawke, and in that position, he dares.

Hawke recalled,

> It was a backs-to-the-wall job. Jim was carrying on about the Vernon Report, which endorsed everything the employers had been saying, and ruined us — knocked off our conceptual approach. Finally I thought, 'God, we've got to do something, or we're going to be battered to death'. We were still getting our ears belted off when the court rose for lunch [on 3 May]. So I went back to the office and I put it to Harold Souter that what we had to do was to call the Vernon Committee and examine them. Albert Monk rejected the idea out of hand, but Harold, to his credit, was positive; he was superb, and finally Albert accepted Harold's arguments. So when the court resumed after lunch I announced that we wanted the Vernon Committee called for cross-examination. Well, Jim and George Polites had kittens, on the spot!

Hawke had asked that the Commission itself call the Vernon Committee; the Bench refused to do so. The next morning Hawke announced his second step: he had prepared subpoenas for the men to be summoned to court. Robinson argued desperately that the Bench should not allow the Vernon Committee to be subpoenaed and questioned by Hawke but as Polites, at least, knew intuitively, there was no chance that Mr Justice Wright would pass up such an opportunity for amusing diversion. The prospect of a rough and tumble union gladiator taking out his net and sword against the lions of the Establishment was too great a temptation for His Honour to resist. Robinson argued on; Wright observed with a note of wicked amusement, 'Sir James . . . may be straining at the bit to get here!' The employers and the Commonwealth, represented by Kerr, continued their objections, for hours, until the Bench announced it would adjourn to consider the matter, but before rising Wright had interjected, 'Mr Robinson, what is so obnoxious about our witness box? You speak of it as though it were in the category of a gaol', and Gallagher had added, 'Or at least a dock'. Again, the decision would hinge upon Gallagher; everyone knew that Moore would not allow Hawke's subpoena because, as he explained later,

> If you had the Vernon Committee subjected to cross-examination the Government might well find it very difficult to get people in public life ever to undertake these tasks. Hawke was a ruthless cross-examiner; there were no holds barred. I thought the Vernon Committee shouldn't be exposed to that kind of thing — for they may well have submerged some of their own views in order to get unanimity. That's what happens with unanimous decisions — you have to learn to yield, but you wouldn't want to be cross-examined on every aspect of it, because you might not agree with every aspect of it. And yet, you've put your name to it.

At 12.20 p.m. on 6 May the judges returned, sat, and two minutes later Mr Justice Wright announced to a packed courtroom that he and Mr Justice Gallagher were in favour of the Vernon Committee being subpoenaed, and that summonses for them were to be issued. The court then adjourned until 17 May, with journalists running for telephones, Hawke and the union people jigging with excitement and the employers' men cursing. Hawke recalled,

> I'd been able to say that here were the employers relying upon this document, this revelation of divine economic truth, and now, Your Honours, they don't want it examined. It was a pretty nice position to be in. When the Bench agreed that the Committee could be called the Government went mad, everyone went mad. There was an enormous

kerfuffle. The Government was pleased with the Vernon Committee's line on wages — the process of disowning the Report had not begun at that stage. When the hearing resumed and Vernon arrived it was unbelievable how many lawyers came in with him: there was Jim Smythe and Hal Wootten — *two* Queen's Counsel to protect him — plus all their juniors. And Kerr. At the Bar table you just couldn't move for silk!

The David-and-Goliath atmosphere was, for Hawke, a pure delight. Kerr was particularly active, supporting Smythe's objections about Hawke's questions to Vernon, objections which came with a leaping to the feet every minute or so. For Hawke there was an added pleasure: Clem and Ellie were in Melbourne on holiday and spent much of each day in the court, which was packed solid. Ellie, aged 67, could not tolerate idleness any better than she could at twelve, and sat in the courtroom knitting like a machine, until a tipstaff ordered her to stop. She was attending adult education lectures and was contemplating travelling abroad, since, officially, she was too old to work. Although her hair was grey, she looked a good fifteen years younger than her age and could still run everyone, except Hawke, to a standstill.

On 27 May, the first morning that Sir James Vernon spent in the witness box, his lawyers were so assiduous in his protection that proceedings became farcical. They jumped up to object to every question of Hawke's which even nudged towards economic matters, claiming that he was cross-examining his own witness. Hawke was unusually polite. He said, 'My blokes were really frustrated; they thought we would be unable to get to Vernon. I told them, "I think you'll find it's different after lunch": at one point Vernon's counsel had objected, "That is like asking a plumber a question about medicine", which I had thought would appal Vernon.' At the luncheon adjournment Sir James joined his counsel at the Windsor Hotel and told them he was prepared to answer Hawke's economic questions. That afternoon Hawke's real examination of the Vernon Committee's wisdom got under way and, as Sir John Moore recalled, 'the people who were worried that Bob would tear Sir James to pieces were left gasping'. Hawke was as gentle as if he had been talking to Clem.

Hawke said,

Essentially, the statistical point upon which the Committee had hung its theoretical argument was that there had been a stability of wages' share of national income over a period of years. Our argument was that because of wrong policies of the Commission, wages' share of national income had declined. Now the Committee, using its figures showing a stability of wages' share, had gone on to argue that the Commission should base its judgments upon economic capacity — in other words, the employers' productivity approach — and that it should not consider productivity *and* prices. Well, if you consider only economic capacity there is always *something* the employers can produce to show that economic capacity will not allow an increase on wages — either farm income is too low or too high, or exports are down or up, or investments are too low, or retail trade is going bad, or secondary industry is wobbly — there is always some bloody thing the employers can pull out of the hat, and say, 'This proves any increase in wages will be a disaster, Your Honours'. Well, we were sure that we could show that the Vernon Committee's basic premise about the share of wages was wrong, and that therefore, the Committee's argument fell apart. And the beautiful thing was that Sir James Vernon was a very honest witness. I took him through the Report's statistics and our statistics, step by step, and he said, 'I'll have to agree that we were wrong'.

By the end of Hawke's questioning of Vernon on Tuesday 31 May Robinson's case was in serious disarray. Hawke recalled, 'The employers were saying, Vernon is not a professional economist; wait until Hawke has to deal with Professor Karmel. Karmel was put in the box and agreed with everything I'd put to Vernon; Myer was next and was almost embarrassingly willing to confirm what had been said by the others.' It was all over for Robinson.
The hearing ended on 16 June and he and Hawke went off for a jubilant spree. During hearings neither of them drank more than a couple of glasses of beer each day and the tradition was now established that when the court finally rose they should set out to get drunk. The party following the 1966 case was famous. Robinson recalled,

We finished early — about 11 a.m. — and decided we would drink nothing but champagne. In those days a lot of people would come down to the Beaufort for after-case celebrations — unionists, Commissioners, people from ICI and TAA — and would want to drink with us. So we made this condition: they were welcome to join us but they had to buy a bottle of champagne — and having done that, they would have the privilege of trying to shoot the champagne cork into a brass pisspot which was up on a ledge in the Beaufort, above the bottles of spirits. The barmaid, Vi, said that if anybody could do it the pub would donate another bottle of champagne. There were scores of people shooting at the po, and on the other side, in the public bar, people were staring at us — in the mid-1960s drinking champagne in a pub was a peculiarity.

By five in the afternoon nobody had succeeded in shooting the po, then, as Hawke recalled, 'A secretary from the Commission walked in, a kid about twenty, and said, "Give me a go" and Bang!, she did it in one'. Festivities continued.
On 8 July, amid a tumult of publicity, the Bench gave its decision. A

136

photograph of Hawke which took up almost all the front page of the Melbourne *Herald* shows him reading the judgment with such intense pleasure that the tip of his tongue is pressed against the corner of his mouth and he looks ready to eat the document. The basic wage had been increased by $2, a disappointingly small amount, but the principle of fixing wages according to prices and productivity had been reinstated. Hawke had burnt down the 1965 judgment. However, he had not destroyed the employers' arguments for a total wage. A minimum wage had been instituted (paving the way for equal pay); the Bench had decided to inquire into the margins system and when its inquiry was completed it would, with certainty, bring in the total wage.

As nobody then realised, the Commission had set in train a fateful process with its decision, in 1966, to inquire into the metal trades (margins) award. There are some things, the *arcana arcanissima* of life, which are very ancient, queer and untidy — like the relativities within the metal trades, the origins of which stretch back to the Middle Ages or perhaps further — and which are safest left alone. To a tidy legal mind, however, the desire to impose logic and order can overwhelm common sense. This happened. The Commission, after its inquiry, tampered with the metal trades and brought not order, but chaos. As Polites remarked, 'When you alter the fitter's margin you start a landslide'. The landslide resulted in the great industrial battle of 1968 which the unions very convincingly won and which sealed the fate, as far as major Australian employers were concerned, of the new Prime Minister, John Gorton. He had not supported them. The victory for militants was followed by the Clarrie O'Shea case of 1969,* and another victory: the penal powers of the Industrial Court, hated by the Left, were transformed into meaningless pieces of paper. Union militancy had won vindication and encouragement in a time of economic boom, when employers were willing to pay higher rates, on a base which was already enhanced (by the total wage) and in a world which was economically over-heating, thanks mostly to that monstrous dollar-making machine, the Vietnam War. Hawke's campaign for the leadership of the trade union movement was to coincide with the greatest surge of industrial militancy for twenty years, and he would be swept into the office of president on a wave of excitement and apparently endless prosperity. The Hawke style — of aggression and optimism — was beautifully matched to the looming hour.

Within a couple of days of the Beaufort celebration Hawke was in Papua New Guinea for the case he considers the most interesting and important of his career. It was called, mildly enough, the Local Officers Case, and was about the pay rates of black members of the Papua New Guinea Public Service

*See Chapter 13, page 161.

Association (PSA). But at heart it was a question of colonialism, independence and racism — above all, racism. 'We truly believed we were part of a crusade. Spontaneously, at parties, we would begin singing that song, "We Shall Overcome" ', a former PSA official, Rod Madgwick, recalled. 'It was an amazingly emotional case.'

Albert Maori Kiki (later Sir Albert) wrote of Papua New Guinea in the mid-1960s:

> . . . we used to have district officers in the Gulf district who brought local girls into their compound, stripped them naked in the garden, hosed them for twenty minutes, then slept with them and kicked them out immediately afterwards . . . What I find most offensive is the way Europeans have native women and despise them at the same time. Even today, in 1967, a former district officer, W. Kennedy, can write in all seriousness: '. . . Few Melanesian women are attractive. On our accepted standards most men would actually find them repugnant.' And he can get this published in a serious magazine like *New Guinea*.⁶

In the small, stifling, white community of Port Moresby, with its neat fibro bungalows and its men servants referred to as Boy to their faces and Rock Ape behind their backs; in the slatternly sprawl of native dwellings, built without kitchens or bathrooms, where only the rich owned a pair of shoes, where a man wearing a suit was regarded with fear — there, in that atmosphere of distrust, racism was the very air people breathed, even in their dreams. Hawke arrived like a wind from the sea on a dead summer afternoon. 'He came into our lives with a great whoosh!' the wife of an Australian journalist said. Madgwick recalled,

> He was bubbly and charmed everyone; he seemed to have no sense of race. He brought a feeling of creativity, of original thought and encouragement. For example, there was something called the Papua New Guinea Society. The atmosphere in Moresby was so conservative that the very word 'union' was embarrassing and unions made sure they never called themselves unions. Bob gave a talk to the Papua New Guinea Society, which was multi-racial, about the Australian trade union movement and people couldn't believe their ears. Their eyes were bulging. Blacks and whites. He was frank and assertive. He dared to talk about things [like the rights of labour] which were unimaginable . . . Bob is a great encourager.

The people whom Hawke encouraged are a Who's Who list of the independence leaders of Papua New Guinea, in politics and the civil service. 'He was a hero there', Madgwick continued. 'I think Bob's work in New Guinea was his finest hour.'

Hawke first went to New Guinea in late 1965 for the opening manoeuvres of the case. As usual, he was initially distrusted by some as 'an outsider', and worse: a man brought in to abort the plans already laid to improve the wages of blacks. Paul Munro, then the industrial advocate of the PSA, said,

> I distrusted Hawke. The PSA was run by whites. Among the local officers there was total disenchantment with it, and splinter groups had formed, outside the PSA. A case had been dragging on about expatriates' territorial allowances and the arbitrator was delaying finishing it. Meanwhile, we were planning the case for the local officers. The Administration [the government in PNG] made an offer on territorial allowances which was unacceptable. Suddenly Bob Hawke arrived to argue the second case and I thought, 'Well, hell, here's the sell-out. It will all be done by reference to the superior expertise of an Australian lawyer. The whites will get a good deal and the blacks will get nothing. And Hawke has been brought in to fix it — to tell everyone that it's got to be like that.' So we went into negotiations with the Administration and Hawke, to the great horror of a couple of us — almost disbelief — threatened the Arbitrator [L.G. Mathews] that if he did not finalise the territorial allowances issues the PSA would *withdraw* the local officers' case. You could have knocked the Administration side over with a feather. I still remember the pause in which people caught their breaths, and the look on Hal Wootten's face [Wootten was the Administration's legal advisor for the wage cases] as he tried to work that one out. But whatever was the shock of our opponents, it was only matched by the shock on our side. What if the Administration said, 'OK, withdraw'? We'd be lost. I was totally convinced, as was everyone else in the room, that Hawke was serious. And it was a bluff. But it was a bluff made possible by his aggression. You see, he dropped it suddenly, unexpectedly and with extraordinary aggression — shouting something like, 'If you don't settle we'll bloody-well withdraw the local officers' claim!' — and it was the aggression that carried, people responded to his anger and were unable to think rationally. After a couple of minutes the Administration buckled and said, 'All right, we'll deal with the territorial allowances'.

If Hawke had any doubts that his opponents in Papua New Guinea — that is, the Government and its representatives — were fools and crooks who required intimidation to bring them to reason and goodness he showed no sign of indecision. Soon after he took over the case, which was part-heard by mid-1966, he established what he called, 'The Pavlovian Treatment' for the Arbitrator, Mathews. As with Kirby and later Gallagher, Hawke set out, in part, to browbeat Mathews into accepting the PSA claim. 'It was a professional tactic', Munro recalled.

Bob's theory was that he would put Mathews on the spot. If he didn't respond in the right way, Bob would have a public altercation with him. If he did respond nicely, Bob would be soft. Mathews used to get discomfitted. He'd twist and show obvious physical embarrassment whenever an uncompromising request was put to him. Another tactic was to have our witnesses present their evidence with aggression, to stand up in court and say how angry they were about their rates of pay. This aggression was not directed at Mathews but at the whole Administration — and, of course, the Press. Bob believed that the decision was going to be taken not in Port Moresby, but in Australia. It wasn't a matter of influencing the local Administration so much as of influencing Barnes, the Minister for Territories, and the Australian population. We [in the PSA] were utterly oblivious to the significance of the Press. Bob flattered, coerced and seduced the local Press men into covering the case, and he was always extremely alert to discover in a statement — or to have someone else discover in a statement — the newsworthy lines. And he got tremendous publicity that way.

One night Rod Madgwick chipped Hawke about the Press coverage he was getting, implying that Hawke was mostly seeking publicity for himself. Hawke was drunk. 'He tore me to shreds', Madgwick recalled. Paul Munro had realised that Hawke was working for a cause larger than (although concentric with) his own ego:

> The publicity affected the courage of our witnesses. By the two things — encouraging them to be assertive and state their grievances in public (and proving to them that they could do that without the sky falling on their heads) and, second, by showing them how to get the news media on side — Bob was training Papuans and New Guineans in basic political tactics. He worked by example, but awarely. And a big group began to pattern around him.

Pangu Pati, the political party which formed the first independent government of Papua New Guinea, had not yet come into being in 1966. But when Pangu did form in mid-1967 every member of it had taken part in the Local Officers Case, either as a witness or as a researcher or as a participant in the sub-culture that the case generated.

An early problem was the local officers' disenchantment with the PSA: they had to be convinced that the union was sincerely concerned about them before they would agree to help. Hawke was taken along to address the most radical and sophisticated group of disillusioned blacks — teachers — and won their trust. 'I loved them and they loved me', he said. Once the teachers were on side, the others followed.

The case itself had come about due to an extraordinarily insensitive

Administration decision: in September 1964 the Administration had imposed salary cuts on black employees; as a result a black doing the same job as a white received about half the pay; in addition, blacks had to pay going prices for house rental, while whites had their rents subsidised. Added up, a white public service employee had at his or her disposal about two to three times as much money as a black colleague of the same sex doing the same work.

The Administration justified its decision on two grounds: the economy could not afford more (for a variety of reasons, including the danger of rural workers leaving plantations to seek higher wages in towns); it was necessary to pay whites higher salaries for without financial inducement they would be unwilling to work in the Territory.

The least skilled public service employees — all blacks — were reduced to penury, unable even to afford a weekly tin of the ubiquitous and loathsome (but nourishing) bully beef. The case which the PSA decided to mount in defence was monumental, based on 'needs' and 'capacity' and embracing in its sweep a mountain of evidence about nutrition, social customs, the state of the economy and regional differences in it, and the danger inherent in allowing resentment to fester in a colony — one which was so central to Australia's defence. There were more than a hundred witnesses for the PSA side and their evidence has provided a transcript that is a goldmine for historians, sociologists and economists. Hawke said,

> It was *immensely* challenging. I arrived cold and had immediately to absorb an enormous quantity of information in areas about which I knew nothing. I had to get on top of a mountain of material about New Guinea's economy, and about sociology and nutrition. I loved that challenge. I worked harder in that case, I think, than I have ever worked in my life. Paul Munro and Rod Madgwick had done the leg-work of finding witnesses and preparing them and for the first few months I was operating as a real barrister, not knowing the witnesses before I had to examine them in the box. For me the exercise idealised the concept of a barrister, mastering a huge mass of material, for a case in which he deeply believed.

The transcript, read fifteen years later, sounds like an account of life in some province of economic disaster, yet the Australian economy and the international commodity market, upon which the Territory's trading income depended, were buoyant in 1966, and the witnesses were all employed. From transcript:

> Nearly all of us trainee information officers have to go without breakfast in the second week after we are paid. Sometimes we have to go without food at lunch-time, because we do not have enough money . . .
> I had no sheets or blankets until Mr Newly bought me some, on the condition that I repay him . . .

I am Thomas Vincent To Bun Bun, a teacher . . . I cannot afford to buy a second-hand VW . . . I am embarrassed by my house . . . I cannot afford to dress my sons properly . . . Australians ask me to their houses, but I cannot reciprocate their hospitality . . .

I am a medical officer . . . we begin to hate our colleagues, the overseas officers, who get much higher salaries than we get . . .

I am Michael Somare, an announcer with Radio Wewak . . . my income is $37.38 a week; my family expenses are $33.80 a week . . . we need decent, neat clothes . . . I have been to Australia and seen houses like the Administration is building for [black] Local Officers, used for cattle sheds or hay stacks on farms . . . In most of the Administration-type houses in Wewak — I am occupying one — there is nothing like stove, sink or proper bathroom and laundry facilities provided. Bathrooms are placed next to the lounge room or entrance to the room, and water has to be carried in buckets to the room: if there were visitors it would be an embarrassing thing or sight to see wife carrying water in it — just walking into the lounge room where you are sitting and getting the bucket into the shower room . . . if wife wants to do washing she has to wash outside and empty dishes just on the grass . . . our toilet stinks. I had some officers from Canberra. I asked them to come in . . . They said, What is smelling? I said, That is toilet . . . I am ashamed to invite [whites] to my home . . . I now have an opinion that many Australian clerks are employed here so that what the Australian taxpayers contribute goes back to their people's own pocket . . . As my friend Albert Maori Kiki puts it, New Guinea is 'whiteman's paradise' . . .

I am Dr Reuben Taureka, District Medical officer for Madang . . . I earn $3,810 . . . I have 386 people working under me, including 45 overseas officers . . . my highest-paid subordinate, a surgeon, earns $10,200 . . . I cannot afford a car, but most of my subordinates own cars . . .

The theme of shame recurs throughout the witnesses' evidence for throughout Melanesian society male self-esteem depends upon ability to give and to repay hospitality, measure for measure, or better. The pay rates and the slum housing of blacks meant that they felt not mere embarrassment, in the Western sense, but unmanned, eunuchs, *vis-à-vis* white males. It's no surprise that rape was a problem in the Territory and that white women lived in fear of it.

Munro said,

Just a few years earlier a deputy administrator, Gunther, had scandalised the white community by inviting Reuben Taureka and his wife to a cocktail party. Drinking at the time was prohibited for blacks and only became legal in 1962-63. It was a totally paternalistic society. White officers wanted and expected the blacks to behave like orderly sons and children, not to swear back or resent white authority. So when a Papuan stood up in court and made these statements of resentment and anger white officers felt terribly wounded and confused.

The Administration was alarmed by the publicity and aggression that had surrounded the case since Hawke had taken over in June 1966 and on 13 July the Arbitrator, Mathews, had rebuked Hawke and the PSA for using the Press. On 30 August the Territory's Treasurer, A.P.J. Newman, announced that if blacks' salaries were increased there would have to be budget cuts: roads and hospitals, for example, would not be built. The case had been adjourned; when it resumed on 12 September Hawke applied his 'Pavlovian Treatment' to the Arbitrator, saying,

> As far as we are concerned in these proceedings we are fighting the Administration, and as far as I am concerned the Administration was having its budget presented through its spokesman, Mr Newman. We ask that . . . you should take the first available opportunity to rebuke the Administration for offending the canons of common courtesy, responsible behaviour and, in fact, your clear observations of 13 July . . . The Treasurer's statement in the House [of Assembly] must be seen, and is seen, as pointing a gun at your head, Mr Arbitrator.

Hawke referred to other statements made by Administration representatives in the House of Assembly and went on to ask Mathews to declare his independence, 'to protect the integrity of the office you hold'. He called the Treasurer's remarks 'contemptuous of this Tribunal', 'political dishonesty' and 'intimidatory of the Arbitrator'. Mathews refused the request. The emotional temperature of the case heightened: Hawke's next witnesses were policemen and Hawke demanded that the tribunal hear them *in camera*, for the men were fearful of speaking out publicly. There had already been acts of insubordination by blacks to whites in the police force, thanks to resentment about pay. Mathews agreed to a closed session. The Administration had not yet made an offer to the PSA on what it would be willing to pay the least skilled black workers; Hawke's tactic was to keep up the heat while the Administration was considering the matter. After the police, he requested permission to include in evidence a document which revealed that district officers (whites) were alarmed by and condemned the blacks' wages. The Administration claimed privilege and Mathews upheld their claim, refusing to accept the document as an exhibit. Hawke demanded higher authority, and the question had to be argued in the Supreme Court. It upheld Mathews' ruling. At this point the Administration made its offer: the lowest paid workers had their salaries increased — from about $7 to about $15 a week. (A chicken in the Rabaul market cost $1.50, and in the Kerowagi market $2.70.)

As Hawke began his summing up of the evidence of the 112 PSA witnesses, he argued fiercely the issues of morality and common sense: that the existing salary structure was improper and immoral and 'positively dangerous'. For this last claim Hawke drew on the police evidence and the work of Dr T.B. Millar, a defence expert, who had written in his book, *Australia's Defence*, that PNG was 'essential', and that the attitude of the local population was a factor in handling any threats to the Territory. Hawke argued that the dissatisfaction created among black public servants opened the possibility of subversion; that the advantages of defence spending in the Territory, which had increased by 10,000% in the past seven years and, in 1966 stood at $20 million, could be negated. His submissions recognised that to attract Australians to work in the Territory, high salaries had to be paid; he sought for the blacks 55% of the white rate, and a single man's rate — thus avoiding the great pitfall in the Harvester Judgment. And then, in repetition of his daring a few months earlier with the Vernon Committee, Hawke dropped a bombshell: he demanded from Mathews permission to put Hal Wootten, Q.C., the counsel for the Administration, in the witness box. What happened next is still remembered by old New Guinea hands as one of the most passionately debated issues of the 1960s; in NSW legal circles, from which Wootten came, Hawke was regarded as a scoundrel. Even Munro, who was as committed to the case as Hawke, 'felt uncomfortable. I had a lawyer's distaste for calling the opposing advocate.'

Wootten [later Mr Justice Wootten] was a liberal and a friend to PNG; he had been concerned about the salary cuts of September 1964 and had written an article, which was published in the *Bulletin* of 27 February 1965, pointing out that there were 'serious implications for race relations' because of the salary cuts. He had then accepted the Administration's brief to argue against significant pay increases for blacks. For Hawke, this was a perfect example of what he had despised since Law I: the advocate as hired hand, arguing for a cause in which he did not believe. Wootten's later career revealed a man of considerable social conscience, and already he was a member of the Association for Cultural Freedom, had done much to develop the Law School in PNG and had many black friends in the Territory — the distinctive mark there of the liberal. Because of Wootten's sympathy the Administration's case was 'probably presented with a little bit more compassion', in Munro's view. Indeed, when Michael Somare was in the box (as Hawke's witness) he had become carried away by his own rhetoric and had added flourishes to what he was saying, under oath. Wootten could have demonstrated that Somare was not a totally reliable witness, but he stopped short in his cross-examination and allowed the issue to slide away. Munro continued,

> None of those things about Hal rated with Bob. Bob was very judg-
> mental: he wasn't a cab-off-the-rank sort of a lawyer, and Hal was. Bob
> caught Hal between his conscience and his professional obligations,

and embarrassed him . . . It was a *political* as well as an industrial case, but I was tremendously naive. I didn't understand that, in such a context, you might call a witness just for effect, or for the *political* argument. Calling Wootten had great significance for it dramatised, it kept the story hot, it demonstrated that even the opponents of the case had misgivings about the propriety and long-term validity of what they were espousing. And that should have an influence on the Arbitrator, but above all it should have an influence on the political system that the Arbitrator represented.

Mathews spent four days considering Hawke's request to put Wootten in the box, during which Wootten's junior, the Sydney barrister R.J. Marr, argued vigorously, claiming that Hawke and the PSA had lied about their purpose and that their real aim was not to elicit evidence from Wootten, but to force him to withdraw from the case. Hawke is enraged whenever he is accused of lying, and indeed throughout his life his only lies have been to women (about other women). His exchanges with Marr were acrimonious; he accused Marr of 'the most vicious personal attack you could conceivably imagine'. Mathews adjourned for a day. On 14 October he announced that Wootten could be sworn.

Wootten's article had said, referring to earlier times: 'Natives felt that "white men" regarded them not as fellow human beings, but as tools or domestic animals, well-cared for and courteously addressed by the enlightened, abused and insulted by the ignorant or neurotic, but accepted as an equal by none', and that these pre-war attitudes were returning.

> Before the recent Public Service salary cuts there was a growing body of natives who could afford homes and meals to which they could invite Europeans without embarrassment, although if present policy continues this advantage will be confined to native politicians, businessmen and private practitioners in the professions. Until these cuts . . . native Public Servants received the same basic salaries as Europeans . . . the general expectation amongst natives was that by hard work and the acquisition of Western skills they could hope to attain something approaching the envied standard of living of the white man. Now they are to receive a markedly lower salary (eg. a fully qualified native medical practitioner will start on about £9 12s. a week), which they are told is related to the economic capacity of their country . . . a round of drinks costs the same for [black and white].

Hawke questioned Wootten with all the power of his own, outraged conscience; Wootten fought back, with dignity:

> The role of barrister is not to assist those with whom they [*sic*] happen to agree, but to provide a service to the community . . . That entails, sir,

a duty on a barrister to accept any brief offered to him, unless he has a good reason for refusing and his personal views on the issues involved are not such a reason.

After a morning of high drama, during which Port Moresby talked of nothing else, it was over: Mathews announced, 'I will now adjourn. I look forward to easier times for all concerned.' Hawke spent the next three days summing up his evidence, then the court went into recess until January 1967, when the Administration was to present its case. While the PSA witnesses, with a few exceptions, had been blacks, the Administration witnesses, without exception, were whites.

For the PSA side one of the most useful occasions for encouragement and display of solidarity had been mixed race parties. Munro recalled, 'Even until 1965 there was still an awkwardness in multi-racial parties. Most of the PSA officials, other than me and Madgwick, were not at all sure about how to go about inviting blacks, or how to serve local people when they came to parties.' As the case progressed blacks and whites overcame their uneasiness and their socialising became euphoric occasions, with laughter and rousing songs. Hawke has always enjoyed singing — he knows scores of hymns and in his drinking days would bellow renditions of 'Abide With Me' or 'Onward Christian Soldiers', champagne or beer bottle in hand. The songs in New Guinea were 'We Shall Overcome' and 'Whose Side Are You On?' Munro recalled the atmosphere of the parties,

> We were all mounted on our white chargers, pursuing truth and justice, and Bob was the hero, the champion of a cause in which we all believed. What people were seeing and experiencing was unique: here was an Australian, an extremely gifted one, fiercely presenting everything we believed in, in a totally uncompromising way, completely committed. There was warmth; there was adulation; there was a collective sense of belonging to a crusade. We were a sub-culture in the community, members of a political-movement-cult.

On the eve of one of Hawke's departures for Australia during a recess, there was a grand celebration which was interrupted by a dog fight. The blacks and wiser whites stood back but Hawke and two other men rushed in to separate the animals. A minute later they retreated: two pairs of spectacles had been smashed, one human leg ripped open and Hawke had a broken wrist. The dogs, looking puzzled, trotted outside to the street to fight in peace. Hawke had involved himself even more recklessly a few months earlier when, walking from his hotel at night, he had come across a large crowd watching two blacks fight; he had broken through the crowd and separated the combatants. As both blacks and whites told him later, it was sheer luck that he had not been set upon by either the fighters or the crowd and beaten to a pulp, for pay-back is central to honour throughout Melanesia and for all he knew, the fight may have been a matter of high principle.

At thirty-six Hawke carried within him still some of the prejudices of his upbringing: one night in PNG he saw a blue movie, an experience he found 'awful' and never repeated. It confirmed his disapproval of pornography. He also scorned gambling. There was little public entertainment in Port Moresby and Saturday afternoons were particularly empty. Munro and the foreign correspondents of the Australian newspapers, with whom Hawke spent much of his leisure time, were keen on punting, and Don Hogg, of the *Australian*, ran a book. The journalists also played one of the favourite card games of South East Asia, variously known as 'Oh, Hell', 'Bum' and, in the more vulgar argot of the Australians in Port Moresby, as 'Fuck Me'. Hawke and Hogg's wife, Gail, were rival champions. On one of his visits to Perth in this period Hawke said excitedly to Ellie, 'I know a tremendous new card game; it's called "F. . . Goodness Gracious Me" ' (which is what journalists later called 'Oh, Hell' in Port Moresby).

When Hawke first saw his friends crouched around the radio on Saturday afternoon listening to the Australian races, he took a step back and repeated the phrase, famous in the Lygon Hotel, of an old Communist trade union man, 'Hush, the workers are at prayer'. At first he refused to take any interest in punting. But one day Munro asked Hawke, who was going to visit Hogg, to place a bet for him there. Hawke asked Hogg for a form guide, picked a horse, and laid a bet himself. With typical bravado he returned to Munro, announcing, '*I've* picked the winner!' He had. Soon afterwards he had a strange experience: he dreamed a race that had not yet been run. 'I saw every detail, and a horse called Pirate Bird winning.' When the race came up it was as he had seen: he won at 16 to 1 on Pirate Bird. Hawke was hooked. Punting became for him what croquet had been to Ellie, a second religion. In 1967, when he returned to Australia and began to keep office diaries, their pages were filled with two categories of name: those of trade unionists he was lobbying in the ACTU presidency campaign, and those of potential race winners.

When he returned for the easier section of the case, during which the Administration would put its arguments, Hazel and the children came too. He had been missing the family, talking frequently to Munro, who was a bachelor and had a bachelor's uninterest in children, about his wonderful offspring. Hazel by now had recovered from her long grief over the death of Robert and was as warm-hearted and jolly as she had been in her twenties; she enrolled the children in a mixed-race school and took them swimming in the afternoons at what was considered 'the black' beach. Years later, when Stephen had refused to attend university, despite his outstanding academic potential, and instead committed himself to working for Australian Aborigines, Hazel suddenly remembered him frolicking in the sea with Melanesian children and caught her breath as she was describing their life in Port Moresby, to say, 'Oh!. . . I've just seen another connection'. Moresby friends recalled, 'Hazel thought Bob was wonderful. She was terrifically proud of what he was doing.'

The key witness for the Administration was Sir Leslie Melville, a distinguished economist, who had made a study of the PNG economy for the case. His evidence embraced three major economic themes: urban drift theory, projections about the Gross National Product in the Territory, and the type of wage structure suitable for the Territorial workers, urban and plantation. Hawke cross-examined him for three days. Munro said, 'I think it was probably Bob's best cross-examination: an absolutely searching analysis with a very guarded, cautious witness, traversing a huge area. People, including all the resident practical and academic economists, were fascinated by it, for it was a very complex debate.' Hawke considers his handling of Melville the high point of his career as an economist-advocate, yet it went virtually unreported in Australia, as complicated matters tend to do. A much more dramatic, newsworthy exchange occurred towards the end of the Administration's case when Dr Roy Scragg, the Director of Public Health in the Territory, appeared. Scragg had been a medical officer in PNG since 1947; he gave evidence that 'a person can physically adapt himself to an intake of 2,000 calories and when this is all the body will receive he can remain a healthy person'. Much PSA evidence had been concerned with the poor nutrition, due to low pay, of blacks. Scragg said that only one in 1,636 native men grew to six feet, and therefore it was wrong to set a calorific allowance, for the food intake suggested by the PSA was only necessary for the exceptional person, and unnecessary for the normal, small one. He said that if blacks' salaries were increased the money would not be spent on food, but 'for other purposes'. (He meant alcohol.) Scragg also said that shoes were not necessary in the Territory — sandals or scuffs were good enough — and that most local officers were 'over-paid'. He added that a salary increase contented only for a short while, then the local officers wanted another increase. Hawke was in a cold rage as he questioned Scragg, so alarming the Arbitrator, Mathews, that he broke in, 'Can you take it quietly, Mr Hawke?' Hawke's cross-examination went on for three days until, at last, Scragg's word was left supported by one thread: assertions about the prevalence of Vitamin A deficiency, as revealed by clinical cases of eye disease in Port Moresby. Hawke cut that thread then abruptly, as he had done before, with Truman, he allowed Scragg to escape. Munro recalled,

Bob would not go in for the *coup de grâce*. He was very gentle. He just stopped. It's such a rare thing for barristers to be able to destroy an important witness, and the most natural self-indulgence is to go for the kill, to ram his lies down his throat and do an exultant dance around him, so that when he steps down he is a totally humiliated person, without self-respect. Now, lesser people — and, in fact, I — would have done that with Scragg. Bob went as far as he had to, then gave quarter. I can still remember the silence in the courtroom as Scragg shuffled his papers together and stepped down.

On 11 May 1967 Mathews gave his decision in an 88 foolscap-page document: while middle-ranking black public servants had some gains, the lowest paid officers had got only an extra $40 a year, leaving their salaries a quarter of the effective base rates for whites. Hawke had been in Australia since the end of the case and had returned for the decision. A party had been arranged for that evening, in anticipation of great news. From the outset the atmosphere was tense.

The party was held in a block of flats and among the blacks were Henry To Robert,* an economist, a Tolai educated at St John's College, Sydney University; and a Tolai friend, Robin Koemina. Munro said,

> There was acute bitterness about disappointed expectations. About 10 o'clock Robin Koemina came in and complained that a white, who'd somehow come to the party, had propositioned his wife as if she were a prostitute. Henry To Robert, who was in his twenties then, about 6 feet tall and very fit, went for the bloke.

What happened next was terrifying: David White, the *Sydney Morning Herald* correspondent, said,

> It took four, maybe five, men to hold Henry down — you can't believe how strong he was. I will never forget the look in Henry's eyes. I grabbed hold of the Australian and said, 'You must leave!' but he was so drunk he didn't understand what was happening, so to save him I pushed him over the balcony and he fell about ten feet to the ground.

Munro and Hawke had not moved. Munro said,

> Robin Koemina, one of my long-time friends, and very friendly with Bob, walked up and stood about a foot in front of us and screamed into our faces, 'That's integration for you!' The racial hatred in the whole room . . . it was horrifying. At that moment, if Bob or I had said or done anything — well, we would have been blasted across the floor. Then somebody, Reuben Taureka, I think, said, 'I think you had better go home'. What made the hatred more unbearable was that it came from and was expressed through people who'd been educated in Australia.

Hawke said of the decision, 'In terms of destroying their witnesses and establishing our witnesses, we won the case *overwhelmingly*. But the tribunal

* Later, Sir Henry, Governor of the Bank of Papua New Guinea.

was predisposed to the Administration's case.' He was angry and now his sense of the dire had been aroused by the passion he had witnessed. He returned to Australia and immediately began publicising the injustices and dangers of the pay scales. He wrote a résumé of the case then persuaded Senator Sam Cohen (Labor), Edward St John (Liberal, MHR) and — such was his commitment — Senator Frank McManus (DLP) to take the matter up in Parliament.

Meanwhile, there was a storm of debate in the Territory's House of Assembly. On 3 June, a Saturday, 1,500 black public servants and a few whites had marched on Government House to present a petition to the Administrator, David Hay. Many carried placards, one of which was a drawing of Mathews holding two blacks down by their necks. Such a demonstration had never happened in the Territory before. The *South Pacific Post* reported the event as 'wildly dangerous' and warned of 'bloodshed', although there had been no violence. When the House of Assembly sat again on 6 June a coffee planter, Ian Downs, Member for the New Guinea Highlands, said that Hawke had fomented and organised the march, referred to him as 'a rabble-rouser' and 'this demagogue' and went on to claim, 'This arrogant advocate was much more concerned that the Arbitrator did not kiss his feet in submissive adulation by meekly succumbing to a racist approach before the Arbitration Court than he was really and genuinely concerned with the result'. Downs also referred to the lack of 'gratitude' shown by New Guineans. He spoke for many white planters and other expatriates, who saw Hawke as close enough to the Devil to make no difference. Back in Australia, Hawke issued a statement to the Press saying he had no supernatural powers and therefore could not organise a march at a distance of 3,000 miles, and invited Downs to repeat his remarks outside the House, so he could sue him. He continued his campaign to swing Australian public opinion behind the local officers. On 7 July the *Australian* ran a story by John Hurst, headlined, 'It's not just a question of salaries, says Mr Hawke . . .' which told of the threat to security from a discontented public service. Hawke appeared on television and radio; he spoke to ALP branch meetings. On 30 September the *Age* had a headline: 'NG Pay Policy a "Tragic Blunder" : Hawke Warns of Bloodshed'. In November he returned to Port Moresby to argue before Mathews for a review, saying, 'a massive section of significant Australian opinion demands that the judgment be reviewed', adverting to the speeches of St John, Cohen and McManus, and adding, 'throughout the political spectrum there is support for a review'. The application was refused. But the Territory would never be the same again. When the case had begun the idea of self-government was discussed, if at all, in terms of something which might be possible in the twenty-first century. By November 1967 self-government, followed by independence, was inevitable. Pangu Pati had been formed. Michael Somare became Chief Minister in 1975 and seven months later, Prime Minister.

The new government left the public service pay scales virtually unchanged. Munro, reflecting on the PSA case later, said, 'We were wrong'. He and Madgwick both made the point that Hawke was unwilling, afterwards, to re-examine the wisdom of the PSA case, in the light of what would be best, economically, for an independent PNG. Hawke commented: 'At the time independence was an unreality, a Sometime-Never discussion. It was futile to discuss the appropriate wage structure for an independent country when the country was, and would be for the foreseeable future, dependent.'

Somare's private secretary, Tony Voutas, said later, 'Hawke had a great influence on Michael'. Hawke had influenced others, too, for he had talked constantly, while in the Territory, of Australian political and trade union events, with such zest and optimism that he inspired enthusiasm where none or little had existed before. One of his close associates in PNG was Ian Macphee, eleven years his junior, a barrister who had presented the early sections of the Local Officers Case while Hawke was in Australia arguing the 1966 basic wage. Hawke talked to Macphee about his ambition eventually to enter — and lead — the Australian Parliament. Munro said, 'Ian told me that if Bob could have those ambitions, so could he'. A decade later Macphee was one of the Fraser Government's most successful and progressive young ministers, and at Hawke's direct urging both Munro and Madgwick had become activists in the Australian labour movement; by the late 1970s Munro was Federal Secretary of the Australian Clerical Officers' Association, and one of the most powerful union leaders in the country.

Meanwhile, Hawke's own parliamentary dreams were once more in abeyance. In 1966 Whitlam had called on Hawke at the ACTU and asked him to run for Corio. Hawke had refused and in the 1966 elections Opperman held the seat. When Opperman resigned the following year Whitlam, who by now had replaced Calwell as Leader, again called on Hawke, who recalled, 'Gough was all over me. "You've got to! You've got to run for Corio!" '

By this time, however, Hawke's campaign for the ACTU presidency was gathering momentum; Labor had been out of office for eighteen years and the trade union movement was, as it has always been except during World War II, a far greater force in the community than its legislative sprig, the federal Australian Labor Party. The State Labor Parties had more power, but Hawke had no ambition to be a premier. He told Whitlam that if he failed to win the presidency of the ACTU he would want to go into federal Parliament immediately; if he did become President of the ACTU he would need about six years in the job, and added that presidency of the ACTU appealed to him more than Parliament, 'because in that job you're making decisions all the time. In Parliament, at best, half the time.' Years later, while recalling the meeting, Whitlam in his tone of voice showed irritation with Hawke for raising such an objection — but by then, they were estranged. At the time they

Justice Alf Foster

Outside the Arbitration Commission
Melbourne, with David McBride, left
and Ted Deverall, right, about 1960

The Corio campaign, 1963: Arthur Calwell, Hawke and George Poyser

'Bob Hawke the Family Man': Corio election, 1963

Jim Robinson and Hawke, about 1964

Albert Monk, 1969

Charlie Fitzgibbon

President-elect of the ACTU: Hawke,
December 1969

Labour leader and Labor Leader: Hawke and Whitlam, 1970

Hawke and Susan returning from Israel (and Russia), 1971

Hawke named Victorian Father of the Year, 1971: Rosslyn, Stephen and Susan greeting him

Hazel helping Hawke work at home, after he collapsed during the oil industry dispute, 1972

Hawke, Mrs Dayan, Moshe Dayan, Israel's
Minister for Defence, and Clyde Holding

Sir John Egerton

Hawke, Alexandre Parodi and Francis Blanchard, (Director General of ILO) at luncheon in Gex, France, June 1975

Lionel Revelman

admired each other's talents and had a warm friendship, based on solidarity in a common cause. It was a friendship that concealed, for years, the under-current of rivalry and disapproval on both sides. Whitlam, a puritan himself, condemned Hawke's boozing and womanising; Hawke thought Whitlam lacked emotional depth and that his compassion was merely intellectual and, ultimately, jejune. They disliked each other's arrogance. Each assumed himself the star around which dimmer constellations moved. Fortunately, both had a sense of the ridiculous. In moments of extreme exasperation with the Leader Hawke would inhale deeply, frown, then burst into a breathy, trochaic Whitlamsque speech — like, 'Whý, have yóu given mé this wrítten in Látin? You knów I ónly read Gréek.'

Whitlam was of the upper middle class and his formal education, though shorter than Hawke's, was superior in breadth and ornament. While the foundation of Hawke's education had been the Bible, the foundation of Whitlam's had been the encyclopaedia. Whitlam loved the elegant — in the arts, in clothes, in food. His mother was a sublime cook, and in adulthood Whitlam's love of elaborate cakes was famous. Hawke has no eye for elegance (he discovered only in his mid-twenties that he is colour blind), and little interest in it. Within his own world, in which the red spectrum does not register, Hawke's taste may be exquisite but to people with normal colour vision he dresses loudly, or did, before he began to take advice from friends. Hawke, whose appetite is small, thinks about food only when he is hungry, and if the ambience is right will relish a take-away hamburger or a tub of chips. His vice is sweets: Violet Crumble, Mars Bars, chocolate almonds, ice cream and strawberries. (As a young child he was seriously rebuked only once, and that was for stealing a sweet from the corner store.) Round the dinner table in Hawke's childhood conversation had been about distress in the parish and the appropriate verses of inspired writing that could offer guidance; in Whitlam's household the discussion had been of literature, classic and contemporary, of national and international issues, with members of the family rearing to their feet to consult reference books to check precisely what Clemenceau or Pericles had said. Whitlam had a vision of Australia as the new Hellas, socially enlightened, flourishing in the arts, an example to the world of intellectual vigour and creativity. Hawke's vision was far more austere and laconic: Sparta, to Whitlam's Greece. He knew the spartan world of pinched finances, hard work and inferiority. It was the common man, not the grandiloquent spirit, at whom Hawke looked and whom, through the trade union movement and, after that, the Parliament, he yearned to rally and uplift.

When he returned from New Guinea in May 1967 he had a national wage case to present, which inevitably he would lose, for his brief was to object to the total wage and, obviously, the Bench was going to introduce it.

(When the Bench did, the ACTU, on Hawke's advice, appealed to the High Court. The appeal was rejected; Hawke then set himself to discover how the trade union movement could use the total wage to its advantage. Apart from Kirby, who thought the total wage was dangerously double-edged, Hawke was the first to recognise that the trade union movement could transform what it believed was a straitjacket on wages into an area of freedom. He was condemned for this insight at first by some union leaders, later by the employers. When Hawke entered Parliament conservative politicians accused him of responsibility for the high level of wages in Australia. They ignored or were ignorant of two facts: that it is the Arbitration Commission which determines wages, and that it was they and theirs who had insisted upon the total wage in the first place. By 1981 Hawke was again arguing that the total wage should be rejected for a return to the basic wage and margins system, or a similar system, under new names. He argued for the cause that was always uppermost in his mind: the well-being of the ordinary worker. The craft unions, highly skilled, highly paid and Left-wing, were furious with him: from them there was much talk about 'a new Billy Hughes' and 'Labor rat'. Indeed, such a system as Hawke proposed would be repulsive to, for example, an AMWSU member earning, as the best-paid did in 1981, $35,000 indexed for inflation.)

By 1967 he was becoming jaded with the wage cases. He had accomplished far more than had seemed possible nine years earlier: the employers now espoused, as their own, half of his argument (productivity increases); the judges acknowledged the importance of prices and were studying economics; and scattered throughout the trade unions there were other, younger advocates who had learned from him and would be able to carry on when he stepped out of the arena. Jim Robinson was so disconsolate at the thought of losing his sparring partner that he decided to abandon advocacy and become a judge. Moore said nostalgically, 'When Bob went, the sting was gone from wage cases'. The heroic age of advocacy was ending. Hawke had agitated and educated. But his focus had been narrow; he wanted now to widen his lens, to take in all the concerns of the union movement.

Albert Monk was in his sixty-seventh year and in poor health but he had as yet given no sign as to when he might retire, held back because the ACTU was without a provident fund for its President. He would certainly not step down before the biennial Congress, to be held in August 1967, but it was unlikely that he would stay on past 1969 for it was a trade union canon that a man *should* retire at sixty-five. If Monk were to retire between Congresses the executive would appoint an acting President; the danger for Hawke's ambitions was that the executive, elected in 1965, was weighted to the Right and would, if unchanged in 1967, appoint a Right-winger. Souter was the Right-wing favourite to succeed Monk — ironically, because in the 1950s he had won the secretaryship thanks to Left-wing support, for in those days he was a radical from whom the Left hoped for great changes in the ACTU. By the mid-1960s he was spurned by the Left. In the words of Sir Jack Egerton (another man in whom political change was later to be observed) Souter had become 'the complete bureaucrat. A big disappointment to us.' Hawke's task of unseating an Acting President Souter would be almost impossible.

As soon as he had returned from New Guinea he launched an offensive to shake the Right's grip on the executive at the 1967 Congress.

That Congress became what Right-wingers called later, in rankling voices, 'the boil-over year'.

Chapter Thirteen

The organisational work that achieved the 'boil-over' of 1967 owes most to the General Secretary of the Miscellaneous Workers' Union (MWU), Ray Gietzelt, of the Left.

Gietzelt, who had trained as a chemist, had, after serving in the AIF, joined his father's chemical company as an employee and become active in the MWU which, in the early 1950s, was under Right-wing control. In 1954 he set out to defeat the union's leadership; he took legal action to have MWU elections declared invalid. Gietzelt's instructing solicitor was Neville Wran and his junior counsel was Lionel Murphy. The action succeeded and Gietzelt became one of the most formidable numbers men in New South Wales; nationally, his union was active throughout the State structures of the ALP. It was on the say-so of the MWU that Wran* was appointed to the Legislative Council in NSW and Murphy‡ was selected for a winnable place on the NSW Senate ticket. By the mid-1960s Gietzelt was on the central executive of the NSW ALP, where moderate and Left-wing colleagues of his were Charlie Fitzgibbon of the Waterside Workers' Federation; Fred Hall, of the Meat Industry Employees' Union; and Joe Anderson of the Painters' Union. That other most important part of NSW machine politics, the Trades and Labour Council, was controlled by a confederacy of Right-wingers: Jim Kenny, the Secretary; Ralph Marsh, the Assistant Secretary; John Ducker, the Organiser and Freddie Brown, the President. Already the Left-Right fight within the NSW machine which, in 1970, led to federal intervention, was being waged and a spirited feud established; Gietzelt and Ducker were learning to dislike each other to the point of detestation.

---

* Later Premier of NSW.
‡ Later Attorney-General; later appointed to the High Court.

Gietzelt had, until the mid-1960s, committed his talents to State politics and to building up his union — which he did with notable success, raising it from 19,000 members in 1955 to more than 60,000 a decade later. In 1965 he had backed a move to have one of the NSW Right's most intelligent and articulate spokesmen, Joe Riordan,* unseated from the ACTU, but had failed on a tied vote. He had held no ambition to be a member of the ACTU executive himself — until the Left's defeats at the 1965 Congress.

In that year the 16-member executive slewed to the Right. The economy was booming; Australia was about to send conscripted, unenfranchised youths to fight in a foreign war; and there were many trade union leaders, Left and centre, who had grown tired of waiting for a federal Labor government to take up causes and who believed that the time had come for the unions to wage major industrial and social campaigns. However, they were held back by a cautious ACTU, and cautious Trades and Labour Councils: the Right had effective control of the trade union movement in New South Wales, Victoria, Tasmania and South Australia, and in Queensland the flabby giant, the Australian Workers' Union, acted as counter-force to the more energetic, Left-wing TLC.

When, soon after the 1965 Congress, Hawke asked Gietzelt to support him in a campaign for the presidency, Gietzelt telephoned his union's federal president, got his blessing, and pledged to run against Joe Riordan in 1967. He worked quietly and efficiently: Hall, Anderson and Fitzgibbon all joined the Gietzelt-Hawke team. Of these, Fitzgibbon was crucial, for the transport group of unions (which he could influence) had a large block of Congress votes and, personally, Fitzgibbon was a man of notable ability, especially in administration and in framing resolutions which would outwit or sidestep ambushes from the Right. His rather frosty manner, his command of language and his capacity for sarcasm caused many to fear him. The AWU hierarchy, with sly Queensland humour, referred to Fitzgibbon as 'The Educated Waterside Worker'. The AWU was another reason why Left and moderate union leaders were prepared to join in the early sparring which would precede the real fighting for the ACTU presidency. After 1965 the AWU began negotiating in earnest to affiliate with the ACTU, a move which for forty years it had resisted. The AWU would bring a large batch of Right-wing votes into the 1967 Congress; it had bargained, as the price of its affiliation, to have its own permanent seat on the ACTU executive. The executive membership would increase to seventeen. (Needless to say, all seventeen would be white males born in Australia or the UK and, with the exception of Gietzelt, not a 'foreign' name among them.) The AWU's decision to affiliate was an irony for Hawke, because the union would stand against his presidential ambitions, yet it was joining the ACTU in part because its

* Later Minister for Housing, Whitlam Government; later, Vice-Chairman of the NSW Electricity Commission.

boss, Tom Dougherty, had been so impressed by Hawke's ability as an advocate.

As the Congress approached the Right felt no frisson of alarm; Souter, although he continued to place restrictions upon Hawke's activities, as an employee, had not yet begun manoeuvres to ensure his own succession. As usual, the executive had allotted Hawke time on the agenda to deliver a major economic policy speech. Like every other Congress there would be Left-Right skirmishing and the Right would end up firmly in control. Or so it was thought.

But to this basic plot a fine Machiavellian twist was added. In February 1967 Whitlam replaced Calwell as Leader of the ALP and from that moment a new type of Labor Party began to reveal itself. Whitlam appealed to large numbers of Australians who had been ignored by both major parties. He appealed to women; Aborigines; immigrants; artists of all types — and to the *arrivistes* of Australian society, the sons and daughters of the working class who had recently climbed in to the middle class. In realising their dreams they had shucked off their parents' class ideologies, but still had a nostalgia for Labor, and were eager for someone to give expression, in modern, materialist terms, to their old family loyalties. The new Labor Party that Whitlam was shaping with such verve and urbanity relegated the rhetoric about Communists and anti-Communists, the very foundation of the DLP, to the level of a barnyard cackle. Riordan said,

> There were those in the DLP who foresaw that with a moderate ALP, under Whitlam, the DLP would disintegrate; it was, therefore, to the DLP's advantage if the ACTU executive could be pushed to the Left, for then the Right could scream, 'Look what's happened! The trade union movement has fallen to the Left!' On the eve of the Congress I knew that something was going on; two very senior officers of the ACTU shared my concern that the extreme-Right had done a deal with the Left for its own, undisclosed political purposes. The size of the vote for Geitzelt confirmed my worst fears . . . It also illustrated that there were forces against Souter being very effectively organised.

In a landslide victory, Gietzelt defeated Riordan for a seat on the ACTU executive by 83 to 56. When all the balloting was over there were six new faces on the ACTU executive, five of them Hawke candidates. The *News Weekly*, organ of the National Civic Council, announced: 'Left-wing march to power', a cry which had already been uttered by sections of the mass media. It was malarkey. The slewing to the Right had simply been adjusted; the victory had been for moderates, and could have been greater if Laurie Short, a Right-winger, had not suddenly contested a seat which he had no chance of winning, split the contest between a Left-winger and the moderate Cliff Dolan, and thereby given another executive place to the Left. At the end of the Congress the numbers on the executive were 9-8 in favour of Souter. Hawke had taken the opportunity offered to him to give a rousing campaign speech to the 'Workers' Parliament', as Congress is called. The federal Budget had been brought down a few days before Congress opened and followed upon a survey which showed that one person in sixteen, in Melbourne, was living in poverty. The Budget had paid scant attention to the poor, as Hawke pointed out.

> It is, in many senses, the most objectionable and grotesquely inequitable budget of the whole postwar period. It is a budget of the privileged, by the privileged, for the privileged. It is contemptuous of the plight of the needy and warrants the utter condemnation of this Congress . . . For the tremendous effort of picking up his telephone and saying one word — 'sell' — to his broker [a speculator] would make a completely tax-free capital gain of $37,000. Compare this with the worker in BHP from whom the Government demands an increasing proportion of his income by way of tax. In one day alone earlier this month . . . the face value of BHP shares rose by $44 million . . . But this Government refuses to tax any part of this unearned income. This sacred right of profit taking must be protected at all costs for the privileged minority.[1]

Having roused passions on this subject Hawke moved to the next stage of a leader's speech: an exhortation for constructive activity to counter the challenge:

> There may be a number of issues which divide us. But let us remember that we are a powerful movement. The substance of economic and wages policies being put before you provides the opportunity, I suggest, for wielding our power unitedly, progressively and without friction . . . Let us unite so as to achieve a rejection of the powers of privilege and, positively, establish that which we are all concerned to establish — a society whose resources will be utilised to the maximum and wherein the reward for labour shall be fair and equitable and the needs of the weak and those unable to fend for themselves shall be our over-riding concern.[2]

His had been a star-turn: aggressive, logical, compassionate, and responsible, a speech structured on the classic formula of 'agitate, educate, legislate' and appealing to the deepest emotions of the trade union movement — envy, sense of pathos, altruism. After two years of very quiet planning — Riordan said later he had no idea that Gietzelt was Hawke's numbers man in NSW — Hawke's challenge for the leadership was now in the open.

Immediately a 'Hawke cell' formed on the ACTU executive, meeting in private and with Hawke present, to plan manoeuvres. Hawke, as an employee, was allowed into executive meetings only if invited to speak on a specific issue, while Souter, by right, was present at all meetings. But Hawke was to have two years' training for running the executive through these private meetings (of which the Right, for some months, remained unaware). During this time he drafted many of the recommendations which his supporters then presented, as their own, to executive meetings. However, before the first gathering of the new executive was held, something happened which polarised the ACTU into bitter factions. Jim Kenny, the Senior Vice-President of the ACTU (and Secretary of the NSW Trades Hall) died. Hawke's supporters proposed that he should be replaced by the moderate Cliff Dolan. The AWU's representative on the executive, Edgar Williams, arriving at his first meeting and expecting that things would continue as they had in the past, with the odd far-Left dissent from a majority view, recalled: 'Now, there must have been an understanding of some importance, some deep appreciation of each other, because a group arrived at the first executive meeting and announced that Cliff Dolan was ready, with his bag packed, to take Jim Kenny's seat. As soon as they proposed that, the meeting deadlocked eight-all.' Ducker, who had been busy in New South Wales, said with relish, 'We chopped off Cliff Dolan's head'. They certainly had: Dolan was never allowed into an official position in the NSW Trades Hall and it was four years before he could enter the ACTU executive. From the moment the Hawke cell had shown its nerve in proposing that a non-Rightist step into a Right's seat, the forces lined up and the ACTU executive was in total deadlock. Every issue, except the most trifling, went to a vote of eight-all. Executive meetings became increasingly acrimonious and irrational, and a cause for hilarity in the Press.

In Hawke, the struggle produced a change, a new seriousness. Ralph Willis recalled,

> I had spent an enormous amount of time with Bob at work and after work, but then, from before the 1967 Congress and onwards, our relationship changed, because he had moved on to a new plane of power-seeking. He was on the telephone all the time, steeling the backbones of people to stand at Congress, and then organising them into a united group against Monk and company. One of Bob's fellows, who was not too brave, worked just around the corner and when ever Bob would see him passing he'd run out and pounce on him. He was doing less and less as research officer because so much of his time was taken up in organising. The phone never stopped ringing, people were popping in and out of our office, distracting me, and Bob had become less fraternal with me. I was intolerant of what he was doing — not because I was doing more of the work — but because I thought he should be concentrating on the area in which he was so outstanding, and which in my view was more important than being President. I guess I was a bit immature.

Willis had five months' leave due, took it and went abroad. The option of simply moving away until Hawke had achieved his mission was closed to Hawke's family. As events turned out, the months they had all passed together in Port Moresby were the last spent in a normal, carefree family manner. Hawke had his job as advocate to continue, his habitual fraternising in the pub, and now the constant need to massage the spirits of his supporters and, increasingly, the Press. He was travelling even more than usual, snatching at every opportunity to talk to meetings of rank-and-file unionists. The Right-wing State machines would not allow him in to talk to their members, the officials of unions, so he was forced into the more time-consuming exercise of addressing individual groups of men. When he was home he was exhausted and stressed, for his skill in public speaking did not alter — and was, perhaps, heightened by — the fact that he was highly-strung. He had the *trac*, the 'nerves', that most good musicians and actors have before a performance and that afterwards the body can only slowly quieten.

He said afterwards, 'In that period when I was constantly politicking for the presidency of the ACTU the family suffered dreadfully — Hazel and the kids . . .' At that stage none of them realised how much greater a price they would pay when he became President.

In late 1968 Hawke was to go to Geneva to attend an International Labour Organisation meeting. Before he left he and Gietzelt discussed the progress they had made and Hawke gave Gietzelt his phone number in Switzerland in case troube arose. After months of pressure the Hawke cell had succeeded in forcing Bill Brown, Secretary of the South Australian United Trades and Labour Council, a Souter supporter, to change sides on the issue of replacing Kenny. Hawke had just arrived in Geneva and was having a shower when Gietzelt telephoned him with the news that Brown had died, and that they now had the chance to replace him with a Left-wing candidate. David Combe's efforts on Hawke's behalf, begun three years earlier, were paying off: the South Australian trade union movement, whipped along by Gietzelt and other federal secretaries of unions from outside the State, elected Jim Shannon of the Amalgamated Engineering Union as the new South Australian Secretary. There had been a technical reason for the Right to refuse to fill the ACTU's vacant vice-presidency (created by Kenny's death) but there was no such technicality to debar Shannon from entering the ACTU executive. He did so in February 1969, the ridiculous 8-8 tie was broken, and from then on the Hawke cell had a 9-7 majority. However, this did not assure Hawke of the presidency; it merely prevented Souter's appointment as Acting President should Monk retire suddenly, and, as yet, Monk had not revealed his plans.

He did so within days of Shannon's entry into the executive. At a Labour Day dinner in Melbourne on 8 March 1969 he announced that he would step down later that year. (A little earlier the executive, in one of its few unanimous decisions, had adopted a decent superannuation scheme for ACTU officers and staff, and had shown Monk that the trade union movement really did love him — although, during rows in the 1950s, it had called him 'Scab!'

— by commissioning a portrait of him for the boardroom.)

Hawke said, 'From the moment of Albert's announcement all the stops were out'.

The next five months were ones of loud and frantic activity in the trade unions, which were already highly stimulated by a different issue: the penal powers of the Industrial Court.

A year earlier, because of a naive decision by the Conciliation and Arbitration Commission following its inquiry into the Metal Trades Award, there had been a huge row between the metal trades unions and their employers, which became known as the Absorption Battle. The employers, with a good deal of vindictiveness, had applied for penal sanctions against their striking employees and had even managed to have unions fined if their members worked normally but refused to work overtime. In the end, after thousands upon thousands of dollars in fines and millions of dollars lost in production, the Commission stepped in, altered its original decision (which had caused the fracas) and thereby awarded victory in the Absorption Battle to the unions. However, this did not solve the problem of the huge costs which victory had incurred; throughout the rest of 1968 and into 1969 the unions were rankling: if they were to obey the law — which the employers had announced they were using as a tool to bankrupt them — they faced fines of more than a quarter of a million dollars, plus towering legal fees.

And there were other, less obvious, discontents. The drums of the mining boom were pounding by 1969. People who would not have known a blue chip from a Smith's chip a few months earlier were holding forth on buses, in trams, wherever two or three gathered together, about portfolios of shares and the fortunes they had happened to make that afternoon. The middle classes were wallowing in paper money. But award wages were being kept down (to guard against further over-heating the economy) so the working class was again locked out of the party. And everywhere, everyone talked of The War — read of it in the newspapers; heard its explosions over the radio; watched on their TV sets as it consumed screaming children with napalm; saw the boys going off, jaunty, grinning, ready for killing that was, under international law, murder — since there had been no declaration of war. What was known of the ancient conflicts of Indo-China was written by historians, in French. A plague of impassioned ignorance, a virus of unknowing, swept the nation. Conservative governments and the Right of the trade union movement were, by definition, eager crusaders against 'the march of Communism'; the extreme-Left of the union movement was, by definition, prepared for counter-crusade. The rest agonised. Government and its institutions of enforcement became increasingly tyrannical. Young men were gaoled for refusing the draft; when war-protestors blocked the roadway in front of the NSW Premier's car, he ordered his chauffeur to 'run the bastards over'.

The Right has always rejected 'political' strikes; it was holding the line against Left-wingers who wanted the unions to swing behind a gathering revulsion for the Indo-Chinese conflict which, in America, was already cleaving the nation. The Right was also only tepid in its objections to the penal powers of the Industrial Court, and secretly liked them. Nevertheless, Left and Right had suffered together during the Absorption Battle and throughout the country Trades Halls were arranging meetings and discussions with industrial lawyers to try to clarify the issue of the penal sanctions. That the same people who most hated 'the war against Communism' also most hated the penal sanctions was an immense confusion for the thinking of the Right, and this discord revealed itself in gathering paranoia.

Then at 11.40 a.m. on 15 May 1969 John Kerr, Q.C., now Mr Justice Kerr of the Industrial Court, gaoled Clarence Lyell O'Shea, an official of the Tramways Union, for one year for contempt of court. It was eighteen years since a union official had been gaoled in connection with his work — and that man, like O'Shea, had been a Communist. When unionists in the courtroom shouted 'Shame!' Kerr threatened to gaol them, too. The union movement was outraged: here was the ultimate tyranny of the penal powers. In fact, O'Shea's gaoling had nothing to do with the penal powers and strikes. The unions either misunderstood — or misrepresented — the truth; the Press from ignorance or mischief misinformed the public; Mr Justice Kerr bumbled the public relations aspect of his job, and a thunder of anger burst. Within hours thousands of Victorian workers were striking and demonstrating and within days the Trades Halls of Queensland, Western Australia and South Australia had announced 24-hour strikes. The Right was severely embarrassed. In Victoria, where O'Shea was remembered as the man whose defiance of the Cain Goverent over penal powers had precipitated The Split in the Victorian branch of the ALP in 1954, the Secretary of the Trades Hall, Mick Jordan, tried to convince people that the whole affair was a Communist plot. About a million unionists struck work over a period of five days — until a friend of Albert Monk paid O'Shea's fine and Kerr, discomfitted, released him.

At any trade union demonstration the chant, like a sudden choiring of cicadas in high summer, can suddenly swell out: 'The worKERS uNITED will NEVer be deFEATED!' It is one of the great truths in democracies — but the workers are, so rarely, united. Over the O'Shea case there had been enough unity to drown the voices, like Jordan's, of the Right. The Government did not dare to try to collect fines and the employers did not dare to seek their imposition again. But despite months of talks with the ACTU the Government refused to remove the penal powers from industrial legislation: there was stalemate. Hawke had been among those who, months before the O'Shea gaoling, had spoken out against the penal sanctions, arguing, 'We are prepared to acknowledge that the trade union movement has to justify its wages before a tribunal, *provided* others do too'. He gave instances of employers (manufacturers) increasing their prices, without hindrance or need for public justification beyond the assertion that a price rise was necessary. 'Give us the same freedom as BHP — or demand that BHP justify its price increases. Give us equality before the law', he had said repeatedly. (The argument that market forces controlled manufacturers was invalid in Australia, for by the 1960s there was a system of monopolies and cartels operating: while free enterprise flourished, free competition was a figment.) Hawke's supporters included those who objected most fiercely to the penal powers; they had no particular interest in achieving a balance in the law; their over-riding concern was to do away with restrictions on the right to strike — and Devil take the hindmost. Hawke was moving towards power in an age of unreason manifest from London (giggling with Indian Messiahs) to Paris (having a 'revolution') to New York (where liberals sang the praises of a Stalinist regime in North Vietnam) to China (where children put dunces caps on their professors and set them to work in the fields) to South Vietnam (where GIs smoked dope on patrols and were blown away). And nearer home, in Hobart, there was unreason to Hawke, in the form of Brian Harradine of the Trades Hall Council. Harradine was convinced that Hawke was an incarnation of Evil. His attacks upon Hawke set the tone of the Right's campaign against him, a campaign that imposed a terrible cost on the trade union movement, for its bitterness ensured that the movement would lack unity, that the President of the ACTU — whoever he was — would be ineffectual. Years later John Ducker, who had fought shoulder-to-shoulder against Hawke, said wistfully, 'I wonder what good the Left-Right fight has done us? When someone comes to write a history of the Australian trade union movement, I wonder if they won't find it's done us no good at all.'

Even before Monk announced his retirement, Harradine in November 1968 had reported to the Tasmanian Trades and Labour Council that an article Hawke had written for the *Federal Law Review* about the total wage was contrary to ACTU policy, and undermined the trade unions. (Monk had read, and approved publication of, the article.) In December 1968 Harradine had laid a complaint about Hawke to Monk; involved the Press in the issue and instructed an industrial advocate to raise Hawke's article unfavourably in a Tasmanian Wages Board case. The upshot had been a story in the Hobart *Mercury* of 25 January 1969: 'ACTU Man Employers' "Weapon": Arguments of Advocate Used Against Unions', its headline said. The national news media picked up this juicy morsel. At the ACTU meeting of March 1969 the executive, by 9 votes to 7, censured Harradine for using the Press to attack Hawke, noting, 'The basis for the attack on Mr Hawke is so unfounded that the only conclusion to be drawn is that Mr Harradine deliberately chose to manufacture a public controversy to further his own purposes within the Labor Movement'. Then on 26 March *News Weekly* ran a headline: 'As deadly as the Mafia', over an assertion from Harradine that 'pressures exerted by certain Left-wing and Communist opponents of Souter contributed to the deaths of two trade union secretaries — Jim Kenny's and Bill Brown's'. Two days later the *Mercury* ran an almost identical story and, the following day, so did the *Age*. Harradine appeared on television and spoke of the 'psychological murder' of Kenny and Brown. Charlie Fitzgibbon, Jim Shannon, and Ray Gietzelt* demanded that Harradine publicly name them as the men whom he was calling 'psychological murderers', so they could sue him. Harradine declined. The *Catholic Worker* of April 1969 wrote of 'the lengths to which Mr Brian Harradine . . . and those associated with him in the extreme Right-wing of the Labor Movement are prepared to go in their desperate attempts to disparage Mr Hawke' and referred to Harradine's 'despicable' assertions about mafias and murderers. Hawke circularised friendly unions with copies of the *Catholic Worker* story, together with a hand-written note which said, 'This is the best possible source as far as we are concerned to combat the Right-wing hysteria about a pro-Communist alliance front. If you can do with more copies please let me know and I will get them to you immediately.' He signed it 'Bob'. His note was soon leaked to the Press and there was further scandal, with headlines asking who had written the note (anybody who had ever seen Hawke's handwriting could recognise it), who was 'Bob', what was going on, and other mysterious foolishness.

Then on 5 June Mick Jordan, the Secretary of the Victorian Trades and Labour Council, died. Jordan had declared that Hawke would become President of the ACTU 'over my dead body'. The claim was not made in writing, or on television, but the implication that the Hawke forces had now psychologically murdered Jordan — who happened to weigh twenty stone, and was a medical miracle in terms of delaying heart disease — was everywhere.

When Monk had made his Labour Day retirement speech he had referred to 'disruptive elements in the trade union movement'. The Souter camp, which had already decided upon a fear campaign, seized upon this reference and the following day, 10 March, Souter issued a 'Declaratory statement . . . on behalf of the non-alliance members of the ACTU executive supporting President Monk's warning to combat disruptive elements . . .' Souter wrote of 'the inherent dangers of the opportunist "alliance front" of the so-called "New Left Movement", which seeks to control the Trade Union Movement to the exclusion of the fundamental inherent rights of trade unionists.' He continued:

> This opportunist front is seeking to gain control through dictatorial pressure tactics by dissident groups rebelling against democratic decisions and self-imposed discipline of the Trade Union Movement and attempting to impose conditions to obtain minority control. Therefore,

---

* Gietzelt laid charges against Harradine which resulted in his expulsion from the ALP in 1975. The trauma in Tasmanian Labor politics, which came to public attention in late 1981, was directly linked to the split which occurred in the State's Labor machine when Harradine was expelled and his supporters in the Trades Hall joined him in exile.

the situation has reached such proportions that we would be failing in our duty . . . not to alert the unions . . . to take effective counter-action . . . Anything done to destroy or assist to destroy the Trade Union Movement . . . is . . . the enemy of the Trade Union Movement . . . Our great Movement cannot be allowed to be fragmented by this senseless thrust for power for individual or sectional gain . . . We therefore call on individual members and union officials to take a more direct and responsible part in union affairs to achieve the objectives of the Trade Union Movement along planned and organised lines determined by the ACTU and its State branches.[3]

It was hardly a frank statement by Souter, for in the full text of 400-odd words he did not mention anywhere that he happened to be fighting for the presidency of the ACTU and that references he made to 'considerable personal sacrifice and hardship over years' and 'planned and organised lines' were covert advertisements for his qualifications for the job. The next day Hawke issued a statement which said:

The [question] has now publicly arisen of who will succeed Albert Monk as President of the ACTU. It seems the main contenders will be Mr Souter and myself. My opponent has seen fit in these circumstances to issue a statement to the Press, and he refers to a 'pro-Communist alliance front' which seeks to take over the trade union movement. I expect I will receive the support of the Left wing of the movement. I know I will receive the support of many unions not normally classified as being on the Left. I expect Mr Souter will receive the support of unions, or branches of unions, under the control of the extreme Right-wing, including the DLP. I don't expect he will reject that support. Nor do I think the fact of that support says anything about his capacities or incapacities relative to my own for the position of President of the ACTU. I hope that the trade union movement will make its decisions on the basis of assessing our respective capacities. I have always regarded the technique of guilt by association and the tactic of the smear as abhorrent, and I refuse to resort to it myself.[4]

He did refuse. His campaign was straightforward, expressed in a Press release he wrote:

Father was a Congregational minister. Hawke is a Socialist by belief, by intellect and because he believes that equality of opportunity should be more than a political slogan. 'If the Australian worker doesn't fairly partake of what he produces then hard work doesn't make any sense to him.' He sees the future of the ACTU as 'unlimited', with closer working-relations between the traditional 'white-and-blue-collar unionists', with scope widened to include all the real needs of the worker. 'There should be no dividing line in the trade unions. We are there to help the worker, so — anything that constitutes discrimination or hardship and in we go.' Hawke holds strong feelings about: Educational opportunity, the Penal provisions of the Arbitration System, Equal Pay for women, shorter working week and the obvious penalties imposed on a low-income family by the exorbitant hire-purchase interest rates on homes and consumer durable goods. Once we broaden into the areas of environmental development, the quality of urban development and town planning, the combined forces of the white-collar movement and the ACTU will have a social significance. We will be better able to make an impact with our combined resources.[5]

He expanded on these themes in public addresses: While socialisation of the means of production, distribution and exchange was the ideal of the labour movement (and the single objective of the ACTU Constitution),

> we have to concentrate on the here and now. We must try to achieve the highest possible living standards for the Australian population . . . The trade union movement has an immense reserve of power. If we are to use that power to improve living standards, we must expand our horizon, broaden our thoughts. We have a responsibility in the here and now to improve things in the society we have.

He called for no campaign against the Vietnam War, nor for the nationalisation of industry. He talked only of improving the lot of the ordinary worker and his/her dependants. However, his opponents could not be persuaded that he meant what he said. Above all, they feared a loss of their own power — which, in theory and in fact, they used, if in a blinkered way, for the same causes he espoused. Ducker, who by now was Assistant Secretary of the NSW Trades and Labour Council, recalled:

> You see, the Communist Party thought it could use Bob. Felt at the very least he was going to smash the Right-wing control of the ACTU. And they were using Bob as an instrument. So it was a fight against Communist Party influence, and against its being increased. And, at that time, it was a legitimate fear. There was a sincerely held belief that a Hawke victory would mean an increase in Communist-Left-wing influence. You couldn't really say that Bob was a Communist, or anywhere near it — although one night I'd got drunk with Hawkey, around the time of the Chinese invasion of Tibet. And he and I had a slanging match about that. He said it was a CIA plot to suggest that the Chinese had done what they did. I said he was just a bloody front-man for the Communist Party. So there was that bit of history between Bob and me.

But, looking back, Bob stood on a policy of reform and modernisation. And there's nothing particularly Left-wing about that.

As the 1969 Congress approached the cries of 'Communist take-over' and 'Red dupe' — that is, Hawke — became more frequent and shrill. The abuse edged perilously close to breaking the male code of honour and self-defence which tabooed public references to a man's sexual life, when an epithet for Hawke, 'Communist lover-boy' — with its neat *double entendre* — was reported in the Press.

While Hawke and, after his initial *faux pas*, Souter, behaved with dignity and sense, both camps engaged in what Ducker later described, with a sigh, as 'gutter-fighting' — for the question of who would be the better man to lead the ACTU had been lost in the shouting and it was now a Left-Right brawl, such as had not occurred for twenty years. It may seem senseless to outsiders, but it should be remembered that trade union officials are politicians and therefore a warrior caste: they love fighting.

There were many small unions which had never bothered to affiliate with the ACTU; they were encouraged — through cajoling and threats — to join it and thereby add their votes to one side or the other at the 1969 Congress election. Unions habitually understated their membership so they could reduce their affiliation fees to the ACTU. But the more members, the more Congress votes: suddenly unions discovered they had hundreds more members than they had thought. Workers who had been retired for years, it was realised, were technically still members if they had taken out life-tickets. (In the Hawke camp Fitzgibbon was the first to discover the benefits of this technicality, his attention drawn to it by a circular that Souter had issued.) Intra-union rows which had seethed for years abruptly stilled on the promise of a vote — and, when promises were broken at the Congress, new feuds began. In 1981 there was still resentment in the AWU against two groups of its delegates who had 'ratted' and given Hawke 12 votes. Ducker said: 'There was standing over people. Threatening them with dismissal. Threatening them with being defeated [as union officials]. A bit of persuasion that life could be better for them.' (For example: pre-selection for a seat in federal or State Parliament, or membership of 'Australia's best club', the Legislative Council, part-time Parliament with a gold pass for travel. A Hawke man who switched allegiance later entered the NSW Legislative Council. In Victoria, there were jobs in the Melbourne Harbour Trust to be awarded to the helpful.) Ducker continued, 'It was said that it might be possible to organise a trip abroad . . . Ray Gietzelt was determined to win and whatever it took, whatever way, that was legit. To some degree it was a fight between me and Ray Gietzelt, and that was an inducement for me: I had the blood in my nostrils.' Gietzelt's opinions of Ducker's tactics are, under Australia's libel laws, unprintable, but along the same lines. Ducker said, 'Ray would say,

"John's a twister, a turner, devious — don't trust him!" It was no afternoon-tea party.'

Ducker is a man of dextrous intelligence and notable charm which, combined, were to make him the colossus of the NSW ALP machine for a decade. He could perform small miracles of persuasion: once, for example, he convinced the NSW ALP Left to waive its claim to a Senate seat, for reasons which seemed lucid when he explained them but which later nobody could quite understand. He created the Labor Government of Neville Wran in New South Wales, when he realised that Wran, although close to and promoted by Gietzelt, was a winner. Gietzelt tried to chop off Ducker's head — as Ducker had 'chopped off' Dolan's and was later, in his own words, to 'do everything, and I mean *everything*' to smash the political career of Gietzelt's brother, Arthur. Gietzelt moved for federal intervention into the NSW ALP and Ducker, with breathtaking nerve, immediately seconded his motion. And survived. Only Ducker's Yorkshire accent debarred him from playing a far more public role in Australian politics. At the ACTU Congress of 1969 he was to use 'every bit of influence and persuasion I could' in pressuring waverers to vote for Souter. The Hawke camp received 51 fewer votes than it had been promised, in part thanks to John Patrick Ducker.

His and other Right-winger's fears about Communist influence on Hawke were not without foundation, for many of Hawke's most active organisers were Communists. One was George Seelaf, then Secretary of the Victorian branch of the meat workers' union and among Hawke's warmest friends. Seelaf is a man of boisterous high spirits — 'Look! A butcher's canary!' he shouted when a blowfly rumbled past — and shines with the boyish optimism that is so often a characteristic of old guard Communists. He had been instrumental in arranging the publication of *Power Without Glory* and was a friend of its author, Frank Hardy, whom he introduced to Hawke. Seelaf and Hawke were working closely during 1969 on the Equal Pay Case. At one of their celebrations the proprietor of Jimmy Watson's, a popular Melbourne wine bar, locked them and a meat industry employer in a back room because of their loud singing of revolutionary songs. Years later, when Hawke had come to detest Communism, he would insist, '*George* isn't a Communist. I never thought of him as a Communist. He just calls himself one.' Seelaf said of his part in the presidency campaign:

> We got the list of delegates for the 1967 Congress and analysed their politics. The committed Right and committed Left we put aside. What remained was a list of eighty or ninety people. We then got to work to lobby them: found out all we could about their political attitudes, who their best friends were, if they were Catholics or Masons. We then chose the most appropriate people to do the lobbying. I don't like to raise the sectarian issue, but if we were dealing with a Catholic, we got a

Left-wing Catholic to do the lobbying; if a Mason, we got a Hawke-committed Mason. I burnt the files, afterwards.

Another Communist Hawke-man was Alec Macdonald, Secretary of the Queensland Trades and Labour Council. Macdonald was a man of extreme gentleness, beloved in the union movement. The AWU aside, he delivered the Queensland vote to Hawke, but died a week before the Congress and Hawke, in the midst of victory, was also in mourning for him. He had loved Macdonald with the extravagant affection he feels for all close friends and years later said that the high edge of excitement in triumph had hurt, because Macdonald was not there to share it.

While Hawke's agents were eliciting votes, his job was to do that at which he excelled: establish rapport with great numbers of people, to project himself as the corporeal form of their hopes. For while the Left would support him, willy-nilly, and sincerely if mistakenly believed that he was their captive — Pat Clancy of the Building Workers' Industrial Union described Hawke as 'a very strong, positive Left force . . . he made many fiery and inspiring speeches . . . and at that stage he was very amenable or susceptible to collective consideration of matters' — it was the large centre ground that would decide the issue. To the centre and, most importantly, to industrial journalists, Hawke had an unacknowledgeable appeal to snobbery: a Rhodes Scholar, a middle-class white-collar man proposing a New Deal for the working class. By 1969 the rush of manual workers' children to the universities was in train. It was still forbidden in trade union circles to admit that middle-class status and values were attractive, but all the behaviour of the working class revealed its yearning. 'Bob had been a Rhodes Scholar — and there's snobbery in everyone', Egerton remarked later, when he had been expelled from the ALP for his own vulnerability to the glitter of status. 'The Rhodes had a big effect on trade unionists.' This was especially relevant, because a decline in blue-collar unionism had already occurred (and was growing) since, with technological change, the workforce had moved away from manufacturing into service industries. Blue was fading into white, and the white-collar sector was little unionised. Union officials knew this, and recognised that Hawke had the social appeal to create regrowth in unionism, among white-collar workers. He talked constantly of the need for the ACTU's one and a half million affiliated members to be joined by the half million public service unionists — a proposition to which both Monk and Souter, and the Left, were opposed. To them, the white-collar public service employees spelt corruption of working-class values. Hawke's committed supporters, when they actually listened to what he was saying, discounted his ideas as the rhetoric of campaigning. And the Right, which had many white-collar members, did not listen at all. From the outset, Hawke was to be at cross-purposes with many of his most ardent admirers, while appealing, increasingly, to the centre ground. And again, it was a problem of style:

Hawke was fiery: when speaking from a platform he used the gestures, the body language, which in Australia, at that time, announced 'Left', and it was necessary to stand at a distance and pay attention to his long, Latinate sentences to understand their meaning. Many did. On 27 June the *Age*, in an editorial headlined, 'The New Unionists', wrote:

> Mr Hawke is articulating, in concrete terms, the problems which will face the trade union movement in the 1970s. He is also proposing solutions to them. Many of Australia's more conservative trade union leaders may be suspicious of his proposals because they call into question all the traditional assumptions about the role of trade unions in society. But the time has come when assumptions must be questioned, when new directions must be sought, if unions are to have an effective future. For this reason alone, Mr Hawke is doing the trade union movement an invaluable service.

Hawke himself knew his appeal was more practical: 'I'd been the wages advocate for ten years and had helped change a situation whereby the basic wage had declined in real value by 5%, to one where, by 1967, it had increased in real value by more than 6%. For that, I had the overwhelming support of the rank and file.'

By the eve of the Congress, which opened on 8 September in the grey, echoing Paddington Town Hall, Sydney — a larger than usual assembly hall was necessary, for, such was the increase in membership and affiliation that there were 101 more delegates than in 1967 — the Hawke camp was confident of victory. Again, the support of Gietzelt was critical, because the services group of unions had the largest Congress vote and Gietzelt had them counted to the last one. Meanwhile, the Souter camp knew they would be hard pressed but believed, from promises made to *them*, that they still had a 50-50 chance. Until a week beforehand George Polites — and all the employers — had been convinced that Hawke could not succeed. In the Conciliation and Arbitration Commission, which was watching events with professional interest, only Sir Richard Kirby had long believed that Hawke would win, 'and my own reason for belief was that Bob was so insistent to me that he would'. Hawke told the Press he would win by 100 votes and, obligingly they reported this. He stood in the doorway of the Paddington Town Hall, hugging his supporters, smiling at and handshaking the non-committed. To his old mentor, Jock Innes, he murmured, 'You've stood by me for twelve years. Stand by me now.' The voting was still three days away. Whips had been appointed to organise the factions on every issue which might, before the election, divide the Congress. The uncommitted would be watching every division on the floor, to calculate in which direction power was flowing. The big unions had marshals for the elections, for they did not allow their delegates to vote according to individual preference, but forced them to vote in accordance with instructions, and the marshals were present to ensure that instructions were followed. Any delegate defying policy could expect to lose his union job. 'We had no slippage', Geitzelt remarked with satisfaction, afterwards; Fitzgibbon said, 'When you asked them later, everybody had voted for the winner'.

On the afternoon before the next morning's election Monk announced that Hawke would speak, as research officer, reporting on economic policy, and would be followed by Souter, who would move the adoption of the executive's official economic policy statement. Both candidates were therefore to have a chance for a last appeal to the electorate. Hawke's address was rousing and fluent (he attacked the latest federal Budget), and lasted exactly thirty minutes. He returned to his seat, Souter took over the microphone — and what happened next was extraordinary. Souter gave up.

As if bored, he stood at the microphone and read out the policy statement, a copy of which every delegate already had, then, although he still had minutes left to rally support, he made a perfunctory gesture — and sat down. The Hawke camp was incredulous. The hall had been silent when Souter began, but after about ten minutes a hum of conversation arose which became so loud that twice Monk had to call the delegates to order. One thing that everyone was talking about was that Hawke had written the economic policy statement, which Souter, instead of speaking to, was reciting. The four-year campaign was over.

Next day Hawke was elected President of the ACTU by 399 to 350.

Over in Washington George Meany, the boss of American labour, heard the wire-service news, 'and nearly had a heart-attack. "The Aussies have gone Communist!" he said.'[6].

It is doubtful that any of the delegates gathered in the Paddington Town Hall and shouting with joy fully understood what they had done: they had created the Australian hero of the 1970s.

When Hawke bounded to his feet to accept victory he moved towards the conclusion of his speech with the declaration:

> Let me make it abundantly clear that I will not be the President merely of those who worked for and voted for me. I will be the President of the whole of the ACTU — equally of those who exercised their democratic right to work for another result. My door will be as open to you, Ralph Marsh, as to you, Jim Shannon. I will seek genuinely to work in harmony with all sections of this movement.[7]

The Right thought he was lying; the Left that he was giving a victor's magnanimous flourish. Their disillusion was to be intense. They spoke later with the sadness of suppressed anger, or made excuses: Hawke was gregarious, he socialised with capitalists and was led astray; he was prepared to be kind, when he should not have been; he was naive and did not understand how vicious the Right was; John Ducker was the complete political animal, and had seduced him; Hawke became bewitched by politics and abandoned the workers — this from the spokesman of the workers of the world, Joe Morris, a Canadian, who had groomed Hawke to succeed him. The Communists said he was a middle-class opportunist all along, who took some time to reveal his true colours. And the National Civic Council, which had thought Hawke a 'Red dupe', said the same thing. Or it was said that he was a Jew. Or that his wife was a Jewess . . . The explanations were as various as the people who gave them. Unionists have always been agreed on one thing; that Hawke is unusually truthful, but they chose to believe that he was not *really* telling the truth about himself.

The fact was, as Hawke had repeatedly said, he wanted to exercise power and to do so in a way that he defined as being in the public good. It was all he had ever wanted and if, to achieve that, he had to do deals with the Right or with millionaires or with conservative politicians, or Communists, he would. He had been a fundamentalist Christian ideologue at nineteen; he had been fed on ideology with his mother's milk; he had lived and breathed the beliefs of the Second Coming, when the righteous dead would rise from their graves to walk in glory with the Lord. And twenty years later, when he became President of the ACTU, he by then believed that a socialist Australia was as distant as the millennium; that what mattered was the justice of the here and now. He had no inner need for the direction to life that ideology gives. He was free. He thought he had been grandiosely enabled to realise his dreams.

As they gathered their papers and prepared to leave the Paddington Town Hall Cliff Dolan said to Hawke, 'Don't rush things, mate. The trade union movement is really very conservative, you know.'

It was years before Hawke would acknowledge the defeats foreshadowed by that acute observation.

Chapter Fourteen

Hawke had won the presidency narrowly. Twenty-five votes would have given the prize to Souter — and in that case one can only speculate on what disruption the disappointed Left would have caused, for 1968-69 marked the beginning of years of industrial unrest. It would be Hawke's job to attempt to harness restlessness, while himself remaining a central figure in the upheaval of change that was altering the old relationships within society. Every generation has its radical alternatives: the difference now was in their extent. Men wore pony-tails; women didn't wear corsets; merchant bankers smoked marijuana; cocaine was the millionaire's snuff; millionaires were cloning, as the property and stock-markets soared; their children ate and dressed in earnest counterfeit of Javanese peasants, or terrorised their professors; or copulated on the university lawn, or dug it up, or sat on it — practically anything, so long as it was forbidden. Psyches were psychedelic. Policemen were pigs; men were soon to become male chauvinist pigs. And vegetarians would inherit the earth — for, underneath the libertine surface, a new puritanism was already assembling its symbolic behaviour. The conservative federal coalition Government was falling to pieces. The boom babies who had been born in the almost forgotten years of war and post-war Labor Governments had grown up, were voters, and in terms of numbers of votes had, in December 1969, voted in Gough Whitlam. The necessary number of seats had eluded him, however. But Whitlam was approaching the height of his powers — and the next election would be his. Hawke had come to lead a trade union movement which, like the wider society it reflected, was excited and unstable. People were looking for leaders to express and channel the huge energies which demographic and technological change had released. His first fan letters began to arrive in late 1969. A man who described himself as non-political wrote: 'I am confident of your personal future and consider your experience will be vital for one day I foresee you worthily filling the office of Prime Minister of Australia. Keep this in mind. Australia needs you, you would be the man for the job.' And another, 'We now have a visionary at the helm!'

Meanwhile, almost half Hawke's crew was sullen, ready for mutiny. The bitterness of the election campaign had bequeathed him an executive that was divided 9-8 in his favour and a Secretary with whom he was barely able to speak. He had gone through a period of hatred for Souter and before the election had told his supporters that he could never again work with him. But when the results were announced Souter had immediately lent forward to shake Hawke's hand and since then there had been an icy civility between them (which Hawke, characteristically flinching from the unpleasant, called later, 'Some tension. But we soon got over it.') It was more than a year before their mutual hostility abated enough for them to speak naturally to each other. On the executive, too, uneasiness was acute for more than a year. Ducker recalled, 'Everybody was extremely suspicious, and bitter'. At Hawke's first experience of chairing the executive, in 1970 (Souter's forces had outwitted his at the Congress on the timing of succession, and delayed Hawke's presidency by four months) Hawke announced that he wanted the trade union movement to join in a huge anti-Vietnam rally which was being organised by the Left of the ALP. He had the numbers. His resolution passed on the mechanical majority. Then Ducker, representing the NSW TLC, announced that, this being an important decision, it would need ratification from a majority of the State branches. Hawke said, 'John left me in no doubt about the outcome of a State branch vote. I'd been rolled.'

The Right feared that Hawke was biding his time, until he could ambush them. It had been widely advertised that Gietzelt was urging Hawke to move in on the Tasmanian Trades Hall and demolish Harradine. There was fear that NSW would be next. Ducker said,

> When Hawke was elected it had been open to him to do what some of his supporters wanted, and that was to lead a thrust head-on against the Right-wing of the trade union movement. He could have elected to try to knock over the leadership of the NSW Labour Council; he could have elected to *actively* organise in unions against Right-wing incumbents. He could have made life very bloody hard — he could have pushed us in NSW a long way. If he'd demanded his right to speak to a Labour Council and said, 'These men here are enemies of the working class' — well, that's the sort of thing that has some impact. And it's the sort of thing we could certainly do without. Because Hawke had such ascendancy, such charisma.

It is an article of faith in the labour movement that the capitalist Press is its enduring enemy, committed to leading hapless readers astray, and that the wise course is to avoid it (except when one can employ it to frighten adversaries in a faction fight). During the penal powers debate Hawke had often referred, in speeches to unionists, to the way the federal Government and the Press were attempting to instil the idea that strikes were illegal; he had complained of public misrepresentation of the activities of the Arbitration Commission, and had always gone on to point out that the trade union movement had taken no action to counter misinformation: 'We as a trade union movement have failed signally to publicise . . . we took it in our stride . . . I don't think a word was said . . . We should be shouting from the roof tops . . .' Monk and Souter had repeatedly warned him against adopting the role of ACTU spokesman: when television channels began, in 1965, to ask him to comment on the federal Budget there was, annually, a row in the office about it. Even before Hawke had formally taken over the presidency in January 1970, he set out to make use of the news media 'to put the message of the trade union movement across'. Hawke said,

> I had the feeling that the big gap in Albert [Monk] in the 1960s was in the area of communications. He didn't get to the people, or even to his own constituents, in a way which explained issues and defended positions. He tended to be very much afraid of the media and I think time after time opportunities were lost to establish positions in the minds of the people and of the Government. It didn't matter what the issue was, Albert wanted to avoid the media. For instance, Budget time: there were clear positions about what the ACTU thought; we [research staff] would prepare stuff for Albert and he'd say a couple of things, but it was under pressure that he would communicate our position. And I used to feel frustrated. We had a lot to say, and could say it effectively, and would prepare material but Albert would perfunctorily — even diffidently — talk to the media and make a point. And then he wouldn't follow that up. He'd done his duty. But there was no *depth* of communication or *persistence* of communication. And there was nobody else who could speak for the ACTU. The ACTU was Albert Monk.

Hawke set out to improve the image of the unions in Australian society.

For a complex of reasons this is extraordinarily difficult. Australia is one of the most unionised countries in the world; because collective bargaining is embryonic (growing in the 1980s) there are numerous short strikes; because of the number of unions demarcation strikes are frequent — and are impossible to justify in terms of social principle; because of the very high level of government and semi-government ownership of utilities — transport, telephone services, postal services, electricity, gas, garbage collection, water supply and so forth — strikes in these areas incur a challenge to legitimate, elected authority and to employers who have a vast supply of money to tough-out strikes and to wage a propaganda war against strikers. In many Western countries strikes in government-owned utilities are illegal. In Australia, they are not. (Fraser Government legislation of the late 1970s restricts them.) Until Hawke became President of the ACTU the unions had never emerged from a strike against the employer-government without being covered in calumny — for no matter how just their cause, their officials had been unable to explain it to an inconvenienced public above the shouting of the politicians. And if workers were forced back without the change they had demanded by drastic action, that seemed to prove that their claim and actions had been unjustified and irresponsible. Anything that fails seems stupid, and it is only in the long-term that many strikes — for example, against shipping pig-iron to Japan just prior to World War II; against supplying material and food to the Dutch counter-revolutionaries in Indonesia — are seen in perspective, and that a new generation can acknowledge that the unions had a stronger grasp of reality than the government. When Hawke became President the 'political' strike — that is, one not concerned with wages and conditions, or demarcation — was popularly presented as a type of trade union terrorism. Eleven years later, when he stepped down, the term had vanished. The unions were no better loved than they had been, but they had learned, from Hawke's example, publicly to present and logically to debate their actions. By the end of the 1970s it was commonplace — almost automatic — for trade union officials to appear on radio and television news to explain why strike action had been taken, something which a decade earlier had been unimaginable. Society at large benefitted. In a decade of social upheaval, had the trade union movement continued its tradition of ignoring public relations the way would have been open for governments — of whatever persuasion — to transform their propaganda superiority into a weapon of repression against the unions. Repression, once begun, has a life of its own.

Hawke was armed with the skills necessary to begin the Herculean task of clearing away the debris of a century of trade union neglect of public relations: he was, as he had dreamed of becoming while still at university, 'articulate, logical and tough' — and an exotic. His Rhodes Scholarship and his swashbuckling personality dazzled the Press. From the moment of his election the news media was mesmerised by Hawke. Within a couple of years his face and brazen voice were among the best-known in the nation; within five they were recorded in the brain cells of the whole society. An image of him had physically entered the Australian people and he could not walk down a street or enter a shop without being besieged by the curious, anxious to verify that part of themselves which he represented. He was constantly

handled — Ducker noted the 'mystical touching of Hawke's clothes' — and
after a day in public would show the signs of extreme nervous stress: his eyes
bright and hard, his movements quick and tense, sweating, hyperactive,
flitting from topic to topic in conversation, argumentative, craving the anaes-
thesia of more alcohol. The distinction between work and leisure blurred,
then vanished. He had become an object of display and was at work at the
races, at work while having a haircut. His close friends all knew the physical
change that overcame Hawke, in a moment, when he was introduced to a
stranger or was in a public place: a sudden tenseness and unnatural vivacity
would envelop him. Friends hated to be present and feel the change but would
accompany Hawke to protect him from the clamorousness of crowds. At
home, the telephone never stopped ringing, for he had set out to make himself
available to the news media and would talk to journalists at any hour of the
day or night, drunk or sober, clothed or undressed. And in this lay a key to his
phenomenal media attention. From early on many newspaper editors were
aware that Hawke was able to 'snow' their reporters and had inchoate
suspicion that he was, in some way they could not quite determine, manipulating them. There was much that was known about Hawke — his drunken
bad temper; his womanising, including outrageously public propositioning
of women when he was drunk — that was never reported and that journalists,
the world's most avid gossips, were unwilling to discuss. The editors were
half-right: Hawke unconsciously inhibited the journalist's inclination to
detract by trusting her or him. He is an unusually trusting man — frequently
naively so, and was to suffer rages of disillusion when people betrayed him or
turned out to be, as others had already recognised intuitively, rogues. The
honesty and honourableness of his upbringing had ill-equipped him for
dealing with the dishonest and devious; it had the benefit that his own
trustfulness inspired trustworthy behaviour: there were only two major
occasions when journalists broke faith and wrote stories about things Hawke
had said when they knew he was talking to them off-the-record. One of the
most effective ways of arousing journalists' hostility is to flatter them by
treating them as powerful: insisting upon questions in advance and on
knowing the content of a story before publication; by trying to control them.
Many public figures make this error: the immediate — and justified —
assumption is that they have something to hide. Hawke worked with
the news media in the opposite way: he *refused* to be told questions
in advance; he did not require reporters to check back with him; he was
boldly open in conversation with them. And he always had something to say.
For most of Hawke's first two years as President, Bill McMahon was the
Prime Minister and was disastrously mishandling the Press, by flattery:
he repeatedly telephoned journalists to give them tips for stories, and
among themselves they treated his eagerness to please with contempt.
Newspaper cartoonists expressed their colleagues' attitudes to the Prime

Minister in drawings of merciless disparagement.*

Ducker said of the result of news media attention to Hawke:

> You weren't dealing with flesh-and-blood. You were fighting a supreme being, and you always expected that you'd come off second best. We'd arrive sometimes at an executive meeting, to discuss something, and find that the newspapers were reporting that we'd decided in a particular way — and we bloody-well hadn't. Bob had just had a few beers with the Press and told them what he thought should happen, and they'd taken that as gospel. Standing up to the ascendancy he'd established, through the Press, wasn't easy and you'd be inclined to roll with the punches.

Since the days of the Groupers the Left and Right wings of the executive have held separate caucuses before and during executive meetings, stayed in separate hotels and drunk in separate pubs. Monk had caucused with the Right and had used various go-betweens to the Left, including George Seelaf for the Communists. Hawke naturally caucused with the Left but he set out to try to calm the fears of the Right on a personal level and to lessen the tension which existed between the factions. The Left was uneasy. Geitzelt said, 'On the question of overseas trips, for example, Bob would say, "We'll give the Right a berth, eh?" If there were five people to go, there would be three places for our blokes and two for theirs. We accommodated the Right. Perhaps too much. The Right never shares — it keeps all the spoils for itself.' And Ducker recalled,

> Bob tried to create a bit of goodwill. One of his constant irritations was that the Right would not drink with the Left. At lunch-time and in the evening Bob repeatedly asked the Right to come and have a drink. I would occasionally break off from my mates and go over and drink

---

* Of the thousands of cartoons of Hawke there has been only one, in a fly-by-night magazine called *Cocaine*, devoted to blasphemy, that has shown him as other than an honest and/or tough man. Leading up to the 1972 elections many large newspapers projected Hawke's toughness as that of a gangster, but this phase did not last long. The *Cocaine* drawing was of violent homosexual acts between an Hasidic Jew (drawn exactly as Jews were portrayed under Nazism), a CIA man, and Hawke. In very small print it carried a disclaimer: 'With apologies to homosexuals and non-Zionist Jews', and was published in 1980, before Hawke entered Parliament, accompanying an article which expressed views in sympathy with some of the Socialist Left in Victoria. Hawke wished to sue for libel by the cartoon, but the magazine disappeared underground.

with Gietzelt and Fitzgibbon. And I think Bob had more than some problems about that, and would have to kid to his blokes: 'Look, suffer him, won't you?' He kept trying to work at it and would come to the Dover and drink with Edgar Williams and Ralph Marsh and others. And it was funny, because when Bob sets out to be charming and interesting and pleasant there are few who can do it better. So they used to enjoy it, although a bit sheepishly. But as soon as he'd gone they'd want to talk about what a bastard he was.

Hawke never stopped hoping that he would be able to heal the ill feeling between Ducker and Gietzelt. He said, 'Ray is a man of tremendous ability and so, obviously, is John. It just seemed so *sensible* to try to get them together.'

The Right's suspicion of Hawke continued through 1970 and 1971. At the Congress of that year there was another dramatic Left-Right clash, and then a sudden ganging up against Hawke. The Right was furious about the leadership he had given to 'political' strikes, most notably, the Springbok tour, and both Left and Right were frightened by the power he had established, through the news media, and outside their control. He had one spot of complete vulnerability: money. Without money his schemes would be difficult to realise, his power limited. Already he had established one enterprise, Bourkes-ACTU, and had been treated to an orgy of publicity and acclaim. At the 1971 Congress the executive was requesting an increase in affiliation fees, necessary, it argued, to carry through the reforms promised in Hawke's election campaign. Delegates voted for no increase. Hawke refused to admit defeat for years, but from that moment his vision of the role the trade union movement could play in Australian society was, effectively, futile. The independence from employers that he sought for it, the loosening of the feudal bonds, would be long delayed, for without money the ACTU could not establish the insurance-superannuation and hire-purchase schemes which would give unionists the freedom to move from one employer to another or to abandon work temporarily for re-training or even to be sick for long. They would have to remain wage slaves, prisoners of the cost of their possessions. The big unions were immensely rich; a few had insurance schemes, a few had credit facilities, but there was nothing coherent; and unions chose to invest their funds conservatively, mostly in real estate. Those who had supported Hawke had paid, as events were to show, only lip-service to his ideas for reform for the whole trade union movement. They preferred the old, familiar ways — the hardship, but also the comforting warmth and solidarity of being victims of capitalism. From the 1971 Congress, Hawke's presidency could only be disappointment after disappointment for him. He had envisaged himself calling forth and directing the blossoming of a newly-awakened force in society. Instead, his job would be what it had been for Monk: bargaining, settling strikes, doing deals with the Government, bullying and cajoling the irrational, being abused as a 'class traitor' — in short, choosing between the unpalatable and the disastrous, and putting a brave face on things. He would clench his fists sometimes and say, 'If *only* we had the sinews of war . . . Money!'

By the time Hawke became President of the ACTU he had been studying and analysing the Australian economy and its institutions for more than a decade and had evolved an elaborate critique of its soggy patches, areas of corruption and injustice. Annually he and Willis had written submissions to Cabinet on the federal Budget. The taxation system was one area Hawke deplored. Trading monopolies and cartels, which maintained artificially high retail prices, was another. Hawke felt passionately affronted on behalf of the ordinary worker that while she or he sold labour according to market forces (with only some protection and much restriction from the arbitration system) manufacturers and shopkeepers, banded together, defeated the laws of free trading and sold their goods at any price which suited them. In the UK and USA this practice had been illegal for years, but in Australia, despite the efforts of the Attorney-General, Garfield Barwick, Menzies had refused to outlaw it. ACTU Budget submissions to the succeeding Holt and Gorton Governments on the issue had been ignored. Then in 1970 Hawke met a retailer who was interested in breaking cartel power in retail trade.

This man was Lionel Revelman, of Lithuanian descent, the youngest of ten children of a widowed mother, who with scholarships and by driving taxis at night had worked his way through Law School and been articled to the trade union legal firm, Maurice Blackburn. At twenty-one Revelman became a barrister and at thirty-three had taken silk. He had voted Liberal throughout the Menzies reign and had switched to Labor when Menzies and Calwell departed from public life. By the time Hawke met him, in the house of Sam Goldbloom — a leading figure in the ALP Left — Revelman was a director, with his brother George, of an electrical store called Bourkes. He was prosperous: he owned a 17-room house in Balwyn, Melbourne, which had a tennis court in its two acres of garden. Tall and fit, with rugged good-looks, Revelman was a taciturn, determined individualist. He was prudish and had never been heard to swear; aloof, courtly, and so loathed social gatherings that he once went abroad to avoid an engagement party. He was a perfectionist, by nature fascinated by detail (Hawke, by nature, is bored with detail) and was so averse to personal emotionalism that he would refuse to watch anything 'emotional' on television. He was eight years older than Hawke. When they met it was as if two half-souls had clicked together. Of all the men Hawke loved in his adulthood, he loved Revelman most: 'He was a father to me', Hawke said. Revelman told his family, 'Bob is the only man I've met to whom I can talk'.

A decade earlier, during the television boom, when Bourkes had been 'selling TV sets day and night', the Revelman brothers had sued every major supplier of television receivers for inhibition of their trade. The big traders, among them Myers, had so pressured manufacturers that they had refused to supply Bourkes, which was undercutting agreed retail prices. The Revelmans lost the case, but had won a two-year breathing space; in this interregnum other discount stores had sprung up in Melbourne. The Revelmans continued to skirmish with big stores and suppliers, and bore particular resentment for Myers. There was an old grudge held by the Revelmans against the Myers; the Revelmans' grandfather had started the first cash-order business in Melbourne with Sidney Myer and, according to Revelman family lore, had advised Myer to open a bargain basement. 'People will steal the stock!' Myer, it is said, objected. He split with Revelman and went on to found the greatest retailing empire in Australia.

In 1970, before he met Hawke, Revelman had involved Bourkes with a group of Left-wing unions which was in revolt against the Victorian Trades Hall Council and which had espoused many fashionable causes. Inflation was already stirring by 1970. The rebel unions had allied themselves with housewives' associations to boycott companies considered to be overcharging. Boycott lists were published in union journals; activists stationed themselves in shopping centres to distribute leaflets advising which brands to avoid — for reasons of price or because they were environmentally damaging. There were big rallies in the Melbourne Town Hall to complain about price racketeering. Revelman thought that high profit and small turn-over was both inefficient and socially objectionable. He saw a useful ally in the rebel unions, but a joint advertising campaign had barely begun when the Trades Hall stepped in and aborted it.

Hawke, at the time he met Revelman, had already widely advertised his dreams of expanding the scope of the ACTU and the horizons of the whole trade union movement. A flood of requests for interviews and to make speeches had swept into the ACTU from soon after the 1969 Congress, and the tide of publicity instead of abating continued to swell. Small companies had written to him suggesting joint-venture schemes, many of them harebrained, some sensible, all of them needing investigation which the ACTU could not afford. It had no money. There were six people on the staff: Hawke; Souter; Willis; an assistant research officer, Jan White; a press officer-personal assistant to Hawke, Geoff Gleghorn; and an education officer, Peter Mathews; plus stenographers. All but the stenographers were underpaid for the hours they worked: Hawke's salary, at $11,000, was a fraction of his counterpart's, George Polites. There was too little space in the Lygon Street building and too few telephones to meet the demand during the week-long executive meetings there, when the executive members would often be called outside from the boardroom to negotiate in strikes that were on in Queensland or Western Australia and would have to do so standing up at somebody's desk. Souter managed the accounting by a method of his own, 'shuffling money backwards and forwards from the International Fund', in the words of Cliff Dolan. 'I never once understood an ACTU balance sheet'.

Neither did others, for Souter was given to secrecy and would become testy when the executive asked for more details. Hawke, with a combination of delicacy and uninterest, never sought to involve himself in the Secretary's domain.

While Hawke had stirred up enthusiasm for the idea of ACTU enterprises he had nothing with which to start them: no capital, no staff and no supply of cash to hire consultants. The most the ACTU could afford was legal opinions. As the central body of the Australian trade union movement the ACTU was already far behind the organised employers in research facilities, even for the basic issue of economics. Research on industrial health was an impossible luxury for it. It had formal ties with trade union groups throughout the world, but when their representatives made fraternal visits or requested information there was only one person available for the job: Hawke. When the head of the West German trade union movement visited Australia in the early 1970s and inquired, bewildered, 'But where is your International Department?' Hawke, who had visited their International Department, with its large staff, spacious offices, library and translation facilities, replied bitterly, 'You're looking at it'. The Australian trade union movement, to the disadvantage of its members, was simply too faction- and envy-ridden to pay its peak council to operate effectively. Of the advanced Western countries — and, one might add, of the Communist countries, where trade unionism is a black joke — the ACTU was the most under-financed peak council. The New Zealand Federation of Labour put it to shame.

Enter Lionel Revelman.

Whether he or Hawke first thought of the scheme, together they developed a plan which swept them both to imaginative heights: the ACTU and Bourkes would establish a joint venture which would have two primary functions — to break retail price maintenance in Melbourne, and to give the ACTU 'the sinews of war'. The former goal anticipated by more than two years *the* problem of political economics of the Whitlam Government: how to reduce prices without reducing the income of workers? Bourkes-ACTU broke retail price maintenance, but the ACTU was not to get the sinews of war.

According to Revelman's calculations, for no capital outlay the ACTU could expect a profit of $750,000 after eighteen months of joint-trading and $3.5 million annually after five years. The money would be kept as internal savings until 1976, when the ACTU could elect to buy out the Revelman family, or to continue in joint-venture. Either way, the staff Hawke needed for trade union education, the scholarships he wanted to give to unionists' children, the economic research he wanted done, even office space — all would be provided. The office space would come early, because Revelman had already planned to expand the store, and would now do so in a way to house the ACTU, rent-free. Hawke believed, and his infectious enthusiasm was shared by Revelman, that unionists would flock to 'their' shop, that the 'brand loyalty' known, for example, among cigarette smokers, would become Bourkes-ACTU loyalty for the ordinary working person. This idea was, for both of them, an astonishing misjudgment. In Hawke it arose from his vast inner optimism, self-confidence and his faith in the workers' loyalty; in Revelman, from rapport with Hawke. Bourkes was situated on the corner of Elizabeth and La Trobe Streets, an ugly, run-down part of town — and as any real estate agent will advise, there are three rules for real estate: locality, locality, locality. Also, shoppers in the early 1970s were housewives; men shopped only for very expensive goods, and working women were notoriously quick, price-careless shoppers for their major concern was time. This pattern did not augur well for trade union loyalty to the store. But more importantly, many unions already had agreements with shops to give discounts to their members. In due course, these unions actively campaigned against Bourkes-ACTU; union journals ran advertisements telling their members NOT to patronise the store. And, overlying all this was the fact that Victoria, as a State, was in an economic decline. Signs of the State's underlying economic weaknesses were disguised, for a time, by the general prosperity that had arisen in Australia from the Johnson administration's misfinancing of the Vietnam War. President Nixon had already created a mild recession, to try to suppress the excess-demand inflation of the war, but inflation had not shrunk in America and unemployment there was growing towards 6%. We felt a shiver in Australia, but it seemed just a cool breeze while we basked on in the sun.

Hawke engaged solicitors and chartered accountants to examine a draft contract for the ACTU. While making no comment on Revelman's projected trading figures, they advised that the ACTU's option to withdraw from the venture after five years and without liability was a 'major safeguard'. The executive invited Revelman to explain his plans at its November 1970 meeting.

There was suspicion in the room. A capitalist had never entered the ACTU boardroom; Revelman was a Jew and the trade union movement, heavily Catholic and of a generation still familiar with that vile disingenuity 'the Jews killed Christ', had the undercurrent of uneasiness which has marked the history of the relationship between Gentiles and Jews. (Years later, trade unionists complained of the ACTU enterprises: 'Why were we always asked by Bob to deal with Jews?') The trade union ethos makes it difficult to think that any capitalists are full members of the human race, have sensibilities, bleed like other men — just as, one must say, middle-class conservatives seem to think that trade unionists are somehow separate from the Australian community, and pernicious. Years of peace, business affluence and conservative government had enforced such views, and of the factors, peace was probably the most important. Even Hawke's very close supporters did not realise the strength of the bond between him and Revelman, that for both there was an intermixture of emotion and pragmatism — that, as another of Hawke's father figures, Sir Peter Abeles, said later of a failed ACTU joint-venture, 'There was so much emotion. Bob and I dreamed dreams together.' Revelman had told Hazel that if he could persuade the ACTU to join the scheme and move into Bourkes' premises, he could help to combat Hawke's drinking problem, for Hawke would be more than a mile away from the Lygon. It is Hazel's belief that a major motivation for Revelman was to get Hawke to moderate his drinking, a subject he discussed only with her. There has usually been a hidden life, a second soul, in Hawke's most intense friendships, as if his animal warmth, boisterousness, indignation, confidence or courage expressed, for the other, a part that lay suppressed — as, in marriage, a cold man will often choose a gregarious, warm-hearted wife.

The ACTU executive quickly grasped the unspoken technicalities of Revelman's proposition: Hawke, using the power of his position in the trade unions and the Press, would out-bully the big retailers should they refuse to supply Bourkes. Manufacturers and distributors would be more frightened of him than, for example, of Myers — and the entire structure of retail price maintenance in Melbourne would come tumbling down. That was straight-forward bargaining, the coin of which is units of anger and determination. All the executive members were experts themselves in the bargaining game. Revelman told the executive that Bourkes' policy was 'to sell the best possible article for the least possible price, coupled with the best possible service', and that 'all the ACTU is putting in is its good name'. But the executive was still uneasy: intuitively some knew there was something unspoken. They feared that Revelman was offering them a Trojan horse — as Fitzgibbon said, 'I don't believe in Santa Claus'. At last Fitzgibbon voiced their fears: 'Why are you doing this? Why are you offering us such a good deal?' Revelman replied, 'If I'm to go broke because of Myers I want to do it roaring like a lion, not squeaking like a mouse'. In such company it was the perfect answer, for it was the businessman's equivalent of deciding to go on strike. However, the extreme-Right was most unhappy, for the whole bargaining exercise to be launched by Hawke would be 'political', not 'industrial'. B.A. Santamaria, a theorist of great acuity, had already warned that Hawke was forming the trade union movement into a political movement of a nature as yet unknown. The extreme-Left, represented by Pat Clancy of the Building Workers' Indus-trial Union, was wildly enthusiastic. Clancy said,

> Hawke made a stunning impact on the thinking of trade unionists. He opened his presidency with a big burst and carried through the positive progressive ideas for which he had campaigned. Bourkes' store was an idea which at that time many people found very new and outgoing — although it was not a new concept, for over the centuries the labour movement has tried similar things, for instance, the Miners' Co-operative Movement. [In the 1950s and 1960s, at Souter's encourage-ment, the ACTU had also considered joint-ventures to try to stimulate a flow of needed cash, but they had amounted to nothing.] I was in favour

of Bourkes. It's essential to bring forward ideas, to broaden the activities of the trade union movement, and Bob Hawke approached this problem with honesty and with great vigour.

The Left and the centre were similarly enthusiastic and John Ducker, who thought ACTU enterprises were 'tinsel', decided not to fight over a popular cause. All of them welcomed the prospect of decent office space: as Ducker said, 'You get bloody sick of living on top of each other for a week, and not being able to have a private phone conversation'.

A month later Bourkes-ACTU opened its doors. The excitement that had surrounded Hawke in his first year of office turned into hysteria. Hawke appeared on one television channel after another, on every radio station — hourly, it seemed — was reported by the yard in the Press, constantly talking of the iniquities of retail price maintenance, the need for legislation against it, the determination of the trade union movement to smash it. In six weeks the store's turn-over increased by 100%. But twenty major manufacturers refused to supply more stock; Myers ran full-page advertisements asking customers to inform it if it was being 'undersold' and promising 'to correct the situation immediately'. Repeatedly, during 1970, conservative politicians had accused Hawke and the unions of causing inflation — Hawke had been a negotiator in some significantly successful wage disputes that year — and suddenly he was turning their argument (which was, at best, only a fraction of the truth) against them and theirs. Retail price maintenance, which was more widespread in Melbourne than in Sydney, was, Hawke argued, the culprit and so was the federal Government for tolerating it: the action of the manufacturers in refusing to supply the public with cheaper goods, via Bourkes-ACTU, was proof. Some of these manufacturers enjoyed tariff protection; Hawke announced that unions which supported tariff protection would reconsider their attitudes. He made it nationally known that there were 13,000 price-fixing agreements currently registered with the Trade Practices Tribunal.

There was a massive swell of public support. However, the Prime Minister, Bill McMahon, took the unwise step of presenting the issue as a trial of strength between himself and Hawke, whom he accused of 'lawlessness', 'ruining the country' and other fancies. McMahon's brother, Sam, who ran a Sydney bond-store, and had a mischievous sense of fun, promptly offered capital for expansion of Bourkes. The NSW Premier, Bob Askin, was loud in his condemnation of Hawke; the Sydney tabloid newspapers referred to 'the power-mad Mr Hawke' and 'this puffed-up Napoleon', and one remarked, 'He is very clearly a socialist who believes in the concept of "class war" '. In Melbourne a Collins Street clubman told the journalist Maximilian Walsh, 'I haven't seen the boys in such a state since Jack Lang's day, forty years ago. They talk about this fellow Hawke now much as their fathers spoke of Lang.' People were confused and exhilarated. Old timers, whose opinions were sought by the news media, said, 'The big money boys will get Hawkey'. Throughout early March Hawke held private talks with the executives of the major manufacturers who were refusing supplies. Then on 17 March he made telephone calls to twenty companies, among them Singer, Julius Marlow, Crestknit, Sheraton, Bata, Tosca Leather, Marathon Footwear, Parker Pens, Onkaparinga . . . his diary records to the minute the hour of conversations. It was time for a show-down. That afternoon Hawke announced that the ACTU was advising its affiliates to stop the movement of all goods to and from the Dunlop group of companies in Victoria. Dunlop had been the most intransigent. It appealed to the federal Government for help against the unions. The Government, after so much threatening talk, refused to guarantee Dunlop that it would fight and twenty-seven hours later it was all over: Eric Dunshea, the Chairman of Dunlop, telephoned Hawke to tell him that his London directors had instructed him, failing Government support, to surrender. Bourkes-ACTU would have supplies. Melbourne talked of nothing else. Many people were now thoroughly frightened of Hawke, among them Dunshea. He had agreed to hold a joint Press conference at which they would announce the news of surrender. Dunshea told his friend, Isi Magid, with whom he lunched every month at their club,

> I was dreading the Press conference. I'm not used to public speaking and Press conferences and that chap Hawke could handle the Press so well, he was so forceful and articulate. I thought he was going to humiliate me and I'd have to sit there while he rubbed salt in my wounds. But he was like a son protecting his own father. He answered most of the questions for me, before the Press could get stuck into me. And he avoided the use of the term 'surrender'. He'd conducted all our negotiations as if we were in a boxing ring — everything was in the open, there were no behind-door deals. Then, in the hour I dreaded most, he was like that — he made it as gentle, easy and honourable as any person could.

Hawke's statement to the news media was: 'The practice of retail price maintenance in Australia has been abolished'. It had been — at least in the eyes of the law.* It meant that Bourkes-ACTU, no longer unique, would now have to battle with the disadvantage of its location, and the ill-will of the unions which had their own discount arrangements with other stores. Revelman, however, was an ingenious retailer. When the first flush of excitement about the store abated later in 1971 he organised

---

* On 25 June 1980 a Federal Court judge fined Dunlop Australia $25,000 for threatening a sports store owner because he discounted a product made by a Dunlop subsidiary. The judge also fined Dunlop's national sales manager $4,000 for trying to enforce retail price maintenance, contrary to the Trade Practices Act.

advertising campaigns in which Hawke was the central spokesman.

They spent much time together, especially from the beginning of 1972, when the ACTU moved from the Lygon Street office into its newly constructed and spacious accommodation above Bourkes. After work and at weekends they played snooker and tennis together. Revelman was a tennis fanatic and when dissatisfied with an aspect of his play, took coaching to correct it. He had suffered two mild heart attacks, but treated such signs of infirmity with disdain; during one of them he pretended he was not in pain at all but had simply bent down to re-tie a shoelace. After recovering from his second heart attack, in February 1972, he announced he was fitter than ever before; indeed, his tennis was at its peak. One evening in May 1972 Hawke asked Revelman to accompany him on a harrowing excursion:

> I'd had some letters from a woman whose husband had cancer and who wanted to meet me before he died. Then I got a message from her saying it was urgent, he had only days to live. His house was near Lionel's place and I asked him to come along. It was a helluva experience: the woman was overcome with emotion . . . So I sat on the bed and talked, and Lionel sat on the end of the bed. Lionel didn't say much, but it was comforting having him there. Then we went back to Lionel's place and had something to eat and he said, 'Let's have a game'. And I said, 'Would you rather play snooker?' And he said, 'No! Tennis!' I won the first set 6-3. I said to Lionel, 'Would you rather go in?' and he said, 'No. It's my serve.' I was walking away from the net, I had my back to him, and I heard a thud.

Hawke rushed to his friend, tried to pick him up, but Revelman died in his arms. Tup, Revelman's widow, recalled, 'Bob came tearing into the house and said, "I think something's wrong with Lionel", then he sat down and burst into tears . . . He couldn't stop crying and he didn't have a handkerchief. I had to find him one — he was weeping like a child.'

The funeral service was held in Revelman's house. It was a very large funeral and Hawke had agreed to give the eulogy. He started to speak but after a few minutes covered his face with his hands and began to sob and Geoff Gleghorn, his personal assistant-Press officer at the ACTU, stepped forward, took him by the elbow and led him outside.

While the death was a horrifying personal blow to Hawke, who agonised that he had caused Revelman's final heart attack by playing tennis too vigorously with him, it was also a blow to Bourkes. George Revelman was heart-broken over his younger brother's death; he did not have Lionel Revelman's flair for retailing. The store began to slide. Hawke consistently refused to tell the ACTU executive what the financial position of Bourkes was, on the grounds that it was a family-owned company and such information was private. Hawke has never mentioned the issue, but it seems that the information may have been difficult for him to obtain. In 1980 when George Revelman was asked for an interview about his brother and Hawke, he replied he had no comment to make, and rang off. Failing information from Hawke, the ACTU executive became increasingly ill-humoured and suspicious about Bourkes. From the latter part of 1980 and through 1981 signs in titanic black letters were painted on the whitewashed windows of Bourkes, announcing baldly: BOURKES-ACTU IS FINISHED. They could be seen two city blocks away, almost from Myers. After a while some wit changed one of the signs to read: HAWKE IS FINISHED. Nobody bothered to erase it. Anyone entering the ACTU or walking down La Trobe Street had to see it.

While Bourkes had not generated for the ACTU the funds Hawke had hoped for, it had provided a substantial financial benefit: in the winding-up of the enterprise it was agreed that the ACTU would continue to have rent-free accommodation until 1988. A general estimate was that sixteen years' rent would have cost the ACTU $1 million. Ironically, just as the store was closing down and Hawke preparing to leave the ACTU, construction had begun on a new train terminal opposite Bourkes and its problem of unfavourable location appeared ready for solution.

From all over the country letters and telegrams had arrived by the bag-full to congratulate Hawke for defeating retail price maintenance, many of them from unions, many from pensioners' associations, many from ALP branches. Those from individual citizens are most revealing of the image which Hawke was establishing in the community:

> At last we have a man of courage, champion of the poor and helpless. God will guide you all the way to a successful end to tyranny.

> You are the Billy Graham of the workers.

> I wish you could be our Prime Minister.

> You are like Ben Chifley and John Curtin.

> Strength to your arm, then, Mr Hawke. There are thousands like me who are looking to you for a better Australia in which to live and bringing to their knees all the powerful business monopolies who would prostitute this country in order to assuage their own gluttonous ends.

> May I say how wonderful it is to see you on television bringing the financial moguls to their knees.

Congratulations on Dunlops. I wonder if you would be interested in sheep drenches, dips, fly dressing and jetting material. Sheep drench is $20 to $27 a gallon . . .

Champion for justice and for a better country . . . you are a leader of courage and principle and hope for a brighter future. To help save Australia the people are grateful to you and proclaim you President of Australia.

Do not work too hard and look after yourself as the little man cannot afford to lose a man like you.

I am an old woman. I am glad I have lived long enough to see this happen.

Permit me, Sir, to say that your obvious sincerity and doggedness of purpose leaves me drained and inadequate . . . May you remain in good health.

We love you.

A couple of years ago I listened to you make a speech at the offices of the Insurance Staff Federation . . . I got the idea you were a somewhat devious gentleman with political ambitions and would promise anything to gain publicity and personal admiration. I used to think, 'Here he goes again on another publicity-seeking self-promotion campaign — what does he care for the worker? As long as he gets to the top, we can go to the Devil.' How completely and utterly wrong I have been. I trust you will accept my apology for being so wrong.

Due to an old injury I have to use Dr Scholls supports in my shoes. The price . . . Could you do something?

Have you ever considered the poor deal the average man receives when he enters the usual superannuation scheme run by a Life Office? Or an ordinary life assurance policy?

I am going to ask you to do something re the abolition of the Means Test. Please, Mr Hawke, try!

I have to wear dentures. Isn't there anything you can do to stop this scandalous dental bill from being introduced?

We bless you.

... the unassuming manner in which you extended mercy to a fallen foe. The charitable way in which you relieved a squirming adversary from his embarrassment will, I doubt not, remain as an inspiration in the minds of many who were privileged to view the programme.

You have stirred me into new hope.

From the hundreds of letters there were only a couple expressing opposition. One said:

Our Australian king of the unions, Hawke by name and nature, the blackmailing, mafia-type, stand-over boss of the workers ... The workers ... go on strike at his commands ... like a lot of sheep. The industries and business houses are frightened of him and the Government is frightened of him ... Hawke's definition of democracy is: 'I do what I like, and everyone else does what I tell them'. (The letter was from a false address.) [1]

Before Hawke had assumed the ACTU presidency he had, in vehement terms, condemned the 1969-70 national wage decision of the Conciliation and Arbitration Commission and had asserted that such decisions would lead to an increase in collective bargaining in Australia. Since 1907, whenever the unions have been angry with arbitrated wages they have threatened to reject arbitration and embrace collective bargaining — which, of course, they then ask the arbitration system to approve, as a 'consent award'. Arbitration judges, conciliation commissioners, union and employer officials, all know the rules of this game and play it with gusto. There are solemn statements, warnings, questions in Parliament — it is all part of the bargaining process to determine who has the largest pile of chips; that is, which party is really most angry and must be assuaged. Unfortunately, it is only the *cognoscenti* of industrial relations who do understand the process, for both the news media and the universities have failed to explain to the public what is really going on behind the rhetoric, and it is in the interests of politicians of all persuasions not to clarify. Only some of them understand it themselves: Sir Richard Kirby said of the years after Harold Holt ceased to be Minister for Labour, 'It was as useful as having Billy the Cat as Minister. The Government put coves in the job who didn't have a clue. I'd see their eyes glazing as I tried to explain things — they literally could not understand what industrial relations was about.' In desperation Kirby would sometimes use the analogy of marriage, in which tension builds up until there is an argument: 'I'd tell them, "That is a strike. It's letting off steam" ... However, they still couldn't grasp the idea that industrial relations operate on the same principles as family relations ...'

It is the job of union leaders to bargain as hard as they can. That is, to express anger. Hawke's unusually developed capacity for the expression of anger in logical terms was to make him the greatest union negotiator there has been in Australia, and, in the opinion of the international trade union community, (represented at the ILO), one of the greatest in the world. Meanwhile the public at large, innocent of the processes of industrial relations and seeing only a very angry man, started to become frightened of Hawke. An early letter to him from a correspondent self-described as 'ex-serviceman, non-striker', said 'Heil Hitler. Why don't you go to Russia, you power-hungry bastard, and take all your stinking Left-wing fascist parasites with you. Australia will be better served by your absence.'

After the showers of congratulations which greeted the Dunlop drama in early 1971 — and which were, notably, less concerned with the economic principle for which Hawke had fought than, in a majority of cases, with revenge — his popularity took an abrupt downturn when he adopted, and in the trade union movement became the leader of, the anti-apartheid cause.

As early as March 1971 students had begun protests against a tour in Australia of a South African rugby union team, due to arrive in June. In early April the South African Government banned the inclusion of two non-white players in the team, the Springboks. A few days later Hawke announced that the ACTU 'had a strong policy against apartheid' and implied that there would be union bans against the Springboks. The ACTU's policy against apartheid had first been stated in 1963, the year in which the Organisation of African Unity was established, and which marked the real beginning of the Third World's struggle against the domination of the First and Second Worlds. On 16 April 1971 Hawke said publicly that South Africa should be isolated from international sport. Labor politicians made similar statements. The Prime Minister, McMahon, said that the ACTU and the ALP were 'ganging up' and that their actions were discreditable. Hawke said the unions would impose bans. The Rand *Daily Mail* ran an editorial headlined, 'An Appeal to Mr Hawke' asking that there be no union action. The Australian news media reported it. The Government and Press editorialists took out their violins and played, fortissimo, what by now was a national refrain: 'Who runs the country? The Government or the unions?'

By late April the parliamentary Labor Party was alarmed that a campaign against the Springboks by the trade unions would damage Labor's electoral chances. The Commonwealth Labor Advisory Council (the formal meeting ground between the ALP and the trade union movement, a body later named the Australian Labor Advisory Council, called ALAC, pronounced Alac) recommended on 27 April that the Government should be pressed to ban the tour on 'moral' grounds and that the unions should not take independent action. Hawke said:

> We were very strong in the position, both in discussions within the ACTU and in all my public statements, that we, the unions, didn't want to be forced into a situation where we had to take action. We wanted the

Government to act. And that was not just a tactical decision — it was what we really believed. But it was 1971 and they were simply slow learners. The standard argument trotted out was that politics should be kept out of sport; that it wasn't appropriate for either governments or trade unions to intrude into sport — which was a pretty funny argument, considering that the exclusion of blacks from sporting teams was a political act, it was the policy of the South African Government. Well, we weren't prepared to accept that argument, either *vis-à-vis* the Government or *vis-à-vis* the Labor Party. There were two aspects to our position *vis-à-vis* the ALP. One, on pragmatic grounds, was that we did not accept that trade union action would damage the Party, come election time — which was more that eighteen months away. Indeed, I believed, as did others in the ACTU, that there were certain issues where, if we were ahead of public opinion and totally convinced of our position, we had an obligation to *act* ahead of public opinion, to act as leaders, in the hope that the public would come to understand. The second aspect was: opposition to apartheid was not merely ACTU policy. The ACTU was part of the international trade union movement and the unequivocal policy of the ICFTU [International Confederation of Free Trade Unions], of which we were part, was opposition to apartheid, and the ICFTU had called upon the ACTU to take action. Therefore we should.

On 5 May Hawke had talks with Charles Blunt, head of the Australian Rugby Union. Hawke recalled:

It was a civilised meeting. He wasn't one of the troglodytes who said we were totally wrong to have an interest in this area, he was a reasonable bloke, but it was quite clear from our conversations that nothing looked like coming out of them to change the head-on situation that was looming in Australia.

On 13 May the ACTU executive met and decided (only the extreme-Right objecting):

to request the Government to inform the Government of South Africa that no team from that country will be received in Australia unless that team has been chosen or has been free to be chosen on a non-discriminatory racial basis . . . to indicate that should positive steps be taken by the South African Government to ensure that [no racial discrimination] is applied to the Rugby Union and cricket teams proposed to be sent to Australia, then the teams would accordingly be welcome. Should these representations prove to be unsuccessful we advise our affiliated unions to take whatever action is necessary as an act of conscience on their part to withhold their services from any activities directly associated with these proposed tours . . .[2]

The executive also instructed Hawke to write directly to the South African Prime Minister, Vorster, stating the ACTU's decision and requesting a non-discriminatory team be sent to Australia. His letter was conveyed by the South African Ambassador and within a few days Hawke had received a rejection. Hawke announced that union action was now inevitable. There was immense publicity; student and civil liberty groups were vociferous. Newspaper editorialists wrang their hands, complained the unions were running the country, apartheid was wrong — BUT politics should not enter sport. The nation was deeply divided, the trade union movement as much as the rest. The Springboks were due to begin their tour in Perth, on 24 June. On 25 May the Western Australian branch of the Transport Workers' Union (TWU) announced that it would not take action; airport refuellers would service the South African Airways plane bringing the team; porters would handle their luggage. The TWU's decision was in part the result of brawling within the union's Western Australian branch, and brawling between the branch and its federal body. The branch was refusing to take orders from the TWU head-office. The Government saw a vulnerable spot. It announced that if other TWU branches prevented aircraft from flying the Springboks around Australia, the RAAF would be used. It commended the Western Australian TWU for being 'responsible'. Then the Western Australian Barmaids' and Barmen's Union announced that it would serve the Springboks. Hawke was due to leave Australia on the day the Springboks were due to arrive, and from Perth. The TWU announced it would blackban his flight out of Perth; at Melbourne airport two men burnt their union cards in front of Hawke. Hawke said that South African Airlines would lose its Australian market if it flew the team into Australia. He telephoned SAA and Qantas to tell their executives that their planes would be black-banned indefinitely — something which never happened. Commenting on this, he revealed the gamesmanship involved: 'Well, you expressed a view as to what you hoped would happen, and certainly put it in terms that it, in fact, would happen. Then you worked in terms of what the unions involved would, in fact, be prepared to do. And, you had to judge how far you could push that.'

In Perth people telephoned Ellie to abuse her. One said, 'Why didn't you strangle him at birth?' Another, 'You gave birth to a monster'. There were repeated claims that Hawke was a Communist.

Hawke was taking his daughter Susan abroad with him. For the first time he was to visit Israel, then would fly on to a conference in Europe, while Susan stayed in Israel on a kibbutz. He was acutely aware that Hazel was rearing the children single-handed, for already his job required him to be overseas or interstate for six months of the year, and when he was in Melbourne he was hardly a normal father: the phone began ringing at 7 a.m. There were Press interviews while they were trying to eat breakfast. Hawke had arranged, at the last minute, that Susan should accompany him abroad. He said:

> There were a group of young fellows, musicians I think, on the flight with us over to Perth. I had some apprehension about what would happen when we landed in Perth and these musicians said, 'We'll walk off with you'. I said to Susan, 'There might be some unpleasantness'. And, indeed, it was a never-to-be-forgotten experience, one of the most unpleasant of the whole time I was President of the ACTU. We got off the plane and there were hundreds and hundreds of people there. Masses of them. And they were screaming abuse and spitting and shouting all sorts of epithets. Susan was frightened, but she was good, she kept cool. We walked through it. The people were there to meet the Springboks. Exquisite timing. We went home to mum and dad's place. We were due to fly out the following night. And there was a lot of talk about that plane being bombed, so there was a very thorough search of baggage. [There was a phalanx of police to escort Hawke and Susan on to the plane.] I said to Susan before we boarded, 'Look, we shouldn't be surprised if once we take off something happens and we have to return to Perth'. It seemed to be sensible to say that to her. Well, we took off and had been flying for about an hour and I said, 'Well, love, it looks as though it's all right'. And the words were hardly out of my mouth when I noticed a change in the altitude of the plane and in the sound of the engines. Then a few minutes later the captain said, 'We are returning to Perth'. He made the usual reassuring noises. So, zoom! We returned to Perth. As we landed and were disembarking some bastard walking past turned to me and said, 'I might have known — you Commie swine', something like that, and I was pretty annoyed, and made a comment back. There was another search, and of course there was no bomb on the plane. It had been a hoax. But it had taken about two hours and I was worried about whether we'd be able to take off again, because of the question of hours for the aircrew. Anyway, off we went again. And after a while the captain came down to talk to me, and not in the friendliest of terms, somewhat cold. He made the point about the aircrew. And I had the distinct impression that he was less than enthusiastic about me. As he turned to go he said, 'By the way, Mr Hawke, it may interest you to know that I am Rhodesian'.

The Springbok riots of 1971 are now a part of Australian history. No apartheid sporting team has visited Australia since, but the principle was established at horrible cost to protestors, and police. The Victorian police force, which bore the brunt of protestor fury, reacted with savagery. Someone threw black paint on Hazel's car. At Sandringham she read letters addressed to Hawke which were filled with vilification. She said, 'Sometimes I'd retch, just reading them'. Twice, inside parcels, there was excrement. At school, the Hawke children were tormented. Rosslyn, the youngest, an affectionate child who adored her father, was made to watch while a group of children symbolically killed Hawke by grinding his photographs into a paste. Hawke had always striven to keep what might be called his woman problem separate from his family life; people, often wearing a mask of sympathy, now took the opportunity to tell Hazel and the children all they knew of Hawke's peccadillos, with flourishes. Hazel said, 'Kids at school and even *adults* said things to the children about their father with a criminal disregard for what effect they would have'. Years of harassment, at first from racists and sadists, later from anti-Zionists and sadists, had begun for the Hawke family.

Peter Coleman, who met Hazel in late 1972 for the first time in a decade, was shocked by the change in her: 'I remembered her as so friendly and open, and here seemed a cold, tough woman. I guessed she must have had a rough spin.' Of necessity, with all but those whom she knew she could trust, Hazel had turned into a tigress. Ducker, who took his family on the same cruise ship as the Hawkes after the 1972 election, said: 'It was a bit difficult for me to get friendly with Hazel. I was the bloke who had tried to knock off her husband — and the iron had entered her soul, as far as I was concerned.' There are scores of stories from journalists and others about tongue-lashings they received from Hazel for criticism of Hawke or for impositions upon the children. She had always been fiercely protective of him; she was now in constant battle for the four of them against what seemed, at times, the entire nation.

Although Hawke's trip to the International Labour Conference was an annual obligation, for he was the workers' spokesman there for Australia and Asia, Brian Harradine publicly accused him of 'skipping out of the country when the going got tough'.

In May 1971 Hawke's popularity had first been tested by a Gallup poll: 42% approved, 30% disapproved of him. By August 1971 the balance had changed: 28% approved, 55% disapproved of him. In the white-collar trade unions only 24% approved, 61% disapproved; in the blue-collar unions 51% approved, 32% disapproved; and in the trade unions as a whole 48% were dissatisfied with him. While Hawke was abroad there were two by-elections in Queensland registering massive swings against the ALP — 18% in Maryborough — and it was generally accepted that Hawke's unpopularity was a major factor. The *Australian* of 22 August announced: 'Hawke is clearly a vote-winner for the coalition parties . . . one of the most unpopular men in the country . . . does not even have the support of a majority of trade unionists'. Hours later Gough Whitlam used the opportunity of his Budget speech-in-reply to defend Hawke (and the ALP's electoral prospects), saying the President of the ACTU had saved the country millions of dollars through strike settlement and the breaking of retail price maintenance. Whitlam pointed out that Hawke had been 'subjected by ministers and the media to a campaign of abuse and denigration unparalleled in Australia's history, except, possibly, for the late Dr Evatt'. A couple of days later a Liberal backbencher described Hawke as 'the arch-enemy of Australia'. On the following Monday, 30 August, the ACTU's 1971 Congress opened — Hawke's first as President.

The Right had its strategy: it would attack Hawke for leading the ACTU to exceed its legitimate functions by authorising industrial action for 'political' ends, and for neglecting to act on other matters of proper concern to the trade unions. The Left had its plans, too. In Victoria, where the State ALP had been a militant industrial party, different from all other Labor machines, Hawke had been transformed from hero (of sorts) to 'traitor', 'Judas' and the like, because of his role in federal intervention in the affairs of the Victorian branch. At the height of excitement over this issue, in late 1970- early 1971, passions had run so high that it had required physical courage to walk into the Lygon Hotel. Many of Hawke's old Left-wing friends in Victoria would never speak to him again, among them Wally Curran, who in earlier days had helped Hawke build a carport and had been assistant to George Seelaf during the ACTU presidency campaign. Hawke had compounded Left-wing anger by settling a strike in the oil industry in 1970. Officials considered that Hawke's intervention had prevented their achievement of a bigger wage increase. By late 1971, although the public was unaware of it, the extreme-Left was extremely cross with Hawke. The Left's Congress strategy was to support his candidates for the executive elections, while attempting to have Congress bind the ACTU to militant action on key issues, specifically wage campaigns and fights against the penal powers.

From this confluence of pressures Hawke and the moderate-Left emerged victors: he was voted an executive which divided 10-7 in his favour and a two-year policy platform that rejected 'massive industrial action' in favour of pragmatism. 'It is not any part of our policy to abandon arbitration', Hawke announced at the opening of Congress, and this attitude was formally accepted by delegates later, as was a resolution on the penal powers which stated that the ACTU was to continue its negotiations with government about them and 'to work out ways and means of ensuring that industrial agreements are honoured by the Trade Union Movement'. This latter statement was significant, for it was an acknowledgment by the unions that relations with employers were a two-way deal — that if the unions demanded to be free of penal sanctions while employers were forced, by the arbitration system, to pay certain wages, the unions would have to give some undertaking that would accept the limitations upon employers as responsibilities upon themselves.

Hawke's Congress success had, however, one fateful set-back: the affiliation fees. Hawke had taken the exceptional step of leaving the chair to second the executive's recommendation for a fee increase of 100%, and had done so angrily. He described the ACTU's staffing position as 'ludicrous' and derided objections to the increase: 'To suggest that 24 cents a member is unreasonable is in itself inexcusable'. He already knew that a compromise between a 100% increase and no increase had been framed, recommending that the extra money be paid over two years; the night before the issue arose numbers men told him they thought this 50-50 amendment could get the votes. Hawke's tactic was to bully the Congress into adopting at least a half-measure. He has an ability to switch on rage: sometimes, before he is to make a telephone call during which he intends to browbeat somebody for being in his opinion a fool or a crook, he will throw an aside, 'This might be a bit rough', then will spend a couple of seconds of intense stillness, like a gymnast collecting his energy for a leap. He then lets fly. The harangue that follows can go on for an hour. (In 1980, over Aboriginal land rights, Hawke was so savage during a telephone conversation with a senior businessman who had not been honest in the matter, that the man had a blackout that night and took three months' leave. Hawke, who liked and otherwise admired him, was mortified.) A verbal Hercules, he often breaks things unintentionally — people, like china ornaments, bewilderingly come apart in his hands. And cut him. Don Dunstan, himself an adept at sudden anger, noted, 'Bob does not have the sensitivity to an audience that, for example, a good actor has'. A group of half a dozen people can be intimidated by Hawke's anger and collapse. At the Congress he was facing 764 men. The delegates voted for no increase.

Perhaps they would have anyway, for there is no end to the wheeling and dealing and last minute reversals of an ACTU Congress. But Hawke had provided his already choleric Left-wing critics with another grudge against him, of the 'Who does he think he is?' variety.

Within hours, however, Congress had endorsed the ACTU's association with Bourkes and the executive's decision to investigate the feasibility of entering consumer credit, insurance and housing finance. Hawke had left the chair to speak on these matters also, and his speech had been moderate. As a chairman, Hawke was both more efficient and fairer than Monk, who would declare votes against executive recommendations lost on the voices, as a matter of course. Hawke actually listened to the voices and declared that the executive had lost, on the voices, seven times. In the old days Congress sessions had never started on time; Hawke managed to open all but two sessions within five minutes of the advertised time and, to the shock of delegates, enforced an extra hour's sitting one day. With individual speakers he was, as Monk had been, impartial and courteous — not an easy matter for anyone, for Congress is *the* arena for unionists to perform and the executive and the President take their share of abuse. During debates at the 1971 Congress, Joe Riordan, Hawke's old adversary, was subjected to some harsh personal attacks by Hawke supporters. Hawke, with great gentleness, called Riordan's attention to the fact that his speaking time had run out. It was a tiny matter, but the Right noticed compassion in a man they had thought too wild for it. Slowly, he was bringing them round. After 1971 the ACTU executive began, for the first time in four years, to vote unanimously, and Hawke began his long reign as a consensus leader.

The Right had realised that Hawke would not, after all, assault them. Ducker said,

> Now that must have been a vast disappointment for, particularly, the Communist Party and the active Left, because it meant that their success was limited. Bob wasn't prepared to factionalise the ACTU to the position where it was split. He was prepared to respect and uphold the constitutional authority of the trade union movement, he was careful to try to work through the structures, the proper procedures. He stood up to the madmen of the Left . . . A lot of it was Bob's gentleness, an ease of manner, being kind to people. Gradually, he and I were getting to know each other and to see in each other something more than we had previously perceived. Fortifying this was our relationship in the Labor Party federal executive. That was neutral ground, and an opportunity for socialising — and we had to get on in the Labor Party because, by late 1971, we were looking at a federal Labor government. We both wanted to assist that. It's difficult to be cordial and friendly in the Labor Party and, often about the same issue, to be at loggerheads in the ACTU . . . I'd seen that the ascendance *was* with Hawke and with the policies and philosophies he was espousing, and I was concerned that the Right could become isolated. That was what the National Civic Council grouping [in the trade union movement] wanted; they wanted total split, in the belief that they would win on that basis. I thought they were bloody mad. So I played my cards carefully. I didn't take the Springbok tour head on. I didn't object to the first 24-hour strike [in 1970] on the Budget, I went with it, and was often able to take a step in advance. And would delight in the fact that I could take a Left position, with Gietzelt following up behind. And I'd tell the Labour Council that, 'despite some reservations by delegate Gietzelt we were able to take a firm, strong, militant position . . .'

On 1 September 1971 Hawke was named Victorian Father of the Year. A photograph of Rosslyn, plaits flying, rushing into his arms, was widely published. It marked the turning point of Hawke's unpopularity. He had been embarrassed by the honour, which he told the news media should properly have gone to Hazel for she was, he said, mother and father — and gardener. Later that month he gave interviews acknowledging that his abrasiveness had alarmed people, implying regret for this. The September Gallup poll showed his public approval had increased by 4% and his disapproval had fallen to 43%. Only 26% of women approved of Hawke.

He had caused serious affront to the burgeoning feminist movement earlier in the year when, appearing on television with Zelda D'Aprano, a leader of the cause, he had felt her shoulder to find out, as he explained, if she were wearing a brassière. D'Aprano was a postal worker; Hawke asked her, 'You do mean M-A-I-L Exchange, don't you?' The feminist magazine *MeJane* named him Male Chauvinist of the Month, and feminists never forgave him. At the time women were just learning to bargain: in Hawke they had encountered an expert, who could have taken up their cause but did not. Back in the early 1960s, when it was unfashionable, he had accepted that women should have equality and had publicly argued for it. His commitment, however, as for many of his generation, lacked a broad conceptual base. He had read Greer's *Female Eunuch* — and in early 1972, when he was working hard on his image, had a lively, genial discussion on television with her — but Greer's work had little effect on those who were not already converted or were psychologically ready-to-be-converted. And Hawke was not. He was in his fiftieth year before he read the seminal text of feminism, de Beauvoir's *Second Sex*, and was appalled by her description of the female condition and by what he had failed to understand. 'It's a disaster! A disaster!' he said. 'I'd not realised . . .' In the meantime, he had showed much hostility to women: his language, his excessively virile swagger, the way he stood — legs straight, calves pushed back, hips forward — his every public gesture revealed dominance, including sexual dominance. Feminists had only to look at Hawke to see The Enemy. Many women found him magnetically attractive. Some daring — and silly — ones pursued him, the more so as his fame grew, and he became their prey rather than the reverse. He would often leave public gatherings in a temper, saying, 'There was a woman there — Christ Almighty! — all over me like a rash'. A certain smugness was always mixed with annoyance. By the late 1970s, when Hawke's womanising had been, at last, publicised, women and girls he had not met would telephone him or write notes suggesting dalliance. Hawke behaved as if he were irresistible to all women and, when drunk, would proposition anyone who caught his eye. He always thought of himself as a man who liked women — as womanisers invariably do; it took him years to acknowledge that his 'liking' was possibly not what it seemed on the surface.

As Ducker noted, by late 1971 a major concern for leaders of the trade union movement was the election of a federal Labor government. Following intervention in Victoria, Hawke had become a member of the ALP federal executive, which had been reformed since the days of the '36 faceless men'. Hawke had his seat as one of two Victorian representatives; Ducker was a NSW representative and Egerton a Queensland one. A major danger for the Party was that the McMahon Government and conservative State premiers were pressing hard on the 'law and order' issue and that strikes, no matter what the political complexion of the unions who staged them, would be blamed on the

ALP. In his first year of office Hawke had given leadership to union opposition to what was deemed unreasonable government action: one celebrated example was a union ban against the export of merino rams which became such a *cause célèbre* that many members of the public revealed, in letters to the newspapers and to Hawke, that they believed the export of rams was illegal, similar to gun-running. Others, of course, saw Hawke as 'dictator', a term applied to him constantly. (All that had happened in the merino rams issue was that the ACTU had responded to requests from farmers' groups to prevent export.) Meanwhile, trade union demonstrations against the Budgets of 1970 and 1971, co-ordinated by the ACTU, had raised an outcry from conservatives. There were many Press assertions that the trade union movement, under Hawke, was the true Opposition, and Hawke the real Leader of the Opposition, dictating to Whitlam — a curious idea, that one.

By the beginning of the election year, 1972, it was essential for the Party's well-being that such imagery be changed. The industrial horse, as it were, had already bolted — and had done so before Hawke became President of the ACTU — but it was his job to try to catch it and put it back in the stable. From the beginning of 1972 Hawke was engaged in strike settlement and in dampening down the pent-up frustrations of a trade union movement that had learned how to live without a federal Labor government. Many union leaders were difficult to convince that it was worth delaying militant action now in the interests of the longer-term goal of 'their' government coming to power. Communist union leaders had even greater reservations: they looked with a jaundiced eye upon Labor and reform. From the beginning of 1972 Hawke, Ducker, and Egerton— a former boilermaker and a man who had a lifetime's experience of the labour movement and 'knew his way in all the little nooks and crannies, better than anyone else', in Ducker's description — began to operate as a triumvirate. All three were wary of each other, but they managed to co-operate quietly and efficiently. Ducker and Egerton (President of the Queensland TLC and President of the Queensland ALP) had real power. Hawke had the illusion of power, through the news media, but ultimately he had only the weapon of oratory, and the fragile 'authority' of the ACTU, while the other two could make threats and promises of substantial nature. 'There were a lot of strikes we stopped', Ducker said; Egerton remarked, 'It always suited me to have Bob up there in front, while I was down shooting the bullets'.

One serious dispute that could not be averted was in the Victorian State Electricity Commission. It had been smouldering for months and the Arbitration Commission had been trying to contain it when, in February 1972, it broke out. The unions rejected arbitration; the VSEC, under pressure from the Victorian Bolte Government, reacted with provocation and intransigence; the unions replied by changing their bans into a strike and chaos was created. Strikes in power generation are the most damaging of all, for they can gallop wildly, stopping industry and throwing hundreds of thousands out of work, within days. This happened. The McMahon and Bolte Governments blamed the ALP and Communists. A quarter of a million people were without work; the federal Minister for Social Security, Bill Wentworth, announced that people put out of work by the strike would not receive dole money. When Hawke announced, after days of private talks with the unions and arbitration judges, that he was formally intervening to try to settle the dispute, someone telephoned the ACTU to say that he would be murdered. Police were put on guard at the Sandringham house and moved around with Hawke.

The strike by now was so critical that Hawke hired an aeroplane to fly to the south coast of NSW to hold discussions with Kirby, who had been ill and was convalescing there. The two men had wanted their meeting to be secret, but the Press had picked up Hawke's movements through car radios, which monitor police radios, and his meeting with Kirby took place in a glare of publicity. As events turned out, the appearance of a break-through that their meeting suggested was the only lever Hawke had when he returned to Melbourne and had to argue to officials of the unions involved that they must recommend a return to arbitration. During strikes there are three internal levels of authority: there are the union officials; the shop stewards; and the rank and file. Frequently, one or two of the groups is in conflict with the third. The most unnerving situation occurs when the shop stewards and the rank and file gang up against the officials. When Hawke returned from his stay with Kirby and entered the Melbourne Trades Hall for talks with officials they told him their fears about the shop stewards: that they would refuse to accept a return to arbitration. Hawke said,

> The officials told me that if I went down to Yallourn the men were going to throw me in the duckpond there. Anyway, I went. There was a police escort. I had to talk to the shop stewards first and really, I barely had a feather to fly with. Dick [Kirby] and I hadn't been able to think of anything much; the whole situation was just a bloody-awful schemozzle, with thousands of people out of work and people going hungry, and the conservatives belting it for all it was worth politically. So I went in to see the shop stewards, and the atmosphere was not exactly warm, and I just told them straight: I could not promise them anything *but* if they would recommend a return to work I would argue the case before the Arbitration Commission. And they accepted that. Then I went out to address the men and there was — oh, you know, some shouting, 'Throw him in the duckpond', 'Sell-out', that sort of thing, but I gave them the same message and they listened, and listened to the shop stewards. And that was it.

The strike had cost an estimated $79 million in lost production. Meanwhile Hawke's action cost him what support he still had in the Left of Victorian Labor politics. There had been a growing estrangement between him and the Left of the Party since about 1966, when the Victorian central executive and its supporters had a renewed seizure of sectarian hatred, directed against Roman Catholics. As Dr Bob Smith, a member of the Victorian branch of those days, recalled, 'The way to prove you were ideologically pure was to be anti-Mick'. The central executive was already authoritarian; there were many in the Party who wanted change, some democracy in the Party. Among them was one of Hawke's closest friends, Barney Williams, who had founded the Australian Council of Salaried and Professional Associations (ACSPA) and who was the Secretary of the Sandringham branch of the ALP, to which Hawke belonged. Hawke said,

> He was the most devoted man I have ever met in the Labor movement. There was not an ounce of selfishness in him. The hard-Left vilified Barney as a Santamaria stooge because he was a Catholic and wanted change. It sickened me. There was an atmosphere of starry-eyed radical socialism in the early 1960s. I began to think it wasn't radical and wasn't socialism, but something else.

Hawke had tried to prevent federal intervention into the Victorian branch but, like others of the centre and Left, had finally agreed to it, and had co-operated with the interveners. The Party was split into three factions: Socialist Left, the Centre Unity, and the Participants (the Right). Hawke became the leader of Centre Unity, which caused the Socialist Left to regard him as a political rat. Following the VSEC dispute, they regarded him as an industrial one as well. However, it took several years for the Socialist Left's hatred of Hawke to become public; they needed an issue.

Within weeks of the electricity dispute Hawke was involved in an even more complicated strike, in the oil industry. It began, on paper, in March and dragged on, through negotiations, breakdowns in negotiations, renewed negotiations, slowly increasing in acrimony. The argument was over a 35-hour week in the oil industry. The claim for a shorter week had a long history, for twenty years earlier an ACTU Congress had endorsed a recommendation that 35 hours should become the normal working week for the entire trade union movement. In the interim little had been done to turn the policy into reality. When the unions presented their claim for a shorter week, in 1972, the oil companies refused to negotiate on the question. The McMahon Government encouraged the companies to stand firm.

By June there were 24-hour strikes. The companies applied for bans clauses which would mean, if flouted, the penal powers would be applied. There were compulsory conferences in the Arbitration Commission; more strikes; when officials recommended a return to work the rank and file refused. By the end of June there were strikes in Queensland, Victoria and New South Wales refineries. Only about a thousand men were involved, but in a high-technology industry massive strikes are unnecessary. The unions made an offer: the companies refused to talk to them. The news media carried stories of a national fuel shortage, which were not denied but instead were encouraged by the Government and the companies, although both knew there were vast, untouched reserves of petroleum. Tanker drivers were thrown out of work; there was panic buying, rationing, bad tempers.

Hawke was in a delicate position: not only were the employers intransigent, the officials themselves were refusing to allow him to enter the dispute. He had been ill during its early stages, stricken with a back injury. Hazel had bought a wig and Hawke had been playing with her and the wig one evening at home, putting it on and parading around the living room; he took it off, threw it down, bent to pick it up and suddenly could not stand. He said,

> Anyone who's had a back injury knows what the pain is like. It's terrible. I was totally incapacitated for three weeks, flat on my back, in traction. When I was able to walk it was awful: I had to hobble along, crouched over. Getting out of the car at the office would take me — well, it seemed like half an hour. I was in pain most of the time and would have to lie on the floor in the office . . . Laurie Carmichael was handling the oil industry dispute for the AMWSU. By this time there was a standard pattern about disputes; union officials had done all the originating work, drawn up the log of claims, and they wanted to handle disputes themselves, without interference from the ACTU. That was valid, in terms of the ACTU constitution. But there came a point where we had to say, we *are* going to be involved. This was the first really dramatic case and we had to be quite tough about it, because while some of the other unions — the Ironworkers and the Australasian Society of Engineers, for example — did not object too strongly, Laurie Carmichael felt very paternalistic. This was his baby, and he was not going to have any paternity suits about it. It was *his*. While I've never been able to agree with Carmichael's political philosophy [Communism], Laurie is straight to deal with. You know where you stand with him and if he gives his word he keeps it. He's tough but reliable. One of the problems on the other side was that the oil companies' industrial officers did not have authority to make decisions. There were two elements to this: in the general scheme of things industrial officers are rarely in the limelight. Suddenly, they are, and they have an almost vested interest in seeing the dispute continue. So one wanted to get to the actual bosses of the companies, to make them face up to their responsibilities. This problem is particularly egregious in the oil industry — the companies' priorities are wrong, and they get themselves in knots. And there was another problem: there was a collusive position between the oil companies and the Government. McMahon was threatening to recall Parliament on the issue, and then to go to the people on it. There was a vested interest in trying to precipitate a position of chaos

and suffering for the community, and using guilt-by-association, to blame the ALP and advantage the McMahon Government.

Hawke decided to play his news media card: he appeared on radio, television and in the Press, announcing collusion. Behind the scenes, he was attempting to split the companies, to persuade one to hive off, and bargain. He was in contact with government, the companies, the Arbitration Commission and the various unions, flying interstate frequently, making hundreds of telephone calls each day. Grudgingly, on 19 July, the men returned to work, on the premise that the companies would resume negotiations. The next day, when they discovered the companies were still intransigent, the men went out again. Hawke had been working for twenty-hour stretches. That night, accompanied by Hazel, he was to launch an art exhibition in Melbourne. He rose, said 'I'm relieved to see this is not an opening in oils. I couldn't stand it', spoke for a minute then murmured, 'I can't go on', and collapsed.

The Hawke children were at home watching *Hogan's Heroes* on television when a message flashed on the screen: HAWKE HAS HEART ATTACK. By the time a family friend arrived at the house the telephone was ringing incessantly with calls from journalists wanting to know if Hawke were still alive, a question the children could not answer, because Hazel had been unable to contact them by telephone. She had taken Hawke to a near-by hotel and put him to bed, and later told the Press that Hawke had not had a heart attack, adding, 'It seems to me that not enough people work hard enough in this world to understand what it's like to be so completely exhausted. He's propped himself up for so long — he keeps propping himself up because he's a man of good faith.' Telegrams and telephone calls streamed into the ACTU. Some read:

Sincere wishes speedy recovery from 27 fork-lift drivers Kent Brewery.

Darwin Telegraph Staff very sorry . . . Welcome to recuperate in sunny Darwin.

Seamen's Union, Melbourne, wishes speedy recovery . . . take a rest . . .

Hotel and motel owners in holiday resorts rang urging Hawke to be their guest; other people offered the relaxation of their sauna baths. Charlie Fitzgibbon, who was familiar with Hawke's overwork-collapse syndrome, and his wildness, sent him a card of a man praying, 'Forgive me now . . . Tomorrow I may not be sorry'.[3]

The next day Hawke had recovered, but his doctor insisted that he take a week's rest. He continued to negotiate from home. The dispute was dragging on; there were queues for petrol; TAA and Ansett were progressively limiting their flights. But Hawke was having some success in splitting the companies and by the last week of July announced an ACTU plan whereby the refineries of certain companies would be exempted from strike action so that essential services, at least, could be maintained. The crisis was near: on 26 July McMahon called an emergency Cabinet meeting, which was to decide if Parliament should be recalled — an extraordinary action for this had occurred before only for the abdication of Edward VIII, the Declaration of War against Japan, and the commitment of troops to Korea. If Parliament were recalled it would be to announce a 'law and order' election.

Hawke said,

> Lynch [the Minister for Labour] had been pleading with me to go to talk to him. I told him, Everything that you've done in this dispute has been pro-company. You haven't been in any sense objective about it, all your pronouncements have come from ignorance of the facts — or, if you've got knowledge, of putting knowledge aside. And you've tried to precipitate a situation so bad that you can go to the country on it. Well, you're not going to bash us into submission. So I won't talk to you. Things got grimmer and Lynch contacted me again and said, Let's talk. I said, Sure. And he said, Come to my office. I said, No bloody way in the world. He said, Let's meet in an independent place — a hotel or something. I said, No way, Phil. You want to talk — you come to the ACTU. I was still in a lot of pain with my back and couldn't stand up properly. Well, McMahon had his Cabinet meeting which was going to frighten us all to death, and what did they decide? That Lynch, Nixon [Minister for Shipping] and Greenwood [the Attorney-General] would come to the ACTU. You've never seen such embarrassed people as those three as they walked into the old ACTU building, past the media. But they faced up to it. And we just belted at them that what they were doing was totally unacceptable, and that was the beginning of the end, in the sense that the Government had collapsed. The oil companies were unbelievably apprehensive about a Labor victory, which, as we moved into 1972, became increasingly likely. There is no doubt in my mind that at an early stage there were a lot of discussions between the oil companies and the Government as to whether the two-year agreement between the oil industry unions and the companies could not be used to take on the labour movement, get sympathy, and divert the thrust towards Labor . . . Later John Gorton, with whom I've always got on well, said to me, If I'd still been Prime Minister I would not have allowed my ministers to call on you!

At mass meetings on 3 August workers decided to return to work while Mr Justice Moore, Acting President of the Arbitration Commission, resumed what he had been forced to abandon a month earlier, chairmanship of discussions. By 21 August a settlement had been reached, and the oil industry was peaceful — for another two years.

There were many telegrams of congratulations to Hawke, among them several from people who signed themselves 'usual Liberals'. They indicated that the flow towards a Labor government was gathering pace, but also something else: Hawke himself had some appeal for the middle-ground of Australian politics. Every time he appeared in a television discussion the channel's switchboard would receive a score of calls demanding to know why 'that Communist' had been allowed air-time. But gradually anti-Labor people were beginning to realise that Hawke did not have horns and cloven hooves, that he actually had the good of the community at heart. Newspaper cartoonists began to draw him as a knight in armour. On 18 October the *Australian* ran a full-page feature, headlined HAWKE — THE MAN ON THE WHITE HORSE, and noting 'his towering intellect' said, 'He is, if it is possible, perhaps too big a man for the job [of ACTU President]'. It also described him as 'the X-factor in Australian politics . . . Many people, quite simply, will vote for or against Bob Hawke [in the federal elections].'

In October Hawke began campaigning. He said:

> I travelled all over the country. I enjoy campaigning. It's unbelievably tiring and for me in those days it was more tiring than for the leading pollies, because I had no support staff, so all the mechanical things that aides can do, I had to do for myself. I think I was good at it — because I really do enjoy meeting people and getting involved with them, and I enjoy the inter-reaction with crowds — and I think I got better at it. I got a technique of reading all the newspapers in the morning and would pick out statements around which I could develop the basic themes of the campaign. One of the problems in campaigning is that you've got to repeat the same stuff, over and over. The audiences don't mind, because they're new audiences every day, but *you* get bored and so does the Press . . . I remember at the official opening, Clyde Cameron [later Minister for Labour] and I were driving out together to the Blacktown Town Hall [in Sydney] and we had a discussion about the head of the Department of Labour. Clyde and I were in agreement that the man had exceeded the role of a public servant, and instead of being a detached expositor had adopted the role of advocate when the ACTU had been in discussions with Lynch about the penal clauses. I'd laid down the law and said to the departmental head that if he were going to behave like that, the ACTU would walk out. Clyde had no time for the man; we were in consensus. And I remember the look on Clyde's face: he's got a special smile he wears when he's holding a knife in his hand, and I thought, Well, that's one decision that has already been taken.

The campaign had barely begun when Hawke was contacted by a stranger who told him that he could supply material about the private life of a senior Liberal minister, for whom the man worked, which was of a scandalous nature and could well cost the minister his seat. Hawke said,

> I don't go in for that stuff. So I said, 'Thank you very much, friend. Put it in writing', and I rang the Liberal bloke and told him . . .
>
> The Party arranged that if Gough was in one city, I'd be in another, but there were a few occasions when we appeared on the same platform, and I think we were a great combination, we enjoyed one another with the natural element of competitiveness — I suppose we were watching one another, listening to all the decibel counts. Without any question the most memorable meeting was the last one, in the St Kilda Town Hall [Melbourne] on the Thursday night before *the* night. By that stage the certainty of victory was there, we knew we were the first Labor government after twenty-three years and the crowds — it was just unbelievable — the Town Hall was packed and there were thousands outside. And I remember we'd arrived and were being prepared in one of the ante-rooms, there was Gough and me and Margaret [Whitlam] and Hazel, and the atmosphere was just electric. Then we moved out to go through the corridors and into the hall, and from the corridors — oh, it was deafening. Almost frightening. I remember thinking that there had been these sorts of meeting throughout the campaign, that there was hysteria, and while that was marvellous for one's ego and flow of adrenalin, I had this sense of — oh, I'm unsure of the word — apprehensiveness. You know, the explosiveness of the hysteria. Walking through that is a very strange experience, an enormously moving experience. The next day, the last day, we had a barbecue on the banks of the Yarra, for supporters and campaign workers, and there was a beautiful feeling of relief that it was all over, and that the next day we would win. It was an emotional feeling I'll never forget.

On 2 December 1972 Labor won government by 7 seats, with a swing of 2.6%. Since Whitlam had become Leader of the Labor Party in 1967 he had achieved a total swing of 9.6%. The euphoria among Labor supporters was mind-splitting; they had returned from exile, led by a king. In the trade union movement it was as if the millennium had been announced: everything that was bad would be swept away. And indeed, within days, without waiting for a Cabinet, Whitlam had begun his reforms, performing coup after coup against his stunned opponents. Draft resisters were freed from gaol, troops ordered to withdraw immediately from Vietnam, Australia's Ambassador to the United Nations was instructed to cease his support for South Africa and to vote with the Third World. Schools would be reformed; there would be changes in social welfare and the arts. For fourteen days edicts poured from the Prime Minister's office. But Whitlam had not won the Senate.

Perhaps Ozymandias had such an Upper House.

Later, David Combe, the Federal Secretary of the ALP, said, 'If only Whitlam had listened to Hawke, we would have survived'.

Chapter Fifteen

The years since 1965 had been a banquet for Hawke. There had been plenty of buffeting in public and in private, but the round of his life, once he had focused upon the presidency of the ACTU, had been a succession of delights. His victory in the leadership of the trade union movement, then three years later the shared victory of a Labor government elected to office, had turned Hawke's world into an Olympus in which he was, unarguably, a senior god. 'Next to Whitlam', he said, 'I'd done more than any other member of the Party to have the Government elected'.

Aged forty-three, his early portrait was complete: he had a mane of glossy dark hair, now touched with grey at the temples, his face had filled out, his neck and torso were powerful, his chest a barrel from the years of exercising, in court and on the hustings, the muscles around his lungs. His eyebrows were thick and expressive, the look in his eyes was friendly but sharp. That aura of vitality which had surrounded Hawke since youth had by this time become something more, a furnace blast of energy and a self-conscious awareness of power. He had often a feline expression of secret triumph. In private he frequently dressed in nothing but a pair of shorts; he would swim naked in the pool at home and once scandalised a group of male trade union officials by doing so, then sitting down and chatting to them, still unclothed, while Hazel poured drinks. Room-service hotel waiters became accustomed, over the years, to seeing Hawke without any clothes and journalists to his giving interviews in a swimming costume. In public Hawke dressed with extreme neatness, in off-the-peg suits which verged on flashiness.

When he was drunk, as he was more often now without the pressure of wage cases — he twitched his eyebrows and had a dangerous, slightly demonic look, like an angry cat. He was as lithe as a cat: the gallons of beer he drank had not produced the usual beer-gut, perhaps because his appetite, which had always been small, was diminished by alcohol, and he took plenty of exercise. He could do twenty-five push-ups without puffing and when in high spirits would issue challenges to other boastful men to stretch out on the floor and try to match him. He weighed twelve stone and stood five feet eleven inches, a good two inches of that accounted for by his hair. He was both smaller and stronger-looking than people who had seen him on television expected — 'like a bantam fighting cock', as a journalist exclaimed. Indeed, Hawke was, as ever, ready for a fight. He was a man who had succeeded dramatically, and yet . . . He had not kept all his promises to himself.

His old dream seemed closer by early 1973; it looked like sunlight standing tiptoe on the horizon, just waiting for dawn. It was a false dawn.

In the middle of 1973 Hawke was offered, and seized, another great prize: he became President of the ALP. 'I'd earned it. I was ambitious for it, I cherished it', he said. And so he did: too well, perhaps.

Hawke said, when he took on the second presidency, that he would hold the job for two years. He held it for five, in the teeth of advice from his political supporters who saw the long-term damage he was doing, within the ALP, to his ambitions. Don Dunstan told him, 'If you want to be prime minister, for God's sake give up the Party presidency. It's a millstone round your neck.' Years later, asked if he had made a great mistake in taking on the job, Hawke's instant reply was, 'No. I enjoyed it.'

Within days of his becoming President of the ALP troubles began. They multiplied. In retrospect the whole period from 1966 to 1980 is cleft in equal parts: seven years' feast, seven years' famine, with mid-1973 as the point of separation. At the conclusion of the time span Hawke looked, when tired, an old man. His hair had turned grey and by 1980 was white in parts; his shoulders hunched; he was shorter for he no longer stood straight; his face, which in profile had become a nutcracker, was marked with lines chiselled by pain and alcohol; his lips had disappeared and what had once been an attractive mouth had become a thin line. The expression in his eyes had changed from sharp curiosity to a baleful suspicion and had that suggestion of emotional damage one sees sometimes in the eyes of intelligent and sensitive men who have been through a war. For Hawke, 1973 opened with joyous enthusiasm and closed with a despair which seemed endless.

He had been in office at the ACTU three years when Labor won the election. In that time he had learned some hard lessons about the limits to power.

Among themselves trade union leaders of the Right had discussed a contingency plan if it should happen that Hawke pressed them too far: they would have him sacked. A president of the ACTU can only be sacked for gross misdemeanour, however once a powerful group is determined upon removing an enemy there is always something that it can find and exaggerate wildly: an expense account does not add up, an office car has been misused. Nobody who spends the money of others and who is busy is ever safe. Ducker said with a grin, 'Y'know, if we'd really wanted to . . .' then added, 'Hawkey had a Law degree — he could have become a judge', and gave a broad, whimsical smile. In the event it was unnecessary for Hawke's enemies to do more than play with the idea of deposing him. He respected the position of the Right; he was given freedom to pursue the goals of his campaign platform. At least, in theory.

In practice, the ACTU's lack of money, the under-financing of the trade union movement as a whole and its many rivalries were to make his task almost impossible. The unions wanted Hawke to carry through the reforms he had promised but only if somebody else would pay.

The problem in Australia was that, except for crises, the idea of consistency in the trade union movement was an ideal rather than a reality; the movement was, and is, as various and conflicting in its parts as the nations of Europe. Outside Europe one may speak of 'the Europeans': in Europe, they do not exist — there are only Spaniards and Dutch, Greeks and Germans. The Clerks Union is as different from, say, the Transport Workers as Poles are from Portuguese.

Besides the frequent reminders Hawke had been given during ACTU executive meetings, the 1971 Congress had made him acutely aware of the difficulties of exercising power, of persuading people to pay for what they said they wanted. He had seen the potential danger for a Labor government: like him, it had a broad programme of reforms; like him, it could be handicapped in implementing them.

In September 1972, at an ALP federal executive meeting in Sydney, Hawke and Clyde Cameron argued that during the forthcoming election campaign there should be no promise that a Whitlam Labor government would not increase taxes. For years Hawke had been advocating that tax loopholes must be closed, that the rich must be made to pay their share of taxes. He recalled,

> By that stage [September 1972] we all believed that we were going to win, so what we were talking about was Labor in government. I was casting my mind ahead and I was quite certain that the Whitlam Labor Government would be judged on its handling of the economy, and that it would be a total tragedy if all that happened was that we came to office and were a one-term government, because we would not be able to do things of a lasting nature in one term. I said this at the federal executive meeting, and privately. I can remember almost my exact words: Whatever great social changes and foreign policy changes were made, we would live or die on our handling of the economy, and that I didn't want to see us unnecessarily constricting ourselves by promising no increase in taxation. Because, if we were to be able to achieve the

things we wanted to regarding redistribution of wealth and positive change, and to do that in the least inflationary way, we *needed to have the revenue available*. The tax system in Australia by 1972 represented twenty-odd years of conservatism, and had been structured in a way which the conservatives regarded as appropriate to their philosophy. I didn't object to that, because they'd been democratically elected, so were entitled to do what they wanted — for example, to make, through the child deduction system, kids worth more to a bloke on $50,000 a year than to a poor person. But that did not mean that we should say, 'Oh, just elect us and we won't change the tax structure and make any greater imposts'. I certainly wasn't arguing that we hit the poor — on the contrary — but I was arguing that the wealthy and upper-income groups should not regard themselves as sacrosanct, and be allowed to think that a generation of conservatism in regard to imposts would continue with a Labor government. My view was that the Australian community was ready for change, and that we should be direct with the community, that we should not get into a position of saying, 'Things won't change regarding imposts'.

What I was saying at the executive meeting was very much related to my concern about the economy, because I believed that the signs were already evident that the economic situation was beginning to change, that we weren't in the situation of limitless vistas of expansion that had characterised, or had seemed to characterise, the 1950s and 1960s. And my concern was related to wages: that in this coming period one of the issues would be wage justice and wages policy. For us to be able, as a labour movement, to get a situation of wage earners accepting restraint the *sine qua non* would be a belief on the part of the trade union movement that Australia had an equitable tax structure. In 1972 there was a belief within the Labor Caucus that growth was still continuing. There wasn't a general perception that the bubble had burst. I didn't realise that myself. But there was, by the latter part of 1972, evidence around that things were getting tougher — overseas, inflation was starting to roar ahead. And it was quite clear that the electorate would be much more astringent in its judgment about the economic performance of Labor than it would be about the conservatives. Even if one's perception of the economy was that we would continue to zoom forward, that there would be low inflation, continued full employment, no international problems — whatever the context — I still would have held the view that we must not tie one hand behind our backs by committing ourselves to an *unnecessary* restriction.

Now, throughout the 1972 campaign, while Whitlam did not promise 'We won't raise taxes', the view was projected to the electorate that we would not. The campaign speeches were carefully written to avoid saying, We Will or We Won't. But the electorate got the message: We Won't. And I thought that was wrong.

Labor's policies on taxation were to be the cause of one of the many rows between Whitlam and Hawke.

During 1972 Hawke had irritated Whitlam by suggesting to him that he should study economics. He said,

> My view was that Gough was such an extraordinarily intelligent man, he had a barrister's ability to get on top of a huge mass of material very quickly, that he could acquaint himself with economics in a couple of months. I offered to arrange for him to have private tuition from economists I knew, who would have made themselves available to him at whatever times suited him. But he wasn't interested. He made the point, 'I have economic advisors'. He just would not accept the points I was making: that economics was going to be central, that it is no use having economic advisors if one could not determine the value of their advice, that the man at the top must be involved.

Perhaps the very suggestion was counter-productive. Someone close to both Whitlam and Hawke observed, 'Bob tried to give Gough advice — and that's fatal'. And Egerton, reflecting on the ALP federal executive years from 1971 to 1976, remarked, 'With Whitlam and Hawke it was the old bull trying to keep the young bull out of his paddock'. The rivalry between them was to become intense.

From early on relations between the Whitlam Government and the ACTU, representative of the Government's largest constituent, were strained. Things had started well: the new Minister for Labour, Clyde Cameron, had attended the first ACTU executive meeting to be held after the election and announced that he intended to make changes to the Conciliation and Arbitration Act. But within weeks, a row blew up between Cameron and the ACTU.

The President of the Conciliation and Arbitration Commission, Sir Richard Kirby, had decided to retire. His obvious successor was Mr Justice Moore, a man whom Kirby had groomed for the job for years and who had proved his ability through his handling of scores of wage cases and dispute negotiations. Moore was trusted by the unions and the employers, and was, after Kirby, the most senior member of the Arbitration Bench. Cameron, however, had promised the job to a barrister, John Sweeney, who had devised the legal means which had allowed federal intervention into the Victorian branch of the ALP. There was outrage in the Commission when Cameron's plan became known. Kirby telephoned Hawke requesting him to persuade Whitlam to tell Cameron to reverse his decision. Moore was appointed. Cameron, however, was so angry that, in the words of Harold Souter, 'for a couple of weeks he stopped talking to me. Relations between the ACTU and the Whitlam Government set off on the wrong foot because of the row over Sweeney, and they worsened because of the failure of ALAC [the Australian Labor Advisory Council] to hold meetings.'

ALAC[1] was the meeting ground between the Labor Party and the trade union movement and leading up to the 1972 election it had convened regularly. It was made up of the four parliamentary Labor leaders; four ALP federal executive members; the President, Secretary and two Vice-Presidents of the ACTU. In the pre-election period ALAC meetings had been the critical area for discussions about how union leaders could defuse potential strikes and how they could defuse the McMahon Government's attempts to explode the 'law and order' issue. It was the forum in which, when Labor was in office, wages policy should have been discussed.

Souter continued,

> When Whitlam came to office there was one punctual meeting of ALAC, but successive meetings went astray. Once we waited an hour and a half for Gough to turn up and he only arrived when Bob threatened to walk out. We [the ACTU] wrote a letter of protest about the falling away of ALAC. Gough was apologetic and he called another meeting, turned up, then left after about fifteen minutes. It was hopeless. We *couldn't talk to the Government*, and eventually ALAC just disappeared.* For the ALP and the ACTU the lack of communication was a disaster. We did have contact through Clyde Cameron but he was an old AWU man and he was always set against the ACTU. In his early days as Minister, Clyde would telephone me every Sunday morning and would talk for an hour or more, often not restricting himself to industrial matters, but going on about his political problems. It got to the stage where I dreaded Sunday mornings. So it was a relief when he was in a temper with us, over Sweeney, and left me alone for a fortnight.

When Cameron was embarrassed over the non-appointment of Sweeney to head the Commission, he appointed him, again without prior consultation with the ACTU, to inquire into industrial relations in Australia. That is rather like inquiring into the sanctity of marriage. Both the ACTU and the organised employers were irritated, and suspicious. Souter recalled,

> Clyde introduced a Bill to amend the Arbitration Act in 1973 and we learned of it only when the Bill had its first reading in the House. Clyde's office then sent us a copy. Frankly, we were better off under the Liberals as far as communications were concerned. If they were going to amend the Act they would show us the draft legislation and, while they would

* ALAC was reincarnated on 11 November 1975.

not introduce changes that the ACTU requested, they would not introduce changes of their own if the ACTU raised strong objections. From very early on the ACTU felt a disillusionment with the Whitlam Government. Our relations reached a nadir over the tariffs cut, and a terrible disillusion spread, not only through the ACTU, but through the whole trade union movement.

George Polites recalled,

Clyde was a great hater. It was as simple as that. He hated the AWU hierarchy and, hell and high water, he was determined to get them. So he introduced a lot of amendments to the Act which were designed to hurt the AWU, but they hurt as well a whole range of other unions. We tried to tell him — I tried, Bob tried, Harold tried. Clyde would not listen. He had his own views about everything, he lived in the past, he pursued old scores and maintained retribution against old enemies. He thought that because he was Labour Minister in a Labor government and came from a trade union background he knew everything and nobody had a right to question anything he did. I made a public statement early on that this was 'a know-all government', that it just doesn't want to talk to you, and if that's the way it's to go on it will commit bloody suicide. And it did. Personally I got on with Clyde — he's a most likeable bloke. He would cuddle up to unions whom he thought were politically useful to him — they could see him any hour of the day or night — but everyone else was Out.

By late 1974 wages were running madly out of control; Cameron (and other ministers) appealed to the trade union movement to restrain itself. The Government had not reformed taxation; its policies had created unemployment. The unions co-operated to restrain wages on terms which suited the highest paid: they agreed to indexation of the total wage. This was a formula for the well paid to be even better paid in relation to the less well-paid; for tax to eat up a larger slice of the increase; therefore, an encouragement for tax avoidance. And, of course, for a massive wages bill to employers, for unemployment and, in due course, for falling government revenues as the world and his wife learned the tricks, once the sport of the upper middle class, of tax evasion. At the time it was the best deal Cameron could strike with the trade union movement and the arbitration system, and there is no doubt that indexation was preferable to the hysterical scramble for higher wages that was going on: unions were badgering the Arbitration Commission with ambit claims as high as $1,000 a week. The treatment, however, while bringing the disease to stability, made it chronic. The problem was, and is, not that unionists are wickedly greedy or that arbitration judges are lunatically extravagant but that the Australian wage fixation system, designed in 1907, had become an inappropriate tool of social and economic policy. Hundreds of people — politicians, unionists, employers and the wage arbitrators themselves — will have to agree before it can be reformed, for it is they themselves who make up the system. However, virtually all members of the system choose to believe differently: 'I am a bird, look at my wings', said the bat. 'I am a mouse, look at my coat', said the other bat.

Cameron, in an article which was published in *Labor Essays 1981* and which when read in full richly confirms the opinions of Polites and Souter, blamed Hawke and the ACTU for the chronic wages mess of the late 1970s. He wrote:

> The reforms I made to the Conciliation and Arbitration Act to ensure that elected union officials properly represented their membership . . . were the finishing touches to a struggle I had waged over many years, first as a member, and later as an elected official, of the large and powerful Australian Workers' Union . . . Some union officials opposed my proposition to outlaw the collegiate system of electing executive officers and for making the embezzlement of union funds an offence against the Crimes Act . . . many union officials disagreed with me. But all of these differences were with union officials over issues on which they, not I, were out of touch with the real trade union movement, ie. its rank and file . . . Tom Dougherty [boss of the AWU] spoke for many of his fellow bureaucrats in the AWU when he used to refer to the rank and file as the 'crank and vile'. He and some of his yes-men literally despised their union's membership . . . [When it came to an agreement about wage indexation] I was unaware of Hawke's plan to bring about an amalgamation between the Australian Council of Salaried and Professional Associations (ACSPA) and the ACTU.* ACSPA was committed to full indexation of total wages irrespective of how high those wages might be. Hawke was anxious that the amalgamation between the two large organisations should take effect. And for this to happen the ACTU would have to tailor its wage indexation policy to accommodate ACSPA demands . . . I believe that the record of the ACTU, in respect of wage indexation, will be viewed by historians as one of the most shameful chapters in the whole history of labour relations in this country.[2]

* Cameron's lack of awareness was astonishing. An amalgamation of blue- and white-collar unions had been a major part of Hawke's campaign for the ACTU presidency; it became one of the most debated issues in the trade union movement for years.

Hawke commented,

> It's just a nasty perversion to explain the ACTU wage indexation decision in terms of Hawke's plans about amalgamation with ACSPA. We had fought for years for a two-tiered wage system, and we'd lost: the trade union movement was confronted by the fact that the system had been turned on its head, against us. And we then had to face up to that reality, and also to the reality that our constituency was a very broad one. The ACTU executive debated at length the possible applications to be put to the Commission — for flat increases; for plateaus; for percentages. We decided to argue strongly for protection of the minimum wage, and for the value of tradesmen's incomes to be protected. Cameron suggests that it did not matter at all if tradesmen's wages were allowed to be eroded. That was not the view of the majority of ACTU executive members. It had nothing to do with ACSPA. Our submissions and theirs were entirely separate and we often had sharp disagreements with them. A reading of ACTU submissions shows that we qualified some of our demands for percentage increases.

Whitlam finally sacked Cameron as Minister for Labour and earned his undying enmity. Unions made polite growls in defence of a fellow trade unionist, while sighing with deepest relief. By then relations between the Government and its largest organised constituent, the unions, were in a shambles. Egerton said later, 'If Whitlam had not been sacked he would have had no option but to have taken the unions on. And I tell you, he would have won, and Hawke would have been finished.'

In early 1973 the public became aware that a Labor government and a trade union movement, while in broad agreement upon ends, do not necessarily agree upon means. The issue was French atmospheric testing of nuclear weapons in the Pacific. The Government, Whitlam in particular, wanted the fight against France's behaviour to be conducted through diplomatic and legal channels; the trade union movement, Hawke in particular, wanted to confront France head on, through a campaign of strikes which would isolate metropolitan France from the rest of the world. Whitlam feared that strike action against France's communications would put Australia in breach of international law and jeopardise the Australian case that had been argued by the Attorney-General, Lionel Murphy, in the International Court. He sent Hawke a long, friendly, admonishing telegram saying, in part, 'Having invoked international law against France . . . it would never do if Australia were herself in breach of obligations . . . under international law', and going on to request the strike action against French communications be halted. Already, without consulting the ACTU, many unions had black-banned French aircraft, shipping, goods and communications, and for once the public was in support of a 'political' strike.

Whitlam had first announced Australia's objection to the tests in January 1973; the ACTU had decided six months earlier to ban French vessels and aircraft, including a planned flight by the new high-speed aeroplane, the Concorde. Public outrage had been gathering. Since the 1960s, when France had begun atmospheric testing in the Pacific, ACTU Congresses had called for strike action against France, but in those days the electorate would not tolerate the trade unions assuming a role that was considered properly to be government's. But in Hawke's time as President his repeated challenge, 'Anything that affects our people — and in we go!' had won, at least in this case, public acceptance. Telegrams and letters poured into the ACTU from June 1972. Some read:

Keep it up, and, as soon as possible, Hawke for Prime Minister!

You are clearly the only one that Australia has with enough guts and determination to . . . stop the French.

Please stop the French.

Australia needs you.

Our Government [McMahon's] has been gutless. You must act. (signed) Staunch Liberal.

And one:
You are destroying the Labor Party because you want to run this country. (signed) Labor Supporter.

By May 1973 concerned citizens were producing pamphlets which said:

Do you WANT
To have deformed children!
To have leukemia!
To be sterile!
To have cancer!
To risk destroying the earth!

In February 1973 Hawke held talks in Geneva with the International Confederation of Free Trade Unions (ICFTU) about the possibility of international action against the French. The ICFTU represents ninety-two million trade unionists, all from non-Communist countries. Its Secretary was Otto Kersten of West Germany, who had been a senior official in the DGB, the Deutscher Gewerkschaftsbund, the largest free trade union organisation in the world. When the DGB speaks the governments of Western Europe listen.

Hawke and Kersten were friends. Kersten told Hawke that the Finance and General Purposes Committee, the highest executive organ (after the Executive Board, which appoints it) of the ICFTU would be meeting in Mexico in late April. He suggested that if, by April, the French still seemed determined, Hawke could approach the ICFTU hierarchy in Mexico — although the French tests were, superficially at least, of no concern to the majority of ICFTU members, since radioactive particles would not fall on *them*.

By 21 April Murphy's mission to the International Court had, in effect, failed for the French announced that they did not recognise the authority of the Court. Hawke talked to Whitlam, but they were unable to reach agreement upon the proper role of the trade unions. He said to the Prime Minister, 'We [the unions] are not tools of government. And the obverse is true.' The Australian trade union movement planned to boycott French cargoes, planes, ships and communications. By itself, such action would be futile: France could hardly be bullied into changing her defence programme because of loss of Australian trade and communications. Hawke, however, had devised a grand strategy, an action unique in the history of the trade union movement, not just in Australia, but in the world: through the ICFTU he planned to involve the workers of the world in action against France. He flew to Cuernavaca:

> I'd been inundated with requests from people to do something, and had had a lot of heart-rending letters from people saying they'd lost contact with their families in France and less heart-rending ones from people complaining that their goods from France were being held up on the wharves and requesting that they be released. It's a problem that always arises — somebody gets hurt. You know, they've bought a Citroen and can't see that waiting for the Citroen might be less important than saving somebody's life. But, overwhelmingly, the public wanted action. A number of scientists had approached me, blokes from Melbourne University and elsewhere, and had offered to tutor me in the scientific and biological questions, so by the time I left for Mexico I had the scientific evidence about dangers to the living and the unborn, and the technical terms pretty well in my head. I've got a limited capacity with science, but I'd been able to master the ideas. The structure of my argument in Mexico was this: the tests were dangerous; it was futile to say, as the French were, that there was no danger, because if this were so why weren't they testing in France? From that base, I went on to argue for international trade union solidarity and demanded that we be given support. It was well received; there was no opposition. But some of the Europeans pointed out that there were legal constraints upon action of the type we talked about. Then others said that, in addition to the ICFTU, we should get the ITS [the International Trade Secretariats] to make their own decisions to join: for example, the International Trans-

port Workers' Federation, the International Metal Workers' Federation, the International Postal and Telecommunications Union. And the ICFTU decided to contact the ITS and ask them formally to support the decision. And that happened. The ICFTU resolved 'to make preparations to take full and appropriate action against French interests throughout the world' to try to stop the tests. Then, I went to Geneva, to the International Labour Organisation. And there was a tremendous response in the ILO.

The International Labour Organisation was established in 1919 as an autonomous institution associated with the League of Nations, its original constitution having been adopted as Part XIII of the Treaty of Versailles. With certain amendments this constitution remains the charter of the ILO today, bringing governments, employers and trade unions together to discuss international labour and social problems. A new declaration of the aims and purposes of the ILO, known as the Declaration of Philadelphia, was added to the constitution at the 1944 session of the International Labour Conference (the ILO's annual meeting) and this asserted the responsibility of the ILO to combat poverty and insecurity. In 1946 the ILO became the first of the specialised agencies of the United Nations Organisation. Over the years the ILO has built up an immense list of recommendations and resolutions about the treatment of workers which its members are required to observe within their own countries. However, unlike the UN, it has no army so it cannot enforce obedience, but it can publicly humiliate disobedient members. If a government withdraws, its workers and employers need not withdraw, for the ILO's unique tripartite structure gives equal authority to each part of a national delegation, that is, the government, the employers, and the workers. If a government wants to re-join the organisation it must promise to observe the rules before it will be re-admitted. Not to belong to the ILO or to be condemned by it is to declare oneself before the international community to be uncivilised and to weaken one's potential for bargaining and lobbying in the United Nations and its other agencies, for example, the World Health Organisation. The game at the ILO is national pride and avoiding injuries to it. Trade union leaders who cannot, in their own countries, criticise their governments for fear of harassment, can do so in the ILO. The Workers' Group, of which Hawke had been a member since he became President of the ACTU, is the cutting edge of ILO debate.

Of its very nature, the ILO is volatile and highly political. The people who run it, the members of the secretariat, must be politicians, diplomats and administrators — skills which are reflected in their wages: currently the Director-General's salary plus allowances is approximately $90,000, after tax. The ILO was founded by white Christians and its rules were inspired by Judeo-Christian ethics; the feasibility of persuading the rest of the world to abide by those ethics and the laws they have formulated is problematic.

When the USSR was expelled from the League of Nations in 1939 it ceased to attend the ILO, but on Stalin's death in 1953 the USSR applied for re-admission, which was granted the following year. Then in 1970 the ILO Director-General, David Morse, decided that it was unrealistic to be without a Communist in the secretariat. He appointed a Soviet diplomat as an Assistant Director-General. Morse's action, just before his retirement, precipitated for his successor, Wilfred Jenks, what became known as 'The Crisis of 1970'.

Like some other international organisations, the ILO is heavily dependent upon the USA for finance. It was unfortunate, therefore, that George Meany, the boss of American labour and a man noted for his fanatical anti-Communism, had flown into a rage over the appointment of a Russian — for Meany had much influence with the US State Department. The American Government drastically cut its financial contributions to the organisation. Hundreds of employees had to be sacked; much of its research work curtailed or abandoned.

Hawke, in 1970, was attending the ILO as a workers' delegate for the first time. The Organisation's legal advisor, Francis Wolf, said, 'Bob took a systematically courageous line in defending the Director-General and in working behind the scenes to soften the anger of the USA. He helped to overcome The Crisis of 1970.' It was particularly difficult for Hawke to work behind the scenes, for George Meany, who was instructing the American workers' delegation, was still convinced that the new President of the ACTU was no better than a Communist. A further problem was Hawke's style — especially for Meany, a devout, moralistic Roman Catholic, whose prejudices were all confirmed by Hawke's swearing, boozing and womanising. There are many cocktail parties for ILO delegates and these were potentially disastrous occasions for the wild colonial boy in those days. Australian diplomats posted in Geneva have anecdotes about muscling a roaring drunk Hawke outside and into a limousine. The story ran like fire that, on being introduced to the Director-General of the ILO, whom others addressed as Mr Jenks, Hawke had said, 'G'day, Wilf', and later in the evening had caused his host, an ambassador, to turn pale, by saying 'That's bullshit, Wilf! And you ought to know it!' The Europeans considered his accent outlandish, while some of the more formal ones, especially the French — and nobody is quite as formal as the genuine French mandarin — referred to him as 'the barbarian'.

However, even the most formal acknowledged, 'He was something extra-ordinary'. In the words of Francis Wolf, 'One was struck by his energy, frankness, dynamic approach, his quick understanding and spontaneous friendliness. He was one of the highest elements, intellectually. And then we saw he had courage.' For his defence of the Director-General, Hawke had won respect and gratitude in the secretariat. The following year he won the admiration and affection of the African delegates for his efforts in Australia to prevent the Springbok tour. Hawke's status with the black African delegations — not only of workers, but of governments and employers — was to be important in later ILO dramas. By 1973 he was an identity in the ILO, still a newcomer, but a man who had aroused the interest of those who had met him. However he had not yet addressed the Conference, where governments, employers and workers all attend, and it was only in the Workers' Group that he was well known.

The International Labour Conference is held annually, in the Palais des Nations on the shores of Lake Geneva. Bold hearts had constructed the Palais des Nations as the meeting place for men whose discussions would save the world. However, the imagination and humanistic optimism of those who founded the League of Nations and had the Palais built somehow escaped its architects. It is a huge, austere building, entirely lacking in charm, the cream and green marble columns of its halls soaring thirty feet to unadorned ceilings. There are some vast, ugly murals of 'Mankind', executed in Socialist Realist style. On a clear day you can stand on the terrace and look across the lake to Mt Blanc, curved like a giant meringue, riding in the sky. The main conference hall seats 2,000; architecturally chilling as it is, its sheer austerity is awe-inspiring.

The most daunting of those who regularly spoke in the conference hall of the Palais des Nations was a Frenchman, Alexandre Parodi, leader of the French Government delegation. Parodi was a septuagenarian by 1973, and a hero. He had been a leader of the French resistance during World War II; when Germany surrendered, France had been handed to Parodi, who became president of the transitional government until de Gaulle could arrive back from exile. Parodi had been close to de Gaulle, who made him Minister for Labour. He had presided over the ILO at its first post-war session in 1945, and was a man of intimidating formality and dignity. At casual weekend gatherings, when others wore sports clothes, Monsieur Parodi dressed in a dark suit and tie. Respect for him was such that nobody in the ILO could remember an occasion when someone had publicly argued with Parodi. Then in 1973, to the thrilled disbelief of the delegates, Hawke leapt to his feet and accused Parodi of hypocrisy in the matter of the French nuclear tests. Hawke did not use that word, his language was suitably tactful, but he conveyed his meaning clearly.

A Spanish delegate, Jose Aguiriano, recalled,

> It was electric. Nobody had ever spoken like that to M. Parodi. People were stunned . . . Hawke was the soul, the engine and the spirit of the international trade union action against the French tests. The French had been using delaying tactics, so that the nuclear testing issue could not be raised in Conference. But Hawke brought on this very high-level controversy.

For several minutes there were sharp exchanges between Hawke and Parodi. Then, as Hawke had already arranged, when the French Minister for Labour rose to speak, two hundred workers, with a noisy shuffling of papers and stamping of feet but not a word said, walked out.

Aguiriano, who was a director of the Geneva office of the ICFTU, said, 'It was the first time ever that a world trade union boycott had been planned. Our boycott failed, because the French exploded their bombs. But for the first time the trade union movement had brought to public awareness, particularly in France, the danger of nuclear testing. And that was all Hawke.'

On 21 July 1973 the French exploded a nuclear device, a second on 29 July and a third on 19 August. On 31 August the French Minister for Defence hinted that future tests would be underground. They were. Two senior French officials — one from the Quai d'Orsay, another the French Consul in Noumea — later told Hawke that the world trade union reaction had accelerated the change in French policy.

Meanwhile Parodi and Hawke, predictably, had become friends. Hawke said, 'I had a great affection for the old bloke. He was a most elegant opponent and we came to respect each other and to have a very very warm friendship.' Parodi, who had referred icily to Hawke in 1973 as 'an interesting man', was soon afterwards calling him, 'my most honourable opponent'. An ILO bureaucrat remarked, 'The French stopped saying, "Monsieur Awk is a barbarian". They said, "Well, he is a strange fellow, but he is a brave fellow".'

Hawke loved attending the ILO. He is strongly attracted to the cosmopolitan and the ILO provided a market-place for ideas. In later years he loved, too, the anonymity he had in the streets of Geneva and would say, 'It's a beautiful feeling to be able to go into a shop or a restaurant and not have people staring at you'. In 1972 Hawke had been appointed to the Governing Body of the ILO and had to go to Geneva three times a year for meetings.

He also had to attend regional meetings of international union organisations and he travelled interstate frequently, often at short notice. He was absent from the ACTU office for a total of six months each year. In early 1973 the executive complained that the President's office was running poorly. One man, Geoff Gleghorn, had been doing the job of two people, working as the ACTU Press officer and as Hawke's personal assistant. The Press office work in itself was nightmarish because Hawke's policy of being available to the news media at all times meant that 'every journalist in Australia knew his private phone number' and Hawke would make statements or give interviews whenever requested, without first checking what other arrangements might have been made. Gleghorn had put in his resignation; the executive decided that two people would be needed to replace him — another journalist and somebody to be personal assistant to Hawke and Souter. The new Press officer was Graham Hardy, a young man who had worked on country newspapers. The personal assistant chosen was Jean Sinclair.

Sinclair was as exotic an employee for the ACTU as Hawke had been himself. She was English-born, the eldest daughter of a comfortable Melbourne family, had attended Merton Hall, one of Australia's best private girls' schools, had an economics degree from Melbourne University and was a director of her family company. She had earlier worked for an investment counsellor, Jim Cowan, analysing the stock market for investors, and later in Australia and the USA, for Rod Carnegie of McKinsey & Co. Her manner is that of a woman not to be trifled with: firm, pleasant, well organised and very quick witted. She and Hawke came to dote upon each other. When Sinclair was on leave Hawke would complain constantly, 'Where's Jean? Where are things? I don't know where anything is. We'll have to wait for Jeanie.' Sinclair became a sort of devil's advocate, scolding him roundly, for example, for appearing on television drunk or giving ill-prepared Press interviews. She would sometimes emerge from his office with her lips pursed, saying, 'We have had words'.

Everyone who has ever been close to Hawke has felt the necessity to give him advice or to criticise him — Hazel said, 'All Bob's life people have been telling him what to do'. It is as if the 'constant teaching' of his childhood has made Hawke an eternal pupil, and yet one who is selectively stubborn. At times, Hawke is deaf; at others, as impressionable as a boy. Since he will not reveal the details of his inner thoughts and what system they follow, even his closest friends do not know in advance how he will react to advice.

Souter interviewed Sinclair for the job, which had appeared as 'a tiny advertisement in the *Age*, saying, Assistant to President and Secretary of the ACTU'. At one point Hawke came in and asked, 'Do you know anything about trade unions?' Sinclair replied, 'No'.

> I thought that would be the end of my chances. I'd given them in writing the details of my background, thinking, They'll accept that or they won't. During the interview Harold had not explained what I was meant to do, so I asked the President, 'What is the job?' And he said, 'Well, I'm away half the year, so you're sort of to look after things'. I didn't see him for the next six weeks ... A couple of days later I reported for work. Harold took me to a room where there was a Clifton Pugh painting of a naked woman on the wall. He waved at the picture and said, 'Don't worry about that, we'll have it removed'. Then he left. What I found was incredible! It was beyond description. There were boxes all over the floor, papers and letters piled up, files which had no indexes and when I opened them there might be inside a letter and a shorthand book with two pages of notes, or just an unused shorthand book. Mail was arriving for the President literally by the bagful each day and there was no system for filing it, or answering it ... There was no airmail paper; the secretaries had typewriters with different type-faces, so that it was impossible to divide, for example, the typing of a report between them. The telephone system, which was new, was useless — I couldn't switch a call through to the President's office.

About 5,000 people knew the President's private phone number, and would ring him direct, so if he were away I'd have to run into his office to answer the phone and half the time it would be some racing friend who had a hot tip, or someone who had met Bob at a party last Thursday and wanted help from him . . . In McKinsey all senior staff were Masters of Business Administration. There were office managers. Efficiency ruled, naturally, because the motive was profit. The ACTU was not stimulated by the profit motive, so nobody had given any thought to efficiency. To get airmail paper, and save on the postage bills, an official request had to be written to Harold. The Secretary of the ACTU was in charge of the stationery! And he had a separate filing system; in seven years I never did discover what was in it. Letters from unions about disputes would arrive and I'd file them, then weeks later discover that the rest of the correspondence was in Harold's files. If we'd had four or five more secretaries we might have been able to answer the correspondence which arrived each day.

There was an incident, very early on, which on reflection, best illustrated what working for Bob was like. He had to address a lawyers' dinner in Geelong, something which Peter Redlich [a President of the Victorian branch of the ALP] had arranged. I looked at the invitation in the morning and noticed that the dinner was black-tie. There was going to be no time for Bob to go home and change, so I said, 'Shall I send a taxi to Sandringham to collect your dress clothes?' I was rather taken aback when he said, 'I haven't got any'. He frowned and added, 'I'll look a bit funny — can you fix that up?' I presumed he meant would I hire him a dinner suit. So at lunch-time I went to a bridal wear shop and picked out a jacket, trousers, shirt, studs and so forth. Bob is an odd size — his chest is much larger than normal for his height. I had a guess at what might fit, thinking that he could try it all on in the afternoon, and I'd have time to change it before the evening. I was young and foolish in those days. Some union discussions went over time, then without warning Bob decided to hold a Press conference, so by the time that was over it was past 5 o'clock and too late to change the clothes. Peter Redlich arrived looking magnificent; Bob saw him and said, 'Gee, you look great! Where are my clothes?' and went off to have a shower. [Hawke's new office, above Bourkes, had a private bathroom.] He reappeared in the trousers, which fitted perfectly and the shirt, which fitted perfectly, and said to me, 'Tie the tie thing, will you?' So I did, then he put on the jacket, and it was extraordinary — the whole outfit could have been made-to-measure. He said to Peter Redlich, 'Now I'm as pretty as you', and off they went. The next morning I said to him, 'Weren't you surprised about the dinner suit?' He said, 'No'. I said, 'Well, I picked it out without any idea about the sizes, and it all fitted — weren't you surprised?' Bob stared at me for a minute, then replied, 'I asked you to fix it, and you fixed it. Why should I be surprised?' . . . It was all like that. You were expected to *know* intuitively what to do. And somehow it worked.

Sinclair became Hawke's fourth arm, in constant battle with what she called 'Bob's third arm — the telephone'. When he was abroad once she had his private number changed, and gave the new number out to

about thirty people with whom he needed to be in contact. But within a month he had given the new number to most of the Australian population, not to mention people overseas, and I realised it was no use arguing: when he needed to have a conference in his room, uninterrupted, I would simply unplug the phone. But it was marvellous fun. I'd set out for work in the morning wondering, what crisis will we have today? A lot of the time we used to get through on laughter.

Hawke returned from the ILO drama about French nuclear tests and had to leave within days for the ALP biennial Conference, which was being held at Surfers Paradise. Just before he left for Queensland he met George Seelaf, who said, 'Don't you take on the presidency of the ALP. The trade union movement has no class conflict, but the ALP does. It's a two-class party. You'll have nothing but conflict if you become President of the Labor Party.' Seelaf parted from Hawke in the belief that he had taken this advice.

There was already some underlying strain in the relationship between the Government and the trade union movement, but the Conference heard none of this. It was the happiest ALP Conference anyone could remember, rather too happy for some, who expressed their joy at Labor's return from exile by celebrating in the Pink Elephant Bar. Part of the get-together was a crying-and-singing Irish wake for Arthur Calwell, who had died while the meeting was in progress. Ministers gave speeches about their magnificent achievements during a mere few months in office, and the wonders that were to come. There was altogether too much sunshine, too much thirst-quenching, too many loud shirts and too many ringing hurrahs. 'We were like kids let loose in the lolly shop', John Ducker said.

Hawke was giddy with euphoria over his election there, unopposed, as President of the Party. Sinclair, who had barely seen him since she had begun working for him, recalled the mood when Hawke returned from Surfers Paradise and came into the ACTU office with Hazel. 'They were on a cloud. They were drinking champagne in Bob's office and telephoning people, calling everyone darling. Hazel was laughing, Bob was laughing. They phoned darling Jack Egerton and darling this and darling that.' Ellie, having heard the news, exclaimed, 'The prophecy of Isaiah has been fulfilled!'

Hawke saw his job as President of the ALP as a powerful symbol to the trade union movement of bonding between it and the Whitlam Government.

In a radio interview he said, 'I was prompted to accept the post by the untidiness of relations between the political members of the socialist movement and the trade union movement ... Lack of communication, gaps, helped defeat the Wilson Government in the UK. I want to bridge those gaps.'

This desire to bridge the gaps, to reconcile opposites, has been a major shaping force throughout Hawke's life: hymn-singer and boozer; family man and philanderer; mate of the manual worker and the millionaire. Sinning saint. But in view of Hawke's longer-term ambition — to be prime minister himself — it is difficult not to agree with George Polites: that taking on, while President of the ACTU, the presidency of the ALP, was 'Bob's greatest mistake. He attempted to straddle two things which simply could not be straddled.'

Within days it became obvious just how difficult life was going to be for him. One morning a couple of weeks after his triumphal return from Queensland, Sinclair entered Hawke's office to find him glaring. He roared at her, 'Get me fucking Whitlam!' Without any warning to the President of the ACTU, Whitlam had announced a 25% tariff cut, which would, the Prime Minister asserted, combat the inflation which had been troubling the Australian economy since the days of the McMahon Government. Hawke was outraged: as he knew, the tariff cuts would cause unemployment. He suspected, too, that they would not reduce inflation. He and Whitlam had a heated discussion on the telephone.

That afternoon Hawke, wearing both presidential hats at once, released a tortured Press statement: '. . . any unemployment effects of the tariff cut will be offset by such factors as the upsurge in consumer demand and export demand, increased government expenditure, the existence of unused tariff and the fact that there is ample room to squeeze the profit-competing producers in Australia'.[3] Of course, a good barrister can assemble arguments to justify anything. But Hawke, while he could produce a defence of the Government's action, could not conceal his bad conscience in arguing for something in which he did not believe. The *Bulletin* reported: 'Hawke was nervous, made simple mistakes and gave the impression of somebody trying to sell an unroadworthy used car'.[4] He admitted to the news conference that he had been 'stunned' by Whitlam's announcement. He added that he had spoken to the Prime Minister who had promised him that anyone put out of work would not be obliged to seek alternative employment at a lower rate. This undertaking in due course was to cause further trouble.

When importers and retailers learned of the tariff cuts they immediately telexed and telephoned exporters and manufacturers in South East Asia and South America, bought cheap and sold dear in Australia. So prices did not fall; Australian manufacturers went broke; their employees were sacked; there was anguish in the trade union movement and much merriment among those over whom the Government had inadvertently poured gold. By 1 August Hawke, again wearing both presidential hats at once, was warning that importers and retailers who did not pass on the tariff cuts to consumers would face industrial action. Meanwhile, an income-maintenance scheme of $25 million had been hastily devised for those who would suffer on account of the tariff cuts. The Government decided that people thrown out of work would be paid at their rate of average weekly earnings. But these were swollen with overtime money, so, unemployed, they earned more than others whose jobs had been saved but who had lost the potential for overtime earnings. Result: the employed resented both their unemployed former workmates and the Government. The unemployed resented the Government. Manufacturers resented the Government. Trade union officials were furious with Hawke for publicly defending the tariff cuts.

And there was more disillusion about 'their' government in store for the trade union movement. The August Budget increased indirect taxes, which hurt the poor, but not direct taxes, which affect the rich. Hawke wore his ACTU hat and publicly condemned the Budget. Result: anger in the Caucus and hilarity in the Opposition parties, the news media and among other wicked people who had a sense of humour. Meanwhile, row number three between the Hawke-union camp and the Whitlam-Caucus camp was brewing. The ACTU executive had asked the Government to take the measure which would have made the tariff cuts work. It had requested that the Government gain power, through a referendum, to control prices. But the Caucus, without consulting the ACTU or discussing the matter in ALAC (which by now was dead anyway, except in name), decided to hold two referenda: one to gain control of prices and one to gain control of incomes. In the trade union movement control of incomes has one meaning: a wage freeze. If the Government had set out to insult and unnerve its largest single constituent it could hardly have done a better job. The ACTU executive decided to campaign against the income referendum, so again the nation was treated to the ironic spectacle of the President of the ALP opposing the policy of the ALP Government. Campaigning went on over several months and in December 1973 the electorate overwhelmingly rejected both referenda. By then relations between Whitlam and Hawke were at their nadir.

The trade union movement never forgave Whitlam for the tariff cuts and Hawke and others on the ACTU executive had to argue vehemently soon afterwards to secure an invitation for the Labor Prime Minister to address the Congress that year.

Meanwhile, Hawke's second presidential hat had caused other problems. It had increased his workload but he had not been given extra staff with which to cope with the extra responsibilities. There were more demands from the news media for interviews; more requests for Hawke to be a guest speaker; more letters from a public already used to treating Hawke as national ombudsman; more lobbying from business and other groups; more meetings to chair, more travelling. More worries. More attacks to field, for Hawke's wearing of the two hats was disliked not only within the ALP

Caucus, but also within the trade union movement. Sinclair said,

> At first there was euphoria. Then this began to change to frenzy. Things became more and more frenzied. It was as if a car had been parked on a hill and the brakes had gone — it began running downhill, slowly at first, then faster and faster . . . We didn't even have the paper for Bob to answer letters to him as ALP President. I had to demand ALP stationery from the federal secretariat, in the end. I was paid by the ACTU, so I could not do ALP work in ACTU time. I would do it after hours, and think of it as a donation to the Party. You could criticise the way Bob chose to play the role of ALP President, that he was very high-profile, but you couldn't criticise him for being half the time in a blur. The work load was intolerable.

Within weeks of the row over the Budget, the 1973 ACTU Congress opened, on Monday 3 September in Sydney. Just beforehand the Communist Party ran a banner headline in its weekly *Tribune* asking, 'Can Hawke's Wings Be Clipped?', for now the rupture between Hawke and his erstwhile far-Left supporters was out in the open. After fifteen years of accusations about being a Communist or a crypto-Communist, and all the weary mischief that had caused, he was at last free of that particular problem. But he faced a new one because the extreme-Left of the union movement and the extreme-Right had formed an alliance against him: smiling hard and, no doubt, holding their ideological noses, the Clerks and the AMWSU hopped into bed together. The 1973 Congress was to see another major challenge to Hawke's personal position in the ACTU.

Things could have been worse for him if the alliance had been more disciplined, but the strength of the extreme-Left was undermined by external events. Within Communist ranks there had been fraternal strife waged quietly, for more than a decade, when in 1972 China had emerged from its long period of weakness to re-issue that challenge to Moscow which dates back to Ghengis Khan. Australian Communists reacted immediately and, at the ACTU Congress of 1973, the supporters of the Middle Kingdom and those of Mother Russia fell to spirited fighting with each other. The result was that Pat Clancy, a Moscow-line Communist, was deposed from his ACTU executive seat by a Mao sympathiser, Norm Gallagher. Gallagher's first act was to refuse to attend the traditional dinner of welcome for new executive members.

Thanks in part to the disarray and misalliances among Hawke's enemies at the Congress, he won handsomely on the personal issue of the ACTU economic enterprises. However, he lost disastrously on the personal issue of an executive vice-president for the ACTU.

Hawke had barely managed to convince his faction on the executive that such a position should be created and that Charlie Fitzgibbon was the man to fill it. He saw a Fitzgibbon vice-presidency as having two functions: to bring administrative order to the chaos of the ACTU office; publicly to promote Fitzgibbon as the next President. He said,

> Charlie was the man who would stand up to me and argue. It was, well, easy for me to establish dominance over a lot of people and I valued Charlie's refusal just to go along with my ideas. And he was immensely capable. My concern was for the good of the ACTU, at the time and in the future.

Fitzgibbon commented,

> I thought it would be good for the ACTU: Bob has no application for administration. And Harold Souter is not a good administrator — although he is almost incomparable in certain areas: dealing with government employment; knowledge of the various Acts; negotiations. I thought I'd end up with a good relationship with Harold. I'd have taken over the pure administrative work and would have provided a link to industrial areas where we could have taken a tougher line — for example, in campaigns and demarcation disputes. Bob would have had more time for the publicity functions . . . All the signs were there that he would eventually want to move from the ACTU to Parliament, but that was not something he and I discussed in relation to the vice-presidential idea. He didn't need to talk openly about Parliament: it was obvious. There was a wide spectrum of trade union movement people who didn't realise that Bob had a desire to enter the parliamentary arena. My colleagues weren't very perceptive.

With Fitzgibbon established as dauphin, Hawke would have been able to abdicate from the ACTU with a minimum of fuss, at a time of his own choosing.

It was not to be.

There was no question that the trade union movement could bear another Left-Right brawl for the presidency like that of 1967-69, so Hawke's failure to secure the succession for Fitzgibbon meant that he would be unable to leave the ACTU for years.

That things turned out this way was in part Hawke's fault, for he failed to try to persuade. Pat Clancy of the Building Workers' Industrial Union, one of Hawke's champions throughout the presidency campaign and later, on the executive, said, 'Bob began to show a lack of understanding for the trade union movement. Increasingly, his approach was a top-level one.' Clancy is a classic-style trade union leader, and is a man of impressive personal dignity and decency. By 1981, when this interview with Clancy took place, he had come to feel betrayed by Hawke, because of Hawke's support for what

Clancy termed, 'that rapacious, bandit government of Israel'. He talked with regret rather than bitterness:

> Bob seemed to have developed a concept that if he proposed something, it would be instantly clear to everyone that what he was saying was quite right. And if there were misunderstanding, and debate revealed that misunderstanding and opposition, in reply he would clear it all up. He's a brilliant debater and certainly a brilliant replier to a debate. In the tactics of the trade union atmosphere, if you can give a good, powerful reply you've got a lot on your side, especially if you hold the position of leader. I think that Bob became deceived by this, thinking that he was all-powerful.

By 1973 Hawke was already severely over-stretched and it was years since he had known solitude or contemplation. He had no time to reflect, no time to consider problems. He was becoming a human pressure-pack: push the button, and Hawke would give a statement or rush into action. Everyone who worked in the ACTU knew what a maelstrom it was.

A few weeks before the Congress, Hawke had his inspiration about Fitzgibbon, who recalled, 'I was unwilling, but Bob got me at a weak moment. We sat down over a bottle of Greek brandy — I had the most terrible hangover next day — and at some stage during the night I agreed that I'd do it. I did not want to move from Sydney, I knew my wife would be unhappy, but . . . well, Bob talked me into it.' Hawke then went into an ACTU executive meeting, rode down opposition — Souter, for one, was sharply against the proposal — and secured from the executive a recommendation to the Congress that Fitzgibbon be elected. Union officials heard of the plan only days before Congress opened. Grumbling began immediately. Hawke had been high-handed, in the opinion of executive members, and they passed on this view to other union leaders. There were also objections to Fitzgibbon himself — industrial and personal. Fitzgibbon has an acute intelligence and a cold manner, and says of himself, 'I can be a very rude man'. Many had felt the lash of Fitzgibbon's sarcasm over the years, and resented him. There was, too, envy of his ability. And complicating everything there was a network of industrial grudges. Fitzgibbon was a moderate. More than a decade earlier he had won the leadership of the Waterside Workers' Federation, once one of the biggest unions in the country, from a Communist. Some of the big Right-wing unions had supported Fitzgibbon's campaign to become Federal Secretary of the WWF, and when he had been travelling around the country to gather votes, at certain places AWU employees, for example, would be waiting to meet him, ready with a car to drive him about. Edgar Williams, the National President of the AWU said, 'We felt, after he was elected, that Charlie didn't show the gratitude that he might have for the fraternal help we gave him'. Fitzgibbon had become the leader of the waterside workers in 1962, during a period of rapid technological change on the waterfront, an upheaval which, in 1982, is still working itself out. The introduction of mechanisation for bulk-loading had been diminishing waterfront work since the 1940s; the trend increased in the 1950s and by the 1960s the WWF was faced with a disastrous novelty: containerisation. Unions, like businesses, thrive or decay according to their adaptability to new products and new processes. Containerisation had fearsome effects upon the WWF: overnight it wiped out the jobs of thousands of wharfies. Before the war there had been 80,000 members of the WWF; by 1956, 27,000. By 1973, five years after the introduction of containers, there were officially 16,000, although other union leaders put the figure at 12,000. Fitzgibbon had adapted the Federation to this dramatic assault upon it: the WWF was very lean, but very tough. He had won for his shrunken membership excellent rates of pay, and job security — something which had not existed in the old days, when wharf labourers had been treated like cattle for auction and overseers would pinch men's biceps before saying, 'OK. You', and giving a day's work. Fitzgibbon stayed on the alert for recruits to the WWF and the union's award made his invitations enticing. Edgar Williams said,

Charlie was not the *beau ideal* of everybody at the 1973 Congress. He had just gone through an exercise of accepting a reduction in the WWF workforce all round Australia and a helluva lot of his people were getting the golden handshake. The membership was right down. Now, in Western Australia, we [the AWU] used to have all the northern ports. And Charlie tried to thieve them off us. When he couldn't do it, he got Clyde Cameron, the Minister for Labour, to refuse to pay the AWU members appearance money. But if they became WWF members, Cameron would have their appearance money paid. So, in their own interests, we had to let them go. Then, on top of that, Charlie commenced his drive to take members not just from the AWU all around the ports in Australia, but to body snatch from every other union he could. He took 160 off his mates in Melbourne. Even the AMWSU. He hooked in and took their members. So, he wasn't exactly a pin-up boy with everybody, he was unpopular even with his so-called friends. And he got knocked over.

When the issue of Fitzgibbon's vice-presidency came before Congress on its second day, Souter spoke strongly against it and was joined in his opposition by the Left's best orator, John Halfpenny of the AMWSU. Hawke, whom observers noticed had been on edge throughout his opening address to Congress, intervened in the debate and 'seemed uncharacteristically nervous'. In response to charges of undue haste about the proposal, Hawke snapped at the 700-odd delegates: 'Aren't you sufficiently mature and intelligent and in touch with your members to make up your minds?' They voted 432 to 352 against him.

On the final day of the Congress, however, Hawke had his victory. The ACTU enterprises were at stake. Throughout 1973 Hawke had made frequent announcements about planned joint-ventures: cheap housing, a holiday village, an insurance company. There had been immense publicity. The enterprises were glamorous in a period when glamour was more than usually attractive, and they seemed to be just around the corner. However, the far-Left had turned sour on the idea of enterprises; the far-Right had never liked it. Fortunately for Hawke the moderate Right and Left were still enthusiastic. On Friday morning he reported to Congress about the progress of the enterprises. He was confident, but low-key. The numbers men had done their work and despite the alliance of far-Left and far-Right, Hawke knew he had the votes. During the debate which followed John Maynes of the Clerks [far-Right] and John Halfpenny [Communist] spoke in opposition. Then Hawke exercised his right-of-reply, and in his first sentence — 'Comrades, don't some debates throw up some strange bedfellows?' — launched into assault upon his enemies. Professor Ross Martin of La Trobe University, whose field is the trade unions, wrote:

> All the stops were out as he soared into a savagely personal attack upon Mr Maynes and Mr Halfpenny, in turn. Delegates were rapturous. The applause was deafening. Yet it is doubtful that many, or any, votes were swung as a result. The big delegations at least were already committed . . . This is not to say that the speech with which Mr Hawke wound up the economic enterprises debate was pointless. It was in fact highly important because it ensured, beyond all doubt, that Congress's favourable decision on the issue would be widely interpreted as a highly personal triumph . . . But, resounding as the triumph was, it could not in the end obliterate memories of the vote three days earlier [about Fitzgibbon] when the President suffered his greatest, though not his first, Congress defeat. Nor was his prestige helped by the confused outcome of the executive elections. On balance, it would seem that Mr Hawke personally lost rather more than he gained . . .[5]

The Press reported that the 1973 Congress was 'cynical, even by the standards of the trade union movement'. The far-Right/far-Left alliance was clearly cynical, but there was more to it than insincerity. From the moment that Hawke opened the week-long meeting, reading his speech, trying to pull applause, nervous — he had been threatened with death by a man purporting to represent the Black September movement a few days earlier — there was a tense undercurrent of disappointment in his audience. It was exactly nine months since Labor had been elected and, strangely, the millennium was not turning out in the way the trade union movement had imagined it would. Indeed the Government, taking its lead from the Leader, had a style which appeared unnervingly middle class. Ministers all had advisors and Press officers; the Press officers and advisors were Party faithful who, in their new jobs, were earning unfamiliarly high salaries. They lunched in restaurants and drank champagne. There were many opinions and many loose tongues. Increasingly Canberra was resembling a *nouveau* expense-account School for Scandal.

Hawke devoted much more than half of his presidential address to the 'implications for the trade union movement' of the Whitlam Government. He spoke of the policy areas in which he saw benefits in line with trade union wishes, placing particular emphasis on the abandonment of the penal clauses; the Government's intervention on the side of the unions in a recent national wage case; the 're-creation of full employment'; and the Government's intention to provide 'advanced facilities' for trade union education. He then turned to the central problem, saying:

> One thing must be made perfectly clear at the outset and whatever may be said by the — of course — dispassionate observers about my various head-gear, I have no difficulty making it. However large the part played by our individual affiliates and by the ACTU itself in the election of the Federal Labor Government, that does not put us in permanent political check to our colleagues in government. The price we were paying for the occupancy of the Treasury benches by an anti-Labor government was extraordinarily high — but no higher price could be paid than the absolute loss of integrity involved for the industrial movement in its becoming the automatic guarantors and endorsers of every action and policy decision of Labor in government. Such a position should be degrading for us, and dangerous for them.[6]

Hawke then elaborated on the differences of opinion over the Budget; the tariffs; and the amendments to the Conciliation and Arbitration Act. Later in the Congress he was able to take a more positive stance, telling delegates of promised Government help for the ACTU enterprises and the possibility of Government help with research costs incurred by the ACTU in connection with hearings on tariff bodies and the Prices Justification Tribunal. But on the whole Congress tended to harp upon the dangers and difficulties in the relationship between the unions and the Government. One man, a timber worker, was fierce in his attack upon the lack of consultation and the tariff decision, shouting bitterly about the loss of jobs in the timber industry — 'and this from a Labor Government I worked my guts out for!'[7]

A few hours later Whitlam strode into the hall, to a standing ovation. They had loved him so much. They wanted to love him. When he showed himself to them they could forget the bad times and re-live the ecstasy — for the time being.

Delegates' support for the enterprises had been so great that opponents had not even bothered to demand a vote for or against them. Hawke now had a mandate to move quickly. For more than a year before the Congress he had been devoting much of his time to discussions with businessmen and State and Federal governments about possible enterprises, and earlier in 1973 had established a second joint-venture, ACTU-New World Travel. The partnership was with Thomas Nationwide Transport, whose managing director (later chairman) was Sir Peter Abeles. Abeles is one of the most intelligent industrialists in the nation, and by 1982 was one of the richest. He is a big man — over six feet two inches — and smokes big cigars. He speaks softly and moves with that unexpected lightness of step which big men sometimes have, while his smoothly plump face reveals little of a complex personality and a sophisticated mind. He wears heavy-framed spectacles, and behind them his dark-brown gypsy eyes are alert, worldly, and passionate. In conversation Abeles describes himself as 'a romantic' and 'just a truckie'. Indeed, his suits are drab and so crumpled sometimes that it seems that he might have thrown them on the floor the night before; his hair looks often as if he has mislaid his comb. In a group, without his magnificent Havanas, one could overlook him. Abeles was born in Budapest in 1924, to a wealthy, totally assimilated Jewish family. His father was a steel merchant. His mother was an excellent pianist, and as a child and youth he studied music and Italian art, though his heart was set, he says, upon becoming a doctor. 'My father was a very strong personality and was all business . . . I had the idea that one could not be a businessman and stay a human being', he said. Abeles' father had insisted that he learn a metal trade. But before he could enter medical school, the war broke out.
  He recalled,

> I survived, at first, because of the trade: I was a specialist welder, so although I was a Jew I got an exemption and was employed in the garage of the German military staff. Then we were all conscripted and put into Jewish labour battalions in the Hungarian Army, under German control. A lot of people in our camp were killed. We lost quite a few during bombing attacks, for instance, because we were not allowed into shelters but were left in the open. And later on it became even worse. But I was young, and I didn't have any notion that I'd perish. We worked very hard, repairing rail lines and doing work behind the troops. While we were not in a concentration camp and weren't behind wire, we were still always under German control, so there wasn't much future in it.

The Hungarian Jewish battalions did not wear uniforms, except for the yellow arm-band. When, in 1944, the Russian army over-ran the Hungarian-German-held position in Czechoslovakia where Abeles was working, he and many other young Jews took their chance and escaped. Officially they were deserters. Abeles' mother-tongue is German; physically, he did not resemble the Nazi stereotype of the Jew. He removed his yellow arm-band and, speaking German, hitched rides back to Budapest with German and Hungarian Gentiles. His family managed to find their way back to Hungary and after the war Abeles' father got his steel business back. Abeles said,

> In 1947, when it was clear that the Communists would take over, I decided to leave Hungary. I had a permit to go to the United States, but in Australia I had some relations, an uncle and a grandmother from my mother's side. I decided to go there first, and have a look. My father gave me £4,000, which was a lot of money in those days. I had married in 1947, so I had to work. I thought I would work for a while, then go to medical school.

European migrants in the late 1940s were like gold from heaven for Australian shysters: a Sydneysider had managed to relieve Abeles of a quarter of his capital within a few weeks of his arrival. Abeles, who was a born entrepreneur, assessed his possibilities and decided to become a salesman. He bought 50,000 paperback novels — remaindered detective stories and westerns — and sold them to Gordon & Gotch newsagencies. He made a profit of £400. He then began to sell knitwear, and was still selling pullovers and cardigans when, in 1950, a Hungarian friend arrived in Australia. This was George Rockey, whose family had owned one of the biggest forwarding agencies in Hungary. Rockey was eight years older than Abeles and had been the particular friend of Abeles' father, with whom he played poker. Rockey, too, had suffered during the war when the authorities had discovered that one of his grandparents was Jewish. He had been brought up as a Catholic. He had been an officer in the Hungarian army, but on the discovery of his Jewish grandmother, 'my uniform was stripped from me', he said. He had worked in his father's business before the war, rather unwillingly. He was a social democrat, in rebellion, he said, against 'the way I was brought up. As a child I was not allowed to fetch a glass of water for myself; I had to ring a bell for the maid'. He, too, had hankered for a medical career and described himself later as 'a frustrated psychiatrist'. At the end of the war he had gone to Vienna, 'and had a complete Jungian analysis', which took about three years. He arrived in Sydney with £150, moved into a boarding house in Neutral Bay and contacted the one friend he had in Australia, Abeles. Abeles said,

> In those days a lot of migrants bought a truck. I said to George, 'Tell me. You know transport. Don't you think we could do something in trans-

port? I've heard if you buy a truck you make a good living.' So we walked around and we finally bought two trucks. They cost £6,000 each, and as a deposit I put down all the money I had. But we didn't know much. George knew forwarding and shipping but not trucks, and within two months the trucks were out of commission, and we were both broke. And we still had to pay off the trucks. So, we decided to become contractors. We got the trucks repaired and hired people who could drive them properly.

Abeles and Rockey founded Alltrans on 11 December 1950. In 1954 they opened Sydney Coal Merchants as well and began to encroach upon the market of the coal giant, Sir Roderick Miller, undercutting his prices. Abeles approached Miller and asked if they might not have agreement about prices, in return for which Sydney Coal Merchants would have one-third of the city's coal market. Miller responded by sending Sydney Coal Merchants and Alltrans broke: he bought every mine that was supplying Sydney Coal. Abeles recalled, 'I am not being facetious: it was only the fact that neither George nor I could read a balance sheet that saved us from going out of business altogether. We'd lost everything we had and everything we didn't have.' Fourteen years later Abeles bought RW Millers. He said, 'Sir Roderick always thought it was my vengeance, to such an extent that one day he sat down with me — we had become friends — and said, "Tell me, how did you plan this? For how long did you plan it?" And truly, I had never considered vengeance: I just saw RW Millers as good business.' In the mid-1960s Abeles moved in on Thomas Nationwide Transport. By the end of the 1970s he had a transport empire stretching around the world.

Until his business interests grew too vast Abeles himself had managed the industrial relations of his various companies. When Hawke became President of the ACTU, Abeles asked for an interview, but on the day of the appointment Hawke was ill with one of his respiratory tract infections. Abeles went to Sandringham, where Hawke was in bed playing rummy with Rosslyn. Abeles said,

He was completely different from what I had expected — I had imagined he would be just an aggressive man, but here was a very human, very nice man. I think we formed an immediate rapport. I think we became friends soon after, and we began to be together a lot. We became trusted friends, and the thing I especially liked — it is best expressed by the German writer, Stefan Zweig, who wrote: There is nothing more beneficial than two people with goodwill towards each other having an argument. Well, Bob and I have been arguing ever since, but always with a feeling of friendship. Bob shows his emotions, and more than his intellect, more than arguing, I find that most attractive about him. It is only the Anglo-Saxons who say a man cannot show his emotions, but I am a European. When I've had personal problems, I cry.

If I've had problems with my children, Bob will listen to me. And I will do that for him.

Abeles, in fact, was Hawke's friend in time of need when, in 1976, there was a family crisis.

The idea of an ACTU-TNT joint-venture grew quickly after this initial rapport had been established. In the ILO Hawke had picked up many ideas about the possibilities for trade union enterprises which confirmed the view he had held for years, that the ACTU had been blind to opportunities for improving services for its members. In West Germany and in Israel he had seen the magnificent achievements of trade union organisations which provided womb to tomb security, plus holidays, housing and other credit, entertainment, education, and sporting contests for their members. There was a big difference, however, between the West German and the Israeli trade union movements and the Australian one: Hitler had destroyed the German unions and, re-born, their unofficial motto is 'Never Again'. Similarly, every citizen of Israel has this motto engraved on her or his heart. On Hawke's invitation representatives of both West Germany's DGB and Israel's General Federation of Labour (Histadrut) visited Australia in early 1972 to study and advise on the possibilities here for trade union enterprises. Both groups expressed very cautious optimism, but offered to help the ACTU if they were asked. The Israelis were astonished that Hawke had such public power — one of the Histadrut delegation said, 'He was treated like a prime minister, people felt honoured when he spoke to them' — yet, because of the structure of unionism in Australia, so little real power: 'He is the prisoner of the national leaders of your big unions'. Both DGB and Histadrut pointed out that the dispersion of capital among the Australian unions was an immense problem for any ACTU undertakings. Abeles had capital.

He recalled of the ACTU-TNT venture:

> It was a case of Bob's and Peter's over-optimism. There is no doubt that the ACTU's affiliated unions represent an enormous market. TNT was inexperienced in travel, but we knew everything about transport and, at the time, that seemed enough. Bob and I talked about it for weeks and weeks and sold the idea to each other more and more. We started to dream and by the time we had finished, we had a huge dream . . . TNT had good industrial relations with all the unions; George and I were very friendly with Bob. We began to see something fantastic in such a joint-venture.

At the ACTU executive meeting of August 1972 Hawke reported on his discussions with Abeles about a joint-venture travel company which would provide travel and holiday packages, general travel and, later, holiday accommodation for trade unionists and their families — all at slightly cheaper than normal rates. The executive, still enthusiastic about ACTU enterprises (with

the exception of the far-Right), was edgy. Earlier in 1972 Abeles had attempted to take over Ansett Transport Industries but the Premier of Victoria, Sir
Henry Bolte, had obliged Sir Reginald Ansett and had had the law changed in
Victoria to thwart the takeover. This had been a *cause célèbre* for
months. Abeles had also been knighted that year. Soon afterwards a very
senior business knight had drawn him aside to say, 'Now that you're one of
us, you really should stop being seen around with that Hawke fellow'. (Sir
Roderick Carnegie had similar warnings when it became known to his
colleagues that he and Hawke were friends.) Whatever the misgivings at that
end of the political and social spectrum about a relationship between Hawke
and Abeles, at the other end, in the labour movement, they were much deeper.
Lionel Revelman had been one thing: he was a businessman battling bigger
businessmen. Abeles was a big businessman and by definition for the trade
union movement, big businessmen are enemies. One can form non-
aggression pacts, even have alliances with them, but beneath politeness and
expediency there is fear and often its cousin, hatred. The Brotherhood of Man
is a limited concept in the labour movement: it is the Brotherhood of Us.
Hawke had been bewitched by this idea himself when younger — there had
been his swaggering contempt for the rich which had so embarrassed Kirby in
the 1960s — but at the same time, creeping through his consciousness, there
had always been a fascination with the Other Side. Abeles fascinated him: he
was subtle, sophisticated, cosmopolitan, immensely wealthy, a foreigner —
his English is good, but non-idiomatic and with Hungarians he speaks their
own language — and had suffered tribulations that Hawke could only guess
at, sympathetically. Hawke's refusal to reject Abeles' friendship, despite
many warnings from his political colleagues that it was viewed as consorting
with the enemy, was to cause him massive political damage. Abeles' companies donated handsomely to Labor campaign funds; he also gave fund-
raising dinners for the Liberal Party, one of them unhappily timed, for it took
place within days of an announcement by Hawke that the ACTU and TNT
were in business together.

A decade after Hawke had formally told his executive that he had a
personal association with Abeles, that he wanted the ACTU to have a
business association, and that Abeles was waiting outside, ready to enter the
boardroom and address the executive himself, people still remembered the
frisson that this created. 'I think Sir Peter found it easier than we did', Ducker
recalled. At first some executive members objected to receiving Abeles, but
others over-rode them. It was, however, a weird moment when 'the very
personification of big monopoly capitalism', as one executive member,
speaking for many, described Abeles, entered the room. (Abeles himself
dislikes being labelled a capitalist and says, 'I am not big capitalism — that is
the Government of Russia. I am big free enterprise.') Ducker recalled, 'There
was a great deal of suspicion and unease'. And Pat Clancy:

November 1975: Hawke addressing dock workers at Williamstown, Victoria

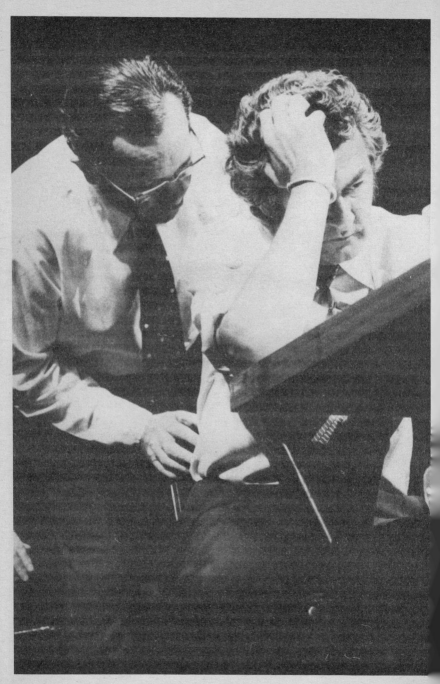

John Ducker comforting Hawke during 1975 election campaign after news of a letter-bomb explosion, attributed to ALP supporters

Sir John Moore, Harold Souter, Hawke, George Polites, Gough Whitlam and Sir Richard Kirby, ACTU 50th anniversary celebrations, 1977

Isi Leibler and Hawke toasting the ACTU-Jetset partnership, 1978

Hawke receiving his Companion of Australia decoration from Sir Zelman Cowen, January 1979

Hawke and Hazel arriving in Rome from Moscow, May 1979

Hawke with Pope John-Paul, June 1979

Hawke shouting at journalists for harassing him, ALP Conference, Adelaide, July 1979

The uranium debate, ACTU Congress, September 1979

The ACTU Executive of 1979: *standing:* Edgar Williams, Ken Stone, Dick Scott, John Morris, Peter Cook, Bob Watling, Barrie Unsworth, Fred Peterson, Norm Gallagher, Keith Lawler, Ray Geitzelt, Ivan Hodgson, Bob Gregory. Harry Hauenschild. *Sitting:* Bill Richardson, Bill Kelty, Peter Nolan, R.J.H., Cliff Dolan, Jim Roulston, Phil Reilly

Hawke, aged 50

I objected to the idea of linking the ACTU with really big business. And I objected to the man. I was all for the enterprises. But I think on the arrangement with Sir Peter Abeles, Bob had moved ahead too quickly, without giving time for proper consultation with the unions, and without understanding the trade union movement. I was the only one opposed outright to the proposition of an ACTU-TNT joint-venture. But since the proposal had to go to the Labour Councils for endorsement I said, 'All right, I won't record any vote against it'. And I think my judgment in doing that was wrong.

Abeles recalled, 'At first I found the executive members sceptical. But they did not seem hostile. Anyway, after about twenty minutes I found them most co-operative and I was surprised by the goodwill they showed and the friendly reception I got.' Ducker commented, 'I always wondered if Sir Peter were not buying himself a bit of industrial relations insurance' — a sentiment voiced by some other executive members also.

ACTU-New World Travel began business in March 1973, as a travel agency. The next step would be a holiday village. From the outset, the enterprise failed to thrive. Right-wing union officials whose members were low-paid objected to it because holiday travel was a luxury beyond the means of their members. The AMWSU and other Left-wing unions objected on various ideological grounds: the 'big capitalism' argument; rejection of any association between the unions and capitalism, big or small, except in a master-servant relationship. Abeles said,

> The Left never felt comfortable with the idea. What should have happened was that we concentrated a lot of energy into it, to make it a success quickly, because if we didn't do that, the Left would say, There's proof it can't work; and then they would begin to make sure that it would not work. Well, we didn't go about things in the right way. I am very critical of TNT, not so much of Bob. TNT was inexperienced in travel, which is a very different industry from transport, as I learned over the years. So, there were unions against us, and travel agents against us. And we did not put the time and energy into it that was necessary. One day Bob told me that Jetset [Australia's largest travel agency] had visited him officially, proposing that it could do things better. So we climbed out.

In 1978 ACTU-Jetset replaced ACTU-New World Travel and was from the beginning a success. The chairman of Jetset, Isi Leibler, is also a successful businessman but he does not have a diverse empire of companies. He had begun work in his father's diamond importing business and, from frustration with the way travel agencies had mismanaged his trips, had founded Jetset.

He had none of Abeles' instincts for an Alexandrian sweep through the business world; his major preoccupation, since student days, was the plight of Jews in the USSR. By the time Hawke was preparing to leave the ACTU it was cash-flow from ACTU-Jetset and, to a lesser extent from ACTU-Solo, a joint-venture founded in 1975 with an independent petrol retailer, David Gold-berger, of Solo, that was keeping the ACTU afloat.

Every ACTU executive meeting during 1973 discussed the enterprises and Hawke maintained enthusiasm for them by constantly publicising the progress of plans. Hot on the heels of an announcement about travel, Hawke would be talking of holiday villages, insurance, cheap housing, consumer credit. Throughout 1973 and into 1974 the news media carried stories of wonders about to be unveiled. Cliff Dolan, the man who succeeded Hawke as ACTU President, said:

> Personally, I thought we were trying to do too much in a hurry, and I didn't completely agree with Bob's enthusiasm. I felt he was forgetting that the trade union movement is very conservative and that there is as much conservatism in the Left as there is in the Right. On the other hand, it was no fault of Bob's that some of the schemes didn't get off the ground: the superannuation and general insurance ideas, for example. We looked long and hard at those and the executive as a whole believed they were goers. But unfortunately, the companies we were dealing with weren't substantial, to put it mildly.

In mid-1973 Hawke was severely embarrassed when, having announced that the ACTU would go into joint-venture with an insurance company, journalists told him the company was under investigation for malpractice. Sinclair, who was unaware of the proposal and had many contacts in the Melbourne business community, said, 'I nearly had a fit when I heard Bob's announcement. I'd been hearing stories about that particular company since I was a schoolgirl. People told you on the tram.' An hour after announcing the ACTU insurance venture was on, Hawke had to announce it was off, saying blame for the error was entirely his. He repeated this explanation to the 1973 Congress. Dolan continued:

> The housing scheme was different. We were to go into partnership with Lend Lease and the MLC. It was a real goer — and I know this, because I finally did the negotiations, and the bloke who stuffed it up was Tom Uren [Minister for Urban and Regional Development in the Whitlam Government]. Uren would not give us the land for the housing scheme, which would have provided good, cheap houses for trade unionists. I think it was just incompetence in the Department of Urban and Regional Development. Tom Uren blamed other people — he said it was Lance Barnard's [Minister for Defence in the Whitlam Government] fault, because the land was part of an old ammunitions complex, at St Mary's,

west of Sydney, and was still under the control of the Department of Defence. But the real problem was inside the bureaucracy, and largely DURD's. Lack of expertise within the ACTU was not an issue because Lend Lease was handling all the expert decisions and had Tony Powell, later the chairman of the National Capital Development Commission, in charge of things. The plans were all drawn up and Lend Lease spent a helluva lot of money. Then Uren and Barnard got cold feet about that particular block of land and offered us some scrub over towards Liverpool, and the Lend Lease people were most unhappy. They pointed out that they would have to entirely re-design. So we went back to Uren and said, 'For God's sake!' One of the other problems was that Gough had made the initial promise of granting land to us, but by then we didn't have very good relations with Gough, so we could not go to him and say, 'Get the whip on to Barnard and Uren'. And he had other problems and wouldn't have done anything, anyway. Then we lost government, so that was the end of the housing.

On the holiday village, Bob was dealing with Askin [Liberal Premier of NSW] and a bloke up at Tweed Heads, and I think they both let Bob down. I told him not to trust Askin too far, but Bob seemed to think there was no real problem with Askin, despite political differences and personal differences, and that Askin would come good on his promise. But he didn't. There was never any decision not to proceed — the holiday village just drifted away.

Then there was the plan for developing a complex in Lygon Street. We owned the old ACTU building there and the idea was we would buy the corner pub [the Lygon] and the building next door, owned by the Builders' Labourers. Bob and Harold were both very keen. But there were problems right from the start. For one thing the Builders' Labourers were snaky and there were doubts that they would sell, and Bob's best mates on the executive were very unhappy about the idea of the ACTU being a pub-owner. Bob and Harold argued that we wouldn't be going into the hotel trade, that we would buy it for the real estate, and keep the pub for just a couple of years, then re-develop the whole block. But we said, 'Oh, no. We won't agree to going into the pub business at all.' And then a certain union heard about the idea and made the publican a bigger bid, which we could not match.

The union's action seems to have been made to undermine the ACTU plan, for when the ACTU rejected the idea of buying the Lygon the union withdrew its bid.

Souter and Hawke, whatever their other differences, were in accord on the need for the ACTU to have enterprises. Souter knew, much better than Hawke, that the ACTU's financial situation was desperate, and in the 1950s had tried to persuade Monk to begin enterprises. Although a teetotaller, he had always been in favour of buying the Lygon Hotel. Hawke said,

When I first went to work in the ACTU I realised that it was pathetically weak financially, but that it had undoubted potential resources. It seemed to me absurd that the unions were pouring money into the Lygon — it was *the* union pub and an awful bloody place, though full of character — and getting, as it were, no return. If the ACTU bought it, the money could be recycled into the union system, and we could make it a better pub. There was also a garage in Victoria Street, across the road from the Trades Hall, which was used by the ACTU and a whole lot of trade union people. I went to Albert and suggested that we should buy both those things. The publican wanted only £30,000, which made the Lygon an unbelievably good investment. But Albert flatly refused. It was never my idea, then or when I became President, that the ACTU should be financed in its traditional areas by income from enterprises, because that would be trade unionism on the cheap. If the union movement wanted the ACTU to function effectively, and if individual members wanted their unions to function effectively, they would have to pay for that. I saw the enterprises as providing better services and cheaper services to unionists and the income for extra activities: like scholarships for kids. My attitude was not a matter of 'socialism in action', as was sometimes reported; it was functional.

At the ACTU Congress of 1971 the executive had recommended that union members pay 1% of their wages as membership fees, to try to overcome the general problem of under-financing of the whole movement. Short-sighted self-interest won the day. Many large unions were holding elections for their leadership positions at that time and, as Edgar Williams put it, 'Nobody was willing to say, Vote for me and I'll put up your membership fees'. The recommendation was rejected. At the 1973 Congress the ACTU again recommended it, this time successfully — in theory. In practice, the majority of unions refused to demand higher fees from their members. A constant fear for union officials is that if fees are too high, their members will resign. 'Union shop' awards are their protection against defection, but there are few union shop awards in Australia and those that exist have been won only after battles with employers *and* other unions.*

Hawke said,

> Until the unions themselves have an adequate fee structure we cannot get the ACTU into financial shape. My error, and there's no point

---

* The obvious solution is amalgamation of Australia's several hundred unions into a half-dozen but not many officials are willing to give up their jobs for the greater good of the movement. Although until 1972 there was nothing in the Arbitration Act to inhibit amalgamations, few had occurred. Since then government fiddling with the Act has made amalgamations difficult. The McMahon Government started the process; cruelly, Clyde Cameron's amendments, while passing through the mincing machine of the Senate, made matters worse.

saying it was anything else, was that I did not understand quickly enough that the ACTU's resources were so pathetic that it was unrealistic for us to try to do more than one or two things. What we needed was a department within the ACTU which would do nothing but run the enterprises: it would have needed a staff of lawyers, economists and finance people. And for too long I was unwilling to accept that we were incapable, because of our limitations, of responding to the opportunities and challenges that arose. We were inundated with proposals, and I worked tremendously long hours on them — and Harold did an immense amount of work, too, but . . .

By 1981 the trade union movement had accepted the principle that 1% of wages was a reasonable membership fee and consequently was willing to increase financial support to the ACTU. Also, the concept that unions should expand their horizons and shift, for example, into superannuation, had been established. Hawke had been a decade too soon, far too optimistic, and much too publicised — for when the movement turned against the enterprises, the main reason given was that they were 'all Hawke's ideas' and that, as years earlier with International House, 'Bob hogged the limelight'.

With Hawke's two hats, publicity was becoming a disadvantage.

A few weeks after the 1973 Congress a Liberal MHR resigned, opening the way for a by-election in the seat of Parramatta. The Liberals had only just managed to hold the seat in 1972; with the new Government still on its honeymoon with the electorate, Labor was confident of winning. Indeed, the Whitlam Government needed to win the seat to confirm its 'mandate'. But suddenly Cabinet performed a miracle of bad timing: it announced that Sydney's second airport would be built at Galston, close to the Parramatta electorate.

Hawke went campaigning in the Parramatta by-election. He recalled, 'I was at a meeting there just after the Federal Government's announcement of the Galston airport. People rushed up to me and complained bitterly about it. They were talking of nothing else.' When asked by the news media for his views, Hawke said that to make such an announcement in the middle of a by-election was 'political insanity' and 'an act of imbecility'. The Liberal Party won Parramatta with a 6% swing and Hawke, again wearing his ALP President's hat, commented, 'I think the Parliamentary Party and the Cabinet have got to be more finely attuned to the electorate. They are becoming removed from the realities of day-to-day politics. They should be keeping their ears open a bit more. They are not keeping in touch with what is happening at the grass roots.' Caucus and Whitlam were irate. Hawke had swallowed his conscience publicly over the tariff cuts, but now, in just a couple of months, he had reverted to form: liberty of conscience is the very foundation of puritanism, and Hawke was, again, exercising it with vigour. The ALP has been for decades a hybrid beast. With Whitlam as its Leader and Hawke as its President it began publicly to resemble something monstrous: a two-headed calf. The Caucus was beginning to hate Hawke, to reject his criticisms of its actions as wilful embarrassment, even traitorous. Other Party faithful disagree. David Combe, the Federal Secretary, said,

> Bob was the bloke who had the courage to stand up and make a bastard of himself by pointing out how crazy some of the Government's decisions were, and trying to get Caucus to change its mind by making a fuss. You would not believe how difficult it was for people who were responsible for the Labor Party to get a hearing from either Caucus or Gough. They just would not listen. After the Parramatta by-election I called on Gough, as Secretary of the Party, to voice my concerns about how we were performing politically, that we'd just had a disastrous by-election, it need not have been a disaster, we could have won the seat, and tiddly-dum. Gough was lying full-length on his settee, reading papers and throwing them over his shoulder as he finished them while various senior public servants danced attendance. He heard me out, still prone. Then he sat bolt upright and stared at me. He said, 'David. You have often told me that this government has one thing going for it. You are wasting its time!' That was the end of our interview. In the whole three years the Caucus never once met as a political caucus, to discuss how it was performing politically.

On 3 November 1973 Whitlam aired his displeasure with Hawke when, at a National Press Club luncheon in Canberra, in reply to a question about Hawke's opinion that income tax should be increased to help combat inflation, the Prime Minister said: 'Mr Hawke's advice was not sought. It will not be sought . . . The President of the federal executive of the Labor Party does not determine such matters — is not consulted in such matters.' As he sat down Whitlam made an aside to journalists, along the lines of 'That will show the little runt'.

He had spoken too soon. A few weeks earlier there had been a dramatic development in international events and on the issues that arose Hawke and Whitlam were to be in disagreement not merely about method — a perennial problem in any reformist party — but about principles. War, said Marx, is the locomotive of history. The Vietnam War had helped to drive Labor in to office; it had showered the nation with gold and good times and good causes. On 6 October 1973, Judaism's Day of Atonement, a period spent in prayer and communion with God, when no fires may be lit nor cars driven nor work performed, the armies of Egypt and Syria had invaded Israel for what later was called, after the Hebrew name for the day, the Yom Kippur War. And in five weeks the world was changed.

Chapter Sixteen

Jerusalem is one of the world's most beautiful cities. It is small, set high in the Judean hills and built from a pale honey-coloured stone which, at certain times of day, glows gold. The desert air is clean. Standing on the Mount of Olives, looking across at Jerusalem's walls and domes, one can pick out the churches which celebrate the life of Jesus, and his last hours — the place of the Last Supper is on a hill to the left, and the Garden of Gethsemane, its foliage surprisingly dark green and luxuriant, is just below, to the right. The sky above Jerusalem as seen from this hilltop has an unusually brilliant, pure light. It is, people say, the outermost garment of the Lord.

Hawke first saw the city in 1971. He came upon it suddenly, rounding a bend in the mountain road. He recalled, 'The physical impact of Jerusalem on me was almost, in the literal sense of the word, indescribable. It conjured up so much from my background, my knowledge of the Bible . . . I don't know how often I've been there since, but every time I've felt a thrill as the car rounds a brow of the hill, and there it is!'

Jerusalem: City of David; execution place of Christ; the town from which Mohammed's soul, resting a moment upon a rock, soared upwards into Heaven. 'Next year in Jerusalem', Jews in the Diaspora prayed for almost two thousand years and, if they were Orthodox, left a part of their houses unbuilt, to signify temporary residence outside the Holy City of the Holy Land.

The city has changed owners often, for it has the sacred sites of three great reformist religions. When Hawke first went there Israelis were still exulting that they had recaptured east Jerusalem and The Wall, all that is left of the Second Temple, from Jordan. The Wall looks like any old wall except that at the height of a man's head and hands, on the left side, and slightly lower — the height of a woman's — on the right, its stones are darkened and have a buttery glaze from the pressing of millions of humans against them. And between all the stones within human reach there are strips of paper, hundreds of thousands of them, each one a prayer. Hawke was taken to The Wall and inserted his own prayer: May Labor win the 1972 election. A few years later at least one Israeli inserted a prayer: May Bob Hawke become Prime Minister of Australia.

Hawke is loved in Israel. Initially, Israelis were sceptical of him.

He went there when he did, and in circumstances that obliged him to take a more than usually active interest in the country, almost by accident. In 1969 the ALP Senator Sam Cohen died during the election campaign. His widow, Judith (later Justice Cohen), and friends wanted to celebrate Cohen's memory and achievements. At the urging of Clyde Holding (Leader of the Opposition in the Victorian Parliament, later Labor MHR), a Gentile with the status of 'a Jew among Jews' in Australia, it was decided to reject a plan that would have made Cohen's memorial some gift to Israel — a building at the Hebrew University in Jerusalem was favoured — and instead to send a trade unionist or a member of the Left-wing of the ALP to visit the country. On return, the visitor would be required to give a Sam Cohen Memorial Lecture about Israel to an invited audience. Holding was of the generation, as was Hawke, that in youth had been stunned by news of the Holocaust and then exhilarated by the founding of the State of Israel, in which H.V. Evatt, as Australia's Minister for External Affairs and Chairman of the General Assembly of the UN, had played a leading role.

Holding showed an uncanny foresight about a change in ALP attitudes to Israel in the 1970s and the need to encourage prominent Labor people to speak out in Israel's defence. He remarked later, 'With the decline of that whole heady, awful business, the Vietnam War, a lot of the younger radicals were a bit lost for a cause. They were on the look-out for the next wretched depressed victims of American capitalism — and there were those benighted Palestinians.'

The choice of Hawke as the first Sam Cohen Memorial Lecturer seems, in retrospect, uncanny also. It is impossible to think of another Australian in public life whose upbringing had made him so open to the appeal and difficulties of the State of Israel and who, at the same time, would be so ready to shout about it from the rooftops — and be heard. Hawke's whole career has been shaped by a sense of indignation. All his successes as a trade union advocate, a strike negotiator and a political campaigner have occurred when he has been able to heat others with his own belly fire — that old Methodist anger he had got from Ellie and from Will Lee before her, and which, as a small, sickly boy intimidated by bigger children, had become concrete and personal in his own life. The institutions and problems of the State of Israel were to seize upon the core of Hawke's being: his admiration for achievement, his capacity for anger, his identification with the 'little man', his instinct to rescue. Israel was — still is — the very image of David defying Goliath.

Israel had not been an issue in Australian politics before the escalation, in 1964, of the Vietnam War. In that year the Palestine Liberation Organisation (PLO) was founded with the major aim of its charter the total destruction of Israel. This aim was inspired by rankling over injustice: the United Nations decision of 1947 to divide British Mandated Palestine, a colony of the Empire, into two countries, allotting one to Palestinians and the other to Jews as a national home, was, from the Arab point of view, both a colonial act of theft and an insult to the whole Arab world. The Arabs had never accepted the Balfour Declaration of 1917 that such a Jewish national home should be created in Palestine; they discounted the fact that already, before World War II, Jews who had been returning to live in Palestine since the 1880s had bought a great deal of land there from Arab and absentee Turkish land-owners. That by 1947 European Jews were desperate for somewhere to live was of little concern to the Arabs for it was not they who had set up the gas chambers and slave camps. They saw the partition of Palestine as a European attempt to assuage European guilt. The Arab policy was to reject half a country and gamble upon winning by force of arms a whole country — or to lose the half they already had. But despite four major wars, 87,000 killed in action, hundreds of thousands wounded, billions of dollars spent on armaments which could have been spent on improving the lives of people, orgies of propaganda to encourage hatred, there is no Palestinian State and Israel has increased its territory.

On the day in 1948 when Israel was declared an independent State the Arabs launched a war and as a result lost territory to Israel. They continued to harass until 1956 when Israel launched a war and won more territory. The Arabs continued to harass, and after 1964 became better organised in their campaign for the total destruction of Israel, which in 1967 made a pre-emptive strike. In six days Israel won a victory which astonished the world. The Arab nations reacted to defeat by increasing the price of oil to what was at the time a staggering $US5 a barrel, more than double the old price. Israel, by now, had the image of permanent military invincibility, and slowly her status as underdog began to change. In the years after 1967 the Arab nations, with a population of 120 million, were able to cast themselves as the plaintiffs against Israel, with a population of three million, as defendants. The Palestinians, refusing to acknowledge the legality or the reality of the State of Israel, lived in refugee camps. In the early 1980s children in the Palestinian camps born there and born of parents who were born there would reply to the question 'Where do you come from?' with the name of a village, now part of Israel, that their grandparents had once lived in and which they had never seen.[1]

The primary attitude of the Left everywhere is an amalgam of fellow feeling (for the weak) and hostility (for the strong). The Palestinian cause was tailored, after 1967, to Left emotions, especially since by then Israel was firmly in the American camp and, partly because of the Vietnam War, America represented All Evil. However, within the ALP the moral stature of Sam Cohen, which was towering, and the activities of other Jews who were active in the ALP Left, had managed to prevent an outbreak of anti-Israel feeling. With Cohen's death and the passing of the heyday of the Vietnam moratorium marches, in which Jews played a leading role, there was a gap. Holding had foreseen that the Party was likely to become increasingly anti-Israel — at least, those Left-wing, and younger members who could not remember newspaper pictures of the Holocaust and the joyful relief that had greeted the founding of the State.

For anyone in the trade unions or the ALP, Israel in 1971 was a fascinating country. It had had Labour governments since its founding in 1948 and it had an egalitarian atmosphere which was an unachieved ideal in Australia. Its trade union council, Histadrut, controlled 25% of Israel's GDP; it was one of the country's largest employers; it had 70% of the population as members; Histadrut had the largest health fund; the second largest bank; the biggest construction company; holiday villas; a shipping line . . . There are no demarcation disputes in Israel because workers — including doctors, diplomats and the President of the country — join Histadrut direct and are then allotted to unions. While other countries have a trade union council, Histadrut got itself a country. It had existed almost thirty years longer than the State of Israel, having begun as a workers' co-operative in British Mandated Palestine, and had provided the first framework of government in the new State. Everybody who was anybody in Israeli politics, aside from the religious, was a member of Histadrut. The Israeli Establishment was, in the broad, Labour.

In 1971 Hawke had, he said, 'a general knowledge about Israel, but no particular interest'. His eldest child, Susan, had recently read the best-selling novel, *Exodus*, and was intrigued by Israel. When he accepted the invitation to be the first Sam Cohen Memorial Lecturer he asked if Susan could accompany him, explaining to the sponsors, with an incuriosity about the thinking of others which, by now, was habitual, 'I don't know why, but she'd like to come'. Arrangements were hastily made for Susan to stay on a kibbutz for six weeks. Hawke was to be in the country only a fortnight, before continuing on to Geneva for an ILO conference. He would collect Susan on the way home.

Dramatic complications to this bland scenario quickly arose. There was the bomb scare on their flight from Perth, because of Hawke's role in the Springbok campaign, but this, as things turned out, was a mere gentle prelude. Hawke's love of Israel and his willingness to fight for it were to cause problems which veered close to wrecking his life and career. Havoc was created in the lives of his children, who became hostages to his public activities. Created, too, were the circumstances for an awful courage.

Hawke recalled his first impressions of the landscape of Israel as if it were reaching out from the books of childhood to embrace him: 'It was as I'd imagined, dusty roads and olive trees'. From the moment of arrival Hawke and Israel were *en rapport*.

Histadrut, which has a large International Department that, among other things, looks after foreign guests, had provided an officer, Michael Siew, and a Tel Aviv taxi driver, Ari Tel-Shahar, to escort him. Relationships, emotional bonds, are everything to Hawke, the rest — including people's names (he could never remember Ari's surname although he loves him) — is detail. The three men formed an immediate bond. Tel-Shahar, who is sandy-haired, as wide as he is high and, in Hawke's words, 'one of the great rogues of all time — would take anyone down', said, 'When the three of us met, it was like a match to petrol'. He and Siew were astonished by Hawke's drinking and his ability to keep going for days with virtually no sleep. 'We learned', Tel-Shahar said later, 'when Bob comes, forget sleep'. Siew, who used to be a BBC journalist and, like Tel-Shahar, was in a tank unit, recalled Hawke at first meeting:

Initially I was impressed by his Mephistophelian eyebrows which he would twitch at me. Then, the fellow was asking too many questions — and very pointed ones, at that. And his arrogance! He actually hinted he was more intelligent than I. And then, his frankness — he told me that while in Oxford he realised one day that he had a prejudice against Jews. Then there was his sardonic impatience with some of our high-sounding, stuffy diplomats, who tried to impress our uncouth guest with Shakespeare. And there was his enthusiasm upon seeing and analysing some of our achievements in social experimentation. And he was a *real* humanitarian: he was disgusted at the suggestion that El Al should fly to Australia via South Africa. There was his sense of humour. His great taste in sheilas. And there was his all-consuming love for Australia, and his grief about the gap between what is and what could be . . . After fourteen harrowing days and nights with him I was so exhausted I could hardly remember the brand of my favourite beer. I volunteered to take him to the airport to make sure he would leave, and en route he had the nerve to assure me he thought I had done my homework on Israel . . . When he left I was besieged by my curious colleagues. They were sceptical about him. After all — shame! — he wasn't Jewish. There must be, they said, some ulterior motive to account for his friendliness — the man has yet to be tested. I told them, You can't even tell a friend when you see one. Until this day people ask me about his blood. I tell them, it's hot, but he's not

Robert James Lee Rosenblum. He is Israel's friend.

Hawke said,

I'm sure I would have developed a love and affection for Israel and its people, but the relationship that was so quickly forged between me, Michael and Ari and has remained ever since, created a beautiful initial environment. The first impression is one that has remained: here was this fantastic blend of informality — in dress [Israel lives in blue jeans], in arranging things; an irreverence, a cocking a snook at authority — *combined with* a very profound awareness of the ever-present threat. It seemed to me that in many people the threat would have produced paranoia, craziness — but here were these people delightfully relaxed in so many ways, and yet sharply attuned. You felt it was like a relaxed spring, that could coil into action very quickly.

The correspondences with his own style were striking.

He had arrived in Israel at a period when the country was exuberantly self-confident: Israelis had the Arabs licked. Or so it was thought. Hawke was taken on a tour of territory captured in three wars: to Sharm-el-Sheik, where Egyptian cannon had once blocked Israeli shipping through the Straits of Tiran; to Syrian bunkers on the Golan Heights from which machine gunners had hosed the Israeli villagers below with bullets. Standing in the bunkers and looking through a slit in the side of the hill one can see, with a pair of binoculars, the faces of Israelis in their houses below and the shelters in which they had slept every night to avoid bullets and mortars. As Hawke's guides told him, 'We fought like Russians, just throwing away lives, to capture these positions'. Lists of the names of Israelis who died to capture a particular bunker are engraved on stones at their entrances. The bunkers themselves, a network of tunnels through the hillsides, are meticulously maintained; around them, above ground, there are heaped in nests old Syrian tank obstacles — great black iron thorns which look like the spiked eggs of some terrible reptile. All Israeli war memorials have the same plain, brutal design of rock and jagged metal. They are horrifying to those with an eye for symbolism, for they all tell one story: this celebrates nothing; there has been no catharsis; this stands not for national glory but as a reminder that the war continues. Hawke quickly realised that the Israelis were deadly serious about the security of their borders.

He was impressed, too, by the achievements of Histadrut, and the argumentativeness and humour of the people he met. For the first time he was encountering a whole nation of individualists — tradition has it that every Jew is 'son of a king' — who had more jokes and as many opinions as he. There is a saying: when three Israelis meet they form eleven political parties;

and another: the only reason I don't make love in Dizengoff Square (the most fashionable area of Tel Aviv) is because every passer-by would give me advice. Hawke said, 'It's the only country I've been to where every citizen reckons that he or she could be Prime Minister and would do a better job'. Hawke's love of all-night arguments had found a permanent home. But, more compelling than these attractions, there was a spot in his consciousness which Israel burnt into, ineradicably. When he was taken to Jerusalem to visit the holy places he was taken to see Yad Vashem.

This is a museum built to the memory of those who died in the Holocaust. It is on a hilltop, with a short avenue of trees leading up to a couple of squat buildings and a bronze mural depicting the Warsaw Ghetto Uprising. Each tree in the avenue has a name beside it and has been planted for a Gentile who, during the Holocaust, defied authority and saved the lives of Jews. Such people are known in Israel and throughout the Diaspora communities as The Righteous. Inside the buildings there is a collection of photographs and objects of surreal horror. They are displayed simply, with low-key, informative captions. Some people walk through the museum, read the captions, look at the display and after half-an-hour continue on the next part of their tour. Others are struck dumb with an inner howl of rage and shame. Hawke was among the latter. Tel-Shahar, who had been waiting in the car outside, said, 'Bob's face was very grave. He sat in the back of the taxi and lent his head against it and couldn't speak. I could see there were tears running out of the sides of his eyes.' Some time later Hawke said, 'The whole of Christendom bears the guilt for that'. He will talk for days about Israel without ever referring to Yad Vashem. For him, finding it always difficult to mention the horrible, the Holocaust is almost taboo in speech, if not in thought. One day in 1981 when the subject arose he said suddenly, 'I can't understand anybody who doesn't weep when they see that. Whenever I think of Israel that's what I have in my mind.'

A few days after Hawke's visit to Jerusalem he, Siew and Tel-Shahar were in Beer-Sheba holding one of their all-night drinking and talking fests, when the question of Israeli-Soviet relations arose. Hawke said,

> The yarning led to my first visit to Moscow on Israel's behalf. I argued to the others that the Israelis hadn't properly explained to the world, but most particularly to the Soviet Union, their position. And the parallel immediately struck me: Israel and the USSR were both creations of the twentieth century. Their viability had been put at issue immediately — there had been an attempt to destroy them at birth, and subsequent attempts. And that the whole concept of the need for security, for recognised boundaries, was something that was uniquely relevant to both countries. As a passing observation I said, You know, I really would love to make those arguments to the Russians.

Hawke had already met the President-to-be of Histadrut, Yerucham Meshel, a man old enough to be his father, who said of Hawke:

> It was love from first looking at each other, from the first sentences. I realised that this man was very open to the tragedy of the Jewish people and the Jewish nation. I realised that he's a dreamer, emotional, spiritual, that he loves people. That he was dedicated to the Labor movement, and the trade union movement, not because he was a real trade union man, but because he wants to improve the standard of living of people in general . . . With all that intellect he has, Bob is also naive. Absolutely naive.

Hawke's desire to 'put those arguments to the Russians' revealed, perhaps more than anything else, the strength of his idealism. It was a combination of naivety — in the sense of his faith in goodness and logic — and his dreaming to improve the human condition, the quality that Bob Rogers had noticed when Hawke returned from India.

The USSR had supported the creation of the State of Israel but this had little to do with goodwill towards Jews. It was stimulated by Soviet desire to hasten the decline of Britain's power in the Middle East, to the advantage of the Soviet Union. Russia's initial expressions of warm feelings for Israel quickly cooled, then chilled and in 1967 became frigid. Soviet disinformation had triggered the Six Day War and the Russians, in high dudgeon of embarrassment, broke diplomatic relations with Israel. Tens of millions of dollars worth of Soviet armaments, sold to Egypt and Syria, had been destroyed by Israel in the War. By 1971 the USSR was massively re-arming Egypt and Syria and had that year signed a Treaty of Friendship with Egypt, which was still formally committed to the total destruction of Israel.

Hawke's initial thinking about the arguments he might put to Moscow had sprung from his deep-seated belief in the Brotherhood of Man and his instinct to find common cause and mediate conflicting positions. On further reflection he realised a more sophisticated debate would be necessary; he proposed to make one of his complicated carrot-and-stick arguments to the Russians, a combination of morality and threats to self-interest: that the USSR, having worked for the creation of Israel, would lose credibility if Russian weaponry caused its destruction; that if Israel were destroyed the Arabs, who hated the Russians on political and religious grounds, would turn away from the Soviet Union, therefore it was in Russian interest that Israel continue to exist so that Arabs would continue to look to the USSR for support. He did not intend to state the too-obvious: that if Russian weapons employed by Arabs destroyed Israel the Jewish lobby in the USA would put an American President under immense pressure to intervene, either against the Arab destroyers or against the USSR.

By 1971 *détente* was under way and the Soviet Union was concerned about international public opinion, so there was some reason for Hawke to be optimistic that the Russians would heed his argument about morality and consistency. But given the freezing relations between Israel and the Soviet Union, it was a long shot. However, Hawke could aim at the bull's eye: he was already friendly with Alexander Shelepin, head of the Soviet trade union movement and a man who was among the top officials in the Soviet hierarchy, spoken of in the Western Press as a potential successor to Brezhnev. Before becoming leader of Soviet workers Shelepin had been head of the KGB.

Siew passed on the word that Hawke was interested in presenting a case for Israel in Moscow. Events started to move quickly. As yet Hawke had not realised what a godsend he was to the Israelis. One country wishing to communicate with another with which it is not on speaking terms must use clandestine methods or envoys from a third nation, usually ambassadors or heads of state who, as a matter of course, extract some payment for their own nation in recompense for the favour they are doing. Hawke had access to one of the highest in the land in the USSR, and his services to Israel cost only the price of his airfares.

He said,

> I was taken to meet Golda Meir, in her Prime Minister's office in Tel Aviv. On the personal side a fascinating dichotomy in her character came out. Susan was with me and had been given the inevitable drink of orangeade. Golda was sitting behind her desk, chain-smoking, and she and I were seriously talking about Israel. Suddenly, Susan knocked over her drink and the glass smashed on the floor. There was an immediate transformation in Golda from a stern stateswoman into a grandmother. She jumped up and came from behind her desk to put her arm around Susan and tell her that it didn't matter about the glass. That spontaneous and unaffected warmth of the human being, the woman, immediately coming out, had a big effect on me.

Hawke's friends said later, 'Bob had the greatest platonic love affair of his life with Golda'. One day, years later, when Hawke was talking to Kate Baillieu about the tribulations Mrs Meir had suffered in childhood, 'he began to weep — he was not drunk'. On their first meeting, scheduled for fifteen minutes, the conversation ran on for more than an hour, and touched on Moscow. Later, Hawke met the Foreign Minister, Abba Eban.

A delicate process of testing Hawke for soundness was in train. A Histadrut official said, 'We couldn't quite believe him — a man with such an intellect, such a forceful personality, a politician . . .' At length, the Israelis were convinced that they had met a rare character: a Righteous Gentile. Whatever the Israeli leaders thought of Hawke's proposed arguments and their chances of success, they had a different submission for him to make in Moscow: they wanted Hawke to argue for the release of Soviet Jews. But for him to do this on Israel's behalf it would be necessary to make him privy to confidential matters of State.

The position of the Soviet Jews, who number three million, is one of the most emotional and diplomatically sensitive issues for Israel and world Jewry. Soviet Jews are known as 'The Silent Jews', 'The Prisoners of Zion' and 'The Beautiful People', and have the status of living martyrs among their co-religionists outside the USSR. Little was heard of them during the 1950s and 1960s in the councils of world Jewry. But following the Six Day War many asked permission to emigrate from the USSR. Anti-Semitism is rife in the Soviet Union. It was pogroms in Russia in the late nineteenth and early twentieth centuries which had forced some Russian Jews to flee to Palestine and dream of establishing a Jewish homeland there. When exit visas were requested more frequently after 1967 some were granted, some were not; some Jews were sacked for asking, some were not; some Jews were harassed by the KGB, some were not. No explanations were given. Two hundred were allowed to emigrate in 1968, 3,000 in 1969, but in 1970 only 1,000. Then on Christmas Eve 1970 a group of three Jews and two Gentiles, who had been refused exit visas and had talked about hijacking an aircraft, were sentenced to terms ranging from fifteen years' imprisonment to death. There was an international outcry. The Queen publicly implored clemency. The hijack plan was so widely-known that Israeli officials were aware of it before its proposed date and in these circumstances it was doomed in advance, for the KGB must have known of it also. However, just as PLO hijacks were raising the national consciousness and indignation of Arabs, the Russian group's very plan and their draconian sentences had a great impact upon the consciousness of Soviet Jewry. Throughout 1971 the demand for visas increased dramatically although, as an Israeli remarked, 'It was like playing Russian roulette'. The Israelis were fearful that a false move would mean a loaded chamber for their kin in the USSR.

Hawke said, 'At some point as the trip went on the Israelis put it to me that they would like me to do a job of representation — in terms that I had proposed to them, to discuss with the Russians the attitude of the Soviet Union towards Israel, and also on the question of the Soviet attitude towards the release of Soviet Jewry'.

Hawke flew to Rome and telephoned Alexander Shelepin. A year earlier Hawke had gone on from an ILO Conference to Moscow on a fraternal visit, as Shelepin's guest. They had taken a liking to each other: Hawke said,

> While I detested all that he stood for, the fantasy about a free trade union movement, and particularly his background in the KGB, I found him a fascinating and likeable bloke. He had an acute intelligence and was extraordinarily well-informed. On my 1970 visit he had brushed aside his aides to ask all his own questions about Australia, revealing an

unusual depth of knowledge and understanding. Physically, Shelepin could have been the twin of [Sir Henry] Harry Bland [former head of the Australian Department of Labour] — short, dark, sharp. We had a strange liking for each other. I had no doubt that in an ultimate sense he was totally ruthless.

One of the pranks Shelepin had played on Hawke in 1970 was to try to trick him into vodka-drinking contests. Hawke said, 'There would be toasts for everything, and suddenly the cry, Bottoms Up! I noticed that I seemed always to have the biggest glass of vodka, and while the two comrades standing closest to me would do a Bottoms Up and would look at me as a challenge to do the same, the real heavies weren't Bottoms Upping at all.'

After a number of international telephone calls it was established that Shelepin, who was on holiday at the Baltic Sea, would be delighted to receive Hawke there. Hawke went on to the European conference, returned to Israel to collect Susan and have further briefings, then flew to Moscow. He arrived there on the evening of 21 July and was met by Boris Averianov, head of the International Department of the USSR trade union movement, and others. Next morning they flew to Palanga, on the Baltic, where Shelepin was waiting in welcome. They had to communicate through translators.

Hawke was extremely cautious, as revealed by the report he dictated as soon as he left the USSR. He spent four hours on a *tour d'horizon* of international events with Shelepin, who opened talks with an exposition about recent USSR-USA discussions in Helsinki; the end of the Cold War; the obstacle of East Germany; the role of Norway, and so on, and set forth an overall view of international relations which was optimistic, in Soviet terms. They had lunch. Hawke then said he wished Shelepin to be under no misapprehension: he wanted to discuss specific issues 'which even by Right-wing standards transcend politics'. Hawke had reduced his arguments to note-form and kept his notes 'on my person for the whole period before and after this'. He made a general introduction, then 'submissions' — first on the Arab-Israeli question. His report says, 'While I put these Shelepin listened with absolute intensity and made copious notes. I proceeded to conclusion without interruption.' He said later,

Often when you're talking to important people from other countries you know it's only a game you're going through, that the exchange of views is a charade of listening. There was no question that Shelepin was just being polite; his attention and seriousness were for real . . . I put the altruistic argument about Soviet consistency, then I tried to impress upon him that the Israelis were just as serious about the security of their borders as the Soviet Union was, and, Christ Almighty, look at what the USSR had done in the cause of its security. It had enslaved the peoples of Eastern Europe, kept its own living standards appallingly low to spend

billions upon armaments — naturally, I did not advert to specifics . . .
Then I moved on to Soviet self-interest in the Middle East — their
capacity to bargain with and keep the Arab States dependent upon
Russia for this very fact: that Israel existed.

Shelepin heard him out and began his reply with an insistence that everything
he said must remain confidential.

In broad terms he tried to justify Soviet sympathy for the Arab cause and
warned Hawke that he and the Israelis ought not to be deceived, that since
their dreadful defeat in 1967, 'the Arab armies have been transformed'. He
assured Hawke that the Soviet Union did not want another war in the Middle
East and had 'expended kilos of salt' in attempting to convince the Arab
States that they must abandon their plans for 'liquidation' of Israel. Hawke
argued to him, 'You are backing the wrong horse', and a year later his remark
was justified, when President Sadat expelled all the USSR advisors from
Egypt. (Five years later Sadat unilaterally broke the Treaty of Friendship and
severed diplomatic relations with the USSR.)

Hawke said in his report,

> What Shelepin really seemed to grasp was my repeated pushing of the
> analogy between the Israeli determination about the security of its
> borders, and the same Russian determination. He emphasised the need
> for time. That he would need time to talk to his peers about this; then, if
> they accepted the point, time for the Russians to talk to the Arabs. I
> believe it is crucial to develop a diplomatic crescendo about the security
> complex — use the German analogy, albeit in muted terms, and create
> the equation: *What is* the difference between the Soviet desire for
> territorial integrity and the steps it has been prepared to take, and the
> position of Israel?

They then moved on to the topic of Soviet Jews. Hawke's report said,

> I put the argument, then Shelepin produced some strained statistics and
> when I pointed out that they were strained, he reacted. He said the exact
> statistics could be provided for me. Then he said, 'The Jews are less than
> 2% of our population, but they constitute at least 15% of our scientific
> people and those with access to State secrets essential to our security'.
> He looked at me across the table and said with his hand raised almost
> plaintively, 'What do we do? You tell me what we do.' My first
> rejoinder was, 'Do these people want to leave?' To which he replied,
> 'Yes!' My answer was, I suppose, inadequate. I certainly gained the
> impression that it was for him. I said, 'These people are merely identify-
> ing with a wider cause. If you are humane to the less important Jews and
> allow them to leave, then the ones you are really concerned about, those

with access to State secrets, will not feel the pressure so much and will not want to leave.' Perhaps you [Jews] pay too high a price for your ability.[2]

In 1971 the USSR allowed 13,000 Jews to emigrate. In 1972, 32,000, in 1973, 35,000. It is widely accepted by Israeli officials that Hawke's 'submissions' to Shelepin had helped to achieve this result. The reason may not be as straightforward as it appears — a matter of Hawke, as advocate, convincing Shelepin, as judge. A senior Australian diplomat who claims expertise on Soviet affairs made the point that because anti-Semitism is so great in the USSR, Soviet officials tend to have paranoid fears about Jews, which include an over-estimation of the power of world Jewry. Further, that the KGB (Shelepin's former field) is especially prone to such attitudes. This certainly would explain the extreme seriousness of Shelepin's behaviour towards Hawke in 1971, for it suggests he would have seen Hawke as the emissary of a mighty and devious foe.

There was immense gratitude to Hawke in Israel. On every trip abroad he began to call in there. A Histadrut official said, 'In Israel, people really cared for Bob. We cared about his drinking problem and his family and his political problems, and he knew it. Here, everyone was his friend.'

But meanwhile, in Australia, relations with Israel were beginning to sour. The Australian Jewish community had donated lavishly to the Whitlam Government's 1972 campaign, much of the money being channelled through Hawke, who, on returning from Israel in 1971, had become a favourite Gentile. Hawke had not told people about his trip to Moscow on Israel's behalf, but news had seeped back from Tel Aviv and Jerusalem that the Government of Israel looked with particular fondness upon Hawke. Australian Jews inclined towards Labor, for it was the Chifley Government which had offered them asylum and Evatt who had helped to establish Israel. They expected great things from the Whitlam Government. During the election campaign Whitlam had promised that Qantas would fly to Tel Aviv. This was especially important for Israelis and their relations abroad because there are many airlines which will not fly to Israel and many countries in which Israelis dare not have stop-overs, so that travelling in and out of the country is a complicated process of picking out routes and airlines which only stop in neutral or friendly nations. Whitlam did not keep his promise about Qantas and the Israeli Government was becoming testy; the Australian Jewish community uneasy.

Given the Government's desire to play an active role in international affairs and to assume leadership of Third World and radical causes, disillusion was inevitable. Power was flowing towards radical Arab nations. There were various reasons: a renaissance of Islam had been under way since the 1920s, world-wide. It had swept through Africa and into the black population of America. The decay of the Christian colonial empires had given it room, and encouragement. Since the end of World War II the world production (and consumption) of oil had expanded from five million barrels a day, in 1945, to about sixty million in the early 1970s and the Arab oil-producers were black with black gold. Their societies were suffering psychic shock from the challenge to traditions that sudden wealth imposed, and were febrile. Importantly, the Palestinians and others were beginning to win the propaganda war against Israel. The world community would not tolerate their assertion that Israel must be obliterated, but to the less dramatic claim, that a great injustice had been done to the people of Palestine, there was growing attention.

Communists of all persuasions were hostile to Israel and in the Left of the ALP hostility was increasing. Hawke widely advertised his plans for Histadrut-ACTU joint-ventures; he was invited to speak at what a leader of Australian Jewry called, 'every Jewish mothers' club in the country'; he was, inevitably, seen as an enemy of the Palestinian cause. His position on Palestine was straightforward: that a Palestinian State should be created; that Israel and her neighbours should recognise Resolution 242* of the United Nations. He complained later, 'I have made my position clear many times and I don't think I have ever been given any credit for it by the supporters of Palestine. They have simply refused to listen to what I have said.'

The problem is that in his speeches on the Middle East, Hawke has devoted only a small percentage, if any, of each one to the plight of the Palestinians, while highlighting the violent physical and verbal assaults upon Israel by her neighbours. He thus projected the impression that, for him, the Palestinians were irrelevant.

By 1973 tension was steadily building in the Middle East. Hawke went to Israel in the first half of the year and by mid-year was convinced that a crisis was looming: 'I felt very tense about it all. Then on the eve of the ACTU Congress there was a death threat, purporting to come from the Black September Movement. I think I was so nervous at the Congress because I had a sense that something was going to break.'

By late 1973 the pace of Hawke's life had turned his life into the panting of a revolving door.

Then on 6 October, the Day of Atonement in Israel, the most holy day of the year, Egyptian forces surged across the Suez Canal and captured the Bar Lev defence line while, simultaneously, Syrian tanks pushed deep into Israeli-held territory north-east of the Golan Heights. It was a massive assault. At

---

* Resolution 242 was promulgated on 22 November 1967, following the Six Day War. It includes these elements: inadmissibility of conquests; need to establish a just and lasting peace; withdrawal of Israeli troops from territories (according to the English text not from "the territories" ie. not necessarily all of them) occupied in 1967; termination of belligerency; acknowledgment of sovereignty; territorial integrity and political independence of all States in the area and their right to live in peace within secure and recognised boundaries; just settlement of the refugee problem and the establishment of demilitarised zones.

first it seemed that Israel had been swept into the sea, but by 12 October it had recaptured territory taken by the advancing Syrians and three days later had thrust between the Egyptian armies on the eastern bank of the Canal, crossed the Canal and established a bridgehead into Africa. On 17 October the Organisation of Arab Petroleum Exporting Countries (OAPEC) announced it would reduce oil production by 5% a month until Israel withdrew from all occupied Arab territories. Saudi Arabia put a total embargo on oil sales to the United States. The war continued. The USA and USSR worked out a ceasefire resolution which was passed by the Security Council of the UN. This broke down immediately, and on 25 October the Israeli forces on the west bank of the Canal surrounded the Egyptian Third Army. Israel now had the Egyptians in checkmate on one front and, on the other, was in a position to destroy Damascus. The USA went on world-wide strategic forces alert, warning both the Israelis against further advances and the Soviet Union against intervention. There was a ceasefire. OAPEC announced further cuts in production of oil. On 6 November the nine members of the European Economic Community endorsed a statement which called for an Israeli withdrawal from the territories occupied in 1967. The long campaign of forcing Israel down to the status of an international pariah had begun.

Hawke had been in Geneva at an ILO Governing Body meeting. He flew to Tel Aviv on 18 November and was met by Tel-Shahar, who was summoned from military duty to escort him. Michael Siew had disappeared, fighting in the Golan Heights. With an army spokesman, a journalist, and Siew's father, they set out for the north, Hawke determined to find Siew. The Golan Heights were 'a cemetery of tanks' — hundreds upon hundreds of them. Bodies had been removed and the barren mountains were eerily quiet, littered with wreckage. Hawke said, 'The tanks were brand-new and had Russian writing on them — inside some of the ones I looked in there were bits and pieces of what had been men'. They drove all day, miles into Syria, stopping at Israeli army camps to ask news of Siew. It was bitterly cold and Hawke sat hunched up and swearing, increasingly distressed as they failed to find his friend.*

Hawke recalled,

> After hours of wandering through this evidence of carnage we drove down to Jerusalem, arrived there late in the afternoon, and I immediately met Golda, in her office. I think that was the most emotional meeting I've ever had in my life with anyone. There was an old woman who had just been through the most unbelievably traumatic experience of having the survival of her country in question — if the Egyptian and Syrian advance had lasted another twenty-four hours Israel would have been finished — and she was tormenting herself. Because, as she said, all the intelligence reports for days before Yom Kippur had indicated a

---

* Siew was alive; he turned up a few days after Hawke left Israel.

massive build-up of Arab forces. So the pressure was on to do what they'd done in 1967 and make a pre-emptive strike. But, as she said, the overwhelming factor was that the Americans had warned they would not tolerate another first strike attack by Israel, and there had been a great fear that if they did attack first they would be left without the sustaining flow of ammunition and replacement weaponry. And she was just emotionally and spiritually shattered, because ultimately she had to make the decision, and she'd lost the lives of 2,500 men. She was blaming herself. There was this great human being, in tears. She hadn't lost control of herself — in fact, the opposite, there was still a great strength in her — but tears were running down her face. It was in that circumstance that she showed me photographs of young Israelis who'd been captured in the Golan Heights by the Syrians, had their hands tied behind their backs and had their heads shot apart. And she was weeping and saying she couldn't understand how people could behave like that. I asked her if I could have copies of the pictures. I made up my mind that I'd do what I could for Israel.

When Hawke emerged from the Prime Minister's office Tel-Shahar said, 'I did not recognise him. He was trembling. Pale.'

Hawke's sense of duty had been stimulated as never before. And probably, too, his belief in his destiny — that he was an instrument which must be used for the good of mankind. He recalled later,

I had been uniquely privileged to have seen what I had — I was the first non-Israeli to have been taken so far into the war-zone to witness what *had* happened and what could have happened. The Israelis were shaken beyond belief by the war, not just emotionally but in the confidence they'd had in their strategic strength. That confidence was gone. But it had been replaced with a determination, which I cannot overemphasise, that, 'This will never happen again'. I must make this point: I have never been told by Israelis either in confidence or out of confidence that they have nuclear weapons, but it was not unreasonable to think in 1973 that they might have them, or might acquire them. In my conversations with people outside the leadership I made the suggestion, based on my observation of their utter determination, 'If Israel had tactical nuclear weapons and was again faced with obliteration, she would use them'. And there was no dissent from this view. So what we were looking at, if there were another round, was the possibility of nuclear war. I had already decided to return to Moscow to talk to Shelepin if the Israelis wanted me to. They did, and had already made arrangements before I talked to Golda. There was no question of the Israelis wanting me to convey the message to Moscow, 'Next time it's nukes'. But by then we knew each other very well — I had a relationship with people there in which the nuances and the unspoken were as significant as the direct and the spoken. I think they knew I would be talking about nuclear war to Shelepin. Certainly, they wanted me to tell him just how much determination there was in Israel, the same message as before, but now even louder. And, of course, they wanted me again to put pressure on him for the release of Soviet Jews.

On 22 November he flew to Moscow and was met at the airport by Shelepin. They talked during the late afternoon and into the night. Hawke recalled,

I had the sense that this was one of the biggest moments in my life, that I was uniquely placed in terms of knowledge and understanding of Israel to try to get this very powerful man, whose country's equipment I had seen smashed to pieces, to understand the enormity of the situation that had loomed and could return. And to try to make him realise that Soviet policy, resulting in the destruction of millions of dollars' worth of its most modern technology, was just insanity! The Arab armies had not been transformed by the USSR. The Israelis had surrounded the Egyptian army, and the bloody Syrians could have lost Damascus. And if it had gone the other way, against Israel, what did he think the USSR would gain? War with America, maybe?

Hawke quickly told Shelepin of his worst fears, the possibility of a nuclear war. Shelepin replied, one can only hope untruthfully, that Egypt had a nuclear device already installed and this could be activated in twenty-four hours. He maintained that the USSR was determined Israel would not be flung into the Mediterranean and that, if this had seemed likely, Moscow would have ordered the Egyptian and Syrian armies to halt their advance. Hawke replied 'rather strongly' — which means, he shouted — that such an assertion was idiotic, that the Arab armies could not have been halted by a command from Moscow and that Shelepin was insulting his intelligence with this assertion.

Hawke recalled,

There was a big difference in Shelepin since 1971. By late 1973 he was totally absorbed, fascinated and worried by China. Australia had a unique position because of Gough's opening of diplomatic relations with China and Shelepin seemed to think that we therefore were able to speak with particular authority. He talked to me as he would talk to very few people. He was paranoid about China. Full of fear and contempt. He said they were rubbish, nothings, but at the same time he manifested an enormous apprehension. He was terrifically concerned by the *rapprochement* between the USA and China and in this context, talking about Nixon, something weird happened. I'd said to him, 'You can stop thinking about Nixon — he's finished'. One did not need to be brilliant to know that by late 1973 Watergate had destroyed Nixon. But Shelepin became vehement that Nixon was safe. He said that the whole Watergate episode was a concoction by 'reactionary capitalist forces who are angry with Nixon because he initiated *détente* with the USSR'. He was totally insistent that Watergate would soon be revealed as a capitalist plot. It shows the strange relationship we had: I said to him, 'Would you care to put your money where your mouth is?' He was puzzled by the translation for a moment, then he realised what I was saying and grinned. We bet two dozen bottles of best vodka.

By the time Hawke had won the bet Shelepin was on the verge of disgrace, so Hawke did not collect his prize. For reasons unknown, Shelepin was removed from the Soviet hierarchy in 1975; there has been speculation since that his fall may have been due, in part, to his meetings with Hawke.

While Hawke was abroad Whitlam had announced that the Australian Government had an 'even-handed policy in the Middle East'. The Party's policy, based on Resolution 242 of the United Nations, and adopted in July 1973 at the Surfers Paradise Conference, stated:

> The situation in the Middle East remains the greatest threat to the peace of the world. There can be no peace until the Arab States respect and recognise Israel's sovereignty and right to exist. Equally, there can be no peace until Israeli forces have withdrawn from occupied territories to secure and recognised boundaries and a just settlement of the refugee problem is achieved.

Hawke returned to Australia on 24 November 1973 and in a Perth news conference made an impassioned plea for Israel. Clem, for the first time in twenty years, was alarmed by the vehemence of his son's manner. Hawke showed to the news media the photographs Golda Meir had given him of murdered prisoners of war. They were screened on nation-wide television. On his part it was an act of questionable wisdom: there is no such thing as a war in which troops maintain military discipline at all times. Hawke's implication that the enemies of Israel had a monopoly upon barbarity was both unjustified — one must recall the activities, just for example, of the Irgun — and reckless, for atrocity feeds upon atrocity.

He said, 'Showing the photographs was, I think, the start of the real hate campaign against me'.

Hawke had said in his news conference: 'For the Australian Government to say our position on the Middle East is one of even-handedness is not an intelligent approach to the situation'. He also made reference to an assumption that the Whitlam Government's attitude was based on fear of loss of oil supplies. He said, 'That's all right for the politicians, but I understand what truth and democracy are all about and I don't put my knees on the same altar as the politicians'. As a result, there were questions in Parliament for Whitlam, and more questions at his weekly Press conference. The Prime Minister said, 'Australia has a bipartisan policy, a policy of neutrality in the Middle East. The ALP policy is substantially the policy which governments have pursued for the last quarter of a century in Australia', and that Hawke was speaking as 'a private citizen', not as President of the Party. The following day the *Sydney Morning Herald* in its editorial wondered, 'How long Mr Hawke, holding the views he does, can sustain his current balancing feat as ALP and ACTU President'. That question was to be tested at the next meeting of the ALP federal executive, due in February 1974.

On 28 November 1973 a senior journalist, Adrian Deamer, delivering the national broadcast, Notes on the News, said:

> This is another vicious attack on the Prime Minister and on the politicians of the Labor Party [by Hawke]. It maintains his early form when he criticised the Government's announcement during the Parramatta by-election that Sydney's airport was to be sited at Galston as 'political imbecility'. He followed this up with his public statement that the trade union movement would not support the Government at the December 8 referendum on prices and incomes, and just before he left for Israel he said that the Government should have increased income tax . . . He has emphasised that on this occasion he is speaking as a private citizen, and this explanation was accepted by Mr Whitlam . . .
>
> The real issue that emerges from this controversy goes far beyond whether Mr Hawke should or should not criticise his party and Mr Whitlam . . . What we need in this country is more information on which we can act, and greater diversity of views, not less. We need to encourage people like Mr Hawke to speak out and to tell us what they know and think, not condemn them for going against the official line . . . Like him or not, Mr Hawke breaks through this apathy and dispels the dullness [of Australian politics], forcing a lot of people to rethink the issues they have taken for granted.[3]

That night Hawke went to see Abeles, who happened to be in Melbourne. Abeles recalled, 'Bob was tremendously upset. He needed to let off steam and talk and talk. He was in an agony. He talked the whole night, until dawn, crying sometimes, and shouting. I was terribly worried. I thought he was at a breaking point.'

Next day in the ACTU office Hawke answered the telephone. A man with a foreign accent said, 'I am from Black September. We are going to kill your children', and hung up. Hawke went into the boardroom to open an executive meeting. His old friends knew from his appearance that something was wrong. After a few minutes Hawke blurted out what had happened and began to weep, saying, 'Must I give up my beliefs to save my children?' The crisis that had been developing all year had been triggered.

A doctor was called. He gave Hawke a sedative injection. Hawke was driven home and put to bed. Police collected the children from school. Police guards were stationed at the house. Terrorism hung over Hawke like an axe. Policemen accompanied the children to and from school and stood guard in their playgrounds. They opened letters which came to the house.

On 5 December the Friends of Palestine published a full-page advertisement in the *Australian* headed, An Open Letter to Bob Hawke. It refuted that the death threat had come from the Black September Movement and went on to say:

> We suggest that Mr Hawke is appallingly ignorant of the real issues in the Middle East dispute. *If he can support Israel on morality grounds, then the traditional meaning of the word 'morality' has ceased.* Mr Hawke is prostituting morality in the services of a fascist regime, sacrificing the noble ideals of the Labor Movement and slaying the Australian 'fair go' principle on the altar of a racist government which imports Jewish citizens from Russia and elsewhere, but consistently denies the indigenous Palestinian Arabs the fundamental right of citizenship in their country of birth.

As soon as Hawke was on his feet again he bought a rifle and would check that all the house windows and doors were locked before going to bed. In the office, 'he looked like death warmed up — he was pretty much a wreck for four months', Cliff Dolan said.

Meanwhile, letters and telegrams had flooded the ACTU. There were hundreds from church-goers, from 'Liberal voters' and, of course, from Jews. Some said:

> God bless you in your work, and as you take this stand I and my church are remembering you in prayer.

> Neither my wife nor I are ALP supporters but we both support your views on Israel . . . delighted that at last a public figure has the courage to state what is morally right even if unpopular.

> In our church service this morning our pastor led us in prayer for you, your wife and family and for the people of Israel . . .

> Australia needs men like you who will stand firm for what they believe to be right . . .

In your role as Trade Union leader, I have never felt there would be
anything in which I could support you, but your public stand on this
matter has changed my views.

I am not on your side politically but loyalty to principles transcends
political differences.

For the first time I find myself in agreement with you.

I beg you to use your position and your voice to pressure the Government into reversing the policy of neutrality . . . I am ashamed to live in a
country which will even *consider* putting economic security before the
right of a brave little country to exist, let alone live in peace . . . I have no
voice. Tell of my anger, I beg you.

I am not normally an ardent supporter of 'Bob Hawke' but . . . after
tonight I think I will be . . . You will have I am sure a multitude of
Australians behind you if they have the opportunity to make their
voices heard.[4]

Many of the letters were from businessmen and academics; some drew
attention to the fact that the writers were not Jewish. The response from the
Jewish community was passionate. The Yom Kippur War had terrified world
Jewry. Jews who had little interest in Israel were suddenly suffocated by the
fear that genocide could recur, and without Israel there would be nowhere to
flee. Saul Same, an ALP member, Chairman of Directors of Glo-Weave and
Chairman of the United Israel Appeal, was one of those in charge of fund-
raising in Australia to help Israel during and after the War. He said,

People who had never given a penny in their lives to Israel came to us.
Money poured in to the United Israel Appeal. There are plenty of poor
Jews in Australia. They sold things to give us money. People mortgaged
their houses, and came to us with their jewellery, even their wedding
rings . . . I can tell you that there were those among us who would give
their lives for Bob Hawke. If anybody had harmed a hair of his head,
that person would have been killed.

Among the letters and telegrams from Jews there were many offering
Hawke their houses and cars as refuges for his family. Non-Jews made similar
offers — a Western Australian businessman telephoned to offer his private
aeroplane to fly the family to safety in the West. A Supreme Court Judge
wrote, '. . . you have had the moral courage . . . while others in high places,
known for their articulate professions of the Brotherhood of Man, have

remained silent'. Another senior lawyer and an ALP member wrote, 'Gough will never know what chills he sent down our spines . . . with that "even-handed neutrality" statement of his. It was so cold and so lacking in insight . . . I suddenly felt insecure here, for the first time in my life.'

There were very few unfavourable letters. Some began, 'Mr Jew Hawke'. A regular critic, who signed himself 'Joe the Worker', wrote on this occasion:

> Your invitation to Zionists to take over your well-planned homes and holidays for the Australian worker is a clear indication that you also support the multi-national corporations and enterprises who [sic] dominate our finances.

Meanwhile, in the trade union movement and in the ALP there was anger:

> You have no right to pursue your personal views about Israel when Australian workers finance your trips overseas.

> You [and Whitlam] have a duty to the people of Australia to control yourselves. Otherwise you will be guilty of sabotaging the Labor Party and the people, as did Billy Hughes and Lyons years ago.[5]

When Hawke returned to work in January 1974 it was to plunge straight in to the predicament within the upper echelons of the ALP which his out-spokenness as President of the Party had caused. He was told that the Prime Minister and other members of the federal executive had exhausted their patience with him, and he would be sacked. 'The phones were running hot, all through January', a senior ALP man remarked. In mid-January Hawke gave a television interview to Mike Schildberger in the office of Eddie Kornhauser, at the time a Melbourne hotel owner. Kornhauser was a shrewd businessman and one of Hawke's close friends. When the interview was over Hawke had a violent argument with Schildberger, a non-Zionist Jew, over Israel. Kornhauser, a strong Zionist, was so astonished by the passion of Hawke's commitment to Israel that, he said, 'For the first time I realised, This man is real. And that night I determined to try to do something for him.' Hawke had told Kornhauser that he was going to be removed from the presidency of the ALP. Kornhauser had a number of IOUs out in the Party, which he had supported handsomely over the years. He decided he would call them in.

Meanwhile, Hawke refused to keep silent on Israel. On 26 January he addressed a conference of the Zionist Federation of Australia and New Zealand in Sydney. He was still being escorted by body guards and the hall where the meeting was held was under heavy police surveillance. Hawke wore the traditional Jewish skull cap as he spoke to a group that was already hyper-charged with emotion. He scorned the even-handed interpretation which Whitlam had given to ALP policy on the Middle East and went on to say,

> Oil is a murky substance and it has, I believe, blurred the vision of men of goodwill . . . We cannot be even-handed in judgment between States, any more than between individuals, when one side is bent upon the physical destruction of the other. In the 1930s appeasement under threat and blackmail permitted, among other things, the holocaust in which six million of our fellow human beings, who happened to be Jews, were exterminated. All mankind was diminished by those events. I do not speak here for my Party or for the industrial movement which I lead. But as an individual Australian, I know that I am not an island and I know that if we allow the bell to be tolled for Israel it will have tolled for me, for us all.[6]

There was a standing ovation.

On 14 February the ALP federal executive was to meet. It would be the first meeting to discuss the Government's failure to win Parramatta and to win the referenda. The Hawke camp had decided to bring up the question of the Middle East. The numbers would be close but within the Party those who were furious with Hawke for his criticisms of the Government and the Prime Minister were confident they could force Hawke to resign. This has been one of the better kept secrets in the ALP. Even in 1981 executive members were unwilling to talk about it, including Hawke, whose only comment is, 'I can't really remember that'. Others too have developed amnesia. However, a letter dated 19 February 1974[7] to Eddie Kornhauser suggests that the move against Hawke was serious and failed because of the hard lobbying conducted by Hawke's supporters. It appears that the attitude of Egerton was critical, for if he would not agree to accept the presidency there could be no smooth transition, but a Party brawl. As it was Egerton (most unwillingly) recalled, 'Gough was saying to me, "Mr President, Mr President". Well . . . I've never had any time for Gough. I stuck by my mates.'

The executive minutes reveal little: merely that on a motion, moved by Egerton and seconded by David Combe, to debate the situation in the Middle East, the executive tied 8-8, and it was therefore resolved in the negative.[8] The voting line-up seems to show that before the meeting opened a Left-Right alliance against the Hawke group had come to an agreement with the latter, and that the alliance itself aborted the plan. One person who reluctantly spoke of the affair gave an explanation which has the ring of *realpolitik* truth:

> They tried to take Bob head on and saw it would be very difficult. So they called that off and went underground against him — used the news

media, the smear campaign in the Party. They're the sort of people who don't much like the light of day and prefer to work in the dark.

The speaker made clear that he did not include Whitlam in this group.

Hawke escaped with a reprimand about his outspokenness. But his problems within the Party were only just beginning for he had now earned the enmity of many Caucus members and all the Left-wingers.

A prominent Left-wing figure on the federal executive was Bill Hartley, former Secretary of the Victorian branch, and as devoted a supporter of the Palestinians as Hawke was of the Israelis. Hartley is a friendly, personable man who, after being a Liberal in his youth, made a change to radical politics. He was active in his opposition to State aid for non-government schools and the Vietnam War and after that turned his attention to the Palestinians. Later he became an employee of the Government of Iraq and championed the 'People's Revolution' in Iran. He and Hawke had fallen out in 1970 over federal intervention into the Victorian branch of the ALP but were still on reasonably friendly terms in 1974. Hartley was, and still remains, at the extreme perimeter of the Socialist Left faction of the Victorian ALP and was for many years the faction's representative on the federal executive, one of the two Victorian delegates to the executive.

Hawke was in such poor shape before the 14 February meeting that Hazel, stalwart as ever, had accompanied him to Canberra. That night Hartley came to their room and he and Hawke had a long 'fairly amicable', Hawke said, argument about the Middle East. It was the last fairly amicable meeting between them. Hawke developed during 1974 a hatred for Hartley because of the latter's published assertions about Israel, which included comments such as 'International Zionism collaborated with the Nazis';* and 'Israel is a huge Ghetto founded on a monstrous injustice [to Palestinians, which] should be replaced by a State containing virtues which Israel has never had, and never could have: an open society, equality, political and religious pluralism, freedom, democracy and amity with its neighbours'. Hartley's notions about the Middle East enjoyed currency in Socialist Left circles, and Hawke's determination to contest them at every opportunity was to intensify his struggle with the Left. The Yom Kippur War, which marked the beginning of Israel's conversion by the international community into a pariah State, was also the beginning of Hawke's pariahdom in the eyes of the Left. By the end of the decade he had, among radicals, the image of a monster: a corrupt and greedy man, a friend to millionaires and a 'fascist regime', an enemy of the poor and weak.

That night in the Canberra Rex Hotel Hawke had drinks with Party

* Without going into the history of the 'Europa Plan' and the Nazi attempt to ransom European Jews for gold from their kinsmen in Palestine, this statement is disingenuous nonsense.

officials and a group of journalists, during which he expressed the views which he had been unable to, earlier that day, in the federal executive. He said,

> I had these feelings: an enormous sense of frustration that people thought that the Yom Kippur War was just another war — so what? I was also horrified by the callousness of attitudes: people were almost blaming Israel for having been in a scrap, and, ho-hum, it might happen again. And following from that, I wanted to try to get home the message that if an attempt to obliterate Israel recurred and if Israel had tactical nuclear weapons, they would be used.

It appears that only Hawke's last point — which he illustrated dramatically by saying that if he were Israel's Prime Minister and were faced with the destruction of his country, he would feel bound to employ tactical nuclear arms in self-defence — got through to his audience. His agitate-and-educate conversation with the group was not an interview, and was therefore off-the-record. But on 16 February Sydney's *Daily Telegraph* carried a front-page story headlined, 'I'D A-BOMB ARABS, SAYS HAWKE'. Three days later the popular television programme, *A Current Affair*, broadcast a jingle to the tune of the Jewish folk song, Hava Nagila, which implied that Hawke was nuclear-bomb happy. He sued on both accounts for libel and won costs against the *Telegraph* and a settlement from *A Current Affair*, but the damage to his reputation had been enormous.

Throughout Hawke's career many of his failures, like this one, have arisen from the same source as his successes: that behind what he says there is an attitude of mind and a system of values which people either grasp spontaneously, or not at all. It is often not the fault of Hawke's audience that he is misunderstood, for he talks in a sort of shorthand, on the assumption that others share his thinking. In conversation with him it is necessary to fill in or to translate much of what he has left unsaid or has stated in his own brand of laconic communication: a twitch of his mouth, a pause, a shrug, a look of puzzlement in return for puzzlement. One early example of the lacunae in his communications was his attitude towards Cecil Rhodes and Rhodes Scholars, which none of his peers understood. A later example came from a very senior public servant who was involved in Hawke's first strike negotiations: the man recalled being initially confounded by Hawke's verbal shorthand. He commented, 'Bob said that "for obvious reasons" such and such could not happen. Those reasons were not at all obvious to me. It was only after lunch that Bob explained. His sincerity, his conviction and his total honesty then came through.' The public servant, who requested anonymity, is a man of unusually sharp intelligence and subtlety; less gifted people are more likely to be bemused by what Hawke says. Good journalists who attempt to maintain objectivity and therefore deliberately resist falling into rapport with Hawke, often achieve this at the expense of understanding of him.

A second aspect, which is both an advantage and a disadvantage, is Hawke's direct expression of anger. Clyde Holding recalled an evening when he and Hawke were arguing about Hugh Gaitskell:

> Bob wanted me to agree with him that Gaitskell was a bastard. I wasn't really interested, but Bob got intense about it. When I wouldn't agree with him he grabbed me and began shaking me or banging my arm on the table, I can't remember which, saying, 'Go on! Say it! Admit Gaitskell's a bastard!' People who aren't used to him, who don't know that's just the bloke's style, get very upset.

Many people are half-deafened by Hawke's intensity and find it difficult to follow what he is saying because their emotional reaction to him has partly shut-down their thinking processes and Hawke's arguments come through to them simplified by the flood of adrenalin he has aroused.

One of those present in the Canberra Rex on the night of 14 February recalled that when Hawke had spoken of nuclear weapons, and had been challenged: 'You cannot justify the use of nuclear weapons under any circumstances', Hawke had replied, 'Why? Because of world morality? Be damned to world morality — the world has stood by for twenty-five years and watched attempts to push Israel into the sea without lifting a finger. If I were the Israeli Prime Minister I wouldn't give a damn about world morality — I would use the atomic bomb to protect my own.'⁹

Had Hawke gone through the steps of his argument, beginning at Yad Vashem and leading on to the Israeli war memorials, his audience may have had a better grasp of his ideas. As it was, he simply expected them to *know* the effect the Holocaust has had upon Israeli attitudes, to *know* that Israelis have never forgiven and, perhaps, will never forgive the rest of the world because of the Holocaust, and to *know* that Israelis regard Gentile morality as bankrupt. They grasped, it seems, none of this background but remembered only the vivid foreground of his anger.

The months from the end of November, when the death threat was made, through to April, when Hawke gathered himself together for a federal election campaign, were terrible ones for the whole family. Hawke had been an absentee father for years; suddenly it had come home to him how dear the children were, and for the first time since his early days at the ACTU he decided he must make time for a family life. A doctor who was a long-term friend and who had treated Hawke after he had been on drinking benders owned a farm in Gippsland and had offered it to the Hawkes as a weekend retreat earlier in 1973. A police guard put on duty there in 1974 noted that Hawke was pitifully overwrought.

There were other symptoms: one night in early 1974 Hawke was drinking in the Boulevard Hotel in Sydney with a friend when he suddenly thought that a waiter, walking towards him, intended assault. Hawke threw a punch at the waiter and had to be forced to leave the bar and go to his room. Next day the friend upbraided Hawke for his behaviour:

> He looked appalled when I told him all the things he'd done the night before. We were having lunch in a restaurant. He said, 'Oh, God, why do I do these things?' and started to cry. But he had the guts to go back to the Boulevard, find the waiter and apologise to him.

The Attorney-General's Department spent months investigating if indeed a terrorist group was operating in Australia and intended to murder the Hawke children. Its officers came to the conclusion that neither Black September guerrillas nor other Arab terrorists had reached Australia, and that the threat was, therefore, probably from a crank — which is not to say that cranks are incapable of murder. Hawke said later with bitter anguish, 'It worried me that, maybe, the kids had been through all of that for nothing'. When questioned further his demeanour becomes threatening, with a look that says, 'I refuse to discuss that'.

By April 1974 the worst period was over. Hawke's recovery was speeded by national political concerns, for the Opposition — emboldened by the Government's failure in Parramatta; with the referenda; and by its misman-agement of an attempt to play political thimble-and-pea (the Gair Affair) — had summoned the nerve to delay supply in the Senate. Whitlam decided to hold a general election. Hawke's popularity rating was very high and the Party decided to use him to the utmost in the election campaign. He was especially useful because of the disillusion with government in the trade union movement, which was so great that a number of unions had disaffiliated from the ALP. This had depleted the Party's campaign funds. Another of Hawke's uses was that he was by now an excellent fund-raiser. David Combe said later,

> I don't know how much Bob has raised for the Party, but it is certainly hundreds of thousands of dollars. We could be confident that he would pack any hall. And he got a lot of dough from businessmen. There was always an irony that the Left would shriek about Hawke's being friendly with big businessmen but when he got big cheques from them there was no suggestion that the money should be sent back, or that he'd done the wrong thing.

During the campaign Hawke was anxious that Whitlam should win back the hearts of the Jewish community. Kornhauser gave a breakfast in his hotel, the Chevron, at which the Prime Minister was to address Melbourne's Jews and calm their fears about the Government's joining the rush away from Israel. Unfortunately, the soothing turned into a confrontation, for during the meeting Whitlam demanded, 'What do you people want?' Years later Jews were still wrathful that Whitlam had called them 'you people'. Saul Same said,

> Gough lost the Jewish vote when he said those words. But people made a distinction for Bob. If there were a fund-raising function and Bob was speaking everyone wanted to come. I remember organising a dinner and being doubtful about approaching a particular man, one of the most senior industrialists in Melbourne. I rang him and he said, 'What! For Bob Hawke? I'll cancel a wedding.' And he did.

Even Hawke's enemies acknowledged that his efforts during the 1974 campaign were heroic and that the Government's victory, with five seats in hand, owed as much to him as to Whitlam.

His determination to spend the weekends undisturbed in the country had of course been abandoned during the campaign. When the election was over his weekend peace was never completely restored. By May 1974 it was obvious that the economy was seriously ill: inflation was surging forward, thanks in large part to *the* sharp weapon in Middle East politics: huge increases in oil prices; there was an epidemic of strikes; wage claims were extraordinary and were feeding back into the inflationary spiral; the Treasury restrictions on money supply were biting too hard on business; and unemployment was increasing. After a while the demands on Hawke were such that a telephone had to be installed at the farm. He was called back to town more and more, and gradually the dream of a 'normal' family life drifted away.

Hawke had cancelled two ILO meetings, fearful that if he were in Europe, where Arab terrorists were most active, he could be killed. But in June he decided he must keep an appointment to address a conference in Oxford. Before he left he called on Kornhauser to ask him to look after Hazel and the children for him if he were murdered. Hawke had no idea what his exact financial situation was, except that he was in debt. He did not know if he had any life insurance policies, for Hazel looked after such matters. Kornhauser recalled,

> Bob was giving me a heart attack! No money, a wife, three children! What am I going to do? It's Saturday night and he's leaving the next morning. We owed him so much . . . I assured Bob that if anything happened to him Hazel and the children would be cared for.

The Israelis also considered it their duty to protect Hawke, and when he arrived there en route for London, a bodyguard was waiting for him. Governments normally provide bodyguards only for ambassadors or heads of state. An Australian diplomat in Israel described the bodyguard as 'nine feet tall and nine feet wide, covered in weapons and muttering into a walkie-talkie all the time. It wasn't very pleasant.' In England Hawke's back gave way again after a two-year remission of trouble and he had to board his aircraft home as an invalid in a wheelchair.

By August he was warning that the Government would not survive unless it brought down the rate of inflation within a year. Meanwhile, throughout 1974, one after another of Hawke's ACTU enterprise schemes had been neglected and the enterprise ideas were fading away. There had been an outright rejection from the unions of any joint-ventures with Histadrut, because of the odium now attached to Israel. Other schemes had vanished because Hawke had been too ill or too distracted with strike negotiations and other work (he was already a member of the Jackson Committee as well as on the Board of the Reserve Bank), to give them time. All round, it had been a miserable twelve months.

Hawke was personally consoled when, in September, he was re-elected unopposed as President of the ALP and the federal executive paid tribute to the efforts he had made to have the Government returned to office. Some office. Inflation for the year was 16.3%, strikes had cost 6,292,500 working days lost and more than a quarter of a million were unemployed. Before the Budget was introduced, a month late, Hawke held pre-Budget discussions with the Government, arguing for cuts in indirect taxes and the income taxes of the less well paid; a reduction in interest rates; the introduction of quarterly wage adjustments to curb wage claims; and indexation of income tax. At a special conference of ACTU affiliated unions he had managed to wring from delegates a commitment to try to pull together with the Government, even to the extent, as the meeting's resolution stated, of giving 'sympathetic consideration to supporting attempts by the Government to acquire ... powers' to deal with economic problems. This was almost a reversal of the unions' previous policy on the incomes referendum.

By October he and Whitlam were friends again, lunching together at The Lodge. It was the calm before the next storm.

Chapter Seventeen

It may be that future historians with a fondness for the convenience of dates will note 6 October 1973 as the day on which the centuries of world domination by the values and laws that arose from Christendom ended. Just a year afterwards, on 13 November 1974, in the General Assembly of the United Nations, Christianity's younger cousin-faith, Islam, revealed the triumph of its reinvigoration: with a gun-holster visible on his hip, Yassar Arafat, leader of the PLO, entered the hall, strode to the podium and said, 'Today I have come bearing an olive branch and a freedom fighter's gun. Do not let the olive branch fall from my hand. I repeat: do not let the olive branch fall from my hand.' The technology was different but the words could have come from the lips of the Last Prophet.

It was the first time a man had addressed the international parliament with such dramatic symbolism. The most dangerous weapon previously displayed there by a speaker was Nikita Khruschchev's shoe, with which he had banged the lectern. Arafat's gun-holster was a sign of the changing times: as a British diplomat had quipped in earlier days, 'The Kingdom of Heaven may run on love, but the Kingdom of Earth runs on oil'. The PLO was admitted to observer status in the UN; before the end of the decade an interesting term had entered common speech: 'The Islamic Bomb'. Nuclear weapons had once been 'American' or 'Russian' or 'Chinese'. Abruptly they were not only national, but religious.

For the rest of the 1970s Hawke fought against the crusades of a new era. He tried to be a mediator: in the PLO, in Israel, in Egypt and Jordan — extraordinary, but futile, efforts. He even tried to meet Yassar Arafat when, in late 1974, a senior Egyptian journalist who had contacts with the PLO visited Australia and offered to sound out the possibilities for such a meeting. However by then the PLO was riding high and had little need or desire to hold discussions with such a committed Zionist as Hawke. The increasingly bitter exchanges between Hawke and Hartley made it all the less likely.

Early in 1975 Hawke learned that, with Hartley's encouragement, a PLO delegation had been invited to visit Australia and that the Government had agreed to issue visas. He was outraged. The Australian Government would not, for example, allow representatives of the Ustashi, dedicated to the overthrow of the Government of Yugoslavia, to enter the country. The PLO visa issue was, for Hawke, another example of the Whitlam Government's dual morality. His diary notes for 29 January 1975: '8.25 a.m. spoke to Whitlam about PLO visas'. Many others spoke, too. The trip was cancelled.

The next day Hawke had to chair an ALP federal executive meeting which would finalise business for the Party's biennial Conference, due the following week, in Terrigal.

Terrigal is a holiday resort town on the north coast of NSW. The choice of a hot weather playground for the Party's meeting was ill advised, for matters of State should never be seen without neck-ties, or in the company of bare shoulders.

Hawke said,

> The Terrigal conference would have been the worst the ALP ever had. The whole thing was a schemozzle. Ministers were writing their policy statements hours before going up to the Conference. The assembling of an economic policy statement was — oh, ludicrous. There was no wages policy debate. There was an unreal air to the whole show; the Government clearly felt that this was an ALP conference that was irrelevant, because *they* were in government, *they* were running things, *they* knew what they were going to do — or didn't know what they were going to do — but at any rate, it was for *them* to decide. So what was the use of this conference? And matters were worsened by the determination of the Press to convey the whole thing as an exercise in hedonism. The photographs of people sitting around the swimming pool, being thrown in the pool . . .

Hawke himself was guilty of playing into the hands of those sections of the Press which were now extremely hostile to the Government and were eager to project an image of it that was undignified. He agreed to assist the promotion of the Government-sponsored Old Sydney Town project and, allotted the part of a convict, was photographed shirtless, his hands bound, and apparently being whipped by an attractive young woman who worked in the office of the new federal Treasurer, Dr Jim Cairns. Egerton complained about the photograph at the time, and said later that Hawke had been distracted from his duties during the Conference by his own streak of hedonism.

Hawke gave the address which opened proceedings, a rallying cry for solidarity, but he was still writing it minutes before he delivered it, so the opportunity for having the speech distributed to the news media was missed. He had the valid excuse that he had no speech writers, no support staff at all, as President of the ALP. Ministers had plenty of hired hands — rather too many, and of the wrong type, in the view of the Press.

For some months the news media had been focusing upon the person and position of a former air hostess and director of some failed companies, Junie Morosi. Morosi, a handsome Eurasian, had in late 1974 become the personal assistant to the Deputy Prime Minister and federal Treasurer, Dr Jim Cairns. Their relationship had aroused curiosity. Cairns had been subjected to a barrage of attack and innuendo, but his fine response to the Cyclone Tracy disaster on Christmas Eve 1974, had served to recoup his prestige. People had temporarily forgotten about Junie Morosi. Then on the second last day of the Conference which, while it had produced little of value in terms of policy, had at least avoided any Left-Right brawls or motions demanding the nationalisation of BHP, Cairns gave a personal interview. The journalist he talked to, Toni McRae, happened to be the wife of an aspiring Liberal politician. He admitted to this woman that he had 'a kind of love' for Junie Morosi. The news media went wild. Only once in a generation can editors hope for a comment as fey as that from a senior politician. The silly photographs aside, the Terrigal Conference had been depicted generally as a dull turn-out, which is how the Government wanted it to be seen. Overnight, Cairns' candid comments turned it into a farce.

George Rockey who, along with Abeles and Kornhauser, had helped to nurse Hawke through 1974, had driven to Terrigal to collect him. Rockey described himself as 'a very low-profile person'. He was small, neat and rather introverted, in marked contrast to his partner's, Abeles', largeness and ebullience. He and Hawke already had the type of easy friendship that Hawke can form in an instant, but between them there was a deeper attraction, an almost shy drawing together of opposites. Rockey was a gambling man and had been 'a bottle of Scotch a night' drinker, but had become teetotal in 1971 because he had reached the stage when every time he drank alcohol he fainted. He was thirteen years Hawke's senior and their relationship, much more than that between Hawke and Abeles, was another father-son affair. For all his gentleness and interest in psychology and metaphysics, Rockey was also worldly, even world-weary. He had worked as an intelligence agent during the war and perhaps because of this, and his later experience as a Jungian analysand, was not inclined to take people on face value. He had known plenty of betrayals. Early in their relationship he had decided to put Hawke's honesty to a test with a 'five-figure cheque', made out to Hawke, mentioning that it was for the ALP campaign fund. Years later he remarked, still with an echo of that first pleasure in his voice, 'And you know, next day I got a receipt for it from the Secretary of the Party'.

When he collected Hawke at Terrigal, Hawke was depressed about the state of the Government and the farcical image which, in the end, the Conference had had forced upon it. Rockey recalled,

I said to Bob the political situation was hopeless and told him that he had better bail out now. I offered him a sort of bribe. I said he could have any job he wanted in industry — he could be earning $100,000 a year, instead of living hand-to-mouth, with not enough money to educate his children. I said, 'Look, leave the Party. Leave the trade unions and think of yourself and Hazel and your children.' He became so angry with me. He said, 'George, stop the car. I'm getting out.' I knew then that I'd met a good man, a person of real honour.

Another matter of honour soon arose for Hawke. In early May 1975 Francis Blanchard, the new Director-General of the ILO, sent his senior assistant, Bernard Fortin, on what Fortin described as 'a secret mission' to Australia to elicit Hawke's help for the ILO. Blanchard had not met Hawke at this stage, so it was a measure of Hawke's reputation within the ILO that the Director-General approached him to assist the organisation — in the affair that was later known as The Crisis of 1975.

The ILO had been the first of the United Nations bodies to feel the sting of Arab vengeance against Israel and the old colonial powers. In June 1974, at the annual conference which Hawke had not attended because of the death threats, delegates had voted overwhelmingly for a resolution condemning 'the policy of discrimination, racism and violation of trade union freedoms and rights practised by the Israeli authorities in Palestine and in the other occupied Arab Territories'. There had been no investigation by the ILO to discover if in fact such abuses existed in Israeli-occupied territory. In the past, when a State had been condemned, there had been a formal ILO investigation beforehand. However times had changed. The Islamic countries of the Middle East, Africa and South East Asia, joined by the Soviet Bloc States and a few Europeans, in this case Spain and Greece, as well as Mexico, had an automatic majority. Having passed a resolution condemning Israel, they then passed a second: to have the ILO investigate conditions of workers in Israel. The resolutions, coming from nations in which trade union freedom was a joke, were staggeringly cynical and, legally, ranked with the adventures of Alice in Wonderland: sentence first, then judge. At the same conference the PLO had submitted a request to the Director-General, Blanchard, to be admitted as an observer to all the activities and meetings of the ILO. The PLO could not request membership because the ILO constitution limits membership to States. The Americans had let it be known that if the PLO were admitted to observer status — a question which would be decided in June 1975 — the USA would withdraw from the ILO. George Meany, who had the chief say on the issue, was intransigent. If the Americans withdrew it was feared that America's allies — for example, West Germany, which had the most important trade union movement in Europe — would also withdraw. Blanchard recalled,

I was desperate to find a solution that would allow the PLO some sort of status in the ILO but which would occur in a way that would not violate the constitution or the standing orders of the International Labour Conference. On one side we had the Arabs saying their demand was absolutely justified; on the other, the Americans, totally intransigent; and in the middle a lot of the European nations very embarrassed. Everything was complicated by Vietnam.

By early 1975, after a decade of American fighting there, North Vietnamese armies were sweeping south; in late April North Vietnamese tanks rumbled into Saigon and, amid horrendous panic, one of the Indo-Chinese wars ended. At home and abroad American morale was at a nadir. Uncle Sam was in an irrational frame of mind, and was not yet accustomed to the idea that the non-Communist global community, ordered about by Washington since the end of World War II, had changed, and that there were, now, many centres of power outside the USA.

Blanchard continued,

> Nations were using the war to insult and attack America and so, of course, the Americans were particularly sensitive. I thought of Bob Hawke as someone who could help because of several factors: he was totally orthodox on Israel and I knew he had a lot of credit in Washington and in the American Federation of Labor. George Meany liked him. I believed Bob was a man to get the Americans to listen, although I must say that Meany, a fascinating man, was absolutely The Chairman, the boss . . . I had the impression, which I later found to be true, that Bob was fascinated by the world at large, beyond the shores of Australia, and fascinated by foreign policy. To me that meant he would not look at problems in a narrow way, but in the wider context of world politics. Bob had criticisms of the ILO, which he would make in private, but at the same time he understood, he had strong feelings about, its importance as an institution. And he could realise what a real crisis, as an institution, it was facing.

Fortin relayed Blanchard's request to Hawke, who agreed to fly to Geneva via Washington. Before arriving in Australia Fortin had gone in secret to Cairo, to ask the leader of the Egyptian workers' delegation, Anwar Salama, a former Minister of Labour, to try to seek a compromise also. Salama had readily agreed. The Yom Kippur War had been a catharsis for the Egyptians, for their armies' vast incursions into Israeli-held territory had exorcised the humiliation of the 1967 war. The Egyptian leadership had announced, and the nation believed, that they had won a great military victory during the 1973 war, and now that Egyptian pride was purring they were thinking more peaceful thoughts. The Egyptians agreed to lean on the Syrians and other hard-line anti-Israel delegations so that a compromise on PLO observer status could be reached in the ILO's Standing Orders Committee. The International Labour Conference would then, automatically, pass the Committee's resolution.

Clyde Cameron was to lead the Australian Government delegation to the International Labour Conference, but on the eve of his departure Whitlam sacked him as Minister for Labour. Cameron, however, refused to be sacked and the Prime Minister had to ask the Governor-General, Sir John Kerr, to withdraw Cameron's commission — a somewhat ironic circumstance, at least for Cameron, in view of later events. His dismissal was one of a growing number of changes in the Whitlam ministry, which added to the Government's appearance of confusion. The drama over Cameron forced Hawke to abandon going first to Washington.

He set out in late May, breaking his journey to Switzerland in Athens, and from there went for a day's sightseeing to Delphi. At Delphi he received the news that Whitlam had performed a second miracle of bad timing.

Lance Barnard, the Defence Minister, had been miserable since he had lost the deputy prime ministership to Cairns. Barnard was a close friend of Whitlam. He had told the Prime Minister he wanted to leave politics and, since the post was becoming vacant, to be the next Ambassador to Stockholm. This would mean a by-election in Barnard's seat, Bass, a Tasmanian electorate which had been egregiously affected by the tariff cuts. Whitlam had conceded to the request of his old friend, and so a by-election would be held in Bass on 26 June 1975. Hawke recalled, stuttering still five years later,

I-I literally couldn't believe it! It was insane. And the reasons why it was insane were just so obvious. You had Malcolm Fraser [the new leader of the Opposition] looking around for a justification to bring the Government down short of its term, and not having a justification — because, simply to assert that a government is doing badly is no reason to force it to the polls. So what do we do? We give a by-election gratuitously which Fraser was obviously going to use to say, 'Here is an opportunity for the nation to express its view about the Whitlam Government'. And what were the circumstances? The economy in bad shape; the unions disaffected generally, but particularly in Bass, where the textile industry had been decimated. On top of that Bass was a rural electorate and the rural lobbies *hated* Whitlam — they'd been throwing tomatoes at him — and further, Bass was not basically a Labor seat, but owed an enormous amount to the personality and position of Lance Barnard. So when you added all those things together, you could guarantee a huge swing. I hoped that if I kicked up enough fuss immediately, and was tough enough, there may have been a chance of turning Gough's decision around. There was no way in the world that I was going to allow, as President of the Party, a position to be established where Whitlam or anyone else could act in a way which conveyed the impression that the ALP or the Labor Government was his possession, in respect of which he could make decisions that could destroy it, and do so without criticism. I believed that the Government was in the process of being destroyed by that decision about Bass, and that the Labor Party was being mortally hurt. The Galston decision had thrown away the seat of Parramatta; Bass was throwing away the Whitlam Labor Government.

Hawke had one of his 'outbursts' to the news media: the Bass by-election was, he said, 'an act of Galstonian madness'. He returned quickly to Athens where the switchboard of his hotel had fifty telephone calls from Australia for him. He repeatedly told the news media that the decision was disastrous. 'Gough', he said later, 'never forgave me. Because what I said then and later, when I returned to Australia, proved to be right. Liberals confirmed my opinion — several of them told me afterwards that it was the Bass result which had made up Fraser's mind to go for our throats.'

By the time Hawke arrived in Geneva he knew that his efforts to have the decision reversed were in vain; he began drinking heavily. People in Geneva who had known him for years and were used to his argumentativeness when drunk were shocked by him, now. He was seething with bitterness and would verbally attack anyone. He bailed up a junior staff member in the Australian Embassy to ask sneeringly, 'Do you ever criticise your boss? Do you just shut up and cop it when you know he's doing something wrong? Have you got any guts?'

He kept working during the week, however, and took part in confidential discussions between the representatives of the United Arab Emirates, Kuwait, Jordan, Egypt, Israel, France, and Australia, represented by him. The discussions were chaired by Blanchard, and were promising, since all the Arab States were from the soft-line camp and all agreed to lobby their hard-line brothers.

On 3 June Blanchard had invited Hawke to a private interview, their first meeting. Hawke had arrived half-drunk and, declining an offer of afternoon tea, had asked for beer and drunk three bottles of it in quick succession. His language had been coarse but fortunately Blanchard, who is very much the dignified French mandarin, had not been able to understand much of Hawke's swearing and Fortin, who was also present and whose English is idiomatic, had not translated for him. Blanchard had formed an unfavourable impression of Hawke from this encounter, but nevertheless was willing to act upon the assurances of others that Hawke was a better man than he appeared. During the interview he had invited Hawke to lunch at his country estate in Gex the following Sunday. By then Hawke had come to terms with his misery over Bass. Barry Watchorn, a senior Australian diplomat in Geneva, recalled, 'On Sunday morning there was a knock on my door early and there was Bob, wreathed in smiles. He was making an apology for the way he had behaved all week.'

At the luncheon in Gex the guests were Hawke, Fortin and Parodi, the leader of the French Government delegation. Their purpose that day was to work out an amendment to the Arab resolution that 'liberation movements be admitted to observer status in the ILO', which would satisfy both the Arabs and the Americans and would not violate the rules of the ILO. The resolution, as it stood, was a monstrous piece of provocation and a precedent which could turn the ILO into a political circus. The PLO was committed, in its charter, to the total destruction of Israel, an 'illegal entity'. But Israel was a member of the ILO and the admission of the PLO — even with observer status only — could reduce the proceedings of the Organization to the level of a bear-baiting spectacle.

Bargaining is necessary for transcending differences of opinion; in Hawke bargaining (a prime political skill) is second nature. It was he who, during the luncheon at Gex, hit upon the words which could force the PLO, if it deeply desired to have observer status at the ILO, to bargain for that status. His amendment to the resolution was: 'that the liberation movement in question recognises the principles of the ILO and its Constitution and the right of all member States to continue in existence and participate in the work of the Organisation'. It was a masterstroke, for if the amendment were passed, the PLO would have to commit itself, before the world community, to rewriting its charter and withdrawing from it the demand that Israel be smashed — or, to abandon its plans to enter the ILO.

The four men were overjoyed. They had two and a half days left to sell the Gex amendment to the opposing camps. Blanchard recalled that by Monday evening, 'We felt we had sealed the thing. The Americans in private conversations accepted our formula, as had many of the Arabs.' The next step was to shepherd the amendment through the Standing Orders Committee of the Governing Body. Then, on 12 June, in plenary session of the International Labour Conference in the Palais des Nations, delegates would make their formal votes, having been advised how to vote by their factional representatives in the Standing Orders Committee, and everybody could get on with the business of the conditions of work, the status of female employees, child labour and other appropriate concerns.

It was the Americans, specifically George Meany, who set in process a chain reaction which ended all hopes. Meany, from Washington, instructed that the American delegation was to reject both the resolution and its amendment. There ensued, in the words of Francis Wolf, the ILO's legal advisor, 'a terrible battle in the Standing Orders Committee'. The Arabs flew into a rage because of the American attitude and announced that, in these circumstances, compromise was anathema. Salama and Hawke tried valiantly to bully and cajole the committee meeting to consider the wider context of its actions, but to no avail.

On the afternoon of 12 June Hawke rose with, as usual, just a few lines of notes, to address the plenary session. The Palais des Nations was packed; all the international galleries were filled; the world Press was overflowing its gallery. After Arafat's triumph in the UN General Assembly six months earlier, this was the second great show of strength by the Islamic world. Tony Street, the shadow Minister for Labour, was attending the ILO for the first time and recalled,

> The atmosphere was electric with tension. Bob Hawke made a truly great speech. And it was like a Greek tragedy, because he stood there and pleaded, on international and humanitarian grounds, with those hundreds of delegates — and yet he knew, we all knew, that it was a lost cause. It was a tremendously moving speech, a magnificent piece of oratory — the best speech I've ever heard Bob make, one of the great speeches I've heard. And all for nothing.

Hawke, as he always does when the numbers are overwhelmingly against him, had wound himself up to believe that if he spoke forcefully enough he would be able to persuade some of the delegates to change their votes. He pressed hard on 'my friends from the continent of Africa', reminding them that 'members of the Australian trade union movement . . . were prepared to face gaol if necessary, in the early 1970s, to take industrial action to support the people of Africa'. He went on to stress that the ALP Government had 'gone beyond sweet words in assisting liberation movements' and referred to the financial contributions the Whitlam Government had made to the liberation movements of Africa. He continued,

> So, I am speaking here with clean hands in terms of an absolute, practical and dedicated commitment to genuine liberation movements. It is in that sense that I plead with this Conference . . . All that we are asking in this amendment is that you say to the PLO, as to any other movement: 'You are welcome to come into the ILO, provided you change your position about the right to exist of an existing member State'. And that is all we ask . . . Delegates, you will never know how close we appeared to come in the work of the Standing Orders Committee to arriving at a position which would recognise Israel's right to existence . . . unfortunately, the reasonableness of [the Egyptians] was overcome by the blind commitment of some people to the destruction of Israel . . . In making a passionate defence of Israel no one is more conscious than I am of the fundamental problems of the Palestinian people and I believe that they have a right to a State, a right to a peaceful existence in that area of the world, but not at the expense of the obliteration of Israel.

Hawke concluded by warning that if the amendment were rejected,

> Delegates, you are going to be the initial actors in the destruction of the
> ILO — no organisation can have its noble purposes emasculated by
> being made a political forum which is going to be used for the purposes
> of advancing the cause of the destruction of a member State. I appeal to
> you as earnestly as I possibly can . . . if you take this step without voting
> for the amendment to the proposal before you, then I repeat that you
> will have taken the first steps down the road to the destruction of the
> ILO.'

The brilliance of the speech had been in Hawke's delivery, in his timing and
intonation, and the passionate conviction he had conveyed through his voice
and body-language. People were unanimous that it was one of the best
speeches ever made in the ILO and ranked with those of Leon Juro. But there
was no clapping at the end of it, just a tense silence. Hawke returned to his
seat beside the other Australians for one of the more bitter moments of his
life: the only countryman who lent forward to shake his hand was his political
opponent, Tony Street. Hawke said,

> I knew the Australian voting position in advance, but it was bloody
> devastating just the same to go and sit down with your mates, with the
> representatives of your Government, and have them all looking the
> other way. I was disgusted by my own Government.* And others. The
> leader of the British Government delegation came up to me, backslap-
> ping and smiling, and said, 'My word, we'd love to vote for that'. And I
> replied rather sharply, 'Well why the hell don't you?' And he backed off
> — 'Oh, dear boy! Our vote would have made no difference . . .' Even a
> Cuban bloke told me and told other people in the ILO that, had he been
> free to make his own decision, he would have voted for the amendment.

Fortin said later of Hawke's warning that rejection of the amendment would
have dire consequences for the ILO, 'Bob said what we — the ILO hierarchy
— wanted to say, but could not'.

The PLO was admitted to observer status in the ILO, without any provisos.
At Blanchard's request Hawke flew to Washington to try to persuade Meany
to change his attitude about American withdrawal. It was fruitless. In November 1975 the US Secretary of State, Henry Kissinger, wrote formally to

---

* In fact, the Australian Government voted for the Hawke amendment. When the
motion was lost (74 in favour; none against; 305 abstentions), Australia voted for
admission of the PLO. Watchorn said, 'Bob lobbied until the last minute: he asked
me to re-interpret my instructions. I told him, "I can't. And it's your Government,
mate".'

Blanchard telling him that the USA was withdrawing.

In 1980, a few weeks after Meany died, America announced that it wished to rejoin the Organisation, but in the interim there had been a second drastic curtailment of ILO functions. Hawke was often the emissary between the ILO and the United States: 'He was one of my main channels of communication', Blanchard said.

While he had been abroad, and Australians at home had known little of his work in Geneva and Washington, a Gallup poll had been published showing that Hawke was now the most popular man in the country. Whitlam's popularity was declining inexorably; every week was bringing a new episode in the saga of the Loans Affair;* politics had turned into a national blood sport, with the Government as frantic, panting fox. On 26 June the electorate in Bass swung by 15% against the ALP, and the Government knew it was done for. The only question now was the time of death.

Within the electorate Hawke became an object of increasing curiosity and, for those sympathetic to Labor, of hope. A month after the Bass by-election he agreed to give Mike Schildberger a national television interview which would focus upon Hawke, The Man. Schildberger had known Hawke for a decade and like most other journalists in the country knew that he was objectionable when drunk, but this had never been publicised. Among journalists themselves there is a tradition of becoming as drunk as princes: perhaps this, and Hawke's reputation as a man who was quick with a libel writ, had inhibited the news media from referring to it. However, by 1975 Hawke's popularity made his heavy drinking a matter of legitimate public interest. Schildberger had drawn up a list of questions, based upon the assumption that Hawke would in the future be Leader of the ALP, questions which covered his political and social ideas and his personal strengths. The penultimate question was 'What are your weaknesses?' The final one, 'It is said you have a drinking problem: comment?' The show was going to air live. Schildberger offered to tell Hawke his questions in advance but, with typical self-confidence, Hawke replied he did not want to see them. When Schildberger arrived at his second last question Hawke hesitated for an instant then, to the horror of his friends and the disbelief of other political observers,

---

* The Loans Affair was the public excuse used by the Opposition to bring down the Whitlam Government. It was an attempt on the part of a group of ministers — including the Prime Minister and led by Rex Connor, the Minister for Minerals and Energy — to borrow billions of dollars from Arab nations to spend on development in Australia. The Loans Affair was inspired by the purest and most benevolent motives but was executed secretly, deviously and with astonishing incompetence. The Opposition managed to drag out details about it over a period of months, presenting each new morsel of information as a fresh scandal. The impression of a huge and sinister conspiracy was created. Once, wary electors had been led to expect Reds under ALP beds; astute politicians that they are, the Liberal-National Country Party leaders had updated the bogeyman model into an Arab banker.

replied that, as for weaknesses, he had a drinking problem. Schildberger could see what the television screens did not show — that Hawke's hands shook with nervousness as he spoke. Schildberger said, 'It was probably the most emotional interview I have ever had'. The cameras were switched off and Schildberger passed Hawke his clip-board with the list of questions, pointing to the last one. Hawke gasped, 'Thank God I told the truth!'

Only those who knew Ellie's detestation for alcohol, and knew that Hawke, even now at forty-five was embarrassed if she saw him drinking, realised what an effort it had been for him to admit that he had a 'problem'. He said later, 'When we were in Maitland, when I was five to nine years old, and my mother first started work for the WCTU, she had made this connection: that alcohol was death and corruption, that it was destruction'. He had defied her and now had publicly admitted the consequences: he was the captive of alcohol. In his reply to Schildberger, Hawke had gone on to say that if he were to become Leader of the ALP he would give up drinking.

The next day and for weeks later the Press was full of the story. Hawke's supporters believed he had made a gaffe equal to Cairns' 'kind of love'. On 31 July, two days after the Schildberger interview, Whitlam arrived at Parliament House. Journalists were used to being brushed off by the Prime Minister on the steps of the Parliament, and held back. But there was a gleam of merriment in the Leader's eye and his imperial head was turning this way and that bestowing smiles of welcome. Reporters realised the Prime Minister wished to say a few words, and approached him. Someone asked about his drinking and Whitlam, with that straight-faced wit of which he is a master, drew a deep breath and replied, 'I intend to turn over a new leaf and undertake steady drinking from now on. I realise, of course, that to hold my position I have to undertake a rigorous programme of social drinking.' He added that he expected future ALP executive meetings to be 'like gatherings of Alcoholics Anonymous'.

The public contempt which Hawke's supporters feared his admission would arouse did not eventuate. Instead, his popularity increased. In a country of heavy drinkers Hawke had admitted to a national sin. A couple of weeks later a record company released 'The Bob Hawke Drinking Song', which referred to him as 'champion of the underdog' and had a chorus, 'Let's drink to Bob Hawke'. His very ordinariness — his flashy suits, flat voice, friendly manner and vulgar humour — had been among his greatest advantages with crowds, because he appeared so like everyone else, only more so: the quintessential Australian, the little Aussie battler. It was an image that was partly true. But as Hawke had told Schildberger and other Jews many times, 'If I were to have my life again, I would want to be born a Jew'. And when in high spirits, talking of Israel, he would say, '*I'm* an Israeli'. He knew himself to have many facets. While at home Australians thought of Hawke as a 'true Australian', abroad people saw him as a cosmopolitan. Blanchard remarked, 'He brought things that were Australian with him — he spoke very fast and used all sorts of expressions which people could not understand — but at the same time he behaved as if he were at home always. I realised he was a man who was at home with the world.'

In July Hawke, in a blaze of publicity, launched ACTU-Solo, a petrol retailing venture which offered large discounts. Souter had done most of the work to establish ACTU-Solo, but left the public relations to Hawke, who reaped immense popularity from it. The petrol discounts saved the motoring public hundreds of millions of dollars — at first, directly, through ACTU-Solo; later because other retailers were forced to discount also. While it is impossible to quantify the effect on prices that the outlawing of retail price maintenance (thanks to Bourkes) achieved, Hawke believes that like ACTU-Solo, Bourkes saved customers hundreds of millions of dollars. He regards these two enterprises as among the major achievements of his presidency.

The public at large, especially a growing number of people who, in letters to Hawke, drew attention to the fact that they were Liberal voters, had come to see him as courageous and concerned for the national interest, and had abandoned the idea — which had been bandied about constantly in his first two years as President of the ACTU — that Hawke was the cause of industrial unrest. However, within the Victorian ALP his problems were increasing. As the membership of the Whitlam ministry continued to change, rumours flew that Hawke would contest this or that seat of a disgruntled or disgraced former minister at the next election, and every bout of speculation about a seat was followed by warnings from representatives of the Socialist Left faction that Hawke could not win pre-selection in Victoria. Hawke said, 'As we moved into 1974-75 I was one who was, perhaps earlier than anyone else in the Party, pointing out the change in economic circumstances and saying that we needed to adapt our thinking and our time-scale of expectations to various objectives. A lot of the Left didn't like that. They thought it was a sell-out position.' There had been row upon row between Hawke and the Socialist Left in Victorian meetings and one in the federal executive when, earlier in the year, Hawke had made what others described as a 'magnificently venomous' attack upon Hartley for an article criticising decisions at the Terrigal Conference. The executive strongly censured Hartley. Significantly, Hawke's major ally in the attack on Hartley was John Ducker. That, in the Left's eyes, was another black mark against Hawke. Quietly, and as yet without a public name, the Stop Hawke campaign was operating.

Meanwhile, in the trade union movement, Hawke's position by late 1975 was one of unequalled authority. At the ACTU Congress which opened in Melbourne on 15 September he was at the height of his strength in the movement. For the first time since the Congress of 1939 there was not a single division involving a count of delegates' votes for or against recommendations by the ACTU executive. In the days leading up to the week-long meeting unionists had been subjected to an unprecedented barrage of comment from the news media and politicians about their responsibilities. Already there was talk that the Opposition, led by Malcolm Fraser, would block supply in the

Senate and thus force Whitlam to the polls again. After the scandals, real and counterfeit, that had dogged the Government since the election of 1974, nobody in the Labor movement imagined that it could win a third time. Congress had assembled in a thoughtful mood.

Hawke's presidential address was an appeal for solidarity couched in sombre, Churchillian terms. He told delegates that since the 1973 Congress unemployment had increased by 266%, that economic growth had declined by 158%, that inflation had risen by 106%, and that

> We ignore these facts at our peril . . . [They are] a reflection in this country of the fundamental malaise which has occurred [since 1973] in varying degrees in every advanced capitalist economic system. Whether their governments have been conservative, as in the United States, or social democratic as in West Germany, all these countries have witnessed acceleration of inflation, rising unemployment and reductions in growth rates.

He devoted nearly all of his speech to developing four themes. First, a defence of the Government, in which he refuted the continual assertions that inflation and unemployment were all the fault of Labor. Second, he addressed the responsibility of the trade union movement, asking union leaders to 'restrain wage pushes well in excess of prices and productivity', and arguing 'our affiliates must recognise the full implications of their actions . . . we must balance the self-interest of particular groups against the interests of workers as a whole'. Third, he spoke of the responsibility of the Government, and in this context argued that it was up to the Government to 'create the conditions within which [union] co-operation can be maximised'. He went on to ask (for the umpteenth time) for tax indexation and that the Government avoid rises in indirect taxes and government charges, and that it expand the Regional Employment Development Scheme if unemployment remained high. And fourth, he spoke of the rights of the unions to free collective bargaining. This is the fundamental tenet and the primary function of trade union movements everywhere. It may seem illogical that Australia has a centralised wage-fixing system while at the same time we have — and have always had — collective bargaining. It is illogical, but then the system has grown haphazardly. Since the introduction of the total wage, in 1967, the illogicality has become more burdensome. Hawke, in reasserting the freedom of the unions to bargain collectively, was soothing their fears that wage indexation would mean a wage freeze. Beneath the surface of his message there lay another appeal: because we are free, we can choose, for a while, to be unfree. It was a skilful piece of manipulation, and it worked.

The Congress followed the sobering tenor of his opening address. In contrast to 1973 there was little open criticism of the Government, while defiance and baiting of the ACTU executive, which is a normal Congress pastime, was at a minimum. As chairman of the meeting of 600 delegates,

Hawke was at his best: decisive, good humoured and gentle, often offering speakers an extension of time instead of telling them to wind up. The Congress elections returned him an executive weighted twelve to six in his favour. He had taken a deliberate decision to play a small role in debates so that Charlie Fitzgibbon could shine. Fitzgibbon did. By the end of the week he was established in people's minds as the heir apparent. As well, Hawke had finally won his argument for extra administrative staff, and the appointment of a full-time assistant-secretary was approved. Also, delegates voted to increase affiliation fees. By 19 September 1975 the ACTU was healthy enough for Hawke, in good conscience, to leave it and at long last to make his transfer to Parliament. The next federal election was due to be held in late 1976 or early 1977.

During the rest of the month and throughout October the crisis in Parliament continued to build. The Opposition, controlling the Senate, was there deferring the Budget bills for supply, and the Government's options for action were decreasing. Hawke's view was that the most prudent method of breaking the impasse would be a half-Senate election. He discussed this with many Labor colleagues. On 10 November he met Whitlam at a ceremony to lay the foundation stone at a club in Broadmeadows, an oppressed suburb of Melbourne. Hawke, Clyde Holding and Bill Landeryou, the Secretary of the Victorian branch of the Storemen and Packers' Union and an active member of the Centre Unity faction of the Victorian ALP, to which Hawke and Holding also belonged, button-holed the Prime Minister. They urged a half-Senate election upon him. When Whitlam left Broadmeadows Hawke, Holding and Landeryou were all satisfied that the following day Whitlam would announce this solution to the constitutional crisis.

Hawke had objected to Whitlam over the appointment of the man he used to call 'Goldilocks', Sir John Kerr, as Governor-General. Several weeks earlier Hawke had asked the Prime Minister and others, 'Can we rely on Kerr?' He recalled, 'From my years of dealing with Kerr in the Commission I had no love for the man. But everyone was sure he was reliable, and I was convinced.'

Hawke had meetings on the morning of 11 November and at 1 p.m. went to lunch at the Hotel Cecil, on the corner of Queen and Lonsdale Streets, with Jack Kornhauser, the brother of Eddie. Hawke said,

> I was feeling a tremendous weight off my shoulders because of the decision, which I thought Gough had made the day before, to break free of the Opposition's bloody-minded obstructionism and hold a half-Senate election. So I went off to lunch in a great mood and had an onion soup, and had ordered a steak to follow. It had just arrived — I can still see it now, a beautiful T-bone — when the telephone rang. We were sitting at a corner table, beside which Jack Kornhauser had a private phone. Jack answered and his face dropped. His voice sounded incredu-

lous. He passed the phone to me and his daughter said, 'Kerr has sacked Whitlam'. She had to repeat it before I took it in. I think I said, 'Oh God' and got up, left the steak and went back to my office. Within an hour I was on a plane to Canberra. We'd gathered up a lot of union blokes and went immediately to John Curtin House, the ALP headquarters, and into an ALAC meeting . . . From the moment the news had spread there had been calls for a national strike. People were ringing me, demanding that I call one. Demands were broadcast on the radio. And I obviously had to think seriously about it. I had to make a judgment very quickly. It was quite clear in my mind that the idea was nonsense — for a couple of reasons: first, we were arguing that the Opposition was violating the constitutional and parliamentary processes of government, therefore, how could one logically take over the processes of government by bringing the nation to a halt? Second, and a more pragmatic consideration, was that I did not believe we could call a successful national strike. And there would have been nothing more futile and counter-productive than calling a national stoppage which failed. So, there was the consideration of principle and of pragmatism. In the ALAC meeting there was a consensus that there should be no national strike, but that we should mobilise the trade union movement to support what we still called The Government. The ALAC meeting was like a group of stunned mullets, stunned by the enormity of what had happened, while at the same time feeling as if it were unreal. Gough was still furious, but he had slipped into a different gear. Now that he had a real fight on his hands the professional campaigner in him came out. So, while he was still tremendously angry, he was talking coolly about tactics for the election campaign. The rest of that day is a bit of a blur — I think we organised a protest rally in Canberra and that I spoke at that. Maybe I went to Sydney . . .

Hawke did go to Sydney, either that evening or the next, and addressed a rally called by the NSW Labour Council at the Town Hall. Pat Clancy, who was already estranged from Hawke, remembered,

Bob gave a magnificent speech: a stinging attack upon capitalism and a declaration in support of socialism, a classic Left speech and beautifully delivered. The Town Hall was packed and when he walked in there was a standing ovation, and throughout the speech people were clapping and cheering. There's no doubt that the workers in NSW hero-worshipped him, Right and Left. I only wish I'd taped it so that I could ask his views about it now.

Hawke recalled, 'I got back to Melbourne and went straight into the process of arranging a campaign'. On the nation-wide radio programme,

AM, on 12 November, Hawke, speaking in a voice described as uncharacteristically 'light and clear' appealed for calm and urged 'controlled and orderly involvement' by the trade unions in the election. He called upon unionists not to strike, but instead to 'give a day's pay for democracy', the same plea he made to the Sydney union rally, and which had been agreed upon at the ALAC meeting. He was in dire fear that the emotional reaction to the Government's sacking could lead to riots. Whitlam, still flushed with rage, had stood on the steps of Parliament House in the early afternoon of 11 November and roared to the crowd that had spontaneously surrounded the entrance to the building, 'Maintain your rage!' Later that afternoon Hawke, in marked contrast to the Prime Minister, had given a news conference, saying, 'Australia could be on the verge of something terrible . . . We don't want to substitute violence in the streets for democracy.' As far as the Left were concerned, Hawke's determination to try to calm the situation was another black mark against him. Even in early 1982 members of the Socialist Left were quoting the leadership Hawke gave to channelling anger into calmer modes of expression as another of his perfidies — although one of their number, Jim Roulston, had been at the ALAC meeting and had expressed no opposing view. In their outrage over the sacking people forget, or perhaps have never known, that it was the massive, botched strike campaign of the 1890s which desolated the Australian trade union movement. Sir Richard Kirby, who by 1975 had a half-century's experience of industrial affairs, said later that Hawke's finest contribution to the union movement was that then and throughout the bitter months which followed, Hawke kept an iron grip on militancy: 'I've no doubt', Kirby said, 'that without the leadership Bob gave, the unions would have pulled on a national strike which would have fallen to pieces and Fraser would have stepped in and smashed them. I don't think the unions have ever realised what Bob saved them from.'

Hawke recalled of the election campaign that began immediately after the dismissal:

> I was up to my ears in it. The things that were most striking were the overflowing, overwhelming enthusiasm of the audiences and the composition of the audiences. They weren't the normal Party faithful, but people from all walks of life who had been deeply insulted by what had happened. Party membership soared. The meetings were the biggest and most enthusiastic of any in the 1970s. From the crowd response I thought right at the beginning that we would win, but the longer the campaign went on the more clear it became that the circumstances surrounding the Government's sacking were being subsumed by disaffection with the Government. By the end of the campaign, I knew that we'd lost.

Again, even Hawke's enemies acknowledged that next to Whitlam he had done more than any other during the campaign to try to win government.

On the evening of polling day, 13 December, Hawke, Hazel and the children all flew to Canberra. Hawke was to be a television commentator on the election result. He said,

> I didn't have any perception of the magnitude of the defeat we were facing. That election night was one of the longest and loneliest nights in my life. I couldn't get up and walk away from the TV cameras, but had to sit there for the whole horrible performance. It was obvious by 9 p.m. that we'd lost, and I conceded defeat very quickly, but then it just piled up and up, defeat after defeat.

At one stage Hawke began to weep and told the television audience, 'We've had the guts ripped out of us'. He said,

> There I was looking out at the shattered remains of all the hopes of 1972 and 1974, and being surrounded by gloating Tories. The only redeeming feature of it was that for quite some time Bill Snedden was the commentator sitting next to me and I was able to point out to him that if he had been a little more patient and not blocked supply in 1974 he perhaps would have been Prime Minister . . .
>
> I remember the moment when Gough arrived in the tally room: when people saw him, a sense of tragedy spread through the hall. I felt terribly sorry for him as a person, a sorrow separate from what had happened to the Labor Party. There was this giant of a man, smashed to pieces — you know, greatness brings its own set of emotions. Including, I suppose, jealousy, envy. Whatever feelings one had about Gough's mistakes at particular times one could not but be enormously sad for him. It wasn't just defeat that night; it was the end. It was a question of time, but he knew it was the end. And he conducted himself admirably: he acknowledged the dimensions of the defeat and then, fairly quickly, withdrew. We drove back from the national tally room and on the way passed The Lodge, where Whitlam was still in residence, and thought about going in and trying to give some consolation. But there was no sign of life there.

Next morning David Combe telephoned Hawke to say that Whitlam wanted to see him at The Lodge. They sat by the swimming pool. Hawke recalled,

> The essence of what Gough said to me was that his leadership had been rejected and that he had to accept that he was finished. And that in his view Bill Hayden was the man to take over as Leader, that he'd spoken to Hayden already, and Hayden had rejected the leadership. So that now I was the person to lead the Party, and that we had to talk about getting a seat for me as quickly as possible. I was surprised, on two

counts: first that he'd so quickly accepted that his leadership should come to an end. I think he was right, but was still surprised that he'd decided so quickly. And I was also surprised that he'd turned so quickly to me. Not because I disagreed with his judgment, but because I wasn't even in Parliament. I thought Gough was quite right in wanting Hayden to take over — Bill had been an excellent minister and had gone through the hard grind of getting Medibank established, then, as Treasurer, had begun to turn the economy around. Gough's jump from Bill to me, while I could see a logic in it, was surprising. I understood quite clearly, as did David Combe, that the leadership was not Gough's to bestow, and that we would face some difficulties. We discussed a few seats. The general thrust of the conversation was that if it was going to be on, then getting a seat would not be an enormous difficulty — that someone would be prepared, in the circumstances, to step aside. Well, things started to go wrong.

The chain of events and actions following Hawke's discussion with Whitlam remains unclear.

Bill Landeryou was in Canberra and returned to Melbourne with Hawke; Landeryou, who strongly supported the idea that Hawke should lead the Party, was anxious to prevent the issue becoming public before detailed plans could be made, and a seat arranged for Hawke. It would seem that Hawke was highly excited, for Landeryou later said that he stayed at Hawke's side that afternoon and evening, and next day, in order to prevent him talking to the Press. He knew Hawke well and was familiar with his impatient over-confidence and his tendency to confide his hopes, as if they were realities, to journalists. Landeryou also knew Hawke's enemies. However, on the after-noon of the Whitlam-Hawke discussions a statement was issued by some-body either on Whitlam's staff or working for the Party in Canberra, to the effect that Hawke would be replacing Whitlam as leader. The following night Hawke was invited to appear on television in Melbourne. There he confirmed that Whitlam wanted him to lead the Party. He went on to say that with his leadership the Party would be back in government in three years. It was an error to have made any comment.

A Caucus outcry greeted the news: indeed, the leadership was not Whit-lam's to confer, nor was it Hawke's to claim. And in Victoria, the place where the notional seat for Hawke should, obviously, be located, the Socialist Left was furious. They had hated Whitlam. But as their actions were to reveal, they now hated Hawke more. After all that Whitlam had been through he was now the underdog and therefore a just object of sympathy. Hawke was pictured as a man snatching at the crown of a mortally-wounded king. At last the Stop Hawke campaign had a name and was out in the open.

Hawke said,

Besides the natural reaction of groups of people in Caucus, Gough himself changed his mind. Quite clearly, what he had said on the day after the election was post-operative shock, and once the patient had settled down he assumed a different view . . . The Left said later that it was wicked of me not to have called the Revolution on 11 November, but the real guts of their dislike for me was my stand on the Middle East. Conversely, Whitlam was their hero, for the stand he had taken on the Middle East. The Left found it convenient to blur their reasons; much of the criticism I copped at that time, on the leadership issue, was a cloak for other things. And, of course, I did not know then, and was in blissful ignorance for another two months, that there had been certain hanky-panky with Iraqi money, and that a number of people must have been apprehensive, by then, about the facts emerging. I think it was very convenient to have a diversion and a figure, me, upon whom to vent hatred.

Whitlam decided he would continue to lead the Party.

His moment of opportunity vanished, Hawke went off for a holiday and returned in late January 1976, 'all fired up', in the words of Jean Sinclair, 'about getting the Liberals out. Bob's view was that politics in Australia were now unstable and that the electorate could easily switch back to Labor at the next election.' It was a widely-held view. What it discounted was that the ALP was now a demoralised, embittered party, led by a man who had lost his self-confidence — the vitals, the heart and liver of political leadership. Commentators made much of the fact that Whitlam had once said, 'You must crash through, or crash', as if such a daring attitude were unique to him, and some fatal flaw, but in fact the words could have come from Curtin, Chifley, Menzies, Gorton, McEwen and, most certainly from Malcolm Fraser. Compared to Fraser, Whitlam had lacked daring.

There was an ALP campaign committee meeting in Canberra on 28 January which was a sad but pedestrian affair. Then, on Thursday 12 February, Hawke noted in his diary: '3.25 — Egerton rang re financial trouble'. Hawke had no time to talk, for he was rushing to catch a flight to Canberra where he was to tape a *Monday Conference* television programme. He went from the airport direct to the ABC studio. When he arrived at his hotel in Canberra at about 9.30 p.m. there were several telephone messages for him, including an urgent one from Egerton. Hawke returned the call. What Egerton had to tell Hawke sounded

like a fairy story. Jack said that Whitlam and Combe had arranged to get $500,000 from the Iraqi Government, to pay our campaign costs. The dough had not arrived, and the Party therefore was in deep financial trouble. David Combe was on a holiday cruise. Ken Bennett, the

Assistant Federal Secretary, was waiting downstairs to see me, in a state of nerves . . . I said we'd have to get Combe off his cruise ship and have a meeting of the senior officers — the President, Vice-Presidents, the Secretary and his assistant, to find out what the hell was going on.

In brief, this is what had happened: some weeks before the Government had been sacked Bill Hartley, who was a Senate candidate, had the idea that the ALP's slender campaign purse could be plumped up with money from the Government of Iraq, for which he worked as a Press correspondent. He had a friend, Henri Fischer, who offered to go to Baghdad and raise the money — between a quarter and half a million dollars. It would not be a loan, but a gift from the Ba'ath Socialist Party, which was in government in Iraq, to the ALP. Had the Ba'ath Socialist Party been composed of seraphim with six wings the idea would have been improper; as it was, the Iraqi Government was notorious for certain blood-curdling executions of its political enemies. For example, in the early 1970s a group of Iraqi citizens who had spied for Great Britain had been hanged by piano wire, in public. Currency black marketeers were shot. Iraq's legal system was different enough from Australia's to make any close association between the ALP and the Ba'ath Party an embarrassment in Australia. However, the more important point was that it was a violation of ALP principles even to consider financial indebtedness to a foreign government, whatever its complexion. But in the confusion and fury that followed the sacking, Whitlam and Combe agreed with Hartley's suggestion that he could tap funds from a special source. It seems that details were vague: the money could come to the ALP, Whitlam was told, via the Reuben Scarf Foundation. Scarf was a respected Sydney clothing manufacturer, who had made donations to the Party in the past. Fischer was associated with the Foundation. He recommended himself to Party officials, and especially to Hartley, as a fund-raiser, because of his often declared loathing for Rupert Murdoch, the news baron and enemy of the Whitlam Government. Fischer was a man of persuasive charm.

By 12 February Combe knew that the money had not arrived from Iraq but neither he nor anyone else knew the reason as yet. Combe assumed he would be sacked for being among those who had agreed to involve the ALP in such an unseemly venture — though, as he commented wryly later, 'I often wondered what view the Party would have taken if the money had arrived and we'd been able to use it to pay our debts'. As it was, the ALP election campaign had been run on the premise that a massive injection of dollars was on its way, and the real budget had been overspent by some $300,000. Hawke took the view that Combe had made an appalling error of judgment but one which, in the Secretary, was forgivable. At first, when Hawke reached Combe by telephone and told him to abandon his holiday and return immediately, Combe refused, saying that since he was going to be sacked anyway, he may as well enjoy himself. Hawke replied that if Combe would co-operate he would do all that he could to save him. Combe said later, 'Bob's a helluva loyal bloke. He'd stood by me in the past. I didn't have much hope about this one, but he was very strong in saying that, while I'd been a stupid bastard, I'd been trying to do my best by the Party in a crisis.' Combe flew to Melbourne and the meeting of senior officers was held in secret, in Hawke's house, on Sunday 15 February.

By then Hawke had heard some more of the fairy story and was dismayed for the ALP. During the meeting he argued that a special conference of the federal executive should be summoned immediately, for two reasons: first, the issue was grave, and second, it was not a matter which could be kept secret long. Already it had been necessary to involve bank officials and employees of the Party's advertising agency, which was owed a fortune, in the affair. Hawke was due to leave a few days later for the ILO. He feared that the story would break in his absence and would be allowed to run wild, worsening the image, created by the Loans Affair, that the Labor Party was of its nature conspiratorial, devious, and incompetent. Egerton and Ducker argued that it was safer to let matters rest for the time being, and to deal with the problem, in secret, at the next scheduled federal executive meeting. Hawke said, 'I was vigorous in replying to them that they were bloody crazy, that there was no way in the world that the news wouldn't leak, and when that happened it would be even worse for the Party, for it would look as if we were trying to cover-up'. Hawke lost the argument, but there was a certain savage pleasure for him in the meeting, for when Combe arrived he told the others that the scheme had originated with Hartley. Hawke saw his chance to have Hartley expelled. Other officers agreed that this should happen; Combe, however, they all agreed, should be allowed to stay on as Secretary. They doubted that the federal executive would want Whitlam to remain leader.

Combe disagreed. He said if the officers were serious in wishing to see him continue as Secretary they must adopt the principle of equal culpability and not distinguish between the gravity of his error on one side, and Hartley's and Whitlam's on the other, and that all should be punished equally. In Hawke's mind, however, Whitlam had for the last time 'played around with the future of the ALP', as he put it. Hawke was convinced that Whitlam should and would be sacked as leader. The discussions broke up with an agreement on secrecy.

That night or the one after, Combe and Egerton went to dinner at Eddie Kornhauser's home and told him of the scandal. Kornhauser was horrified: by the facts, because he was fearful that the story would break in the Press and he could be blamed as the leak; and for another, special reason. After the argument between Schildberger and Hawke in Kornhauser's office two years earlier, Kornhauser had decided that Hawke should be given a lasting honour in Israel and had hit upon the idea of a forest. After months of planning he had arranged for a gathering of distinguished members of Australian Jewry, who had pledged to contribute to the cost of the forest which would be planted in

Israel and named after Hawke. The gathering at which the plan for a Hawke forest would be formally unveiled was to be held on Thursday 19 February. Kornhauser feared that if it became known in the interim that the ALP had been prepared to accept $500,000 from Iraq, a country which demanded the obliteration of Israel, his guests would think twice about donations for the President of the Party.

Kornhauser recalled,

> Bob said nothing to me and I didn't tell him that I knew about it already. I was having heart attacks on Tuesday, Wednesday, Thursday. Finally Thursday night came and there had been no story in the newspapers. Bob came to the function and was very subdued. He had to make a speech to all the people I'd invited to be supporters. He gave his speech without once lifting his eyes to the audience. People thought he was reading from a prepared speech, but I was sitting behind him and could see that he had no speech, just one line of notes. Later, when the story broke, he told me: 'I was too ashamed to look at them. That my Party had done that . . .'

A day or so later Hawke left for the ILO, stopping first in Singapore, where he lunched with an Australian diplomat, Richard Butler. Butler told Hawke, in confidence, that he had applied for the job of Whitlam's private secretary. Hawke told Butler, in confidence, that he had better reconsider before resigning from Foreign Affairs, for Whitlam was unlikely to be leader much longer. He told Butler why. Hawke continued his journey towards Geneva, stopping next in Israel.

The morning after his arrival in Jerusalem he was in the lobby of his hotel chatting to a group of students who were the first beneficiaries of another eponymous honour in Israel: Hawke was one of the twenty-four Gentiles in the world, up to the time of writing, after whom a research fund at the Hebrew University in Jerusalem has been named. He was summoned away from the students to take a telephone call from, he thinks, London, from Rupert Murdoch. Hawke said,

> I thought, Oh, just as I predicted. I didn't feel smart about having been right; it was just so bloody obvious that the story would break. Murdoch said enough to me for it to be clear beyond question: he knew. He asked me to comment and I told him I had no comment. At that stage I didn't know where he'd got the story, but as we discovered later, Henri Fischer had told him. I thought, Well, we're done for — it will be in the Australian Press in a day or so. I was going to lunch with a group of senior Israeli Labour Party people and decided that now the cat was out there was no point in pretending.

One of the Israelis at the luncheon, which was at a famous restaurant in Jerusalem, was the Defence Minister and later leader of the Labour Party, Shimon Peres. He recalled,

> When Bob told us, we could not believe that a fraternal party would do such a thing. Bob was depressed about the state the Australian Labor Party had reached. He said it had lost its character and ideology, and that he would stand for Parliament soon because he wanted to bring back character and ideology to the Party. But, he had personal problems . . .

Hawke contacted Blanchard in Geneva to tell him he could not, now, attend the International Labour Conference, and caught a plane to Athens that evening. From there he telephoned 'either one or all of Combe, Ducker and Egerton'. They confirmed that Murdoch's flagship newspaper, the *Australian*, had a front-page story about what was already known as 'The Iraqi Money Scandal'. Hawke returned to Australia, arriving back during the final week of February.

The senior officers of the Party had a succession of discussions to decide upon a recommendation to the federal executive, a special meeting of which had been summoned for 5 and 6 March. The Iraqi Money Scandal was, beyond debate, a genuine scandal. For more defensible errors Whitlam had sacked Rex Connor and Jim Cairns from his ministry. The officers recommended that the federal executive of the ALP should expel Bill Hartley from the Party and severely reprimand Combe and Whitlam.

Then, on the weekend before the federal executive was due to meet, Hawke made a *faux pas*. He allowed a news conference to be held at his house and after his tight-lipped formal announcement of a thorough inquiry, continued to talk, off the record, to a few journalists who stayed on, drinking. During the conversation Hawke, in conveying the common belief of the officers that Whitlam would not survive as Leader, remarked, 'Gough's gone a million'. The next morning Sydney's largest-circulation daily newspaper, the *Telegraph*, had a front-page story headlined 'Hawke to Axe Whitlam'. It was the second breach of journalistic ethics from which Hawke suffered. Matters were made worse by the fact that he was seen as pre-empting the decision of the federal executive. The reporting of Hawke's remarks helped to create a surge of sympathy from ALP branches for Whitlam, who suddenly was the very image of pathos: sacked as Prime Minister and now to be sacked as Leader of the Opposition. The Party, wallowing in self-pity for its defeat, transferred that pity to Whitlam — and not without logic. For if he were sacked as Leader that would seem to justify his sacking as Prime Minister. For the second time in less than three months Hawke appeared to be overstating his importance, and this time deliberately humiliating further a humiliated man. Already, back in January, he had stimulated a frenzy of paranoia in the Left by calling on Fraser in Canberra, wearing his ACTU President's hat. It was proper for Hawke to do this, as ACTU President. It was, however, objectionable that the ALP President be photographed smiling and chatting to the new Prime Minister. Under a Liberal government, Hawke's two hats were as difficult to wear as under a Labor one.

Whitlam's staff made many photostats of the 'Hawke to Axe Whitlam' story, and distributed them widely. Hawke was harassed by the news media to confirm or deny. 'It was a very windy moment for Bob', John Ducker recalled. Hawke made a statement which came perilously close to tarnishing his deserved reputation for truthfulness. Meanwhile, Hartley rushed in to the breach. During interviews with the print and electronic media he suggested that it was Hawke who had leaked the story to Murdoch, and went on to imply that the CIA and Israeli Intelligence were really behind the whole thing. The public could be forgiven for thinking, from what Hartley said, that Hawke was an agent of the CIA or Israeli Intelligence, or both, and had at their instigation set up Hartley and Whitlam for a phony deal, in order to bring them down, which he had then tried to accomplish by using Rupert Murdoch. It is a measure of the paranoia which the names 'Murdoch' and 'Hawke' could arouse in the Left that many believed this demonological nonsense, for years.

A further complication was that on 25 February, the same day as the Murdoch story had broken, the Melbourne *Sun News-Pictorial* also had a version of the scandal, written by a political journalist and author, Laurie Oakes. It was well-known that Oakes and Hawke were friendly. Hartley announced, 'I know who gave the story to Oakes', which suggested to many ALP people that Hawke had. However, from certain details in Oakes' story, Combe and Ducker were convinced that an official of a State branch had been responsible, especially because the man had been overheard talking to Oakes. The man later left his job in the ALP, with a little help from John Ducker.

The federal executive met in Canberra on 5 March in an atmosphere of acute distrust. David Combe, since returning to his home, Canberra, had been besieged by the news media. He recalled,

> We had journalists camped on the front lawn and were under police custody for the best part of a week, with paddy wagons out the front and the family unable to leave the house. It was terrific! I first went out on the night of 4 March, for the officers' meeting. Then the next morning, when the federal executive meeting opened, everyone was as jumpy as hell. There was a buzzing noise. We were all so spook-conscious that we thought the room must be bugged. Bill Hartley clambered around trying to find bugs. After a while [Senator] Arthur Gietzelt owned up. He had a new hearing-aid and he didn't quite know how to work the thing, and it was that which was making the noise. I

moved that the meeting be taped, because X was there and I knew he had dudded me to Oakes. In case I was going to be dismissed, I wanted the tapes as an accurate record of proceedings. The meeting rejected my request, but as things started to unfold Egerton made one of his masterful interjections. He said, 'The Secretary asked us to tape proceedings. We refused. We should have bloody-well sold the film rights!'

Indeed, with a theme song and some special effects, the story that emerged could have been 'A-L-P, The Musical'.

Hawke recalled,

It was a meeting that defied imagination. People were punch-drunk by the revelations. For instance: during the election campaign Frank Crean was still occupying the rooms of the Deputy Prime Minister of Australia, and Hartley had installed in this office the telex machine he used as the Iraqi Press correspondent in Australia. So while the election campaign is going on, telex messages from Iraq about hundreds of thousands of dollars are pouring into the office of the Deputy Prime Minister. We heard all this, then I said, 'Are there any more questions?' and there was one, directed to Hartley, who then told us that the telex messages started going astray — to some major business office. Messages about the ALP were coming off a machine in Westinghouse! Then there were the stories about Henri Fischer. They were told to ring him in London; London said he was in New York; New York said he was in South America. It was Keystone Cops! That the Labor Party's future was being played around with, like that! We gave each of the three people involved, Combe, Hartley and Whitlam, the opportunity of making a full statement.

Combe said,

Hartley, in his statement, said things like, 'But I don't think the Leader would have been aware of that' and 'I'm sure the Leader didn't know . . .' It became obvious from fairly early on that a deal had been done to save Gough and to dump me. During Gough's statement he said, 'It was perfectly proper for Reuben Scarf to give a donation. I thought we were only talking about ten, twenty or twenty-five thousand dollars.' I went white, and gawped. We broke for morning tea. Bob and I were furious. Bob called Ducker over and I said, 'If we're breaking from the principle of equal culpability, then the gloves are off. I'm going in to give fresh evidence.' Ducker said, 'I'll talk to Gough'.

So a great earnest discussion between Ducker and Whitlam took place, then Whitlam came over and said, 'Well, Comrades, John seems to think that you're concerned about the amounts'. I said, 'Yes, Gough.

You've conveyed the impression to the executive that it was just a normal donation. I must insist that you knew that we were talking about a very large sum of money.' Gough replied, 'I should clarify that'. So from then on the whole thing was run on equal culpability. Each of the three of us was as guilty as hell of gross lack of judgment . . . I should mention that I don't think Reuben Scarf ever knew about the Iraqi money . . .

The motions ranged from the officers' recommendation that Hartley be expelled, to one from Neil Batt and Ken Wriedt that we all three be expelled, through various alternatives. From the time that the principle was established that we must all be truthful and tell the whole truth the executive operated magnificently. There was a genuine endeavour on the part of everyone to face up to the problem and resolve it, and to forget about factional differences. Bob played a big role in preventing a faction-feud. While he had strong personal views about Hartley, and while he would have liked to pursue them, he didn't. He backed off very quickly from the idea that Hartley be expelled. He kept that executive under a tight rein for two days, determined to elicit all possible information about what had happened, determined to get a genuine, non-factional discussion. If only Whitlam had handled the Loans Affair in the same way that Hawke handled that executive — getting everything out in the open, admitting there had been an error — then the Loans Affair would never have damaged us the way it did, with bits and pieces of information dragged out like teeth, and the suspicion in everyone's mind that the full story was never revealed.

Within two days the drama was over. The Party knew all that it could know from Whitlam, Hartley and Combe about what had happened. The federal executive decided that the three men be severely reprimanded for what they had done and that it should tell the nation the facts. After some discussion about whether it was safe to allow Hawke to speak about Hartley, the executive decided that Hawke's sense of justice could be trusted, and he was given the task of divulging information to the public. The news conference was the biggest ever held by the ALP, and Hawke was at his best: he was frank, decisive and just. He did not go into any of the *opéra bouffe* details but revealed all the important elements of the affair. The paper on which was written the officers' recommendation to the executive that Hartley be expelled had been shredded, as had other pieces of paper recommending expulsion for all three. Hawke was alert in his handling of the news media: the best journalists in the country did not sense that there was a chink in the armour-plating of Party solidarity which Hawke projected, or if any did, none had a chance to ask questions which would expose it. Hartley attended the news conference and at the end of it congratulated and thanked Hawke, saying he could not have wished for fairer treatment.

Hawke said,

> I had no doubt about the integrity of Combe and Whitlam, I merely
> thought they had been stupid beyond belief. But I believed one could
> distinguish between their actions, and Hartley's. I think there were
> other considerations in Hartley's mind. The surprising thing was that he
> seemed unable to comprehend the magnitude of his actions. When he
> told us those Keystone Cops stories people began to laugh, they
> couldn't help themselves. And Bill joined in the laughter, but he did not
> seem to know that we were laughing at him, and not with him. I realised
> that he honestly did not understand what he'd done ... I was quite
> happy to go along with those who thought that it was unfair to make a
> distinction between the three. I didn't feel, as I have on some occasions,
> that those opposed to me were just wrong and stupid.

The Iraqi Money Scandal was, literally, a nine-day wonder. The *Australian*
story appeared on 25 February; Hawke's Press conference was held on
6 March. The speed with which the federal executive had dealt with the issue
had minimised the public damage to the Party. But within the upper echelons
of the ALP the little self-confidence that remained had suffered further
attrition, for members of the federal executive suspected that as with the
Loans Affair, the Gair Affair and the Kerr sacking, the Whitlam Government
had been the naive player in a very sharp poker school. They believed that the
Iraqis had donated about $250,000 to the ALP, the money had been sent via
Beirut to Tokyo for laundering, and got lost in the laundry.

The whole affair had affected Hawke much more deeply than he cared to
admit later or, publicly, at the time. He loved the Party and felt keenly
protective of it. Privately, he was outraged that Hartley had remained an ALP
member. He began to think of Hartley and other extreme members of the
Socialist Left as malignant growths within the body of Labor politics, and
among friends would have outbursts of invective against Hartley, during
which he shouted, 'I will destroy him!'

Hawke fell ill with a respiratory tract infection soon after the special
federal executive meeting. David Combe and his wife, Caroline, sent him
some flowers and a message thanking him for all he had done on their behalf.
Combe recalled,

> Next time I spoke to Bob he mentioned the flowers and then went into a
> *tirade* about how unfair it all was, that the only person who'd suffered
> out of the whole deal was himself. What had happened was that the
> Murdoch Press had run a massive campaign promoting Bob, against
> Gough. Within the Party anybody who was in favour of the Murdoch
> Press was, *ipso facto*, a louse. In those days it was not only purists who

refused to buy Murdoch newspapers — ALP members in general boy-cotted them.

Murdoch had barracked hard for Whitlam in 1972. During one of the campaign meetings Hawke had said to Whitlam, 'You're going to regret the day you got into bed with Rupert', a prophecy which was speedily fulfilled. Murdoch's news empire became the nemesis of the Government it had once promoted and Murdoch himself was elevated, in the Party, to membership of a trilogy of demons, the other two being Malcolm Fraser and Sir John Kerr. As Combe remarked, 'To be a friend of Murdoch was a sin'.

Hawke did not stop buying Murdoch newspapers, but few Party loyalists knew this. All were aware, however, that Hawke was opposed to the Party's obsessional hatred of Kerr. On several occasions early in the year he said publicly that he believed it was futile to dwell upon the past, and that the Party should be concerning itself with the future. But Hell hath no fury like a true believer scorned. Hawke's attempts at encouraging the ALP away from negativism towards a positive and expansive frame of mind were more black marks against him. Stroke by stroke, the picture of a traitor was growing. Hawke was now, for the Left, protagonist in a play plotted by unknown forces, all his actions taking place under a lurid light, or in deep, sinister shadows. For them he was turning into a Demon King himself.

Since he had become President of the ACTU Hawke had sometimes, when in his cups, shown exaggerated sensitivity to slights. For example, Richard Carleton, the television journalist, recalled Hawke arriving late and drunk at the Taiping Restaurant in Sydney for a dinner celebrating the 1972 election victory, and asking loudly of the Chinese waiter who blocked his path, 'Don't you know who I am?' His sense of power had grown bigger when he became President of the Party in government, so much so that Hazel was worried that he had lost his sense of perspective in relation to others. An air of vulgar self-importance often surrounded him, and was accompanied by a discounting of people around him. He had come to treat much criticism as humbug; he was habituated to flattery. Few had the temerity to object to Hawke's face when he was rude to them, but when, very rarely, someone would tell him afterwards of some outrageous act of his, he would at first refuse to believe he had behaved so badly, asserting, 'That's not me!' If he could be convinced he would slump into melancholic silence.

When Rupert Murdoch invited Hawke to dine with him in early 1976, in a Sydney restaurant, Hawke did not feel inhibited about accepting, although they were destined to be overseen. The meeting was widely reported and caused a scandal within the ALP. There was a detectable whiff of oppor-tunism in Hawke's reception of the Press baron's overtures, but his meetings with Murdoch were also an example of Hawke's consistent behaviour pat-tern of attempting to transcend differences and to reconcile opposites. He wanted Murdoch's support not merely for himself, but for the institution which Murdoch had so mercilessly savaged, the ALP.

By late March, Whitlam had made public his change of mind about the leadership, saying that Hawke's support in Caucus had declined in the past fifteen months and that, 'He is not, I believe, as intellectually well-equipped for leadership as I know Bill Hayden to be'. By April, Hawke's popularity rating was 62%, compared with 53% for Fraser and 41% for Whitlam.

For pragmatists within the Party the figures spoke for themselves: if the ALP were to win back government, Hawke would have to enter Parliament. A pressure campaign upon him began, and was to last for the next three years. Countering it, there was now the openly declared Stop Hawke campaign of the Socialist Left. The period between 14 December 1975 and 23 September 1979 were the most difficult years of Hawke's life. He was severely over-stretched physically; emotionally he was becoming unstable from physical exhaustion, political battles and a deteriorating personal life; intellectually, he was weary.

He read at least four newspapers every day and stacks of committee reports, but it was years since he had read thought-provoking books, and the effect of a barrage of shallow ideas and trivial facts was becoming obvious — in his speeches, for example, at the National Press Club in June 1976; in the few articles he wrote, for example, in *Heyday or Doomsday: Australia 2000*;[2] and in his conversation. His mind was still extraordinarily quick and logical, and he could still perform astonishing feats of absorbing and analysing quantities of information at a speed which awed those who worked with him. However, his natural inclination to solve immediate, practical problems had caused a narrowing of interests. Hawke fell silent, or looked bored, when discussion moved away from current events or politics. Paul Munro, Hawke's friend from New Guinea days, said,

> Bob is without small talk. If people can't talk to him about things he's interested in, he can't talk to them about things they are interested in — you know, theatre, books. He's often plain awkward in company until he's figured out what role he can play. He needs to have a defined purpose in any social situation.

Hawke's social values were sound — like second nature to him — but his ideas often flimsy. A major cause of his physical, emotional and intellectual weakening was his gregarious drinking. Hawke would rarely drink alone, but he spent hours drinking with mates and he had come to depend upon alcohol to help him relax. Hours that could have been passed in thought were given over to the bogus intellectual stimulation of boozy argument. The fact that the Anglo-Australian legal system is one based upon debate about right and wrong in the eyes of the law and not, as for example in the French system, upon determining truth, encouraged in Hawke, as it has in all our lawyer-politicians, a love of scoring points in arguments.

While the forces upon him to enter Parliament — and those threatening him against trying — built up, the more serious dilemma for Hawke was a private one: alcohol. He had made a public promise to eschew it were he to become Leader of the ALP, and his sense of honour made fulfilling the promise unavoidable. But with or without a promise, he knew that he could not achieve his dream unless he moderated his drinking. Already television interviewers were covering up for Hawke, by scrapping film of him recorded when he was drunk. When he was to be broadcast live, or to take part in important pre-recorded debates, Hawke by 1976 would sometimes mutter, 'No. I mustn't drink. I mustn't drink.' He had arrived at a stage when he had to confront a conflict that was as old as he was: his relationship with Ellie. It was she who had inspired him to seek power, to seek the prime ministership; it was she who had instilled in him an image of the bottle as black god.

By June 1976 he had replied to the importunate Press that 'this might be the year' he would enter Parliament. A week later he led an ACTU delegation to Canberra for talks with Fraser and the Cabinet, held in the Cabinet room. Out of the meeting sprang one of the most unfair of the Socialist Left attacks upon Hawke. He said, in the presence of ACTU executive members, the Prime Minister and some senior Cabinet Ministers, that if wage claims were to be moderated the trade union movement would require a reform of taxation, to guard its spendable income; Hawke proposed that if the Government would change the taxation structure it could anticipate a lessening of wage claims. Fitzgibbon, a member of the delegation, turned to another ACTU executive member, Jim Roulston of the AMWSU, a leader of the Socialist Left in Victoria and Fitzgibbon's senior in the ACTU executive hierarchy, and asked, 'Do you know about this? Do you agree with it?' Roulston replied he did not. Fitzgibbon asked, 'As a senior officer of the ACTU are you going to say something?' and Roulston replied he would not. Fitzgibbon then addressed the meeting, saying he disagreed with Hawke's proposal, that it would be difficult to persuade the rank and file to accept such a trade-off. Fraser, the Cabinet Ministers, Hawke and others formally took note of Fitzgibbon's warning. That evening Fraser invited Hawke, Ducker and Dolan to dine at The Lodge.

Earlier in the day the ACTU team had learned, from a note sent in to the Cabinet room from David Combe, that Egerton, President of the Queensland branch of the Party, had accepted a knighthood from the Fraser Government. The news was another stunning blow to Labor morale. John Ducker was so distressed that he drank a good deal before dinner; he, Dolan and the other guest, Tony Street, who was now Minister for Labour, all left The Lodge early. Hawke stayed on, drinking with Fraser, engaged by the Prime Minister in what Hawke believed was a challenge to last the distance with bottle after bottle of port. At last Mrs Fraser appeared in a dressing gown and said to her husband, 'Dear, it's time you went to bed'. Hawke recalled, 'Tamie Fraser was the most beautiful sight in the world. By then my legs were pretty wobbly, but I'd been determined not to give up.'

The next day Roulston announced that Hawke had cooked up a $650 million tax-wage trade-off with the Prime Minister. The story was spread, and reported, that this had been done *tête-à-tête* over dinner at The Lodge. It was even believed by some more gullible members of the Party, and hinted at by the Press, that Hawke's meeting with Fraser had occurred in secret, without the knowledge of the ACTU. At the next ACTU executive meeting Fitzgibbon angrily denounced Roulston and recounted Roulston's refusal to speak against the proposal when he had had the chance to do so in the Cabinet room. But the damage to Hawke had been done. In the next major meeting of the Victorian ALP the Socialist Left faction was joined by the Right faction to pass a motion condemning Hawke for his supposed 'deal' with Fraser. Handbills appeared in Victoria headlined, 'HAWKE HAS SECRET MEETINGS WITH FRASER AND MURDOCH TO BETRAY WORKING PEOPLE' and saying:

> Hawke is a most despicable person. Hawke cannot be called a 'traitor' because he has never belonged to or supported the working class. He was selected by the capitalist class to be President of the ACTU in order to strengthen the control of that class over the trade unions. Hawke is a close confidant of US labor attaches (CIA) and the greater part of his activity is secret. Who knows — apart from his bosses — what he does overseas? Who knows his precise relations with the fascist Israeli leaders? Who knows what he talks about with Fraser? Who knows what he talks about with Murdoch? Who really knows what his business connections are? This despicable person whose rotten outlook is reflected in his private life should be exposed for what he is . . . DRIVE HAWKE OUT!³

The garbage bins at his house were searched for evidence about Hawke's life-style and the readers of a radical newspaper were informed that Hawke had 'disgusting' rubbish: cartoned orange juice, for example. The house itself excited a frenzy of condemnation for its size, location and the fact that it had a tennis court and swimming pool. One night in mid-1976 somebody painted in black on its front wall: WEALTHY PIGS LIVE IN LUXURY.

Such sentiments were not confined to the new breed of semi-educated baby puritans, bearded-up like Victorian curates, whom the 1970s had spawned. One evening in 1980 a clean-shaven, middle-aged professor of history from a Melbourne university delivered himself of the opinion that it was 'disgraceful' that Hawke lived in Brighton. When informed that Hawke lived in the less expensive suburb of Sandringham, the professor replied that made no difference: Hawke's life was luxurious. Upon inquiry, the professor divulged that he lived in the fashionable and expensive suburb of Kew, adding, 'But I'm only renting'.[4] Whatever that reveals about the quality of intellect of a senior academic, it is a demonstration of the success of the smear campaign against Hawke, who, until the end of the decade, was continuously in overdraft. Only when Hazel began working full-time could they afford to hire somebody to do the heavy household cleaning and the ironing.

The paranoia of radicals about Hawke was matched by enthusiasm among non-radicals. In July 1976 the Rev. Lillian Livingstone, a Congregational minister, asserted during a sermon in Sydney that Jesus Christ resembled Bob Hawke more than 'the gentle Jesus meek and mild' of popular fancy. Letters and telegrams arrived at the ACTU urging upon Hawke various actions:

> Should you enter Parliament the people of Australia will be exposed to the risk of having their greatest hope taken hostage. The Australian has needed a mate for nearly half a century.

> Although opposed to your political views I sincerely believe your destiny is on the world scene, for God and the Good of all kind.

> You have got a definite spiritual character about you that is hard to define . . . I say a special prayer for you each Sunday at church . . . I've got a photo of you from a local newspaper and I always carry it with me wherever I go. It gives me spiritual and emotional strength . . . I'd gladly die for you, if I had to. It's guys like you who make the Labor Party a great party.

> For the sake of your Party and the country I urge you to go for pre-selection.[5]

By September 1976 speculation about when and if Hawke would enter Parliament had reached such outlandish proportions that he decided to hold a news conference on the issue. The Victorian branch of the ALP had forced a show-down by deciding that nominations for pre-selection for the election due in December 1978 must be lodged by 30 September 1976. Normal practice was to call for nominations twelve months before an election was due. The rule change was designed to nobble Hawke, because if he put himself forward as a parliamentary candidate he would be a 'lame-duck' President of the ACTU for — as it was then believed — two years. (As events turned out, Fraser held the election one year early.) Two days before his news conference was scheduled the Socialist Left announced, presumably in case some deaf person had not heard the sound of the grinding of axes, that they would 'oppose completely any bid of Hawke's for pre-selection'.

Fifty journalists gathered in the Melbourne Trades Hall on 15 September to learn Hawke's decision: Not this time. The *Age* commented editorially,

> Mr Hawke said . . . his move would create a lame-duck ACTU presidency for the next two years. We suggest the logic of that argument can be taken a step further: if his effectiveness as the leader of the trade union movement would be destroyed by his becoming an officially declared candidate, it will surely be at least diminished by his remaining a potential candidate.

It was a perspicacious comment. Hawke had been standing, unchallenged and unchallengeable, on a mountain top of trade union support: beneath his feet the rock was to subside.

By late 1976 senior officers of the ACTU were so alarmed by the campaign against him, and by Hawke's drinking, that they agreed he needed a chauffeur-bodyguard. The ACTU had no funds for such an extra staff member, so it was arranged that a job be found in ACTU-Solo, and that the man employed would work for the petrol discounting company when not driving and protecting Hawke. The person chosen was Chris Crellin, a young, physically beautiful giant — he weighed 17 stone — who had been a policeman. While still a member of the force he had been chosen as a bodyguard for Fraser during the 1975 election campaign, which was cause for hilarity among police, since Crellin was known for his Labor sympathies. He speaks quietly and moves with the silent grace and menace of a panther. He told Hawke he would feel honoured to work for him, then when Hawke asked him to wear a pistol, refused — 'with passive resistance, and after a while Bob didn't mention it any more'. Hawke doted upon Crellin; when Crellin would appear noiselessly in a doorway Hawke's eyes would soften. 'Chris. Chris . . . he loves me', Hawke would say sometimes.

Hawke has always craved love, and those he loves he trusts wholeheartedly. Kirby remarked, 'Once Bob accepts you, that's it. I could say to him I thought the earth was flat and he wouldn't fly off the handle at me, but would say, "Well, Dick, I'm sure you have some reason for believing that". There's a special quality in his friendship.'

By the end of 1976 John Ducker and Hawke were friends. It was a friendship which saved Hawke's political life in 1977.

Chapter Eighteen

The broad challenge to authority that had begun in the 1960s had brought liberty. And liberty had brought confusion: by the mid-1970s Australian society was divided by a host of issues. Especially painful was the fight over the rights and status of women, an upheaval that had affected the whole community. There were questions about Australia's moral authority *vis-à-vis* her closest neighbour, Indonesia; education — for academic excellence or for personality development? permissiveness — in sexuality, dress, manners; debate about the citizen's duties to society — was unemployment 'dole bludging'? — and the Government's duties to the citizen: should it artificially create jobs, and if so, how much should it spend? In private lives there were discovered, afresh, old arguments about emotions and awareness versus logic and cogitation: guidance for conduct was sought in astrology, and clearer perception through inhaling, injecting or eating vegetable extracts. Senior members of society despaired of the nation's youth. Preservation of the environment (an economic question dressed up as a moral one), was pitted against a frank economic question: jobs; there were demands for ethnic distinctions in Australia versus demands for a coherent cultural core; there was abortion: murder or mercy or none of your business? What to do about the Aborigines? We could not even agree upon a national anthem.

Malcolm Fraser had been elected to change all that. He was an authoritarian, with an authoritarian's disdain for human frailty, and he inspired confidence among the confused. While few people liked him millions were willing to vote for him because Fraser promised a return to certainties, however unpalatable. He had the strength of a political leader who knows that his personality is matched to the inchoate yearnings of the electorate: frightened by liberty and uncertainty, people wanted a patriarch who would put an end to the bickering of national life and point them in the right direction for the Promised Land. He had won 57% of first preference votes in the 1975 election, with a kind of decalogue, the first commandment being 'sound economic management' and the second 'fight inflation first'. The corollary of the first meant breaking up the handiwork, the great public spending programmes, of the Whitlam years, while that of the second meant worsening unemployment. In theory, unemployment would worsen only in the short term; within a few years prosperity would return to all. In practice, the Government found its programme was as difficult to implement as that other one engraved on tablets of stone. Years of economic meandering began.

The percentage of votes cast for the conservative Government in 1975 showed that a goodly number of those who would define themselves as working class, or who were members of blue-collar unions, had rejected Labor and chosen Fraser. Of itself this suggested that within the labour movement a period of self-hatred had begun. What the voting figures suggested was further revealed by the behaviour of the ALP and its demoralised representatives in federal Parliament — they cursed the name of John Kerr, they maintained their rage, in the end a rage at themselves for having been tricked — and by the angry dejection and confusion within the trade union movement.

The unions had won great gains in the 1960s in wages and in liberty, culminating in the sweeping away of the penal powers in 1969, thanks, finally, to Kerr's mishandling of the O'Shea case. Fraser was determined to reintroduce 'pains and penalties', as the unions called them, into Australian industrial life. Hawke's jobs, as President of the ALP and of the ACTU, became exquisitely difficult. For the former he had to take the role of optimistic, inspirational leader to a group which had, as he observed, 'had the guts ripped out' of it. He had to stand as a Party signpost pointing expansively forward. But as leader of the unions he had to demand a diminution of hope and an increase in self-discipline, in the pursuit of survival. He needed to be cheerful and soothing, and aggressively determined, by turns. His personality equipped him for the performance of both roles.

Fraser's vote in 1975 was, unlike Whitlam's 1972 poll of 49.6% of primary votes, a genuine mandate, which gave the new Prime Minister the right to pursue whatever policies he chose. Once the new Government was safely in office it began a campaign of 'union bashing', a procedure made easier by the fact that the Whitlam Government itself had, in its confusion and panic, led the way. There had been Cameron's famous remark, when he was still Minister for Labour, about public service 'fat cats', and scores of speeches from Labor ministers inveighing against wage demands and strikes. Fraser was determined to take the issue much further, to mount a direct assault upon union freedoms.

To aid the process, the new Government needed to bring the trade union movement into disrepute. Beginning in mid-1976 Fraser's ministry progressively introduced a legislative programme designed to weaken the unions financially and, especially, to undo the liberty of action they had enjoyed since the O'Shea case. He and his ministers took every opportunity to blame inflation upon union greed and irresponsibility. Their assertions about wage claims causing inflation were not wholly true but nor were they entirely false — they were, rather, a confusion, similar to confusing a fever, symptom of disease, with its cause. Wage claims were a fever and, fed back through the arbitration system, were making inflation worse. They were not the cause of inflation but a response to it.

Fraser had not been elected for nice debate or for stating the facts — indeed, his disregard for the facts was already well-known in Canberra and was to become a national by-word. Yet from him, this was acceptable to the electorate, at least until the period of acute fear had passed. The damage done by the electorate's acceptance that its federal government was led by a man who did not regard veracity as necessary in political life cannot be overestimated, for such behaviour in a leader generates cynicism and cynicism leads to apathy. And, it must be added, the Whitlam Government's record in this matter was checkered: the Fraser Government bulldozed along a track which had already been marked out by its predecessor. By November 1975, the electorate had countless examples of the mendacity of politicians and their contempt for the people at large. The old anarchist saying, 'Whoever you vote for, a politician will get in', had come to have particular relevance.

It was Hawke's job to protect the trade union movement from the Prime Minister, and to carry the flag for honesty.

Fending off the attacks upon the trade union movement launched by the Fraser Government required of Hawke all the political skill and authority he had, for the legislative wing of the labour movement, the federal ALP Caucus, had been reduced to a stump and was unable to assist the industrial branch. Souter recalled, 'The Party could give us no help at all in Parliament against Fraser's legislation. We were fighting it on our own and the ACTU just had to push and pull the best way it could.' Hawke needed to push at the Government with one hand and to pull in the unions with the other; his life became a series of dramatic public threats to the Government and private efforts at conciliation.

In mid-1976 when it became obvious that the Fraser Government, in the teeth of its election promise, intended to dismantle the Whitlam Government's most popular bequest, Medibank, the ALP Caucus was powerless to prevent the attrition of Medibank and the struggle to preserve the national health scheme became the responsibility of the union movement. Hawke was loud in his public denunciations of the Government while privately he was trying to hold back the more radical unions from rushing to strike action, and behind the scenes was attempting to force the Government to bargain with the ACTU over the issue. A large section of the Left of both the unions and the Party thought it shameful to negotiate with the Fraser Government at all, and wanted immediate confrontation. Hawke had no doubt who would win: the Government would, for the voting figures alone had told him that the union movement was deeply divided in its attitudes to Fraser and could not be relied upon to stand shoulder-to-shoulder in a confrontation. He stalled for weeks, requesting longer talks and more debates with the Government before the ACTU could make a decision. At length, the activities of radicals sabotaged him. Fraser perceived the vulnerability of Hawke's position and decided to challenge the unions to defy the Government. Very unwillingly, with no room left to manoeuvre, Hawke called the first national stoppage in Australia's history, in June 1976, to protest for one day about the changes to Medibank. It went quietly. The Government proclaimed the Medibank strike had been a failure, and took courage.

Hawke was extremely bitter. A few weeks later he used the opportunity of a meeting with union representatives in the Brisbane Trades Hall to upbraid radicals and to try to beat into their consciousness the danger to hard-won wages and liberty that the unions now faced, and the consequent need for disciplined action. He told them:

> In the Cabinet room — and this was a rotten, terrible bloody experience I had to go through — I had the Prime Minister saying to me, 'Mr Hawke, if we move to your position on Medibank, even if we do so because we are persuaded that you are right and that yours is a better position, we would possibly have the worst of both worlds, because you couldn't say to us that your trade union movement would accept it'. And that happened because *you* in your lack of wisdom and your snuggling under slogans and your non-thinking, tried to lead the trade union movement. You jumped the gun. You hadn't done your homework, you wouldn't know anything about what it was about. We [the ACTU] had done our homework, we'd got the Government to the edge of agreeing to a better deal on Medibank. Then, you jumped in. And so, we had the Prime Minister saying, 'All right, the Government won't agree for one reason: because, Mr Hawke, you can't control the trade union movement'. It wasn't the vast membership of the trade union movement who behaved in a way to enable the Prime Minister to say that. It was you!

Hawke knew from his meetings with Fraser how formidable he was in willpower, if not in intellect and, being only an average-sized man himself, was particularly impressed by Fraser's massive 6 foot 5 inch frame. 'You ought to see his thighs!' Hawke exclaimed. 'They're like tree trunks! . . . The man is a bastard — he's a liar and he's got a second-rate mind, as was noted at Oxford. He needs to work tremendously hard to get on top of information. But he's a fascinating bastard . . .' Hawke's remarks revealed as much about himself as about the Prime Minister: he adores intelligence — 'the God-given brain' which, in childhood and youth, he had been constantly urged to use — and his commitment to truthfulness was almost equal to Ellie's, but in much more difficult circumstances than any she had needed to withstand. Hawke spoke so often of his intellectual prowess that Chris Crellin, his chauffeur, picked up what *he* referred to as 'Bob's belief in his God-given brain and his duty to use it'.

It was many more months before the unions realised that they now faced a Prime Minister more intimidating than any in living memory and that if their lives were not to become harder, Hawke was their major hope. His public esteem was crucial, for it was the one weapon he had to use in bargaining with the Government on one hand and, on the other, with those more wild-eyed sections of the union movement which did not admit that *vis-à-vis* the new Government, the trade union movement was weak. Hawke became known as The Fireman, because of his constant rushing around and hosing down disputes, for which he enlisted the assistance of George Polites and other leaders of the organised employers, and of Sir John Moore and other arbitration judges. He also set out to establish rapport with the new Minister for Labour, Tony Street. Publicly, Hawke and Street would snap at each other. Privately, they were becoming warm friends.

In 1976 and 1977 Hawke made several public relations trips abroad to seek to improve the image of the Australian unions with our major trading partners, particularly Japan, urging that contracts for iron ore and other goods be signed, for the cargoes would be delivered, not held up by strikes. It was the Government's own tactic of reviling the unions which had, in part, necessitated such exercises by Hawke: at home ministers abused the trade union movement for irresponsibility and ruining the country, and their speeches were reported in Japan and elsewhere. They would then arrive in Tokyo and expect Japanese business leaders to believe the truth: that since the appalling year of 1974, Australia's strike record had moderated,* although, unlike America, the timing of strikes was unpredictable. However, the Government's constant harping upon the wickedness and greed of the unions was having its effect: the electorate at large, which had once accepted that the unions, for all their faults, had done more for decency, honesty and the betterment of society than most other organised bodies of men, was changing its mind. The unions *were* falling into disrepute.

In January 1977 Hawke began publicly to call for a meeting of unions, employers and Government to discuss, without inhibition or party political considerations, the state of the Australian economy, and from such discussions to agree upon methods of improving it. He was convinced that the Government was mishandling the economy; he knew that the employers were far from happy; and he knew that the unions could never be persuaded to co-operate in a national economic revival until the Government had won their trust. So far it had only won their mistrust. The Government and its

* 1974: 6,292,500 days lost; 1975: 3,509,900; 1976: 3,799,200, of which 55% of days lost were due to the Medibank strike; 1977: 1,654,800.

institutions — such as the Reserve Bank and Treasury — had access to a wealth of information on the national and international situation: if only they could be persuaded to share it with the employers and the unions simultaneously, and in an atmosphere of frankness, the first step towards reform would have been taken. Hawke repeatedly demanded a consensus approach to the nation's economic problems. But politics is too often a game of Winner Take All, and his pleas and demands were rejected. Years earlier Albert Monk, who as ACTU President had co-operated with the Curtin, Chifley and Menzies Governments to help to achieve and maintain full employment in Australia, had remarked to Sir Richard Kirby, 'You know, people say now that Hawke is a mad radical. Wait a few years. They'll be saying, "Dear old Bob — he's trying to get a consensus. He's turning out to be just as conservative as Albert was." There'll always be unemployment, and Bob's a responsible fellow. Wait and see.' Monk was dead by now; Hawke's commitment to seeking consensus was regarded as something new and within the ALP, if not in the trade union movement, was much disliked. The Prime Minister did not like it himself: a senior employers' representative who knew Fraser well remarked, 'Every time Malcolm looked at Bob he saw the President of the ALP and he just could not bring himself to trust Hawke'. There were no tripartite discussions. Instead, in March 1977, the Government agreed eagerly to a half-formulated plan from the premiers to put a brake upon wages and prices. Don Dunstan, the Premier of South Australia, said, 'Being party to that was one of my errors. Bob Hawke came in and stitched up a compromise which saved the bacon of us Labor premiers.' After a few weeks the scheme was abandoned and wages, prices and unemployment all increased. The Government blamed the unions.

Hawke was already so adept at strike negotiations that some unions had reached the stage of planning strike campaigns — without Hawke's knowledge — around him: they would calculate that they could reach a certain point in the bargaining process by themselves, but would then get stuck and would need to call upon Hawke to be their negotiator. This was a major change from the old days, under Monk, when officials would only turn to the ACTU as a desperate and unplanned measure. To resort to the Council was to seek to distribute the humiliation of a lost campaign: throughout the trade union movement the ACTU had been known in those days as The Graveyard of Strikes. Now, in a period when the unions were weakening, as unemployment continued to rise inexorably, month by month, and their membership figures were static or decreasing, Hawke's ability to bargain and win settlements for them was of major importance in keeping up morale. His mystique increased. He was seen to be the real Labor leader while Whitlam, in Parliament, sat seemingly brooding — isolated and resentful.

As Hawke became in the public's eyes the equal of the Prime Minister, and far more popular than either the Leader of the Government or the Leader of the Opposition, the Left's and the ALP Caucus' grudges against him grew.

For as conservative politics — Labor, Liberal, Communist or whatever — has its dark form in bullying, the vice of reform is envy.

By mid-1977 Hawke was supremely enviable in Labor eyes. Alone of their leaders he had survived November 1975 with all his titles and privileges intact, and his prestige — now that Whitlam was off centre-stage and a mere shade of the Olympian he once was — had increased. The sweet perquisites of office had been ripped from the Caucus without ceremony. But Hawke now had a personal chauffeur and an LTD limousine (both paid for by ACTU-Solo), with a desk in the back seat where he could work. Even Hawke's supporters on the ACTU executive had been embarrassed by the size of the car — although the alternative, his continuing to drive the ACTU-supplied Holden, was both a waste of his time and a risk to his life, considering his drinking. There had been spirited criticism about the new car in an executive meeting, and much muttering within the Party: Hawke looked too grand for a Labor man. And he was treated like a grandee. Crowds fawned upon him; mobs of *nouveaux riches* rowdies attached themselves to him as cheer squads and Hawke did not discourage them — to the annoyance of his older and more serious-minded friends, who complained that he was surrounding himself with toadies who lacked both social virtues and intellect. Hawke has always been indiscriminately friendly, giving and receiving love and admiration in lavish quantities. In the years when his career was particularly stressful and when his future was uncertain he seemed to need his band of hero-worshippers to shore him up with yea-saying. His real friends were not afraid to disagree with him and often reproached him when they thought he behaved intemperately. Abeles frequently prefaced remarks to Hawke, 'I must say to you, Bob, you are being stupid'; Rockey, as host of a reception, had once asked Hawke to leave when he was rude to another guest. Hawke's closest friend in Melbourne was Colin Cunningham, a small businessman, an excellent golfer, a good snooker player and a keen punter. Racegoers describe Cunningham as 'a character out of Damon Runyon'; he calls himself 'a knock-about bloke'. He is long-limbed and laconic. Cunningham grew up, son of a taxi-driver, in the slums of Melbourne — 'a Labor supporter all my life' — and has a working class wiseguy's sense of irony. He is a couple of years younger than Hawke and said of their relationship,

> Bob sort of latched on to me — it was big deal for me, back in 1972 when everybody was staring at him — because, I think, he hadn't been out in the world all that much. He wanted to know more about life . . . general knowledge, sayings. He loves sportsmen, and I knew a few: Frank Sedgman, Neil Fraser, Gary Sobers — I'd take them round to his house. I had golfing friends like Bruce Devlin and Jack Newton playing over in America, and I'd tell Bob what was going on . . . I love the guy. He's a free-giving person . . . I like looking after him, you know? Years ago I said to him, 'Pal, you're going to kill yourself — you need a

chauffeur'. He wanted me to do it, to look after him. I was tempted. But my wife said, 'Do that, and don't bother coming home' . . . He was very anti-Establishment, back in 1974 or 1975. He and I were on holiday in Surfers Paradise, and went for dinner in a famous restaurant there. Bob gave the owner a helluva time — he was really misbehaving. I said, 'Pal, I'm going home. You can do what you like, but I'm not putting up with this situation.' We both packed our bags and left Surfers Paradise at 6.30 the next morning.

Recognised wherever he went, Hawke moved in an aura of power. Foreign dignitaries who visited Australia wanted to meet him: an official of the American Embassy commented, 'We had to make a cut-off point of seniority. For those below the line we would not even consider trying to arrange an appointment with Bob.' Any news release of his was reported, while Labor shadow ministers had to cajole journalists for attention. People hurried to serve him in shops; chefs emerged from restaurant kitchens to ask if he were enjoying his food and would prepare dishes, at his request, that were not on the menu; airline staff shepherded him into VIP lounges; bowls of fruit and flowers, with a note from the manager, welcomed him in hotels (and one regularly supplied book matches with Hawke's name printed on them); artists of variable talent dedicated songs, books and paintings to him. Hawke was always immaculately dressed in public; he wore a single piece of jewellery: a gold ring set with a large topaz on his left hand. By his late forties he had grown handsome, much better looking than he appeared to be on television. His face was chiselled with character and his hair was grey, gleaming and luxuriant. One could often catch middle-aged men eyeing it enviously.

While sections of the ALP hierarchy could find reasons for condemnation of the Party President in his style, there was now a special area for argument with him: uranium. The Whitlam Government's policy had been to mine and sell uranium ore, but since losing office the ALP had been rethinking its attitude. The Left of the Party, plus a large minority of people outside the Labor movement, formed into protest groups and were intense in their fear of the mineral and its uses. They demanded that it should be allowed to lie sleeping in the bosom of the earth, its only safe guardian. Attitudes to uranium seem to be determined by personality and individuals' attitudes to humankind: is human nature trustworthy or unreliable? Is history tragic and impersonal, or a progress towards enlightenment, or a divine comedy of errors and angelic leaps? Or none of these?

Depending upon their answers to such questions some people were convinced that uranium would be misused and were passionately opposed to disturbing it; others believed it could help to solve the world's energy problems and thereby return the prosperity enjoyed before the Yom Kippur War; others were simply baffled. There was also the argument, ever-fashionable,

for venality — from those who owned uranium leases, from those who were
highly-paid to mine yellowcake, and from governments avid to collect revenues from it. By 1977 the uranium debate had become radiantly hot on the
side of the objectors and, on the side of the supporters, sullen and suave by
turns. A large section of the community was agnostic.

Hawke had publicly said that he 'wished the bloody stuff had never been
discovered', but since it had and since, whatever Australia did or did not do
about its massive deposits of uranium ore, yellowcake elsewhere would be
mined, refined and used, he thought it futile to take an isolationist position.
Therefore, he believed that, given safeguards about its handling and use,
Australia's uranium should be mined. His was the pragmatic agnostic's
position. However, agnosticism is invariably confused with atheism in the
minds of excited true believers, and with timid theism in the minds of excited
atheists. Hawke had earned himself another bunch of black marks in the Left
of the Party and among radicals outside it.

Some of his closest supporters, including Clyde Holding and Bill Landeryou, two of the leaders of the Centre Unity faction in the Victorian ALP, were
opposed to his view that uranium mining should continue in Australia, as was
one of his best friends on the ACTU executive, Cliff Dolan.

For Hawke, much more distressing than disagreements with his friends
were arguments with his children on the issue.

His household was unusually liberal. Other teenagers had been astonished
by the subjects, taboo to them, that the Hawke children raised with their
parents and by the atmosphere of freedom in the house. Adult visitors were
often shocked by the liberties in speech allowed to the children. Hawke was
the obverse of an authoritarian father; as well, he was determined that his
offspring would not suffer the tight social constrictions of his parents' milieu,
against which he had spent half a lifetime in rebellion, and with which he had
yet to come to terms. His son, Stephen, was opposed to uranium mining and
his elder daughter, Susan, was an anti-uranium activist. Susan, who had
resembled Ellie so much in infancy, now, aged twenty, looked uncannily like
her father and had his fiery debating style and acute intelligence. He was
extravagant in his admiration for her and had been boasting since she turned
fourteen that he could have more stimulating discussions with her than with
many of his adult male colleagues. However, as a Law student at Monash
University, Susan Hawke's politics had taken a radical turn. Her arguments
with him were becoming embittered as, increasingly, their social views
diverged. Hawke was dismayed by the rift that was opening between them.
He was also anguished by his arguments with Stephen, whose personality was
calm and full of tenderness, like Clem's. Family friends said, 'Bob would put
his head on the railway line for Stephen'. Just before the ALP Conference of
1977 Hawke flew to Tasmania to talk to Stephen, who had matriculated with
excellent marks but was resisting the idea of going to university. Stephen
wrote a ten-page letter imploring his father to change his attitudes to uranium

mining. Hawke caught a plane for Perth on 29 June, agonising over his looming estrangement from the older children. There was no question that he would change his mind about uranium to please them.

For the time being, however, uranium was the least of his problems. Unbeknown to Hawke, he was about to be deposed as President of the ALP.

He was still extraordinarily selfish. He said of himself a couple of years later, with misery, 'I'm the most selfish man in the world'. He had selfishness' assumption that people would do as he wanted them to, and so was incurious about the wishes of others. If he thought about such matters at all, it was to assume that most people had the same good motives as he did.

Unfortunately, trust in good nature, applied in politics, frequently translates as naivety. Hawke had been trapped by naivety in the past; travelling to Perth, he was flying straight into an elegantly constructed ambush.

When he had become President of the Party in 1973 he had said he thought he would hold the job for only one term (until the 1975 Conference) but he had already held it for two and had been shilly-shallying — assuming, again, that others would be in accord with his wishes whatever they turned out to be — about how much longer he wanted it. There were many arguments for his stepping down. A major new one was that his ALP presidency stimulated the combative spirit of the Prime Minister. The senior employers' representative who noted that Fraser could not help seeing Hawke as a political enemy because of Hat II added, 'A lot of things Malcolm did were to get after Bob as ALP President, and that meant getting after him as President of the ACTU as well'. Hawke, however, cherished the extra prestige that came with his second hat. Although the way he wore it continued to damage him within the Caucus, it was of great benefit to him personally, as a public figure, and, he believed, beneficial to the Party. Hat II doubled his potential for publicity; he was the most popular man in the country. These two facts were interdependent and, he thought, generated a third: national affection for the ALP. He wanted all of these things. He had, therefore, decided to continue on as Party President. He was especially keen to be chairman of this Conference, in Perth, for that would give particular pleasure to Clem and Ellie. It had not occurred to Hawke that anyone would stand against him.

The ALP federal executive of eighteen members began its traditional pre-Conference meeting on the morning of Thursday 30 June, at the Sheraton Hotel, with Hawke in the chair. Executive elections would be held the following day; over the weekend interstate delegates would arrive and on Monday the Conference proper would get underway.

At the morning-tea break on Thursday, New South Welshman Tom Uren, the leader of the Left in Caucus, deputy leader to Whitlam, and a champion of the anti-uranium cause, took David Combe aside. Combe recalled:

Tom was very chummy. He said, 'You and I agree on this uranium question. You know, you're not a bad bloke. I don't always agree with you, but you're not a bad operator. You've got a bastard of a job.' I said, 'Oh, sometimes, Tom. But I enjoy it.' He said, 'Yeah. Sometimes you've got to do things you mightn't like.' I said that was true. He said, 'Well now, you're a good mate of Bob's. A few of us have been having a talk and we've decided we want Mick Young* to be President. And we've got twelve votes to say he becomes President. You're the bloke to pass the message on to Bob.' I said, 'Bob's going to run again'. Tom said, 'We think it would be bad for the Party if he did. He doesn't want to run and get knocked off. We've got twelve votes to say he shouldn't try — the whole of the Left, plus some others. It's not even close: Bob has had his chips. He's to step down and make way for Mick.'

Then Tom added, 'It's not a one-way street: we're going to support John Ducker for senior vice-president'. That was no concession at all, because Ducker was going to win anyway. Tom said, 'We're telling John the same thing. You're to tell Bob not to run.' I said, 'Why don't you tell him yourself?' Morning tea was over. There was no time to say anything to Bob.

We returned to the meeting and John [Ducker] and I exchanged sign language to indicate that we both had been spoken to, then we passed a note to each other saying we would give Bob the word at lunch-time. As soon as we broke for lunch John and I told Bob we had to talk to him. When we told him what had happened, Bob was devastated. It was inconceivable to him to be treated like that. He became very quiet. He was obviously terribly hurt. I guess what was going through his mind was *who* the twelve people were. Some were pretty obvious, but there were others he'd thought were friends. He was very distressed that Mick Young was involved, because Mick was his mate. Anyway, we agreed to talk it over when the afternoon session had closed. Bob was extremely subdued after lunch, visibly so. At afternoon-tea time Uren came up to me with a grin from ear to ear and said, 'Well done! You've obviously told him. How did he react?' I replied, 'He hasn't decided yet if he'll run or not. We'll discuss it later.'

That evening Hawke, Combe and Ducker assembled in either Combe's or Ducker's hotel room. Ducker took up the story:

---

* Mick Young had been a shearer and AWU organiser, Secretary of the South Australian branch of the ALP, then Federal Secretary during the traumatic period of intervention into the Victorian branch, in which he had played a leading role. He entered Parliament as Member for Port Adelaide in 1974 and in 1977 became President of the South Australian branch of the Party and shadow Minister for Industry and Commerce. He is an avid punter and he and Hawke had a regular Saturday morning telephone conference about which horses they would back.

I didn't realise that Bob was going to go under, because I'd got used to the fact that Hawke never went under. I think it was Graham Richardson [Secretary of the NSW branch of the ALP] who told me the facts of life. Bob was saying, 'The West Australians are on side — they won't do me over'. He was very upset — overwrought — not in tears, but so close to tears it was indistinguishable — and still clinging to hope. So I had to say to him, 'Bob, you're done. Please understand that you are *finished*. Please understand the consequences of that: *you are a failed leader*. You're out!' And he replied, 'After all I've done for the Party! Worked my arse off, battled and struggled. Sacrificed my family. And that's what they're going to do to me!' So I said to him, 'You've helped to create this yourself. You've been playing footsie, saying maybe I will continue, maybe I won't. You've got to make up your mind. Do you want to be President of the ALP?' And he said, 'Yes! Just for one more term.' So I said, 'Right. Let's get the list [of executive members]. You get on to your mates, and leave the rest to me. We'll call in every bloody IOU you ever had.'

There were two thoughts uppermost in my mind: one was friendship and loyalty to Bob. The other was the absolute disaster for the labour movement of his standing and being defeated. As well, I had my blood up, because in the final analysis, this was a fight between the Left and the Right. So for all those reasons I was willing to go to the wall . . . Looking back, I think I was already wondering if the worst came and we were done, if that would be such a bad thing. Because, we'd live to fight another day, and on a pretty good platform: those for Hawke, and those against him. At that time especially Bob was a saintly figure in the labour movement — he was a figure of awe, of reverence, tremendously strong. Even among the Left in New South Wales. A helluva lot of the younger Left there had unbounded admiration and affection for him. So there was a potential in that. Now my thoughts about the possibilities for the future were not at the front of my head, but knowing myself, they were there in the back somewhere.

Time was critical: it was already about 6 p.m. and the federal executive would meet at 9.30 the following morning. Hawke is unused to fighting for himself, as distinct from fighting for others: the battle for the ACTU presidency had been a power bloc battle; when he had almost been sacked as ALP President in 1974, it was the trade union faction on the ALP executive that had weighed in to save him. Except for the most malicious, nobody doubted that Hawke had courage, but he was known as a man who was courageous in pursuing causes, while expecting fraternal generosity for himself. In the Victorian Left it was a frequent complaint that Hawke expected pre-selection for a winnable parliamentary seat, 'on a plate'. Indeed, the Socialist Left's ability to frighten Hawke off, apparently, from a fight over pre-selection had convinced people that he was a man who would not fight for himself. Therefore, if only he could be demoralised (by being treated shabbily), he would quail and give up. Ducker and Combe both feared that this would be his reaction. Combe said,

> I learned that night that Bob was a fighter. I think it was the first time that he had been forced to get into that grimy arena in which Ducker and I, for example, had to operate often, the nasty nitty-gritty of actually getting on the phone himself and asking for support. He had always had such a machine working for him. His intellect and his stature were such that he'd never had to get down to that level that the rest of us were used to. Other people had always done it for him . . . Ducker said to him, 'Listen, you're to get on the telephone to these buggers and say that you are running for President and can you count on them for support. Don't listen to how they hedge. You've got to force a commitment out of them — Yes or No.'
>
> So we began running a couple of phones at once. Joan Taggart [executive delegate from the ACT] had joined us early on, and was on side. We had people all over the joint, finding other people. Poor old John Waters, the delegate from the Northern Territory, had just arrived and was checking in at the reception desk when we barrelled him and said, 'We want to talk to you. As soon as you get to your room, ring this number.' And upstairs Bob was on the blower, saying, 'I understand there's going to be a contest for the presidency tomorrow. I want you to know that I'm running for a final term. Can I count on you for support?' He got some pretty funny responses. You know, people who *obviously* had promised Uren that they would go along with the Young move, and who were now backing and filling to Bob.

Essentially, Hawke's lobbying was soft, an appeal to old colleagues to stand by him. The leaders of the move against him, Uren and Senator Arthur Gietzelt (brother of Ray) had not, it seems, counted on his lobbying at all. Their more serious miscalculation was that they had not counted on the loyalty of that wily myrmidon, John Ducker. It was well known that Ducker was keen to become senior vice-president of the Party, so it was thought that Ducker would do nothing to ruin his own chances. But while Hawke was appealing to the sweeter instincts of his colleagues, Ducker, elsewhere in the hotel, was verbally thumping them witless.

He recalled,

> I said to people, 'You realise that this will be a fundamental split between the Party and the ACTU? You realise that we're dealing with the most popular man in the country and we are going to dump him,

publicly?' And they came back with, 'Oh, can't we persuade him not to run? He hasn't said he's going to run yet.' And I said, 'Well, he's going to. And the Party will be seen to have knocked him off — the President of the ACTU, a man with the esteem he's got. And if you're happy to wear that, OK. But I want you to know that we'll make sure you are personally accounted for, in terms of the part *you've* played in getting rid of Hawke, and you can go back and talk to your mates in the Trades Hall about the fact that you sold out the trade union movement . . . Haven't we had a thousand bloody battles about the trade union movement's right to have a fair go in the Labor Party? And *you're* going to be one of the people who've destroyed that!' And I'd get the arguments: 'Hey, listen. You know he's gone off the deep end. You remember when he bucketed the [Whitlam] Government! You remember the number of times when all of us were bloody angry about the things he did. Why have we got to cop that, forever?' And I'd say, 'Well, he's been going a lot quieter, hasn't he? And if you do the balance sheet adjustment about Bob, which way does it go?' And to that I'd get, 'Yeah. All right — he's done more good than bad.' So then I'd be nice and friendly, and would say, 'Do you carry as much bloody stress and pressure as that bloke does? Look what it's done to his wife and kids. And he's done it for the Party and the trade union movement. Now, where do you stand?' And, then I'd have to say, 'I'm a reasonable man. But I'll make sure that the lines are drawn in this bloody Party and trade union movement between who stands for Hawke and who is against him. And I'll be on one side of that fence, and you'll be on the other, chum. And if you're satisfied that the rank and file will support you for stabbing Hawke in the back, have a go, mate!'

And to Mick: 'Mick. You want to stuff yourself for all time? You're a man with many ambitions. Don't forget that Hawke, in intervention in Victoria, stood up for what was right. Just count your debts, Mick. Just count the number of times he's been a mate for you. Just consider how you'll feel about cutting his throat. Do you think, after that, you'll be able to ring him up and talk about which horses to back, like in the old days?'

And then I had another point to make to a few people: 'If you want the Parliamentary Party to be seen as anti-trade union, if you want to run the risk of an absolute split — because, I tell you something, friend, the trade union movement and the workers of this country are getting to a point where they're wondering whether they can afford the bloody Labor Party. And it wouldn't be all that bloody impossible to see the trade union movement decide to go independent. You realise that, I hope? And I hope you realise that if the trade unions were to abandon the Labor Party, well . . . You haven't got too many resources left, have you?' It was a friendly sort of light chatter . . . To the people from New

South Wales I had a particular message. I told them, 'We've always in the end had a bit of tolerance in New South Wales with the factions. There will be *none* if this happens. I'm prepared to go all the way on this one. Because, quite frankly, I don't altogether mind a situation in which the Left has destroyed Hawke and the Right has backed him. If you want the battle lines drawn on that basis, then I'm prepared to go to our next [NSW ALP] Conference and have a bit of cleaning up.' Well, they didn't like that sort of proposal.

Not surprisingly, for Ducker was threatening a frontal assault by the Right on the Left in NSW, and there could be no doubt about who would win that. The outcome could be a split in NSW. If the Party split there it would almost certainly split in Victoria as well.

By about 8 p.m. Hawke had spoken to those whom he knew were not his sworn enemies and Ducker had bailed up the same people and many others for his friendly chat. But Hawke was still far from safe: promises are one thing, votes another. More importantly they wanted to avoid, for the Labor movement's sake, a brawl on the eve of the Conference. Obviously Uren also wanted to protect the Party from a brawl. David Combe said, 'I think *we* finished up with about twelve votes', but Ducker was not convinced and said later, 'I wasn't confident that when the moment of truth came the numbers would be there'. The Hawke camp, now a Gang of Four — Hawke, Ducker, Combe and Taggart — decided that they had to seize the weapon of their opponents and turn it against them. Uren had tried to use psywar to frighten Hawke out of standing for the presidency: the trick now was to frighten Uren out of attempting to execute his plan for running Young as President. Combe recalled:

We had to decide how to get the message through to Uren. We tried to find him and he'd gone into bloody hiding. So had Gietzelt. We tried to telephone him several times and there was no answer, then we got on to the hotel switchboard who told us that Mr Uren was not taking any calls. So we came up with what was a brilliant strategy: everyone would be listening to [the national ABC radio broadcast] AM. We'd give John Highfield of AM an exclusive interview. We'd get him to do an interview with Bob, ostensibly about the Conference and then — I would have primed Highfield up — he'd throw in a question at the end asking, 'By the way, Mr Hawke, have you decided yet whether you're running for the presidency?' And Bob would say, 'Well, John, you've caught me at a weak moment. Yes, I am going to run.' It would be obvious to anybody who heard it that he had the numbers. The important people would know that Hawke was fighting back. So we tried to get Highfield but he'd gone out to visit relations. We left messages everywhere for him. We were all feeling absolutely euphoric about our brilliant plan and went and had a marvellous dinner to celebrate. By the time High-field got back to the Sheraton we were as full as boots. Bob was no worse than the rest of us: we were all full, with the exception of Joan Taggart, who has an amazing capacity to hold her liquor. It was a tremendous dinner! The interview with Highfield took place at 1 a.m., on John Ducker's bed. And then we rollicked on for the rest of the night: I don't think any of us went to bed at all — maybe we had an hour's sleep. Uren complained later to the executive that he'd been harassed at 4 a.m. — he claimed he looked through the peep-hole in his door and there was a little bloke with crinkly hair and a big bloke with curly hair standing outside, thumping on the door. Joan Taggart swears it's not true. She stayed with us all night, and is positive that Bob and I didn't do that to Tom.

Before 8 o'clock, when AM is broadcast, the Hawke camp had reassembled around a radio. Combe said,

I remember the AM linkman saying, when the interview was over, 'that was an obviously tired and emotional Bob Hawke telling John High-field . . .' Well, we needed a bit of a heart-starter. I think Bob had a brandy for breakfast. Then we went into the executive meeting. And they were furious! You could have cut the air with a knife. They'd all listened to AM and knew they were done. So the vote was taken quickly. Ducker nominated Hawke as President of the Party — there were no other nominations — and that was it. Unanimous re-election for Hawke. The whole episode was one of the most exciting I've been involved in.

Hawke's comment about the affair was:

It was all a bit nebulous. There was a brief push that developed around Mick Young. By the time we arrived in Perth it was clear that there was a move to try to get Mick up and knock me off. I didn't want to hold on to the ALP presidency forever, but I particularly wanted to chair the Conference in my home State . . . Oh, but a bit of talking here and there and we were able to fix things up.

This description was given years later, when Hawke's barricade of defence mechanisms was in place. He especially wanted to forget that Mick Young, of whom he is very fond, had been a party to the plan. In 1978, when Hawke voluntarily stepped down as ALP President, he lobbied hard for Young to succeed him, but the numbers for Young could not be raised a second time and Neil Batt from Tasmania won the position. Talking of other matters, Hawke remarked in the early 1980s, 'I suppose that thinking the best of people has done me a lot of harm over the years. But I still believe it's the right way.'

On Friday 1 July 1977 he was scheduled to address a luncheon at the Perth Press Club, and set off in an elated mood, positively swaggering with renewed self-confidence. He began his speech to the news media, assembled from all over the country, and all aware that there had been moves afoot to oust him, by announcing his unopposed re-election as President of the ALP. Earlier he had told journalists that he might have an 'important announcement' to make about his future, creating the impression that he was about to announce his move to Parliament. There was some surprise that his speech — which was peppered with jokes, including one about the Queen's horse breaking wind — had no mention of this. During question time journalists raised the matter. Hawke replied, 'If I am going to change from a position which I enjoy and do well [the presidency of ACTU], it would not be sensible for me to put my bum on a backbench seat', and went on to say that, were he to enter Parliament, he would want to be Leader.

There was an instant scandal. The *Sydney Morning Herald*'s headline of 4 July best summarised the Caucus reaction: HAWKE SELF-DESTRUCTS. The country's major political commentators announced that day and for weeks afterwards that Hawke, by implicitly demanding the Leadership of the Opposition as the price of his entry to Parliament, had destroyed his political future.

On the same day, under a headline, 'Hawke hogs the spotlight again', Michelle Grattan of the *Age*, in a long, thoughtful analysis of the Party's mood, wrote:

> . . . he is putting the terms of his entry so high [people are saying] that they cannot be met within the Labor Party's democratic norms. There- fore he can explain his failure to enter Parliament as due to factors outside his control. Friday's behaviour can also be seen as showing the essential Hawke style . . . An unmistakable Hawke characteristic — both a limitation and a strength — is the so-called larrikin streak, the recurring tendency of the Congregational minister's son to break out and say 'to hell with the niceties' . . . [Like] Whitlam, Hawke also uses [the] device of appealing over the heads of his immediate circle to a wider audience. Mr Hawke must know Caucus's knee-jerk anger and resentment at anyone's attempt to claim the leadership as some sort of right (or destiny). But perhaps he believes, consciously or not, that the electorate sees it as refreshing honesty, a willingness to dispense with the false modesty politicians assume . . .

Phillip Adams, the humorist and social critic, wrote in the *Sydney Morning Herald* of 7 July,

Mr Hawke said today he would only enter the Catholic Church if he became Pope. 'I'm in a pretty powerful position now, as spiritual advisor to the Butchers' Union, and wouldn't want to waste my time going to the Vatican unless my colleagues in the College of Cardinals promised to come across with the puff of white smoke. Similarly, I don't propose dying unless suitable arrangements are made in heaven. I'm not knocking God. He's done a pretty good job in recent aeons. But it's about time he stood down in favour of a younger, more talented bloke.'

There was a consensus among political journalists that Hawke's parliamentary political career was finished before it had a chance to begin. Combe remarked in late 1981, 'I wonder how those characters can live with themselves, having written him off so often, now saying that he is the best thing the ALP has going for it?'

The Conference, which opened on Monday 4 July, was not a happy one for Hawke. Conferences are traditionally occasions for social drinking; a number of women — delegates and journalists — complained later that Hawke, drink-taken, had propositioned them with his usual frankness and on rebuff had become sarcastic. He was bad tempered for much of the week. He had been prevented from speaking on the uranium issue but had made a vehement speech in support of the building of the Omega navigation base in Victoria — to which the Left was strongly opposed, believing it to be linked with the darker side of American international defence capabilities. The Conference decided by one vote that Omega should be constructed. Hawke took satisfaction from this, for Peter Cook, a delegate from Western Australia, told Hawke later that he had been persuaded by Hawke's speech to vote for Omega, in defiance of his instructions. Hawke is probably justified in believing that his intervention decided the policy. The uranium policy which was proposed stated that there should be a ban upon uranium mining and export 'until the ALP national conference so determines'. But Clyde Holding, Don Dunstan, Combe and others conceived an ingenious amendment, which they persuaded the Left to support. It was that uranium mining should be banned 'until the ALP so determines, recognising that the authority of the Australian Labor Party can be vested in: the Conference, the executive, the Caucus'. Combe said, 'It was very bloody clever. While Bob and I and the others knew what it meant, the Left didn't quite realise what it was getting itself into — because, should we win government, it would be a very simple proposition for the Caucus to say "the ALP has now decided . . ." ' Most of the news media also did not quite realise that there was a loophole in the wording of the ALP ban on uranium, which would allow a future Labor government to overturn it. The policy was widely reported at face-value, as an unlimited ban on uranium.

Hawke's argument, which was stated privately to the executive then restated by him publicly, to an ALP gathering, was:

> I am not convinced as a matter of intellectual integrity by the arguments for leaving uranium in the ground. If we leave it in the ground we have done nothing about the dangers — the disposal of nuclear waste, terrorists acquiring weapons — nothing about the people occupied in the generating plants in West Germany, Japan and the United States. We have done nothing about that, except to make it more expensive, and in the process, it seems to me that what we have done is to forgo the opportunity as Australians to have a voice in safeguarding the world in the processes of the utilisation of uranium.

The anti-uranium lobby was furious. When the Conference was over the Socialist Left's newspaper, *Labor Star*, ran a story asserting that 'some prominent ALP people believed themselves immune to policy' and that they could 'please themselves what they said publicly'. It singled out Hawke as a major offender, then concluded, 'If our leaders do not wish to accept this principle [of loyalty to policy] they should get out or be removed. The Party cannot afford this luxury.'[1]

A few days later Hawke was addressing a public meeting in the Town Hall Square, Sydney, attacking the latest federal Budget, when a demonstration organised by the NSW Teachers' Federation was staged. People bearing placards which read NO NUCLEAR HAWKS marched on to the platform and others in the audience began to boo and heckle him. Hawke lost his temper. Indeed, the anti-uranium propaganda campaign had grossly misrepresented his views on the issue, and over a period of months had suggested that Hawke was in cahoots with captains of the mining industry, among them Sir Roderick Carnegie, to assist them in their uranium ventures. (An irony was that Carnegie and Hawke disagreed about the virtues of uranium: Carnegie found Hawke's lack of enthusiasm irritating. But the anti-uranium forces did not know that and were scandalised to have recently discovered, twenty years after the event, that Hawke and Carnegie were friends. Vile motives were read into their relationship.) Hawke accused the protestors of being 'enemies of the working class' and 'henchmen of Fraser and Lynch' (then Deputy Prime Minister) and stormed off the platform.

On 25 August the Government announced that mining and export of uranium could go ahead. The ACTU Congress was due to open just over a fortnight later, in Sydney, and the uranium issue would be paramount, whether Hawke liked it or not. He did not.

Hawke's ability, learned in childhood, to put out of his mind matters which he found unpleasant has been a major factor in sustaining him physically and psychologically over the years. Under pressures which would have caused others to have nervous breakdowns, heart attacks, or to give up in despair, he

Sir Peter Abeles and Rupert Murdoch

Hawke and Ian Macphee, 1980

Hawke auctioning a pressed ham left over from his election celebration at the Coburg Town Hall, October 1980

Shadow minister for Industrial Relations, addressing rally, Canberra, 1981

Hawke and Speaker of the House, Sir Bill Snedden, 1981

Hawke bowling in the Crusaders v Australian Politicians match, Scotch College, 1981

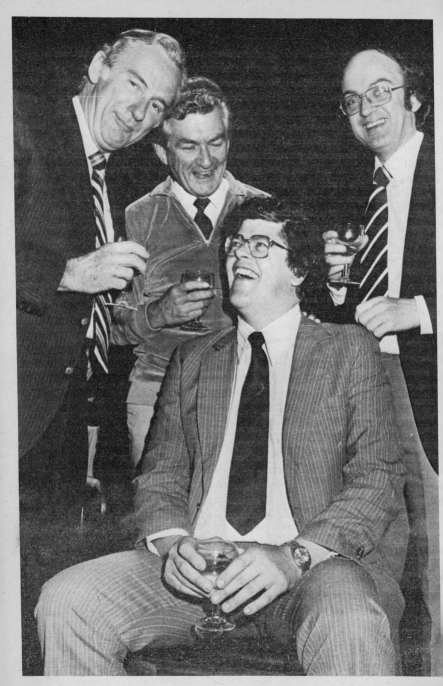

Bill Hayden, Hawke, David Combe and Bob McMullan, the successor to Combe as federal Secretary of the ALP, 1981

Hawke and George Rockey, May 1981, five months before his death

Hawke working in the sun beside a car lent to him by Col Cunningham, before visiting
Odyssey House, Eltham, Victoria, 1981

Hawke, 1981

has remained cheerful or, when he has suffered some serious reversal of fortune, has recovered quickly. He banishes the negative, as Ellie banished any doubts about divine mercy when Neil met his horrible death. Uranium was a factor in the tensions of Hawke's private life — while the ALP Conference was in progress Susan had been in an anti-uranium demonstration that was ridden down by mounted police — and of his public one. Colleagues in the Party had warned him that, as President, he must either remain silent or toe the Party line. He wanted to be allowed to forget yellowcake.

At the ACTU executive meeting which preceded the Congress, Charlie Fitzgibbon read through the agenda of recommendations to be put to delegates and was taken aback to see that there was no mention of uranium. He said to Hawke, 'We have to formulate a policy on uranium. No matter what it says, *we've got to have one*. And Bob replied, "It's not an issue. Don't worry about it." ' The ACTU executive prepared for the 1977 Congress without a uranium policy, but was then forced to accept a motion from delegates that the uranium issue be added to the agenda. As well, forty ALP Caucus members signed a petition to the ACTU requesting that it uphold ALP policy. The executive scrambled together a recommendation demanding, first, that the federal Government agree, within two months, to hold a referendum on uranium mining; second, if no referendum undertaking were given, that the unions 'after proper reference to rank and file meetings and subject to their endorsement' place a ban on the mining and transport of uranium. This double-barrelled recommendation did not amount to an ACTU point of view about uranium. It was, rather, a barrister's argument against the Government, which had chosen to adopt some of the recommendations of the Fox Inquiry into uranium, while rejecting others. The ACTU's recommendation wore the hallmarks of Hawke's legalistic carrot-and-stick puritanism. It was logically watertight, morally spotless and evaded the big issue: emotional prejudice. It also evaded ALP policy. The Party has no right to order the trade union movement around, but it often behaves as if it thinks it should have.

Hawke was supremely confident about the ACTU Congress. Since he had been written off as a future parliamentarian in June, his status as leader of the trade union movement had strengthened. Unionists were not at all dismayed that Hawke had offended most of the ALP Caucus, for the ancient hostility of workers for 'their' politicians is a constant undercurrent in labour movement affairs, and becomes a rip tide whenever 'their' politicians are seen to be useless in protecting the workers against legislative assaults by anti-Labor governments. Hawke had been fighting against the Fraser Government's industrial relations legislation for a year, with some success, for while the Bills were being introduced, their laws were not being enforced. The Government was arming itself against the unions, but so far had not summoned the nerve to launch a material, as distinct from verbal, attack. As well, 1977 was the fiftieth anniversary of the founding of the ACTU, and a cause for general good humour, sentimentality, and congratulations.

Hawke's confidence was well-founded: the 1977 Congress turned out to be his most resounding personal success. After eight years he managed, in that Congress, to achieve a major aim of his election platform — agreement to the merger of white-collar unions with the ACTU. As well, he trounced the extreme Left, which had been harassing him since the moment he had been elected President. And he got a new Secretary.

Souter was retiring. A new Secretary and a new Assistant Secretary would mean that ACTU administration would be different in future, run by younger and less strict men. Souter's replacement was the Assistant Secretary, Peter Nolan; Bill Kelty, who had been a research officer, would move up to become Assistant Secretary, and was to become the most significant element in ACTU administrative affairs. Kelty was from a working-class Melbourne family, university educated, and like Hawke had rejected a promising academic career — Kelty's Professor of Political Science said he was one of the brightest students he had ever had — to work for the trade union movement. He had first joined the Storemen and Packers' Union. In Lygon circles that union had once been known as the Poormen and Slackers, but the leadership of Bill Landeryou was transforming it into one of the best organised and most progressive unions in the country. Landeryou himself was a product of the New Look unionism which Hawke, by his successes as ACTU advocate, had helped to create. Kelty was Landeryou's protégé. Souter, whose eye for good staff was unusually sharp, had hired him in 1974 and had trained him. Kelty was justly described as 'a little factory' because of his capacity for work.

By 1977 Hawke and Souter were reconciled to each other and there was even the warmth of nostalgia between them, but their working methods still drove each other mad, and their mutual irritation affected other ACTU employees. Souter and Jean Sinclair, Hawke's right arm, had not been able to work easily together, but Sinclair and Kelty were buddies.

The new Secretary, Peter Nolan, had a traditional trade union background — he had been a printer — and was a large, well-dressed and agreeable man whose personality and appearance equipped him to take some of the burden of public performance from Hawke's shoulders. Souter had eschewed the news media and speech-giving. Nolan's relaxed manner fitted him for public appearances of all sorts; he projected the image of a modern, reasonable union leader. Even Tories could not dislike Peter Nolan, while Hawke still sent them into fits of anger.

In Hawke's opening address to the 632 delegates (representing, because of a new card-voting system, 864 votes) he devoted most of his time to an attack on the Government's policies and made only fleeting reference to uranium. It was not one of his better speeches, being spangled with superlatives, many of them theatrical-sounding exaggerations. Since the election of the Fraser

Government there had been a notable change in Hawke's speeches to union audiences, a reversion to the dramatic oratory he had used in his early days as ACTU President when, with anti-Labor governments in office, he had described every federal Budget as 'the worst', 'the most hypocritical', 'the most blatant . . . '

It was his role to fire the troops with conviction. His own conviction — that the new Government's policies were socially disastrous and economically futile — was deeply felt, but his speeches by 1977 were running against the social current: people were fatigued by political drama, the electorate at large did not possess his emotional stamina to continue arguing. The Press, affected like others, was wearied by Hawke's language of crisis. Andrew Clark of the *National Times* reported, 'Hawke showed during the conference that the considerable intellectual fat he built up during his days as a student at Oxford, and later the ANU. . . is diminishing . . . Hawke's opening speech was verbose and sloppy . . .'[2]

Indisputably, however, Hawke's speeches during the uranium debate, which took up most of Thursday 15 September, were brilliant displays of the jury barrister's art. By the time the uranium issue arose it was clear that the ACTU executive was in deep trouble with its recommendation, for the Left and Centre had organised and were determined to force the executive to argue on a different ground — not on legalities, but on the emotional issue: the dangers of uranium. Charlie Fitzgibbon quickly drafted an addendum to the executive's recommendation to try to save the leadership, and specifically Hawke, from defeat. A major problem for the executive was that members of the AWU and the Federated Ironworkers were already employed in uranium mining at Mary Kathleen.They were very well-paid. No matter what the Congress decided, they or other men would mine yellowcake, for the money was too good to resist. If the unions of which they were members decided they must obey a ban on uranium mining and removed the uranium miners from their books, other unions would move in and sign them up, or non-union labour would be used. All of this opened the way for bitterness, demarcation disputes between different unions vying for members, and, worse, a public demonstration that the ACTU was incapable of enforcing its policies upon its affiliates. It would, in short, be a show of weakness, of division, and to a Government already determined to weaken the union movement. Tony Street had told Hawke that if the trade union movement barred transport of uranium, the Government would use troops to do the work.

The Left's amendment was moved by Ralph Taylor of the Australian Railways Union and seconded by Jim Roulston of the AMWSU. Their proposal echoed ALP policy and went on to demand an early meeting of unions 'involved in uranium mining . . . for the purpose of seeking the endorsement of the union members concerned' of a total ban to prevent the Mary Kathleen mine from filling existing contracts. Hawke, in his first speech, emphasized that the issue before Congress was not uranium mining as such, but the ACTU executive's recommendation about a referendum. The anti-uranium faction refused to be side-tracked and four hours of vehement debate, most of it from the Left, ensued. Their speakers included Taylor; Roulston; P. Cavanagh of the Northern Territory Trades and Labour Council; and the Left's lion, John Halfpenny, who provided a 'brilliant piece of atmospheric oratory'.

There is no contest between the oratory of the trade unions and that of the federal Parliament: as public speakers, union officials excel parliamentarians in their sincerity of feeling and their robustness of language, and an ACTU Congress battling over a serious issue is one of the great pieces of theatre in Australian political life. Unhappily, it is all allowed to dissipate, unrecorded, except for a paragraph here and there which is reported by the news media.

Hawke, having moved the executive's recommendation, had the right-of-reply. He had taken some notes of his opponents' arguments during the preceding hours of debate. When he took the rostrum he spoke for almost an hour, pouring out refutations of the major points of those who had supported the Taylor-Roulston amendment. Professor Ross Martin of La Trobe University, who had attended ACTU Congresses for two decades, wrote:

> His reply in the uranium debate was a *tour de force*. [I] could not recall any Congress contribution during the last twenty years in which a range of opponents was attacked in terms of their own remarks quite so cuttingly and with such command ... If there were any votes still swinging at the end of that debate, Mr Hawke must surely have swung them his way ... It is impossible adequately to summarise such a long and complex speech ... but its varied flavour may be suggested by a sample of comments (necessarily abbreviated) on specific points made by opposition speakers:
>
> The 'people should examine the issue' (Taylor): [Hawke] 'Examine but not decide; this is a nonsensical position'.
>
> Anti-uranium demonstrators are not 'louts or long-hairs' (Taylor): [Hawke] 'Don't use this argument to me, Ralph Taylor', a reproof administered with evident emotion and followed by remarks about 'Those sincere young people', involving an implicit reference to the President's own daughter.
>
> Likening a referendum on uranium to one on heroin (Taylor): [Hawke] 'an absurd analogy', the distinction between uranium and heroin, in terms of views about their consequences, being elaborated [by Hawke].
>
> The unions should not leave it to others to determine their position (Halfpenny): [Hawke] 'Don't put up that nonsense that we're dodging the issue'; the executive recommendation committed the ACTU to campaign for a 'continuing moratorium'.

The task is to protect workers and Aborigines (Halfpenny): [Hawke] 'We'll be in an infinitely stronger position to protect the trade union movement' if, when the Government tries 'to put troops on the wharves and on to the railways . . . we can be seen to have adopted the processes of democracy'.

Statistics of worker fatalities in North American uranium mines (Cavanagh): [Hawke] a 'bad and improper argument' because the figures related to underground mining not open-cut, as in Australia.

A written account, let alone a short one, cannot hope to convey all the nuances of such a speech — the changes of tone and tempo, the flashes of raillery, sarcasm and jocularity, the spurts of emotion and the calm appeals to reason. It was a speech that drew jeers as well as applause, boos as well as cheers. It also drew blood in unusual quantity . . . Irrespective of reaction, however, the President held his audience completely captive for the entire forty-nine minutes of his speech. At the end he reiterated that there were 'people of integrity' on both sides of the uranium issue, and quietly asserted that there had been 'no more important decision in our whole fifty years of history . . . and about the sort of society in which this trade union movement operates'.

Fourteen minutes later, Congress had made that decision. The Taylor/ Roulston amendment was defeated by 493 votes to 371 . . . The great issue was settled — for the time being.[3]

Martin's final comment was prophetic: the uranium issue was to resurface at the Congress of 1979 and to provide Hawke with his most devastating defeat as leader of the union movement. He had, in 1977, although he did not yet know it, made his last great speech to Congress as President of the ACTU.

The executive that Congress elected was weighted 13-5 in Hawke's favour; the significance of this lay in the new meaning of 'in Hawke's favour'. Once it had meant a coalition of Centre to extreme-Left supporters: now it was an amalgam of old friends and former enemies, stretching from the Left to the Right. Ducker was Hawke's candidate for the junior vice-presidency of the ACTU, in contest with the Left's candidate, Jim Roulston. Ducker won. The alliance that had brought Hawke to victory in 1969 was, by 1977, formally broken, and Hawke had bid goodbye to the hard Left for good. The parting was not of his making, but rather that of the Socialist Left faction in Victoria: Labor politics in that State had forced him in to alliance with the Right.

Hawke could now choose to continue as President of the ACTU for the rest of his working life, or he could seek to enter Parliament. The impediment to this latter course was, as it had been in the early 1960s when it had first been suggested to him that he should aim for the presidency of the ACTU, that he did not have many feathers to fly with. He had no effective power base, no machine, only — as then — the affection and admiration of ordinary men and women. By 1977 there were millions of Australians who held him in high regard. But millions of citizens could not guarantee that seventy people, members of the Victorian ALP's electoral committee, would vote for Hawke's pre-selection as a Labor parliamentary candidate.

He had little time to consider his future, for from the time the Congress ended he was busy with dispute negotiations and continued arguments about the uranium problem. The Government had rejected the idea of a referendum on uranium within days of its adoption by Congress; Hawke entered negotiations with Street and the Government on one hand, and the unions on the other, searching for a compromise. He over-worked and by the first week of October was in bed with a respiratory infection, so severe that some newspapers reported he had pneumonia. While he was still convalescent another federal election was called.

Hawke rallied his energy and set out on the campaign trail. The Party had arranged an electioneering schedule for him that, just to read, creates a sensation of fatigue: 15 November: Goulburn; 16-17 November: ALP campaign, Sydney; 18 November: Perth; 19 November: Kalgoorlie; 20 November: Brisbane; 21 November: Sydney and Melbourne; 22-23 November: Sydney; 24 November: Brisbane; 25 November: Queensland; 26 November: Melbourne; 27 November: Launceston and Hobart; 28 November: Hobart and Burnie; 29 November: Melbourne, Australian Farmers' Union; factory gate meeting, Melbourne Ports; lunch Windsor Hotel; Box Hill Town Hall; 5 December: Melbourne, Canberra, Orange; 6 December: white-collar rally, Her Majesty's Theatre; Kadmiah Hall, Elsternwick; 7 December: Melbourne, Hobart, Melbourne; 8 December: Sydney Chamber of Commerce; book launch; Fitzroy Town Hall; ethnic meeting.[4]

In fact, his electioneering began three weeks before this formal schedule. Senior Party officials commented during the campaign that Hawke was working so hard they feared he would drop dead. He recalled:

> As the campaigning went on I knew that we were not going to win, and that has a physical as well as an emotional impact. I was — you know — miserable inside . . . From early on I was very apprehensive about our economic policy. I remember sitting in my office at the ACTU, not long before Whitlam was due to deliver our policy speech, when Ralph Willis [who had left the ACTU in 1973 and been elected Member for Gellibrand] telephoned me. He said, 'Have you heard what's happening?' And I said, 'No, what do you mean? And he told me that Whitlam, in the policy speech, was going to announce that Labor would not give tax cuts — which Fraser had promised, and which the Libs were using in their advertisements, with photographs of a fistful of dollars — but instead of that Gough would promise to abolish payroll tax. Gough was going to say that abolition of payroll tax would stimulate economic recovery and provide more jobs. I said to Ralph, 'You're bloody joking!' And he replied 'I'm not. You'd better ring Bill

Hayden, because Bill is not opposing it.' So I rang Bill and he said that he'd talked to Whitlam and Whitlam seemed absolutely committed to it, so there was nothing Bill could do. That was about Tuesday. On Thursday or Friday, Whitlam was to launch our campaign at the Sydney Opera House. The night before I flew to Sydney and stayed in the Boulevard Hotel. Gough's Sydney office was next door, in the Westfield Tower. I spent about half an hour with his advisors, explaining to them that this was just *lunacy*, unbelievable lunacy — that if they thought they could persuade people that abolition of payroll tax was better than tax cuts, and get the electorate to believe that, they were just bloody crazy. I persuaded them that I was right. So off they went to talk to Gough about it — he was closeted upstairs somewhere. After about half an hour they came back and said, 'Aw, we're sorry, Bob', and I'll never forget the next words, 'We're sorry, but Gough feels that he must have something dramatic'. And I replied, 'Well, you can tell him that he's got it!'

Then we went out on that campaign trail and everywhere I went I was hit between the eyes with the payroll tax. I remember one particular meeting in Tasmania, at a factory. It got a good reception and when the crowd had dispersed one of the shop stewards, a stalwart Labor bloke, came up to me and said, 'That was a great speech, Bob. But it's tough. This tax thing — they just won't buy it. Not half of them are going to vote for the Party.' At a factory meeting! The more I went around the country, the more I knew we were gone. Gough was a giant in so many respects, but in terms of understanding the political implications of decisions . . . Even so, I was surprised by the enormity of our defeat. It was a gruelling night in Canberra, in the tally room. The defeat was even worse in terms of votes than 1975.

Labor polled only 39.6 per cent of primary votes, its worst result since 1931. Whitlam's political career was dust and ashes and it seemed he was leaving behind him crippled heirs, a Party whose sense of failure was such that it would espouse defeat as romantic, its inevitable fate. David Combe, seated in a corner of the tally room was almost in tears. Earlier in the evening Kate Baillieu, who was reporting on the election for a television network, had asked him to comment when the results were clear and Combe had agreed to do so. When she returned with her cameraman Combe dissuaded her from going through with the interview by saying, 'Do you really want me to show my humiliation to the people of Australia?'

Baillieu recalled,

A while later Bob left his chair in front of the TV cameras and I saw him go over to Combe, who was alone, and put his arms around him . . . At the end of the night Bob, Hazel, I and Geoff Gleghorn [who had returned to the ACTU as Press Officer] all went out to get in the car and be driven to the Canberra Rex. Geoff was so upset that he began banging the roof of the car with his fist, then beating his head on it. Bob was very depressed, but his reaction was extraordinary. He immediately started to cheer Geoff up, and to talk about the future. He said, 'Come on. We mustn't despair. We've got to think about the future, about winning.' And he went on talking like that for the rest of the night.

Hawke said,

As President of the Party I had the obligation to attempt to counterbalance the proportions of the defeat. I had to say, Look, we're down — but we can win from here. And I believed that. Also I thought it was imperative that we prevent people from thinking, Oh, Labor's out of office most of the time, and now it's out for another twenty-three years.

It was a foregone conclusion that Whitlam would resign as Leader and be replaced by Bill Hayden. Hayden had been the most able of Whitlam's ministers; he had displayed true grit as Minister for Social Security, in his negotiations with the medical profession over the introduction of Medibank; in the few months he had been Treasurer he had shown decisiveness and an understanding of economics otherwise lacking in the Cabinet; he was a hard worker; reserved, pleasant. Political journalists respected him. But Hayden was not a forceful speaker, and he had neither Whitlam's grandeur of vision and wit, not Hawke's larrikin panache and large sympathies. Whether Hayden would be able to compete successfully with the bull-like strength and monkey cunning of Malcolm Fraser and lead the Party back to office, was debatable. The popularity polls said that Hawke could.

Hawke had been delaying his dream now for fourteen years, since the Corio election. Since 1974 he had frustrated his political supporters and his numbers man in Victoria, Bill Landeryou, by refusing to make a decision about Parliament. There are yards of newspaper cuttings, from 1974 onwards, reporting that Hawke had or would decide to became a candidate for one safe Labor seat after another. Landeryou and others had been scurrying around behind the scenes, negotiating on Hawke's behalf, only to discover that he was not, today, as keen on the idea as he had been yesterday. For all Hawke's impetuosity in small matters, in large ventures — for example, finding employment, running for the ACTU presidency — he can take an interminably long time to act. In the interim 'he blows hot and cold', as Jean Sinclair noted. She had learned to discount Hawke's sudden spurts of enthusiasm, knowing that by the following day, he would as likely as not have thought of reasons why a certain course was unwise.

But now the time for decision making was running out. Hawke would have to make his parliamentary move before the next federal election, or not at all. And the problems he faced were daunting.

Politically he was a man under siege, hated by the best-organised and most disciplined faction of the Victorian ALP, the Socialist Left. The Right faction was in its social complexion and attitudes a very different group from the NSW Right, which was solidly working class and union. The Victorian Right was middle class and professional and had no great love for the trade union movement. It had often joined forces with the Socialist Left to defeat Hawke's Centre Unity faction, and to attack Hawke. The Right regarded the Centre as 'lacking in principles', mere pragmatists.

Hawke had never cared for the time-consuming niceties of local politics: he did not attend branch meetings; he rarely went to the weekly Labour Council meetings in the Trades Hall, as Monk had done, religiously. People complained Hawke operated 'at the top level', and resented this. It was conceivable, given the neurotic and vengeful nature of much of Victorian Labor politics, that the branch would reject him if he put himself forward for pre-selection. The Victorian Party would make itself a national laughing stock if it took such action — but it had done some impractical things in the past.

Pre-selection for a winnable seat was only the first impediment to Hawke's ambitions. In the federal Caucus he had a mere handful of supporters, too few to carry him within touching distance of Party leadership. He could abandon leadership of the trade unions and all that meant in terms of power, prestige and striving for the public good, only to sink into obscurity. His other problem was personal: alcohol. The difficulty was not that Hawke drank but that he was and had been for years a loathsome drunk — poisoned, savage, a man possessed. He was not like this every time, or even a quarter of the time when he was drink-taken. Usually, especially if he drank only beer, he would remain a boisterous, good-natured man. But it happened often enough, noticeably if he drank too much champagne, that Hawke would transform. A colleague of the 1960s recalled,

> You could never tell when it would happen. Bob could be his beautiful self, then suddenly he'd take a dislike to someone. It might be a taxi-driver or a lift-attendant, anybody at all, a face or a voice or some remark a person made — I never knew what it was that would affect him — and he would launch into horrible abuse. There was nothing one could do to stop him. As far as I know he was never like that with anybody he was fond of — he could be aggressive, of course, but that was part of the excitement of debate . . . By the mid-1970s I'd see Bob ringing up Jean [Sinclair] to ask her if there were any cocktail parties or dinners that he had been invited to, and had turned down, which he could attend. Partly, it was his gregariousness. But really, he was looking for opportunities to drink.

Another colleague remarked, 'I can remember Jean going almost mad with anxiety because Bob was setting out for some public performance, and she knew he was drunk or was going to get drunk, and she'd be trying to head him off'. Hawke could live with his drinking problem as head of the ACTU, in Melbourne. He could not live with it in Canberra. It is a small, sharp-eyed town, with a limited number of restaurants and bars, where political and social gossip runs from tongue to tongue as quickly as the news of a miscarriage runs through a village. Behaviour tolerated in a trade union leader would, if he were a parliamentarian, incite the Canberra Press gallery to pillory him.

In November 1977, during the federal election campaign, Ellie had had a stroke. A couple of weeks later Hawke went on the wagon. He had taken the first step of what was to be a traumatic, three-year struggle with the very roots of his personality. Of all Hawke's battles this one was to be the most harrowing, for the enemy was himself. As an act of will he had to smash up the old Bob Hawke and create a new one, stalked by the anxiety that if he succeeded it may be at the cost of his magic touch — his popularity, his enthusiasm for life, his expansive sympathies — and that the new Hawke may be colourless and empty, denatured. He set off whistling loudly, in the dark. He announced at every opportunity that he was not drinking, and the Press duly reported this astounding news.

By early 1978 he was recidivist: just a glass of wine with dinner had become just a glass a lunchtime also. Then two. Then a bottle. Then cognac with coffee. Ellie had partially recovered from her stroke and Hawke had partially recovered from shock and remorse. His mother had a magnificent constitution: in the early 1970s she had suffered a heart attack but one week after she had been released from hospital Ellie was so spry that, conducting her favourite niece on a tour of the University of Western Australia, her headlong rush had forced the niece, almost thirty years Ellie's junior, to beg to be allowed to rest. Ellie had spent a couple of weeks in hospital after her stroke then had returned home and begun to recuperate. She continued to attend church, but she had to walk on a frame. It was tragic to see this lioness of a woman dragging herself around, wounded.

Hawke telephoned his parents at least once a week and took every chance to fly to Perth; during the 1977-78 Christmas holiday period he and Hazel went there together. Ellie, who had prayed daily since 1949 that he would give up alcohol, saw that he was drinking again. She was very distressed and talked privately to Hazel about her anxiety. From this point on Ellie's health declined, so sharply that Clem began to despair of his capacity to care for her. He was a competent housekeeper, but he was in his eightieth year. In late January or early February 1978 he told Ellie, 'I'm sorry, my dear, but it looks as if you'll have to go into a nursing home'.

Some weeks later, following several days of heavy drinking, Hawke again became teetotal. Then on the eve of Mother's Day, 1978, he learned that Ellie had suffered a second stroke and was not expected to survive until dawn. He went immediately to Perth, where his mother was alive by a thread, sometimes conscious, sometimes not. There would be no recovery this time, and no easy death. Ellie was moved into the Home of Peace for the terminally ill, in Subiaco, and there entered a long twilight. Hawke drank less during 1978 and into the early part of 1979 than he had for years, sobered perhaps by thoughts of mortality. In 1979 when he was visiting his mother one day he knelt by her bedside and said, 'I want to thank you, Mum, for everything you've done for me'. She had recognised him, but he was not sure if she had heard him. Ellie suddenly spoke. 'It was a pleasure son', she replied. Those were her final words to him.

The change in Hawke on his second attempt to give up drinking was remarkable. During his five teetotal months in 1978 a man whom many had never seen began to emerge: Hawke was considerate, sweet tempered and serious-minded. These qualities had always been in him, but too often blurred out by the roller-coaster speed at which he lived. Sober, the rush of his life eased in pace and noise. The change was especially evident to those who saw him infrequently and whose attitudes to him were not shaped by the Australian news media and Australian political life. An official of an international trade union federation based in Geneva recalled:

> I had first met Bob in 1975 when I was on a union visit to Australia, and had not liked him. I'd found his behaviour most unimpressive. In 1978 I began to talk to him seriously. He was a different man from the one I'd met before. He was a man with a great heart and a great strength . . . At the time I was going through a crisis, with my job and my personal life. I don't know how, but somehow Bob Hawke gave me strength. I think if it hadn't been for him I may not have survived. He said once, 'In Geneva, you can see me as a human being. In Australia, people don't see me as human any more — politics has distorted everyone's vision.' He was sad about it, because he loves people, and he'd been for years in a position of power, never allowed to forget that he was important. Even his close friends, maybe even his family, could never forget that he was important.

However on that or a later visit to Geneva during 1978 he angered the senior ILO official, Bernard Fortin, by aggressively questioning an American guest of Fortin. Hawke demanded that the American state his ideas about American society in the year 2000. The Frenchman said, 'I wanted to poke Bob in the eyes, by making him answer a difficult question. I asked, in the same tone he had used, "What do you enjoy most?" ' Hawke answered, 'Power!' The remarks of the union official, above, and Hawke's reply to Fortin reveal the depths of his ambivalence — his dislike of the effects of power and his craving for it.

He and Fortin then moved on to a discussion of personal power, its uses and the limits to exercising it, Fortin questioning whether Hawke had ever, in fact, been able to exercise power as an individual, as distinct from the power of a group-representative. Fortin recalled that Hawke reflected for a while before replying. He then said that he thought his speeches during the ACTU Congress of 1977 in the uranium debate had been an example of personal power exercised for the public good. He offered Fortin no other example, which suggests a weighty discontent with the balance sheet of his career.

On a different visit to Geneva, when Hawke was drunk, he told Fortin 'that when he was Prime Minister he would appoint me to his Cabinet. Bob said I could become an Australian citizen quickly', Fortin recalled. This assertion of Hawke's was more than a little outlandish, one of many examples during the 1970s of his attacks of grandiosity which would infuriate colleagues and irritate friends, whose complaints ranged from 'Bob thinks he's God' to 'He's behaving as if he were Superman'. Essentially, they were attacks of childishness: the child believes, until it learns not to, that wanting something will, magically, make that something materialise — a bicycle; a cricket bat. The adored child of Bordertown, Maitland and Perth was still alive inside the adult, and another of Hawke's problems. But the boy — affectionate, daring, vulnerable and imaginative — was also the charm of the man, and one of his strengths, for through him Hawke had kept the capacity to dream. He dreamed of reform. His remark to Fortin about appointment to Cabinet was indicative of the continuing growth of Hawke's ideas about parliamentary reform which he was to take up in the Boyer Lectures of 1979.

Despite his talk about Parliament during 1978 — which included telling close friends, categorically, that he would stand at the next election, and assuring non-Australians that he would be the next Labor Prime Minister — he had not yet made up his mind. He would jump forward a few steps then dart backwards again, like a juggler. The four hoops he was juggling were his prime minister dream; the pleasures of life at the top of the union movement; the Stop Hawke forces; and drinking-teetotalism. He was able to relieve the tension of mental acrobatics by undertaking during 1978 more international work: the Crown Prince of Jordan had invited Hawke to Amman to discuss Middle East affairs.

In mid-1977 the Israeli Labour Party, after twenty-nine years in office, had lost government to the Right-wing Likud Party, in coalition with minor groups. The new Prime Minister, Menachem Begin, was loathed in Israeli Labour circles. As a leader of the Irgun he had planned, among other atrocities, the bombing of the King David Hotel in Jerusalem in 1948. He was a man known still to harbour the terrorist's attitude of mind: that history can be changed by dramatic, manipulative actions. The world was amazed when in November 1977 Begin was co-author of another dramatic event. President Sadat of Egypt had announced, with that theatrical flourish so popular in non-democratic societies, that he would go 'even to Jerusalem' to seek peace in the Middle East. Begin instantly responded and days later the two were kissing each other, in the holy city. The door to peace had been unbolted, by a most unlikely pair.

Hawke had met Begin in late 1977 or early 1978. He has no comment to make on the Israeli Prime Minister. However, an Israeli who was Hawke's escort during his first meeting with Begin said afterwards,

> I knew our new Prime Minister was crazy. But even I could not believe the things he said. I felt embarrassed and ashamed, as an Israeli, by what Begin told Bob. When we came out I was bowing my head. Bob put his arm around my shoulders and said, 'Don't worry. I'll still support Israel, no matter what your Prime Minister says.'

Hawke discussed the Crown Prince's invitation with Israeli officials, some of whom were alarmed. Fear of betrayal eddies in the depths of Israeli consciousness, for six million good reasons. Since the Yom Kippur War one former friend after another had abandoned the country: embassies and consulates had been closed, votes in the UN, the ILO and other international bodies had switched to abstentions or to open support for the Arab side. A senior Israeli said, 'We feared that Bob would fall under the charm of Arab hospitality'. In diplomatic parlance 'hospitality' can mean seduction and blackmail, although this may not have been what the Israelis feared, for throughout the world Arab charm is justly famous. The Israelis put aside their concern and primed Hawke up 'to convey to the Jordanians the *mood* in Israel'. Hawke is one of fewer than half a dozen non-Israelis who have undertaken such an unofficial Israeli-Arab go-between role. Another was the Austrian Chancellor, Kreisky, and a third the former British Prime Minister, Jim Callaghan. Hawke was to be the houseguest in Jordan of a leading businessman, Rauf Sa'd Abujaber, who was a supporter of the Palestinian cause and was close to the royal family.

Hawke entered Jordan by walking across the Allenby Bridge,

> with very strange feelings: I just did not know what sort of reception I would get on the other side. I was met by a chap who was equivalent to the Secretary of the Department of Labour, a very bright young man who had been trained in the United States, and we formed a close relationship immediately. We drove up to Amman, and there and elsewhere I had meetings with the Crown Prince, Hassan, who was in charge of the country, because his brother, the King, was abroad. I made a crack to my escort that the King was probably out looking for a new wife, and as I learned later, the guess was right: Hussein was away courting the daughter of the Jordanian head of Pan-Am. The first meeting I had with Hassan was in the palace, and I was very very favourably impressed. He was enormously well-informed and involved with his people. Clearly there was a division of labour between him and the King, with the Crown Prince predominantly concerned with the

internal economy, the operation of the country and its development. He talked in great detail about sectors of the economy and plans for development in rural and secondary production, and was particularly worried by the bleeding of talent — of skilled labour and professional people — out of Jordan and into other higher-paying countries in the Arab world. The following day he invited me to lunch at a big oil refinery town about eighty kilometres north of the capital. There was a lavish luncheon for a group of foreign guests, but Hassan and I had a chance to continue talking during lunch, then he invited me to drive back with him to Amman. He drove himself; there were just two of us in a big Mercedes, the bodyguards were somewhere behind. After a while he said he wanted to show me something, and what happened next was fascinating. He drove into a refugee camp.

There were hundreds of thousands of Palestinian refugees in Jordan. Sporadically, from the mid-1960s up to late 1970, the PLO had launched attacks on Israel from its bases in Jordan, until the Israelis told the King if it happened again Israel would retaliate not just against the PLO, but against Jordan itself. In September that year Hussein expelled the PLO from his country. The Black September Movement, in whose name so much mischief had been done to Hawke's life, formed in revenge. King Hussein was at the top of the Black September assassination list. When it had been announced that Hawke was going to Jordan there were reports that, in Australia, Hawke was No. 1 candidate for murder. He was astonished that the Crown Prince, without a bodyguard, had stopped his car and was about to enter a refugee camp where there could be Black September agents. He recalled,

The camp was extremely crowded and squalid. He just walked in and started talking to people, and two things struck me immediately: he was very popular with them, and totally fearless. When we got back in the car I said, 'Well, you and your brother have a reputation for fearlessness, and certainly that was evidence of it'. He replied, 'Oh, well, Mr Hawke, I am the President of the London Jujitsu Club'. And I remember I said, 'I don't know what good that might do you, in terms of stopping a bullet', but he just laughed and shrugged it off. So we returned to the palace and had another very long yarn, about the whole situation in the Middle East. By this time the process that led to the Camp David talks*

---

* The Camp David talks were complicated peace negotiations between Israel and Egypt, mediated by the USA. They succeeded in achieving agreement for Israeli withdrawal from all occupied Egyptian territory, an act completed by April 1982. But because Jordan could not join the talks, the problem of Israeli occupation of the West Bank remained without solution. Egypt's willingness to seek peace with Israel infuriated other States in the region. In October 1981 President Sadat was assassinated.

was underway. Part of the documentation of Camp David referred to Jordan and expressed the desire that Jordan would join in negotiations.

There was no question about Hassan's commitment to the desirability of peace. Also, he accepted without question the right of Israel to exist. But Jordan has no oil of its own and is totally dependent upon subventions from Saudi Arabia for its economy, so quite clearly cannot take any significant initiatives, independent of the Saudis. The Crown Prince was forthright in saying that Jordan could not afford to associate itself with the processes that were emerging from Sadat's visit to Jerusalem. The Israelis had asked me to find out just what the Jordanian attitude was, and it boiled down to this: existence of Israel; commitment to a Palestinian entity; and, long-term, the possibility of an economic federation between Israel and Jordan while leaving open the possibility of a relationship between that potential Palestinian entity and Jordan. Naturally, he expressed some apprehension that an enlarged Jordan would become the new Palestine.* His position about the borders of a Palestinian entity was that Israel would have to withdraw to its pre-1967 boundaries. He accepted that Jerusalem [which until 1967 had been divided by barbed wire, with its eastern sector and — most significantly — The Wall, belonging to Jordan] would prove to be the most difficult part of the negotiations. In total, I thought the reaction from him was very positive. And, arising from that, I began to turn over in my mind the crucial question of security for Israel's borders.

Her great fear was that if she withdrew to pre-1967 lines, which meant reducing her territory to just a few miles in width at its narrowest point, over-running the country would be easy — much easier in the 1980s, with more modern armaments, than ever before. The Egyptians were saying that Israel need have no anxiety, that Egypt would not use the territory returned to it as a launching pad against Israel. Hassan said the same thing to me about the West Bank. So it occurred to me sometime in late 1978 or early 1979 that an undertaking should be written in to the peace treaties, but in this form: should Israeli-occupied territory, returned to its pre-1967 owners, be used as a launching pad for assault upon Israel, any gain in territory that Israel made as a result of going to war would be non-negotiable. Israel would keep the lot, and there could be no argy-bargy afterwards, with the Arabs saying, 'Aw,

---

* Fifty-six per cent of the population of Jordan is Palestinian. For many years one of the proposed 'solutions' to the Middle East problem has been that the Israeli army should overthrow the monarchy in Jordan and 'give' the country to the Palestinians. The Jordanian royal family, a creation of the British Empire, is understandably unenthusiastic about this idea. Kings tend to stick together: the Saudi royal family also finds such a proposal objectionable. Importantly, so too does the PLO.

come on, give it back to us'. There would be a clear agreement on ground rules: if this happens, then that follows. I elaborated it a bit more in my own mind, going into the details of non-military zones and what would constitute *casus belli*. I thought that if the major parties could be persuaded to accept this concept formally, and before the world community, there would be a magnificent opportunity for establishing peace in the region.

Hawke's idea was constructive. Maybe one day it will be a protocol in a peace treaty between Israel and Jordan or Palestine-Jordan, and between Israel and Syria, but that day has not yet dawned.

He did not have an opportunity to discuss his proposal with Israelis until early 1979, and it was another year before he could advocate it to the Egyptians and Crown Prince Hassan.

Meanwhile, this first trip to Jordan had stirred up his instinct to help people; he thought up a modest, easy to implement scheme. In Jordan he had been impressed that

there was something in the country which you could reasonably, genuinely, think of as a trade union movement. Not in our sense, but there was a Department of Labour, and there was a concern to improve the conditions under which people worked. Not free collective bargaining or anything like that, but there was more reality in the relationship between employers and employed than in many other non-democracies. It struck me that it would make a lot of sense if Australia attempted to help the Jordanians. The Crown Prince and the Department of Labour people had talked in particular about industrial accidents — the prevalence of them — and industrial health. I thought it would be worthwhile for Australia to provide one or more mobile industrial health units. The Jordanians were enormously responsive. There were two elements in my thinking: first, the intrinsic value of improving industrial health;* second, that Australia had good relations with Israel, that Jordan was a critically important State in the Arab-Israeli situation, and therefore it would be useful for Australia to have a practical and warm relationship with Jordan. And that this would be one way of establishing it. When I got back to Australia I talked to Tony Street. He was totally responsive and arranged for me to see Fraser, and the three of us had a long yarn in the Prime Minister's suite about it. I've got to give the Government full marks: Fraser was *perfect* about it: he

---

* As a direct result of a speech Hawke gave at Sydney University on occupational health in Australia, a leading Sydney hospital decided in 1982 to establish an occupational health unit.

saw the point and responded positively, without any equivocation. He said it could go ahead.

As often happens, the politicians were willing but the bureaucrats were weak. Hawke's Jordanian scheme echoed one he had evolved on his first visit to Indonesia, in 1970, when he had been appalled by the lack of training facilities for skilled tradesmen and the resultant impediment to Indonesia's economic progress. He had suggested, then, that Australia could strengthen her friendship with Indonesia and improve life in a country where unemployment was, at a conservative estimate, 30 per cent, if the Australian Government established a large skilled-trades school in Java. Nothing happened. Similarly, the Jordanian scheme was allowed to lapse: it seems there was a bureaucratic power struggle in Amman and Jordanian responsiveness to the proposal dissipated.

Hawke's great success during 1978 was in the ILO.

Namibia had requested membership of the Organisation. Namibia was also known as South West Africa, and was controlled by South Africa — illegally. In 1966 the United Nations had terminated the old League of Nations mandate given to South Africa over Namibia, and in 1967 had created the UN Council for Namibia and established this as the legal administering authority for Namibia. South Africa ignored the UN, and continued to occupy the country. In 1971 the International Court of Justice declared that, its presence being illegal, South Africa was under obligation to put an end to its occupation. South Africa ignored the International Court of Justice. Finally, in resolution 32/9E of 4 November 1977, the United Nations asked all its specialised agencies as well as all international conferences to admit Namibia as a full member.

When the UN Council for Namibia requested that the country be admitted as a full member of the ILO, the Organisation's Selection Committee sought advice from the International Labour Conference's Legal Counsel, Francis Wolf. Wolf gave a long written opinion, the key phrase being 'that Namibia cannot be admitted as a member of the ILO until it attains independence'. He had drawn on the precedent of the Free City of Danzig (now known as Gdansk, the birth-place of Solidarity), which had been created by the Treaty of Versailles in 1919 and in 1930 had applied for membership of the ILO. The matter had been referred to the Permanent Court of International Justice for an opinion; the Court had held that the Free City of Danzig could not participate as a member of the ILO. Danzig was not admitted.

Wolf's opinion on Namibia was circulated on Monday 12 June to members of the Selection Committee, of which Hawke was Workers' Vice-Chairman. Wolf recalled,

By any legal definition, Namibia was not a State, and only States may be members of the ILO. The difficulty was that virtually all members of the ILO wanted Namibia to be admitted — many of them passionately so, for one-third of our members are Africans. The problem appeared insoluble and for the ILO secretariat was an extreme embarrassment. Bob Hawke accepted that my legal opinion was correct; he appreciated that a political disaster was looming for the Organisation. He got himself elected to a small sub-committee of the Selection Committee, which organises the work of the International Labour Conference, and there he produced a draft proposal of great ingenuity: it did not refute the ILO's formal legal opinion, but stepped around it. The crux of Bob's draft was that the ILO 'should not let the illegal action of South Africa frustrate the aspirations of the Namibian people'. It was a master-stroke! From the abstract legal point of view there was no solution, but Bob had the imagination to break the impasse. His formula was one of the best examples of constructive imagination we have seen in an international body. What he had done was to change the question around: instead of being asked to vote *for* an illegality [violation of the ILO Constitution, by calling a non-State a State], the Conference would be asked to vote *against* an illegality [South African occupation].

Hawke gained unanimous agreement from the Workers' Group for his Namibian proposal. On Friday morning, 23 June, he made a stirring speech to the plenary session, assuring delegates of the uniqueness of the situation:

I ask you to note the words [of the resolution] . . . 'That Namibia is the only remaining case of a former mandate of the League of Nations where the former mandatory Power is still in occupation'. I stress that, should there still be any delegates who are legitimately concerned that in passing this resolution we may be creating some precedent for the future, they should have confidence in the fact that the resolution itself quite clearly and specifically spells out why this [decision] is absolutely and totally unique and cannot in any way constitute a precedent for any other set of circumstances . . .[5]

The Conference voted 368 in favour, none against, with 50 abstentions, to admit Namibia.

Another major step towards freeing the people of Namibia from South Africa had been taken, and African gratitude to Hawke was lavish. The same International Labour Conference had before it a resolution condemning Israel. When the vote was taken it was the Africans who defeated it. Oscar de Vries Reilingh, a former Secretary of the Dutch trade union movement and later the Secretary of the Workers' Group in the ILO, said,

Bob swayed the Africans back from condemnation of Israel. He could influence not only the African Workers, but African Governments. His influence was very great — much greater than his presence. He exercised influence on the Chairman of the Workers, Joe Morris; on the British; the Anglophone Africans; the Commonwealth delegates; the Asian Anglophones; the Caribbean Anglophones; the Americans — sometimes even the Russians because of his personal friendship with Peter Pimenov of the USSR. He was the best orator in the ILO and he flowered in conferences, before a big audience. He electrified the atmosphere.

By 1978 Hawke was the most popular Worker delegate. The Workers' Chairman, a big gruff Canadian, Joe Morris, was one of Hawke's closest friends in the ILO and another of his father figures. Morris was due to retire and in 1978 he began to urge Hawke to declare himself a candidate for the post of Workers' Chairman — that is, to be the spokesman of the workers of the world. Morris said,

> Bob had everything — an analytic mind, courage to fight, qualities of leadership, and capacity as a speaker. But he was torn by the conflict of where he could make the greatest contribution: in the trade union movement, or in politics. I think he'd become mesmerised by politics. I kept at him, though. That year and all the next.

The temptation that Morris held out to Hawke was an additional complication to the decision he had to make, soon, about his future. Were he to become Workers' Chairman, Hawke could press forward on an issue of international importance that, in the past few years, had been occupying much of his attention: the hypocrisy of the Soviet Bloc trade union system.

Hawke had a minimal interest in the technical work of the ILO. Many people noted that he was 'bored to tears in Governing Body meetings and during technical discussions, and would often sit there reading the Australian newspapers, or taking a nap'. Much of the ILO's most creative work takes place informally — at the receptions and dinners that are a permanent accompaniment to Conference life, and during breaks for conversation in the coffee bars that are scattered throughout the ILO headquarters building. The place is a market for ideas. Hawke was one of those who had noted that the Russian tripartite team of government, employer and worker was an artificiality: the government delegate could just as easily announce he was the worker, or the employer. People had become used to this, but in doing so had overlooked a major principle; a legal convention of the ILO; and a matter that lay at the heart of trade unionism: freedom of association. Clearly, freedom of association did not exist in the USSR or in other

Soviet Bloc countries. For several years Hawke had been taking the opportunity of informal discussions to draw attention to the fact that the USSR was violating ILO conventions about the treatment of workers and human rights, which it had promised to honour. Tony Street said,

> In my view Bob had a significant influence on people's thinking about the meaning of ILO conventions. He identified with great precision the inherent contradictions in the Soviet Bloc ratifications of those conventions, and the Soviet performance. He talked constantly about the Soviet system — and that became crucially relevant in relation to Solidarity, in Poland.

In 1978 the ICFTU, within which Hawke was highly respected, submitted a complaint to the ILO about trade union rights in Poland. The Polish Government said it would apply ILO standards. In May 1980 the ILO sent a delegation to Poland to investigate the application of ILO standards in the country. In August 1980 Solidarity was formed, with a major aim of forcing the Polish Government to implement ILO conventions. In November 1980, after a long court battle, Solidarity was registered as an official trade union body and included in the documentation of registration were ILO Conventions 87 (on freedom of association) and 98 (on the rights of collective bargaining). Nobody makes the claim, least of all Hawke, that he was involved in any way with the birth of Solidarity and the revolution in Poland that followed. However, his efforts as an agitator and educator in the ILO helped to create an atmosphere in which recognition of rottenness could surface. Heribert Maier, the General Secretary of FIET (the International Federation of Commercial, Clerical and Technical Employees) remarked, 'Hawke was very active during his eight years on the Governing Body as an advocate for applying the basic human rights conventions of the ILO — that is, 87, 98, 100 (equal pay) 111 (non-discrimination in employment) and 105 (forced labour). His major concern was that human rights be respected.' In 1981 the ILO Application of Standards Committee took an extraordinary step: without putting the issue to a vote the Committee condemned the fact that Soviet Union law does not allow freedom of association. If ever the workers of the USSR have the nerve to challenge Big Brother, that international condemnation of the Soviet system will be one of their most telling arguments. Street commented, 'In my view George Polites, the leader of Australia's employers' delegation, was the greatest single influence. Hawke, in the workers' delegation, also played an important role in bringing about that finding by the Application of Standards Committee'.

Hawke's work in the ILO was unknown in Australia. Nevertheless, his stature at home was growing. Earlier in 1978 he had been a negotiator in one of the most ugly industrial disputes in the nation's life this century: a row between meat workers and farmers over the export of live sheep. Once more, the origins of the problem lay in the Middle East. Islam requires special methods of slaughtering animals for food (*hallal* in Arabic) and, for some major festivals, the sacrifice of animals. The massive oil wealth of Middle East countries had created an upsurge in demand for meat there for everyday eating, and for sheep to be slaughtered in religious observances. Although meat-exporting countries, like Australia, gave assurances that carcases were being prepared in accordance with Islamic requirements, there was an understandable preference in Middle Eastern countries for meat that was killed by Islamic butchers. What is more, *hallal* meat should be freshly slaughtered. For these reasons a live animal could fetch a far higher price than a dead one. The Australian rural industry had been severely depressed for several years: the sudden demand for live sheep was a life-raft for them. But for meat workers, it was disastrous: it meant a loss of work. Negotiations between farmers and unionists had been dragging on for more than a year without any resolution to the argument about how many live sheep, in relation to sheep carcases, could be exported.

Hawke happened to be in Canberra, continuing discussion with the Government on the uranium question, when he was given a message asking him to go urgently to Street's office in Parliament House. The dispute had abruptly shifted towards flash-point. Unionists were picketing wharves in Western Australia and South Australia to prevent sheep export. In South Australia a convoy of sheep trucks had already set out and was only a few hours away from arriving at the wharves; both the picketers and the farmers were carrying weapons. Hawke recalled,

> I got to Tony's office and he told me what the position was: we had only a couple of hours. The situation was appalling — the union blokes and the farmers were armed, and when the trucks arrived at the wharves that was going to be it. We got on the telephones and managed to get a message to Ian McLachlan, who was the leader of the farmers' group in South Australia. McLachlan is a very able bloke and one of the toughest I've ever had to deal with in negotiations. Finally, we were able to talk to him in a telephone box at Wallaroo. I had a very tough conversation with him — I pleaded then demanded that he had to call his people off because otherwise there would be bloodshed, maybe death, and if that happened then there was no way the thing could be unravelled, and at any rate, it was just too horrible to contemplate that people might be killing each other. He was very tough — his side undeniably had a case: the farmers were really scratching financially and were fighting for their livelihood — but to his credit he responded. He called his men off. That was just the first step.

The next was to try to resolve the conflict. He, Street, I and [Sir] Sam Burston [President of the Australian Woolgrowers and Graziers Council], who was magnificent in his co-operation, then had to work something out. We set up an inquiry. Everything happens in such a rush in these situations — you're going on television and flying backwards and forwards — I think I flew to Sydney and to Adelaide once or twice, and then in Canberra I was operating out of Street's office for a couple of days. Fortunately, the Government had given Street a free hand in reality, although I think for public consumption there was a bit of nonsense going on, requiring Tony and me to argue with each other on TV. But Doug Anthony [Leader of the National Country Party] had flown up in the air, and was a damned nuisance. You can always rely on Doug to do his block and start blazing away from the hip. Fortunately Burston, for the farmers' side, understood the enormous danger of the situation, and he's a generous-minded man: he could understand the union side, that the meat workers were fearful that they would lose their jobs. Another man who was very helpful in calming things down was Wal Fife, who was acting as Attorney-General.

I must add that the whole situation was made more difficult by two facts: there was an internal blue in the Meat Industry Employees' Union, and there was an element within the union which was violently anti-Hawke. The South Australian branch of the union was unhappy with the way the federal body was handling the dispute: there was a background of intra-union rivalry and jealousy. Then Wally Curran, the Victorian Secretary, [an activist in the Socialist Left and ardent supporter of the PLO] was pathologically anti-Hawke. He and his group, at a meeting we had in Adelaide, paraded gross absurdities and falsehoods and prejudices — that I was selling out the unions, enemy of the working class — all the usual stuff. It wouldn't matter what I was doing or what the issue was, those blokes would misrepresent it. Then we had the Western Australian Government, and the ever-unhelpful [Premier] Sir Charles Court.

A senior government official, who requested anonymity, said later that Hawke's handling of the dispute had averted not just a brawl on a wharf in South Australia but the development of a widespread violent confrontation. Both sides had access to weapons — the farmers were carrying iron clubs and batons gnarled with barbed wire, and are rifle owners while the meat workers could lay their hands upon a murderous variety of skinning and boning knives. The live sheep dispute is generally regarded in industrial relations circles as the most potentially dangerous since the Depression. Sir Richard Kirby commented. 'The only dispute that I remember being anything like as serious was the Rothbury Disaster of 1929. I think for the country as a whole, we had a very lucky escape in 1978.'

Hawke was the negotiator in two other major but less dramatic disputes in 1978: one was a six-week Utah miners' strike; the second was a month-long dispute between Telecom and its employees that silenced telephones throughout the nation.

He had just returned from the International Labour Conference when he was pitched in to the Utah row, which was a straightforward argument over wages. Utah's profit had risen from $8 million in 1971 to $158 million in 1977. As the Queensland Coal Board noted in its 26th annual report, each of Utah's 2,000 employees had contributed $79,150 to the company's profit for 1977. Yet Utah, which exported most of its profits for 1977 to the USA, had refused to negotiate a new award with its miners since 1972. By 1978 Utah miners needed an extra $50 a week to be in the same position as they had been six years earlier. If their pay were increased by $75 a week, that would merely restore to them the $23 award loading of 1972. They worked in harsh conditions on remote sites and were now demanding a $100 a week increase, and had already rejected an offer from Utah of $83.30. Hawke proposed that, in return for a 5 per cent increase in coal production at Utah's mines, the company pay an increase of $95 a week, made up of a $63 production bonus; a work clothes allowance; money for medical and dental expenses; an accident contribution scheme; and a Christmas bonus. After three days of talks, both sides agreed to the package deal. The company had sought Government approval before committing itself to the new award, since $95 a week sounded an outrageously large sum when stated baldly, and out of the context of Utah miners' conditions. The Government agreed that the increase was reasonable. But as soon as it had been announced the Prime Minister publicly attacked Hawke, referred to the 'outrageous' size of the award, asserted that union greed was rampant and that Hawke was its instrument. Hawke was furious. Fraser's remarks were one of the clearer examples of his somewhat paranoid attacks upon Hawke, the potential prime minister, under the guise of attacking Hawke, the President of the ACTU.

By this stage the Telecom dispute was underway, grinding slowly forward through a series of bans and limitations, and little by little Australia's tele-communications system was breaking down. Hawke had already arranged to go to the Northern Territory to discuss with Aboriginal leaders the issues of land rights and uranium mining. He was particularly anxious to spend some time alone there with his son, who was working for the Aborigines.

Stephen Hawke was following the tradition of social commitment which had marked out the Lees and the Hawkes for generations and which, in each generation, had required a rebellion against parental values. Will Lee had rebuffed the clannishness of the Cornish miners; Ellie had fought for the right to be educated; Clem had rejected his ancestral church. Stephen was rejecting his parents' urgings that he attend university. Clem had ministered to Aboriginal communities in South Australia in the 1920s and 1930s; Hawke, as a student at the University of Western Australia, had agitated for Aboriginal rights and throughout his presidency of the ACTU had highlighted the plight of Aborigines. He was delighted that Stephen had decided to take up the cause of Australian blacks, but he disagreed strongly with his son's methods: 'I wanted Steve to be properly — as I thought then — equipped', he said. Hawke was hoping to persuade Stephen to enrol for a university course the following year. He wanted, too, in the calm of the outback, to reflect on the question of his future career: he could be spokesman for the workers of the world; or he could be Australian Prime Minister; or he could lose the lot. Before he set out he remarked to a friend, 'Let's see how that fount of industrial wisdom, the Prime Minister, handles the Telecom dispute. I've not forgiven the bastard for what he did to me over Utah.'

By the time the Telecom dispute had reached a crisis, Stephen Hawke had convinced his father that further arguments about attending university were futile, and that he was going to pursue his chosen career in his own way. The seriousness of the rift that had existed between them was revealed in Hawke's comment to journalists, 'I think we got closer then than we have been for a long time'. Hawke had also taken another step forward: he had decided — almost — to enter Parliament.

He recalled,

I was at an ALP fund-raising dinner in Darwin, where I was to be guest speaker, when a telephone call came through from Street's office, asking me to return to Melbourne for a National Labour Consultative Council [NLCC]* meeting next day. The Government had got itself into a fine mess. It had not allowed Telecom management to negotiate with the union, which is the first ingredient for disaster. Fraser was doing his tough guy act, 'We shall never surrender'. Meanwhile, there were two pertinent facts: the union had a valid case and one which concerned the community, for its argument was over the introduction of new technology. There were millions of citizens who were frightened by the surge of technological change that was sweeping through Australia and that was, obviously, going to put tens of thousands of jobs at risk. Word processors, electronic cash registers, massive changes in banking — the technological revolution was starting to rumble over people in the while-collar sectors, and here, with Telecom, was the first real fight about it. The ATEA [Australian Telecommunications Employees' Association] leadership had very effectively got this message through to the public: It's our jobs today — it'll be yours tomorrow. So there was public sympathy for the union. The second thing was that the business community was going berserk, and was

---

* The NLCC is a tripartite body, the meeting ground of Government, labour and employers. At times of particular tension between the Government and the ACTU, the ACTU has refused to attend NLCC meetings.

screaming at the Government to do something. But Fraser was carrying on with his Tarzan act. So now the Government was saying: Come back, talk.

We met on Saturday morning [26 August] in the Department of Labour Building in Bourke Street. Tony Street was sitting in the middle with his people around him, and I was seated opposite, with my blokes. And it was beautiful: Tony gave a run-down on the dispute, then said, 'We must be able to talk about this'. I grabbed hold of that sentence and replied, 'You say, "Talk". The guts of it is that Telecom management is not being allowed to talk to the union. Now, will you say to me unequivocally that Telecom management is allowed to talk, to negotiate?' There was a silence. Then Tony turned round to his advisors and they all whispered to each other.* At last Tony said, 'Yes'. And I said, 'Right. Let's close this meeting. We're going to Telecom.' So my mob went round to the Telecom office, to talk to top management, including Jack Curtis, the Managing Director. The atmosphere was very taut, because Telecom believed that the introduction of new technology was a management prerogative, and rejected the idea that the workers should have any say in how it was to be introduced. Telecom management had welcomed the Government's support; they were feeling undermined by the change of Government position which I'd forced from Street. We had some pretty tough talking: I had to put it hard and clear to Telecom that it was facing a Luddite position, that if it went ahead and introduced the new equipment in disregard of the wishes of its employees that the danger of sabotage was real. My second argument was that this was a fundamental social issue, and that the trade union movement was *not going to budge*. Ducker was with me, but he had to leave early. Just as he reached the door he turned back to the room, put his hand on his heart and said to the Telecom people, with that marvellous, rueful look he can assume, 'Please, please don't make me pull out New South Wales'.

By Saturday afternoon Telecom had agreed to conciliation and arbitration by Justice Mary Gaudron of the Commission. Hawke again was the union's tactician, while its Federal Secretary, Bill Mansfield, presented the complicated technical submissions. After thirteen hours of argument the month-long dispute was ended, but for the formality of mass meetings to endorse the agreement between ATEA and Telecom about the manner in which new technology would be introduced and jobs protected.

The news media covered Hawke in glory. By this stage his reputation as a strike settler was such that the mere announcement that Hawke was about to

---

* Street said, 'My aim in calling NLCC together was to break the industrial impasse. Hawke's question appeared to provide the opportunity to do so.'

intervene in a dispute created an expectation in the parties that their troubles would soon be over and, psychologically brightened, they were already prepared to consider a compromise. His skill as a negotiator arose from those aspects of his personality that he had inherited from Clem — capacity to listen, patience, and soothing diplomacy — and those inherited from Ellie — honesty and determination. He was often asked by business groups to tell them the secrets of successful dispute negotiation, and singled out three basics: patience, honesty and authority to make decisions.

Although Hawke was awarded the kudos for ending a strike which had caused appalling public inconvenience and had seriously disrupted the business community he said later that Justice Gaudron, the first female federal arbitration judge, deserved much of the credit.

> We all knew she was an extraordinarily intelligent woman, but she has an unnerving manner: she giggles. It was even more unsettling for management than it was for our side, I think. However, everyone soon realised that the Judge knew exactly what she was doing. In fact, her sense of humour was a big help in keeping things together. In conferences of that length fatigue and frustration cause short tempers, and often the whole thing breaks down. It's a tremendous plus if the mediator can keep the atmosphere light.

Two years later Hawke for the union side (which is consulted on appointments to the Conciliation and Arbitration Commission), championed Judith Cohen, widow of Sam, to become a federal judge.

He had never doubted that women are as intelligent as men; from the time he had joined the ACTU he had publicly espoused the principle of equal pay for females. In his first year as President he had excited comment by hiring for wage-case research a young woman graduate, Jan White, (later known by her married name, Marsh) who, like Jean Sinclair, had also worked for the investment counsellor, Jim Cowan. Hawke was promoting her as the next ACTU advocate, an idea to which many members of the trade union movement were still having difficulty accustoming themselves. Distrust of female competence runs deep in the unions. At ACTU Congresses in the 1970s whenever one of the handful of female delegates spoke, male delegates would leave in droves and broad grins would spread across the faces of those who remained. At the end of her speech — however good, bad or indifferent — there would be long, indulgent applause. Few if any of the clapping men realised how insulting it was to treat a speech made by a woman as something extraordinary. Hawke, on one hand, had a strong sense of justice but, on the other, his attitude was trammelled by the effects of his milieu.

His intellectual conviction about the equality, or potential for equality, of women was one thing: emotionally, he was yet to come to terms with his old ambivalence of simultaneous love and resentment for the other sex. Women who worked with Hawke often feared him, for his general impatience was (and remained) more noticeable with females than with males and he seemed to find conventionally feminine women irritating. He paid a sincere compliment when he remarked of a woman, 'She's got balls'. It would appear that the pressures upon him in early childhood and later, at school, caused him to exaggerate his virility. By the time he was in his early thirties masculinity was so strongly established in him that he had the freedom to behave in conventionally 'unmanly' ways — crying, for example, or kissing his men friends. Once on a long aeroplane trip, accompanied by Bill Landeryou, Hawke noticed that a child, whose mother was asleep, had vomited. Without waking the mother, Hawke cleaned up the child himself. His friends have scores of examples of his kindness, many of them, like this one, 'unmasculine'.

During his months without alcohol in 1978 he had been, at some unconscious level, sorting out the turmoil of his attitudes to women. Again, it was people abroad who noticed more quickly than those in Australia that he was now less aggressive with women.

In his own odd way Hawke was a faithful man, devoted to Hazel. By her late forties she was a strikingly handsome woman, her gaiety and quick wit melded with strength of character, warmth and a certain worldliness. People who met her for the first time remarked that she reminded them of the French actress, Simone Signoret, when she was in her forties. When, very rarely, he broke his silence about intimate matters, he spoke of Hazel with Biblical passion: 'Out of *her* loins she has borne me children'. One had the clear impression that any man who dared to look speculatively at Hazel in the presence of her husband would be in trouble. However, his own refusal to behave as the possession of any one woman evoked female anger and jealousy, and within the ALP it was widely asserted that 'Hawke treats women shamefully'. One long-term friend, a mystically religious woman, remarked, 'People crave to own Bob, but he is a Big Soul and cannot be owned by anyone else'. Abeles made a similar point: 'Bob is such a blithe spirit'.

Moreover, Hawke's artless self-relevation as a harem male was a social affront, especially in the extremely prudish atmosphere of traditional Labor circles. There was much prurient gossip. Newspaper editorials had been referring for several years to his 'flamboyant life-style', a euphemism for philandering, and articles about him were now more often using the term 'playboy'. By late 1978 Hawke had come to recognise that, if he were to enter Parliament, he would have to conform to accepted mores about women as well as drink. The two were linked, of course. He had managed to deport himself staidly during his teetotal months but in September 1978, on a trip to China, he began to drink again. He assured everyone that he was drinking now only in moderation — and so he was, for a while.

The new year opened on a high note for him, as a public figure: on Australia Day he was to be made a Companion of Australia. Another source of satisfaction was that he and others had worked out a scheme for having Bill

Hartley expelled from the ALP. But in Hawke's private life forces were gathering that were to make 1979 the nadir of his existence.

Hazel, who said later, 'At home we mostly saw Bob when he was beat', had been to see a divorce lawyer. The story that the Hawkes were going to be divorced was around Melbourne and soon reached Sydney. Bob-and-Hazel were still the bonded pair they had been since they were teenagers, but their relationship had been under acute strain for years and now that the children had left home they had both come to terms with changed circumstances. Doing so was traumatic: Hawke, the great negotiator in other people's affairs, was helpless to re-negotiate with Hazel the shape of their marriage now that the enforced stability of parenthood was removed. Fortunately George Rockey, who had been married three times, was as close to Hazel as he was to Hawke, and was a source of sympathetic advice. He had no doubt that beneath the turbulence their marriage was sound; that they were, as he put it, 'still deeply in love'. Rockey set out, patiently and quietly, to help them both. Hazel referred to him as 'my father confessor' and Hawke as 'Uncle George'. Other friends were supportive: Sir Roderick Carnegie, who had perceived that Hawke was in bad shape emotionally, gave him a copy of *Seasons of a Man's Life*, a major study of patterns of change in male existence, which set out to demonstrate that, at certain ages, crises are inevitable.

All Hawke's behaviour, from September 1978 when he abandoned tee-totalism, to September 1979, when he formally made his decision about Parliament, was affected by the dramas of his personal life — the upheaval in his marriage, his sense of inadequacy as a father, Ellie's slow dying, fears for Clem's health and, perhaps most of all and arising from these pressures, the beginnings of a long-delayed introspection.

He had stepped down as ALP President in mid-1978 but was still a Victorian delegate to the federal executive. Its first meeting for 1979 was due in late January, in Canberra.

Hawke arrived a few days beforehand in a buoyant mood, for everything was arranged for the federal executive to expel Bill Hartley of the Socialist Left. In 1978 there had been a row in the Western Australian branch of the Party into which Hartley had intervened, making accusations about the State Secretary, Bob McMullan, other branch officials, and Hawke. Leaders of the Centre Unity faction in Victoria saw their chance. Hawke said,

> Hartley had been an electoral albatross around the Party's neck for years but the argument always was, That's Victoria's problem. Here was a matter of sufficient significance and relevance for the federal executive to be involved. A number of Centre Unity unions in Victoria talked it over and Bill Landeryou decided that the Storemen and Packers would lay a formal complaint against Hartley with the federal executive. We got the numbers. But a State election was due some time in the

first half of 1979, so in the circumstances it was only fair and appropriate that Frank Wilkes, the Victorian leader of the ALP, be informed and have right of veto. The argument would be: If you expel Hartley you could split the Victorian branch, and Wilkes, with an election coming up, might adjudge that as a net minus. And if that were his judgment, we wouldn't go ahead. Also, if Wilkes lost the election the blame could be laid on those who had expelled Hartley and created Party strife just before polling. So I invited Wilkes to my office. Landeryou was also present. Wilkes' response was simple and, I think, right. He said, 'Have you got the numbers?' I said, 'Yes' — I'd spoken to Hayden about it and a number of other people, and there was no doubt. Wilkes said, 'If you've got the numbers, that's good. The worst thing would be to have a go and miss.' So we accepted that. I went to Canberra and had lunch at the Lobby with Landeryou and his secretary, and they had the letter to the federal executive with them, typed out. It was to come up next day.

Meanwhile, plans had begun to go awry in Melbourne. The Victorian branch of the ALP somewhat resembles in its intrigues the courts of the medieval popes. The Socialist Left faction is not, as many outsiders think, composed entirely of wild-eye radicals but has, rather, an extreme wing more interested in ideology than in forming a government, and a pragmatic wing concerned with winning elections. The State Secretary, Bob Hogg, a former engineer, was among the pragmatists of the Socialist Left. On Boxing Day 1978 he had heard of a move involving Hawke, Landeryou, Combe and others to expel Hartley, but had discounted it as 'Christmas drinking'. Then on Monday 15 January he had been asked by someone he did not name to come to a 'private meeting' in, curiously, the Lygon Hotel. There are few places less private than the Lygon: the windows of the Trades Hall overlook its door; one walks past the old ACTU building, which is now the headquarters of the Storemen and Packers' Union, to enter the pub. Inside, there are no private rooms. Hogg realised that he was being observed by a group of union officials and that the 'private meeting' was designed to be a public one. In the hotel he was told that the numbers were there for Hartley to be expelled. The next day the agenda for the ALP federal executive meeting would be finalised and Hartley's expulsion would be an item. Hogg said,

Those who wanted Hartley expelled gave as their reason that it would be worth a 3 per cent electoral swing in the forthcoming State elections. This was a simplistic argument, for it ignored the behaviour of the Left wing of the ALP, both in Victoria and elsewhere. The Left would have united: there would have been a Save Hartley campaign. The Victorian branch would have talked and thought of nothing else for six months. It was exactly what we didn't need, with a State election looming. I rang Combe and a few others. The NSW people, including Ducker, had a meeting. On 15 January the Expel Hartley forces had the numbers. By 16 January, they didn't.

On 16 January Wilkes told Landeryou and Hawke that the situation was too dangerous. The agenda for the federal executive meeting was drawn up, without any mention of Hartley, who once again had survived. Hogg was criticised for his 'policies of containment'; loathing for Hawke increased. Frank Wilkes failed to win the election, and in due course was replaced as leader by John Cain. Hawke has maintained since that

> If Wilkes had not made his misjudgment, or the people around him hadn't made the misjudgment, he may well have become Premier of Victoria. The Nervous Nellies! I thought all the talk about a schism was rubbish and that expelling Hartley would have won us seats. Once Wilkes had told us the deal was off I just put the thing out of my mind.

Defeated, Hawke had decided to fight another day.

The ALP Victorian State Conference was held in late March. Its Industrial Affairs Policy Committee presented a report to which a very long amendment, moved by Percy Johnson and seconded by Bill Hartley, had been added. Item 3 of their amendment read: 'The revolt of the Third World as reflected in the events in Iran is likely to intensify these [economic] contradictions which are an inherent part of the contemporary capitalist system'. The Shah of Iran had recently gone into exile and an elderly Islamic religious leader, the Ayatollah Khomeini, had returned from exile to become Head of State. Iran was in the early stages of chaos, a massive social bilious attack brought on by the nation's inability to digest an overdose of oil wealth, and other problems. Hartley and other extreme members of the Socialist Left were hearty in their applause for the Iranian Revolution, which increased Hawke's contempt for them: he swept into the Fitzroy Town Hall, where the conference was held, exhaling fumes of sulphur. Hawke's speech during the industrial affairs policy debate, delivered off the cuff, was in the tradition of the hellfire-and-brimstone harangues of his Methodist ancestors. He described the Hartley group as 'a canker' and, in lighter vein, 'a telephone box minority'. He recalled,

> There was *unbelievable* stupidity during the debate. The mad Left had bans on the building of Newport power station — yet Newport was being built, growing each week. So when were they going to remove the bans? The day Newport's doors opened? But people got up and endorsed a continuation of bans. That is the sort of lunacy which does nothing but bring the Party into disrepute and create divisiveness within the trade union movement. Then Hartley, this great expert on foreign affairs, made a speech about Iran — that here was a marvellous example

of revolution in the Third World, another case of the democratic forces in the Third World bursting forth. And, oh my God, it would make you sick! The whole thing stuck in my gullet. So I gave them a bit of a serve, and asked in passing whether Hartley's female supporters, the Joan Coxedges of this world, would, as members of the women's movement, find the Iranian Revolution such a glorious event. Returned to purdah; civil liberties, human rights, stripped from them. It was so obvious what was happening in Iran, but there they were cuddling up with their warm little slogans. And again, some of our weak brothers and sisters thought I'd done the wrong thing. Centre Unity people came up to me after and said, 'That was a very good speech, but you shouldn't have done it'. I said, 'Why not? They're bastards — but you don't tell them?' It was just too much, part of this weakness syndrome: You're allowed to *see* the canker, but you're not to say or do anything about it. For a decade we'd been putting up with the SL and I was sick and tired of the number of times I'd been told that they were changing, they were becoming more reasonable; but every time they opened their mouths they became less reasonable.

Peter Blazey, the political biographer and journalist, described Hawke's 'bit of a serve' as 'one of the most excoriating attacks heard within the Labor movement since the 1955 split. It was more contemptuous and satirical than speeches made by Whitlam against Hartley's Victorian Central Executive in the late 1960s and historically represented the destruction of the [Socialist Left's] ability publicly to embarrass the Parliamentary wing [of the Victorian ALP].'[6] But the headline of Blazey's double-page analysis of the Victorian conference read: SUPERHAWKE PROVES HE IS NO HEAVYWEIGHT, and was accompanied by a cartoon of Hawke as a demonic Superman, hitting Bill Hartley over the head with a phallic-shaped weapon, in a telephone box.

The speech, and the amalgam of praise and condemnation which it evoked, both from commentators like Blazey and from Centre Unity faction members like Gareth Evans [later the federal shadow Attorney-General], who took Hawke to task about it, encapsulated Hawke's difficulties within the Victorian ALP. Many have remarked that Hawke does not understand the Victorian branch, that he is unfamiliar with the intricate web of friendships, hostilities, grudges and debts that twine through the factions and across the factions, and that therefore an intervention like the one he had just made, disturbed, unbeknown to him, both enemies and friends. The point which even Hawke's close friends in the branch were slow to recognise was that, if a principle were at stake, Hawke would not give a damn about whom he offended. His speech had done the Party a service by damning a foolish proposal close to a State election. Labor's chances of winning Victoria in 1979 were enhanced by his assault upon the Socialist Left, for Hawke had been addressing the electorate at large when he described Hartley's group as a 'telephone box minority'. But simultaneously Hawke had injured himself: the very force of his assault helped to create unity in the Socialist Left, when it had had a chance to recover from shock. As well, people were uneasy that Hawke expended so much passion on what, to them, was a trifling cause. Yet passion had been a feature of the Hawke style for his twenty years as a public figure. Blazey wrote:

> At the Napier pub everyone was crowded around Hawke congratulating him on his speech. He was beaming, drinking and filling the air with contempt for the Socialist Left. Surrounded by admirers, he had got such an adrenalin blast from the speech that it was obvious he would love to be back in the fray . . . There was almost a sexual glamour to him in the Napier pub . . . He had just 'done over' his worst enemy in the most humiliating manner possible. And everyone approved — they had to. But his victory was too easy, too set up. It was beneath him in a way — or perhaps it wasn't . . . Really classy fighters don't fight out of their class.[7]

Blazey's observations were a fair example of the sort of ambivalence that Hawke's outsized passions aroused. They suggested an apprehension that people had felt since he was a small child that in some way which they could not quite express, he was uncontainable, like a genie escaped from its bottle. Blazey's article also predicted that Hawke would not enter Parliament because he lacked the character to do so:

> He lacks . . . the one characteristic by which all his other brilliances are reduced to histrionics or mere charm — it is the quality in leaders which Churchill called mettle. Menzies, Stalin and Mao had mettle. So do Whitlam and Fraser, but not Bob Hawke. All have done their lonely, unpopular long marches in politics. But Hawke, at the age of 50, is not prepared to undertake such an uncertain slog. Why should he? He's the most popular politician in the country without really being one. He loves the applause too much to give it up now.[8]

It was a widely-held view. In 1982 political journalists and Hawke's colleagues in the Caucus were still harping upon this theme: 'Hawke is always looking in the mirror of the polls — he's only interested in his popularity' and 'he has no self-discipline' were the expressions used. (Even Hawke's closest friends had been convinced that he would be unable to give up alcohol.) People sneered at some of his fixed indignations; they were derisive, for instance, about his passionate hostility for the Minister for Industrial Relations, Ian Viner; there was a Canberra Press gallery jest: 'Not another Hawke statement about Ian Viner's lies!'

He spent much of April campaigning in the Victorian election and in May flew to Israel for briefings in a venture that was, as events turned out, to tear him in half. He had agreed to go to the USSR for a third time, to plead for the release of Soviet Jews. On this occasion he would not be making a general submission, but would go requesting that twelve people in gaol or Siberian exile, and their families, plus other Jewish families who for more than five years had been refused exit visas from the USSR, should be allowed to leave the country. For the first time he would be meeting, face to face, Soviet Jews who were forbidden to leave the USSR. Hawke had never contemplated suicide: he was to do so after leaving Moscow.

Some hint of what was happening to Soviet Jewish dissidents came in snippets of information that seeped out. A letter to Hawke in 1979:

> I beseech you to take up my cousin's cause . . . In January this year I sent a parcel of new winter clothes for X, who is in exile, to his mother's address. It was returned in May with a stamp 'Forbidden' on it . . . He has been sentenced to seven years' hard labour and three years' exile.[9]

A radio broadcast from London, also in 1979, incorporating tapes smuggled out of the USSR:

> A, who displayed a banner reading, 'Allow me to join my family in Israel', was sentenced to four years' exile for 'malicious hooliganism'. There she lived in a hut with sixty former male convicts who 'behaved like apes' and attacked her in the night. She fortressed herself in one room, with a dog for company. 'Sometimes I don't know what to do — to cry or laugh. My life here is so miserable, so meaningless . . . Even the children when they played with my dog were questioned by police.'[10]

A report smuggled out to Australia, following interviews in the late 1970s with 'refuseniks', as those who are forbidden visas, are called:

> She appeared pale, sad and desperate. Her husband is in gaol, living in a room with three others in temperatures 50 degrees below freezing. He has been convicted of 'parasitism'. He spent two years in exile, returned to Moscow, then was sentenced to three more years' exile to the Far North. It took two months' travelling to get there.

> B was sacked from his job as an electrical engineer after applying for a visa to Israel. He was gaoled for drunkenness, although he is a teetotaller. He now drives a lift.

> C said, 'If they deny my sons a visa again I think that by September no matter how terrible it must sound to you, I will leave without them. I

cannot take it any longer. I don't want to die here. The problem we ask ourselves all the time is who makes decisions? We don't know. Probably Brezhnev himself.'

D said, 'When the US Senators were here the authorities permitted Yiddish theatre performances, which are usually forbidden, to take place in major urban centres. It was incredible. One couldn't get tickets . . . It was a great occasion for Moscow Jews, it was a holiday, people were excited and cried.'

Mrs E queued for four hours to buy fish for my [kosher] lunch. They were so hospitable. We loathed eating any of the food they offered us.

F, a cyberneticist, author of twelve books and a total of 160 scientific works, some of which have been translated into English, German, French, Chinese and Japanese. World renowned in cybernetics. Applied for a visa in September 1971. Refused on the grounds of 'State interest'. Dismissed from all his elected bodies and duties. His name has been deleted from all his publications in the Soviet Union, he was forbidden to teach and deprived of membership of the Communist Party. Medical aid facilities at the Academy of Sciences were also withdrawn. His children were expelled from post-graduate studies.

G, H and J have been sacked for applying for exit visas. They are teaching Jewish culture, Hebrew, and so on, but have had to find menial work, because they are not allowed to declare their tax on earnings from teaching Jewish culture, and if one does not pay tax one can be gaoled for 'parasitism'. This is the only country in the world where people desperately fight the bureaucracy to be allowed to pay tax.

The temperature was below freezing on the Sabbath, but an extraordinary number of people gathered in the synagogue. The KGB stood around, watching and taking notes . . . I have been trailed by the KGB all the time, even at the ballet. I had had a drink and was a little light-headed. I walked up to him and showed him my ballet tickets. He shouted at me and then walked off. I paid for my foolishness later that night: every hour the telephone rang and when I answered it, they slammed down the receiver at the other end . . . I feared being charged with 'hooliganism'.[11]

Hawke was to meet some of these people and hear from them much more about their lives. Among them are the most famous names in world Jewry, people who in Israel and the Diaspora communities have the status of supernatural beings because of the persecutions they have suffered over many years, and their refusal to surrender.

Hawke had a long-standing invitation from the Soviet Government to pay another visit to the country. It was Isi Leibler, the head of Jetset and a world activist on behalf of Soviet Jews, who persuaded him that 1979 was the time to return to Moscow and while there to apply pressure on the authorities for the release of refuseniks. The hour seemed ripe: the USSR had recently allowed some Jews, who had been in gaol, to leave the country. Rumour said that this was done in exchange for Soviet spies held in the USA. Strategic Arms Limitation Talks (SALT) II between the USA and USSR were in progress; there was a Bill before the American Senate which could veto Most Favoured Nation treatment in trade with the USSR unless it observed human rights. Since the initiation of *détente* the Soviet bloc economy had become intertwined with Western economies and the trading partnership with the USA was of special importance to the USSR. Another vulnerable area was the Olympic Games, to be held in Moscow in 1980. It was known that the Kremlin was anxious that the Games should not be marred by demonstrations about human rights.

The Australian Olympic Federation had awarded Leibler's company, Jetset, accreditation as the official Australian tourist organiser for the Moscow Olympics, in recognition of its handling of the Montreal Olympics in 1976. Leibler had gone twice to Moscow in 1978 on Olympic business and while there had quietly suggested that the Olympic Games could progress more smoothly if the Russian Government would allow exit visas to Soviet Jews. A senior Australian diplomat remarked, 'The Russians were furious. They saw that Leibler had a lever over them, and they regarded that as a dirty trick.' Leibler wanted to accompany Hawke to the USSR in 1979, but he had been refused an entry visa. 'I am, of course, an agent of the International Jewish Conspiracy', he remarked with a weary smile.

By 1979 Isi Leibler was one of Hawke's closest friends, although for many years he had deliberately remained distant from Hawke out of political delicacy. Leibler had been born in Belgium, the eldest son of a diamond merchant who had escaped from Europe just in time. The Leiblers had arrived in Australia in 1938, when Isi was four years old. By his early twenties he was working towards an academic career in political science, his special study being Marxism, when he became aware of the plight of Soviet Jews. In those days and for years afterwards conventional wisdom had it that since the Revolution Jews in Russia had suffered no discrimination. The ALP Left, including Sam Cohen, was committed to this view, as was the World Jewish Congress. Leibler became the *enfant terrible* of the Australian Jewish community and alarmed international Jewish leaders because of his audacious insistence that Soviet Jews were harassed as a policy of State. He was saved from being dismissed as public relations chairman of the Victorian Jewish

Board of Deputies only by the intervention of the communal leader, Maurice Ashkanasy. His continuing fight for his kinsmen in the USSR led him in to close contact with the Menzies Government: Australia was the first country in the world to raise in the United Nations, in 1962, the question of Soviet anti-Semitism, and this occurred thanks to Leibler's tireless lobbying of Liberal politicians, especially the Minister for External Affairs, Garfield Barwick. Because of his heresies about the Soviet Union at a time when the ALP Left was sympathetic to it and his contacts with the Menzies Government, Leibler was regarded as an enemy of Labor.

In 1965 he published a Marxist analysis of the plight of Soviet Jewry which Rex Mortimer, a leader of the Australian Community Party, and other important Communists, publicly endorsed. The book and its endorsement caused a furore in the CP; more importantly, it influenced pro-Soviet groups throughout the world. They used its information and conclusions to dissociate themselves from Russian anti-Semitism.

Leibler's social manner is mild and charming but manifestly determined. On first meeting he could be mistaken for an ordinary, agreeable, successful businessman, who has carried over into middle-age an interest from his youth. In fact he is a man of extravagant feelings. Of all Hawke's friends, Leibler is the one who most resembles him in passionate commitment. By 1979 he was the President of the Executive Council of Australian Jewry.

Leibler knew of the turmoil in Hawke's private life in 1979 and insisted that Hazel accompany her husband to Moscow, to look after him and to share what Leibler guessed would be a harrowing experience for Hawke — who, by April, was again drinking as heavily as ever. He said,

> Bob is a genuine ideological social democrat and I think only an ideological social democrat can be truly appalled by the Soviet Union. He understands the extent to which the system has moulded the country, that beneath the pseudo-civilised mask there is a very ugly animal, that you have there a world of pretence — fake history, fake unions . . . Bob *hates* the Soviet system. I think the only time he is ever frightened is when he is in the USSR. On something like this there was nothing in it for him, politically — which is a totally different situation from that of the American Senators who have lent their support to the cause. There are votes in it, for them — but the Jewish vote in Australia . . . ? It's inconsequential. I knew he would be deeply affected by actually meeting the refuseniks — Bob makes life such a passionate experience, all the time. He is incapable of neutrality.

The three of them flew to Israel, where Hawke had briefings and again met with Begin, then the Hawkes continued on to Moscow and Leibler went to Rome for a meeting of the Praesidium on Soviet Jewry.

Before he left Australia Hawke had told the Soviet Ambassador that he would be raising the refusenik issue — 'I thought it was better to be frank with them' — and had discussed it with Andrew Peacock, the Minister for Foreign Affairs. Peacock had been sympathetic and promised Australian Embassy support in Moscow. A further oddity in the bizarre nightmare of life for the refuseniks is that, while they live under surveillance, they have contact with the outside world — one woman has a telephone, others use public telephones to make reverse charge calls. They had been alerted to Hawke's arrival. He had the address of a flat in Moscow in which they gathered, but given the circumstances he did not want to travel there in a Soviet Government car. Something peculiar had recently happened to an Australian diplomat posted to Moscow, and it appeared that he had been drugged. Peacock arranged for Embassy transport.

It was only in the evenings that Hawke and Hazel had a chance to meet the refuseniks: during the day he had a rigorous programme of talks. One of these was a lengthy discussion with Professor M.S. Kapitsa, Head of the First Far Eastern Department of the Soviet Foreign Office, and an expert on Asian affairs. The summary of their meeting, made by an Australian diplomat who accompanied Hawke, fills twelve pages and covers Sino-Soviet relations, Soviet perceptions of future Chinese development, USSR-USA relations, political developments in Western Europe, China's role in South East Asia, Vietnam and Kampuchea. The record of conversation concludes: 'Professor Kapitsa . . . complimented Mr Hawke on his wide knowledge of international affairs. He added he now knew why knowledgeable people were saying Mr Hawke was the future Prime Minister of Australia.'[12] Hawke was gratified by the Professor's final remarks, for they encouraged him to think that elsewhere in the Soviet hierarchy his reputation would be enhanced and the real purpose of his visit moved forward.

He had already had one meeting with the refuseniks, and had given his heart to them. They called him 'Bobba' and later asked Leibler: 'Isn't Bobba really Jewish? How could anybody understand us and have such rapport with us after such a short time, and not be Jewish?' 'He made a tremendous impact on them — they are not naive simpletons, those people the USSR is holding back, but are men and women of unusual intellect, probably encompassing some of the most outstanding Jews living in the world', Leibler said.

Even before he arrived in Moscow Hawke was tense with anxiety about what he was attempting to do. Once he had met the refuseniks his anxiety twisted tight. On the next day of his visit Hawke broached the subject with Alexei Shibayev, Shelepin's successor as head of the Soviet trade union movement, and with Peter Pimenov, another senior official. They said that a decision would have to be taken 'at a high level'. Hawke made a second evening visit to the little flat on the outskirts of Moscow; on the final day of his visit to the USSR, in the late afternoon of Friday 25 May, he went for a third time with astonishing news: one of the Soviet officials had said that Hawke's requests would be met. The gathering that night was euphoric.

People wept with joy. Hawke drank a lot of vodka and was in tears on and off. It was, the refuseniks told Leibler afterwards, 'like a family reunion'. At some stage during the celebration it was suggested that a Press statement should be prepared because, as Hawke said, 'The refuseniks and I thought this change of Soviet policy should be presented to the West as a *good* decision, and the West should be invited to welcome it'. At 7 o'clock next morning one of the refuseniks, Professor Alexander Lerner, arrived at the Hawkes' room in the Sputnik Hotel with the news release already typed out. It read:

> We welcome the position which we believe has been conveyed on behalf of the Soviet Authorities in regard to the emigration of Jews from their country. Our understanding of this position, as conveyed at the end of last week to an Australian Trade Union Official, Mr Bob Hawke, was summarized to three issues. First, people who have had their application for visas denied for more than five years will be granted exit permits. Second, the twelve in prison or in exile will be released. Third, as to the future, five years will be recognized as the maximum period for refusal of exit permits, consistent with the concern of the Soviet Authorities for security in regard to State secrets. We understand that the processes necessary to give effect to these changes are to be initiated in the near future. These changes are of profound importance and when given effect to, will call for appropriate positive response on our part.[13]

Hawke took a copy of the statement and showed it to Pimenov, who had come to the airport to farewell him. In the presence of a number of Russian and Australian officials, including the Ambassador, Hawke asked Pimenov, 'What should I do with this?' to which Pimenov replied, 'Do as you will'. Hawke had earlier asked if he might telephone a friend to convey the good news, and Russian officials had agreed that he could and should, and had arranged the call. It was, of course, to Leibler in Rome, who said, 'I was frightened. I thought, oh, Christ! It's too much! Bob said to me on the phone, "This is the greatest contribution to a humanitarian cause I've ever achieved". He was intensely emotional.' When, next morning, Pimenov read the Press statement and raised no objections to it, Hawke — who said 'I still felt staggered by the whole thing' — was convinced that the matter was sealed.

It was inconceivable to Hawke that Pimenov would allow a public promise to be made, through a Press statement, and then retract it because, as he reasoned, 'They would be revealed to the world as liars. And with the international situation as it then was, that could only harm them.' At the airport Murray Bourchier, the Australian Ambassador, warily agreed with Hawke that it appeared he had pulled off a magnificent coup. What became known in Moscow as 'The Hawke Incident' was just unfolding.

Chapter Nineteen

A photograph published on the front pages of Australian newspapers and in other papers around the world tells some of the story: Hawke had just disembarked from his aeroplane in Rome, six hours after leaving Moscow. He is walking towards the photographer with Hazel beside him. His expression is angry and confused. Hazel has turned towards him, her eyes full of alarm.

Unknown to Hawke, Professor Lerner had distributed the news statement to the Moscow Press corps that morning, convinced that Hawke had authorised him to do so.* By the time Hawke arrived in Rome journalists from all over the world were waiting for him. Hawke barged through them, saying only that the Moscow statement was correct. It was an embarrassment that the story had broken before Hawke had had a chance to talk to Leibler and other international Jewish leaders on publicity tactics.

Leibler recalled, 'I've never seen Bob quite as shattered as he was when he got off that plane in Rome. He looked like a dead man. I've never seen a person so completely pulverised as he was, his emotions were smashed in. He was out for twenty-four hours.'

Much of Hawke's exhaustion was due to vodka. He said, 'I was absolutely whacked. The Russians entertain extremely hard and I'd made a point of staying with them — there was no way I was not going to be entirely with them — so I was tired and worn-out by the time I got to Rome.' By the next day he had slept off the effects of six days of entertainment and tension, and was brimming with optimism. At a lunch given by the world Jewish leaders he reported in detail on what had transpired in Moscow, his personal conviction so intense that it swayed his audience. Zvi Netzer, a senior official of the

* There is no satisfactory explanation for the communications confusion between Hawke and Lerner. It may have been due to over-excitement.

Israeli Foreign Office, whose ancestors were Russian Jews and who had served as a diplomat in the USSR before the 1967 war, happened to be in Rome and recalled, 'I *knew* the Soviet system, but even I was convinced. We were all very optimistic.' Even the premature Press release appeared an advantage: Hawke argued that it would lock the Russians in to their promise. His view was accepted. The President of the World Jewish Congress, Phil Klutznick; the President of the Jewish Agency and the world Zionist Organisation, Leon Dulzin; and the Chairman of the United States Jewish Presidents' Conference, Theodore Mann, all publicly expressed their appreciation for Hawke's efforts. In Australia the Victorian Jewish Board of Deputies unanimously passed a vote of thanks to Hawke 'for his extraordinary and courageous efforts on behalf of our brethren in the Soviet Union'.[1] There was an atmosphere of exhilaration, not just in Rome but for Jews around the world. In the same week as the refusenik announcement, Egypt had opened its borders to Israel — for the first time in thirty-one years.

The next step was to take place in Geneva, at the ILO: there Peter Pimenov, the leader of the trade union delegation, would give Hawke a list of those who were to be issued with visas.

Hawke arrived in Geneva at the end of May in an exalted frame of mind. George Rockey, who had resigned from TNT when it became a public company (he complained, 'A public company! Every time you wanted to have a pee you had to ask the Secretary'), was a resident in Switzerland now. He met Hawke in Geneva and they went off to France for a few days to indulge Rockey's passion, gambling. Rockey had introduced Hawke to casinos in 1977; by 1979 Hawke was a blackjack fan. He refused to play roulette, but he had 'a system' for blackjack and for the third year in succession won handsomely.

When he returned to Geneva and saw Pimenov he had the first inkling that his winning streak had run out: Pimenov, on catching sight of Hawke, dodged him.

The following day the international Press carried a story quoting Pimenov as saying that Hawke had 'misunderstood' what had been said in Moscow. He conveyed the impression to journalists, and Soviet officials in Moscow made similar suggestions to foreign diplomats, that Hawke had gone to the Soviet Union resolved on some stratagem the depths of which were unknown, and had finished up leaving the innocent Russians in a state of honest perplexity. The conclusion to be drawn was that Hawke was a devious customer.

Then on 7 June at the opening of an ILO Governing Body meeting, Pimenov arrived with a translator. His English had been satisfactory in the past: suddenly, it seemed, he could only speak Russian. Hawke bailed him up but Pimenov, using sign language, indicated that the situation was too delicate to discuss in the presence of the translator. Hawke appealed to Joe Morris, Chairman of the Workers, to intervene. Morris, too, discovered that

Pimenov could not understand English. Later that day, in the Governing Body meeting, Hawke sent Pimenov a sharp note, stating that while they had in the past had disagreements, he regarded as 'monstrous the suggestion that I have in any way misrepresented the unequivocal commitments made to me in Moscow'.[2] He demanded a private discussion with Pimenov. The Russian read the note (without the assistance of his translator), rose and left the meeting. Hawke could not find him.

A day or so later Boris Averianov, the man who had accompanied Hawke on his visits to Shelepin in 1971 and 1973, approached Hawke. Averianov was a senior official of the World Federation of Trade Unions, the Soviet-dominated version of ICFTU. Averianov had with him a document relating to the SALT II talks, and asked Hawke to endorse it. Hawke replied, 'Before asking me for any favours, consult Pimenov'.

A few days later the Soviet delegation to the ILO was giving a cocktail party, which Hawke attended. He was standing alone, willing Pimenov to stop ignoring him, when he was approached by a smiling, personable young man who introduced himself as Eugene Arapov. Arapov explained that he was based in Geneva as a Soviet ILO liaison officer with the news media. When Hawke questioned Arapov further the Russian said, 'I have been here for four years. You don't think we would have someone insignificant in this position, do you?' In plain English this meant, I am from the KGB.* He suggested that it would be useful if he and Hawke could talk to each other, soon.

By this stage Hawke was growing desperate. On Friday 15 June, following a session of the Resolutions Committee which he was chairing, he was approached once more by Arapov who invited him to go outside the building 'for a confidential discussion'. They went out to the Russian's car and as soon as they were inside Arapov switched on the radio loudly, remarking, 'You know why I'm doing that, don't you?' The cat was playing with its mouse. Arapov said he wanted to speak to Hawke privately and confidentially, at a place where neither the Soviets nor Hawke's colleagues could see them. However, driving Hawke around in his own car, in daylight, was hardly the right way to begin what is known in the trade as 'a deniable meeting'. With one part of his mind Hawke realised that what was happening was fantastic, but by now he was so anxious that he was willing to suspend his incredulity. Arapov drove to a small restaurant in Geneva, the Monte Cristo, and there they talked for three hours.

A transcript of Hawke's oral report to Jewish leaders, made soon afterwards, says:

Arapov advised Hawke that . . . It would be counter-productive for

---

* Senior ILO officials later told Hawke they believed that Arapov was, indeed, a KGB officer.

Hawke to have any further discussions with Pimenov about the Soviet Jews unless Pimenov himself raised it, which was highly unlikely. All future discussions should be directed to him. Secondly, he asked Hawke to recapitulate everything that had transpired, although it was quite clear that he was fully in the picture. Thirdly, he advised Hawke that the matter was of such a nature that he would have to revert to Moscow and possibly go to Moscow personally for discussions.[3]

Arapov then raised the SALT II meeting in Vienna between Presidents Carter and Brezhnev. He emphasised the importance of SALT II and asked Hawke if he believed, in the event of exit visas being granted to Soviet Jews, that it could be guaranteed that the American Jewish lobby would 'give a positive response' — that is, pressure the Congress to ratify the SALT II agreement which Carter and Brezhnev had signed in Vienna. He ended by telling Hawke that he must wait until discussions with Moscow had been finalized, when he would again make contact.

Hawke's anxiety and misery brought on a bout of heavy drinking. A couple of nights later he telephoned a friend in Australia and talked for more than an hour, expressing his fears that he had, all along, been duped. At one stage he said, 'If I've let those people down — I've never thought of this before — I think I'll kill myself. I really think I could commit suicide.' Leibler, with whom Hawke was keeping in contact, said later,

> It was heart-breaking. Bob was in the weakest negotiating position he's ever been in, and he was clutching at every little straw, every little word. Intuitively, I felt the Russians were playing a game just to keep him quiet, to prevent him from attacking them in the ILO. But like him I was also looking for miracles.

Already General Vladimir Grigorievich Borisenko, the head of the Passport and Visa Office of the USSR Interior Ministry, had given an interview in Moscow saying that Hawke had no authority to broadcast reports that refuseniks would be released, and nor did Alexei Shibayev have any authority to make such claims. Borisenko added, 'We in the Interior Ministry have not authorised anyone to make a statement about decisions coming within the competence of the Ministry of the Interior. No maximum period for refusing exit visas has been set. We will never set any.'[4]

After his first long discussion with Arapov, Hawke had twelve days left in Geneva, time in which he could cause severe embarrassment to the Soviet delegation by publicly attacking the USSR on the general issue of human rights and on the particular question of the refuseniks. Arapov, however, had adroitly silenced Hawke: he had warned him that he should say nothing, lest he jeopardise the delicate, secret process now underway. Leibler confirmed Hawke's belief that he must avoid a confrontation with the Russians. Then on 26 June, the day before Hawke was due to leave Geneva, Arapov invited Hawke for lunch — again at the Monte Cristo.* Their luncheon lasted almost two hours. According to Hawke's report, Arapov told him that

> He had been advised by Moscow that there was a probability of Brezhnev becoming personally involved in the situation, but that the most important prerequisite from the Soviet viewpoint . . . would be a *quid pro quo* if the Soviets delivered.
>
> Arapov stated that he would still have to get final authorisation (presumably on the level of Brezhnev) and if that were forthcoming, Hawke would be contacted either directly from Geneva or via the Russian Embassy (in Canberra) with a message stating, 'Go on Bob'. If such a message were received it would mean that the following *quid pro quo* situation would come into effect:
>
> a. Hawke would have to go to the United States and convince the American Jewish lobby to support strongly the [view] that the SALT II talks were beneficial, and ensure that key Jews would be prepared to lobby (openly) for Senate ratification, without amendments.
>
> b. If SALT II were to be fully ratified without changes, the Soviets on the day of ratification would release the fifty refuseniks and twelve prisoners and their families and provide them with a special flight.
>
> Hawke pointed out to Arapov that it was more than feasible that even if Jewish groups could be persuaded to lobby for SALT ratification, it could still fail because of other factors. Arapov responded that ratification was imperative; that Soviet delivery of the package would be more difficult but still possible in the event of Jewish lobbying failing to succeed in ratification. After ratification of SALT II [which would be followed by] the release of the fifty refusenik families and the twelve prisoners, Jews should then extend support for Most Favoured Nation status for the Soviet Union, and extension of credits to the USSR. If this succeeded, the Russians would then formally ratify their commitment regarding a maximum five-year term for all Jewish emigrants denied visas on grounds of their having had access to State secrets.
>
> Arapov also discussed at length the Olympics and stated that in the event of the above scenario moving smoothly, the Russians would expect an undertaking that there would be no problems encountered during the Olympic Games.

The oral report made by Hawke continued:

* If Arapov were having his meetings with Hawke monitored by more senior KGB officers, someone in a car parked near the restaurant or in a building across the road would have been able to listen to and record their conversation. Or it may be that a familiar place was chosen simply for its soothing effect.

Arapov was evasive and embarrassed as to reasons for Soviet repudiation of promises made in Moscow, although at no stage did he suggest that Hawke was misrepresenting what had been conveyed to him. He emphasised that [the *quid pro quo*] scenario still had to be confirmed through discussions on the highest level, involving contact with Brezhnev. He indicated that he considered the likelihood of package endorsement at the highest level to be very good and he hoped to revert to Hawke in the not too distant future.[5]

Hawke told Arapov that he would give him until the end of June to make contact. If he had heard nothing by then he would make one final effort to contact Arapov through a Geneva intermediary.

The message 'Go on Bob' never came. It is unlikely that anyone outside the USSR will ever know what happened, but there are some interesting points to The Hawke Incident. An Australian diplomat's comment: 'Hawke was trapped between two powerful forces — the KGB and International Zionism which, in the Russian mind, because of Russian anti-Semitism, is a huge and dangerous adversary'. From an Israeli diplomat:

> The Russians had not been serious from the beginning, but had been anxious to avoid embarrassment — a denunciation of them by Hawke in the ILO — so had kidded him along in Moscow, then in Geneva, playing for time. The Russians require payment, and Jews are bargaining chips. Australia, an insignificant country, was in no position to 'pay' for the Jews. SALT II was the payment and Hawke was unable to deliver on that.

It was almost a year, and one of the chessmen in the game was dead, before a more complex analysis of what had happened emerged. Another very senior Australian observer of the Soviet scene wrote to Hawke:

> . . . the 'nekrolog'* of Peter Pimenov [published in *Pravda* on 30 May 1980] . . . confirms the views of those who said that [Pimenov] was personally very close to Brezhnev . . . This suggests that Pimenov who was, it seems, stage-managing developments during your visit was pursuing a stratagem known to very few others. My tentative conclusion . . . is that everything turned out exactly as intended by the Soviet side. I think they may well have been worried that the meeting between Brezhnev and Carter in Vienna on 1 June 1979 might have been made the occasion of a demonstration by Jews dissatisfied with aspects of Soviet policy. Pimenov may have been told to do something which would make a Jewish demonstration in Vienna less likely, for

* English: necrologue.

instance to get a credible report circulating that good news for the Jews was on the way, leading them to think that a demonstration might be not only unnecessary but actually against their interests. If my supposition is right then one can only say that as a disinformation operation it was cleverly done — at some cost perhaps to the USSR's future relations with Australia, but meeting the demands of the moment very well![6]

Hawke was comforted by this 'tentative conclusion', since it vindicated his integrity. But if the analysis is correct he had been victim of a most subtle undermining and the worst traducement of his career, for the Soviet Union had successfully portrayed him as a devious incompetent — to the world: the refusenik release story had made the front pages of all the great newspapers of the West. There is no suggestion of any malice towards Hawke: the issues at stake were too important. He had simply arrived in Moscow at a convenient time, making a convenient request.

Meanwhile, the effect of these experiences on his morale was grave. He was both wrenched with guilt for having falsely raised the hopes of Soviet Jews, and fearful that because of the incident they might be punished. He felt humiliated before his Diaspora and Israeli friends. Leibler was staunch and did not doubt that Hawke had got his facts straight, but there were others, especially non-Jews and Australian journalists, who made Hawke their butt and tormented him about what he had failed to do for the Russian Jews. The most distressing result was that the episode brought fear and distrust to the surface of Hawke's mind. In the past paranoia had risen occasionally when he was drunk, but even roaring drunk Hawke had remained affectionate and trusting with friends. In the period after his sojourn in Geneva in 1979 up to the time he became a teetotaller, Hawke, when drunk, made accusations of treachery to some of his best mates.

He left Geneva on 27 June 1979 in an agony of hope and despair. As usual he was able to disguise his feelings with his public mask of *bonhomie*, but misery was having its effect and within two months, his life complicated by other problems, he felt 'relieved' when told he might have a brain tumour.

Hawke flew from Geneva to Rome, where he was to have a private audience with Pope John-Paul. His Holiness was keen to talk about Australia, Poland, the USSR and trade union matters and their interview over-ran its allotted time. Hawke has never lost his simplicity of heart: as Ducker remarked of him, 'a giant in many ways, and also in many ways an ordinary bloke'. He felt deeply honoured by the Pontiff's interest in what he had to say. The audience had been arranged at short notice by Hawke's friend, John Hogan, a much-loved figure in the NSW ALP, who farmed in the Tweed River district and was nicknamed The Planter. Hawke had been reading without break on the flight back from Rome but then, as the plane approached Jakarta,

I put my book down and began thinking about John, wondering about my schedule and how I could get to see him to express my enormous gratitude. I was filled with very warm feelings for him. When we landed in Perth I rang Hazel, who told me that John had died a few hours earlier. It had happened at the very time I had begun thinking about him, coming into Jakarta. I was terribly upset — and I couldn't go to the funeral because there was a dispute on Christmas Island that I had to fly out to immediately. I sent a long telegram from Perth and Hazel went to the funeral, representing both of us.

On Christmas Island the workers garlanded his shoulders with flowers in thanks for what he had done for them. But in Australia miseries and problems were awaiting him. In Perth he visited Ellie. A few weeks earlier she had spoken to him; she was now beyond speech. In Melbourne his domestic life was still strained: a front-page newspaper photograph of Hawke and Hazel, at home, published a few weeks later beside a quote from Hawke saying that 'lack of privacy had also affected his family' hinted at the difficulties.[7] The children had all left home and were living in various States, Stephen using a fictitious surname. Furthermore, there was discontent within the ACTU, for Hawke's continuing inability to reach a formal decision about Parliament was unsettling to staff and executive members, who complained that he was often distracted from the real concerns of the presidency. There were complaints that he did not fully have his mind on the job and that the Council was not functioning properly because he was absent from his office so often — frequently because the burden of his normal representation of the trade union movement on a wide range of committees was increased, at this time, by his membership of the Crawford Committee.

On return to Melbourne from Christmas Island he went straight into a new Telecom dispute and was still engaged in a rush of travelling to and from Canberra for negotiations with the Government, which had proclaimed the Commonwealth Employees (Employment Provisions) Act and was threatening to sack tens of thousands of public servants, when the ALP biennial Conference opened in Adelaide.

It was Bill Hayden's first Conference as Leader of the ALP and naturally enough he wanted to make an impressive showing. Hayden was in an invidious situation: he was Leader of a demoralised Party and his own position was being continually undermined by news media speculation that Hawke would enter Parliament, usurp Hayden's leadership and sweep Labor to victory at the polls. Barely a day passed without the news media goading Hayden about his leadership, vis-à-vis Hawke, while Hawke was constantly pinched and prodded with questions about his political career, causing him, around this time, to exclaim to journalists, 'If the reindeer were moulting in Lapland you would want to know how that affected my attitudes to entering Parliament!' The result was inevitable: two men who had liked each other and worked amiably together had forced upon them the roles of antagonists. If the news media did not exist this would have happened anyway. The difference the media, especially television, made was that it transformed political rivalry into a Roman circus, at once creating and catering to an appetite for blood.

While Hawke had been abroad Hayden had made a veiled public attack upon him; the Deputy-Leader, Lionel Bowen, had followed up with a less veiled one. In the days prior to the ALP's Conference there was much broadcast speculation that Hawke would give a more dazzling performance than Hayden.

For more than a year Hawke had been chairman of the ALP's federal economic policy committee, among whose members was Ralph Willis, now the shadow Treasurer. They had drawn up a series of recommendations to put to the Conference, the most controversial being that a future Labor government would hold a referendum to gain control over prices and incomes. Six years earlier the Whitlam Government had failed to convince the trade union movement to support government control over incomes, but at the time the idea had been presented to the unions brutally, without consultation, and during a period of booming employment — the last loud flash, as people had come to realise, before a twilight stillness descended upon the economy. Had the Whitlam Government been empowered in December 1973 to restrain prices and incomes its handling of the economic crisis of 1974-75 would have been easier; it may even have survived.

Hawke and Willis were now convinced that a future Labor government must have such powers. However, persuading the trade union movement, even six years later, to agree to such a proposal would be difficult. Hawke's strategy was to have the ALP adopt as policy a prices and incomes referendum at its July Conference in Adelaide. He would then be well armed, at the ACTU Congress in September, to argue to the unions that they, too, should adopt this policy. By September 1979 the ACTU would have two million affiliated members; if such a large number of citizens were morally bound to the referendum proposal, a future Labor government would have the best chance any government has ever had of winning a controversial referendum.

The matter was scheduled for debate on Monday 16 July in Adelaide. Meanwhile it was known that the Left had drawn up seventy amendments to the ALP's economic policy recommendations, and that it would reject outright the referendum.

The ALP federal executive held its pre-Conference meeting in Adelaide on Thursday and Friday, 12 and 13 July, but because of the Telecom dispute Hawke could not attend. He said,

> On Sunday night Neil Batt [the ALP President] telephoned me and begged me to come over to Adelaide because of the wages policy debate that was coming up the following week. He said it was absolutely vital

that Bill have a good win at the Conference on this issue, which would be so important to a future Labor government. Then on Monday night Batt rang me again and handed the phone to Bill who said, 'We've got the numbers, but we want to make sure we win well'. He said he really wanted me to come to Adelaide, although as I'd explained the Telecom dispute was at such a stage that I felt I should stay with it, and that there was a danger that I'd have to pull myself out of Adelaide to return to negotiations. The federal executive had decided to put the economic debate off by a day to give themselves more time to lobby delegates for support. I told Bill on Monday night that I'd get over to Adelaide on Tuesday morning. The debate was due to begin at 9.30 a.m., but there was no flight that would get me there early enough. So it was agreed that Ralph Willis would open the session and when I arrived, around 11 o'clock, I'd take over. I had a speech prepared, attacking the Left's position on the issue, which would have devastated them and shown up what a pack of bastards they were. When I arrived Ralph was already speaking. I went up on the platform and sat down behind him. Hayden was seated in the audience, on the left of the hall. We broke for lunch and I went down to say g'day to Bill. He made an extraordinary remark. He said, 'This was never my idea', referring to the recommendation on wages. I was in a hurry to get to a luncheon at State Parliament. I said, 'What are you talking about?' I was staggered by what he had said, but I just thought, Oh Jesus. When I returned from lunch I was given the message that Hayden had done a deal with the Left. They had an amendment to the wages policy and Hayden was going to support it.

Unbeknown to Hawke, his old adversaries Tom Uren and Jim Roulston had buttonholed Hayden the day before to tell him that the unions would not accept the referendum proposal. Uren had said, 'We've got the numbers to roll you'.[8] On Tuesday morning Hayden had called a breakfast meeting with about nineteen delegates to lobby them to support the referendum proposal. By lunch-time Tuesday Hayden had come to the conclusion that he could not muster the numbers to have the referendum idea passed: he was therefore, as Leader of the Party, forced to choose between defeat at his first Conference, or a compromise. He chose to compromise. Unhappily — in the broader view — he did not warn Hawke that he believed himself trapped and was therefore changing his tactics. Instead, he embarrassed Hawke, who had only two minutes warning before the debate resumed after lunch that the Leader had dumped him and the economic policy committee recommendation. Willis and Mick Young, the shadow Minister for Industrial Relations, were similarly caught off-guard for they, too, had been given no warning. Neither had the NSW Right. Hawke believes that members of Hayden's staff had persuaded him that a sudden undercutting of the President of the ACTU was a smart tactic to strengthen his leadership of the Party. He was furious — on his own account, and on the larger issue of what he believed was best for the labour movement and the Australian economy.

He asked Neil Batt, 'What will I do now?' Batt told him to say nothing, to avoid confrontation. Ducker, who was beside Hawke, gave the same advice: there were only seconds in which to confer, then Ralph Willis had the unpalatable job of continuing the debate, deserted by Hayden and unsupported by Hawke, who was seated behind him, fuming but silent. The amendment, which committed the Party to a 'dialogue' with the unions, but not to an incomes referendum, was duly moved, supported by Hayden, and passed into ALP policy — as formidable as a resolution in favour of motherhood. Hawke did not speak all afternoon.

At the end of the session journalists asked Hayden when Hawke had been told, of the compromise. He replied, 'After lunch', then added heatedly, 'Listen, I make up my own mind in these matters and I carried the Conference. I think that's the thing that counts and it's not such a bad result' — remarks that revealed, unwittingly, the Leader's jittery feelings about Hawke.

Hawke himself was already raw-nerved and deeply fatigued. The previous week, during the Telecom dispute, he had slept on average only three hours a night. He was vulnerable, especially at this stage when he was still throbbing with pain from the duplicity of the Russians, to exaggerated feelings of betrayal. Add an atmosphere of hostility towards him, then alcohol, and he would be primed for an outburst of self-righteous anger. Unhappily his old protector, John Ducker, was not well enough to force Hawke to evade danger. Ducker said later, 'If only I'd been able to persuade Hawkey to come upstairs with me to talk to the Queenslanders. He could have said what he liked to them, got it all out of his system. But he wanted to go and sound off in the bar.' Ducker, after years of 'fighting and struggling for purity and goodness', as he referred later, with a cherub's smile, to life in ALP politics, was going through a period of traumatic emotional change: 'a tremendous pressure of contradictions — trying to keep oneself afloat and do something useful'. His blood pressure was high; his doctors had ordered him to have more rest; he was torn, he said, between his political career and wanting to spend time with his family.

Ducker had spoken vehemently against the amendment inside the Conference, stating the view of the NSW Right, which was furious about the deal. When the session ended he joined Hawke in a makeshift television studio only a few feet from the Conference floor. Journalists had not yet realised what complicated emotions had been unleashed: at Bill Hayden's Conference, Bob Hawke was being cold-shouldered. Ducker said, 'Everybody walked away from Bob. I was the bloke who stuck with him. Others simply found they were engaged elsewhere.' Hawke gave a low-key television interview, saying that the compromise 'was something which occurred over lunch-time. I haven't had time to consider it.' Asked about his political future he replied that if delegates thought he could serve the Party better in another capacity he would expect them to come to him and express their view 'and so far they haven't'. At the end of the interview Ducker and Hawke hugged each other. Paul Kelly and Stuart Simpson of the *National Times* continued:

> The ABC, sensing they might be on to a story, brought in some bottles of beer to keep the duo around . . . Hawke and Ducker stayed in the studio watching replays of the Hawke interview, punctuating their stay with frequent displays of comradeship, as more and more people, sensing the drama of discontent, came into the studio.* But after an hour or so John Ducker, realising Hawke's capacity to exaggerate was leading to over-kill, began to play down the incident, telling colleagues, 'It will all be over after a good night's sleep'. But to no avail. Sleep was low on Bob Hawke's priorities. He walked into the Rotunda Bar of the Gateway Inn at 9.10 p.m. Journalists, delegates and other hotel guests were sitting around in the plush red chairs of the small bar. Hawke was quiet at first, mingling with delegates . . . But his temper warmed when he spotted Hugh McBride, original author of the amendment moved by Bill Hayden, and Simon Crean, also a member of the Victorian delegation.[9]

Hawke called out to McBride and Crean, both Centre Unity faction members, 'You're all bloody gutless!' He added, 'As far as I am concerned Hayden is dead'. Limbering up he went on to describe Hayden as a liar with a limited future.[10]

The next morning Hawke's outburst was national news. His potential career as a parliamentarian was written off, comprehensively, by the Press. The *National Times* devoted its whole front page, plus pages 3 and 4, to a cover story: HAWKE: THE END OF THE ROAD?, remarking,

> His behaviour probably rules out any chance he will ever have of becoming Leader and suggests that he will never run for Parliament anyway . . . The most significant point of the Adelaide Conference was that it brought on prematurely the long simmering, inevitable clash between Hayden and Hawke . . . [and] resolved [it] in Hayden's favour . . . The irony of Adelaide was that Hawke's undoing was entirely his own . . . Hawke, through dint of sheer perseverance, transformed a minor setback for himself into a major one . . . despite his brittleness and lack of political nous, Hayden emerged with the imprimatur of leadership. He put his own indelible stamp on Labor's future direction,

---

* Either at this point or a while later, in the Rotunda Bar, a journalist taunted Hawke, 'What about those Jews you were going to get released from Moscow, eh?' Neither he nor anyone else present realised what anguish such questions caused, because Hawke had refused to reveal what had actually happened in Geneva.

formally ended the era of Whitlamism, and ushered in a new era of his own based on the twin themes of sound management and limited reform.[11]

The page 3 headline read: HOW BOB HAWKE BLEW IT — AGAIN, above a cartoon by Patrick Cook of Hawke, pacing, hands behind his back, thinking to himself, 'And some have self-destruction thrust upon them'.

By the next day Hawke was very shaken. When harried by a TV crew while trying to telephone Jean Sinclair about the Telecom dispute he shouted, 'Piss off!' and film of this remark, with Hawke flailing his arms at the cameras, was put to air. He recouped some of his ground with mild television interviews, given later on Wednesday, and broadcast on the evening news, but he was hunched up and haggard. He had to return that night to Melbourne for the Telecom dispute, and arrived back at the ACTU office at 8 p.m. He recalled, 'The staff were beaut. They gathered around me, sort of protecting me . . .' He had been in the office only a few minutes when Rosslyn telephoned from interstate to comfort him. Hawke was so upset that when she had rung off he left his desk and went to a corner of the room, pretending to look out the window, so that those gathered in his office would not see the tears in his eyes. His miseries, however, were not over yet.

Publicly, he had recovered his poise within a few days. By the end of the following week an amiable, cheerful Hawke was launching a book at the National Press Club in Canberra and announcing that a future Labor Government would limit the powers of the Governor-General. Ten days was time enough for the news media to forget that Hawke's political career was ruined, and speculation on the topic resurged. Every major article evoked a flood of letters from the public. Throughout 1979 hundreds, maybe thousands, of people wrote to him, urging him to enter Parliament; a small number asked him to remain with the ACTU. It was years since he had had time to read his mail; he relied on Jean Sinclair to tell him the trend of opinions. Excerpts from individual letters give some hint of his standing with the electorate by mid-1979:

I have always looked on you as a kind of Messiah . . . God bless you.

When you become Prime Minister you will enrich our lives and inspire our hearts.

You have been a strong leader of men.

You are the saving grace for our country.

There are hundreds of people who pray for you and your family.

> You can be likened to a type of Christ.
>
> As I was working through the day's work called 'Confidence and Faith' your name kept coming into my mind. The possibility for Australia of a Prime Minister living his life to the limit of the potential given by the Creator and without limit when lived in perfect harmony with the Creator made my heart leap for joy.
>
> You are such a brilliant, honest and humane man.
>
> You are the hope of Australia and the future of our land lies in your greatness.
>
> I cannot compare your style of English, *the matchless words,* to anyone but to the late Sir Winston Churchill, who used very choice words in times of crisis.
>
> At present there are many thousands who do not know where to turn. You are the one . . .
>
> The young people of Australia need you.

Old people, recalling the Depression and stating that they found Hawke a source of hope in new, harsh economic times, wrote many of these notes as, obviously, did the religious. Despite the discounting of political commentators the Australian public continued to believe in Hawke, for somehow, through the miasma of information, misinformation, gossip, myth, scandal and simplification he had managed to reach out and touch the people. In a selfish epoch of shrinking opportunities and insecure status Hawke's generosity of mind and his confidence were a balm for mass anxieties.

A remarkable number of letters expressed patriotic fervour — 'this great country', 'this beautiful country' were phrases that recurred — and revealed a link in correspondents' minds between Australia and Hawke: that he was the authentic expression of our society. This was particularly interesting sociologically, given Hawke's public commitment to Israel and to such an abstruse issue, for the majority of Australians, as Soviet refuseniks. Mick Young noted, after Hawke had wept in Parliament in late 1981 when a Liberal backbencher had accused him of deserting Israel to please the ALP,

> If I'd cried I wouldn't have had the nerve to return to my electorate. I would have been dead, politically. Soon afterwards I went with Hawkey to a public meeting. You would have thought that people would give him a roasting but they were trying to touch his hair, touch the sleeve of his jacket. There isn't another politician in this country who could arouse that response.

Perhaps the explanation is that Hawke is not a politician in the sense in which this label is generally understood.

Sir John Crawford, who first began advising Australian prime ministers in the 1940s, knew Hawke well by 1979, having met him regularly for more than a year on the inquiry into manufacturing, of which he was chairman and Hawke one of three committee members. He saw striking correspondences between Hawke and John Curtin, the Labor leader whom Hawke most reveres and who, like him, was a bad drunk. However, it was another quality, common to both men, that Crawford singled out: 'Sensitivity and associated deep feeling'. He said,

> Curtin was not a professional politician — and for that matter, neither was Ben Chifley when he started out as Prime Minister — Curtin was a humane man, a man of very deep feeling, but not a professional in politics. Neither is Bob Hawke. Compared with someone like [Sir] Phillip Lynch [the former Deputy-Leader of the Liberal Party] Bob is a novice politician. But he could get the people behind him, like Curtin did, for a great national effort. My fear, and I choose my words advisedly, is that the strain of office would prove too much for Bob Hawke, as, in my view, it did for John Curtin.

There is a curious resonance between Crawford's sober concern and the ecstatic outpourings from ordinary men and women, describing Hawke in their letters as 'Messiah' and 'type of Christ': the ultimate purpose of such figures is that they be destroyed, for the community.

Skimming through Hawke's fan mail, the poetry and prayers sent to him, observing hands yearning to touch him, one begins to suspect that some ancient, inchoate force is at work in Hawke's relationship with the Australian public and that this middle-aged boyish man represents something else — perhaps something lost but cherished, and recognised in him. It is curious that in a period when the trade unions were falling in public esteem Hawke, their representative, continued to rise: in the community's mind he was placed apart.

By August 1979 his inner struggle with what he was and what he could become was moving towards a point of critical decision: he had only a few weeks left to declare his candidature for Parliament. The seat which his Centre Unity supporters had marked out for him was Wills, in the industrial heart of Melbourne, a blue-ribbon Labor electorate. But within the Victorian ALP Hawke's opponents begrudged him a safe seat: it was widely asserted that he should stand for a marginal electorate, and that he had no right to demand special treatment from the Party. His insistence that he would consider only a safe seat (which would leave him freer to meet the demands of electioneering for the Party as a whole and for national issues) was said to be another example of Hawke's 'top level' attitudes.

Meanwhile, he had other problems. Since he had returned from Geneva he had been having trouble with his hearing, which he had thought at first was due to the effects of a head-cold, and flying. When the cold had cleared he had remained partly deaf. In the third week of August Hawke sought medical advice and was told he might have a brain tumour. By this stage he was so intensely miserable, in such a state of conflict over his private life and his future, that he said on hearing the news, 'I almost felt relieved'. It was another week before further tests revealed that he had nothing physiological wrong with him. In the interim, and for weeks afterwards, Melbourne buzzed with the rumour that: 'Hawke is dying of cancer'.

He was dying of indecision. Night after night he was awake until the early morning, drinking, talking, driving himself and his friends mad about his future career. Many of them believed he should not enter Parliament: they feared that he would go to Canberra only to be torn apart by the Press and the Party. Michael Elitzur, the Israeli Ambassador to Australia at the time, a man who was very close to Hawke, told him, 'You would be like Uriah with David. I didn't have to remind him of his Sunday school lessons; he understood immediately.'*

The Stop Hawke campaign was now in full gear. The Socialist Left had decided to try to frighten Hawke out of standing for pre-selection, and handbills, called by those who produced them 'shit sheets', were circulating in Melbourne. Some made their way interstate to other Left-wing branches. They elaborated the familiar themes that Hawke was an enemy of the working class, the stooge of big capitalism and Rupert Murdoch, lived in luxury, and would betray Labor principles. One had a drawing of a large, cigar-smoking 'capitalist' who bore some resemblance to Sir Peter Abeles. The drawing suggested that whoever it was, Hawke in Parliament would be his creature.

Abeles himself was strongly opposed to Hawke's standing for pre-selection. He had been abroad for some weeks but had learnt of the Adelaide débâcle. On 5 September he visited Hawke, who was in Sydney to attend the next day a Reserve Bank board meeting. Abeles pleaded with him not to run, for the same reasons as Elitzur had given. George Rockey accompanied Abeles and similarly urged Hawke not to abandon the safety of the trade unions. Elsewhere, pressures on Hawke's few supporters in Caucus were already intense. Clyde Holding, who had moved from Leader of the Opposition in Victoria in 1977 to federal Parliament, recalled,

> The kind of pressures that were placed upon me were amazing. Bob and
> I were old friends, our kids had grown up together, we have a very close

---

* King David wanted to marry Bethsheba, wife of Uriah. He sent Uriah into the front line of battle against the Ammonites, with secret orders that the rest of the unit suddenly withdraw, leaving Uriah surrounded and defenceless. Joab, David's commander of the army, had to lose a battle in order to get Uriah killed, but even at this expense the King was satisfied.

relationship, we'd gone through God knows how many battles together. It was said to me, 'You've got to stop him getting in to Parliament'. In Canberra I was adopting political positions which were very attractive to the Left. Lots of my ideological positions I would regard as more progressive than, say, Uren's and the Left's. I was also getting, I suppose, a lot of promotion from the Leader. It was put to me quite directly and very hard that I would have a crucial role, that it was not in the interests of the Party that Hawke should be in Parliament, and as I was someone from Victoria I could make that clear. I was told — it's demonstrable — if you go through the pages of Hansard you'll see a whole range of debates on important issues: there would be the shadow Minister or the Leader, and me; the Leader, and me. All of a sudden, nothing. I was told subsequently that I had behaved in an awful way — the implication of the carrot was always there. There were all those pressures to keep Bob out, and much of that has carried over. There's an example: one of the issues that Bob and I don't agree on is uranium. He knows my position; I know his. I believe that within the framework of his position he has behaved with integrity. Certainly, during the 1980 election, he *didn't put a foot wrong*. But during that election, as soon as we started looking like winning, who were the blokes up in the Northern Territory and South Australia and elsewhere, who were saying, 'Well, if we're the Government we will have to look at our uranium policy'? It wasn't Hawke. He'd played it straight down the line: he'd had his argument, and he'd lost, and that was it. The blokes who were proposing to throw out Labor policy were the people in the leadership. But that doesn't stop people saying, today,* 'Aw, you couldn't trust the bastard'.

Hawke's supporters in Caucus numbered about twenty and there was no aid to be sought now from John Ducker. A few weeks after the Adelaide Conference Ducker had resigned from all his positions in the ALP and the trade union movement.

Meanwhile, Hawke refused to fight those campaigning against him. He said later, with scorn, 'Personally, I did nothing about it. I regarded it as ridiculous bastardy. My own people in the electorate were working on numbers, doing the job, so I left it to them.'

The Socialist Left's candidate for Wills was an energetic young SL organiser, Gerry Hand.

By 6 September Hawke, still in Sydney, had decided that he would not run. He telephoned Jean Sinclair, who was convinced that he should enter Parliament, to obtain Bill Landeryou's telephone number so that he could alert Landeryou, his chief organiser, to halt his lobbying efforts. A few days earlier

* March 1981 interview.

Lord Mountbatten had been murdered by the IRA; it was publicly admitted that some IRA assassins were trained in their craft by the PLO. While explaining his change of mind to Sinclair, Hawke said, 'I'm the guy who's copping everything and I'm expected to go on copping everything, including the proposal that I must justify myself as an ALP candidate to the pre-selection committee in preference to the likes of that unknown Gerry Hand'. He went on to say that the SL formed 'a party within a Party' and that this had been sufficient in the 1950s to cause the Split: why was a party within a Party tolerated now? He added,

> I hate Hartley more than I hate Fraser and yet I'm expected to appear on platforms with him and others, as brothers. Mountbatten was assassinated with the help of people [the PLO] whom Hartley supports, and I find that abhorrent . . . I'm worried about the State of Denmark. The ALP has got to begin a process of self-criticism; it's got to purge itself of this rottenness.

He had cheered up as soon as he had decided against standing. For the first time he cancelled, without notice, his Reserve Bank board meeting, saying 'I can't come today, I'm celebrating'. This was a figure of speech, for he went immediately into a meeting with representatives of the Seamen's Union, attempting to persuade them to agree to reduce crew sizes in return for an expansion of employment through the founding of an Australian-owned overseas shipping line, in which the ACTU would be a partner. For sixteen years, since the Corio election, Hawke had urged a reform of Australia's maritime transport; in the early 1970s he had made strenuous efforts to form a shipping partnership between Don Dunstan's South Australian Government, the ACTU and Israel's ZIM, a shipping subsidiary of Histadrut, but the Australian trade union movement's rejection of things Israeli and other difficulties foiled the plan. Hawke continued to dream of it and in 1979 had a new burst of optimism when George Rockey, retired from TNT and equipped with a wealth of experience in the industry, agreed to act as an agent. It was, and is, extraordinary that Australia, economically reliant upon overseas trade, operates only a handful of international cargo vessels: a major problem is that Australian crew costs are so high. Hawke had been arguing for weeks with shipping union officials that if they would accept a reduction in employment per ship they would have guarantees of greater employment in future because there were companies ready to expand our international shipping, if the price was right. He was so exhilarated that before going to the meeting he said, 'I'll fix this in half an hour'. After two hours he had been unable to clinch his argument. However, his spirits were still buoyant.

The next day, Friday, he appeared at the opening of an ALP electoral office in the Melbourne suburb of Coburg, smiling and relaxed. He stood on a butcher's box so that those at the back of the hall could see him and remarked, 'I got a box. I thought it might have been a seat, but they're hard to come by.' When journalists asked him if he would seek pre-selection he grinned and replied, 'I may'. This was taken to mean that he would. Late that evening he was at home in Sandringham when Hazel, who had answered the telephone, approached him softly. 'I have some bad news', she said. Ellie was dead.

For almost two years he had been mentally preparing for this blow to fall, even saying sometimes, 'I almost wish she could die — what's the use of living in the state she's in? Just breathing . . .' Now that it had happened, he was stricken. Over the weekend, during which he had been scheduled to work on final preparations for the ACTU biennial Congress which would open on Monday, he spoke to many of his friends about Ellie's death, and was frequently in tears. Rockey said later, 'Bob couldn't believe his mother was dead. It was weeks, at least, before he began to accept that she'd gone.'

There was much rearranging to be done: Hawke would deliver his opening Presidential address to Congress on Monday then he and Hazel would fly immediately to Perth for the funeral, on Tuesday.

Harold Souter, retired now, had come for the opening day of the Congress, which was held in the Dallas Brooks Hall in Melbourne. He seemed to be one of the few people there who realised what Hawke was suffering, and who sorrowed for him. As delegates milled around in the foyer, laughing, joking and lobbying, Souter stood aside, shaking his head. 'This is a sad day for Bob', he said. 'For a great man like him . . . his mother's death.' When Hawke walked on to the platform to address the 755 delegates he looked an old man, stooped, grey, haggard. But for his luxuriant hair, he could have been seventy — and he was not yet fifty. Hazel had come to the Congress and sat in the visitors' gallery watching him roaring out hope and determination to the audience below, his feet dancing, his hands gesturing with light, dramatic movements. From his words there was no hint that he was grieving. He was like a toy figure on the stage: wound up, he worked. 'A millionaire with words', someone sneered loudly. Already the atmosphere was hostile.

In Perth, he spent the whole night talking to Clem and the next day kissed Ellie goodbye. He murmured to Hazel, 'She's so cold'. Hazel tried to comfort him but the chill of death preyed on his mind and for the next few days he referred to it, grimacing. Straight after the funeral he flew back to Melbourne, for the worst fortnight in his life: in Adelaide Hawke had been sent to coventry by his Party, but at the 1979 ACTU Congress he was rejected by the trade union movment.

On the night he arrived back from Perth, Tuesday, there was an ACTU concert at which a range of prominent artists were performing, free. Unfortunately the audience was small. Ray Gietzelt was worried by Hawke's appearance and at about 9.30 p.m. told him, 'People will understand if you leave early. You're exhausted. Go and get some sleep.' Hawke replied, 'I can't walk out'; he had about three hours sleep that night.

Had his mind been at ease; had he not been exhausted; had he not lost four days of Congress organising time because of Ellie's death . . . disaster may have been averted. Hawke failed on everything at the 1979 ACTU Congress: he failed on the executive elections, on the uranium debate, and on affiliation fees. By the afternoon of Friday 15 September he was left standing alone on the stage of the Dallas Brooks Hall from which the roaring crowd of men had vanished, contemplating the losses: the ACTU was facing a cash shortfall of $400,000 and Charlie Fitzgibbon, arguably the most able ACTU executive member, had been tipped out of office. It was, however, the uranium debate that had occasioned his worst defeat.

The debate, the most controversial issue before Congress, was scheduled for Thursday 14 September. By Wednesday morning the thrill of a rout for Hawke was in the air: the executive elections were in progress and news was spreading that there were two Left-Centre tickets, both entitled 'Official Progressive', but one coloured white, the other yellow. The 'Hawke ticket' was white; the yellow ticket was a ring-in. The vice-presidents, senior and junior, of the ACTU are elected by a complicated system of preferential voting: first the senior vice-presidency is established, then through an exhaustive method of distribution of preferences, the junior vice-presidency quota is reached. The two 'Official Progressive' tickets, one of them not official at all, and the Right-Centre ticket all nominated Cliff Dolan as senior vice-president. The Hawke ticket nominated Charlie Fitzgibbon as junior vice-president. The ring-in ticket nominated Jim Roulston of the AMWSU. There were yellow and white Official Progressive tickets for other elections, also. The far-Left and the Right had done a deal to support Roulston — although he was a member of the Socialist Left — in favour of Fitzgibbon, who was an ALP moderate. Part of the background to the Left-Right deal was that the Right was angry because it had failed to get extra ACTU executive seats for its bigger unions, like the Clerks and the Shop Assistants, while the middle-class ACSPA group was to be rewarded for joining the ACTU with special executive positions. As well, a faction fight was stirring in the New South Wales ALP, where a middle-class New Left was gathering strength, to the irritation of the industrial Old Left and the fury of the industrial Right. And importantly, Fitzgibbon was a more intelligent and strong-willed man than Roulston. Gietzelt commented, 'The Right knew it couldn't control Charlie, while Jim Roulston would be much easier to deal with'.

It was the familiar story of strange bedmates. Until too late Hawke's camp was unaware of the yellow tickets which, as Gietzelt noted, had been carefully designed to take advantage of this complex preferential voting system: 'I believe that —, from the AMWSU, used the union's computer to calculate how preferences must be distributed to defeat Fitzgibbon.* The yellow tickets were handed out by marshals to trusted delegates who then voted according to instructions', he said. By midday Wednesday Fitzgibbon was gone, running last in the race. Simon Crean, a very able Centre-Left Hawke candidate, had also been defeated, in favour of a Right nominee.

The elections were a stunning setback for the Hawke camp and for Hawke personally. He had lobbied hard on Tuesday evening for support for Fitzgibbon who, besides being one of the most capable union leaders in the country, and therefore a desirable member of the ACTU executive, was the man Hawke wanted to succeed him as President. If Hawke were to change his mind about Parliament, he now had no obvious successor as ACTU President. Dolan, although next in line, lived in Sydney, and did not want the job.

The Left was ecstatic about its cleverness in the elections. By Wednesday evening Hawke had been told that the executive's recommendation on uranium mining would be defeated. He had three choices: to dump the executive's policy; to run dead; to fight.

The ACTU's recommendation was that delegates accept the existing and future operation of uranium mining at the Ranger, Mary Kathleen and Narbalek sites, while opposing any further development. There was nothing, in reality, that the ACTU could do to prevent mining at those sites: if union labour were withdrawn, blackleg labour would move in. The transport of uranium ore could, perhaps, be prevented: but the Government had already said that it would use troops to move yellow cake, if necessary. Military trucks could carry the mineral just as effectively as the railways; it could be loaded on to ships berthed at naval wharves. The executive's recommendation recognised these facts of national life — plus a harsher truth: in Hawke's words, 'If you want to damage the trade union movement, commit yourself to a policy that you can't deliver; ban mining, then watch unionists go in and mine it, and unions fight each other to get the miners on their books. My major concern was an industrial one, a concern for the movement.'

---

* The Right-Centre ticket nominated P. McMahon as junior vice-president. A total of 892 formal votes were cast, yielding a quota of 447. Dolan won the senior vice-presidency with a primary vote of 556; Fitzgibbon got 42 primaries, McMahon 275 and Roulston 19. Dolan's second preferences went 208 to Fitzgibbon, giving him a total of 250; 72 to McMahon, giving him a total of 347; and 276 to Roulston, giving him a total of 295. Fitzgibbon was therefore out of the race. The second preference of his 42 first-preference votes split evenly, 21-21 to McMahon and Roulston. Fitzgibbon's third preferences (that is, the third preferences of the 208 voters who gave their first preferences to Dolan and their second to Fitzgibbon) were distributed. The Hawke ticket had Roulston as third choice. Of the 208, 75 went to McMahon and 133 to Roulston. Roulston won the junior vice-presidency by 449 to 443, on Hawke ticket preferences.

I am indebted to Professor Ross Martin of La Trobe University for these figures — B.d'A.

The crucial amendment to the executive's proposal came from the Left; it demanded 'continuing opposition to the mining and export of uranium and the present programme of development'. Late on Wednesday night the Assistant Secretary, Bill Kelty, said to Hawke, 'They've got the numbers and we're going to get done. Let me lead the debate so that it's not a defeat for you, personally.' Hawke replied, 'You know I don't operate like that. If we are going to be done, I won't walk away from it.' He would move the executive's recommendation and would thereby have the mover's right-of-reply. As usual he screwed up his optimism to a point where he was declaring, 'It's worth a go!' It was, again, David against Goliath.

Outside the hall there was a large crowd of anti-uranium demonstrators; a room inside the building had an anti-uranium display. Susan Hawke was among the volunteer workers there, in what was called by delegates 'Sue's Room'.

Hawke gave a fiery, three-quarter hour speech on Thursday morning, emphasising the impracticality of outright opposition. He characterised this attitude as 'a sloppy exercise in ineffective morality'; he stressed the divisions among unions and their members on the issue; the failure of the unions to prevent uranium mining so far; and the doubtful impact on the international use of nuclear energy of even an effective Australian union embargo: if Australia would not supply uranium, South Africa, Gabon, and the USA would. When the open debate began there were hours of splendid oratory but this time, although there was a sense of *déjà vu*, the atmosphere was more hostile, both to the executive and to Hawke personally. When Kelty rose to support Hawke's motion, Jack Marks, a swashbuckling grey-beard from the AMWSU in Western Australia, shouted, 'The sorcerer's apprentice!'

It was an inspired interjection — for when Hawke came roaring back to the microphones to make his speech-in-reply he seemed transformed into some blood-curdling spirit escaped from the underworld, cursing men on earth. The glinting sword-play of his address-in-reply in 1977 was abandoned: Hawke was swinging an axe. He was like a man possessed of holy rage — shouting, taunting, his feet in a boxer's dance, his arms flailing the air, his fists banging the rostrum to emphasise points. Had he turned aside and spat on the people who were yelling back at him his contempt and fury could not have been more savagely stated. As a performance it was, literally, stunning: the force of his harangue, which went on for almost an hour, at deafening volume, had people pressed back in their seats. And at no point had he lost control of himself, although he attacked opposition speakers in personal terms which would take them months to forgive. He assaulted one of his dearest friends, 'Cliffie Dolan', and his young supporter from Western Australia, Peter Cook, both of whom had spoken in favour of the Left amendment. Cook had privately told Hawke that he did not believe in the anti-uranium case. Hawke hurled this back at him, scornfully, and from the visitor's gallery people could see that tears were standing in Cook's eyes. It was as if all the anger and frustration that had been building up in Hawke for months were now being given catharsis. The experience was frightening for observers, the more so because it was directed by a mind which had not stopped thinking, but which was in the grip of inflamed audacity, of moral outrage and logic locked together.

He sat down, the vote was taken and lost 512 to 318 — the executive's defeat was even greater than it would have been had he not intervened. Hawke grimaced as if in agony. Then as the hall erupted into cheering he dropped his head in his hands. People seated above the dais could see what delegates could not: he had gone to sleep. He slept for about a minute then woke up, looking relaxed. A few minutes later he was imperturbably telling journalists, 'You win some, you lose some. I cop it sweet.' The public mask was back in place and stayed there that night when Hawke was host to a large reception, and next day when the executive was rebuffed on the question of affiliation fees: the Left and the Right combined to defeat a recommendation that fees be increased by 75 cents a member, and indexed to rises in average award wages, in favour of an amendment to increase them by only 6 cents, without indexation. That meant the ACTU would be deeply in debt within a few months. *Tribune*, the Communist Party of Australia newspaper, celebrated the Congress with a front-page announcement that 'Left and centre forces scored important victories'.[12]

Judged by the prejudices and preoccupations of the hour the 1979 Congress was a slashing defeat for Hawke. But in the longer view it blazoned a major achievement. In his opening address he had said, 'This is an historic Congress, for it marks the definite emergence of one central trade union organisation in this country'. And so it did, for after ten years as President Hawke had accomplished the major aim of his campaign platform of 1969, a goal he had described then as 'some form of organic co-operation' between the ACTU and the white-collar union councils. At the 1979 Congress the Australian Council of Salaried and Professional Associations (ACSPA) had formally affiliated with the ACTU; at the next Congress the Commonwealth and Goverment Employees' Organisations (CAGEO) would do so.

Ironically, it was the Left-wing ACSPA votes in 1979 that had decided the uranium issue: temporarily. By early 1982 the ACTU executive had been forced to accept that Hawke's exposition of the problems of banning uranium mining and export was accurate, and had acknowledged the policy he had espoused two and a half years earlier by waiving export bans. Meanwhile, the affiliation fee decision had been overturned, in favour of the executive's original proposal, and Charlie Fitzgibbon had returned to the executive.

Before these reversals of Hawke's 'defeats' had occurred Professor Martin wrote:

. . . once the dust of contemporary controversies has settled, the 1979 Congress is likely to be remembered principally as marking the beginning of the end of the independent existence of the two main white-collar peak councils . . . the effective incorporation in the ACTU of the Australian Council of Salaried and Professional Associations . . . for the first time took the ACTU's official total of affiliated unionists to more than two million . . .

In his 1969 acceptance speech, Mr Hawke had also spoken of expanding both the policy concerns of the ACTU and its administrative expertise. A decade later, Congress considered executive recommendations which not only covered an unprecedented range of policy issues, but were formulated with a care and an eye to detail that owed most to a greatly enlarged and highly qualified full-time staff . . .

The 1979 Congress was also distinguished by two noteworthy innovations, both of which reflected the President's inclinations. One was the invitation extended to M. Young, shadow Minister of Industrial Relations in the federal Parliamentary Labor Party, to address Congress. Mr Young is the first Labor parliamentarian, other than a prime minister, to be accorded this privilege in at least twenty years. The other innovation was the special effort made . . . to encourage the attendance of observers at the Congress. This is in line with what is, perhaps, Mr Hawke's most remarkable talent, his extraordinary flair for publicity. There can be little doubt that it will be in relation to projecting a public image of the ACTU that his successor as president will find him most difficult to follow.[13]

In the week following Congress, Hawke's schedule was that he would set to work writing the Boyer Lectures. These are an annual series of ABC radio broadcasts given by eminent Australians, the majority of them scientists. It was a unique honour that Hawke, a party political figure, had been invited to be the Boyer Lecturer of 1979. He had accepted eagerly early in the year and nominated his subject, the Resolution of Conflict, but had as usual delayed writing his talks. He was due to record the programmes in mid-October. Mid-September, when he was to begin writing, could not have been a worse time for him to attempt calm reflection. He was exhausted physically and was daily flaying his spirit with doubts: the closing date for parliamentary pre-selection was 1 October — which happened to be Ellie's birthday. Earlier in the year, when she was still alive, he had mentioned this coincidence of dates to journalists: descendants of the Lee family, who read his remark in the newspapers, saw in it an unconscious statement of how firmly, still, Ellie's hand rested on her son's shoulder.

He spent the week from the end of Congress to Saturday 22 September in an agony of irresolution, drawing up lists for and against daring the Parliament, becoming increasingly distracted and self-pitying. Finally, it was Hazel who persuaded Hawke that he must come to terms with the forces that had shaped him and his career. She knew, as Hawke later also acknowledged, that he would live the rest of his life with a sense of failure if he 'squibbed it', as Uncle Bert had done in 1945.

He had arranged a Press conference to announce his decision on 23 September; on 22 September he telephoned Eddie Kornhauser and asked him to come to Sandringham. It was Saturday, and the Jewish New Year, when the orthodox may not drive cars. Kornhauser had to organize a ride to Hawke's house. When he arrived Hawke asked his opinion. Kornhauser urged him to run. Hawke replied, 'That's my decision'.

Following his experience in Adelaide with Hayden, Hawke's distrust of the Leader was acute: he feared to give Hayden advance warning. However, Kornhauser insisted that he telephone Hayden immediately and tell him. Hawke rang Hayden, told him he thought he had made up his mind, and would be announcing his decision at 3 p.m. on Sunday. On Sunday morning he rang Hayden again and told him he would be standing.

There were sixty journalists gathered in the ACTU boardroom that afternoon and Hawke's voice was trembling as he announced, 'I have done what I believe is best in all the circumstances . . . I will be a candidate for preselection for the seat of Wills . . .' Hazel had accompanied him to the ACTU and sat in the boardroom composed, beautifully groomed, her expression revealing nothing of what they had both endured before this moment had arrived.

Hawke continued, plainly stating his position in the centre ground of politics, 'I want now through the [ALP] to help provide a position which will match the thoughts and aspirations of the great majority of Australian men and women, which will help weld Australians together', then added a swipe at the Socialist Left, 'We cannot be a vehicle for advancing the fantasies of any extremist group'. .

When the news was broadcast his trade union colleagues had mixed feelings. Joe Morris of the ILO said, 'I thought it was a tragedy'. Charlie Fitzgibbon said to Ray Gietzelt, 'If he thinks he must, I suppose he must'. Both men had known for year that Hawke's dream was to become prime minister. They doubted that he could achieve it: he had alientated the Left of the Party and it was questionable that the Right would support him. Unlike his drive for the ACTU presidency, Hawke had no major power-base within the ALP.

The support he did have was from the people. They wrote:

I gave three cheers when I heard [the news]. It's just wonderful . . . you may be emotional, but emotions are sincere and deep.

I'm quite excited and have gone up and down the corridors of this large hotel broadcasting the good news — and the response? 'Good on him' and from others — Liberals, too — 'Really, well that is good news for all of us'.

A born Liberal voter . . . but your Party will certainly get my votes from here on.

You will be a great Prime Minister, for a great country.

Your actions are Christ-like — helping those who need help, labouring for the betterment of our nation and, above all, a peacemaker.

Our Party desperately needs practical leadership by men with a wide mental horizon and the ability to gauge what the electorate requires — and I believe you are one of the very few with those qualities.

Thank you for being a Christian leader, who stands up for the right.

Once the fever of indecision had broken he began to recover. But he had burned many bridges in the Party and in the trade union movement — the uranium speech-in-reply was generally held to be 'the worst speech Bob ever made' — and he had yet to conquer alcohol. His friends nagged and cajoled him to stop drinking; they telephoned Hazel and Jean Sinclair to propose stratagems for persuading Hawke to give up grog. Abeles told him, 'I will always be your friend, but if you won't stop drinking I will cease to speak in support of you'. Hawke continued to drink.

Meanwhile he had to undo some of the harm he had done to himself and, with a very little time left, write the Boyer Lectures. His diary records that at 5.45 p.m. on 2 October he 'spoke to Peter Cook' — that is, apologised to Cook for his remarks during the uranium debate. He had also to make peace with Dolan, who was now the most likely successor to the ACTU presidency. Dolan accepted Hawke's apology; he rejected the presidency. In early October the final drama of pre-selection closed. The Socialist Left waged a spirited campaign for Gerry Hand, but Hand was sunk and they knew it. Bob Hogg, the Victorian Secretary, and an SL member, said later, 'Once Hawke had decided to nominate, the matter was decided. The Party could not afford to defeat him.' On 14 October, following interviews with the selection panel, Hawke won ALP endorsement for Wills by 38 votes to Hand's 29.

In between all this politicking, and distractions like continued negotiations with the Seamen's Union and Press conferences, Hawke had been trying to write, in the Boyer Lectures, a major statement of his social and political ideas. The Boyer Lectures of 1979 have been lauded as visionary and scorned as glib. They were the work of a man who was very tired and short of time.

For twenty years Hawke had been making speeches about Constitutional reform; be began his series of talks with two that were concerned with the question, 'How We Are Governed'. These were the lectures which most excited commentators to praise or condemnation. In them Hawke proposed an adventurous re-thinking of Australia's political system in the light of changes that had occurred since 1901:

> We are daily witnesses to the fact and impact of change unparalleled in our memory, change which is being reflected in the structure of our economy, our capacity to provide employment and in the very cohesiveness of our society. And yet we are constitutionally and institutionally immobilised — in the framework for the conduct of our affairs, nothing changes. It is not change itself of which we should be afraid, it is this paradox of change/no change, the total lack of symmetry between our innovative capacities as technical and political human beings, that should cause us alarm . . . no one is more conscious than I of our tendency to conservatism, as a people, and of the need, therefore, for those who would advocate change to temper their fervour with a sense of gradualism . . . no one . . . would believe that the men and women with the best available administrative capacity for the government of the country repose exclusively in the two Houses of Parliament . . . I would advocate that as an initial step one quarter of the positions in the Ministry should be open to be filled by persons not elected to the Parliament . . . These Ministers would not be members of the Parliament but would be responsible *to* Parliament . . .

Hawke developed his theme of parliamentary reform at length. A reviewer, Professor G.S. Reid of the University of Western Australia, writing in *Quadrant*, asked:

> What would a government do if a strongly held opinion of an appointed Minister was electorally unpopular — would the Government defer to the Minister and run the risk of political annihilation; or would it reject the Minister's point of view and run the risk of his resignation? If the Government took the former course the public would ask — why have electorates or elections? And if it took the latter view the public would ask — why appoint expert Ministers? Mr Hawke does not appear to have thought through the problems his scheme would create.[14]

He went on to say:

> From the scholarly point of view Hawke's best lectures were the two called 'Australia In Crisis' (his third and fourth). In these he discussed the nation's unemployment crisis, the problems of equality for women, alternative lifestyles and industrial relations. These chapters reduced

the flow of [his] rhetoric in favour of a few statistics . . . These two lectures rescued the intellectual standing of the series . . . Hawke's lectures on *The Resolution of Conflict* were interesting for the conflicts they ignored. For example, there is nothing in them about uranium exports, nuclear power, mining, Aboriginal landrights, law and order, environmental crises, defence expenditure, the American alliance, abortion law-reform, the structure of taxation and so on — subjects which attract the major social and political conflicts in Australia today. They were ignored in favour of subjects more amenable to the projection of a positive man. Hawke chose his subjects with precision.

In conclusion, Professor Reid commented:

Bob Hawke's Boyer Lectures did not measure up to a scholar's predilection for tight logical thinking . . . The former Rhodes Scholar obviously decided he was speaking to an audience which would not demand precision and exactitude in argument . . . [The] 1979 Boyer Lectures were obviously designed to foster the speaker's public profile. In that respect the lectures were highly successful.[15]

Reid's conclusions were an accurate assessment of Hawke's political strategy, beleaguered as he was in the ALP: he was addressing the group who could, perhaps, outweigh the Caucus — the Australian people. Reid had also identified the shortcomings in Hawke's working habits, shortcomings which George Rockey complained of as 'Bob's leaping from A to Z, without worrying about the details'. Changing his habits — from thriving on pressure to dreary diligence; from painting in bold brush to paying attention to *petit point*; from relying on quickness of wit to resigning himself to the tedium of background reading — were problems Hawke would have to face in Parliament. The job of ACTU advocate had forced him to develop steady working habits, contrary though they were to his impatience, his confidence in heroic energy, and his 'streak of hedonism'. The question was whether, in his fifties, after a decade of riding a roller-coaster, he would have the strength of will to discipline himself once more. If he could stop drinking, that would be the first sign.

By December 1979 he was talking about resigning from the ACTU around Easter 1980. This would give him about six months before the next federal election in which he could rest, read, think and, he said, learn Italian. There are many Italians in the Wills electorate: Hawke's desire to learn their language had little to do with winning votes, since the seat was unchallengably Labor's, but it had everything to do with his instinct to be *en rapport* with people. He had time for none of this, least of all learning Italian. Jean Sinclair, who had to cope with Hawke's estimation that every day contained forty-eight hours and that he should be awake and occupied for all of them, remarked that a good week for her was one in which she dissuaded him from committing himself to a major scheme: agreeing to write a book, for example. In late 1979 she took six months' holiday to accompany her husband on sabbatical leave. Hawke had thought he would need Sinclair's help when he moved to Canberra. The experience of being six months without her convinced him. He also wanted Bill Kelty to accompany him to Canberra as a research assistant and administrator, but at length Kelty decided he could not abandon the trade union movement. He was in tears as he made the farewell speech to Hawke at an office party.

Hawke had to delay his departure from the ACTU until two major difficulties were solved: finance and the presidency. By December 1979 the ACTU's financial difficulties — a cash shortfall of $400,000 — had become public. Two years earlier, when Peter Nolan had taken over as Secretary he had reported to the executive that by 1979 there would be a deficit of $27,000. Just before the 1979 Congress some executive members who were familiar with balance sheets suspected that the financial situation was much worse than anyone realised, but it was not until after the Congress and further auditing that the seriousness of the position became clear. Hawke, Nolan and Kelty knew that delegates' refusal to increase affiliation fees by a reasonable amount was due largely to two factors: the mis-timing of the fee debate — which was held the day after the uranium debate — and the traditional Congress caper of plaguing the executive. Once tempers had cooled they were confident that the ACTU's State branches, the Trades and Labour Councils, would vote for the 150% fee increase needed. By the end of the year this process was under way. On Christmas Day 1979 Hawke turned his attention to the presidency. He telephoned Ray Gietzelt, asking him to have dinner in Sydney the following week to discuss what could be done. Gietzelt recalled, 'I'd had dinner with Cliffie Dolan the week before Christmas and he'd told me he was not interested in the job. Between Christmas Day and 2 January Bob had changed Cliff's mind.'

When Hawke had become President of the ACTU it had a membership of 1.4 million, 107 affiliates and a total staff of eleven. Dolan would be taking over an organisation with 139 affiliates, two million members and a staff of forty. In 1970 its income had been $162,000; by 1980 it was more than $1 million. In a decade the ACTU had established a social welfare research unit; a legal department; an occupational health unit; an industrial information co-operative; a migrant workers' office; a union child-care centre; a working women's charter; an arts department; ninety petrol discount outlets; and a travel branch which had catered for 20,000 people. Bourke's-ACTU had forced the introduction of legislation banning retail price maintenance, which saved Australian shoppers untold millions of dollars and saved the ACTU $1.2 million in rent. The Council's research staff no longer had to devote nearly all its energy to preparing wage cases, with a little time left over for Budget submissions. During Hawke's final year as President the research staff wrote forty-seven separate submissions and background papers to government departments and government-sponsored enquiries and authorities. The executive had been reorganised into a committee system; the committees were supplied with background papers in advance of meetings. In Monk's day there had rarely been an agenda for executive meetings. During Hawke's presidency the ACTU had helped to establish the Commonwealth Trade Union Council and the Australian-New Zealand Trade Union Co-ordinating Council; it had also joined the Trade Union Advisory Committee of the OECD. Perhaps the greatest difference that Hawke had made to the ACTU was in its image: he had firmly established it as a major institution in Australian public life. Yet in a spasm of invective or ignorance the *Financial Review* editorially summed up the years of Hawke's leadership of the Australian trade union movement as 'a decade of barren failure. He leaves the ACTU with nothing more than he brought to it.'[16]

In February 1980 Hawke left for Geneva to make his last major contribution to the ILO. On Christmas Eve 1979 the Soviet Union had invaded Afghanistan, an action which, among other things, spelt doom for hopes of early recovery in Western economies, for it quickly stimulated a diversion of capital into armaments, at a time when industrial nations were just surmounting the financial disaster that had ensued from the Yom Kippur War. Hawke had been appalled by the invasion and the consequences he foresaw, but he was out of step with the major trend of ALP thinking, which inclined to the view that the USSR's activities were of little concern in the antipodes. In Geneva he had an opportunity, denied — or, at least, muted — in Australia, to express his thoughts, and did so in a speech to the Governing Body. He was the first Governing Body member to raise the Afghanistan invasion, for the matter was not on the agenda and was, in fact, irrelevant to the business in hand. Observers described Hawke's speech as 'electrifying'. Having damned the invasion he went on to inveigh against the USSR's refusal of human rights to its citizens and its flouting of ILO Conventions: one more step had been taken towards the formal ILO condemnation of the Soviet Union that was to follow, in 1981.

While Hawke was tidying up the loose ends of his public life, his private life remained badly frayed. Alcohol. And not alcohol *tout court*.

He had been trying to ameliorate his problem by drinking only white wine, but whenever he was in a public place in Australia where alcohol was served people would press him to drink; strangers would send drinks to his table — sometimes triple whiskies. One could see the struggle on his face as he stared at a glass of spirits; suddenly he would reach for it.

By May 1980 his drinking problem was as bad as ever — he was drinking less but was a more unpleasant drunk. He looked ill. In three years his face had aged many more; his cheeks were deeply scored with lines and his complexion, when he had been a week or so without sun, had an unhealthy sallowness. He had been used to be able to go to sleep as if throwing a light switch, but during 1979 he had become insomniac and this had persisted. Waking, he moved in a deepening shadow: George Rockey, the man he loved almost as much as he loved Clem, had just learned that he had a malignant secondary tumour on his brain and Hawke had been affected by this news as if Rockey were, indeed, his father. Neither of them was able to articulate his feelings for the other — Rockey said, 'My little daughter, she's three years old, I called her Roberta ...' Hawke turned much of his psychological energy into schemes of diversion for Rockey's last months of life: for example, that Rockey should collaborate in writing a company history of TNT; that they go travelling together to exciting and unknown places. Hawke spent time he could not afford, professionally, with Rockey, flying to Sydney frequently to visit him and accompanying him on trips to the Wrest Point Casino in Hobart. Rockey was a true gambler: he returned to the tables until he was too weak to walk; on their final trip Hawke had to carry him back to bed in the hotel. Every meeting and conversation with Rockey would bring on a fit of gloom in Hawke. He complained frequently of fatigue and talked about taking a holiday — on Hayman Island, on a yacht in the Mediterranean, 'just somewhere where I can lie in the sunshine and *sleep*'.

At the beginning of the third week of May he flew to Hobart for an ACTU executive meeting and was joined there, later in the week, by Rockey. On 21 May they went to the casino together. Hawke had a good win on the blackjack table, slept for a couple of hours then returned to Melbourne to appear before the Conciliation and Arbitration Commission as advocate in the ACTU's national wage case. The more radical metal trades unions were campaigning for a 35-hour week and the Bench had threatened to discontinue the national wage case hearing unless the strike and bans campaign stopped. Hawke had less than two hours to assimilate the ACTU's arguments about why the Bench should continue with the case. Ranged against him, asserting that the Bench should carry out its threat, were more than half a dozen advocates, representing the employers, the federal Government and State Governments. Hawke succeeded in persuading the Bench to delay its decision about hearing the case until he had negotiated with the metal unions. Next evening he flew to Canberra and instead of resting, went to a journalists' party, where he stayed until about 1 a.m. The following morning he had to go shopping early to buy curtains for the apartment he had bought in Canberra, then fly on to Sydney for talks with the metal unions. He was ashen when he set out for Sydney, but successfully negotiated a change of tactics on the 35-hour week campaign, thus opening the way for the Bench to decide to proceed with the national wage case.

Hawke returned to Melbourne that evening. He was to leave the next day for Egypt and Geneva. He recalled,

> Sometime that night I was having a leak and I said to myself, 'Well, bugger it. You'd be better off not drinking. Why don't you give it up?'

So I went and washed my hands, and that was it . . . I never thought of myself as an alcoholic and I don't think I was in the sense that I could not do without it. I didn't get up in the morning and have a drink. There were days when I did go without it. It didn't have hold of me in that sense, but it was really too much of a crutch to me. I'd gone through enormous pressures about making up my mind about what I was going to do — it was driving me absolutely bloody crazy. That year, 1979, was an awful one; a terrible year . . . I couldn't quantify this, but the whole thing about my mother dying was gnawing away at me, the uranium question was driving me mad, and all of that horrible period had spilled over into 1980. I suppose the very fact of deciding to go into Parliament started to do things inside me. I knew I would have a big, new set of pressures on me and a lot of people wanting to destroy me if they could . . . I didn't relish life without grog. I embraced Churchill's observation: I've taken more out of grog than grog has taken out of me. I enjoyed especially the way it could break down barriers with people — I've got close to a helluva lot of people through drinking. I loved it. But I knew what the minuses were, and I just had to admit to them.

For months he had been, as he called it later, 'climbing the mountain': abruptly he had wrenched himself up to the summit. By curious coincidence it had taken nine months and two weeks since Ellie's death for Hawke to struggle his way out of drunkenness — curious because he had earlier lived nine months and two weeks unborn: it was as if an intimate, slow rhythm of growth had pulsed through him, unhurriable, its span determined, and now here he was, delivered at fifty, as unprepared as any new creature after butting its head for an eternity in the dark — to meet day-light.

From the time he had decided that his drinking days were over he had 'a total certitude' that he would not fall back again. Others were sceptical, waiting for a collapse of will: there were constant rumours that, 'Hawke's back on the grog', despite the fact that one only had to see him to know that he was not. However, in time even the cynics were convinced that Hawke had climbed a mountain. Within months he was looking younger, his gestures and expression lightened by a surge of vitality. The glowering, demon-possessed demeanour that had been familiar by late or early evenings when he was boozing had gone — although he still appeared older and tougher than other men of his years. Standing beside contemporaries who had become academics, judges and senior executives in business or the public service Hawke could have been a generation older than they, but he had an animation and vigour that contradicted the impression one first gained from a gnarled, grey head. His manner was more gentle and more often light-hearted. He had always been a kind man; however it had often been difficult for people to perceive it, on the other side of the intelligence in his eyes and his raspy voice. Men and women who met Hawke for the first time in the early 1980s frequently remarked, their tone incredulous, 'He's so nice. He was polite; he didn't snap . . .' A Labor feminist, who shared the sisterhood's hostility to Hawke in the 1970s, said in early 1982, after he had given a paper on the economic problems of women, 'He understands it. Broadly. He actually understands the social and economic implications of sexism. The radicals almost fell off their chairs . . . I talked to him later and got the impression that he was a man who was at peace with himself.'

Almost as soon as Hawke stopped drinking he started sleeping properly and began eating, on his estimate, 'twice as much'. In the early months of teetotalism his craving for sugar was so strong that he ate kilos of confectionary, but in time this need decreased to 'normal' — for a sweet tooth. (Hazel said later she thought he had always been allergic to alcohol; scientists are only beginning to decipher the cryptograms of biochemistry: it may be that a physiological cause and effect relationship existed between Hawke's appetite for sugar and his later abuse of alcohol.*) In the early months, too, he suffered acute discomfort when in the company of drinkers: he was bored, ribbed, and needed to explain repeatedly why he wanted orange juice or mineral water. He said afterwards, 'The first months were pretty rough. The worst thing would be sitting through dinners where people were drinking beautiful wines, talking about vintages and bouquets, and I'd be hanging on to a glass of mineral water — surely the most boring drink ever created.' He began to turn up at social functions with his own two-litre container of orange juice, until his new condition was widely enough known for hosts and hostesses to have on hand soft drinks for him. He avoided pubs and left dinners early, at first because of discomfiture, later because he had, after a lifetime of gregariousness, come to value solitude. At home, his teetotalism was a revolution; Hazel often confided to friends her admiration for what he had achieved.

In late August Hawke stepped down as President of the ACTU and within a fortnight was campaigning for the federal election. Since the Adelaide Conference ALP officials, especially the Victorian Secretary, Bob Hogg, and the national Secretary, David Combe, had worked hard behind the scenes to achieve a *rapprochement* between Hayden and Hawke, and had succeeded.

---

* It may also be that Hawke's emotionalism, most apparent when he was boozing, is in part caused by physiology: his lack of a spleen. A Sydney naturopath, Dorothy Hall, who claims expertise in the functions of the spleen and liver, said that to be without a spleen is to be without a barrier to the expression of anger; that while other people naturally coop up anger, Hawke naturally releases it. She also held the opinion that he was born with a large, active liver which had grown bigger and more active when his spleen was removed, and that this allowed him to drink heavily for years with much less effect than such drinking would have on a person with an ordinary liver. I could not find a physician who was willing to give a medical opinion on these matters — B.d'A.

Before the campaign was launched the Leader and the candidate had established a working relationship and a degree of intimacy. Hayden had promised that Hawke could go straight to the front bench (Caucus permitting); Hawke that he would campaign as hard as he could to make Bill Hayden the next prime minister. The Party's national campaign team was Hayden, Hawke and Neville Wran, the new ALP President and the most popular State premier in the country. During the election period Hawke had an unexpected bonus from teetotalism: 'I travelled as much and I made as many speeches, but physically it was the easiest campaign I've done. Instead of staying up after meetings, talking and on the grog, I went to bed early.' Ten days before the poll, due on 18 October, it seemed as if the unimagined were happening and that the swing to Labor would bring them back to office. Hawke was wildly excited, although a Labor victory in 1980 would have ruled out for years, or forever, his own chance of the prime ministership. However, when the counting was finished Labor had lost — by only several thousand votes in a dozen electorates, but by 23 seats in the House. Hawke was the Member for Wills and a couple of weeks later became the shadow Minister for Industrial Relations.

Parliament resumed in November 1980. On the evening of the 26th the galleries of the House of Representatives were full: word had spread that Hawke would, sometime that night, make his maiden speech. Clem and Hazel were seated in the visitors' gallery. At 8.52 p.m. the Deputy-Speaker called on Hawke and reminded the House that, because this was a maiden speech, interjections were out of order. His reminder added to the slightly unreal atmosphere: maiden speakers are supposed to be hesitant and to need protection from the experienced, tougher members. Listening to maiden speeches is one of the tiresome duties of a new Parliament, from which Ministers usually excuse themselves. Hawke had just risen and approached the mace when Malcolm Fraser and the rest of the Government front bench strode into the chamber. In the Press gallery above journalists came hurrying in.

He began lightly, saying to the Deputy-Speaker, 'As one of the tardier maidens to appear before you I express the hope that I shall do nothing in the future to upset unduly the even tenor of your ways'. He then moved on to his reasons for entering Parliament:

> I come to this House after twenty-two years with the Australian trade union movement, an organisation often denigrated by our opponents in this Parliament . . . but the existence of which is a *sine qua non* of a free and democratic society . . . I have become increasingly conscious that in such a democracy ultimately it is only in and through the Parliament that decisions can be made which will fashion for all our people the opportunities to release their talents in work and in leisure — the

opportunities to be well-rounded, constructive human beings, the opportunities for happiness for themselves and in relation to others, which seems to me what government should be about.

He then turned to the theme he would pursue relentlessly:

In his election policy speech of 30 September the Prime Minister, in describing a situation where over 100,000 kids between fifteen and nineteen could not find work, found it sufficient to say of those who leave school: 'Some move smoothly into a job; others have difficulty'. Even more insidious is the attempt to blame the victims, to make them appear indeed the victims of their own inadequacies . . . the crying need is to create cohesion, a sense of common purpose leavened by a constructive compassion for that growing body of our fellow Australians who are underprivileged . . .

As we have moved into the 1980s under this Government, we have moved inexorably towards that destabilised and dangerous position described by Disraeli as 'two nations', the nation of the privileged and the nation of the poor . . . we face an enormous challenge to combine those human and natural resources in an economically and socially productive manner, in a manner which will eliminate the pathetic spectacle of the importing of skilled and semi-skilled labour while our young in growing numbers are untrained and unemployed, and in a manner which will eradicate the canker of poverty in the midst of opulence . . . Our tragedy is not that we, as Australians, do not have the capacity to meet this challenge. It is that we have a Prime Minister and a Government whose natural instincts are not for cohesion but confrontation, not for truthful exposition to serve as a basis for mutual understanding but for partisan propaganda calculated to set Australian against and apart from Australian . . .

We will, from this day, work to provide Australia with an alternative government which will match not only the resources and the challenge but also what we believe to be the innate sense of fair play of the great majority of the Australian people.[17]

It was a grand beginning yet soon it seemed, as pundits had maintained for years, that Hawke had delayed too long — that he should have entered Parliament in 1974 or 1976, in a by-election, for now he would have to serve years of apprenticeship and in the interim his ambitions would be withered by forces he could not control. In Government, Fraser's giant frame overshadowed political life; in Opposition, Bill Hayden had earned respect for rebuilding the Party since 1977, plus the prestige of almost toppling Fraser in their first contest. And increasingly, the opinion polls showed a trend towards

Labor so that, at the next election an ALP led by Bill Hayden seemed likely to win. Most importantly, while the Australian people continued to admire Hawke and stated consistently that he was their preferred political leader, Hawke was failing to impress the would-be king-makers of the Press gallery and the real king-makers: his colleagues in Parliament.

His public speaking style, which for more than a decade had been shaped by the robust requirements of the union leader, sounded overly hot and aggressive in the cooler, jacket-and-tie atmosphere of the House. In Caucus meetings he was often fidgety and distracted, or bored. His supporters, a group of about ten, mostly Victorians, were bewildered by his patchy performances as a parliamentarian and complained privately that Hawke 'simply isn't contributing in Caucus'. When challenged later (but before he had become ALP Leader) that he seemed to be 'idling, not in gear' during his first two years in Parliament, Hawke acknowledged that his showing during that time was uninspiring: 'I don't *have* a gear for being in that position, unable to make decisions', he said. 'All my adult life, since I was at university and became President of the Guild, I've been used to leadership or being my own boss — as I was all the years as ACTU advocate, when I made the decisions about conducting cases, and took responsibility for them. I've felt at a loss . . .' For the period from November 1980 to May 1982 Hawke nominated (for this book) three personal successes in Parliament which at first seem curious, even shallow, but which in the light of later events reveal how soundly his political intuition works. One success was a straightforward matter of performing effectively in his job as shadow minister: Hawke helped take the scalp of the real Minister for Industrial Relations, Ian Viner, a man whose sobriquet was Sid Vicious, and whom Hawke loathed. Viner was moved to a minor portfolio. The other two 'successes' were much less obviously cause for satisfaction: Hawke had forced the establishment in Hansard of his description of the Prime Minister — 'a liar'. This label, applied to an MHR, had never before been allowed to stand and Hawke's pleasure in it arose in large part from the intuition that he had dealt Fraser, a man whose assertions of rectitude were immensely important to his self-respect, a piercing psychological blow. The third success Hawke nominated was this: Lionel Bowen, the Deputy-Leader of the Labor Party, had declared in Parliament, 'It appears that whenever the Honourable Member for Wills, Mr Hawke, decides to do anything in this House, the Government takes fright'. In the daily vilification of parliamentary debate Bowen's remark sounds little more than a throw-away line. But Lionel Bowen had the power, finally, to decide who would lead the Labor Party; at the time his loyalty to Hayden was unquestioned. When Hawke signalled out this trifling comment of Bowen's as a personal achievement, he was doing so as one who has seen a straw in the wind.

With nothing of great moment to point to from his first year as a parliamentarian Hawke added to the uneasiness about his capacities in the new arena by a classic gaffe, in late 1981. The ALP had decided to oppose the Government's decision to send an Australian contribution of men and helicopters to the American-sponsored peace-keeping force in Sinai, the establishment of which was a protocol of the Camp David Accords. The Australian public objected to contributing to the force and it was in large part this objection that determined Labor's attitude. Hawke did not share the public's or the Party's view. He argued against it in Caucus, accepted defeat, then admitted openly that he had changed his mind because public opinion was set against him. It was the first test of his relationship with Israel under the strains of parliamentary life and Hawke was less than happy with himself about it. As he left his office to go into the House where the issue was to be debated and where, he knew, Government members would take the opportunity to attack him personally, he said to Jean Sinclair, 'I hope I'm going to get through this'. He did not. When a Liberal backbencher taunted him with abandoning Israel — a gross overstatement but a very accurate emotional dart — Hawke became so distressed that he walked out of the room, in tears. The only other case of weeping in the Chamber in MHR's memories had occurred twenty years earlier when Garfield Barwick had witnessed one of his prize pieces of legislation being destroyed, and even then he had only appeared to be weeping, people could not say for sure. Hawke's tears made front-page headlines. One year in Parliament, it seemed, had ended his ambitions, in the light of two accepted truths: that leaders must be strong men and that strong men don't cry. Hawke's support in Caucus waned immediately; politicians of both sides, with blood-curdling hypocrisy, declared they had been disgusted or appalled. But then, after a few weeks, it became plain that the people were less mesmerised by some laws of masculine mystique than had been supposed.

Hawke was downcast and shaken by the incident for about a fortnight but by Christmas 1981 he had recouped his self-confidence and began telling friends that he could be the leader within six months. It was an assertion he had been making privately for almost eighteen months, to increasingly sceptical listeners. Only those who were prepared to believe that if Hawke said something, it must be so, or those who, like Kirby years before, had realised that the sheer force of Hawke's conviction had the power to penetrate a power structure and crack it internally, gave much credence to his claims. But just as his drive for the ACTU Presidency was founded upon his certainty that unionists would reward him for his work as advocate, winning increased rates of pay, so, in considering the ALP leadership and his position *vis-à-vis* Bill Hayden, Hawke's confidence owed less to wishful thinking than it seemed. Before the 1980 election Hayden had told Hawke of a conversation between himself and his wife, Dallas: Hayden had said to Dallas that, in the 'most horrible circumstance' of Labor losing the election by 'only two seats' he would step aside for Hawke. Hawke had taken this anecdote to be

Hayden's pledge that he would abdicate immediately on failing to win government, but in twelve months Hayden had shown no sign of doing so, and rather, the reverse. However, the conversation of 1980, kept confidential by both men, had cast a psychological die — indisputably for Hawke and apparently, too, for Hayden, in the light of later events. Hawke was indignant that Hayden, by his silence, had seemingly forgotten the intimacy.

During 1981 he had taken stock of Hayden's attitude and of his own meagre support in Caucus and had decided upon a tactic of using the popularity polls as a psychological weapon to gain the leadership. He did not have a moment's doubt that, if he were the ALP Leader, he would beat Malcolm Fraser in an encounter at the polls. His conviction about this was so strong that he mentioned it only in passing, as a matter too obvious for discussion, or in irritation that all his political colleagues and political journalists had not come to the same conclusion. But he was less certain about the necessary first step — the leadership — because his electors in that competition would not be the Australian people, with whom he felt en rapport, but that raw-nerved small group of men and women, prey to melancholy and wild swings of mood, who make up political Opposition.

By May 1982 he believed he had a 50-50 chance of displacing Hayden before the end of the year: that month Hawke learned the results of a poll which showed that on a range of personal qualities he rated in public esteem well ahead of both Hayden and Fraser. Importantly, although the ALP was outpolling the Government, its figures were not so handsome as to assure a labor electoral victory.

In the latter part of May, Hawke supporters gave the poll findings to selected newspaper journalists, members of Caucus and senior officials of the ALP: throughout June a movement to make Hawke Leader gathered speed, its initial impetus given energy by other opinion polls, publicity, and Left-wing anger with Hayden because of his determination to soften Labor's objection to the mining and export of uranium. There were few policy differences between Hayden and Hawke. The Hawke challenge was based on a single blunt argument: with Bill Hayden as Leader a Labor Government is not guaranteed; with Bob Hawke, it is. By the beginning of July there was mounting excitement within the Party and the news media about the possibility of a leadership contest.

On 5 July the Party's national policy-making conference opened in Canberra under a theatrical glare of television lights, in a conference room made portentous, even jingoistic, by giant displays of national and Party symbols. The motto of the conference was 'Preparing for Government' and the policies it espoused were mild — for there was in the air an impatience with the impotence of Opposition and an unfamiliarly pragmatic, even crafty, mood that said, 'The head must rule the heart'. But glaring over the words, in red, white and vivid blue were the extravagantly large symbols of a resurgent nationalism. They announced an unspoken and seductive message: Patriotic

Australians Vote Labor. (Within nine months this conference's symbols would be haunting the Fraser Government: knowing his Party would lose the election of 1983, a Liberal official complained, 'And Labor has taken over the Australian flag'.) The Canberra gathering was so well-dressed and sensible that some wits wondered loudly about the difference, these days, between a Liberal and a Labor Party conference. Indeed, with business progressing smoothly, with such decorousness and sobriety, the ALP's 1982 conference could have been boring. But from its opening day it was febrile with tension, for hour by hour the Hawke challenge was growing, under a momentum of its own, now that television and radio had taken up the issue.

On Wednesday 7 July the *Bulletin* published a new poll which showed that Hayden's popularity had slipped sharply while Fraser's had increased somewhat, and that 50 per cent of people questioned thought Fraser would be a better Prime Minister than Hayden, while only 31 per cent thought the reverse. Early that morning, asked to comment on television, Hawke remarked that the poll results were worrying for the Labor Party. His implied criticism of Hayden's leadership ended the weeks of shadow boxing.

The next afternoon, following thirty hours of wild surmise, Hayden acted. At 3 o'clock, just as Hawke was to deliver his major speech of the conference — on industrial relations — Hayden issued a statement which complained of 'a deliberate campaign . . . to de-stabilise' the Party, 'serious damage to [its] morale and credibility', 'this destructive exercise' and 'insidious de-stabilisation'; he then called a special meeting of Caucus for the following week 'to put an end to this matter'. Journalists had rushed from the conference room at the news of Hayden's statement and Hawke was left addressing a small audience which was too distracted to listen to him and had to be called to order. If prizes were to be given for upstaging tactics, Hayden had won hands down.

On Friday 9 July the editorials of the country's major newspapers declared for Hayden; throughout the week the Press mounted a hostile campaign against Hawke, reverting to fears and suspicions about him which it had first expressed, using different epithets, in the early 1960s (Mr Inflation, Communist) and early 1970s (Napoleon, Dictator). The *Bulletin* had gone to the trouble of mocking up a photograph of Hawke's head upon the opulently-gowned body of an actor who was posing imperiously and dressed as the Emperor of Rome.

There were alliances and broken alliances all week. Within days the Left, which had pledged itself to Hawke before 7 July, had deserted and for twenty-four hours Hawke faced an ignominious defeat — until some trade union leaders of the extreme Left made the astonishing error of publicly demanding a Hayden victory. At this, questions about how the NSW Right would vote were resolved: it swung behind Hawke. By the morning of 16 July both camps were claiming they would win, although Hayden told Hawke later that he thought he — Hayden — would lose, and Mick Young, on

Hawke's team, had 'a feeling in his bones' the night before that some of the promised votes would not be honoured, and that Hawke would 'just miss'. Young's Celtic bones were right: three people switched sides and soon after 11 a.m. the Caucus, by 42 votes to 37, re-elected Hayden as Leader.

Praising Hawke's 'honourable ambition' to lead the Party, Hayden was as magnanimous in victory as Hawke, who had immediately declared his loyalty, was gracious in defeat. But within two hours, in Hayden's presence, Hawke had told a news conference that his ambition for leadership remained.

After the challenge many Caucus members complained that they did not know Hawke, they had never spent any time with him socially, and that they were puzzled or offended by the fact that he had not lobbied them for support but had delegated the soliciting of votes to lieutenants, or had simply relied upon a belief that they would 'do the right thing' by him. This behaviour was unconventional, but from Hawke to be expected. It had a singular advantage for any leader-to-be: by holding himself aloof, Hawke had very few debts in the Caucus. Meanwhile, the eruption of hostile publicity had taught him and his supporters a lesson about silence. The challenge damaged relationships within Caucus, for after the first relief of victory, the victors had set to, punishing the vanquished: at least two shadow ministers who had supported Hawke became seriously ill from stress; a poisonous bitterness infected the air.

Some time after his defeat Hawke was alone in a washroom in the Commonwealth offices in Sydney when John Button happened to walk through the door. Button was, and is, Labor leader in the Senate and the head of the Victorian Independents. The Independents are descendants of the Participants, the right-wing group which forced federal intervention into the Victorian branch a decade earlier; with a new name they were now celebrated as the faction that had organised a coup in Victoria to install John Cain as State Labor Leader — and soon after, Premier. The Independents characterise themselves as pragmatists-with-principles. Button had been Hayden's most senior marshall in beating off Hawke's challenge. Suddenly alone together, Button said to Hawke, 'Before the vote I'd told Bill that a close win wasn't enough. As soon as the vote was over Bill said to me "Are five votes enough?" and I replied "No."' Hawke responded coolly, replying merely, as he remembered, 'Is that so?' Despite his show of indifference Hawke saw the exchange as of great significance and during the next six months recalled it, in private, as a pillar for his next challenge: Button had served notice on Hayden that it was only a matter of time before he would be displaced.

In more than eighty years in federal politics Labor had never dumped a leader. However, the mood of professionalism that had distinguished the national conference had marked a turning point in the ALP: the conference had revealed that, after its long night of anguish caused by the events of 1975, the Australian Labor Party had returned to life and the world, a tougher creature than before.

Politically, the latter half of 1982 was entirely taken up with Government and social scandals, speculation about an early election, and, from September, concern about an acutely worsening economic situation that boded to deteriorate further during 1983. Despite this, Labor made little headway against the Government in Parliament and in the public mind, in part because Hayden mishandled the Opposition's attack on the Government over tax evasion. Information about massive public fraud and sharp practice came to light in the second six months of the year and proved, at length, what Labor politicians had realised for some years but had felt helpless to change: that the nation's communal values were decaying. Safe, fat and on the edge of the world, the country was sliding into carelessness. The trade union movement was becoming increasingly selfish and bloody-minded; the rich were selfish and bloody-minded; the petit-bourgeois aspired to be rich and selfish, tax evasion and disregard for the poverty-stricken unemployed were symptoms of a national disease. Successive governments, beginning with Whitlam's, had educated the public to realise that the Australian economy was a pawn on the table of international economics, but the reaction to this perception of over-riding, alien forces had been, 'Every man for himself'. Some renewed sense of community, of national solidarity, was essential if Australia was to halt its degeneration into a nation of white-collar criminals, thuggish labour bosses, sharp lawyers, pettifogging tax cheats and a mass of ordinary people enervated by cynicism. Inchoately, perhaps, those who had designed the symbols for the ALP conference had realised that an appeal to nationalism would be a string to pull the country around. However, it was Malcolm Fraser who, by November 1982, had clearly understood the mood of self-disgust and who devised a policy to capitalise on it. That month, before a by-election in the Victorian seat of Flinders set for 4 December, he proposed a wage freeze which would, he announced, help the economy and therefore the unemployed. Using logic and statistics, economists quickly advanced arguments which proved that the wage freeze was *a*. the perfect solution or *b*. useless and damaging. The correct answer belonged to the Prime Minister who, as ever, had calculated on the political abacus of psychology. The wage freeze was welcomed by the electorate, for it gave a sense of national purification through suffering.

Labor had expected to win the Flinders by-election. It lost. A mood of inevitable defeat, if Hayden continued as Leader, set in. The Canberra Press gallery invited Hawke to its Christmas party at the Lobby restaurant, 'where I laid it all out for them. I said, if you want to understand current Australian politics you've got to think of two famous explorers — Bass and Flinders.' Several influential journalists were convinced that somehow Hawke would become Leader but only one, Greg Hywood of the *Financial Review*, had enough information to present a factual story: just before Christmas he wrote that John Button had gone on holiday to Fiji, where he would decide whether or not he and his group would continue to support Hayden. It was unknown to the Press that the issue was much further advanced than that: a disciplined Hawke machine was already at work, and barring bad luck and bad management, Hawke *would be* the Leader by February. The Hawke machine had decided upon secrecy: Hawke himself was to take merely a passive role and was informed of achievements or set-backs only when necessary. One reason for secrecy was to maintain in the Prime Minister and the Government the sense of security that had undertaken them on winning the Flinders by-election. Speed was also essential. When Hawke learned the Flinders result and considered it in combination with the forseeable trade union reaction to the wage freeze, he was convinced that Fraser would hold the earliest possible election. By mid-December he was forecasting in private that the wage freeze, opposed by the ACTU, would give rise to a big strike, 'perhaps in Telecom', as soon as the Christmas holidays were over, and Fraser would thereby have a popular issue to take to the country. (Telecom, along with the oil industry, is the area of industrial disputation that most enrages the public. As events turned out, it was the oil industry which obliged — or disobliged — Malcolm Fraser.) Hawke also believed that if ALP leadership did not improve Fraser would win such an election and that, because of the likely upturn in the world economy during 1984, the Liberals could win the next election after that, and possibly another, thanks to the national good-temper arising from the bi-centenary celebrations of 1988. What the Australian Labor Party was facing by December 1982 was the possibility of its disintegration into futility.

The Prime Minister, who had spent the final weeks of 1982 convalescing from an operation on his back, returned to work in the second week of January with a vigour that astonished. In his weeks of recuperation he had refined still further his intuitive grasp of the public mood, its yearning for solidarity and purposefulness. Within days of returning to his desk he had abandoned the rhetoric of small government, announced an array of grand national building projects and had articulated the concept, magnificent in its flourish, 'Australia won't wait for the world!' President Sukarno of Indonesia — 'Go to hell with your aid, America!' — would have been proud of him, and could have offered a little extra advice about coups. On 6 January, before Fraser had returned to work, John Button had flown to Brisbane and asked Bill Hayden to step down. Hayden had refused. On 19 January, while Fraser was still in the process of announcing nation-building schemes, Lionel Bowen, by his demeanour in a Labor executive meeting, had indicated that he, too, now rejected Hayden. By this date Hayden had mishandled ALP-ACTU dealings over the wage freeze. Without consultation, he had switched from the agreed position of opposition, to one of cautious support when it appeared he was backing a politically unpopular cause. The ACTU was extremely angry and demanded, through Hawke, that Hayden switch back again — or the Party's prices and incomes agreement with the trade union movement would be scuttled. Hayden and Hawke had a blazing row in the executive meeting. While Hayden was defending his actions, Lionel Bowen rolled his eyes. Hawke, watching Bowen's face, knew that the last domino had fallen. It was abruptly a contest between the cunning of Hawke's machine, and the Prime Minister. The Hawke group had to persuade Hayden to abdicate quickly and silently, for as soon as the Prime Minister got wind of upheaval in the ALP, he would make a sprint for Yarralumla. For months the Government had had the Constitutional reasons for an early election — from thirteen sales tax Bills rejected by the Senate — and a strike in the oil industry was threatening on cue. Senior members of the Labor Party believed that Fraser had already planned an election for 19 March, so by mid-February at the latest the leadership change would need to be made. Caucus was not due to meet until 21 February.

The twelve days from 19 January moved in tantalising slow-motion for Hawke: he thought he had the numbers, Hayden thought Hawke had the numbers, but Hayden was refusing to resign and was proposing to force the issue to a party-room fight. The consequences of that could be disastrous for Labor's electoral prospects. By the last weekend in January Hawke's machine had decided that, beginning on Monday 31 January, Hayden was to be systematically pressured by the other parliamentary leaders to desist and go quickly. Button had already written to Hayden telling him he should step down: the latest opinion polls showed that at a time when Labor could expect to be ten or fifteen points ahead of the Government, it was only four; under such circumstances, it would lose the unannounced but imminent election. The context, by this stage, was that inflation was running at 10 per cent and almost 650,000 people were unemployed. The Australian Labor Party hardly had any business in politics if it could not beat a Government which had such a blighted record.

It was not until 31 January that the seriousness of the leadership struggle moved from the shadows of journalists' guesses and snippets of information, into the glare of publicity. That morning Bowen, asked if he supported Hayden's leadership, gave a non-committal answer to the Press. The next day Button flew to Brisbane to talk to Hayden again. He gained the impression that Hayden would resign if he were guaranteed the Foreign Affairs portfolio. This shadow ministry was held and cherished by Lionel Bowen who, in a separate conversation with Button, agreed to relinquish it. The day afterwards, Wednesday 2 February, Hawke and Button met in Melbourne. Button said, 'It's going to happen, but not until the weekend.'

None of these events was known to the news media, the Prime Minister or, indeed, to any but a tiny group of senior Labor people and some of their staff members. However, on the evening of 2 February, somebody apparently hoping to change Hayden's mind, informed Fraser's office of what was afoot. The Prime Minister decided to call an election the next day, thereby expecting either to short-circuit Hayden's resignation, or to catch the ALP, once more, 'with its pants down'.

Early on 3 February, before Fraser had made *his* plans public, Hawke flew to Brisbane for what he believed would be a routine ALP executive meeting. He had just arrived at the Commonwealth offices, venue for the meeting, when Button beckoned him aside. 'It's going to happen this morning. Hayden wants to see you,' Button said. Then the meeting began. Hawke recalled, 'There was an unreal atmosphere. Hayden chaired the morning session during which people were coming in with rumours from Canberra. Then, at morning tea I, Button and Bowen went up to Hayden's office. Bill said he was resigning immediately.'

By 11.15 Queensland time, that is, a quarter past midday Eastern Australian summer time, there was an eerie feeling of crisis around Parliament House, an atmosphere that revived memories of 11 November 1975. Rumours from the news media in Brisbane had reached the capital that something momentous was happening inside the ALP meeting there, while the Prime Minister had just set out in his official limousine for Yarralumla, having told the Press he soon would have an announcement to make. Fraser, as he had done before, was dashing off to use the Governor-General, but this time nothing went smoothly: fifteen minutes earlier, in Brisbane, Hayden had formally told the ALP executive that he was resigning immediately; in Canberra the new Governor-General, Fraser's own appointment, had not been informed of the Prime Minister's visit and when Fraser arrived at Government House he was told he would have to leave his letter requesting an election until the duties of a diplomatic luncheon had been fulfilled. By the end of lunch-time on 3 February Fraser had, like Whitlam at the end of lunch-time seven years earlier, thrown away his Government and his career. Hawke, by then, had taken over the ALP.

On election day, 5 March, having campaigned on a slogan which expressed his own struggle away from a divided personality, towards wholeness — 'Bob Hawke, Bringing Australia Together' — Robert James Lee Hawke became the Prime Minister.

With only two years in Parliament and three weeks as Leader of the Opposition, his rise to power is the most spectacular in the history of Australian politics.

Endnotes

The primary source of information in this book is R.J. Hawke. I made many hours of tape-recordings with him, which are stored in the Australian National Library. Copyright is jointly held by Hawke, d'Alpuget and the Library. The majority of quotes from Hawke are taken from these tapes; however, there are many other, briefer quotes from him drawn from notes of conversations I had with him. A major secondary source has been interviews with the people listed under Acknowledgments at the front of the book. My notes and transcripts of taped interviews with them are stored in the Library, but access cannot be granted for some years. The written page would be a thicket of numbers if a reference note were given for every oral source: I have decided to avoid that. Unless otherwise indicated in the text, all quotes in the book have been made during interviews with me. I list other references below.

Chapter One
  1. Pryor, *op. cit.*, pp. 106-7.

Chapter Two
  1. Jules Zanetti, to B. d'A.

Chapter Five
  1. Pullan, *op. cit.*, gives a different emphasis to Hawke's role. See pp. 38-9.

Chapter Six
  1. *Pelican*, 4 April 1952.
  2. *Ibid.*, 1 August 1952.
  3. Letter to author.

Chapter Seven
  1. Letter to author.
  2. *Ibid.*

Chapter Eight
  1. Letter to author.
  2. Freudenberg, *op. cit.*, p. 176.

3. Letter from R.J. Hawke to Geoff Brown, Maitland.
4. *Ibid*.
5. Letter from Dr Clark to author.
6. Letter from R.J. Hawke to Geoff Brown.
7. *Ibid*.
8. Interview with Terry Winter, former member of the ACTU executive, former Commissioner of the Conciliation and Arbitration Commission. This interview was given when Winter was literally on his death bed and too weak to talk for more than a few minutes at a time. I wish to thank his widow, Beryl, for allowing me to see her husband.
9. Hawke, B.Litt. thesis, p. 283.

Chapter Nine
1. Hurst, *op. cit.*, p. 26.
2. It is generally thought that the Boilermakers' Case was the reason for splitting the jurisdiction, but see d'Alpuget, *op. cit.*, p. 143.
3. Kirby kept the title of Chief Judge; it lapsed when he retired from the Commission, see d'Alpuget, *op. cit.*, pp. 147-8.
4. The *Observer*, 30 April 1960.

Chapter Ten
1. Hagan, *op. cit.*, p. 319.
2. My thanks to Mrs Jennie McLellan for allowing me to copy this poem.
3. Transcript, p. 180.

Chapter Eleven
1. Hawke's personal papers, ACTU files.
2. *Ibid*.
3. *Ibid*.
4. Transcript, p. 1135.

Chapter Twelve
1. Hagan, *op. cit.*, p. 135.
2. Transcript, p. 343.
3. *Ibid*, p. 453.
4. *Ibid*, p. 454.
5. *Ibid*, pp. 558-9.
6. Kiki, *op. cit.*, p. 94.

Chapter Thirteen
1. Hawke's personal papers, ACTU files.
2. *Ibid*.
3. *Ibid*.
4. *Ibid*.
5. *Ibid*.
6. Interview with Jim Shea, former offical of AFL-CIO and colleague of Meany.
7. Hurst, *op. cit.*, p. 81.

Chapter Fourteen
1. Hawke's personal papers, ACTU files.
2. ACTU Press release, ACTU library.
3. Hawke's personal papers, ACTU files.

412

Chapter Fifteen

1. ALAC was known as CLAC, the Commonwealth Labor Advisory Council, before the election of the Whitlam Government.
2. *Op. cit.*, pp. 13-25, *passim.*
3. Hawke's personal papers, ACTU files.
4. The *Bulletin*, 28 July 1973.
5. Ross Martin, 'The ACTU Congress of 1973' in *Journal of Industrial Relations*, December 1973, p. 414.
6. Hawke's personal papers, ACTU files.
7. Ross Martin, 'The ACTU Congress of 1973' in *Journal of Industrial Relations*, December 1973, p. 415.

Chapter Sixteen

1. Briefing to author in Tel Aviv by staff of Australian Embassy.
2. Hawke's personal papers, ACTU files.
3. Transcript, current information section, Parliamentary Library, 'Hawke' files.
4. Hawke's personal papers, ACTU files.
5. *Ibid.*
6. *Hawke on Israel*, pp. 53-4.
7. Shown to author by E. Kornhauser.
8. The voting for the Egerton-Combe motion was: in favour — Innes, Hartley, O'Byrne, Wriedt, Lourigan, Egerton, Ducker, McMullan; against — Whitlam, Barnard, Murphy, Enderby, O'Neill, Young, Geitzelt, Bryce. Neither Combe nor Hawke had voting rights.
9. Pullan, *op. cit.*, p. 135.

Chapter Seventeen

1. Report of International Labour Conference, 1975, pp. 236-7.
2. ed. Patrick Tennison. Hill of Content, Melbourne, 1977.
3. Hawke's personal papers, ACTU files.
4. Conversation with author.
5. Hawke's personal papers, ACTU files.

Chapter Eighteen

1. *Labor Star*, 16 August 1977.
2. *National Times*, 24 September 1977.
3. Ross Martin, 'The ACTU Congress of 1977', in *Journal of Industrial Relations*, December 1977, pp. 427-30 *passim.*
4. Hawke's diary, 1977.
5. Report of International Labour Conference, 1978, p. 28/7.
6. *Nation Review*, 12 April 1979.
7. *Ibid.*
8. *Ibid.*
9. Hawke's personal papers, ACTU files.
10. *Ibid.*
11. Report by Isi Leibler.
12. Copy of Department of Foreign Affairs record of conversation; Hawke's personal papers, ACTU files.
13. Hawke's personal papers, ACTU files.

Chapter Nineteen

1. *Jewish News*, Melbourne, 8 June 1979. Resolution was passed on 4 June.

2. Hawke's report to Isi Leibler; copy in Hawke's personal papers, ACTU files.
3. *Ibid.*
4. *Jewish News*, Melbourne, 15 June 1979.
5. Hawke's report to Leibler; copy in Hawke's personal papers, ACTU files.
6. Letter in Hawke's personal papers, ACTU files; anonymity requested.
7. *Sun-Herald*, 22 July 1979.
8. Hurst, *op. cit.*, p. 240.
9. *National Times*, 28 July 1979.
10. Hawke's actual words were reported to have been: 'a lying cunt with a limited future'.
11. *National Times*, 28 July 1979.
12. *Tribune*, 19 September 1979.
13. Ross Martin, 'The ACTU Congress of 1979' in *Journal of Industrial Relations*, December 1979, pp. 485-96 *passim*.
14. *Quadrant*, May 1980.
15. *Ibid.*
16. *Financial Review*, 21 August 1980.
17. *Hansard*, 26 November 1980, pp. 97-101 *passim*.

Bibliography

Alexander, Fred. *Campus at Crawley*. Cheshire, 1963.

Australian Labor Party. 'National Committee of Inquiry Report and Recommendations to the National Executive', March 1979.

Barber, J.D. 'Strategies for Understanding Politicians', *American Journal of Political Science*, 18, No. 2.

— *Power to the Citizen*. Markham Publishing Company, Chicago, 1972.

— *The Presidential Character: Predicting Performance in the White House*. Prentice-Hall, New Jersey, 1972.

Brasher, Rev. F.W. *Methodism in the Maitland District*. South Australian Historical Society, 1958.

Clark, Claire. 'The Middle East since 1973: the Difficult Path to Peace', *World Review*, Vol. 17, No. 3.

Comay, Michael. *Zionism, Israel and the Palestinian Arabs*. Keter Books, Jerusalem, 1981.

d'Alpuget, Blanche. *Mediator, a Biography of Sir Richard Kirby*. Melbourne University Press, 1977.

Davies, A.F. *Skills, Outlooks and Passions, a Psychoanalytic Contribution to the Study of Politics*. Cambridge University Press, 1980.

Evans, G. and Reeves, J., eds. *Labor Essays 1980*. Drummond, Melbourne, 1980.

— and Malbon, J., eds. *Labor Essays 1981*. Drummond, Melbourne, 1981.

Evatt, H.V. *William Holman, Australian Labour Leader*. Angus & Robertson, Sydney, 1979.

Freudenberg, Graham. *A Certain Grandeur: Gough Whitlam in Politics*. Sun Books, Melbourne, 1978.

Gabbay, Dr Rony. 'Israeli Interests in the Middle East', paper given to the Australian Institute of International Affairs, March 1980.

Giblin, L.F. *The Growth of the Central Bank*. Melbourne University Press, 1951.

Hagan, Jim. *The History of the ACTU*. Longman Cheshire, Melbourne, 1981.

Hawke, R.J.L. 'An Appraisal of the Role of the Australian Commonwealth Court of Conciliation and Arbitration with special reference to the development of the concept of the Basic Wage', Bachelor of Letters thesis, University of Oxford, December 1955.

— *Hawke on Israel*. Australian Friends of Labour Israel, Melbourne, 1977.

415

— *The Resolution of Conflict, 1979 Boyer Lectures.* Australian Broadcasting Commission, Sydney, 1979.

Hevrat Ha'Ovdim, The Labour Cooperative Sector in Israel. Logos Ltd, Tel Aviv.

Histadrut, The General Federation of Labour in Israel. Histadrut, Tel Aviv, 1976.

Hurst, John. *Hawke, The Definitive Biography.* Angus & Robertson, Sydney, 1979.

Hyslop, Anthea. 'Christian Temperance and Social Reform: The Women's Christian Temperance Union of Victoria, 1887-1912' in *Women, Faith and Fetes,* edited by Sabine Willis. Dove Communications, Melbourne, 1977.

Industries Assistance Commission. *Structural Change in Australia.* Canberra, June 1977.

Innes, J. *Jock Innes: The Man — His Message.* Electrical Trades Union, 1965.

Israel, History from 1880. Israel Pocket Library, Keter Books, Jerusalem, 1973.

Jupp, J. 'The Victorian ALP', draft chapter for *Machine Politics in the Australian Labor Party.* In press for Allen & Unwin, Sydney, 1982.

Kiki, Albert Maori. *Kiki, Ten Thousand Years in a Lifetime.* Cheshire, Melbourne, 1968.

Killek, Teddy and Pearlman, Moshe. *Jerusalem.* Steimatsky's Agency Ltd, Jerusalem, 1975.

King's College, 1924-1944, The Friendly Years. King's College, Adelaide, 1944.

Kohut, Heinz. 'Forms and Transformations of Narcissism', *Journal of the American Psychoanalytic Association,* No. 2, 1966.

— 'Thoughts on Narcissism and Narcissistic Rage', *The Psychoanalytic Study of the Child,* 27, 1972.

— 'Creativeness, Charisma, Group Psychology: Reflections of the Self-analysis of Freud', *Psychological Issues,* 9, Nos. 2-3, 1976.

Lasswell, H.D. *Psychopathology and Politics.* University of Chicago Press, 1930.

— 'The Selective Effect of Personality on Political Participation' in *The Authoritarian Personality,* edited by R. Christie and M. Jahoda. The Free Press, Illinois, 1954.

Latourette, Kenneth Scott. *A History of Christianity.* Eyre and Spottiswoode Ltd, London, 1955.

Levinson, Daniel J. *The Seasons of a Man's Life.* Ballantine Books, New York, 1979.

Little, Graham. 'Leaders and Followers: A Psychosocial Prospectus', *Melbourne Journal of Politics,* No. 12, 1980.

— 'The Liminal Character', paper given to an informal seminar on philosophy and psychoanalysis, University of Melbourne, June 1981.

Lloyd, Clem. 'The Federal ALP', draft chapter for *Machine Politics in the Australian Labor Party.* In press for Allen & Unwin, Sydney, 1982.

McCorkindale, Mrs, ed. *Torch-Bearers, The Women's Christian Temperance Union of South Australia, 1886-1948.* WCTU of South Australia, 1949.

McKinlay, Brian. *The ALP, A Short History.* Drummond, Melbourne, 1981.

McLeod, Jeanette and Carmichael, Ern. *Yorke Peninsula Sketchbook.* Rigby, Adelaide, 1974.

McVey, Margaret E. 'Australia's Middle East Foreign Policy', *World Review,* Vol. 17, No. 3.

Mann, Peggy. *Golda: The Life of Israel's Prime Minister.* Coward McCann, New York, 1971.

Martin, R.M. *Trade Unions in Australia.* Penguin, Melbourne, 1980.

— 'The ACTU Congress of 1961'

— 'The ACTU Congress of 1963'

— 'The ACTU Congress of 1965'

— 'The ACTU Congress of 1967'

— 'The ACTU Congress of 1969'

416

— 'The ACTU Congress of 1971'
— 'The ACTU Congress of 1973'
— 'The ACTU Congress of 1975'
— 'The ACTU Congress of 1977'
—- 'The ACTU Congress of 1979'
    All in *Journal of Industrial Relations*, December issue of relevant year.
Murphy, D.J. *Hayden, A Political Biography*. Angus & Robertson, Sydney, 1980.
—, ed. *Labor in Politics*. University of Queensland Press, Brisbane, 1975.
Murray, Robert. *The Split, Australian Labor in the Fifties*. Cheshire, Melbourne, 1970.
Nelson, Hank. *Papua New Guinea*. Pelican, Melbourne, 1972.
O'Farrell, P.J. 'The History of the New South Wales Labour Movement, 1880-1910: A Religious Interpretation', *Journal of Religious History*, Vol. 2, No. 2, 1962.
Olden, Christie. 'About the Fascinating Effect of the Narcissistic Personality', *Imago*, Vol. 2, No. 4, 1941.
Ormonde, Paul. *A Foolish, Passionate Man, A Biography of Jim Cairns*. Penguin, Melbourne, 1981.
Oxford University Handbook. Clarendon Press, 1950.
Parkin, Andrew. 'Party Organisation and Machine Politics: The ALP in Perspective', draft chapter for *Machine Politics in the Australian Labor Party*. In press for Allen & Unwin, Sydney, 1982.
Plowman, David. 'Unions in Conflict: The Victorian Trades Hall Split 1967-1973', paper given to the ANZAAS Conference, 1977.
Pryor, Oswald. *Australia's Little Cornwall*. Rigby, Adelaide, 1962.
Pullan, Robert. *Bob Hawke, A Portrait*. Methuen, Sydney, 1980.
Rawson, D.W. *The Impact of the Trade Unions*. AIPS Monograph: 3.
— 'Victoria 1910-1966', *Historical Studies*, Vol. 13, No. 49.
Renwick, A.M. *The Story of the Church*. Inter-Varsity Fellowship, London, 1958.
Reserve Bank of Australia, Functions and Operations. Reserve Bank, Sydney, 1975.
Ross, Lloyd. *John Curtin, A Biography*. Macmillan, Melbourne, 1977.
Rydon, Joan. 'Victoria 1910-1966', *Historical Studies*, Vol. 13, No. 50.
Sammi, Michael. *Refuge*. Am Oved Publishing House, Israel, 1981.
Santamaria, B.A. *Against the Tide*. Oxford University Press, London, 1981.
Sexton, Michael. *Illusions of Power, The Fate of a Reform Government*. Allen & Unwin, Sydney, 1979.
Sheehan, Peter. *Crisis in Abundance*. Penguin, Melbourne, 1980.
Shoeck, Helmut. *Envy*, translated by Michael Glenny and Betty Ross. Harcourt Brace & World, New York, 1970.
Smith, Rev. L.P.G. *Centennial of Christ Church, Kapunda 1856-1958*. Kapunda, 1958.
Somare, Michael. *Sana, an Autobiography*. Niugini Press, Port Moresby, 1975.
Stevens, Bron and Weller, Pat, eds. *The Australian Labor Party and Federal Politics*. Melbourne University Press, 1976.
Study Group on Structural Adjustment Report. The Crawford Committee, Canberra, 1979.
Tatiara, the Good Country. Tatiara Pastoral, Agricultural and Industrial Society, 1976.
Tennison, Patrick, ed. *Heyday or Doomsday: Australia 2000*. Hill of Content, Melbourne, 1977.
Thurow, Lester C. *The Zero-Sum Society, Distribution and the Possibilities for Economic Change*. Basic Books Inc., New York, 1980.
van Sommers, Tess. *Religions in Australia*. Rigby, Adelaide, 1966.

Walker, Judith. 'Restructuring the ALP — NSW and Victoria', *Australian Quarterly*, Vol. 43, No. 4.

Walker, Robin. *Congregationalism in South Australia, 1837-1900*. Royal Geographical Society of Australasia, South Australian Branch 1967-68, Vol. 69.

The Wallaroo and Moonta Mines. Hussey and Gillingham Ltd, 1914.

Walsh, Eric. 'Broken Hill and After, an Exercise in Self-Destruction', *Australian Quarterly*, Vol. 42, No. 4.

Walter, James. *The Leader: A Political Biography of Gough Whitlam*. University of Queensland Press, Brisbane, 1980.

Waters, Frank. *Postal Unions and Politics*. University of Queensland Press, Brisbane, 1978.

Wheelwright, Tom. 'The NSW Labor Party Machine', draft chapter for *Machine Politics in the Australian Labor Party*. In press for Allen & Unwin, Sydney, 1982.

Wilner, Ann Ruth. *Charismatic Political Leadership, a Theory*. Centre for International Studies, Princeton University, 1968.

Yehoshua, A.B. *Between Right and Right — Israel: Problem or Solution*. Doubleday, New York, 1981.

Zionism. Israel Pocket Library, Keter Books, Jerusalem, 1973.

Other printed sources:

All Australian newspapers, as clipped by the current information section of the Parliamentary Library, Canberra.

Transcripts of Australian radio and television broadcasts, as held by the current information section of the Parliamentary Library, Canberra.

ACTU Executive Minutes, 1970-80.

Hawke's personal papers, ACTU files, 1959-80.

Hawke's diaries, 1967-81.

Hawke's speeches, ACTU files.

Commonwealth Arbitration transcripts of wage cases of 1959, 1961, 1965, 1966.

Transcript of the Local Officers' Case, Territory of Papua New Guinea.

Commonwealth Arbitration Reports.

Index

Note:

1. The index entry for Bob Hawke is meant to serve mainly as a list of contents; obviously the whole work is about Hawke.
2. The form of names in the text, often somewhat informal, has been used in the index. It is expected that readers using a more formal approach will recognize the name from its context; for example, a reader who has located in *Who's who in Australia 1980* the entry for Urquhart Edward Innes will recognize him as the Ted Innes of this index.

420

MORE ABOUT PENGUINS, PELICANS
AND PUFFINS

For further information about books available from Penguins please write to Dept EP, Penguin Books Ltd, Harmondsworth, Middlesex UB7 ODA.

In the U.S.A.: For a complete list of books available from Penguins in the United States write to Dept DG, Penguin Books, 299 Murray Hill Parkway, East Rutherford, New Jersey 07073.

In Canada: For a complete list of books available from Penguins in Canada write to Penguin Books Canada Ltd, 2801 John Street, Markham, Ontario L3R 1B4.

In Australia: For a complete list of books available from Penguins in Australia write to the Marketing Department, Penguin Books Australia Ltd, P.O. Box 257, Ringwood, Victoria 3134.

In New Zealand: For a complete list of books available from Penguins in New Zealand write to the Marketing Department, Penguin Books (N.Z.) Ltd, Private Bag, Takapuna, Auckland 9.

In India: For a complete list of books available from Penguins in India write to Penguin Overseas Ltd, 706 Eros Apartments, 56 Nehru Place, New Delhi 110019.

A Penguin Special

PRIESTS ON TRIAL
Alfred W. McCoy

In 1982 the Philippine Army filed criminal charges of murder and rebellion against an improbable group of Catholic conspirators – a Filipino parish priest, Irish missionary Fr Niall O'Brien, and Australian missionary Fr Brian Gore. Using perjured testimony from paid witnesses, the Army pursued them with prosecution and imprisonment for two years. Pressured by international protests, President Marcos finally ordered the charges dismissed and the priests deported.

Gore and O'Brien were victims of the growing conflict between Church and State in the Philippines. For over a decade, they worked to shatter the subservience of peasants on Negros Island, the poorest of Third World poor. In revenge, the island's wealthy sugar planters persecuted the priests to silence the Church.

This book is both a detailed and disturbing account of what happened, and a penetrating insight into the position of the Church in the Third World today, caught in a cross-fire between dictatorship and revolution.

THE TWYBORN AFFAIR

Eddie Twyborn is bisexual and beautiful, the son of a Judge and a drunken mother. With this androgynous hero – Eudoxia/Eddie/Eadith Twyborn – and through his search for identity, for self-affirmation and love in its many forms, Patrick White takes us on a journey into the ambiguous landscapes, sexual, psychological and spiritual, of the human condition.

'It challenges comparison with some of the world's most bizarre masterpieces. – Isobel Murray in the *Financial Times*

THE VIVISECTOR

Hurtle Duffield loves only what he paints. The men and women who court him during his long life are, above all, the materials of his art. He is the Vivisector, dissecting their weaknesses with cruel precision: his sister's deformity, a grocer's moonlight indiscretion, the passionate illusions of such women as the sugar heiress Boo Davenport, and his mistress Hero Pavoussi, wife of a Greek shipping magnate. Only the egocentric adolescent he sees as his spiritual child elicits from him a deeper, more treacherous emotion.

FLAWS IN THE GLASS
A Self-Portrait

With force, candour and emotion, Patrick White writes of his youth in Australia, his English boarding school, his life at Cambridge and trips to Germany, London during the Blitz, RAF wartime intelligence in the Middle East and his first meeting with the man who was to become the central focus of his life.

'A singularly penetrating act of self-scrutiny, a cold, calculating stare into the mirror of the artist's life' – David Lodge in the *Sunday Times*

'One of the most interesting and absorbing novelists writing in English today ... One of the great magicians of fiction ... White's scope is vast and his invention endless' – Angus Wilson in the *Observer*

A Choice of Penguins by David Malouf

CHILD'S PLAY

In the streets of an ordinary Italian town, the people go about their everyday lives. In an old apartment block above them, a young man pores over photographs and plans, dedicated to his life's most important project.

Day by day, in imagination he is rehearsing for his greatest performance. Yet when his moment comes, nothing could have prepared him for what happens . . .

'One of the most effective and penetrating studies of the mind and being of a fanatic' – *Financial Times*

'Written with the beautiful clarity and sharp edges of a cut crystal' – *Sunday Telegraph*

FLY AWAY PETER

For three very different people brought together by their love for birds, life on the Queensland coast in 1914 is the timeless and idyllic world of sandpipers, ibises and kingfishers.

In another hemisphere civilization rushes headlong into a brutal conflict. Life there is lived from moment to moment.

Inevitably, the two young men – sanctuary owner and employee – are drawn to the war, and into the mud and horror of the trenches of Armentieres. Alone on the beach, their friend Imogen, the middle-aged wildlife photographer, must acknowledge for all three of them that the past cannot be held.

'The continuities of nature are set against the obscenities of war . . . to construct a memorable book' – *Sunday Telegraph*

'The novel of a poet without a single trace of overwriting' – *Daily Telegraph*

Published in Penguins

SISTER KATE

Jean Bedford

Kate Kelly grew up in a house of women: when the Kelly men were not in jail, they were outlaws. Kate's loyalty to her family becomes a bitter obsession: 'They were bent on destroying us – like a nest of rats the farmer comes on with his plough – not caring that they hurt women and children but only wanting to root us out completely.'

Inevitably the police take brutal revenge on the Kelly Gang at Glenrowan. Kate must watch as the scorched body of her lover is strung up for public display.

Neither wandering nor marriage, time nor drink, can blot out this gruesome climax of her young life.

Until the ashes of their heroism turns her mind to darkness.

MEG

Maurice Gee

Meg is the younger of the Plumb children. Emotionally dominated by her family – the terrifying George Plumb, a man driven to extremity by his wayward conscience; a loving, exhausted mother; her flawed and contradictory brothers and sisters – Meg is the one who cares best.

For fifty years she watches as they grow up into a New Zealand of the Depression and post-war boom, lovingly gathering up the harvest of their lives – and deaths – in this harshly tender, passionate quest to uncover the truth about them ... and herself.

'Maurice Gee's trilogy is shaping towards the realization of as rich a tapestry as we have had so far of contemporary social life' – *Auckland Star*

Published in Penguins

SUCH PLEASURE

Martin Boyd

Bridget Malwyn, the illegitimate daughter of a wild Irish peer, is brought to live amongst the decaying splendours of his castle in County Galway, until his death in her sixteenth year. When his puritanical successor turns her out, penniless, she is forced to work in a draper's shop in Bedfordshire. The restrictions and humiliations of her new status give Bridget an exaggerated sense of the value of the life she has left, and she is determined – with an intensity that later betrays her – to recapture the spirit and status of her early years.

'Pure pleasure reading, exquisitely accomplished and light as air, a joy' – Pamela Hansford Johnson in the *Daily Telegraph*

MILK

Beverley Farmer

Whether writing about being an Australian woman in love in Greece, or waiting at the airport for a small son, or being old and embedded in everything that has gone before, Beverly Farmer isolates moments of human experience with almost unbearable clarity. She charts the distances between people, their place in light and landscape, their failures to love and be loved or even to sustain each other more than momentarily.

Set in Greece and Australia, these are remarkable stories by a writer acclaimed in *Age* as 'an extraordinarily gifted and original talent'.

Published in King Penguin

JUST RELATIONS
Rodney Hall

The residents of Whitey's Fall are aged between 80 and 114. In this remote Australian mining town they are a bastion against the empty promise of progress. In fact they are the guardians of the land's unfulfilled dream, a mountain of gold awaiting the gentle kiss of gelignite.

'*Just Relations* is of the school of Patrick White with a bow to Bellow, Marquez, Pynchon, old Uncle James Joyce and all ... Hall is a protean writer, varying between the crude, the comic, the lusty and the poetic' – Andrew Sinclair in *The Times* (London)

'Out of foibles and squabbles, dreams and nightmares, Hall fashions a hilarious, yet moving, study' – *Washington Post*

'The most exciting book I have read in a long time ... its lusty, vigorous prose, full of the joy of words, takes it looping and humming along, and makes exhilarating demands on the reader' – Marion Halligan in *The Times* (Canberra)

TOURMALINE
Randolph Stow

Sun-baked, red and barren, Tourmaline is not a ghost town: it simply lies in a coma.

Then from the surrounding Western Australian desert comes the diviner, Michael Random. He offers salvation – on his terms. And before he leaves again, a broken man, the strange characters of Tourmaline have been stirred into life by hate and love.

'The strongest piece of atmospheric landscaping I've read for a long time ... there is no denying its power' – Norman Shrapnel in the *Guardian*

'Poetic accuracy is the only one aspect of a rich talent. Mr Stow has narrative gift as well ... He is, in fact, a real novelist' – John Davenport in the *Observer*